THE PRESS

THE
PRESS

Geneva Overholser
Kathleen Hall Jamieson

EDITORS

THE **A**NNENBERG **F**OUNDATION **T**RUST
AT **S**UNNYLANDS

OXFORD
UNIVERSITY PRESS

OXFORD

UNIVERSITY PRESS

Oxford University Press, Inc., publishes works that further
Oxford University's objective of excellence
in research, scholarship, and education.

Oxford   New York
Auckland   Cape Town   Dar es Salaam   Hong Kong   Karachi
Kuala Lumpur   Madrid   Melbourne   Mexico City   Nairobi
New Delhi   Shanghai   Taipei   Toronto

With offices in
Argentina   Austria   Brazil   Chile   Czech Republic   France   Greece
Guatemala   Hungary   Italy   Japan   Poland   Portugal   Singapore
South Korea   Switzerland   Thailand   Turkey   Ukraine   Vietnam

Copyright © 2005 by Oxford University Press, Inc.

Published by Oxford University Press, Inc.
198 Madison Avenue, New York, New York, 10016
http://www.oup.com/us

Oxford is a registered trademark of Oxford University Press

Library of Congress Cataloging-in-Publication Data

The press / Geneva Overholser, Kathleen Hall Jamieson, editors.
   p. cm. — (Institutions of American democracy series)
   Includes bibliographical references and index.
   ISBN   978-0-19-517283-6 (alk. paper, cloth)
   ISBN   978-0-19-530914-0 (alk. paper, pbk.)
   1. Press and politics—United States.   2. Democracy—United States.
3. Freedom of the press—United States.   4. Government and the press—United States.
   I. Overholser, Geneva.   II. Jamieson, Kathleen Hall.   III. Series.
           PN4888.P6P64   2005
       071´.3—dc22   2004029861

Book design by Joan Greenfield
Copyedited by Melissa A. Dobson

3   5   7   9   10   8   6   4

Printed in the United States of America
on acid-free paper

CONTENTS

DIRECTORY OF CONTRIBUTORS

Geneva Overholser (Editor)

Curtis B. Hurley Chair in Public Affairs Reporting, Missouri School of Journalism
Washington Bureau

Ms. Overholser, a former ombudsman and syndicated columnist for *The Washington Post* and editorial board member of the *New York Times*, was editor of the *Des Moines Register* from 1988 to 1995, leading the paper to its 1991 Pulitzer Prize Gold Medal for Public Service. She was named best in the business by American Journalism Review and editor of the year by the National Press Foundation. She served on the Pulitzer Prize board and is a former officer of the American Society of Newspaper Editors and Nieman fellow. She is a fellow of the American Academy of Arts and Sciences and of the Society of Professional Journalists.

Kathleen Hall Jamieson (Editor)

Elizabeth Ware Packard Professor of Communication, Annenberg School for Communication at the University of Pennsylvania;
Director, Annenberg Public Policy Center

Dr. Jamieson is the author or coauthor of ten books including *Everything You Think You Know About Politics . . . and Why You're Wrong, The Press Effect,* and *Eloquence in an Electronic Age,* for which she received the Winans-Wichelns Book Award. She has received numerous teaching and service awards including the Christian R. and Mary F. Lindback Award for Distinguished Teaching and the Public Education Award of the American Foundation for Suicide Prevention. She is an elected fellow of the International Communication Association and a member of the American Philosophical Society and the American Academy of Arts and Sciences. During the fall 2004 presidential campaign, Dr. Jamieson appeared regularly on *The NewsHour* with Jim Lehrer and *NOW* with Bill Moyers.

W. Lance Bennett

Professor of Communication and Professor of Political Science, University of Washington;
Founder and Director, Center for Communication and Civic Engagement, University of Washington

Dr. Bennett is author, coauthor, or editor of numerous books including *News: The Politics of Illusion*, *Mediated Politics: Communication in the Future of Democracy*, and *Taken by Storm: The Media, Public Opinion, and U.S. Foreign Policy in the Gulf War*. He has served on the editorial boards of *Journal of Communication*, *Political Communication*, and *Press/Politics*. He received the Murray Edelman Career Achievement Award in political communication of the American Political Science Association and the Ithiel de Sola Pool Award and Lectureship of the American Political Science Association.

John Carey

Professor, Communications and Media Management, Fordham Business School;
Managing Director, Greystone Communications

Dr. Carey's research focuses on the adoption and use of new media, media ethnography, public broadcasting, and telecommunications policy. Dr. Carey has conducted research studies for A&E Television Networks, Cablevision, Consumers Union, CPB, General Electric, The Markle Foundation, NBC, the *New York Times*, NTIA, PBS, Primedia, Scholastic, WNET, and XM Satellite radio, among others. He is widely published in the areas of new media and interactive media, and serves on the board of the Adult Literacy Media Alliance.

Timothy E. Cook

Professor of Mass Communication and Political Science in the Kevin P. Reilly Sr. Chair of
Political Communication, Manship School of Mass Communication, Louisiana State
University

Dr. Cook was first to serve as the Laurence Lombard Chair at Harvard University's Joan Shorenstein Center on the Press, Politics, and Public Policy. He came to LSU after twenty years on the faculty at Williams College, where he was Fairleigh Dickinson, Jr., Professor of Political Science, and recurring stints as a visiting professor of public policy at Harvard's Kennedy School of Government. Among the books he has authored, co-authored or edited are *Freeing the Presses: The First Amendment in Action* (2005), *Governing with the News: The News Media as a Political Institution* (1998) and *Crosstalk: Candidates, Media, and Citizens in a Presidential Campaign* (1996), which won the Doris Graber prize for outstanding book in political communication from the American Political Science Association.

James Curran

Professor of Communications, Goldsmiths College, University of London

Appointed to London University's first Chair of Communications in 1989, Mr. Curran is the author or editor—some with others—of 16 books about the mass media. These include *Power Without Responsibility*; *Media and Power*; *Contesting Media Power*; *Mass Media and Society*; *Media, Ritual and Identity*; and *De-Westernizing Media Studies*. He was an academic adviser to the last Royal Commission on the Press (U.K.), and is a former columnist for *The Times* (London).

Robert M. Entman

Professor, Communication and Political Science, North Carolina State University

Dr. Entman is author of *Projections of Power: Framing News, Public Opinion, and U.S. Foreign Policy*; *Democracy Without Citizens: Media and the Decay of American Politics*; and coauthor of the award-winning *The Black Image in the White Mind: Media and Race in America*. Currently working on a new book about media bias and presidential scandals, he received the Alumni Outstanding Research Award from North Carolina State in 2002.

Robert Giles

Curator, Nieman Foundation for Journalism, Harvard University

Mr. Giles was senior vice president of the Freedom Forum and editor in chief of its *Media Studies Journal*. Mr. Giles began his career as a newspaper reporter and editor, eventually becoming executive editor of the *Beacon Journal* and editor and publisher of *The Detroit News*. Both newspapers received Pulitzer Prizes under his leadership. Mr. Giles has authored or co-authored such books as *What's Fair? The Problem of Equity in Journalism* and *Newsroom Management: A Guide to Theory and Practice*.

Theodore L. Glasser

Professor, Communication, Stanford University;
Director, Graduate Program in Journalism, Stanford University

Dr. Glasser's several books include *Custodians of Conscience: Investigative Journalism and Public Virtue*, written with James Ettema, which won the Society of Professional Journalists' Sigma Delta Chi award for best research on journalism. His research and commentaries have appeared in variety of publications, including *Journal of Communication, Critical Studies in Mass Communication, Journal of American History*, the *New York Times Book Review* and *Nieman Reports*. He has held visiting faculty appointments in Finland, Singapore and Israel. In 2002-2003, Dr. Glasser served as president of the Association for Education in Journalism and Mass Communication.

Marc Gunther

Senior Writer, FORTUNE Magazine

Mr. Gunther reports on the media industry, business, and social issues. Before joining *FORTUNE*, he served as a television writer and critic at Knight Ridder, the *Detroit News*, and the *Hartford Courant*. Mr. Gunther is author of several books, including *The House That Roone Built: The Inside Story of ABC News* and, most recently, *Faith and Fortune: The Quiet Revolution to Reform American Business*.

Daniel C. Hallin

Professor, Communication, University of California, San Diego;
Adjunct Professor, Political Science, University of California, San Diego

Dr. Hallin's research focuses on political communication and the role of the news media in democratic politics. His writings address such topics as the media and war, television coverage of elections, the development of professionalism in journalism, and comparative studies of the media's role in the public sphere, particularly in Europe and Latin America. His books include *The "Uncensored War": The Media and Vietnam, We Keep America on Top of the World: Television Journalism and the Public Sphere* and, most recently *Comparing Media Systems: Three Models of Media and Politics* (with Paolo Mancini).

James T. Hamilton

Professor of Public Policy, Sanford Institute of Public Policy, Duke University

Dr. Hamilton has served as visiting associate professor in global communications at Harvard University's Kennedy School of Government and was director of Duke University's Program on Violence and the Media from 1993-2000. His recent publications include *All the News That's Fit to Sell: How the Market Transforms Information into News*. Dr. Hamilton received the 2001 David N. Kershaw Award of the Association for Public Policy Analysis and Management.

Robert B. Horwitz

Professor and Chair of the Department of Communication, University of California, San Diego

Professor Horwitz is the author of *The Irony of Regulatory Reform: The Deregulation of American Telecommunications* and several articles on communications media and free speech law in the United States. He also is the author of *Communication and Democratic Reform in South Africa*, a study of the transition from apartheid to democratic structures in the South African communications sector.

Alex Jones

Laurence M. Lombard Lecturer in Public Policy, Harvard University;
Director, the Joan Shorenstein Center on the Press, Politics, and Public Policy, Harvard University

A Pulitzer Prize-winning journalist, Mr. Jones has coauthored *The Patriarch: The Rise and Fall of the Bingham Dynasty* and *The Trust: The Private and Powerful Family Behind the New York Times*, a finalist for the National Book Critics Circle Award. He has hosted National Public Radio's "On the Media" and has been host and executive editor of PBS's "Media Matters." Mr. Jones has served three times as a juror for the Pulitzer Prize competition, and was Nieman Fellow at Harvard. He is on the advisory boards of the *Columbia Journalism Review*; the International Center for Journalists; the Committee of Concerned Journalists; the Center for Strategic International Studies; the Institute for Politics, Democracy & the Internet; the Nieman Foundation for Journalism; *Harvard Magazine*; and the International Institute of Modern Letters.

John Keane

Professor of Politics at the University of Westminster and the Wissenschaftszentrum Berlin;
Founder of the Centre for the Study of Democracy in London

John Keane's research interests include the future of the public sphere and freedom of communication, new forms of violence, citizenship in Europe, the philosophy and politics of Islam, and the contemporary growth of global civil society. He is currently preparing a history of democracy—the first for over a century. His works, which have been translated into many languages, include *Vaclav Havel: A Political Tragedy in Six Acts; Civil Society: Old Images, New Visions; Global Civil Society?;* and *Violence and Democracy*.

Jane E. Kirtley

Professor, Media Ethics and Law, University of Minnesota;
Director, Silha Center for the Study of Media Ethics and Law, University of Minnesota

Ms. Kirtley has been a reporter, a practicing attorney, and has served as executive director of The Reporters Committee for Freedom of the Press. She serves on the board of the

Sigma Delta Chi Foundation and writes the "First Amendment Watch" column for *American Journalism Review*. Her distinguished honors include induction into the Medill School of Journalism's Hall of Achievement, the John Peter Zenger Award for Freedom of the Press, and the Matrix Foundation's First Amendment Award. She is a member of the Freedom of Information Hall of Fame.

Martha Joynt Kumar

Professor, Political Science, Towson University

Dr. Kumar is coeditor or coauthor of such books as *Portraying the President: The White House and the News Media* and *The White House World: Transitions, Organization, and Office Operations*, which came from her work as director of the White House 2001 Project. She recently received a Wilson H. Elkins Professorship awarded by the University System of Maryland.

Maxwell McCombs

Chair in Communication, University of Texas

Dr. McCombs is coeditor of *Communication and Democracy: Exploring the Intellectual Frontiers in Agenda-Setting Theory* and coauthor of *Research in Mass Communication*. He is past president of the World Association for Public Opinion Research, a fellow of the International Communication Association, and past director of the News Research Center of the American Newspaper Publishers Association. Among his honors are The American Political Association's Murray Edelman Award and an honorary doctorate from the University of Antwerp.

Carolyn Marvin

Frances Yates Professor at the Annenberg School for Communication at the University of Pennsylvania

Dr. Marvin is the author of *When Old Technologies Were New* (1988) and *Blood Sacrifice and the Nation: Totem Rituals and the American Flag* (1999), as well as many articles on cultural communication. She was formerly a journalist at the *Atlanta Journal-Constitution*.

Nancy Hicks Maynard

President, Maynard Partners, LLC.

Ms. Maynard is president of Maynard Partners, LLC. She is the former co-owner and publisher of the *Oakland (CA) Tribune*. She has covered domestic policy for the *New York Times* in New York and Washington, and education for the *New York Post*. She has served as senior vice president of The Freedom Forum and chair of its Media Studies Center. Ms. Maynard is the author of *MEGA MEDIA: How Market Forces Are Transforming News*. She has served on the boards of Tribune Company, PBS, The Maynard Institute for Journalism Education, among other organizations. She is director of Editors' World, a project designed to redefine and improve coverage of international news in mid-sized media markets.

Philip Meyer

Knight Professor of Journalism, School of Journalism and Mass Communication, University of North Carolina, Chapel Hill

Mr. Meyer is the author of *The Vanishing Newspaper: Saving Journalism in the Information Age* (2004). He is a member of the board of contributors of *USA Today* and has published in a wide range of periodicals from *Esquire* to *Public Opinion Quarterly*. Several organizations have honored him with career achievement awards, including the Newspaper Association of America Research Federation and the American Association for Public Opinion Research. His first book, *Precision Journalism*, was published in 1973 and is now in its fourth edition (2002).

David T. Z. Mindich

Associate Professor and Chair, Journalism and Mass Communication, St. Michael's College

Dr. Mindich is a former assignment editor for CNN. He is author of *Just the Facts: How "Objectivity" Came to Define American Journalism* and *Tuned Out: Why Americans Under 40 Don't Follow the News*. His writings have appeared in the *Wall Street Journal*, *New York* magazine, and elsewhere. Dr. Mindich is founder of Jhistory, an Internet group for journalism historians. In 2002, he received the Krieghbaum Under-40 Award for Outstanding Achievement in Research, Teaching and Public Service from the Association for Education in Journalism and Mass Communication.

Pamela Newkirk

Associate Professor, Department of Journalism, New York University

Ms. Newkirk is the author of *Within the Veil: Black Journalists, White Media*, which received the 2001 National Press Club Award for Media Criticism. She is widely quoted about media diversity and African American portrayals. Her articles have appeared in the *Washington Post*, the *New York Times*, the *Columbia Journalism Review*, *The Nation*, the *Media Studies Journal*, and *ARTnews*. Ms. Newkirk has worked as a reporter at news organizations including *New York Newsday*, where she was part of a Pulitzer Prize-winning reporting team. She is the editor of *A Love No Less: Two Centuries of African American Love Letters*. Ms. Newkirk was also named the 2004/2005 Alfred Knobler Fellow at the Nation Institute.

Thomas Patterson

Professor, Government and the Press, the John F. Kennedy School of Government and the Shorenstein Center on the Press, Politics, and Public Policy, Harvard University

Dr. Patterson's articles have appeared in numerous journals including *Political Communication* and *Journal of Communication*. His books include *Out of Order*, which received the American Political Science Association's Graber Award for best book in political communication, and *The Unseeing Eye*, which was named one of the 50 most influential books on public opinion in the past half century by the American Association for Public Opinion Research. He codirected the Shorenstein Center's study on the 2000 presidential campaign and shared its results in his 2002 book *The Vanishing Voter: Public Involvement in an Age of Uncertainty*.

Robert G. Picard

Hamrin Professor of Media Economics, Jönköping International Business School, Jönköping University, Sweden;
Director, Media Management and Transition Centre, Jönköping International Business School, Jönköping University, Sweden

Dr. Picard has authored more than 200 articles and authored or edited 19 books, which include *The Economics and Financing of Media Firms* and *The Newspaper Publishing*

Industry. He was founding editor of the *Journal of Media Economics*. Dr. Picard serves as a media issues consultant to many newspaper and broadcasting companies. His honors include the Journal of Media Economics Award of Honor for lifetime contributions to media economics scholarship and the Clinton F. Denman Freedom of Information Award.

William Prochnau

Contributing Editor, Vanity Fair

Mr. Prochnau is a former national correspondent for the *Washington Post* and a contributing editor for *Vanity Fair*. He reported from Vietnam for several months in 1965 and again in 1967 while serving as the Washington bureau chief for the *Seattle Times*. His writings include the acclaimed books *Once Upon a Distant War* and *Trinity's Child* and such articles as "Adventures in the Ransom Trade," upon which the film *Proof of Life* was based.

Bruce W. Sanford

Partner, Baker & Hostetler LLP

A First Amendment and corporate lawyer, Mr. Sanford has received accolades including being named one of the 100 most influential lawyers in America by the *National Law Journal* and one of the most accomplished press lawyers in the nation by *American Journalism Review*. He was elected to the Freedom of Information Hall of Fame by a coalition of major press organizations. He is author of *Libel and Privacy* and *Don't Shoot the Messenger: How Our Growing Hatred of the Media Threatens Free Speech for All of Us*. Mr. Sanford is a charter trustee and chairman of the board of the Thomas Jefferson Center for the Protection of Free Expression at the University of Virginia.

Robert Schmuhl

Professor, American Studies, University of Notre Dame;
Director, John W. Gallivan Program in Journalism, Ethics, & Democracy, University of Notre Dame

Dr. Schmuhl has published essays in *Critical Studies in Mass Communication*, *SOCIETY*, the *Review of Politics*, the *Chicago Tribune*, the *Boston Globe*, and the *Washington Post*. Among the nine books Dr. Schmuhl has written or edited are *Statecraft and Stagecraft: American Political Life in the Age of Personality* and *The Responsibilities of Journalism*, which has been published in several foreign editions. In 1996 he was named a participant in the U.S. Department of Education's "Democracy at Risk" project.

Daniel Schorr

Senior News Analyst, National Public Radio

Mr. Schorr's career in journalism has spanned more than six decades and earned him numerous distinguished awards including three Emmys, the Alfred I. DuPont–Columbia University Golden Baton award, the George Foster Peabody personal award for "a lifetime of uncompromising reporting of the highest integrity," and decorations from European heads of state. In 2002, he was elected to the American Academy of Arts and Sciences. A renowned national and international correspondent for more than 30 years, Mr. Schorr remains a regular contributor and analyst at NPR.

Michael Schudson

Professor of Communication and Adjunct Professor of Sociology, University of California, San Diego

Dr. Schudson has authored and edited numerous publications, including such books as *The Sociology of News; Rethinking Popular Culture;* and *The Good Citizen: A History of American Public Life.* Among his honors are fellowships from the Guggenheim and the Russell Sage Foundation and the "genius" award from the MacArthur Foundation. He has written about the media and civic participation for popular as well as professional journals, including the *Los Angeles Times, Newsday,* the *Financial Times, Columbia Journalism Review,* and *Wilson Quarterly.*

Philip Seib

Professor, Journalism, Marquette University

Mr. Seib holds the Lucius W. Nieman Chair and teaches courses about media ethics and the news media and international relations. His recent books include *Beyond the Front Lines: How the News Media Cover a World Shaped by War; Going Live: Getting the News Right in a Real-time, Online World;* and *The Global Journalist: News and Conscience in a World of Conflict.* He is a former print and broadcast journalist, and his coverage of social issues and politics won numerous awards.

William Serrin

Associate Professor, Journalism & Mass Communication, New York University

A former labor and workplace correspondent for the *New York Times,* Mr. Serrin has also been a reporter for *Newsweek* and the *Detroit Free Press,* where he was one of the team of reporters who won a Pulitzer Prize for their coverage of the 1967 Detroit riots. Mr. Serrin authored *Homestead: The Glory and Tragedy of an American Steel Town,* edited *The Business of Journalism,* and has contributed to numerous publications including the *Atlantic Monthly* and *Columbia Journalism Review.*

Mitchell Stephens

Professor, Journalism and Mass Communication, New York University

Mr. Stephens' work includes *A History of News; The Rise of the Image the Fall of the Word* and the widely used textbook *Broadcast News.* He has written for the the *New York Times,* the *Los Angeles Times,* and the *Washington Post.* Mr. Stephens recently traveled around the world and reported and wrote essays for the radio program "Marketplace," the online magazine *Feed,* and for Lonelyplanet.com. He is a history consultant to the Newseum.

Esther Thorson

Associate Dean for Graduate Studies, Missouri School of Journalism, University of Missouri-Columbia;
Professor, Missouri School of Journalism, University of Missouri-Columbia

Dr. Thorson has published extensively in advertising, news effects, and health communication. Her scholarly work has won a variety of research and writing awards and she has advised nearly 40 doctoral dissertations. She applies research, both hers and that of her colleagues, in newsrooms and advertising agencies across the U.S. and abroad. Dr. Thorson serves on an extensive list of editorial boards. Her administrative focus is on bringing together theory and practice in graduate journalism and persuasion education.

Susan E. Tifft

Eugene C. Patterson Professor of the Practice of Journalism and Public Policy Studies, Duke University

Before joining *TIME* magazine as a writer and editor, Ms. Tifft was a press secretary for the Federal Election Commission and speechwriter for the Carter-Mondale reelection campaign, as well as director of public affairs for the Urban Institute. She coauthored *The Patriarch: The Rise and Fall of the Bingham Dynasty* and *The Trust: The Private and Powerful Family Behind the New York Times*, which was a finalist for the National Book Critics Circle award in biography. She has served as an election analyst for NBC News, and her work has appeared in the *New Yorker*, the *New York Times*, the *Los Angeles Times*, the *Chicago Tribune*, the *Wall Street Journal*, and *Columbia Journalism Review*.

Barbie Zelizer

Professor, Communication, University of Pennsylvania

Dr. Zelizer, a former journalist, is the author or editor of seven books, including *Journalism After September 11; Taking Journalism Seriously: News and the Academy;* and *Reporting War: Journalism in Wartime. Remembering to Forget: Holocaust Memory Through the Camera's Eye* received numerous awards, including the Best Book Award from the International Communication Association and the Simon Wiesenthal Center's Bruno Brand Tolerance Book Award. A former Guggenheim Fellow, Media Studies Center Research Fellow and Fellow at Harvard University's Joan Shorenstein Center on the Press, Politics, and Public Policy, Zelizer is founder and coeditor of *Journalism: Theory, Practice and Criticism* and Director of the Annenberg Scholars Program in Culture and Communication.

GENERAL INTRODUCTION:
THE PRESS AS AN INSTITUTION
OF AMERICAN CONSTITUTIONAL DEMOCRACY

Jaroslav Pelikan

IT HAS BEEN A NOVEL AND ENLIGHTENING EXPERIENCE FOR a historical scholar whose typical unit of chronological measurement is a century (in my case, indeed, the twenty centuries of the development of Christian doctrine) to work closely with a group of colleagues who, quite literally, "take it one day at a time"—the etymological root of the English word *journalism* is the French word *jour*—and in the process to enrich (or at any rate, to enlarge) my vocabulary with such more or less euphonious neologisms as *the CNN effect* and *bloggers*.

But when, in the final sentence of the first chapter of her *Pride and Prejudice,* Jane Austen says of the "invariably silly" Mrs. Bennet, "The business of her life was to get her daughters married; its solace was visiting and *news*,"[1] she is not using the word *news* in the journalistic sense in which it is being used throughout this volume, but in the sense of gossip, pure and simple (although, to paraphrase Oscar Wilde, gossip is not often pure and often not simple). Moving now to the opposite end of the nineteenth century and to the opposite end of Europe: when, in the eighth and final part of *Anna Karenina,* which performs some of the same philosophizing and moralizing function as the more notorious "epilogue" of his *War and Peace* does, Leo Tolstoy has Prince Alexander Dimitrievich Shcherbatsky grumble, "It's the newspapers that all say the same thing. That's true. And it's so much the same that it's like frogs before a thunderstorm. You can't hear anything on account of them,"[2] he obviously is speaking about journalists. With its echoes of the choruses of the comedy *The Frogs* by Aristophanes, this denunciation of journalistic chatter as the cacophony of "frogs before a thunderstorm" is an indication of the growing prominence of newspapers in Tsarist Russia during the second half of the nineteenth century.³ It is, moreover, an idiosyncratic and rather crotchety expression of the critical and self-critical attitude toward the press that comes through in most of the chapters, both by working journalists and by scholars of the press, that make up this volume.

Yet the most remarkable journalistic statistic that I have encountered during these years of participating in the preparation of this volume and in the work of the Commission on the Press that produced it did not in fact come from any of the scholarly books of the professors or any of the analytic articles of the journalists, but from the biography of the racehorse Seabiscuit. At the end of 1938, the year that would "live in infamy" in our Slovak American household because of the Munich Pact and the sellout of Czechoslovakia by England and France, "when the number of newspaper column inches devoted to public figures was tallied up, it was announced that the little horse had drawn more newspaper coverage in 1938 than Roosevelt, who was second, Hitler (third), Mussolini (fourth), or any other newsmaker. His match with War Admiral was almost certainly the single biggest news story of the year,"⁴ bigger apparently than Munich. That statistic raises with dramatic force an issue that is touched upon explicitly several times in this volume and implicitly throughout: the relation of news to entertainment, including what Robert G. Picard calls "mindless entertainment." In principle there would probably be wide agreement that it is important for both the press and the public not to confuse the two, and therefore not to allow sensationalism and titillation to skew the amount and the kind of attention that a story receives. But from the trial of Bruno Hauptmann for the kidnap-murder of the Lindbergh baby to the O. J. Simpson trial to whatever may be the sensation du jour during the week when this volume is published, that is repeatedly what has happened. As James T. Hamilton points out in his chapter, "The Market and the Media," "since the 1970s news coverage has shifted to an increasing emphasis on what people want to know and away from information that they may need as voters." Here it is helpful to retain the historical perspective that informs several of the chapters, from which it becomes evident that periodically throughout its history the press has been willing to sacrifice its primary responsibility to the idols of voyeurism and the marketplace, and at least sometimes no less flagrantly than it has in recent decades.

As its appearance several times in various chapters suggests, "the marketplace" has become, especially in the expanded formula "the marketplace of ideas," a key metaphor for defining the context and the mission of the press as an institution of democracy. It owes its currency in considerable measure to a celebrated dissenting opinion of Supreme Court Justice Oliver Wendell Holmes, Jr., issued in 1919: "When men have realized that time has upset many fighting faiths, they may come to believe even more than they believe the very foundations of their own conduct that the ultimate good desired is better reached by free trade in ideas—that the best test of truth is the power of the thought to get itself accepted in the competition of the market, and *that* truth is the only ground upon which their wishes safely can be carried out."[5] Justice Holmes had articulated this relativistic understanding of truth and of law even before being appointed to the Supreme Court, in the chilling axiom, formulated half a century before Hitler and the Nazis would come to power, that "the first requirement of a sound body of law is that it should correspond with the actual feelings and demands of the community, *right or wrong.*"[6]

More broadly, to be sure, "the marketplace" is a way of talking here about what sells newspapers. One of the deepest concerns voiced in *A Free and Responsible Press,* the report of the Commission on Freedom of the Press chaired by Robert Maynard Hutchins of the University of Chicago in the 1940s, was the fear, as it had been formulated by William Allen White, Pulitzer Prize–winning editor of the *Emporia (Kansas) Gazette,* that newspapers "have veered from their traditional position as leaders of public opinion to mere peddlers and purveyors of news," with the result that "the newspapers have become commercial enterprises and hence fall into the current which is merging commercial enterprises along mercantile lines."[7] More than half a century, and dozens of media mergers—and hundreds of millions of television receivers—later, the authors of several of these chapters believe that there is more reason than ever to fear the influence of the invisible hand of commerce and of advertising on the identification, selection, interpretation, and distribution of what is deemed newsworthy, and therefore to ask, in the words of Robert G. Picard, "how to ensure that democratic functions are served by commercial enterprises." All of these developments have been accompanied meanwhile by a rising wave of public cynicism both about the press itself and about the political process it reports (or sometimes fails to report adequately). "An old-time journalist finds it a matter of sorrow," the veteran Daniel Schorr observes, "that the press, at the height of its influence, is at a depth of its public approval."

Central to that "crisis," which, as the historical chapters of this volume explain, is by no means unprecedented, is the second component of the title of the report by the Hutchins Commission. Although it was a "Commission on Freedom of the Press" that Hutchins had assembled in response to the urging and the funding of Henry Luce, founder-publisher of *Time* magazine, the report incorporates, in its title and throughout, the moral imperative of "a responsible press," to counterbalance the seemingly constant drumming on the demand for "a free press." The two do not necessarily go together; nor is it accurate, several of these chapters properly remind us, to suppose that the traditional American systems for ordering the relation of "free press" to "responsible press" in a democratic society are the only ones. Yet James Carey has been quoted as observing, on the basis of considerable experience, that "to raise any ethical question with journalists is to invite the response that the First Amendment is being violated in even considering the issue."

The most important such ethical question is, of course, the question of fairness, honesty, and objectivity. It may be, as Mitchell Stephens and David T. Z. Mindich put it, that "journalism has remained the last redoubt of the nineteenth-century faith in realism," in a "postmodern" intellectual climate where social scientists, historians, and sometimes even natural scientists have begun to give up on it as a naive and unattainable ideal. But the new discovery—or, at least sometimes, the reluctant admission—that everyone has a viewpoint and that this viewpoint does inevitably affect how one reports on the stock market or on baseball or on an election can have the effect of making any effort at meeting the standard of fairness or objectivity seem to be only an illusion at best, and a delusion at worst. It can have that effect, but it need not have it. As the standard of objectivity was formulated in the course of the discussions of all five of the commissions of the Sunnylands Institutions of American Democracy project, and specifically in those of the Commission on the Press, it can be defined functionally as meaning the following: that even and especially in news articles that reflect the political or philosophical presuppositions of the writer it should be possible for a reader to find the narrative and the data (if any) on which a different set of conclusions and an opposing view could also be based. The special situation of the press in time of war is the particular topic of William Prochnau's chapter, in which he quotes the classic paradox of Winston Churchill: "In wartime truth is so precious that she should always be attended by a bodyguard of lies," which highlights unforgettably the practical complexity and the moral ambiguity even of the standard of journalistic honesty.

In part, the issue of standards is also tied to the repeated efforts in this volume to answer the question whether journalism should be defined as a "profession." Whatever other components there may be to such a definition, among them the forming of professional associations and the definition of agreed-upon professional norms of conduct, it does seem that to qualify as a profession a field of activity, including the preparation of its future practitioners, ought to have been the subject of systematic and ordered, even philosophic, reflection about its nature and goals as well as about its standards, and that such critical reflection ought to have produced a substantial scholarly literature and the intellectual debate that goes with the development of such a body of literature.

For the relation of journalism as a profession to American constitutional democracy, that reflective literature has been shaped above all by the debates and research dealing with the First Amendment to the Constitution, which, in addition to the chapter directly about it by Bruce W. Sanford and Jane E. Kirtley, is cited and discussed here in one chapter after another. That is not surprising, in view of the striking circumstance that, in words of Justice Potter Stewart from 1975 that are quoted here both with and without attribution, "The publishing business is . . . the only private business that is given explicit constitutional protection." It is intriguing, and perhaps also significant, to note that practically without exception these various chapters quote the First Amendment with ellipsis points as: "Congress shall make no law . . . abridging the freedom of speech, or of the press." The full text of the First Amendment of course reads this way: "Congress shall make no law respecting an establishment of religion, or prohibiting the free exercise thereof; or abridging the freedom of speech, or of the press; or the right of the people peaceably to assemble, and to petition the Government for a redress of grievances." Supreme Court justices Robert Jackson and Harry Blackmun laid great emphasis on the heavy symbolism of the "firstness" of the First Amendment within the Bill of Rights as a whole.[8] The significance of the "firstness" within the First Amendment of the freedom of religion, with its matching and carefully balanced prohibition of "establishment" and protection of "free exercise," has, however, been less clear. In 1938, for example, the Supreme Court could protect the right of the Jehovah's Witnesses to distribute their tracts on the basis of the freedom of expression rather than of the freedom of religion, treating such evangelistic literature therefore as one species among others of protected print rather than as a "free exercise" of religious faith.[9] At the very least, the firstness of the establishment clause and the free exercise clause, coming before there is any mention of these other freedoms, would seem to suggest that for the freedom of speech, of the press, and of assembly, too, the First Amendment is extending to those other forms of expression, whether printed or oral, its original and fundamental condemnation of "prohibiting the free exercise thereof."

Even with all these protections and with all this appropriate emphasis on its "responsible" position, it is difficult to avoid the impression that is voiced by Geneva Overholser and Kathleen Hall Jamieson, the editors of this volume, in their introduction, that "maybe the press is being asked to do too much, making up for problems in education, government, and civil life"—as well as in the family and organized religion. With its privileged position among private businesses of being the only one enjoying explicit constitutional protection, the press is nevertheless only one of the several "institutions of democracy." For there are some things it does not do very well. For example, Aristotle rightly recognized that he had to embed the teachings of his *Politics* in the larger and more profound context of his *Ethics,* relating the exercise of the public virtues to the cultivation of the private virtues overall.[10] Where there does not exist a general agreement about the ethical context, whether religious or even secular, as does seem to be the case in contemporary Western societies including our own, discourse about politics, including the discourse of the press about the politics of constitutional democracy, is often called upon to provide it. That may be understandable, but the results are frequently quite dismaying and shallow. A newspaper article, even an op-ed column or a Web site, is no substitute for the classic definitions of the moral life as we have inherited them from masters like Aristotle or Augustine or Maimonides.

Not only does the practice of democracy have its ethical and philosophical foundations, moreover, but its grounding in an educated citizenry is indispensable to its thoughtful exercise. It would sometimes be amusing, if it were not more often depressing, to watch some of the attempts of the press and other media, well meaning though they undoubtedly are, to fill that particular vacuum. If the two academic subjects most fundamental to an educated citizenry in American democracy are history and civics, including at least a basic literacy about the Constitution, years of neglect and mountains of ignorance are too massive an obstacle for sound bites to overcome them. This series includes a volume on the schools as institutions of democracy, because the twin tasks of educating the young and reeducating their elders in the rights and responsibilities of the civic life are central to the mission of the schools. In that mission, to be sure, the schools can collaborate also with the press and other media, as various experiments in various school systems have been documenting in highly gratifying and effective ways—and as the teaching materials being prepared in support of each of the five volumes of Institutions of American Democracy are also demonstrating. But it takes time and teaching to lay these foundations. By themselves, the media cannot do the job, and it is unfair to lay it on them. Once the foundations are there, the ongoing deliberations are an assignment that the media can, and at least sometimes do, handle superbly.

Surely it is not merely a symptom of the preoccupation of our time with electronic gadgetry when several of these chapters address the opportunities and the temptations that have come to the press through technological progress. Even superficial attention to the historical setting of the First Amendment will show that "the press," whose freedom it seeks to protect against abridgement, was a very specific kind of machine, associated with the technological prowess and entrepreneurial genius of Benjamin Franklin. Of the many stages in the technology of communication since that time as it has decisively shaped the history of successive understandings of the press, three from the twentieth century seem to be most on the minds of the authors of these chapters: radio, television, and the Internet.

Foundational to the other two was the development of radio, from the experiments of Marconi to the evolution of the great international shortwave stations and longwave broadcast networks. Perhaps I may be permitted a personal reminiscence here. Ever since early boyhood I have always had a shortwave radio of some kind. My father had long been an avid listener, so that my first conscious memory of a public event was of him rushing into my room shouting (in Slovak), "The young man has made it!" when Charles A. Lindbergh crossed the Atlantic in May of 1927. During the mid-1930s, while I was intensely studying German and coming of age with at least an elementary grasp of international relations, it was the shortwave radio that gave me a sense of direct contact with both. The speeches of Adolf Hitler on "Kurzwellensender Berlin" introduced me for the first time to the demonic power of rhetoric; and then the gutturals of Winston Churchill as (in Edward R. Murrow's phrase) he marshaled the English language and sent it to war, supplied me with its antidote. As several of these chapters observe, President Franklin Delano Roosevelt, in those same years, was creating a whole new modality of the relation between communication and democracy, in ways for which many of us are still nostalgic. Radio was also responsible for a decisive shift in the legal and constitutional standing of the press. For although postal subsidies had long been a way for government to give indirect aid to newspapers and magazines, the need to assign radio frequencies as a scarce *public* resource meant that government, by granting or withholding a license, could exercise a new and powerful control.

With the advent of television journalism, the motto "You are there!" (title of a popular series) acquired a new immediacy, but the competition and the confusion between news and entertainment reached new levels of complexity. Historians of the media, and of their relation to the functioning of democracy, have focused considerable attention on the Vietnam War as a laboratory. The polemics of those politicians who blamed the media for having manipulated public disaffection with the war must certainly be rejected as oversimplified; but the fundamental change in the manner and the mode of war coverage, evident in the transition from Ernie Pyle in the press and Edward R. Murrow on the air to the indelible scenes, now visible in every living room during prime time, of bombing and carnage did represent a genuine case of Thomas Kuhn's brilliant but by now somewhat hackneyed concept of "paradigm shift."

Yet clearly that shift was nothing to compare with the effect of the Internet. This is due in considerable measure to its interactive possibilities, which, in conjunction with modern sophisticated polling techniques, raise the prospect—hopeful sign or specter, depending on one's interpretation—of an ongoing day-by-day referendum on the issues of the day or a rolling plebiscite, a kind of electronic town meeting (24-7, as the buzz word says), as a new institution of a new democracy. What this would mean, what it already does mean, for the future of constitutional *representative* democracy is one of the most troubling questions coming out of this entire enterprise.

Notes

1. Jane Austen, *Pride and Prejudice* (1813), edited by Tony Tanner (New York: Penguin Classics, 1985), 53; italics added.
2. Leo Tolstoy, *Anna Karenina* (1875–77), translated by Richard Pevear and Larissa Volokhonsky (New York: Viking, 2001), 808.
3. Louise McReynolds, *The News under Russia's Old Regime: The Development of a Mass-Circulation Press* (Princeton, N.J.: Princeton University Press, 1991).
4. Laura Hillenbrand, *Seabiscuit: An American Legend* (New York: Ballantine, 2002), 284–85.

5. Oliver Wendell Holmes, Jr., dissenting, *Abrams v. United States,* 250 U.S. 630 (1919); italics added for clarification.

6. Oliver Wendell Holmes, Jr., *The Common Law* (London: Macmillan, 1881), 41; italics added for emphasis.

7. Commission on Freedom of the Press, *A Free and Responsible Press; A General Report on Mass Communication: Newspapers, Radio, Motion Picture, Magazines, and Books,* edited by Robert D. Leigh (Chicago: University of Chicago Press, 1947), 60.

8. Quoted in Akhil Reed Amar, *The Bill of Rights: Creation and Reconstruction* (New Haven, Conn.: Yale University Press, 1998), 257.

9. Chief Justice Charles Evans Hughes, for the Court, *Lovell v. City of Griffin,* 303 U.S. 444 (1938), 450–52.

10. Werner Jaeger, *Aristotle: Fundamentals of the History of His Development,* translated by Richard Robinson, 2nd ed. (Oxford, U.K.: Clarendon, 1948), 275–77.

INTRODUCTION

Geneva Overholser and Kathleen Hall Jamieson

O N A STEAMY JULY MORNING IN 2003, AN UNLIKELY gathering assembled at the University of Pennsylvania to talk about the press as an institution of American democracy. The unlikeliness lay in this fact: Among the fifty convened by the Annenberg Foundation Trust at Sunnylands for an intensive two days of discussion were two groups more accustomed to critiquing one another than to joining forces. Here were scholars who have spent their careers studying journalism, and journalists who have spent theirs practicing it. The commingling was purposeful. This volume's coeditors, in putting together the commission that produced the work, sought to synthesize the best thinking from several different academic disciplines—and to ground it in the practical experience of longtime editors, reporters, and broadcasters. It worked. The discussions revealed a deepening awareness on the part of the journalists of just how much enrichment lay in the thoughtful analysis the scholars brought to bear. The scholars, for their part, saw more clearly than ever the complexities of the challenges facing the media, and the passion in the journalists' attempts to respond.

All agreed that this moment in American journalism and, indeed, in American democracy, is a critical one. The group struggled with such questions as: Is journalism necessary for an informed citizenry? What *kind* of journalism is essential to democracy? How can that journalism be sustained? They discussed the relationship between the press and government, and how the public and the press view one another. Does journalism give citizens the information they need, in a way that they can use it? "Journalism is the means," said one participant. "The end is democracy." Yet journalism is "a quasi profession trapped in a market-driven business," said another, citing an irreconcilable conflict between the economics of journalism and its mission. No, said a third: "The practice of journalism doesn't have to be lodged in the industry." But what are the responsibilities of "the big media powers"? And what of the relative powerlessness of journalists themselves, with only some 6 percent belonging to even the largest professional organization? What about government's interest in controlling information? And the disruptiveness—as well as the promise—of new technologies?

On that first day of the commission's work, the air-conditioning broke down but the talk never flagged. How do we measure how well the press is doing? How might successes be spotlighted? How can the public be made aware of the challenges confronting the press? "In this age of media plenty, a citizen has to work harder for civic knowledge," said one commission member. How does U.S. hegemony affect citizens' need to know? What does the shift of power toward a transnational, corporate system mean for journalism? Maybe the press is being asked to do too much, making up for problems in education, government, and civic life.

The goal, the group agreed, was a thorough examination of the role of journalism and its impact on American democracy at the beginning of the twenty-first century. By the second meeting, six months later in the drier and cooler climes of Rancho Mirage, California, chapter drafts had been prepared. Another two days of lively debate ensued, followed by months of polishing, merging, adding, and eliminating.

Four sections emerged, and four distinguished experts agreed to edit them. Michael Schudson, a historian, communication scholar, and sociologist, supervised the writing of the essays in the section that orients the volume. Timothy Cook, a political scientist who studies the relationship of government and the news, superintended the essays on the functions of the press. The presidential communication scholar Martha Joynt Kumar edited the essays on government and the press, and the journalism scholar Theodore Glasser was responsible for the final section, on the structure of the press. Each section is introduced by a brief essay written by the section editor. We are particularly grateful to these exceptional scholars for their hard work, and we thank each of the commission's participants for their contributions.

THE PRESS

ORIENTATIONS: THE PRESS AND DEMOCRACY IN TIME AND SPACE

Michael Schudson

THREE COMMON PITFALLS MUST BE AVOIDED IN SEEKING to understand American journalism and its relationship to democracy. First, it is important to recognize that there are multiple types of American journalism, with multiple purposes, diverse audiences, and varying relationships to democracy. It is a mistake to identify American journalism exclusively with the dominant mainstream–television–network news and high-circulation metropolitan daily newspapers. This error is compounded if, in examining these dominant news outlets, attention is paid exclusively to leading hard-news reporting, and features, editorials, news analysis, opinion columns, and other elements of the journalistic mix are ignored. In this section, the essays by Robert Entman, Pamela Newkirk, and Barbie Zelizer warn us away from this tendency.

Entman's essay distinguishes among the commitments, values, contents of, and audiences for, four different types of journalism—traditional mainstream journalism, advocacy journalism, tabloid journalism, and entertainment journalism. Clearly, as Entman observes, it is rare to find a "pure type" of any of these forms. But we are perfectly able to categorize most news outlets as falling predominantly into one category or another. Newkirk reminds us that in the United States, ethnic and racial minorities have historically produced newspapers and, more recently, television, radio, and Internet news by and for their own communities. Some of these news organizations have had huge audiences; some of them with small circulations have nonetheless had enormous influence. Newkirk focuses in particular on the African American press, with some attention to Native American, Latino, and various Asian American media outlets as well. And she insists on the importance of the advocacy role of this press. Zelizer's essay on how journalism is defined takes on the same problem from another angle, noting how much the "definition" of journalism is a work in progress, one that has favored some versions of journalism over others, and that in its canonized form misleadingly represents one version of journalism as the whole of journalism. She calls attention to the variety of definitions of journalism and metaphors for the journalistic enterprise that are in active use by both journalists and journalism scholars.

If the first error is to consider mainstream conventional journalism as the only "legitimate" journalism, the second error is to limit one's understanding of journalism to present-day American journalism, a view that is obviously provincial. Even if we confine our attention to democratic societies globally, there are various types of journalism—and various democracies. This point is well made in the chapter by Daniel Hallin and Robert Giles, who compare three separate democratic media systems (and variations within them) in the liberal democratic world today. Understanding journalism in a democracy requires an understanding of the different ways that the news media are integrated in or intersect with different democratic party systems, electoral systems, and political cultures. Meanwhile, Michael Schudson and Susan Tifft demonstrate that the character of American journalism has changed from colonial days to the present, moving from a determinedly apolitical adjunct to the printing business in the colonial world, to a vibrantly and sometimes viciously partisan subdivision of political parties for much of the nineteenth century, to a twentieth-century model shaped by both commercial pressures for profit and professional efforts at nonpartisan reporting—and the tension between these forces. Together, these two essays help to locate the distinctive features of contemporary American journalism by placing them in comparative and historical perspective.

There is a third error that Americans are particularly likely to commit, and in this case a non-American, John Keane, points it out: American journalism today is not cordoned off from the rest of the world but is shaped increasingly by the forces of globalization. This is true, Keane emphasizes, not only because of technological and economic relationships that span national borders, but because of the growing presence of an international civil society; that is, transnational discussions and transnational organizations of people are building a new moral framework within which journalism operates. The forces of globalization are complex, and at the turn of the twenty-first century the extent of a "globalized" experience and "globalized" access to information omitted some two-thirds of the peoples of the world, but Keane nonetheless offers an optimistic assessment of how globalization might enrich the connections between journalism and democracy—might indeed make journalism more important for democracy than ever before.

There are many ways to be parochial. Americans, unconsciously arrogant because we live in what is temporarily the most powerful nation on the planet, adopt all of them. We tend to think that we invented the world, and just yesterday. We tend to think that the First Amendment is the only mechanism for the protection of free speech and the press and that other democracies, without it, must be deficient (rather than different). Those who teach journalism and work in news organizations are likewise parochial in evaluating some forms of news as better than others, even when we do not know in fact if "hard news" or news analysis, or investigative reporting, or soft features, or editorials, or advocacy publications, or political satire and jokes are best at communicating significantly with the public and fostering a desirable quality, quantity, and diversity of public discourse and informed decision-making.

Any volume appears at a particular moment in time and cannot help but be influenced by that moment. But it will not serve us well to presume, without evidence, that journalism is in crisis. We need to avoid writing as part of a moral panic—as if we were members of a religious cult walking up and down the street with signs reading "The End [of journalism] Is at Hand!" It is not. Journalism is changing. There are some forces, particularly in the advent of computer communications, the abundance of cable television, and the global interconnectedness of communications, that clearly signal powerful change, but so did the telegraph, the transatlantic cable, and the first wire services with a global reach, all emerging in the same thirty-odd years in the mid-nineteenth century. It is not that there is nothing new under the sun. It is just that we are not in a very good seat to see which of the social changes of the past five or ten or twenty-five years is likely to seem earth-shattering several decades from now. And maybe these changes are not shattering the earth so much as reshaping it.

1

PRESSES AND DEMOCRACIES

Daniel C. Hallin and Robert Giles

O N MARCH 14, 1982, THE FRONT PAGE OF *LE MONDE* WAS
dedicated mainly to a decline in the value of the franc. A brief summary of the facts (which French journalists call the *chapeau,* or "hat"),
including comments from principal political figures, appeared below the headline, along with two articles. One began like this:

> The franc will not be able to avoid a certain amount of "seasickness."
> But the defense of its parity has become an imperative for the govern-
> ment. This is the thing that is perhaps most difficult for those who
> brought Mr. Mitterrand to power to understand. How can a politics of
> social justice and expansion be shackled by "speculators" or by faceless
> international bankers, who govern through their strange balances the
> destiny of currencies?
>   It is necessary to leave behind this infantile mythology. . . .

The article cited not a single source, nor did it report any particular event or
fact. Like the other article that followed the *chapeau,* it was from beginning to
end a political argument, addressed by the journalists to the readers, the majority
of whom could be presumed to be among those who put the Socialist prime
minister François Mitterrand in power. It featured long paragraphs, complex,
stylish language, and, like several of the other articles on the front page, footnotes.
This randomly selected issue of the leading French newspaper is more or less
typical of the French national press of the period.

News media around the world vary considerably in their styles, structures,
and social and political roles. The differences are less dramatic in 2004 than they
were a generation ago. "Globalization" has resulted in a considerable degree of
homogenization of media systems, as a similar, mainly commercial structure and
a common culture of journalism have increasingly spread around the world.
However, the differences among media systems continue to be striking.

Until recently, media scholars had done little to understand the nature of these differences or the reasons they exist. The study of journalism has always had a tight relationship to professional education, and has focused heavily on normative models, models of what journalism "should be," rather than of what it is and why. The weakness of comparative research in communication is illustrated by the reality that *Four Theories of the Press,* the classic text by Fred Siebert, Theodore Peterson, and Wilbur Schramm, is still influential, despite many critiques directed against it over the years. Written in the 1950s, it proposed four models of "what the media should be and do": the "authoritarian," "libertarian," "social responsibility," and "communist" models. The two models that apply to democratic systems, the libertarian and social responsibility models, both had their roots in U.S. journalism, and have not been very useful for understanding variations among democratic systems. They tell us little about why *Le Monde* seems so different from the major metropolitan American newspaper; both would have to be considered examples of the "social responsibility" model, which sees the press as bound by ethical obligations to the reading public.

It would not be productive to re-create *Four Theories of the Press*—that is, to develop a global classification scheme for world media systems—even if we confined ourselves to democratic systems. Too little substantive comparative research has been done on most of the world's media systems to provide a basis for any such scheme. But we will try here to offer an overview of the kinds of media systems that evolved in the countries on which there is the most extensive research, those primarily of Europe and North America.[1] In doing so, we hope also to illustrate more generally the differences that exist among media systems and the ways in which these differences are connected with other characteristics of political and social systems, and with differences in political and social history.

Western Media Systems

In general terms, we can identify three models of media systems in the Western world:

1. The liberal model, which finds its purest expression in the United States, but also prevails in modified form in Britain and other former British colonies such as Ireland, Canada, Australia, and New Zealand.
2. The "polarized pluralist" model, borrowing a term from comparative politics, which prevails in southern European countries that had relatively long and conflicted transitions from feudalism and patrimonialism to capitalism and representative democracy. This is a characteristic they share with most of the rest of the world.

3. The "democratic corporatist" model (again borrowing a term from comparative politics), which prevails in northern and central European countries that are characterized by strong welfare states and political systems based on compromises among highly organized social groups.

These systems differ from one another in many ways, but four major dimensions are worth identifying:

1. The emergence of a mass-circulation press. True mass-circulation newspapers developed only in a few places in the world, mainly northern Europe, North America, and parts of East Asia. In other regions, electronic media became the first real mass media, while newspapers remain an elite medium that reaches a relatively small audience, usually one engaged in the world of politics.
2. The degree and nature of state involvement in the media.
3. The degree of "political parallelism." The term "party-press" parallelism has been used for many years to refer to the degree to which the structure of the media system is organized along the same lines as the political party system, with different news organizations reflecting the views of different parties. This is also referred to as "external pluralism." Political parallelism can involve actual organizational relationships between media and political parties, but this is not always the case. Even commercial papers often reflect partisan affinities in their content, in their recruitment of journalists, and in the political preferences of their readerships. The number of newspapers with close connections to a single political party is smaller today than in the past, but in many countries, media organizations still reflect different political tendencies; hence the broader term "political parallelism."
4. The degree of professionalization. The notion of journalism as a "profession" has always been contested, but we define it here in terms of three characteristics: the degree to which journalism develops a distinct set of values and standards of practice, separate from those of other areas of social life (e.g., standards of newsworthiness distinct from those that arise out of party politics); the degree of autonomy that journalists exercise in managing news operations; and the degree to which journalists see themselves as trustees serving "the public good" rather than particular interests. As we shall see, professionalization of journalism can be centered in formal institutions such as professional associations and press councils, or it can be embedded in the traditions, norms, and routines of news organizations.

The Liberal Model

The liberal model is distinguished primarily by three closely interrelated characteristics. First, commercial newspapers developed early and displaced other forms of media that, as we shall see, played more central roles in other media systems. Second, state intervention in the media system is limited compared with other systems. Third, a strong form of journalistic professionalism developed in the liberal system, centered around the "objectivity norm"—the idea that journalists should be politically neutral and separated from attachments to political parties and organized social groups. The degree of political parallelism is thus low.

The liberal model finds its purest expression in the United States. A commercial newspaper industry began to develop in the United States in the 1830s, earlier than in any other country. Commercial newspapers displaced newspapers connected with political parties or other organized social groups; this contrasts, as we shall see, with other systems where newspapers developed more as a part of the world of politics than the world of business. In the twentieth century, the United States was the only country to develop a primarily commercial broadcasting system. Until recently, most other economically advanced democracies depended upon public broadcasting systems. In most of these countries, public broadcasting remains a significant institution. Typically, public broadcasting has a 30 percent to 40 percent share of the television audience, compared with 2 percent in the United States.

The role of the state is complex in the United States as it is everywhere in the world. It would be inaccurate to say that the state has historically played no significant role in the development of the U.S. media system. The federal government built the postal system on which early newspapers depended, and provided such subsidies as printing contracts and jobs for editors, which were critical to the economic stability of the commercial press in the first half of the nineteenth century. In the twentieth century, broadcasting developed as a federally regulated industry. The state played an important role in the expansion of global media markets for U.S. firms, the development of the Internet, and in many other ways. Still, government's role is limited compared with other democracies: public broadcasting reaches a small but significant audience compared with commercial network and cable outlets, subsidies to the press are marginal today, and the legal tradition of the First Amendment bars forms of regulation that are typical in other systems. Right-of-reply laws, for example, are common in many democracies, as are regulations banning paid political advertising in favor of free airtime for party broadcasts; such regulations have been considered unconstitutional in the United States.

The government's limited role as owner, funder, and regulator of the media in liberal systems does not necessarily mean that the state has less influence on media content. Though the "watchdog" role of checking government power is certainly part of liberal media culture, research on Anglo-American media has often made the point that the media have evolved, in Douglass Cater's words, as a kind of fourth branch of government,[2] and that official influence on the news agenda and how stories are framed is considerable. A significant influence in the relationship between government and the press is that the United States and Britain are world powers that have histories dating to World War II of voluntary cooperation between state and media in time of conflict.

Finally, a strong form of professionalism has evolved in U.S. journalism centered on such norms as "objectivity," balance, and fairness, as well as other ethical norms. These norms became consolidated by about the mid-twentieth century, gradually limiting the role of powerful newspaper owners such as William Randolph Hearst and Robert McCormick, who used their newspapers for partisan political purposes. Journalists came to see their role as detached observers, providing information to readers and viewers on a "nonpartisan" basis. The kind of external pluralism that characterizes the press in other systems, where news organizations reflect ideological tendencies, has mostly disappeared from the U.S. press. One study by the American political scientist Thomas Patterson and the German communication researcher Wolfgang Donsbach surveyed journalists in the United States, Britain, Sweden, Germany, and Italy, asking them to place political parties and news organizations on a Left–Right scale in their respective countries.[3] In all the European countries, journalists placed the media over a wide spectrum, wider, in fact, than the spectrum of parties. In the United States they placed all the news organizations in a narrow band between the Republican and Democratic parties. One exception to the political neutrality of the United States through much of the twentieth century was the ethnic press, particularly the black press, which served readers not addressed by the mainstream commercial press.

The United States shares this pattern with Britain and some former British colonies, though the common practice of speaking of an "Anglo-American" model of journalism is a bit misleading. Britain shares many media characteristics with the United States: the commercial press became dominant relatively early in Britain; commercial television was introduced earlier than in most countries; the state does not subsidize newspapers; and the journalistic culture places heavy emphasis on information and narrative rather than political commentary (of the sort that has historically characterized the French press). In other ways, it is quite different and looks more like continental European systems. It has one of the strongest public broadcasting systems in the world. British newspapers also exhibit a high level of party-press parallelism—the term actually originated in Britain—with a media market that reflects the major political divisions in society. British tabloids are actually as partisan as newspapers anywhere in Europe; in 1997, for example, the *Daily Mirror,* the only tabloid that normally supports the

Labour Party, devoted most of its political content to Tony Blair's election campaign; even the "page three girls" (scantily clad models) became " Blair babes," who told readers each day why they were voting Labour. The objectivity norm mainly applies, in the British case, to broadcasting, which is legally required to observe "due impartiality" in news coverage.

Two factors may explain the higher level of political parallelism in the British press. First, the British political system is characterized by more unified, ideologically distinct parties, rooted in divisions of social class. Second, the British newspaper market is a competitive national market. Politically neutral newspapers tend to develop in monopoly or near-monopoly markets, such as in the United States in the mid-twentieth century, where the press is mainly local rather than national. In more competitive markets, media often differentiate themselves by appealing to particular political orientations. This is beginning to happen in the cable television market in the United States with the emergence of FOX News as a politically distinct voice, although there is no evidence at this time that CNN, MSNBC, or network news organizations will follow.

The Polarized Pluralist Model

A significantly different media system from that embraced by the liberal-model states evolved across the Mediterranean countries of Europe. The press in southern Europe emerged more as a part of the worlds of literature and of politics than of the market. Commercial media industries were established only near the end of the twentieth century, and newspapers remained primarily vehicles for expression of ideas and for intervention in the political realm. Mass-circulation newspapers did not develop in southern Europe, except for the sports press and weekly human-interest magazines directed at women. The Italian journalist Enzo Forcella wrote in a famous essay in the 1950s that the audience for political journalism in Italy consisted of "fifteen hundred readers," including top politicians, business leaders, and members of the clergy. More market-oriented newspapers began to develop in the 1970s, but their readers are still a relatively small percent of the public, well educated, urban, politically engaged, and considerably more male than female. As the Italian scholar Paolo Mancini has put it, newspapers in southern Europe are engaged more in a process of horizontal communication among political elites than in a vertical process of mediating between elites and the mass public.[4]

The state has generally played an interventionist role in the media systems of southern Europe. Through much of the history of the region it has been a censor, reflecting long periods of dictatorship. Since the transition to democracy, the state has continued to have some ownership control of media, sometimes through state-owned companies such as the Italian oil company ENI, whose director founded the newspaper *Il Giorno*. State subsidies for the press and state involvement in the financing of newspaper sales are also common practices. On the other hand, the welfare state is weaker in parts of southern Europe than in northern Europe, and political factionalism and clientelism tend to reduce the effectiveness of state regulation. Public broadcasting is relatively weak in Portugal, Spain, and Greece, and in Italy, Silvio Berlusconi built a commercial television empire during a long period when the Italian state was unable to agree on a system of media regulation.

Political parallelism is high in southern Europe. When Eugenio Scalfari started the tabloid newspaper *La Repubblica* in the 1970s, it was seen as a pioneering entry into the market-oriented form of journalism that began to develop during that period. In the first issue of the new paper (June 14, 1976), Scalfari wrote, "This newspaper is a bit different from others: it is a journal of information that doesn't pretend to follow an illusory political neutrality, but declares explicitly that it has taken a side in the political battle. It is made by men who belong to the vast arc of the Italian left."

Spain, meanwhile, is one of the few countries in the Western world where newspaper sales have increased in recent decades; at the same time, the Spanish media, print and broadcast, have become increasingly divided into two political camps, one close to the Socialist party and one close to the right-of-center Popular Party. Newspaper owners and journalists in southern Europe customarily have political alliances, although this is less true of younger journalists, who are more influenced by a global media culture based on the liberal model. The role of the press in democracy has traditionally been conceived in southern Europe not in terms of providing information to individual citizen-consumers, but in terms of the process of bargaining among political factions. The latter are numerous, and the press is quite diverse politically.

Journalistic professionalism, as defined above, is not as deeply rooted in the polarized pluralist system. This does not mean that journalists in southern Europe are not good at what they do, or that they lack education or prestige. Journalism has been an elite occupation in southern Europe, at least at the top of the media hierarchy. The quality of writing and political analysis at papers such as *La Repubblica* and *Corriere della Sera* in Italy, *El Pais* in Spain, and *Le Monde* in France is extremely high, serving an intended audience of well-educated readers. Still, according to the criteria of professionalization introduced above—the emergence of norms and practices distinct to journalism, the autonomy of journalists, and the strength of an ethic of public service—professionalization has developed more slowly, and not as fully, as in other systems. With their historical roots in the worlds of politics and literature, as the Spanish researchers Félix Ortega and M. Luisa Humanes put it, newspapers "valued more highly writers, politicians and intellectuals," and journalism was regarded in Spain until recently as "a secondary occupation, poorly paid, to which one came often as a 'springboard' to a career in politics" or in literature.[5] Writers and editors were political actors above all, and their commitment to strictly journalistic standards of practice, to the extent that these existed, was weaker than their commitment to political factions and principles. Codes of ethics have developed slowly in southern Europe, and the only press council in the region is in Spanish Catalonia. Autonomy is limited; news organizations have often been controlled by actors outside of journalism—political parties (especially in the case of public broadcasting) or businesspeople with political ties who intend to use media outlets for purposes of intervention in politics.

Differences in media systems between southern Europe and the systems of North America and northern Europe are explained by different historical patterns. Liberal institutions, including the press, became dominant early in northern Europe and in North America, especially the United States, which, as the political scientist Louis Hartz pointed out, was "born liberal" rather than undergoing a transition from feudalism.[6] In southern Europe, on the other hand, the institutions of the ancien régime—the monarchy, the landed aristocracy, and the Catholic and Orthodox churches—were powerful forces. The institutions and culture of liberal society—the market, urbanism, literacy, representative democracy—emerged later, out of protracted political conflict. As a result, the political systems of southern Europe moved toward the model that the Italian political scientist Giovanni Sartori called "polarized pluralism," characterized by many parties with sharply conflicting ideologies. In this context, the state and political parties have played a strong role in society, and the media were closely tied to those institutions. Advocacy journalism tended to be the rule, and political neutrality was dismissed as naive or opportunistic. As the media scholar Jean Chalaby puts it, in contrasting Anglo-American journalism with that of France:

> In [the United States and Britain] political struggles were confined within the limits of parliamentary bipartism. Journalists could claim to be "neutral" simply by proclaiming to support neither of the political parties and to be "impartial" by giving an equal amount of attention to both parties. This efficient codification of the political struggle facilitated the development of a discourse based on news and information rather than political opinions. . . . During much of the [French] Third Republic, political positions spanned from communism to royalism. The principles these parties put into question (private property and universal suffrage) were both taken for granted in Washington and London.[7]

France is actually a mixed case in many ways, sharing characteristics of both the polarized pluralist and democratic corporatist models. Journalists at *Le Monde* have a particularly high level of autonomy, as *Le Monde* was originally set up as a journalist-run organization; autonomy is something they share with journalists in the democratic corporatist system. But French journalism historically provided the model for the "journalism of ideas" that prevailed in southern Europe, in contrast to the "journalism of information" that characterizes the United States and Britain.

The Democratic Corporatist Model

In northern continental Europe, yet another media system developed. It is a model that has historically combined characteristics often assumed to be incompatible—in part because assumptions about how media systems "naturally" develop have been influenced by the liberal model. First, the countries of northern and north-central Europe combine strong principles of press freedom with active state intervention in the media. Like the liberal-model countries of the North Atlantic, northern European societies introduced principles of press freedom relatively early, beginning with Sweden in 1766. On the other hand, this region also is characterized by strong welfare states, and by an assumption that the state has a responsibility to intervene in society to promote a variety of social values. This is reflected in strong public broadcasting systems, press subsidies, and relatively strong regulation of media industries.

Second, while commercial media industries developed as strongly in the democratic corporatist states as in the liberal countries, they coexisted in northern Europe with media linked to political parties, religious communities, and trade unions, media whose central purpose was to represent a point of view within society rather than to make money or to provide "neutral" information. This role of the press originated in the religious and political conflicts of the Thirty Years War (1618–1648) and continued through most of the twentieth century. In the 1970s, a Swedish government committee listed the following four functions of the press:

1. To give information to citizens so that they can form views on social questions
2. To comment on events in society either independently or as a representative for organized social groups
3. As a representative of the public, to scrutinize the activities exercised by those holding power in society
4. To promote communication within and between political groups, trade unions, and other voluntary groups in society[8]

This definition combines the liberal view of the press as a "watchdog" on the actions of the government and those in power and as an information provider, and the democratic corporatist view of the press as a representative of groups in civil society.

The democratic-corporatist-model countries—including all of Scandinavia, the Netherlands, Belgium, Germany, Austria, and Switzerland—are characterized by strong political parties and strong, unified organizations representing different segments of society. They share with the liberal-model countries a pattern of historical development in which conservative forces were relatively weak in contrast to liberal forces, represented by small, independent producers such as merchants, artisans, and independent farmers. In this environment, liberal institutions developed early. Where the democratic-corporatist-model countries differ from liberal-model countries like the United States and Britain is in their segmentation into communities divided by religion, social class, and ideology. The term *democratic corporatism* refers to a political system that was created in most of the small countries of northern Europe early in the twentieth century in an effort to prevent polarization and the collapse of democracy. It was a system that rested on the incorporation of organized groups into a process of bargaining and power sharing. (Austria and Germany had histories of greater political polarization, but moved toward the democratic corporatist model after World War II.) News media linked to these social groups served this process of bargaining by reinforcing the internal coherence of these groups, by facilitating their exchange of views in the public sphere, and by building public consensus around the bargains that they reached.

Party and other "representative" newspapers combined with the commercial press to produce extraordinarily high rates of newspaper readership in northern Europe. Newspaper reading became an important component of people's sense of belonging to their own social group. Seven hundred twenty newspapers are sold per 1,000 population in Norway, as compared with 260 per 1,000 in the United States and 120 per 1,000 in Italy. Northern European countries have the highest newspaper readership rates in the world, along with a few East Asian countries, including Japan.

By the end of the twentieth century, the party press and other group-linked media had all but died out, but their legacy survived in the relatively high degree of political parallelism that persists in northern Europe, with different newspapers and, to some degree, different television stations representing different political tendencies.

Finally, the democratic corporatist system combines political parallelism with a high degree of journalistic professionalization. As external pluralism prevailed, with much of the press linked to parties and social groups, journalists have often had political attachments. The role of commentary in their jobs has been more significant than in the liberal system, and they have understood it as their responsibility to report the news from a point of view. At the same time, the level of professionalization is high. Effective norms for journalistic practice evolved in the democratic corporatist countries, which have been received with a solid consensus among journalists, regardless of their political point of view. Journalistic autonomy is the equal of that in the liberal-model countries. Surveys in some countries suggest it may actually be higher; certainly it is more formally recognized as an issue. German journalists, for example, have long pressed for what they call "internal press freedom"; many news organizations in northern

Europe have "editorial statutes" intended to protect the autonomy of professionals within the news organization; in some cases these are mandated by law. There is also an ethic affirming that news organizations should serve society as a whole, and not simply particular interests within it. Though it may seem paradoxical on the surface, as the political scientist Peter Katzenstein notes, democratic corporatism combines ideological diversity with social partnership, and is characterized at all levels by a strong sense of, and commitment to, common norms.[9]

The form of journalistic professionalism that evolved in the democratic corporatist countries differs from that of the liberal system not only because it is less tied to the objectivity norm, but also because it involves a higher level of formal institutionalization. Journalists' unions are strong in northern Europe—consistent with the strength of social organizations in these countries. And most have formalized systems of self-regulation of the media, in the form of press councils, for example. In the 1980s, when the Swedish prime minister Olof Palme was assassinated, Swedish media withheld the name of the suspect through years of legal proceedings, something impossible to imagine in the United States, Britain, or Italy.

Convergence of Media Systems

The differences among the three systems outlined above have diminished considerably over the last decades of the twentieth century. This has resulted in part from the global influence of the liberal model, but it is rooted more deeply in what could be called the "secularization" of European society, the decline of people's attachments to separate religious and ideological "faiths" and of the social organizations once connected with these. It is also related to the expansion of commercial media, particularly since the turn toward neoliberalism and the introduction of commercial television in Europe in the 1980s. One way to characterize this change is to say that media systems in Europe have become less closely related to the world of politics, and more deeply rooted in the market. Some predict an end of media history in which all systems converge toward the liberal model. But that may be too simplistic. Political cultures and political systems still differ considerably, even among the relatively similar countries of North America and western Europe. In southern Europe, attempts to create politically neutral media have generally failed. In northern Europe convergence has gone further, but multiparty political systems, with their significant ideological diversity, are still different from a two-party system, and this continues to affect the practice of journalism and the preferences of readers. European legal systems are also unlikely to adopt the kind of "First Amendment absolutism" that characterizes the United States. In the United States, meanwhile, changes in market structure are leading to a reemergence of political parallelism in the media, and in that sense a convergence toward the pattern of the European media systems.

The changes that have taken place in media systems at the end of the twentieth century have been substantial, and raise important questions about their implications for democracy, questions that are not easy for scholarship to answer. Will the decline of media linked to organized social groups in Europe decrease the diversity of views represented in the public sphere, and lead to greater imbalances in the access of different social groups? Will the level of political knowledge, which is generally higher in Europe than in the United States, decline in a more commercialized system, where public affairs content might not get the emphasis that it once did? And in the United States, as partisan media reemerge, is it possible that the issue of political control by media owners, prominent in the era of the old press barons but less so after the shift toward professionalization, will also reemerge as a central concern?

Notes

1. The analysis presented here is based primarily on Hallin and Mancini, *Comparing Media Systems*. There are a number of works that deal with media systems in other parts of the world, including Chappell H. Lawson, *Building the Fourth Estate: Democratization and the Rise of a Free Press in Mexico* (Berkeley: University of California Press, 2002); Susan J. Pharr and Ellis S. Krauss, eds., *Media and Politics in Japan* (Honolulu: University of Hawaii Press, 1996); Silvio Waisbord, *Watchdog Journalism in South America: News, Accountability, and Democracy* (New York: Columbia University Press, 2000); and Yuezhi Zhao, *Media, Market, and Democracy in China: Between the Party Line and the Bottom Line* (Urbana: University of Illinois Press, 1998).
2. Douglass Cater, *The Fourth Branch of Government* (Boston: Houghton Mifflin, 1959).
3. Thomas E. Patterson and Wolfgang Donsbach, "Press-Party Parallelism: A Cross-National Comparison." Paper presented at the annual meeting of the International Communication Association, Washington, D.C., 1993.
4. Enzo Forcella, "Millecinquecento lettori." *Tempo Presente*, no. 6, 1959; Paolo Mancini, "The Public Sphere and the Use of News in a 'Coalition' System of Government," in *Communication and Citizenship: Journalism and the Public Sphere in the New Media Age*, edited by Peter Dahlgren and Colin Sparks (London and New York: Routledge, 1991), 137–54.
5. Félix Ortega and M. Luisa Humanes, *Algo más que periodistas: Sociología de una profesión* (Barcelona: Editorial Ariel, 2000), 125. (Translated by Dan Hallin and Robert Giles.)
6. Hartz, Louis, *The Liberal Tradition in America*. (New York: Harcourt Brace & World, 1955), 16.
7. Jean K. Chalaby, "Journalism as an Anglo-American Invention: A Comparison of the Development of French and Anglo-American Journalism, 1830's–1920's," *European Journal of Communication* 11, no. 3 (1996): 310.
8. Quoted in Karl-Erik Gustafsson, "The Press Subsidies of Sweden: A Decade of Experiment," in Anthony Smith, ed., *Newspapers and Democracy: International Essays on a Changing Medium* (Cambridge: MIT Press, 1980), 105.

9. Peter J. Katzenstein, *Small States in World Markets: Industrial Policy in Europe* (Ithaca, N.Y.: Cornell University Press, 1985).

Bibliography

Curran, James, and Myung-Jin Park, eds. *De-Westernizing Media Studies*. London and New York: Routledge, 2000. A collection covering many parts of the world, making distinctions between authoritarian and democratic and between neoliberal and regulated societies.

Gunther, Richard, and Anthony Mughan, eds. *Democracy and the Media: A Comparative Perspective*. Cambridge, U.K., and New York: Cambridge University Press, 2000. A collection covering eastern and western Europe, plus Japan and Chile, focusing on media and politics.

Hallin, Daniel C., and Paolo Mancini. *Comparing Media Systems: Three Models of Media and Politics*. Cambridge, U.K., and New York: Cambridge University Press, 2004. The principal source for the analysis presented here.

Humphreys, Peter. *Mass Media and Media Policy in Western Europe*. Manchester, U.K., and New York: Manchester University Press, 1996. An excellent overview of West European media.

Semetko, Holli A., et al. *The Formation of Campaign Agendas: A Comparative Analysis of Party and Media Roles in Recent American and British Elections*. Hillsdale, N.J.: Lawrence Erlbaum, 1991. A comparison of U.S. and British election campaigns, and their coverage by the media.

Siebert, Fred S., Theodore Peterson, and Wilbur Schramm. *Four Theories of the Press: The Authoritarian, Libertarian, Social Responsibility, and Soviet Communist Concepts of What the Press Should Be and Do*. Urbana: University of Illinois Press, 1956. The old classic; flawed but still influential.

2

AMERICAN JOURNALISM IN
HISTORICAL PERSPECTIVE

Michael Schudson and Susan E. Tifft

JOURNALISTS HAVE OFTEN CLAIMED TO SERVE TIMELESS longings, to be the storytellers of the world, the bards and troubadours of everyday life for everyday people. They lay this claim to universal relevance atop a belief that a thirst for news is all but innate to human nature. People throughout history have demonstrated a curiosity about their world. They are curious about novel things as well as perennial concerns, especially things that have come to be called sensational—blood, gore, violence, sex, betrayal, and perfidy, the moral frailty and dissipation of the rich and powerful, the stuff of Greek tragedy and of Italian opera.[1]

Even if a thirst for news *were* somehow wired into the human psyche, however, almost all questions about the news media concern differences among competing styles and principles of journalism, alternative institutional structures of news organizations, or different systems of political control of news. Why do states censor news in some countries more than in others? Why do journalists write literary essays in some journalistic traditions and fact-centered reports in others? Why are sensational stories on the front page in some newspapers and not in others, even in the same city? Why are some countries dominated by commercial TV and others by public television? What difference, if any, does it make? Why is one story more interesting than another? Why is a sports reporter free to favor the home team and the political reporter not equally free to cheer for the favorite son? What is better for our civic life, news that gives politicians more room to state their own views without interruption or tightly edited news, a succession of short sound bites where the journalists identify and highlight the politician's key points?

None of these questions can be answered by an appeal to universal human nature. Most of them can be informed by a historical understanding of the development of news institutions; in fact, some of them cannot be understood at all without placing journalism in historical perspective. In the past two centuries, news has become a professionally created and commercially distributed product in most parts of the world. It is important to know how that happened, how the development of news has varied across national cultures and disparate political systems, and how the different forms this development has taken have had varying outcomes. Exactly what is commercialization and what are its consequences? The profit motive, like, say, sexual desire, can have terrible consequences, but it is one of the forces in life powerful enough to push people ahead in the face of risk, tyranny, and physical and moral hazard. What have been its costs and benefits and its variations across national traditions with respect to the news media?

The same questions should be asked of a development parallel to commercialization: professionalization—the differentiation of journalists as a distinct occupational group with distinctive norms and traditions and, depending on the time and place, some degree of autonomy from political parties and publishers. How has this varied across nations? What have been its sources? What have been its consequences?

The primary institutional and cultural features of contemporary news have a relatively brief—four hundred years at the outside—history. The occupation in which people get paid to write true stories about current events and publish them on a regular basis is about 250 years old and in many places only 150 years old. The normative commitment of this occupational group to writing political news in order to inform the citizens of a democracy is of course no older than contemporary democracies, a history of roughly two centuries. The idea that this same group of people, journalists, should try to write news in a nonpartisan and professional manner emerged in the past one hundred years. All of these features of contemporary journalism take a different shape in different national traditions. This essay will focus on the history of news in the United States, where the two master trends of commercialization and professionalization come into sharp focus.

The Invention of News, 1690–1850

In colonial America, printers were small-businesspeople, not journalists. They pretty much invented the newspaper as they went along, amid their efforts to make money selling stationery, printing wedding announcements, running the post office, or even selling from their print shops such sundries as chocolate, tea, snuff, rum, beaver hats, patent medicines, and musical instruments. Their newspapers were four-page weekly journals designed initially to advertise their print shops. Their contents, after a time, tended toward a common model: an assortment of local advertising, occasional small paragraphs of local hearsay, and large chunks of European political and economic intelligence lifted directly from London newspapers. Political news of other colonies rarely appeared. Local political news was nearly nonexistent. If a newspaper proprietor happened to attack the royal governor or, for that matter, the colonial legislature, he was likely to find himself indicted for seditious libel. When two historians examined a sample of nineteen hundred items that Benjamin Franklin's *Pennsylvania Gazette* printed from 1728 to 1765, they found only thirty-four that touched on politics in Philadelphia or Pennsylvania.[2] Eighteenth-century printers avoided controversy when they could, and printed primarily foreign news because it afforded local readers and local authorities no grounds for grumbling.

As conflict with England heated up after 1765, politics entered the press, and printerly "fairness" went by the board. It became more troublesome for printers to be neutral than to be partisan; nearly everyone felt compelled to take sides. Print shops became hives of political activity. In the late seventeenth and early eighteenth centuries, colonial politics had been ordinarily limited to a small circle of gentlemen. When an occasional pamphlet took up a political issue, it addressed itself to the colonial assembly, not the general population. Pamphleteers became more active in political campaigning in the 1740s in New York, Philadelphia, and Boston, but pamphlet publication reached its height later, especially with Thomas Paine's publication of *Common Sense* in 1776. Where the typical pamphlet was printed once or twice in editions of a few thousand, *Common Sense* sold an estimated 150,000 and was reprinted in newspapers up and down the coast. Paine, like other professional pamphleteers of his generation, addressed the general populace, but he extended and perfected the practice, dropping esoteric classical references for familiar biblical ones, seeking a common language.[3]

In the same era, the newspaper began its long career as the mouthpiece of political parties and factions. Patriots had no tolerance for the pro-British press, and the new states passed and enforced treason and sedition statutes in the 1770s and 1780s. By the time of the state-by-state debates over ratification of the Constitution in 1787–88, Federalists, those leaders who supported a strong national government, dominated the press and squeezed Antifederalists out of public debate. In Pennsylvania, leading papers tended not to report Antifederalist speeches at the ratification convention. When unusual newspapers in Philadelphia, New York, and Boston sought to report views on both sides, Federalists stopped their subscriptions and forced the papers to end their attempt at evenhandedness.[4]

Some of the nation's founders believed that outspoken political criticism was well justified so long as the American colonists were fighting a monarchy for their independence, but that open critique of a duly elected republican government could be legitimately curtailed. Samuel Adams, the famed Boston agitator during the struggle for independence, changed his views on political action once republican government was established. This great advocate of open talk, committees of correspondence, an outspoken press, and voluntary associations of citizens now opposed all hint of public associations and public criticism that operated outside the regular channels of government.[5] As one contemporary observed, it did no harm for writers to mislead the people when the people were powerless, but "to mislead the judgement of the people, where they have *all* power, must produce the greatest possible mischief."[6] The Sedition Act of 1798 forbade criticism of the government, making it a criminal offense to print "any false, scandalous and malicious writing . . . against the government of the United States." As many as one in four editors of opposition papers were brought up on charges under this law. But this went further than many Americans of the day could stomach. Federalist propaganda notwithstanding, Thomas Jefferson won the presidency in 1800, the Sedition Act expired, and party opposition began to be grudgingly accepted. Only at that point did the famous First Amendment declaration of 1791 that "Congress shall make no law . . . abridging the freedom of speech, or of the press" begin to accrue a legal tradition consistent with the broad protections of its language. Until then, in fact, it could be argued that the First Amendment was more of a protection of states' rights than the rights of individuals or the press. After all, it prohibited the federal government—but not the state governments—from abridging freedom of speech and of the press.

The Press and Political Parties: 1800–1890

In the first decades of the new nation, intensely partisan newspapers were frequently founded as weapons for a party or faction, such as Alexander Hamilton's *New York Evening Post*, begun in 1801 to recoup Federalist power after the loss of the presidency to Jefferson. Jefferson, well remembered for his 1787 statement that he would prefer newspapers without a government to a government without newspapers, was as president a prime target for the vituperation of the Federalist press. So it is perhaps not surprising that, while president, he wrote more caustically about newspapers, telling a friend in 1807, "The man who never looks into a newspaper is better informed than he who reads them, inasmuch as he who knows nothing is nearer the truth than he whose mind is filled with falsehoods and errors."[7] Editors attacked one another as viciously as they attacked politicians, and sometimes they carried rivalries into fistfights and duels. Reporting of news was incidental, unorganized, and obviously subordinated to editorial partisanship. Politicians complained bitterly about the other party's papers but they still offered favors to the press as a whole. The Postal Acts of 1792 and 1794 provided newspapers preferential mailing rates, so from the republic's first days the press was the beneficiary of laws that enriched and enlarged the newspaper business.

As late as 1830 the largest paper in the country had a circulation of only forty-five hundred, and that was more than double a typical city paper's reach. Newspapers were differentiated by that time from the post office and the print shop, at least in leading cities, but they were not clearly distinguished from the party, faction, church, or other organization they served. Journalism was not an identifiable occupational path. Few papers hired reporters. A "correspondent" was just that, a friend or acquaintance of the editor whose writing was that of an unpaid amateur.

But like other institutions in Jacksonian America, newspapers were about to undergo a democratic revolution. In the 1820s, several New York papers began to send small boats out to incoming ships to get the London news more quickly. Beginning with the *New York Sun* in 1833, a new breed of newspaper sought commercial success and a mass readership. Between 1833 and 1835 in New York, Boston, Baltimore, and Philadelphia, venturesome entrepreneurs began "penny papers" selling for a penny an issue rather than six cents.[8] The new papers were hawked on the street by newsboys rather than being sold exclusively by subscription or at the newspaper office. The penny press aggressively sought out local news, assigning reporters to the courts and even to coverage of "society." They also actively solicited advertising and engaged in vigorous competition to get the "latest" news as fast as they could.

The penny papers' business-minded assertiveness made them the earliest organizations to adopt new technologies. In 1835, already selling twenty thousand copies a day, the *New York Sun* became the first newspaper in the country to purchase a steam-driven press. Another penny paper, the *Baltimore Sun*, made early use of the telegraph and helped encourage its public acceptance. During the war with Mexico in 1846, penny papers in New York and Philadelphia made the first and fullest use of the telegraph. Technology was available but it took the peculiar disposition of the competitive, news-hungry, circulation-building penny papers to make quick use of it. What the penny papers brought to American journalism was a broadened, robust sense of what counts as news and an assertive dedication to making profits (through news) more than promoting policies or politicians.

The penny papers were at the leading edge of journalistic innovation before the Civil War, but the most widely circulated papers of the time were still country weeklies or other nondailies with local circulations. These papers were invariably boosters of economic development in their own towns and regions. A newspaper career often included employment at both country and city papers. Horace Greeley, like many other journalists of his day, began his career on a small town weekly. He moved from Vermont to Pennsylvania to what was already fast becoming journalism's mecca, New York. There he first issued a literary magazine, then in 1840 ran the Whig Party's campaign newspaper, and in 1841 began a penny paper of his own, the *New York Tribune*. The *Tribune* became one of the most influential papers of mid-century, and while it never rivaled the circulation of the *New York Herald*, James Gordon Bennett's penny paper, its weekly edition established a significant circulation beyond

New York City. It was widely known in rural communities throughout New York, New England, and the West.

The pluralism of American society was reflected in the press. There was a flourishing German-language press in the antebellum years when Germans represented a quarter of all foreign-born citizens. In 1828 the *Cherokee Phoenix* began as the first Native American newspaper, published bilingually in English and Cherokee. The African American press began with *Freedom's Journal* in New York in 1827. Frederick Douglass began *The North Star* in Rochester in 1847. African American–run papers before the Civil War were a part of the abolitionist movement, whose most famous journalistic leader, apart from Douglass, was William Lloyd Garrison with his Boston-based *Liberator,* first published in 1831. The abolitionist press served as a vital part of a growing social movement.

In the conventional daily press, newsgathering grew as the papers' central function, but this was not as obvious a development as one might imagine. As late as 1846, only Baltimore and Washington papers assigned special correspondents to cover Congress. Only as politics heated up in the 1850s did this change, with more than fifty papers hiring Washington correspondents. The correspondents typically wrote for a half dozen or more papers and earned further salary as clerks for congressional committees or speechwriters for the politicians they were covering. They often lived at the same boardinghouses as congressmen, and the boardinghouses tended to divide along party lines. The occupational world of journalism was thinly differentiated from politics. Despite the proud, independent commercial-mindedness of the penny papers, for most of the nineteenth century most important journals were political, financially supported by one party or another, and dedicated to rousing the party faithful as much as to reporting the news. Not only did parties sponsor newspapers, but factions of parties and sometimes individual politicians did so, too.[9]

But the connection between party and paper began to weaken late in the nineteenth century. After the Civil War, newspapers rapidly expanded as profitable businesses, the biggest of them larger than all but a few other industrial operations. By 1870, every major daily in New York, which was already the nation's media capital, had at least one hundred employees. Advertising became a more central source of income and new advertisers, notably the urban department stores, became a major source of revenue.

Competition for news grew intense; so did competition for readers. Promotional campaigns and stunts aggressively courted new audiences, particularly women. Simpler language, larger headlines, and more lavish illustrations helped to extend readership to immigrants and others whose abilities with written English were limited. By 1880, New York City had half a million foreign-born citizens; a decade later 40 percent of the city's population was foreign born. For ambitious publishers, economic changes made a new mass journalism possible, the prospect of profit made it desirable, and the changing habits and inhabitants of the cities made it necessary.

At the turn of the century, the most celebrated publishers of the big mass-circulation daily newspapers were Joseph Pulitzer (at the *New York World*) and William Randolph Hearst (at the *New York Journal*). Pulitzer pioneered most of the new crowd-pleasing developments when he came to New York journalism in the 1880s. When Hearst arrived in 1895 from San Francisco, he bought a faltering paper and quickly introduced comics, sensational news coverage, and a self-promoting crusading spirit as he battled Pulitzer for the biggest share of the city's circulation. Hearst, followed somewhat more gingerly by Pulitzer, pushed for a war with Spain in the late 1890s and sent correspondents to Cuba, then a Spanish colony, to cover the developing crisis there. The warmongering was a high-water mark of sensationalism. Still, the common view that this so-called yellow journalism "caused" American intervention owes a lot to Hearst's delight in taking credit for the war. Many other leading papers, including those with the greatest influence in elite circles, opposed American intervention.

The pull of dollars and the popularity of sensationalism helped move newspapers away from parties. So, too, did a growing reform movement that questioned the worth of parties altogether. In the 1870s and 1880s, liberal reformers, first among Republicans and then Democrats, began to criticize the very notion of party loyalty. They promoted new forms of political campaigning, urging an educational rather than participatory or "spectacular" campaign, moving from parades to pamphlets. They urged that citizens, in the exercise of the franchise, make an informed choice among candidates, parties, and policies rather than demonstrate an emotional allegiance to a party label. Newspapers became more willing to take an independent stand. By 1890 a quarter of daily newspapers in the North, where antiparty reforms were most advanced, claimed independence of party.

As late as the 1890s, when a standard Republican paper covered a presidential election, it not only deplored and derided Democratic candidates, very often it simply neglected to mention them. In the days before public-opinion polling, the size of partisan rallies was taken as a proxy for likely electoral results. Republican rallies would be described as "monster meetings" in the Republican papers, while Democratic rallies would often not be covered at all. For Democratic papers, it was just the reverse. Partisanship ran deep in nineteenth-century American journalism and well into the twentieth century. At the same time, the independent spirit of reform, and the economic excesses and political corruption of the Gilded Age, produced an activist brand of journalism known as muckraking. Its exemplars—Jacob Riis, Ida Tarbell, and Lincoln Steffens—attacked the privileges of class and wealth and made no apologies about advocating change. Although newspapers participated in this reform journalism, the most notable muckrakers wrote for a new set of monthly magazines that addressed a national, middle-class audience.

Although journalism at the turn of the twentieth century could not be called a professional field, professionalizing tendencies were at work. First, antiparty reforms and the growing commercial strength of newspapers loosened the hold of parties on the press. Second, reporters came increasingly to enjoy a culture of their own, independent of political parties. They developed their own mythologies (reveling in their intimacy with the urban underworld), their own clubs and watering holes, and their own professional practices. Reporters' status, income, and esprit de corps rose at the end of the century. Popular acclaim for dashing reporters—Elizabeth Cochrane (Nellie Bly) going around the world in eighty days, Henry Morton Stanley finding David Livingston in Africa, the handsome Richard Harding Davis reporting on war and on football, added to the appeal of the field.

Third, the work of reporting began to involve more than stenography or observations and sketches. Interviewing, all but unknown in 1865, was widely practiced by 1900 and was the mainstay of American journalism by World War I, when it was still rare in Europe. The rapid diffusion of this new practice among American journalists seems to have been unaccompanied by any ideological rationale. It fit effortlessly into a journalism already fact-centered and news-centered rather than devoted primarily to political commentary or preoccupied with literary aspirations.[10] It was one of the growing number of practices that identified journalists as a distinct occupational group with distinct patterns of behavior.

The growing corporate coherence of that occupational group would soon produce a self-conscious professionalism and ethic of objectivity.

The Growing Commercialization of News: 1900–1945

The industrial, educational, and technological expansion of the early twentieth century swept newspapers along with it. The number of daily newspapers peaked in 1910 at about twenty-six hundred, and foreign-language papers flourished. In 1900 more than a quarter of the literate population subscribed to a newspaper— a figure that would grow to 45 percent thirty years later.[11] Photographs, which had been included occasionally in publications as far back as the Civil War, became commonplace in news reporting, while other visual elements, such as comics and rotogravure sections, provided entertaining relief from the gray dullness of earlier eras. But even as individual newspapers thrived, the seeds of consolidation were taking root. By the early 1920s, chain ownership would be increasingly common, driven by the speed and productivity made possible by the Linotype machine and the rotary press, the growth of national advertising, and the business and political ambitions of Pulitzer, Hearst, and other press barons.

Newspapers had attempted to cut costs through cooperative news gathering as early as the 1830s, but chains in the modern sense did not emerge until sixty years later. The first large chain in the United States was assembled by an eccentric populist named Edward W. Scripps, who in addition to founding, merging, acquiring, and selling dozens of papers during his lifetime, launched the United Press Association, the precursor of United Press International, in 1907. William Randolph Hearst's empire, which consisted of six newspapers in 1904, swelled to twenty daily and eleven Sunday newspapers, two wire services, six magazines, and a newsreel company by 1922.[12] Frank Gannett, whose first acquisition was a half-interest in the tiny *Elmira* (NY) *Gazette* in 1906, owned a stable of twenty-one newspapers and seven radio stations two decades later. The political and financial clout of chains made it increasingly difficult for single newspapers to compete, and the number of papers declined dramatically. New York City, once home to twenty dailies, had just eight in 1940.[13] By the early 1930s, the six largest chains—Hearst, Patterson-McCormick, Scripps-Howard, Paul Block, Ridder, and Gannett—controlled more than two-thirds of the daily-newspaper circulation in the country. The publisher Frank Munsey—known to critics as "the great executioner of newspapers"—had predicted in 1903 that "it will not be many years . . . before the publishing business of this country will be done by a few concerns."[14] Now, Munsey's prediction seemed to be coming true. On the eve of the United States' entry into World War II, twenty-five of the country's largest cities had just one daily, and that paper was increasingly likely to be controlled by a chain.

Meanwhile, magazines came to play a larger role in news gathering and reporting. With the launch of Time in 1923, founders Henry Luce and Briton Hadden introduced a revolutionary concept in news magazines. Unlike the *Nation, Harper's Weekly*, the *Atlantic Monthly*, and other nineteenth-century models, *Time* relied on "group journalism," synthesizing information from the previous week's newspaper and wire service reports in lively and heavily opinionated stories that appeared without bylines, giving the impression that a single person, with a single sensibility, had written the entire magazine. *Time*'s success inspired competitors, including *Newsweek* and *U.S. News & World Report* (both founded in 1933), and *Business Week*, launched, ironically, in a year that became synonymous with financial ruin—1929. Eventually, Luce (Hadden died in 1929) sat atop a diversified publishing empire that included a successful photojournalism magazine (*Life*), a business magazine (*Fortune*), and a radio program and a newsreel both called *The March of Time*.[15]

That press barons such as Luce and Gannett sought to be players in radio is no accident. The reach of newspapers and magazines was by definition tied to the transportation system; the number of people who read Luce's *Time* or Gannett's *Rochester-Times Union* was limited by how many copies could be distributed over a defined geographic area. Radio technology, which had become more sophisticated as a result of war-related research during World War I, made it possible for the first time to reach a mass audience—with all the power and influence that implied. Indeed, throughout the 1920s debate raged about who would control the new medium, how it would be funded, and whether it should be used for educational, cultural, political, public service, or commercial purposes.

In 1919 General Electric, at the urging of U.S. Navy officials, bought out British Marconi Wireless's American subsidiary, ostensibly to prevent foreign takeovers of U.S. broadcasting facilities. Then, together with American Telegraph & Telephone, United Fruit, and Westinghouse Electric, the company pooled all American radio patents in a new entity called the Radio Corporation of America (RCA). The move was anticompetitive, possibly even illegal, and helped ensure business domination of the airwaves for years to come. But RCA's initial mission—manufacturing radio equipment and perfecting radio technology— was only the beginning. Companies soon realized that radio could reach a popular market for a relatively small investment. When the first modern broadcast went on the air on November 2, 1920—KDKA, a Westinghouse station in Pittsburgh, announced the results of the presidential race between Warren G. Harding and James M. Cox—the company's goal was not so much to disseminate news as to get listeners to tune in so they would buy radio receiving sets. Barely two years later, WEAF in New York City charged a Queens realtor fifty dollars to deliver a ten-minute pitch for his new apartment complex. Thus was born the first "commercial," gradually changing radio from a service supported by the sale of sets to one supported largely by advertising.[16]

As the United States entered the 1930s, the contours of a modern broadcasting structure had begun to emerge, with radio firmly controlled by commercial interests and loosely regulated by the federal government—a departure from the traditional hands-off relationship between government and the print press. The Radio Act of 1927 had declared the airwaves public property subject to government licensing, and called on the Commerce Department and the Interstate Commerce Commission to share regulation "in the public interest, convenience, or necessity." With the passage of the federal Communications Act of 1934, regulation was consolidated in a single new agency—the Federal Communications Commission (FCC)—which came to symbolize the new alliance between government and private industry. As the number of radio stations grew (there were five in 1921, seven hundred in 1927), so did the global reach of radio news. In 1929 Americans heard a symphony broadcast from Queen's Hall in London, and an account of Admiral Richard Byrd's exploits in Antarctica. Politicians were quick to exploit radio's ability to bypass reporters and editors and go straight to the people. Franklin Delano Roosevelt, first elected to the White House in 1932, became known as the "Radio President" because of his Fireside Chats. "Radio has given to the president a weapon such as no ruler has ever known," wrote the editor of *Radio Guide* in 1934. "It enables him instantaneously to answer, overthrow and defeat any false statement concerning himself, the government, or his plans."[17]

The Depression was unkind to newspapers, in part because many advertisers switched their business to radio. Adolph S. Ochs, publisher of the *New York Times,* cut the size of the paper and slashed executive bonuses; Hearst poured his own personal fortune into his papers to keep them alive. But the real toll was on reporters, who in 1933 made an average wage of barely $30 a week—if they were lucky enough to work at all. Spurred on by Roosevelt's National Recovery Act, which allowed employees to organize and bargain collectively, news reporters for the first time banded together in a union: the American Newspaper Guild. Many publishers—and some reporters, as well—worried that unionizing journalists was anathema to the very notion of an independent press. Objectivity would suffer, they said, especially in stories about business and labor. In part to answer such criticisms, the guild in 1934 adopted a code of ethics calling for accurate and unbiased reporting, guided "only by fact and fairness." Newspapermen and women clearly considered themselves members of a profession with distinct norms and standards, but by unionizing, they also aligned themselves with labor, not white-collar workers.

While most reporters aspired to objectivity as an ideal, some press owners openly rejected it. Henry Luce used his publications to spread his pro-business, muscularly American views, while Robert McCormick's *Chicago Tribune* published unabashedly biased coverage of Roosevelt's reelection campaigns and thumped the tub for isolationism in the years leading up to World War II. When America finally entered the conflict in 1941, print and radio correspondents stationed abroad and at home acceded to government censorship as a wartime necessity. At the same time, they had remarkably open access to military action that allowed them to produce firsthand accounts from the battlefront, including the invasion of Normandy. In radio, Edward R. Murrow of CBS provided some of the war's most memorable reporting with his "This . . . is London" broadcasts from the British capital during the blitzkrieg. Although such coverage was expensive—at the war's peak, news outlets had twenty-six hundred American correspondents stationed overseas—the public benefited from its front-row seat at world events.

The Limits of Objectivity: The 1950s

As the country entered the postwar era, objectivity was universally acknowledged to be the spine of the journalist's moral code. It was asserted in the textbooks used in journalism schools, it was asserted in codes of ethics of professional associations. It was at last a code of professional honor and a set of rules to give professionals both guidance and cover. Members of the American Society of Newspaper Editors had adopted a code of ethics or "Canons of Journalism" at their first convention in 1923 that included a principle of "Sincerity, Truthfulness, Accuracy" and another of "Impartiality," the latter including the declaration, "News reports should be free from opinion or bias of any kind."[18] At the time, objectivity was a kind of industrial discipline to help keep reporters in line, but it was also a natural and progressive ideology for an aspiring occupational group during an era when science was god, efficiency was cherished, and increasingly prominent elites judged partisanship a vestige of the tribal nineteenth century. It was also a way to disaffiliate from the new "profession" of public relations, which had gotten a great boost from President Woodrow Wilson's efforts to "sell" World War I to the American public.

At the very moment that journalists claimed "objectivity" as their ideal, they also worked around its limits. In the 1930s there was a vogue for what contemporaries called "interpretive journalism." Leading journalists and journalism educators insisted that the world had grown increasingly complex and needed not only to be reported but explained. Political columnists such as Walter Lippmann, David Lawrence, Frank Kent, and Mark Sullivan came into their own during this era. Journalists insisted that their task was to help readers not only know but understand. They took it for granted that understanding in any sense they could admire had nothing to do with party or partisan sentiment.

Even so, for most working journalists, the rule of objectivity remained cardinal. But with the ascension of Joseph R. McCarthy, the limits of objectivity became more apparent. McCarthy, a junior senator from Wisconsin, first made headlines in February 1950, with his sensational claims that there were hundreds of Communists in the U.S. State Department. Over the next four years, his drumbeat of allegations, often aimed at specific government officials and even military officers, grew louder. Although McCarthy rarely provided supporting evidence, the mere fact that a U.S. senator was making these charges made news, while digging deeper to find out whether they were true took more time and effort than most reporters could spare. McCarthy, well attuned to the ways of the press, exploited the newspapers' competitive search for a hot story, the pressure of deadlines, the practice of objectivity, and the deference routinely granted a U.S. senator. Some papers—the *Washington Post* and the *Milwaukee Journal,* for example—investigated the veracity of his claims, and columnists such as Drew Pearson and Joseph Alsop gave McCarthy no quarter.

But it took television finally to show that this emperor wore no clothes, even if, by that point, McCarthy's influence was waning. On March 9, 1954, on his popular *See It Now* program, Edward R. Murrow broadcast a half-hour of film clips showing McCarthy at his worst. When McCarthy made false charges or contradicted himself, Murrow pointed it out. At the end of the broadcast, Murrow spoke directly to the television audience in what amounted to an impassioned editorial against "McCarthyism": "The actions of the junior senator from Wisconsin have caused alarm and dismay amongst our allies abroad and given considerable comfort to our enemies," he said. "And whose fault is that? Not really his. He didn't create this situation of fear, he merely exploited it—and rather successfully. Cassius was right: 'The fault, dear Brutus, lies not in our stars but in ourselves.'"[19] McCarthy continued his crusade, but the broadcast had mortally wounded him. Then in April and May, television helped McCarthy expose his own bullying in live broadcasts of six weeks of McCarthy's investigation of Communist subversion in the U.S. Army. Republicans sought, but failed, to block the television coverage because they could see what television was doing to their wayward colleague. James Reston of the *New York Times* summed it up in saying that McCarthy, on television, "demonstrated with appalling clarity precisely what kind of man he is."[20] On December 2, 1954, the Senate officially censured McCarthy; three years later, he was dead.

The incident demonstrated the growing power of television. Sets had been available as early as 1938 (they were a big hit at the 1939 World's Fair), but World War II had diverted the electronics industry from fully developing the medium. By 1948, however, television was on its way, with 172,000 homes equipped to receive programming—a figure that would climb to 42 million just ten years later.[21] At first, TV programming seemed to be little more than radio with pictures; indeed, many of the first TV announcers and anchors came from radio. But by the early 1950s, TV offered its own entertainment series and nightly news broadcasts, prompting the creation of what would become one of the most successful magazines ever—*TV Guide*. The 1952 presidential race between Dwight D. Eisenhower and Adlai Stevenson was the first to provide advertiser-sponsored campaign coverage; that same year, Eisenhower's running mate, Richard M. Nixon, resorted to a TV appearance to defend himself against charges of corruption and save his political career with an address that became famous as the "Checkers" speech. By 1960, when Nixon squared off with John F. Kennedy in a series of decisive televised debates, the medium's ability to influence public opinion was indisputable—and not always applauded.

The money to be made through television advertising was not lost on media owners, who continued to acquire, merge, and consolidate properties after the war. At the urging of *Time* magazine founder Henry Luce, who feared that too much media concentration would invite government regulation, the president of the University of Chicago, Robert M. Hutchins, formed a commission to "look into the present state and future prospects of freedom of the press." The commission was a collection of "great men," none of them journalists, but its report, *A Free and Responsible Press,* issued in 1947, is remarkably prescient in its anticipation of troubling trends in journalism. In particular, the commission singled out the increasingly monopolistic nature of the press as a danger to democracy. "Throughout the communications industry the little fellow exists on very narrow margins, and the opportunities for initiating new ventures are strictly limited," the report said.[22] Predictably, press owners reacted negatively, and over the ensuing two decades kept up a brisk pace of acquisitions.

The nature of reporting changed, too, after the mid-century point. Correspondents had frequently cooperated with government during World War II and the early postwar years. Now a new, more adversarial generation was working its way up through the ranks. The *New York Times'* decision to play down the imminence of an invasion of Communist Cuba by Cuban exiles, eliminating all references to sponsorship of the operation by the U.S. Central Intelligence Agency, generated angry debate at the paper. When the April 17, 1961, invasion, known as the Bay of Pigs, failed, resulting in 1,000 captives, 114 dead, and embarrassment for the White House, President Kennedy himself commented that he wished that the *Times* had published all it knew.

The apotheosis of the changed relationship between government and the press was the war in Vietnam—sometimes called the first "television war." At first, most journalists, like most Americans, subscribed to the domino theory, which held that if one nation becomes Communist controlled, neighboring nations will follow, and accepted the White House position that it was vital to defend South Vietnam against the Communist North. But as American casualties mounted, and the perception grew that victory was unlikely, both the press and the public became more skeptical. The policy that the Kennedy administration and that of its successor, Lyndon Johnson, followed in Vietnam set them a devilish media problem—how to convey to the enemy their resolve to pursue the war to victory while communicating to the American public their assurance that the war would require a limited commitment.

Nothing shattered the precarious success of that communication effort more than the Tet Offensive in late January 1968, which involved surprise attacks by the North Vietnamese fighters, the Vietcong, on more than half the provincial capitals of South Vietnam. While in strictly military terms, the Vietcong suffered heavy losses in the assault, the Communist North gained a great psychological victory by taking the war into the streets of Saigon and making it clear that the United States did not by any account have the fighting under control. Barely a month later, the CBS anchorman Walter Cronkite, just back from a visit to Vietnam, shed his trademark neutrality and delivered a blunt on-air critique. "It seems now more certain than ever that the bloody experience of Vietnam is to end in a stalemate," he said. The only "rational way out" for the United States was to negotiate.[23] Objectivity, at least in this instance, had given way to advocacy, something the conflicts of the 1960s—Vietnam, the civil rights movement, the assassinations of President Kennedy, his brother Robert Kennedy, and the Reverend Martin Luther King Jr.—seemed to demand.

The Adversarial Press: The 1970s

As more and more Americans, both in the general public and in Congress, came to doubt the chances of military success, journalists began to reflect the country's lack of consensus about the war. Increasingly, the news emphasized policy divisions and conflict in Washington. Even adhering to the standards of objectivity produced a portrait much more varied, and much less flattering to the administration's policy pronouncements than before. To counter the growing swell of bad news, the Nixon White House successfully promoted the notion that contrary to their profession's own dogma, journalists were not public-spirited surrogates for citizens. Instead, they were an independent and dangerously irresponsible source of power.[24] Vice President Spiro Agnew denounced intellectuals who attacked American policy as "nattering nabobs of negativism," while the White House, eager to stop damaging leaks to the press, illegally wiretapped journalists, including *New York Times* reporter Hedrick Smith and CBS newsman Marvin Kalb.

It was in this atmosphere of acrimony and growing disillusion with the war in Vietnam that the *New York Times* published what came to be known as the Pentagon Papers. Secretary of Defense Robert S. McNamara had commissioned the study of U.S. involvement in Southeast Asia during the final year of the Johnson administration. When it was completed, the forty-seven-volume top-secret study, much of it from classified material, showed a pattern of government arrogance, missteps, and outright lies about the extent of U.S. military engagement. On June 13, 1971, the *Times* began publishing a series of articles based on the study, portions of which had been made available to the paper by Daniel Ellsberg, an analyst who had worked on the project. Two days later, the Nixon Justice Department, arguing violation of national security, obtained a temporary restraining order to halt further installments—the first time in the nation's history that a newspaper was prevented in advance by a court from publishing a specific article. In defiance, the *Washington Post* began running stories based on the documents, followed by the *Boston Globe*. The government moved against both papers as it had against the *Times*. On June 30, in a historic 6 to 3 decision, the U.S. Supreme Court ruled that the constitutional guarantee of a free press overrode the government's concerns, and allowed further publication. For its daring exposé of the government's decades-long record of duplicity, the *New York Times* was awarded the Pulitzer Prize for Meritorious Public Service, journalism's highest honor.

A year later, the *Washington Post* won the same award for what has become an iconic example of modern investigative reporting: Watergate, a scandal of political intrigue and obstruction of justice that eventually led to Nixon's resignation. The stories made celebrities of Bob Woodward and Carl Bernstein, the rookie reporters who wrote them, although even *Post* publisher Katharine Graham later admitted that it wasn't the press that brought down the president. As Edward Jay Epstein observed in a 1974 article in *Commentary,* the "agencies of government itself"—the courts, the FBI, and congressional committees—played a pivotal role.[25] Nevertheless, the morality tale that was Watergate *did* have an effect on journalism, exacerbating the already adversarial relationship between the White House and reporters, underscoring the "character issue" in politics, making the pursuit of scandal synonymous with news, and lionizing investigative reporters in ways that their forebears, the muckrakers, could never have imagined.

By the mid-1970s, public confidence in national leadership had crumbled under the cumulative weight of Vietnam, the Pentagon Papers, and Watergate. An increasingly critical culture, even an "adversary culture," had expanded from the groves of academe to the halls of Congress itself, while the explosion of news as a cultural commodity on television underscored doubts that the line between journalism and business or news and entertainment could stand. One thing was certain: broadcast news, once a prestigious add-on to network programming that was not expected to turn a profit, had begun to make money. In 1961 the FCC chairman, Newton N. Minow, had memorably declared television to be a "vast wasteland," and urged the networks to produce more news programming. They did. In 1963 NBC and CBS increased the time devoted to nightly news from fifteen minutes to thirty (ABC later followed suit). That same year, a Roper poll found for the first time that more Americans said they relied on television than newspapers as their primary source of news. When *60 Minutes* debuted in 1968, it became the most highly rated program in the country and put the CBS news division in the black for the first time. Imitators such as *20/20, Dateline NBC,* and *Prime Time Live* soon followed. For the first time, TV news was not only central to American life, it was central in the thinking of the broadcasting companies themselves.

At the same time, despite the steady drumbeat of history-making events during the 1970s, most daily newspapers reduced the amount of strictly political and economic news they covered. One reason was the entry into adulthood of the baby boomers, who, as the first TV generation, never developed the newspaper-reading habits of their elders. Women who in earlier eras had been full-time homemakers streamed into the work force, with less time for newspapers, while the post–World War II suburban lifestyle meant longer hours commuting to work. Surveys showed readers wanted more information about entertainment, leisure, and daily living concerns. Publishers complied by reconfiguring newspapers to attract a younger, time-conscious audience. Features about food, home, and fashion that had once been relegated to the "women's page" were now welcomed under the ever-expanding umbrella of what was considered "news." Even the *New York Times,* which prided itself on comprehensive national and foreign coverage, launched a "Living" section, while news magazines, unable to match the immediacy of television, ran reader-friendly cover stories on ice cream, back pain, and cats. Emblematic of the phenomenon was *People,* which went from a regular light feature in *Time* to a stand-alone magazine in 1974, and the national newspaper *USA Today,* created in 1982 on the assumption that brief stories and bright graphics would prove alluring to mobile, visually oriented readers.

Rather than merely an addition of fluff, the new content amounted to a long-overdue expansion of what counted as news to include a wide range of vital aspects of public and private life that conventional political and economic coverage had generally neglected. While media companies' eagerness to please advertisers and investors helped this expansion take hold, what fueled it in the first place was a changed cultural atmosphere. The emerging women's movement, for instance, made a variety of issues related to health and medicine more newsworthy. The controversy over abortion in the 1970s made aspects of both medicine and domestic life a central public issue, as did the AIDS epidemic some years later. When "identity politics" became more central to public life, that is, when what united people with common economic interests became less important than issues that divided them according to their racial, ethnic, gender, social, and religious identities, and when it entered into the politics and personnel of American newsrooms themselves, the pressures for changing news judgments became palpable; market demand made these changes easily digestible for news organizations, but it did not create them.

The drift away from hard news and toward features also occurred on network news programs, but for different reasons: the advent of cable and satellite technologies, and the changing economics of broadcasting. In 1970 ABC, CBS, and NBC had no competition; only 10 percent of American homes had cable. By 1989 that figure was 53 percent.[26] At the same time, local news stations, their range expanded by vans equipped with satellite dishes, were able to cover national events that had once been the exclusive preserve of the networks. The result was a gradual drop in the audience for network news. To reverse falling ratings, the networks pared back serious policy coverage and expensive reporting from overseas—so much so that when the political scientist Robert M. Entman compared two months of network newscasts in 1975 and 1986 he found that the number of domestic policy stories had dropped by 37 percent while features increased 50 percent.[27] The pace of stories became faster as well. The average sound bite, or uninterrupted excerpt from a news maker, in election coverage fell from an average of 43.1 seconds in 1968 to a mere 8.9 seconds in 1988,[28] leading to an increase in what the media scholar Daniel C. Hallin has called "mediated" news, stories in which journalists intervene to provide context, meaning, and analysis. This was a far cry from the conventional ideal of "objectivity" that insisted on greater deference to government officials and other news sources judged to be authoritative.

Ironically, while cable greatly multiplied the number of channels available to Americans, it also made it easier to opt out of the national conversation. Prior to cable, viewers had two choices on the evenings of presidential addresses and debates: they could watch them or they could watch nothing at all. The networks honored most White House requests for airtime, but cable treated such programming as elective, which allowed Americans to avoid the increasingly few moments television still had to serve as the collective campfire around which citizens gathered. Seventy-one percent of all TV households tuned in to the presidential debate between Jimmy Carter and Ronald Reagan in 1980, according to Nielsen estimates. Eight years later, only 38 percent watched George H. W. Bush square off against Michael Dukakis. "All in all," observed the communications historian James L. Baughman, "cable's spread had not promoted democracy."[29] The introduction of remote-control devices, which allowed bored viewers to switch channels without leaving their seats, and VCRs, which permitted the audience to delay watching programs until it suited them, only accelerated the retreat from a shared civic experience.

To be sure, some in the cable industry tried to encourage democratic engagement. When C-SPAN was introduced in 1979, with its fixed-camera trained on congressional debates, the hope was that it would bestir Americans to witness their elected representatives in action. In fact, the audience for such fare was minute. Viewers were more interested in human interest pieces, such as the 1987 rescue of "Baby Jessica," a little girl trapped in a Texas well, which garnered CNN its highest rating (7.4 percent) during the 1980s.[30] Politicians soon found nonnetwork television to be an effective way to reach voters. In 1992 the Texas billionaire H. Ross Perot announced his independent run for the presidency on CNN's *Larry King Live,* and kept up the momentum in subsequent appearances, despite the networks virtually ignoring him. The live interview and call-in format allowed the candidate to avoid the tough questions of trained reporters and instead speak directly to voters, creating what some hailed (and others decried) as "talk-show democracy." The traditional gatekeeper function the networks had performed in deciding who was worthy of coverage, and in what manner, had come to an end.

Technology and Consolidation: 1980s–1990s

As the 1980s dawned, it became increasingly apparent that innovations in communications technology, which historically had expanded coverage from the days of the telegraph onward, now held the potential to diminish its depth and quality. Portable videotape, first used in the 1976 presidential campaign, pushed deadlines back nearly to news time, increasing the pressure on reporters to rush stories onto the air. Portable satellite uplinks, called "flyaways," permitted producers to "go live" from around the globe, bringing viewers dramatic images of everything from the toppling of the Berlin Wall to the first hail of bombs and missiles in Baghdad at the start of the Persian Gulf War. But the emphasis on "real time" reporting meant that the technical side of television was often ready to tell a story before the correspondent was. "Putting someone on the air while an event is unfolding is clearly a technological tour de force," said the ABC correspondent Ted Koppel, "but it is an impediment, not an aid, to good journalism. To simply train a camera on a complicated event is not journalism, any more than taking someone out on a boat and showing them a stretch of coastline is cartography."[31]

Good or bad, the demand for "you are there" journalism grew, fed in no small part by the introduction in 1980 of CNN, the first twenty-four-hour cable news network. In an earlier era producers had worried whether there was enough news to fill a thirty-minute evening broadcast; now, the "news hole"—the amount of time allotted to reporting the day's events—was huge. The network got a ratings boost in January 1991, when three of its correspondents, huddled in a Baghdad hotel room, provided the first and only live link between Americans and the U.S. military's initial aerial attacks in Iraq. In the ensuing years, CNN's ratings would soar and slump with the ebb and flow of events; Americans rarely tuned in unless there was a blockbuster event like a war or a verdict in a high-profile crime case. What the cable upstart had that its network counterparts could not match, however, was its global reach, a feature that had a profound effect on international diplomacy. Suddenly, presidents and prime ministers witnessed world events at the same time as any citizen with access to a television and a cable hookup. As the journalist Johanna Neuman noted about CNN's coverage of the first Gulf War: "Governments watched history with their publics, losing the luxury of time to deliberate in private before the imperative to 'do something' stood on their doorsteps."[32] The urgency reporters experienced as a result of advances in communications technology was now shared by those they covered.

The capacity to bring the world into the nation's living rooms was not matched by a thirst for foreign news. Historically, Americans' interest in international affairs had been weak and episodic, spiking in times of war or the threat of war and waning in times of peace. As Garrick Utley, a former foreign correspondent for NBC and ABC News, has observed, it is no coincidence that the growth of television news occurred during the period of the longest of the country's global conflicts, the cold war, when Americans had self-interested reasons to be attentive.[33] The consequence was that, with the end of the cold war, foreign news reporting both at newspapers and on television, where production costs for international reporting are particularly high, shrank steadily. According to the *Tyndall Report,* which monitors the networks' weekly nightly newscasts, total foreign policy coverage at NBC plummeted from 674 minutes in 1988 to 320 minutes in 1996; reports from the network's foreign bureaus fell from 1,013 minutes to just 327 minutes. Even the leader, ABC, experienced a precipitous drop, from 1,158 minutes of foreign bureau reports in 1988 to 577 minutes in 1996.[34]

The paradox was clear: even as American popular culture saturated the world, American business extended its reach across borders, and more and more Americans worked and traveled overseas, broad viewer interest in foreign affairs declined. While many in journalism saw it as their professional duty to expand citizens' notions of the public sphere, changes in the economics of news made fulfillment of that goal increasingly elusive.

The corporate ownership of news organizations, firmly entrenched by mid-century, continued its relentless march, intensifying the tension between news values and commercial values. Local ownership of newspapers became increasingly rare as punishing inheritance laws made it hard for family papers to be passed on to succeeding generations. Some families, like the Grahams at the *Washington Post* and the Sulzbergers at the *New York Times,* devised schemes that allowed them to take their companies public while still retaining control. But others sold out to chains, with the result that the share of American dailies that could be considered independently owned fell from 68 percent in 1960 to 30 percent in 1986.[35] By 2000 the nation had 292 fewer daily newspapers than it had in 1950; by 1992, only thirty-seven cities in the United States had separately owned, competing dailies. At the beginning of the new millennium, most of the country's papers were owned by seven national chains, ranging from Gannett, the largest in total circulation with 101 dailies, including *USA Today,* to Hearst, with 12. Ninety-nine percent of chain-owned papers were monopolies in the cities in which they operated. Still, some papers improved after being bought by out-of-town owners, and the newspaper industry as a whole remained surprisingly diverse. Even Gannett's outsized share represented only about 6 percent of the nation's 1,500 dailies.

More troubling for journalism's editorial mission was the growing trend toward public ownership and the merger of media companies into hydra-headed conglomerates. When Dow Jones, Inc., publisher of the *Wall Street Journal,* issued publicly traded stock in the early 1960s, it was the first media company to do so. By the late 1980s, at least fifteen publicly traded corporations owned papers.[36] The change brought clear financial benefits: newspapers could use company shares to acquire other properties; they could attract and retain top talent with stock-ownership plans; and they could use proceeds from stock sales to update plants and equipment. But it also meant that newspapers now had a new commercial interest other than advertisers to take into consideration: shareholders, who invested in newspaper companies for the same reason they invested in General Motors: to make a profit. No longer was it possible to have the patience of a Eugene Meyer, the longtime publisher of the *Washington Post,* who lost a million dollars or more every year for the first twenty years of ownership.[37] Many in journalism agreed with the sentiment that James Reston, the legendary *New York Times* correspondent and columnist, had expressed to Wall Street analysts in the early 1970s: "I think the time we begin thinking about the news in terms of how *you* look at it, that's the day . . . we begin to go down the drain."[38]

The deregulation of other industries that had begun in the 1970s picked up speed under President Ronald Reagan, whose administration favored less involvement by the FCC in the media business. In 1985 the FCC, under chairman Mark Fowler (who had once described television as "a toaster with pictures," implying that it deserved no more regulation than an appliance), rolled back the so-called 7-7-7 rule, which barred an owner of TV and FM and AM radio stations from having more than seven of each. The new limit was "12-12-12," as long as no one company's stations reached more than a quarter of the nation's homes. The change made possible what at the time was the largest media merger in U.S. history: the union of ABC (owner of a national network as well as numerous local stations) with Capital Cities Communications (owner of the *Kansas City Star* and the *Fort Worth Star-Telegram,* as well as broadcast stations). Less than ten years later, Capital Cities/ABC reclaimed that record when it merged with the Disney Company. In between, General Electric acquired RCA Corporation and, along with it, NBC, while Westinghouse took over CBS, only to sell the network four years later to Viacom.

In the meantime, the media world was in the midst of a revolution brought about by a new technology—the Internet—which began as a cold war project and moved ahead as a mechanism to connect scientists across universities and research labs around the world. By the early 1990s it had evolved into competitive private network services with subscribers. Companies such as America Online and Yahoo collected and distributed news, they did not report it, but as the use of personal computers spread, and more and more people hooked up to "the Net," traditional news organizations launched Web editions that allowed news not only to be interactive, but updated continuously throughout the day. When AOL and Time-Warner announced their merger in January 2000, it was hailed as the ultimate in "synergy," a word that, as the media critic Ken Auletta said, implied that "one plus one will add up to four."[39] Suddenly, the content of *Time, Fortune, Sports Illustrated,* and other Time, Inc., publications could be distributed across several media "platforms"—traditional print magazines; the Internet; and CNN, which the company had acquired in 1996. Journalism could even serve as the basis for Warner books and movies. While the anticipated arithmetic never fully materialized and AOL Time Warner stock plummeted, prompting the eventual removal of "AOL" from the company's name, the merger was emblematic of America's transformed media landscape. In an earlier era, press lords like Hearst and Luce dominated a single medium on a single continent. By the mid- to late 1990s, modern-day magnates were diversified; the Australian Rupert Murdoch, the controlling owner of News Corporation, sat atop an empire that spanned six continents and nine different media, including newspapers, books, magazines, broadcasting, direct-broadcast satellite TV, and a movie studio.[40]

Media conglomerates generated impressive revenues. Whether they were good for journalism, or democracy, however, was a matter of spirited debate. Critics such as Robert W. McChesney and Ben H. Bagdikian argued that consolidation fostered a numbing sameness in news selection and presentation, reduced the number of distinct editorial voices, and multiplied the opportunities for conflicts of interest. In 1998, for example, ABC killed a story critical of the hiring and safety practices at a theme park owned by Disney, its parent company. Likewise, during the nine months that it took to debate and pass the Telecommunications Act of 1996—legislation that FCC chairman Reed Hundt called "the biggest corporate giveaway of the century"—Americans learned little about the details. No more than nineteen minutes about the proposal managed to get on the three major networks, whose owning companies stood to benefit from the changes, and what did make the air failed to mention one of the bill's most controversial aspects: the debate over whether broadcasters should pay for use of the digital spectrum.[41]

Journalism had always been a business, but professional norms and traditions had kept a sharp separation between the "church" of reporting and the "state" of the countinghouse. Now the wall between the two seemed to be lowering. The phenomenon was apparent in 1999 when the *Los Angeles Times,* under the corporate leadership of chairman and CEO Mark Willes, a former General Mills executive, agreed to share the profits of a special Sunday magazine about the opening of the Staples Center, a downtown arena, with the owners of the new facility. The stock price of Times-Mirror, the paper's parent company, had tripled under Willes, who displayed it on a screen in the *Times's* lobby where reporters saw it before their morning elevator ride.[42] But the paper's credibility had been dangerously compromised. In short order, the "cereal killer," as Willes was derisively known, was sent packing. The Staples incident became a scandal, the *Times's* editorial staff was publicly and loudly up in arms, and the embarrassment for the paper was severe.

But the momentum toward business involvement on the news side was powerful. News magazines such as *Time* used focus groups to determine which cover stories readers would find most compelling. The *Today Show,* NBC's morning news program, spent almost as many minutes each day in "cross-promotion"—soft-selling the network's prime-time lineup in interviews and features—as it did on breaking events. The line between news and entertainment, already blurred, became fuzzier still. Because cost cutting was an easy way to boost profits, some newsrooms lacked adequate resources to pursue complex stories. Others replaced older, more experienced staff with younger, less expensive reporters. Some practiced triage, closing statehouse bureaus and leaving certain agencies of the federal government uncovered. The trend toward "convergence"—the replacement of competition between different kinds of media with cooperation—meant that reporters at some news organizations were called upon to file stories for their company's newspaper, TV station, and Web page, raising questions about quality and completeness. Wall Street, by its nature conservative, sought regular, positive, predictable results and disliked the risk associated with tough investigative stories that might require time-consuming Freedom of Information requests or invite lawsuits and negative publicity. "Although journalism is important," a research analyst for Bank of America Securities told a *New York Times* reporter, "at the end of the day, investors care more about the number of newspapers you sell and the ad rate increases you get, rather than the number of Pulitzer Prizes."[43] Increasingly, reporters, editors, and producers struggled to maintain what many argued was journalism's greatest public function—its watchdog role—in the face of the profession's private masters.

Even public broadcasting, begun in 1967 to serve as a civic and cultural counterweight to commercial programming, felt the hot breath of financial pressure. While the Public Broadcasting Service's evening newscast, *The MacNeil-Lehrer News Hour* (retitled *The NewsHour with Jim Lehrer* after coanchor Robert MacNeil left the show) drew an educated elite to its in-depth interviews and analysis, and National Public Radio's audience surged, fickle government funding left PBS continually in search of corporate underwriters and advertisers. It also made PBS vulnerable to conservative politicians like Senator Newt Gingrich, who in 1995 as Speaker of the House, denounced public broadcasting as "this little sandbox for the rich" and sought to cut off federal subsidies. By 2004, the Right had pragmatically given up trying to eliminate PBS and settled for a stronger role in shaping its programming.[44]

The power of economic pressures and incentives could not be denied. Still, at the beginning of the twenty-first century, reporters and editors operated with resources for good journalism that they did not command a generation earlier. The capacities in both print and television for graphic display of visual and statistical information were much improved. The multitude of databases, available online, including easy access to news stories in every major and most minor newspapers around the country, simplified and enriched the research that reporters could master in a short time. Even more important than these technological changes, the cultural transformations in politics and the media since the 1960s provided a new openness to government sources. The Freedom of Information Act (enacted in 1967 and expanded and toughened in 1974) provided a valuable new tool to journalists seeking information that government agencies were reluctant to share. The data collected by the Federal Election Commission (established in 1974) on campaign contributors and campaign finances created a way to "follow the money" in elections—imperfectly, to be sure, but much more carefully (and readily) than ever before. The movement toward open committee meetings and roll-call votes in Congress, part of a general wave of open government reforms in the 1970s at both federal and state levels, also made journalism a better partner to democracy than had been previously possible.

More Information, Less News: The Challenge of the Present

Today, Americans are saturated with images, interviews, facts, and analysis, yet have a surprisingly superficial knowledge of the machinery of democracy or the rest of the world. Paradoxically, there is more quality news available than ever before, but it is often overwhelmed by the sheer volume of entertainment, consumer features, crime, and sensation. While this may rivet the attention of those who otherwise might not see or read much of anything, it has come at a price. Media scholar Thomas E. Patterson has argued that, the trend toward "infotainment" and news that is more critical in tone, born largely of the drive for profits, has actually contributed to a declining interest in the news.[45]

Indeed, "news" has become so conflated with opinion and other cultural commodities that a one-size-fits-all definition no longer applies. "Truth, fact and information seemed fairly straightforward concepts to most people in the news business a quarter century ago," wrote Marc Fisher in *The American Journalism Review.* "Today, they're entirely up for grabs."[46] Americans, fragmented across hundreds of outlets with varying standards and agendas, rarely come together around news events unless there is a crisis (such as September 11), a scandal (Monica Lewinsky), a sports spectacle (the Super Bowl) or a sensational trial (O.J. Simpson). Even the notion of who is a journalist is remarkably fluid, with many, especially the young, giving equal credence to Matt Drudge, who posts unverified items on his eponymous Web site; comedian Jon Stewart of *The Daily Show;* late-night talk show host Jay Leno; and NBC anchor Tom Brokaw. While some decry the dumbing down of news, and berate the audience for having grown less discriminating, others contend that editors and producers are only giving Americans what they want, and still others suggest that the blurring of rigid definitions of news rightly takes conventional journalists down a peg and usefully broadens the ways that knowledge of contemporary affairs is distributed.

This market model of journalism, ascendant in the twentieth century, has taken on new meaning because of the Internet. While only a fraction of the ten thousand Web sites that are reportedly created each day can be considered "news" sites, the Internet has greatly expanded the number of places one can go to get news; it has made news available instantaneously and around the clock; and it has effectively dismantled the barrier between journalist and reader. Now anyone with a computer and a modem can be a "publisher," an argument that the FCC chairman Michael Powell has repeatedly invoked to make his case that government regulations constraining further media consolidation should be further relaxed. Whether such "publishers" are journalists, however, is a matter of contention. Most "bloggers"—authors of Web logs or creators of online journals—

concede (and occasionally crow) that they don't adhere to the prevailing standards of the profession, including accuracy, verification, balance, and fairness. But that doesn't mean that what bloggers produce doesn't sometimes look like news. It was bloggers who in December 2002 took note of a brief item on ABC News's Web site about Senate Majority Leader Trent Lott's racist remarks at a one-hundredth birthday party for South Carolina senator Strom Thurmond and sent outraged posts racing around the Web. The items caught the attention of the mainstream media, which belatedly turned its full wattage on a story that until then they had largely ignored. Within two weeks Lott resigned as majority leader.[47] In this case, the bloggers' function bridged that of a journalist (several of the key bloggers in this case were well-connected former magazine journalists) and that of a concerned citizen calling up the hometown paper to complain that a local scandal had been overlooked. As the press critic Jay Rosen put it on his own blog, PressThink: "Reactions and rumblings from across the blogs were . . . a kind of proxy for public reaction that had not been able to emerge."[48] Historically, the press had mobilized citizens; now, it was citizens who mobilized the press.

Bloggers are hardly alone in their rejection of reportorial conventions. With the explosion of cable channels, Internet Web sites, and radio talk shows has come a kind of cafeteria-style approach to news consumption. Readers, viewers, and listeners now have access to a wide array of news-oriented programming and commentary, much of it sharply partisan, from FOX News and radio talk show host Rush Limbaugh on the right to comedian Al Franken and Air America on the left. Just as the economic need to appeal to a broad audience in the nineteenth century encouraged the press to gradually wring political invective from the news, so the economic appeal of niche audiences in the twenty-first century has prompted the press to restore it. While objectivity remains a dominant professional norm for journalists—a 1999 Pew Research Center survey found that some 75 percent of reporters and news executives said it was possible to obtain a true, accurate, and widely agreed upon account of an event—a significant number of Americans believe the media are biased.[49] Surveys showing that moderates and liberals make up a disproportionate share of those in newsrooms only reinforce this view, although hard evidence that journalists push a left-wing agenda is hard to come by. As Brent Cunningham noted in the *Columbia Journalism Review,* "Mostly . . . we are biased in favor of getting the story, regardless of whose ox is gored."[50]

Indignant about charges of liberal bias—the columnist Geneva Overholser, a professor at the University of Missouri school of journalism, calls them "largely hooey, and dangerous hooey at that"[51]—some journalists have begun to push back. In a May 2004 speech at the University of Oregon journalism school, the *Los Angeles Times* editor John Carroll denounced the "cold cynicism" of what he called "pseudo-journalism"—outlets such as *The O'Reilly Factor* that take on the trappings of newsrooms but whose chief aim is to manipulate the audience. "We live in changed times," Carroll said. "Never has falsehood in America had such a large megaphone."[52] Citizens, however, continue to gravitate in large numbers to programs that express views with which they agree. More than half of those who regularly watch FOX News, for example, describe themselves as politically conservative, and the audience for Rush Limbaugh's radio show is overwhelmingly so. CNN, which more closely mirrors the general population ideologically, nevertheless has more Democrat-leaning viewers in 2004 than it did in the past.[53] As the columnist John Leo observed, "Now we can all go to a TV channel, a radio show or a web site that will protect us from those aliens across the moat who disagree with us."[54] Fewer Americans appeared to value the media's role as surrogates for the public or its function as a filter through which inaccuracy, imbalance, and unfairness are sifted out.

President George W. Bush claimed that he rarely reads newspapers, preferring to "go over the head of the filter and speak directly to the American people." Like Nixon, Bush views the press, in the words of the media critic Ken Auletta, as "special pleaders—pleaders for more access and better headlines—as if the press were simply another interest group."[55] Many Americans no doubt would agree. Yet at the same time, the government, after effectively hampering journalists from covering the first Gulf War and the war in Afghanistan, instituted a policy of "embedding" some six hundred reporters with the troops during the 2003 war with Iraq—the first time since Vietnam that the press traveled side by side with the military during combat. In the atmosphere of heightened patriotism after September 11, news outlets were alternately castigated for their lack of skepticism about the purported reasons for invading Iraq, and criticized for their tough reporting on prison abuses and the messy aftermath of the war. With both national leadership and popular opinion deeply divided about the war, there was little the press could do to please everyone.

The attacks on journalistic objectivity came at a time, ironically, when the people entering the field were better educated than ever. In 2002 nearly 90 percent of all journalists had at least a four-year bachelor's degree, up from 58 percent in 1971.[56] But that has not shielded the profession from ethical lapses that have only deepened the public's distrust. Plagiarism, fabricated stories, and outright lies have tainted news organizations as esteemed as the *New York Times* (whose reporter Jayson Blair repeatedly faked stories and plagiarized others' work) and *USA Today* (where the foreign correspondent Jack Kelley concocted portions of stories and lifted quotes from competing publications). At both papers, top editors resigned as a result of the scandals; the *Times* also hired its first ombudsman, or "readers' representative," while other mainstream news organizations updated their ethics policies and training practices.

Today, journalism is in the midst of what the Project for Excellence in Journalism (PEJ) calls "an epochal transformation, as momentous probably as the invention of the telegraph or television."[57] Contradictions abound. The journalist's role as the arbiter of information has diminished, yet the need to alert citizens to the misleading, the false, and the propagandistic has never been greater. Americans have more control over when and how they get their news, yet they know little about the normal processes and common pitfalls of new production. Media companies report record profits, yet with the advent of TIVO, a commercial-skipping technology, and shrinking audiences for traditional news outlets, the advertising that has supported news since the late nineteenth century is under threat. While most Americans still turn to local, cable, and network television for their news, the percentage who say they read a daily paper has slipped from 58 percent in 1994 to 42 percent a decade later, and the majority of those readers are older—a red flare that has motivated several large urban papers to experiment with free youth-oriented tabloids.[58] Meanwhile, the audience for online news is growing steadily, despite the lack of a clear economic model to sustain it. In short, what is the future of news? For that matter, what is the future of democracy? The only thing clear is that they are intertwined. "Journalism . . . is not becoming irrelevant," declared the Project for Excellence in Journalism. "It is becoming more complex."[59] On that point, at least, there is consensus.

Notes

1. For an ardent advocate of this view, see Stephens, *A History of News.* See also Richard Streckfuss, "News before Newspapers," *Journalism and Mass Communication Quarterly* 75 (1998): 84–97.
2. Charles E. Clark and Charles Wetherell, "The Measure of Maturity: *The Pennsylvania Gazette,* 1728–1765," *William and Mary Quarterly* 3rd series, 46 (1989): 292.
3. Eric Foner, *Tom Paine and Revolutionary America* (New York: Oxford University Press, 1976), 83. On the growth of political pamphlets in the leading cities, see Gary Nash, "The Transformation of Urban Politics, 1700–1765," *Journal of American History* 60 (1973): 616, 618. The best general history of the colonial press is Clark, *The Public Prints.*
4. Jackson Turner Main, *The Antifederalists: Critics of the Constitution, 1781–1788* (Chapel Hill: University of North Carolina Press, 1961), 209, 250–51.
5. Pauline Maier, *The Old Revolutionaries: Political Lives in the Age of Samuel Adams* (New York: Knopf, 1980), 30.
6. Pennsylvania jurist Alexander Addison, as quoted in Richard Buel Jr., "Freedom of the Press in Revolutionary America: The Evolution of Libertarianism, 1760–1820," in *The Press and the American Revolution,* edited by Bailyn and Hench, 85–86.
7. Thomas Jefferson, letter to John Norvell, June 11, 1807, in *The Life and Selected Writings of Thomas Jefferson,* edited by Adrienne Koch and William Peden (New York: Modern Library, 1944), 581–82.
8. On the emergence of the penny press and on nineteenth-century U.S. newspaper history generally, see Schudson, *Discovering the News.*
9. Ritchie, *Press Gallery,* 60–63; Michael Schudson, *The Good Citizen: A History of American Civic Life* (Cambridge, Mass.: Harvard University Press, 1999), 177–82; and

Michael E. McGerr, *The Decline of Popular Politics: The American North, 1865–1928* (New York: Oxford University Press, 1986), 107–37.

10. See Schudson, *Discovering the News,* and Michael Schudson, "The Objectivity Norm in American Journalism," *Journalism* 2 (August 2001): 149–70.

11. Figures from Alfred McClung Lee, *The Daily Newspaper in America: The Evolution of a Social Instrument* (New York: Macmillan, 1937), and Leonard, *The Power of the Press.*

12. Stephens, *A History of News,* 209.

13. Kenneth T. Jackson, ed., *The Encyclopedia of New York City* (New Haven, Conn.: Yale University Press, 1995), 813.

14. Stephens, *A History of News,* 203.

15. George N. Gordon, *The Communications Revolution: A History of Mass Media in the United States* (New York: Hastings House, 1977), 192–93.

16. Gordon, *The Communications Revolution,* 127–32; Folkerts and Teeter, *Voices of a Nation,* 387–93; and Stephens, *A History of News,* 276–78.

17. Donna L. Halper, "Radio in 1934," Original Old Time Radio WWW Pages, www.old-time.com/halper/halper34.html.

18. Michael Schudson, *The Sociology of News* (New York: Norton, 2003), 82.

19. Folkerts and Teeter, *Voices of a Nation,* 492.

20. As quoted in Westbrook Pegler column, *New York Journal-American,* June 3, 1954.

21. Folkerts and Teeter, *Voices of a Nation,* 480–83.

22. Robert D. Leigh, ed., *A Free and Responsible Press: A General Report on Mass Communication: Newspapers, Radio, Motion Pictures, Magazines, and Books by the Commission on Freedom of the Press* (Chicago: University of Chicago Press, 1947), 37.

23. As quoted in *Reporting Vietnam: American Journalism 1959–1969,* vol. 1 (New York: Library of America, 1998), 581–82.

24. As quoted in Schudson, *The Power of News,* 144.

25. Ibid., 144.

26. Ibid., 173.

27. Entman research referenced in Baughman, *The Republic of Mass Culture,* 216.

28. Baughman, *The Republic of Mass Culture;* sound bite research in Daniel C. Hallin, "Soundbite News: Television Coverage of Elections, 1968–1988," *Journal of Communication* 42 (1992): 5–24.

29. Baughman, *The Republic of Mass Culture,* 213.

30. Ibid.

31. As quoted in Michael Murrie, "Communication Technology and the Correspondent," in *Live from the Trenches: The Changing Role of the Television News Correspondent,* edited by Joe S. Foote (Carbondale: University of Illinois Press, 1998), 97.

32. Johanna Neuman, *Lights, Camera, War: Is Media Technology Driving International Politics?* (New York: St. Martin's, 1996), 3.

33. Garrick Utley, "The Shrinking of Foreign News: From Broadcast to Narrowcast," in *Live from the Trenches,* edited by Foote, 87.

34. Ibid., 85.

35. Baughman, *The Republic of Mass Culture,* 165.

36. Folkerts and Teeter, *Voices of a Nation,* 542.

37. Leonard Downie Jr. and Robert G. Kaiser, *The News about the News: American Journalism in Peril* (New York: Knopf, 2002), 118.
38. As quoted in Tifft and Jones, *The Trust,* 471.
39. Ken Auletta, *The Highwaymen: Warriors of the Information Superhighway* (New York: Random House, 1997), 180.
40. Ibid., 260.
41. Dean Alger, *Megamedia: How Giant Corporations Dominate Mass Media, Distort Competition, and Endanger Democracy* (Lanham, Md.: Rowman and Littlefield, 1998), 109.
42. Brent Cunningham, "Two Brothers, Two Worlds," *Columbia Journalism Review* 40 (July/August 2001): 34–39.
43. Jacques Steinberg, "After the Peaks of Journalism, Budget Realities," *New York Times,* June 14, 2004.
44. Ken Auletta, "Big Bird Flies Right," *New Yorker,* June 7, 2004, 42–48.
45. Thomas E. Patterson, "Doing Well and Doing Good: How Soft News and Critical Journalism Are Shrinking the News Audience and Weakening Democracy—And What News Outlets Can Do about It" (working paper, Joan Shorenstein Center on Press, Politics and Public Policy, Kennedy School of Government, Harvard University, Cambridge, Mass., 2000), available at http://www.ksg.harvard.edu/presspol/Research_Publications/Reports/softnews.pdf.
46. Marc Fisher, "Metamorphosis," *American Journalism Review* 24 (November 2002): 20.
47. Esther Scott, "'Big Media' Meets the 'Bloggers': Coverage of Trent Lott's Remarks at Strom Thurmond's Birthday Party," KSG Case Study C14-04-1731.0 (Cambridge, Mass.: John F. Kennedy School of Government, Harvard University, 2004).
48. Jay Rosen, "The Legend of Trent Lott and the Weblogs," PressThink, March 15, 2004.
49. "Bottom-Line Pressures Now Hurting Coverage, Say Journalists," survey report, May 23, 2004 (Washington, D.C.: Pew Research Center for the People and the Press), available at http://people-press.org.
50. Brent Cunningham, "Re-Thinking Objectivity," *Columbia Journalism Review* 42, no. 2 (July/August 2003): 24–32.
51. Geneva Overholser, "Liberal Media: Could the Charge Have Had Its Run?" Poynteronline, June 11, 2004, http://www.poynter.org/column.asp?id= 54&aid= 66983.
52. John S. Carroll, "Pseudo-Journalists Betray the Public Trust," *Los Angeles Times,* May 16, 2004; the article was adapted from his speech entitled "The Wolf in Reporter's Clothing: The Rise of Pseudo-Journalism in America," delivered at the University of Oregon, May 6, 2004.
53. "News Audiences Increasingly Politicized," survey report, June 8, 2004 (Washington, D.C.: Pew Research Center for the People and the Press), available at http://people-press.org.
54. John Leo, "Instead of Arguments, We Get Shouts & Insults," *(NY) Daily News,* June 15, 2004.
55. Ken Auletta, "Fortress Bush," *New Yorker,* January 19, 2004.

56. *The American Journalist in the 21st Century* (St. Petersburg, Fla.: Poynter Institute, 2003), http://www.knightfdn.org/publications/americanjournalist/aj_keyfindings.pdf.
57. Introduction to *The State of the News Media 2004: An Annual Report on American Journalism* (Washington, D.C.: Project for Excellence in Journalism, 2004), http://www.stateofthenewsmedia.org.
58. "News Audiences Increasingly Politicized."
59. *The State of the News Media 2004: An Annual Report on American Journalism* (Washington, D.C.: Project for Excellence in Journalism, 2004), http://www. stateofthenewsmedia.org.

Bibliography

Bailyn, Bernard, and John B. Hench, eds. *The Press and the American Revolution.* Worcester, Mass.: American Antiquarian Society, 1980. Excellent collection on that crucial era.

Baughman, James L. *The Republic of Mass Culture: Journalism, Filmmaking, and Broadcasting in America since 1941.* 2nd ed. Baltimore: Johns Hopkins University Press, 1997. An astute and approachable study of the recent era.

Clark, Charles E. *The Public Prints: The Newspaper in Anglo-American Culture, 1665–1740.* New York: Oxford University Press, 1994. The best overall account of colonial newspapers.

Emery, Michael, Edwin Emery, and Nancy L. Roberts. *The Press and America: An Interpretive History of the Mass Media.* 9th ed. Boston: Allyn and Bacon, 2000. Along with Folkerts and Teeter, a useful textbook on American journalism history.

Folkerts, Jean, and Dwight L. Teeter Jr. *Voices of a Nation: A History of Media in the United States.* New York: Macmillan, 1989.

Graham, Katharine. *Personal History.* New York: Knopf, 1997. Personal account by long-time publisher of the *Washington Post.*

Greenfield, Meg. *Washington.* New York: Public Affairs, 2001. Illuminating memoir by a journalist who served as editor of the *Washington Post's* editorial page.

Leonard, Thomas C. *The Power of the Press: The Birth of American Political Reporting.* New York: Oxford University Press, 1986.

Nasaw, David. *The Chief: The Life of William Randolph Hearst.* Boston: Houghton Mifflin, 2000.

Nord, David Paul. *Communities of Journalism: A History of American Newspapers and Their Readers.* Urbana: University of Illinois Press, 2001.

Ritchie, Donald A. *Press Gallery: Congress and the Washington Correspondents.* Cambridge, Mass.: Harvard University Press, 1991. Particularly illuminating on the nineteenth and early twentieth centuries.

Schudson, Michael. *Discovering the News: A Social History of American Newspapers.* New York: Basic Books, 1978. With Stephens, a useful general work on the history of U.S. journalism.

Schudson, Michael. *The Power of News.* Cambridge, Mass.: Harvard University Press, 1995.

Stephens, Mitchell. *A History of News: From the Drum to the Satellite.* New York: Viking, 1988.

Tifft, Susan E., and Alex S. Jones. *The Patriarch: The Rise and Fall of the Bingham Dynasty.* New York: Summit Books, 1991.
Tifft, Susan E., and Alex S. Jones. *The Trust: The Private and Powerful Family behind the New York Times.* Boston: Little, Brown, 1999.

3

THE NATURE AND SOURCES OF NEWS

Robert M. Entman

THE IDEAL GOAL OF TRADITIONAL JOURNALISM HAS been to make power accountable: to keep ordinary citizens apprised of what government is doing, and how it affects them both individually and with respect to the groups and values that they care about. Journalism thereby fosters in the public informed, rational opinions about politics and candidates. Many observers now fear that a shift toward soft news and entertainment ("infotainment") diminishes the mass public's ability to hold government to account. They foresee a downward spiral of diminishing demand for and a dwindling supply of what has been called "accountability news."[1] This is news that enables even the typically inattentive citizen to understand at least some of the impacts that government decisions are having on their lives and values. With less accountability news, citizens' recognition of the very need to watch TV news or read newspapers may weaken. When this happens, the market sends signals to media organizations: ramp up production of soft news, infotainment, and "reality" TV—making it still less likely that citizens will stumble across accountability news.

Yet all is not lost. For one thing, traditional journalism has not fulfilled the key democracy-enhancing purposes of news as consistently as might be thought. For another, media that do not label their products as "news" can nonetheless achieve some of the objectives traditionally associated with news. The aim of this essay is to outline the core democratizing roles of journalism and to explore the ways in which the full range of media products may now be fulfilling at least some of these "news functions." The ultimate aim is to acknowledge and nurture the contributions made to democracy across the entire media landscape.

Core Function of News

Although news has always contained elements of entertainment and vice versa, most observers would agree that the rise of competition from cable and satellite

48

television, the Internet, and other forms of electronic media has changed the way in which journalists go about their business. Perhaps less fully recognized is how and with what effects those not denominated or identifying as journalists nonetheless provide audiences with insights into society's important events, issues, problems, and relationships. Intuitively one can perceive differences between the *New York Times* and the *New York Post,* or among Rush Limbaugh's syndicated radio commentary, *The Oprah Winfrey Show, 60 Minutes,* and *The West Wing.* But these differences do not necessarily translate into distinctions made by audiences as they process information and respond to these media. Audience members who hear about problems faced by families without health insurance on *The Oprah Winfrey Show* or who read in the *National Enquirer* that the First Lady is going to divorce the president do not, and perhaps should not, entirely discount or ignore this information and only consider what they read or hear from outlets certified as "news" media.

In other words, media not bound by the canons and practices of traditional journalism can serve the core democratizing functions of news, the functions that help citizens hold government to account. These news functions involve illuminating four areas of knowledge vital to effective democratic citizenship:

1. Policy (specific public policy issues)
2. Power (the actions of individuals [especially public officials] and groups exerting political power)
3. Ideology (the philosophical perspectives that shape decisions on allocating wealth, status and other valued resources)
4. Self-interest (individuals' own political interests and stakes in policy issues and elections, and their roles in society)

Almost any media organization irrespective of how it labels its products and defines its missions can convey useful information on these four matters and thus help citizens operate more effectively at holding government to account. In this sense, a diverse range of media can fulfill these core democratizing functions of news. Media outlets and products that can assist citizenship range from the traditional journalism as practiced by, say, the *New York Times* or *CBS Evening News,* to the advocacy journalism of the *Nation* or the *Weekly Standard,* to the tabloid journalism of the *New York Post* or the *National Enquirer* (themselves rather different from each other), and finally to more or less pure "entertainment." The first three categories are produced by organizations and personnel that identify primarily with the journalistic profession, and audiences regard their messages as non-fictional accounts of social actors, events, and issues. For now, we can distinguish advocacy journalism as news influenced by the organization's commitment more to advancing particular political or policy agendas than to enhancing citizenship in general. Tabloid journalism is news shaped more by commercial considerations and by mass audiences' presumed tastes for sensation and emotion than by the commitment to democratic purposes. Entertainment, in contrast, is neither produced by journalists nor consciously consumed as news. Audiences generally regard entertainment as fictional, or as artificial and disconnected from real social processes (e.g., so-called *reality* TV, which throws "real" people into situations created only for the program). However, these classifications are subject to many exceptions and ambiguities. For instance, some segments of 60 Minutes and *20/20* arguably function as advocacy journalism even as other segments merely celebrate celebrities. We need to probe these distinctions further.

Once we acknowledge that greatly differing organizations now produce material that audiences *use* as news—that is, material that influences audiences' thinking with respect to policy, power, ideology or self-interest—seeing more precisely *how* these sources of mediated communication differ illuminates the nature of news in the early twenty-first century. These distinctions reveal the more varied character of news as it is now frequently composed under constraints and norms only distantly related to those taught in journalism schools or honored in traditional news organizations. This in turn helps us chart directions for research and issues for public policy while developing a fuller understanding of how to improve the contributions of a "press"—that is, a news-production apparatus—that encompasses far more than the traditional journalistic enterprises that formed the focus of the Commission on Freedom of the Press (the so-called Hutchins Commission) in 1947, and similar normative discussions since.

This said, however, traditional newspapers, broadcast news programs, and newsweeklies are thought to perform the core news functions most thoroughly, directly, responsibly and consistently. These media put illumination of policy, power, ideology, and self-interest at the center of their productions and do so in every issue or edition. This is not to say that the traditional news outlets always or even usually augment democracy; an enormous literature documents the gap between journalistic ideals and traditional journalism's actual contributions to democratic life.[2] It is merely to say that the media in this category are generally regarded as having the highest probability of contributing to democratic citizenship.

For many critics, achievement of the core news functions is jeopardized as "entertainment" displaces "news" and "soft" news displaces "hard"—as audiences choose to spend less time with media content that presumably assists democratic citizenship effectively, and as media produce less of such content. Herbert Gans, in *Democracy and the News,* defines soft news as:

> a very heterogeneous residual category, including human interest, scandal, entertainment, and the celebrity stories that now appear even in the most elite newspapers. Another . . . form of soft news is the feature story that provides people with helpful information for everyday life, for example about heart attack prevention, healthy diets, and new lifestyles

and leisure activities that are thought to enhance the quality of public life. (p. 28)

As this definition suggests, soft news bleeds into entertainment, but both can sometimes fulfill news functions. Baleful as the ascendance of soft news might be, it appears to be an unstoppable feature of twenty-first-century journalism.[3]

Distinguishing among Media

Journalists, scholars, and the educated public have long thought of news as a more or less self-evident category of media product—the stuff that appears in newspapers, newsmagazines, or on TV shows that have the word "news" in their titles. Yet audiences increasingly appear inclined to use other products as news, products that do not fit this traditional conception. This trend demands a new look at just what is meant by "news" and how to differentiate among various media and their products. The approach here is to distinguish media outlets (and segments within them) based not merely on how the organizations label their products, but on how they produce them. Table 1 illustrates a taxonomy.[4] No strict line separates the categories, but we can usefully distinguish traditional journalism; advocacy journalism; tabloid journalism; and entertainment. The main areas of difference in how these media outlets go about their business are listed across the top of the table:

- Degree of commitment to key journalistic standards
- Core organizational values and missions
- Target audiences and market constraints
- Prototypical message content

In a fifth column, the table also suggests the differences in media outlets' performing of news functions.

The categories on both horizontal and vertical dimensions of the table are imprecise. Beyond differences among the four types of outlets, the very same outlet can differ from program to program (on television or radio), section to section (newspaper or magazine) or Web page to Web page. Even within the most prestigious journalistic media, individual stories or segments differ. The *New York Times* offers plenty of sports, lifestyle, and celebrity coverage that does not fit definitions of traditional news. (Not to mention that the *Times*, like almost every other medium, devotes large chunks of its space to advertising.) And *Times* readers may use some of the material not appearing in the guise of traditional hard, political news in developing their thinking and feelings about policy issues, government officials, social problems, or their own interests in politics and society (for instance, in their roles as working women or wealthy men). In the same way, different organizations will show greater or lesser differences on the traits listed across the top of the table. Again, no clear lines exist.

Media category	Commitment to key journalistic standards	Core organizational values and missions	Target analysis and market constraints	Prototypical message content	Performance of news functions
Traditional journalism *NYT/LAT/Chi. Tribune* ↓ *CBS Evening News* ↓ *Meet the Press* ↓ *Time/Newsweek*	All 5 key standards of traditional journalism (accuracy, balance, etc.)	1. Democratic watchdog 2. Profit 3. Give useful information for monitoring and coping with the world	1. Politically interested citizens 2. Upscale and midscale consumers 3. At apex (*NYT, WSJ*) driven by national, not local, audiences	1. News story about a top government official's actions/proposals 2. Opinion column on current policy issue 3. More detailed news story or full interview transcript on Web site	Performed most consistently and overtly
Advocacy journalism *The Nation/Weekly Standard* ↓ Documentary film ↓ Nonfiction books by Michael Moore, Ann Coulter et al.	Commitment to only 3–4 standards	1. Democratic watchdog 2. Agenda setting and policy impact	1. Politically informed, ideologically committed citizens 2. Upscale and midscale consumers	1. Investigative story probing hidden consequences 2. Opinion/analytical essay or polemic 3. One-sided, aggressive interview	Performed, but how well depends on one's ideological perspective
Tabloid journalism Local television news ↓ *America's Most Wanted* ↓ *O'Reilly Factor/ New York Post* ↓ Matt Drudge Web site *National Enquirer*	Commitment to 0–2 standards	1. Profit 2. Amusement and diversion 3. Agenda setting and policy impact	1. Downscale consumers 2. Ideologically committed citizens	1. Local news: crime, accidents, fires, soft news. 2. Other tabloids: unusual crime or sensational scandal 3. Ideologically driven polemics	Rarely performed
Entertainment Infotainment TV (*Oprah/Today Show*) ↓ Infotainment magazines (*People*) ↓ Television and film drama; novels	Commitment to 0–4 standards	1. Profit 2. Amusement and diversion	Everyone, with segmentation of specific target audiences in many cases	1. Fictional dramatic narrative 2. Interview or documentary nonfiction narrative of good vs. evil, or personal redemption 3. Comedic monologue or situation comedy	Indirectly performed

Then there are questions about the degree to which the content of seemingly pure entertainment outlets—say, Jay Leno's or Jon Stewart's topical jokes or *People* magazine's celebrity profiles—always differs from that of news organizations in actually fulfilling commitments to journalistic standards. It is now widely recognized that the late-night comedy monologues, for instance, are quite political. During Leno's first ten years as host of *The Tonight Show* he told over eighteen thousand political jokes, thirty-seven hundred about Bill Clinton alone.[5]

Consider the feedback loops among news and entertainment outlets, and the potential impacts on public opinion, of the following case: President Clinton's purported $200 haircut in 1993. This alleged extravagance was widely reported to have taken place while *Air Force One* was parked at Los Angeles International Airport, reportedly causing major delays for LAX passengers. Seen as symbolizing Clinton's arrogance and hypocrisy, the haircut, according to a *Washington Post* ombudsman story, actually did not cause air traffic delays,[6] nor did it cost $200. In fact it cost less than $150, perhaps far less (the hairdresser charged $150 for a first-time haircut, but Clinton was an established customer and thus paid less[7]). Nonetheless, according to the Pew Research Center for the People and the Press, the story of Clinton's $200 haircut ranked as a major news story of mid-1993 in terms of public interest, with 18 percent of survey respondents saying that they followed the story "very closely"—as compared with 26 percent who followed the Bosnia situation very closely, and 12 percent who followed the story of Clinton's deficit-closing budget.[8]

This kind of news story often provides fodder for the politically charged jokes told on late-night television. Jay Leno, as one example, offered the following joke months after the putative hair session took place: "Remember the good old days when Miss America had a two-hundred-dollar hairstyle and the president did his own?" In 1993 President Clinton was the most joked-about politician on late-night talk shows, far outdistancing Ross Perot, who ranked second (761 jokes to 100 jokes).[9] The *Washington Post,* which broke the haircut allegations on May 20, 1993, and mentioned "the most famous haircut since Samson's" in nine front-page stories over six weeks, itself never prominently corrected its original allegations,[10] so it hardly seems fair to castigate comedians for using the original, false tale as a launchpad for jokes. Even after the facts came out in June—that *Air Force One* caused no delays at LAX and the haircut cost much less than $200—many prominent newspapers continued to treat the "$200 haircut" as real. The mythical $200 haircut lived on for years; in July 2004, the *Times* of London mentioned it as if factual.[11] Indeed, the *Washington Post* ombudsman story did not itself correct the $200 figure even as it criticized the *Post* and other media for repeating the falsehood about airport delays.

This example suggests that the differences in factual accuracy between non-fictional news and fictional entertainment are not always as great as journalists might like to believe. Perhaps the $200 haircut was so useful as a symbol of Clinton's asserted personal flaws that neither journalists nor comedians could let go of it. Given the fallibility of individual journalists and of news organizations, there are unavoidably many other examples, ranging from the Patriot missile's mythical effectiveness in the first Gulf War[12] to the rarely contradicted images (at least while in office) of John F. Kennedy and Ronald Reagan as devoted family men.

With this warning that the distinctions are fluid, the borders between categories murky, let us consider in greater detail how the four types of media performing news functions can be distinguished using the criteria listed across the top of Table 1.

Commitment to Key Journalistic Standards

The key differences among the four types of media enterprise arise from differing levels of commitment to five key standards in the production of texts. Professionals and scholars consider these the defining standards and behavioral traits of traditional journalistic activity:

1. Accuracy. News organizations devote great resources and energy to assuring the factual basis of factual claims in news columns. In practice this usually means reliance on legitimate sources: those persons affiliated with, and documents produced by, prestigious, credible, powerful institutions.

2. Balance. Journalists attempt to provide roughly equivalent treatment to contending sides in disputes (most often, spokespersons of both major parties) and keep personal views of issues and persons involved in news from coloring reports.

3. Checks on pure profit maximization. Decisions on stories to cover, how to play them, how much to follow up, and the like are made more on grounds of professional news judgment than on immediate profit calculations.

4. Democratic accountability. Traditional news organizations attempt to hold government to account by maintaining a high level of surveillance of public officials and promoting monitorial citizenship.[13] Highest priority (page-one placement, most prestigious/skilled journalists assigned) is therefore accorded to major policy issues and decisions by executive (especially), legislative, and judicial branches of government.

5. Editorial separation. News and editorial staffs are largely separate and positions endorsed on editorial pages do not consciously influence balance on news pages. Story selection, placement, and followups are determined by news judgments, not by editorial positions

Note that level of commitment can vary from profound to nil. For each standard, we might imagine a hypothetical scale from 0 to 100 measuring the intensity of the conscious commitment among media organizations and the individuals who constitute them, as well as their actual importance in guiding behavior. At one end of the hypothetical spectrum of commitment, scoring nearest 100 on each standard, are traditional news organizations and journalists. Strong attachment to these standards best characterizes the prototypical mainstream daily newspaper. At newspapers from the *New York Times, Wall Street Journal,* or *Los Angeles Times,* through the quality regional papers (*Atlanta Journal-Constitution, Chicago Tribune, Minneapolis Star Tribune*), to the quality local papers (*Raleigh News & Observer, Des Moines Register*), these norms hold fairly strong sway throughout. These organs adhere to a more or less strict partition of news from editorials, and of both from advertising. Among these media, profit maximizing is tempered by professional commitment to standards of quality and responsibility. The national, daily evening news shows on ABC, CBS, and NBC announce the same principles. These are closest to the pure types that come to mind when we think of traditional journalism. Slightly less "pure" would be the newsweeklies such as *Time* and *Newsweek,* and the Sunday morning interview shows. Both mix reporting with a bit more editorializing, and the hybrid is a part of their identities and marketing images.

Thus, some media organizations and personnel might score near 100, others at or near zero, and still others somewhere in between, on each of these standards. A hypothetical formula might be based on an algebraic summation of empirically measured intensities of commitment and behavioral influence on each of the five standards, multiplied by the number of people in the organization, with greater weight assigned the scores of those at the top of the organization than the bottom. (Where 100 percent of the people in the organization had absolutely no commitment to the standards, the score would be zero; where only a few people at the bottom had such a commitment, the score might be 10; and so forth.)

Although some of the media organizations of interest here make no pretense at seeing themselves as conveyors of truth or institutions of democracy, some of these standards play at least a *potential* role in the thinking and behavior of all media organizations, at least in some of the production decisions that they make. For instance, libel laws and commercial calculations about verisimilitude sometimes make standard 1, accuracy, relevant even to makers of entertainment products. Other entertainment makers actually do care about contributing to genuine democratic deliberation and responsiveness (standard 4), perhaps more than some working in news organizations that have a narrow ideological agenda that subordinates democracy to control over policy outcomes. Still, the advocacy, tabloid, and entertainment categories are not simply failed or insufficiently committed versions of traditional journalism but, especially as we move further away from traditional daily journalism and particularly when we get to tabloid and entertainment, different genres with quite distinct purposes in their own right.

It is change in adherence to the third standard that is perhaps the most striking trend among traditional journalistic outlets. The French sociologist Pierre Bourdieu has written persuasively of the two "fields" of power that contend for influence over the behavior and outputs of media personnel, one representing market pressures and the other cultural norms that include professional autonomy.[14] In our terms, Bourdieu would see the sway of the market field growing. Even among the quality daily news outlets, the sway of the cultural field is under assault, mainly due to growing economic pressures to keep profits rising in the face of shrinking audience interest in traditional news, particularly among younger Americans.[15] In particular, standards 3, 4, and 5, all of which imply a degree of insulation from or balancing against economic pressure to maximize circulation or ratings, are diminishing in impact on the behavior of media organizations and personnel, as even traditional news outlets turn increasingly to stories of crime, sex scandal, natural disaster, and celebrity, stories that are assumed to attract audiences (and revenue) more reliably than "boring" stories about government. Coverage of state government is one area that has suffered particularly in response to heightened economic pressures, even as state governments face growing responsibilities in the wake of federal budget cutbacks.[16]

Journalists and researchers report a growing tendency toward "high impact" stories, those presumably more attractive to audiences than pieces concerning less colorful, more complicated government officials and institutions. As we move to the smaller daily papers and the electronic or nondaily news media, journalistic standards generally exert still less force over news content. A growing proportion of news therefore has little to do with the core, citizenship-enhancing functions of traditional news, and this trend has been the subject of considerable criticism.[17] Yet, as several scholars reveal,[18] softer news and infotainment do possess some political content, and offer some potentially beneficial political effects.

Moving down the typology of media outlets, advocacy journalism does not hold strongly to standards 2 and 5, balance and editorial separation. Depending on the specific organization and journalist, the level of commitment to these standards might be at or close to zero on our hypothetical scale. However, a good case can be made that advocacy journalism contributes as much or even more than traditional journalism to the core news functions, in part precisely because of its willingness to violate those standards of balance and separation of editorial viewpoints from news.[19] On the other hand, there are many who believe that advocacy journalism tends toward irresponsibility and distortion, especially as it moves toward the boundary with tabloid journalism, where accuracy may be sacrificed to scoring ideological points and exerting influence over policy[20]—where commitment to standard 1 is near zero.

Indeed, many in the tabloid media feel little obligation to follow any of the standards, particularly when it comes to the supermarket tabloids and many Web logs (blogs) and Web sites. Although local television news does generally prize accuracy and avoid editorializing, it is highly if not exclusively profit-driven and typically accords crime, accidents, fires, and other disasters far greater priority than all but the most extraordinary political news—and thus belongs in the tabloid group. Little on a typical local television news program fulfills the core news functions.

Distinguishing tabloid journalism from the entertainment category can be surprisingly difficult. "Infotainment" programs such as *Good Morning America* and *The Today Show,* and even *The Oprah Winfrey Show* and *The View* (with Barbara Walters and others) may well have stronger commitments to accurate use of legitimate sources and other news standards in their interviews than do many tabloid news outlets. They often deal with personal issues that are relevant to public policy in ways far more compelling and arguably no less factual and balanced than many traditional print or television news stories.[21] Most of the news on these programs may be soft, but it is often still recognizably news. They may therefore illuminate the four areas of knowledge vital to citizenship—policy, power, ideology, and self-interest—with surprising regularity.

Although situation comedies, cartoons, dramas, and other more or less purely fictional productions obviously have little to no formal commitment to any of these standards, "real world" events and issues do show up with increasing frequency as the basis of entertainment episodes. How closely the plotlines adhere to the known facts of the situation varies. *The West Wing* occasionally incorporates a barely disguised, untrustworthy Middle Eastern ally obviously based on Saudi Arabia. Called "Qumar" in the show, the nation creates problems for the fictional President Bartlett that in some ways arguably reflect the true status of United States–Saudi relations more accurately than many news reports that paper over the complexities and frustrations of this particular alliance.[22]

As one example of the core news functions performed by media content that is produced by people other than traditional journalists, consider again the late-night television talk shows. A survey by the Pew Research Center for the People and the Press during the early part of the 2004 campaign showed that 28 percent of respondents "sometimes" or "regularly" got news about the election from late-night TV shows, such as those hosted by David Letterman and Jay Leno. These sources are particularly important for younger Americans (under age thirty), who are more than twice as likely to cite Leno and Letterman as news sources, and to say that they regularly learn something from these sources, compared with older citizens.[23] Although this appears troubling, it is worth noting that politically oriented comedians and satirists have been with us for centuries. Mark Twain, Will Rogers, even Benjamin Franklin are some of the rather distinguished progenitors of today's Bill Maher and Jon Stewart. It is also worth noting that in some cases, in part because such commentators are not bound by news conventions (timeliness, balance) that can turn journalists into tools of spin doctors and public relations operatives, they have the ability to speak truths that elude the front page or the network news.

Of course, the political role of nonjournalistic media goes well beyond late-night monologues. Scholars have documented other sources of information potentially relevant to political thinking and behavior that originates from personnel and organizations not bound by the traditional canons of journalism. For example, Matthew Baum, in the 2003 text *Soft News Goes to War,* demonstrates that television infotainment such as *The Oprah Winfrey Show* responds to major news events, particularly foreign crises, and shows that soft, human-interest content emphasizing talk—such as emotional interviews of American soldiers' spouses and children—affects public opinion. Infotainment outlets also influence straight news production. Thus an examination of news coverage of the sex scandals involving President Clinton reflects how traditional media outlets adapted and reacted to nontraditional formats (such as Internet Web sites, entertainment media, and even motion pictures) in deciding which stories to report and how to report them.[24] The production processes of the media are in some senses converging, but important distinctions remain.

Core Organizational Values and Missions

Traditional daily newspapers and the national daily broadcast news programs generally claim roughly the same two core missions: (1) reporting on important events, people, and issues, particularly those involving governmental institutions and actors, in ways that are accurate and balanced, and (2) generating sufficient advertising and circulation revenue to make a profit regarded by the stock market or private owners as acceptable. Standards for acceptable profit levels are rising; that is, profit pressures are increasing, with negative effects on news quality, according to many observers.[25] The two additional core missions that distinguish among media are influencing public policy, and amusing and diverting mass audiences.

Advocacy journalism does not attempt or pretend to be balanced or "fair," though it does claim to be accurate. The ideological or issue agendas of those running the advocacy organs are usually proclaimed plainly, up front, and they do not shy away from allowing their own analyses to shape the emphases, vocabulary, and questions that inform their coverage. Profits tend to be of less concern among these media; indeed, many are chartered as nonprofit organizations. What drives them is ideological commitment and hopes of influencing policy.

At tabloid journalistic outlets, profit concerns override those of serving democratic citizenship. At the extreme, some have less commitment to realism and factual accuracy than many entertainment vehicles. Tabloid outlets are not always honest about their products and projects. Such media as FOX News and the *New York Post,* while behaving in distinctly different ways from traditional journalism and often like blends between advocacy outlets and entertainment, proclaim their adherence to more or less traditional canons. Like advocacy journalists they seek to influence policy, and like entertainment outlets, to maximize profit. Note that tabloid-formatted newspapers do not necessarily fall into the "tabloid" group. Such papers as the *Chicago Sun Times* and the *New York Daily News* meet most or all of the standards for traditional journalistic outlets.

Finally, the core mission of entertainment media is "merely" to amuse and divert as a path to maximum profit. A secondary purpose is to serve as expressive outlets for the ideas, imaginations, and fantasies of a large, ambitious creative community. Nonetheless, research shows that entertainment is often rife with political implications, some of them consciously understood and considered by producers, others unconscious.[26]

As Table 1 suggests, the difference between entertainment and tabloid journalism is minimal, consisting mainly in the prototypical message content they offer. Tabloid journalism does deal in the activities (or alleged activities) of actual persons, whereas much entertainment (excepting the infotainment of *The Oprah Winfrey Show* and other talk shows and television magazine shows such as *20/20*) typically concerns the imagined activities of imagined persons. But despite the fictitious nature of entertainment personae, entertainment products may sometimes yield information relevant to citizenship, and as we have seen, real-life politicians and policies are often the subjects of comedic monologues and some other entertainment forms. Some entertainment media organizations—for instance, Oprah Winfrey's—clearly feel some commitment or responsibility to serving larger social goals aside from mere profit. Women's magazines have long sought to combine profitability with serving in some senses to empower females in a male-dominated society.[27] By the same token, although local television news deals with real persons and events, their civic significance is rarely substantial, and the stories of car crashes, fires, crimes, and other calamities function more like fictional narratives than news, arousing sufficient fear, pity, and catharsis to keep audiences tuned in throughout the commercials. On our hypothetical 0–100 scale, then, the folks who bring us *The Oprah Winfrey Show* and even *Martha Stewart Living* might score higher, at least on some dimensions, than those working for our local "Action 5 News Team" and its many clones around the country.

Target Audiences and Market Constraints

As Table 1 suggests, the different types of media organizations do target somewhat different audiences or, perhaps, different components of the same individuals' tastes. A media organization's market positioning affects what it does and how it does it. For instance, the *New York Times, Wall Street Journal,* and *Washington Post* achieve much of their economic value by refusing to cater to the average member of the public's limited interest in political and policy details. These papers assign reporters and allocate resources on the assumption that their core audiences want such fare. At the other end of the spectrum, *Average Joe* and *Fear Factor* attain their considerable profits by catering to audiences' tastes for titillation and escapism. Between these extremes, too, audience expectations and demands and marketing strategies differ systematically among the four categories of media. There is considerable overlap, since most people actually consume both news and entertainment and many consume some of each of the four categories. Most *New York Times* readers go to the movies and watch television entertainment, as indicated by the extensive coverage the *Times* gives to these media, and fans of *The Bachelor* and *Survivor* may also read the daily newspaper—perhaps even the *Times*—and the *Weekly Standard,* and watch the *O'Reilly Factor* and *ABC World News,* too.

Nonetheless, when all is said and done, the four media categories can be distinguished by the central market demands and constraints they face. Traditional daily newspapers cannot begin knowingly running fictional narratives about fictional characters on their news pages (comics and Sunday magazine short stories notwithstanding).[28] They face both legal and market-driven constraints to value factuality and accuracy. Nor could daily papers simply imitate local television news—or vice versa. If a paper decided to become a print analogue of local TV, in order to fill its news hole and still leave room for advertising, it would have to report and hype every fender bender in the area, every brushfire and false alarm, every stolen bicycle, every bar fight. The paper would promptly lose much of its audience. By the same token, in the unlikely event that local television news were to attempt replicating a local newspaper, it would have to provide long, talking-head reports on county board and zoning commission meetings rather than interviews of traumatized victims or witnesses of fire and crime, graphics of budget figures and property lines rather than images of leaping flames and perp walks. Although traditional newspapers can make moves toward tabloid journalism, and local TV can in theory provide more traditional news of government and politics, the market niches each occupies limits their range of choices and the nature of the products they offer.

Prototypical Message Content

Table 1 illustrates the different types of content typically produced by the four media categories. As suggested earlier, this listing should not be read as establishing rigid boundaries between the various media outlets. On the contrary, even for the major daily newspapers and TV news shows, prototypical news content is quite normally mixed in with material that performs little or no discernable civic function. In light of the intermingling of formats and subjects, how can we best distinguish messages that might function as news from those that do not? We can rate a given media outlet for how consistently it carries out the core democratizing functions of news (informing citizens with respect to policy, power, ideology, and self-interest as discussed above), and we can rate any particular story on these criteria as well.

Observers' general concern is that traditional and advocacy journalism possess more consistent potential to augment democracy, but also are under economic pressure to move toward softer, more entertaining, audience-pleasing content, and that this may undermine democratic citizenship and government responsiveness. However, identifying the prototypical "news properties"—those traits of traditional news coverage that are implicitly associated with the ideal forms of democracy-augmenting journalism—suggests two complications in this somewhat pessimistic picture. First, much of the content produced by traditional journalistic outlets, even those at the top of the chart—the prestige newspapers and network news—frequently falls short of achieving these ideal news properties. Second, specific products of entertainment outlets can sometimes rank higher on these properties than expected. The more of these properties a particular story has, or a particular media outlet offers during a typical year, the more likely that story or media outlet would be to serve the core democratizing functions of illuminating policy, power, ideology, and self-interest.

What follows is an illustrative rather than exhaustive list of news properties that might help in assessing the civic value and effects of media content across the ever-growing array of media products serving news functions:

- Focuses on the substantive goals and activities of those holding power in government or those outside government who influence government decisions
- Provides insight into the distribution of power, wealth, and status in society
- Illuminates impacts of public policies and proposed policies on the lives and opportunities of various groups of citizens—for example, those with lower incomes or limited education, those facing ethnic discrimination, or, alternately, those enjoying wealth and ethnic privilege
- Penetrates the hype and spin to reveal the true policy stands, key support groups and advisers, and demonstrated records of action and inaction of candidates for office

Looking at this list we can see that a lot of news that occupies page one or the network news possesses one or more of such ideal news properties, but much does not. Much is routine coverage of the president's speeches, partisan maneuvering, or natural disasters, crimes, and other events that have little bearing on power, policy, ideology, or self-interest. Many stories cover media events, photo ops, and other manifestations of managed news or public relations. At the same time, entertaining anecdotes told by Jon Stewart or Jay Leno, episodes of prime-time dramas such as *The West Wing* and *Law and Order,* and Hollywood movies such as *Wag the Dog* and *Bamboozled* can provide deep and accessible insights into the impacts of policies, the prevarications and real goals of public officials, and the distribution of wealth and power.

This observation does *not* imply that traditional journalism and entertainment are nowadays equally effective or ineffective at performing news functions. Among the features that make traditional and, often, advocacy journalism generally superior to tabloid journalism and entertainment at assisting democratic citizenship are:

- The credibility attributed to news by audiences as factual
- The timeliness of news reports
- The focus of many news stories on identified government officials and other powerful individuals who can be held accountable
- The frequent reliance of journalists on well-documented factual reports or well-grounded analyses by experts rather than on anecdotes and hunches

Therefore, while acknowledging that soft news, tabloid news, infotainment, and straight-out entertainment can sometimes execute news functions, we should not lose sight of the particular strengths and continuing potential of traditional and advocacy journalism.

Conclusion

Traditional journalism faces growing pressure to change, in ways that potentially threaten its ability to execute the core news functions as effectively as it once did. At the same time, the nature of news is changing, and the sources from which Americans receive messages that are potentially relevant to their political thinking are more abundant than ever. Scholars and other observers must establish the precise character of the threats to the ability of the media, broadly considered, to carry out the vital democratic missions long at the core of journalists' ideal self-images. This chapter suggests the particular need for scholars and media professionals to identify more precisely just what democracy-enhancing news functions they would like to see nurtured and maximized, and how those functions can be accomplished by specific textual choices across the full range of media.

Notes

1. Entman, *Democracy without Citizens.* See also Patterson, *The Vanishing Voter,* and Thomas E. Patterson, "The Search for a Standard: Markets and Media," *Political Communication* 20, no. 2 (April–June 2003): 139–43.
2. See, for example, Entman, *Democracy without Citizens;* Schudson, *The Good Citizen;* Bennett, *News;* and Gans, *Democracy and the News.*

3. See Patterson, "The Search for a Standard"; Markus Prior, "Any Good News in Soft News?: The Impact of Soft News Preference on Political Knowledge," *Political Communication* 20, no. 2 (April–June 2003): 149–71; and John Zaller, "A New Standard of News Quality: Burglar Alarms for the Monitorial Citizen," *Political Communication* 20, no. 2 (April–June 2003): 109–30.

4. The classification in Table 1 grew out of a working group discussion, chaired by Professor Theodore Glasser, at the July 2003 meeting of the Annenberg Press Commission in Philadelphia.

5. Center for Media and Public Affairs, "Jay Leno's Greatest Hits: 10th Anniversary Finds Political Jokes Approaching 19,000, Clinton Biggest Laugh," http://www.cmpa.com/pressReleases/JayLenosGreatestHits.htm.

6. Joann Byrd, "The Most Famous Haircut since Samson's," *Washington Post,* July 11, 1993, C6.

7. Amy Wallace, "Clinton's Hair Stylist Defends His Presidential Clip Job," *Houston Chronicle,* June 20, 1993, A9.

8. Pew Research Center for the People and the Press, survey report, "Support for Independent Candidate in '96 Up Again," August 24, 1995, http://people-press.org/reports/print.php3?PageID=414.

9. Center for Media and Public Affairs, "1993 Top Ten Joke Targets," http://www.cmpa.com.

10. Byrd, "The Most Famous Haircut since Samson's."

11. See, for example, William Safire's *New York Times* column of July 11, 1993; for the *Times* of London story see Nicholas Wapshott, "Let Us Spray: How to Get Ahead in American Politics" (July 14, 2004), p. 16.

12. Weeks, 1992.

13. Zaller, "A New Standard of News Quality"; Schudson, *The Good Citizen.*

14. Bourdieu, *On Television.* See also Rodney Benson, "News Media as a Journalistic Field: What Bourdieu Adds to New Institutionalism, and Vice Versa," *Political Communication,* forthcoming.

15. Roberts and Kunkel, eds., *Breach of Faith*; Andrew Kohut, "Young People Are Reading—Everything but Newspapers," *Columbia Journalism Review* 41 (July 2002): 77.

16. Walton and Layton, "Missing the Story at the Statehouse."

17. Gans, *Democracy and the News;* Patterson, *The Vanishing Voter;* Kaniss, *Making Local News.*

18. Baum, *Soft News Goes to War;* Zaller, "A New Standard of News Quality"; Gamson, *Freaks Talk Back.*

19. On investigative journalism, see Ettema and Glasser, *Custodians of Conscience;* Protess et al., *The Journalism of Outrage.*

20. See Brock, *Blinded by the Right;* Conason, *Big Lies.*

21. See Gamson, *Freaks Talk Back.*

22. See Entman, *Projections of Power,* and Baum, *Soft News Goes to War.*

23. Pew Research Center for the People and the Press, survey report, "Cable and Internet Loom Large in Fragmented Political News Universe," January 11, 2004, http://people-press.org/reports/display.php3?ReportID=20.

24. Delli Carpini and Williams, "Let Us Infotain You"; Kalb, *One Scandalous Story.*
25. See Roberts and Kunkel, eds., *Breach of Faith.*
26. See Bourdieu, *On Television.* On the racial politics of prime-time dramas, see Entman and Rojecki, *The Black Image in the White Mind.*
27. Laurie Ouellette, "Inventing the Cosmo Girl"; and Ann Mason and Marian Meyers, "Living with Martha Stewart Media: Chosen Domesticity in the Experience of Fans," *Journal of Communications* 51, no. 4 (December 2001): 801–23.
28. Some might argue that newspapers unknowingly do report fiction as truth in some cases, citing as examples the sometimes credulous reporting on weapons of mass destruction in Iraq in 2002–3, or the hagiography that passed as news in the days following former President Ronald Reagan's death in 2004. But journalists usually, eventually, recognize and repudiate these deviations from the cherished norms.

Bibliography

Baum, Matthew. *Soft News Goes to War: Public Opinion and American Foreign Policy in the New Media Age.* Princeton, N.J.: Princeton University Press, 2003.

Bennett, W. Lance. *News: The Politics of Illusion.* 5th ed. New York: Longman, 2002.

Bourdieu, Pierre. *On Television.* Translated by Priscilla Parkhurst Ferguson. New York: New Press, 1998.

Brock, David. *Blinded by the Right: The Conscience of an Ex-Conservative.* New York: Crown Publishers, 2002.

Conason, Joe. *Big Lies: The Right-Wing Propaganda Machine and How It Distorts the Truth.* New York: St. Martin's, 2003.

Delli Carpini, Michael X., and Bruce Williams. "Let Us Infotain You." In *Mediated Politics: Communication in the Future of Democracy,* edited by W. Lance Bennett and Robert M. Entman. Cambridge, U.K., and New York: Cambridge University Press, 2001.

Entman, Robert M. *Democracy without Citizens: Media and the Decay of American Politics.* New York: Oxford University Press, 1989.

Entman, Robert M. *Projections of Power: Framing News, Public Opinion, and U.S. Foreign Policy.* Chicago: University of Chicago Press, 2004.

Entman, Robert M., and Andrew Rojecki. *The Black Image in the White Mind: Media and Race in America.* Chicago: University of Chicago Press, 2000.

Ettema, James S., and Theodore L. Glasser. *Custodians of Conscience: Investigative Journalism and Public Virtue.* New York: Columbia University Press, 1998.

Gamson, Joshua. *Freaks Talk Back: Tabloid Talk Shows and Sexual Nonconformity.* Chicago: University of Chicago Press, 1998.

Gans, Herbert J. *Democracy and the News.* New York: Oxford University Press, 2003.

Kalb, Marvin. *One Scandalous Story: Clinton, Lewinsky, and Thirteen Days That Tarnished American Journalism.* New York: Free Press, 2001.

Kaniss, Phyllis. *Making Local News.* Chicago: University of Chicago Press, 1991.

Ouellette, Laurie. "Inventing the Cosmo Girl." In *Gender, Race and Class in Media,* edited by Gail Dines and Jean M. Humez, 116–28. Thousand Oaks, Calif.: Sage, 1995.

Patterson, Thomas E. *The Vanishing Voter: Public Involvement in an Age of Uncertainty.* New York: Knopf, 2002.

Protess, David L., et al. *The Journalism of Outrage: Investigative Reporting and Agenda Building in America.* New York: Guilford, 1991.

Roberts, Gene, and Thomas Kunkel, eds. *Breach of Faith: A Crisis of Coverage in the Age of Corporate Newspapering.* Fayetteville: University of Arkansas Press, 2002.

Schudson, Michael. *The Good Citizen: A History of American Civic Life.* New York: Free Press, 1998.

Walton, Mary, and Charles Layton. "Missing the Story at the Statehouse." In *Breach of Faith: A Crisis of Coverage in the Age of Corporate Newspapering,* edited by Gene Roberts and Thomas Kunkel, 1–48. Little Rock: University of Arkansas Press, 2002.

Weeks, Patricia. "Patriot Games: What Did We See on Desert Storm TV?" *Columbia Journalism Review* 31, no. 2 (July/August 1992): 13.

4

DEFINITIONS OF JOURNALISM

Barbie Zelizer

AS JOURNALISM HAS COME TO BE THOUGHT OF AS A PROfession, an industry, a phenomenon, and a culture, definitions have emerged that reflect various concerns and goals.[1] Journalists, journalism educators, and journalism scholars all take different pathways in thinking productively about the subject, and the effort to define journalism consequently goes in various directions. Naming, labeling, evaluating, and critiquing journalism and journalistic practice reflect the populations from which individuals come, the type of news work, medium, and technology being referenced, and the relevant historical time period and geographical setting. No wonder, then, that the distinguished broadcast journalist Daniel Schorr noted that reporting was not only a livelihood for him but "a frame of mind."[2] By extension, journalism as a frame of mind varies from individual to individual.

Thinking about Journalism

The various terms of *news, the press, the news media,* and *information* and *communication* themselves suggest profound differences in what individuals consider journalism to mean and what expectations they have of journalists. Although the term *journalist* initially denoted someone who systematically kept a public record of events in a given time frame, today it is applied to individuals with a range of skills, including publishers, photographers, field producers, Internet providers, and bloggers. Largely associated with journalism's craft dimensions, the term tends to reference the evolving skills, routines, and conventions involved in making news. The term *news*—originally derived from the word *new* during the late sixteenth century—tends to signal a commercial aura that surrounds the ongoing provision of information about current events. *News media,* by contrast, and *the press* as one of its forms, came into use in association with the industrial, institutional, and technological settings in which journalists began to work in the eighteenth century, while more recently, a focus on *communication* and *informa-*

tion—an outgrowth of the ascent of academic curricula in communications that took over journalism training programs—created a sense that journalists are above all information providers, setting aside the other roles that they fill.

None of these ways of understanding journalism provides the complete picture of what journalism is. Nor do any reflect all of the expectations we might have of the press in a democracy. Each instead underscores a tendency to argue for the universal nature of what we call news work. And yet journalism is anything but universal: we need only recognize that Dan Rather, Matt Drudge, and Jon Stewart—a professional broadcast journalist, an Internet scoopster and columnist, and a popular television satirist—all convey authentic news of contemporary affairs to a general public, despite the questions raised about whether they are all journalists and all do journalism.

These different terms for journalism have not been equally invoked, either by journalists themselves, those who educate budding reporters, or those who study journalism. Although journalism today reflects many contradictory sets of people, dimensions, practices, and functions, discussions of journalism tend to be reduced to one variant of practice—that connected with hard news in primarily mainstream establishments. This growing gap between "the realities of journalism and its official presentation of self"[3] has grown more severe as journalism continues to be responsible for shaping public events.

How Journalists Talk about Journalism

Journalists are notorious for knowing what news is but not being able to explain it to others. More prone to talking about writing or getting the story than providing definitions of what news actually is, journalists easily trade sayings such as, "News is what the editor says it is" or, "News is what sells papers or drives up ratings." As one journalistic textbook commented in the 1940s, "It is easier to recognize news than define it."[4]

Nonetheless, journalists do repair to collective ideas about what news is. Although not typically mentioned in the literature on journalism—for as Theodore Glasser and James Ettema argued in 1989, there remains a "widening gap between how journalists know what they know and what students are told about how journalists know what they know"[5]—journalists talk about journalism in patterned ways. Revealing what the sociologist Robert Park called "synthetic knowledge"—the kind of tacit knowledge that is "embodied in habit and custom" rather than that which forms the core of a formalized knowledge system[6]—journalists display much of how they think about journalism in journalistic guidebooks, how-to manuals, columns, autobiographies, and catchphrases associated with journalism's practice. The cues that they invoke metaphorically address potentially problematic, and not altogether revered, dimensions of journalistic practice, providing a venue to talk about journalism in ways that are true to experience but not necessarily respected by the professional community. Six such references prominent in journalists' discussions of their craft are explored here.

Journalism as a Sixth Sense

Journalists make frequent mention of what they call a "news sense," suggesting a natural, seemingly inborn talent or skill for locating and ferreting out news. "News" refers to both a phenomenon out there in the world and a report of that phenomenon, and sometimes a news sense is said to have olfactory qualities, as in having "a nose for news," being able to "smell out news," or, as stipulated in a 2003 directive from the Poynter Institute, "writing with your nose." As the Poynter guideline reminded its readers: "Good reporters have a nose for news. They can sniff out a story. Smell a scandal. Give them a whiff of corruption and they'll root it out like a pig diving for truffles."[7]

The news instinct is so central to the journalistic endeavor that it has been referenced in campaigns to recruit new reporters, and in the development of Web sites for news organizations, new modes of reporting, and public relations strategies for institutions dealing with the news media. Journalists often maintain that one is either born with a news sense or not. Lord Riddell, a longtime newspaper editor in both the United Kingdom and Australia, wrote in 1932 that all "true journalists" possess an itch to communicate the news.[8] Having "a nose for news" was so important to the U.S. journalism educator Curtis MacDougall that he used the expression to title a section in the many editions of his text *Interpretative Reporting.*[9] It also prompted the *Washington Post* editor Ben Bradlee to explain why he decided to publish Seymour Hersh's exposé of the My Lai massacre, the 1968 massacre of unarmed civilians by U.S. troops during the Vietnam War: "This smells right," Bradlee was rumored to have said.[10]

Conversely, when journalism falls short, it is often blamed on the failings of its positioning as a sixth sense. Journalists are said to have missed the scent trail of a story or to have "underdeveloped noses."[11]

Journalism as a Container

Journalists talk about journalism as a phenomenon with volume, materiality, dimension, depth, and complexity. Thought "to contain" the day's news, journalistic vehicles are said to hold information for the public until it can appraise what has happened. "Containing" in this regard has two meanings—keeping the news intact and keeping the news within limits, or checking its untoward expansion. Journalism as a container thus both facilitates access to information while putting limits on the information that can be accessed.

Seeing journalism as a container requires a certain degree of attention to the material that fills it, and a corresponding notion of the "news hole"—or the capacity of a newspaper or newscast in delivering the news—concerns journalists faced with more information than can be processed on any given day. The news hole presumes that a day's news must fill a number of predetermined empty spaces—in a newspaper edition or newscast lineup—on a regular and predictable basis. One early U.S. textbook provided novice practitioners with the following example: "'We're filling up,' the news editor warns. 'Boil hard.' The copy editor hears this warning often. There is almost always more news than space."[12] A large news hole suggests that journalists need to find more news; a tight one indicates an inability to take new copy.

The material in this container is unevenly valued. It is shadowed by concerns, borne out by research, that the news hole has been continually shrinking to accommodate more advertising, though the Internet offers what many regard as a bottomless offset to the hole's constriction.[13] Reduction of the news hole has many implications—the shortening of news articles or items, closing of foreign bureaus, lessened assignment of complicated investigative pieces. Conversely, the journalistic "scoop," or the advantage gained by being first on an important news story, always rises to the top of the container. Made famous as the title of Evelyn Waugh's book-length lampoon of England's newspaper business during the 1930s, the "scoop" references not only the victorious activity of filing a story before anyone else but also the news items themselves, positioning them as evidence of journalistic triumph over usually adverse circumstances.

The idea of journalism as a container also figures into the idea of "journalistic depth." Good journalism is said to be that which plays to the volume and materiality of information out there in the world, and journalism's role is to reflect that depth by making complex events and issues into simple and understandable stories. Good journalism is expected to tackle the complicated, unobvious, and often embedded angles of seemingly straightforward happenings. Certain modes of journalistic practice—investigative journalism, muckraking, journalistic reformers, news sleuths, and exposés, to name a few—are premised on the notion that journalists dig deep to find their stories. No wonder, then, that events and issues are said to be "*in* the news," and journalists "*in* the know."

Journalism as a Mirror

Journalists see journalism as the work of observation, tantamount to gazing on reality or the objective happenings taking place in the real world. News is equated here to all that happens, without any filtering activity on the part of journalists. Journalism as a mirror is central to professional notions of objectivity, still prominent in the United States, and it presumes that journalists function primarily as recorders, observers, and scribes, reliably taking account of events as they unfold.

A central part of existing journalistic lore, the idea of journalism as a mirror surfaces among some of the most highly regarded reporters. Lincoln Steffens remembered his years on the *New York Evening Post* by recounting that "reporters were to report the news as it happened, like machines, without prejudice, color, or style."[14] Ernie Pyle's dispatches from the foxholes of World War II were said to have a "worm's eye" point of view, and Walter Cronkite's famous nightly sign-off on CBS—"And that's the way it is"—was built on the notion of journalism as a mirror. As Daniel Schorr told it, "the word 'reporting' was always closely associated in my mind with 'reality.'"[15]

The notion of journalism as a mirror figures prominently in how journalists and news organizations present themselves to the public. It surfaces in catchphrases by which journalists describe their work—providing "a lens on the world," producing "newspaper copy," compiling "journalistic relays," offering "all the news that's fit to print." Publishers choose names for newspapers that play to the idea of journalism as a mirror of events, likening them to a sentinel, beacon, emblem, herald, standard, reflector, or chronicle.

The conception of journalism as a mirror also has particular resonance for the visual side of journalism. Not only do catchphrases like "having an eye on the news," or relying on "the camera as reporter" crop up, but the epithet for many local television news stations—"eyewitness news"—builds on the idea that journalists are able to reflect what they see into the processing of news. The camera is said to be a reliable and objective recorder of reality, with noted photographer Robert Capa saying that "if your pictures aren't good enough, you aren't close enough." As news photographer Don McCullin said of his time in Vietnam, Biafra, and Lebanon, "Many people ask me, 'why do you take these pictures?' It's because I know the feeling of the people I photograph. It's not a case of 'There but for the grace of God go I'; it's a case of 'I've been there.' . . . My eyes [seem] to be the greatest benefactor I had."[16]

And yet, the notion of journalism as a mirror is seen by many contemporary reporters as a less than viable way of explaining journalism. Recognizing the metaphor's limitations as a way of thinking about journalistic practice, Pete Hamill noted the following rules of journalism: "Things ain't always what they seem to be. . . . If you want it to be true, it usually isn't . . . [and] in the first twenty-four hours of a big story, about half the facts are wrong."[17]

Journalism as a Story

Journalism, for many journalists, is reflected in notions of the "news story." The "story" describes what journalists produce when gathering and presenting news. Journalists refer to different kinds of news stories—items, briefs, reports, series, records, chronicles, accounts, and features—and have different expectations about the kinds of information each highlights, the style in which it is written, the position that it occupies in the newscast or newspaper, and the role it plays.

Journalists distinguish most frequently between the kinds of stories typical of hard and soft news, with the front pages of newspapers and top items of broadcast lineups commonly favoring the former over the latter. As Michael Schudson demonstrated in his history of American newspapers, practices of storytelling have long been central to distinctions made between journalism that informs and journalism that tells a gripping tale.[18] Among journalists, hard news has long been associated with an absence of storytelling, involving no narrative technique whatsoever, though that notion is complicated by an increasing degree of attention to what Hugh Kenner called "the plain style"—a storytelling mode that strategically involves brevity, simplicity, and explicitness.[19] Soft news, by contrast, uses a variety of narrative techniques to produce dramatic and heartrending stories, moral lessons, and compelling plotlines.

Getting the story is the imperative of every reporter. As one editor commented in 2003, "There are so many times when I hear reporters gripe about the fact that 'there just isn't a story there.' And that 'they can't believe they have to make a story out of this; nothing happened.' And yet, there in the paper the next morning is 12 inches of informative non-story."[20] Journalists aspire to producing a "top or lead story," often a "special report"; in-depth efforts get labeled as the "story behind the story" or a "news series." And yet, good stories often come at the expense of good journalism. As the National Public Radio reporter Nina Totenberg said in reference to stories that she worked on and then threw away, "I've had more good stories ruined by facts."[21]

Certain kinds of journalism are characterized by the kinds of stories they provide: human interest news, New Journalism, and literary journalism each take on storytelling forms that distinguish them from the larger world of journalistic relays. Hunter S. Thompson, credited with founding "gonzo journalism," consciously turned his writing into a blend of fact and fiction because "the best fiction is far more true than any kind of journalism—and the best journalists have always known this."[22]

The downside of seeing journalism as a story has been the various violations involving storytelling—plagiarism, fabrication, misquotation. The plight of journalists who lost their jobs and reputation for such violations—Janet Cooke, Jayson Blair, Mike Barnicle—is often said to have developed on the backs of their strong storytelling skills.

Journalism as a Child

For many journalists, the news requires careful nurturing, and they position themselves as its caretakers. Journalism is seen as not only fragile and vulnerable—a phenomenon in need of attention, supervision, and care—but it often demands an unreasonable and unpredictable on-call status. No surprise, then, that journalists can and do adopt a parental stance, by which they necessarily attend to the news at all times. That position, which according to professional lore has been variously held responsible for journalists' fabled premature professional burnout, high divorce rates, and uneven social lives, tends to figure prominently in popular cultural representations of journalists in fiction, television, and cinema.

This conception of journalism forces on journalists a watchdog role, by which they stand guard over the shaping of news, and at other times calls for a gentler nurturing role. Catchphrases like "putting the paper to bed"—which involves closing the press for the night, "sitting on a story"—which involves taking care of a story until it is time for publication, and "pampering" or "coddling" a story—which refers to elaborating a "thin" or unsubstantiated story line all build on this idea. And "feeding the beast," a reference to an always hungry press, describes a reaction to situations in which journalism's demands are excessive and go too far, not unlike those of an overly demanding child.

Journalism as a Service

Journalists think of journalism as a service in the public interest, one that is shaped with an eye toward the needs of healthy citizenship. A notion of service both to the profession and community permeates the language that journalists use in referencing journalism: news *service,* wire *services,* and news as being *in the general interest.* Journalists are said to "serve" London, Washington, and Beijing.

Serving the public surfaces frequently in journalists' discussions of their craft. Addressing journalists' isolation from the lives of poor and working-class individuals, *Columbia Journalism Review* reminded its readers that "we in the press have a responsibility to engage everyone."[23] The *Washington Post* ombudsman Michael Getler complained that the tendency of newspaper chains to "work on the cheap" shortchanges "readers and our democratic foundations."[24] Awards— the Pulitzer Prizes, National Magazine Awards, and Dupont Awards, to name a few—are regularly given for journalistic service.

The idea of journalism as a service has received renewed attention with the ascent of the public journalism movement, which defines journalism in conjunction with its ability to serve the public. Journalists' willingness to break with old routines, a desire to reconnect with citizens, an emphasis on serious discussions as the foundation of politics, and a focus on citizens as actors rather than spectators all position journalism squarely in the service mode.[25]

How Scholars Talk about Journalism

Scholars borrow from various disciplinary interests in talking about journalism. Five definitional sets, none of them mutually exclusive, prevail in the scholarly literature.

Journalism as a Profession

Many scholars regard journalism, first of all, as a set of professional activities by which one qualifies to be called a "journalist." The designation was helpful for organizing a basically disorganized group of writers in the 1900s into a consolidated group, but today journalists display few of the traits by which sociologists tend to identify professions—certain levels of skill, autonomy, service orientation, licensing procedures, testing of competence, organization, codes of conduct, and training and educational programs.[26] In David Weaver and G. Cleveland Wilhoit's words, "The modern journalist is *of* a profession but not *in* one. . . . The institutional forms of professionalism likely will always elude the journalist."[27]

But other ways of understanding journalism as a profession point toward the term's broader resonance. Scholars argue that it provides a body of knowledge or ideological orientation about what to do and avoid in any given circumstance or that it constitutes an organizational and institutional firewall for reporters, safeguarding against change, loss of control, and possible rebellion.[28] Certain scholars are critical of the idea. Thomas Patterson explains the failure of journalists to energize a robust political sphere by pointing toward one of the long-standing supports for U.S. professionalism, the idea that journalists could and should be politically neutral. James Carey brands journalism's professional orientation "the great danger in modern journalism," because the client-professional relationship it implies leaves the public no real control over information and thus dependent on journalism for knowledge about the real world.[29]

Nonetheless, the idea of journalism as a profession lives on, if unevenly so. Many quarters of the academy readily include the norms, values, and practices associated with professionalism as part of their curriculum, and concerns over professionalism remain implicit in much of the journalistic trade literature. Trade journals as wide-ranging as the *American Journalism Review, Quill,* and *Editor & Publisher* invoke journalistic professionalism in discussions over breaches of consensual journalistic practice and ongoing conversations about the need for stronger journalistic ethics. The outcries in 2003 over Jayson Blair and the *New York Times'* attempts to cleanse itself of his unethical behavior were shaped around invocations to professionalism.

Journalism as an Institution

Scholars often regard journalism as an institutional setting, characterized by social, political, economic, and cultural privilege. Journalism is seen here as a large-scale and complex phenomenon, whose primary effect is wielding power, shaping public opinion, and controlling the distribution of informational or symbolic resources in society. Although the institution simultaneously means the setting, the behaviors that constitute the setting, and the values by which the setting is organized, including organizations or formal groups that work according to collective standards of action, regarding journalism as an institution is by definition to address the historical and situational contingencies against which journalism performs a range of social, cultural, economic, and political tasks or functions. That said, journalism by this view must exist institutionally, if it is to exist at all.

In thinking about journalism as an institution, scholars tend to search for the interfaces by which it links with other institutions, facilitating connections between journalism and the government, the market, culture, the educational system, and the religious establishment. Primary here has been work devoted to the study of the intersection between journalism and economics, highlighting patterns of ownership and convergence, corporate influences, deregulation and privatization, as well as journalism's impact upon the production and distribution of material goods and wealth.[30] Other scholars have targeted the meeting point of journalism and politics, focusing on journalism's impact on public opinion, its blurring of public and private spheres, and its role in changing conventions of citizenship.[31]

Adopting an institutional lens has facilitated global and comparative analyses of the news. Institutional pressures vary as nation-states jockey for power with the interests of broader economic corporations and global concerns.[32]

Journalism as a Text

Scholars interested in the patterned relay of news see journalism as a text. The texts of journalism tend to have agreed-upon features—a concern with certain types of events (a fire, a summit conference, a murder), currency or timeliness, and factuality. In the United States, they also tend to display less readily articulated features—an anonymous third-person author, a generally reasoned and unemotional accounting of events, and an uncritical gravitation to the middle of the road on issues of contested public interest. In David Halberstam's view, such features have "required the journalist to be much dumber and more innocent than in fact he [is]."[33]

Seeing journalism as a text considers the public use of words, images, and sounds in patterned ways, and key here has been the evolving notion of different kinds of news styles—print and broadcast, mainstream and alternative, elite and tabloid. Scholarship over decades of research—produced by Helen Hughes, Robert Darnton, Roger Fowler, and G. Stuart Adam, to name a few—paved the way for thinking critically about the various ways in which a news text can be put together.[34] As the role of journalism has been claimed by an increasingly varied register of venues—the news magazine, the Internet, reality television, the comedy show—a focus on the texts they use shows how they resemble and differ from more traditional modes of reportage.[35] Seeing journalism as a text has also produced discussion of the frames through which journalists and news organizations structure their presentation of events, using story presentation as the prism for considering the lack of neutrality in U.S. news.[36]

But scholars have not agreed about which journalistic features to analyze— words tend to take prominence over either images or sounds. Neither have they agreed about which texts to appraise—one issue of a newspaper, one segment of a broadcast, or all existing coverage of a given event.

Journalism as People

Defining journalism through the people who work as journalists has been common since journalism's initial days of academic study. Although Walter Lippmann was first to note that "anybody can be a journalist—and usually is,"[37] others have offered more elaborated descriptions of the attributes of the journalistic community. In one view, journalists need

> a knack with telephones, trains and petty officials; a good digestion and a steady head; total recall; enough idealism to inspire indignant prose (but not enough to inhibit detached professionalism); a paranoid temperament; an ability to behave passionately in second-rate projects; well-placed relatives; good luck; the willingness to betray, if not friends, acquaintances; a reluctance to understand too much too well (because *tout comprendre c'est tout pardoner* and *tout pardoner* makes dull copy); an implacable hatred of spokesmen, administrators, lawyers, public relations men and all those who would rather purvey words than policies; and the strength of character to lead a disrupted life without going absolutely haywire.[38]

Scholars have made substantial effort at defining the wide range of traits characterizing the people we call journalists. J. W. Johnstone and his colleagues and David Weaver and G. Cleveland Wilhoit in their stead were instrumental in conducting wide-ranging surveys of journalists in the U.S. context, providing a comprehensive picture of who they are, where they were educated, their values and beliefs, and the kinds of experiences they have as journalists.[39] Such work focused primarily on high-ranking individuals employed by recognized and elite mainstream news institutions.

A certain degree of residual disagreement over who is a journalist has lingered alongside the ongoing attempts to define the journalistic community. Early ambivalence over consideration of print setters, proofreaders, and copyeditors as journalists has given way to an ambivalence directed at individuals engaged in page layout, graphic design, video-camera editing, fact checking, and provision of Internet access. A common focus on the most prestigious national news organizations, and primarily on top editors and national reporters even there, has minimized academic attention to women, minorities, and holders of nonmainstream political views, all of whom have been employed more often in the ethnic press, weekly journals of opinion, and local and regional media.

Journalism as a Practice

Scholars also envision journalism as a set of practices. How to gather, present, and disseminate the news has been a key target of this lens, which has produced a flow of scholarly work on "getting the news," "writing the news," "breaking news," "making news," "news-making strategies," and "newsroom practices."

Thinking about journalism as a set of practices focuses on the practical and symbolic dimensions of news practice. Not only does journalism have pragmatic effects, such as information relay and agenda setting, but it is ascribed a crucial role in shaping consensus by relying upon tested routines, practices, and formulas for gathering and presenting the news. Scholarship by Gaye Tuchman, Herbert Gans, and Todd Gitlin, among others, established the register of features that characterize what we today recognize as news work.[40]

As journalism has expanded into new technological frames, the set of practices involved in doing news work continues to change. Typesetting skills of the print room have given way to a demand for computer literacy, and an increasingly diverse list of sources necessitates changes in news practice, making journalism a more collective operation: using teams for fact checking, for instance, lends news making a collaborative dimension that it did not have in earlier days.

Still in need of attention are the alternative ways for thinking about journalistic practices. Those following the tenets of muckraking would be hard-pressed to deliver their relays through wire-service briefs. Literary journalism ranks the actions of journalists differently than does investigative journalism, a difference made more marked by the preferences of the Anglo-American tradition, which sides with briefer, fact-based chronicles, and its French counterpart, which prefers a more elaborated prose style.

The Usefulness of Definitions

Journalism is a phenomenon that can be seen in many ways—as a sixth sense, a container, a mirror, a story, a child, a service, a profession, an institution, a text, people, a set of practices. These ways of thinking about journalism suggest various routes through which we might approach journalism, the press, and the news media. They are useful here because each offers a way to think about how the press could work better than it does today. And in considering its role in democracy, the stated intent of this volume, there can be no more suitable aim.

How might the press serve democracy more effectively? Much is suggested by the broad range of terms through which journalism is defined here. We might remember that no one definitional set has been capable of conveying all there is to know about journalism. But taken together, they offer a glimpse of a phenomenon that is rich, contradictory, complex, and often inexplicable. That richness, those internal contradictions and complexities, and the fact that we cannot explain all of journalism's workings in one way at any given point in time all need to be sustained and nurtured. For recognizing their uneasy coexistence can help us see how the press might work better in contemporary democracy. Thomas

Paine is rumored to have said long ago that journalism helps us "see with other eyes, hear with other ears, and think with other thoughts than those we formerly used." In thinking about journalism, we might do well to heed his advice.

Notes

1. The discussion here is adapted from and extends upon Zelizer, *Taking Journalism Seriously.*
2. Daniel Schorr, *Clearing the Air* (Boston: Houghton Mifflin, 1977), vii.
3. Dahlgren, introduction to *Journalism and Popular Culture,* edited by Dahlgren and Sparks, 7.
4. Stanley Johnson and Julian Harris, *The Complete Reporter: A General Text in News Writing and Editing, Complete with Exercises* (New York: Macmillan, 1942), 19.
5. Theodore L. Glasser and James S. Ettema, "Common Sense and the Education of Young Journalists," *Journalism Educator* 44 (summer 1989): 18.
6. Robert E. Park, "News as a Form of Knowledge: A Chapter in the Sociology of Knowledge," *American Journal of Sociology* 45, no. 5 (1940): 669–86.
7. Chip Scanlan, "Writing for Your Nose," www.poynter.org, July 28, 2003.
8. Lord Riddell, "The Psychology of the Journalist" (1932), in *A Journalism Reader,* edited by Michael Bromley and Tom O'Malley (London and New York: Routledge, 1997), 110.
9. Curtis D. MacDougall and Robert D. Reid, *Interpretative Reporting,* 9th ed. (New York: Macmillan, 1987).
10. Cited in Glasser and Ettema, "Common Sense," 25.
11. Stephen W. Gibson, "Entrepreneur Must Have a Sixth Sense," *Deseret News Archives,* February 15, 1998. Also see Geneva Overholser, "Our Nose for News Fails Us When the Smell Is Close to Home," *Columbia Journalism Review* 40 (July 2001), and Alice Cherbonnier, "The *Sun* Shows No Nose for News," *Baltimore Chronicle & Sentinel,* January 8, 2003, www.baltimorechronicle.com/media_joblessrpt_jan03.html.
12. Robert Miller Neal, *Newspaper Desk Work* (New York and London: D. Appleton, 1933), 27.
13. *The State of the News Media, 2004: An Annual Report on American Journalism* (Washington, D.C.: Project for Excellence in Journalism, 2004).
14. Lincoln Steffens, *The Autobiography of Lincoln Steffens* (New York: Harcourt Brace, 1931), 171.
15. Schorr, *Clearing the Air,* viii.
16. Don McCullin, "Notes by a Photographer," in *The Photographic Memory: Press Photography—Twelve Insights,* edited by Émile Meijer and Joop Swart (London: Quiller Press, 1987), 11, 13.
17. Pete Hamill, *News Is a Verb: Journalism at the End of the Twentieth Century* (New York: Ballantine, 1998), 89.
18. Schudson, *Discovering the News.*
19. Kenner, "The Politics of the Plain Style." Also see Adam, *Notes towards a Definition of Journalism.*
20. Josh Awtry, "There Just Isn't a Story There," www.poynter.org, October 15, 2003.

21 Cited in Eric Newton, ed., *Crusaders, Scoundrels, Journalists: The Newseum's Most Intriguing Newspeople* (New York: Times Books, 1999), 143.

22. Ibid, 2.

23. Brent Cunningham, "Across the Great Divide: Class," *Columbia Journalism Review* (May/June 2004): 32.

24. Cited in Laurie Kelliher, "Brits vs Yanks: Who Does Journalism Right?" *Columbia Journalism Review* (May/June 2004): 49.

25. See Rosen, *What Are Journalists For?;* Charity, *Doing Public Journalism;* and Merritt, *Public Journalism and Public Life.*

26. See Schudson, *Discovering the News;* Schiller, *Objectivity and the News;* and Gaye Tuchman, "Professionalism as an Agent of Legitimation," *Journal of Communication* 28, no. 2 (1978): 111.

27. Weaver and Wilhoit, *The American Journalist,* 145.

28. Everett C. Hughes, *Men and Their Work* (Glencoe, Ill.: Free Press, 1958); Magali Sarfatti Larson, *The Rise of Professionalism: A Sociological Analysis* (Berkeley: University of California Press, 1977); Eliot Freidson, *Professional Powers: A Study of the Institutionalization of Formal Knowledge* (Chicago: University of Chicago Press, 1986); Schiller, *Objectivity and the News;* John Soloski, "News Reporting and Professionalism: Some Constraints on the Reporting of the News," *Media, Culture and Society* 11, no. 4 (1989): 207–28.

29. Patterson, *Out of Order;* James W. Carey, "A Plea for the University Tradition," *Journalism Quarterly* 55, no. 4 (1978): 846–55.

30. Oscar H. Gandy Jr., *Beyond Agenda Setting: Information Subsidies and Public Policy* (Norwood, N.J.: Ablex, 1982); Peter Golding and Graham Murdock, "Culture, Communications, and Political Economy," in *Mass Media and Society,* edited by James Curran and Michael Gurevitch (London and New York: Edward Arnold, 1991), 70–92; McManus, *Market-Driven Journalism;* Ben H. Bagdikian, *The Media Monopoly,* 5th ed. (Boston: Beacon, 1997).

31. Paddy Scannell, *Radio, Television, and Modern Life: A Phenomenological Approach* (Oxford, U.K., and Cambridge, Mass.: Blackwell, 1996); Blumler and Gurevitch, *The Crisis of Public Communication.*

32. Nancy Morris and Silvio Waisbord, eds., *Media and Globalization: Why the State Matters* (Lanham, Md.: Rowman and Littlefield, 2001).

33. Cited in Michael Parenti, *Inventing Reality: The Politics of the Mass Media* (New York: St. Martin's, 1986), 53.

34. Hughes, *News and the Human Interest Story;* Robert Darnton, "Writing News and Telling Stories," *Daedalus* 104, no. 2 (1975): 175–94; Roger Fowler, *Language in the News: Discourse and Ideology in the Press* (London and New York: Routledge, 1991); Adam, *Notes towards a Definition of Journalism.*

35. Campbell, *60 Minutes and the News;* Bird, *For Enquiring Minds;* Kevin Glynn, *Tabloid Culture: Trash Taste, Popular Power, and the Transformation of American Television* (Durham, N.C.: Duke University Press, 2000).

36. William Gamson, "News as Framing," *American Behavioral Scientist* 33, no. 2 (1989): 157–61; Robert Entman, "Framing: Towards Clarification of a Fractured Paradigm," *Journal of Communication* 43, no. 4 (1993): 51–58; Vincent Price and David

Tewksbury, "News Values and Public Opinion: A Theoretical Account of Media Priming and Framing," in *Progress in the Communication Sciences,* edited by George Barnett and Franklin J. Boster (Norwood, N.J.: Ablex, 1997), 173–212.

37. Cited in Newton, ed., *Crusaders, Scoundrels, Journalists,* v.
38. Nicholas Tomalin, "Stop the Press, I Want to Get On," *Sunday Times Magazine,* October 26, 1969; reprinted in *A Journalism Reader,* edited by Bromley and O'Malley, 174.
39. For example, John W. C. Johnstone, Edward J. Slawski, and William W. Bowman, *The News People* (Urbana: University of Illinois Press, 1976); Weaver and Wilhoit, *The American Journalist;* David H. Weaver and G. Cleveland Wilhoit, *The American Journalist in the 1990s: U.S. News People at the End of an Era* (Mahwah, N.J.: Lawrence Erlbaum, 1996).
40. Tuchman, *Making News;* Gans, *Discovering What's News;* Gitlin, *The Whole World Is Watching.*

Bibliography

Adam, G. Stuart. *Notes towards a Definition of Journalism: Understanding an Old Craft as an Art Form.* St. Petersburg, Fla.: Poynter Institute, 1993.

Allan, Stuart. *News Culture.* Buckingham, U.K., and Philadelphia: Open University Press, 1999.

Bennett, W. Lance. *News: The Politics of Illusion.* 2nd ed. New York: Longman, 1988.

Bird, S. Elizabeth. *For Enquiring Minds: A Cultural Study of Supermarket Tabloids.* Knoxville: University of Tennessee Press, 1992.

Blumler, Jay G., and Michael Gurevitch. *The Crisis of Public Communication.* London and New York: Routledge, 1995.

Campbell, Richard. *60 Minutes and the News: A Mythology for Middle America.* Urbana: University of Illinois Press, 1991.

Carey, James W. "The Dark Continent of American Journalism." In *Reading the News: A Pantheon Guide to Popular Culture,* edited by Robert Karl Manoff and Michael Schudson, pp. 146–96. New York: Pantheon, 1986.

Charity, Arthur. *Doing Public Journalism.* New York: Guilford, 1995.

Cohen, Stanley, and Jock Young, eds. *The Manufacture of News: A Reader.* Beverly Hills, Calif.: Sage, 1973.

Cook, Timothy E. *Governing with the News: The News Media as a Political Institution.* Chicago: University of Chicago Press, 1998.

Dahlgren, Peter, and Colin Sparks. *Journalism and Popular Culture.* London and Newbury Park, Calif.: Sage, 1992.

Epstein, Edward J. *News from Nowhere: Television and the News.* New York: Random House, 1973.

Ettema, James S., and Theodore L. Glasser. *Custodians of Conscience: Investigative Journalism and Public Virtue.* New York: Columbia University Press, 1998.

Fishman, Mark. *Manufacturing the News.* Austin: University of Texas Press, 1980.

Gans, Herbert J. *Discovering What's News: A Study of CBS Evening News, NBC Nightly News, Newsweek, and Time.* New York: Pantheon, 1979.

Gans, Herbert J. *Democracy and the News.* Oxford, U.K., and New York: Oxford University Press, 2003.

Gitlin, Todd. *The Whole World Is Watching: Mass Media in the Marketing and Unmaking of the New Left.* Berkeley: University of California Press, 1980.

Hall, Stuart. "The Determinations of News Photographs." In *The Manufacture of News: A Reader,* edited by Stanley Cohen and Jock Young. Beverly Hills, Calif.: Sage, 1973.

Hardt, Hanno, and Bonnie Brennen, eds. *Newsworkers: Toward a History of the Rank and File.* Minneapolis: University of Minnesota Press, 1995.

Hartley, John. *Understanding News.* London and New York: Methuen, 1982.

Hughes, Helen MacGill. *News and the Human Interest Story.* Chicago: University of Chicago Press, 1940.

Kenner, Hugh. "The Politics of the Plain Style." In *Literary Journalism in the Twentieth Century,* edited by Norman Sims, pp. 183–90. New York: Oxford University Press, 1990.

McManus, John. *Market-Driven Journalism: Let the Citizen Beware?* Thousand Oaks, Calif.: Sage, 1994.

Merritt, Davis. *Public Journalism and Public Life: Why Telling the News Is Not Enough.* Hillsdale, N.J.: Lawrence Erlbaum, 1995.

Patterson, Thomas E. *Out of Order.* New York: Knopf, 1993.

Rosen, Jay. *What Are Journalists For?* New Haven, Conn.: Yale University Press, 1999.

Schiller, Dan. *Objectivity and the News: The Public and the Rise of Commercial Journalism.* Philadelphia: University of Pennsylvania Press, 1981.

Schudson, Michael. *Discovering the News: A Social History of American Newspapers.* New York: Basic Books, 1978.

Schudson, Michael. *The Power of News.* Cambridge, Mass.: Harvard University Press, 1995.

Schudson, Michael. *The Sociology of News.* New York: Norton, 2003.

Tuchman, Gaye. *Making News: A Study in the Construction of Reality.* New York: Free Press, 1978.

Weaver, David H., and G. Cleveland Wilhoit. *The American Journalist: A Portrait of U.S. News People and Their Work.* Bloomington: Indiana University Press, 1986.

Zelizer, Barbie. *Taking Journalism Seriously: News and the Academy.* Thousand Oaks, Calif.: Sage, 2004.

5

THE MINORITY PRESS:
PLEADING OUR OWN CAUSE

Pamela Newkirk

IT HAS BEEN NEARLY TWO CENTURIES SINCE THE EDITORS of *Freedom's Journal* affirmed in their inaugural newspaper editorial that

> [African Americans] wish to plead our own cause. Too long have others spoken for us. Too long has the public been deceived by misrepresentations, in things which concern us dearly. . . . From the press and the pulpit we have suffered much by being incorrectly represented. Our vices and our degradation are ever arrayed against us, but our virtues are passed by unnoticed."[1]

This declaration of self-determination came as slave revolts threatened the viability of African servitude and the nation's leaders debated a plan to repatriate black Americans to Africa. It was also a time when African Americans were widely portrayed as savages and buffoons in the white press and even free African Americans were denied full citizenship. For the purposes of apportionment, the Constitution counted African American slaves as three-fifths of a person. *Freedom's Journal* and the succession of black newspapers that followed provided a prominent platform from which African Americans opposed slavery, the widespread lynching of blacks, and other measures deemed harmful to blacks. Alongside the black press were a string of Native American newspapers, beginning with the *Cherokee Phoenix,* published in Georgia from 1828 to 1835. Like the black press, the Native American press stressed cultural pride and civil rights for Native Americans, who in the 1820s faced mounting pressure from President James Monroe's administration to relinquish aboriginal title to Georgia. A number of laws were passed in the 1820s and 1830s to dissolve Cherokee sovereignty. In 1828, after the discovery of gold in Georgia, a state law forbade Cherokees from mining, even on their own land.

In a speech to raise money for the new paper, the first editor, Elias Boudinot, said: "To obtain a correct and complete knowledge of these people, there must exist a vehicle of Indian intelligence, altogether different from those which have heretofore been employed." In the first issue of the paper, Boudinot stressed that the objective of the paper was to serve the Cherokee Nation.[2]

These alternative newspapers, published by racial minorities denied the rights of full citizenship, raised the bar on American democracy by exposing the hypocrisy of a nation founded on principles of liberty and justice, but that somehow rationalized the enslavement of African people, the subjugation of Native Americans, and the fierce discrimination against Asians. By the 1870s rabid anti-Chinese sentiment on the West Coast resulted in the yellow peril, during which mobs burned the homes and businesses, and lynched hundreds, of Chinese residents. The Chinese Exclusion Act, in effect from 1882 until 1943, was the first federal law to ban immigration of a single nationality.[3]

While the nation's racial landscape has radically changed between then and now, and the mainstream press—including television, radio, newspapers, and the Internet—is more diverse than ever, many believe the need for a racial minority press "to plead our own cause" persists. In 2004, while racial minorities represented more than 31 percent of the population, they held about 12 percent of newspaper, 18 percent of television, and 8 percent of radio positions. When attention turns to management, the landscape becomes even whiter. People of color held 9.7 percent of newspaper, 9.2 percent of television, and 5 percent of radio news management jobs.[4] And numbers tell only part of the story. Numerous studies conducted in the early 2000s show that many racial minorities believe they continue to be stereotyped or ignored by the mainstream media, which largely appeal to a white audience. Content analysis of major newspapers by four Native American Journalists Association members in 2003 found that most stories concerning Native Americans fell into predictable categories, such as casino gambling, sports mascots, reservation affairs, and entertainment.[5] A 2003 study on media coverage of Latinos found that Latinos continued to be marginalized on the evening newscasts and that out of 16,000 stories that aired in 2002, only 120—or less than 1 percent—were about Latinos.[6] Similar studies have found that the media routinely stereotyped Asian and African Americans and was slow to hire and promote them in the newsroom.[7] A 2000 Freedom Forum study noted that while an average of 550 journalists of color were hired each year by the newspaper industry between 1994 and 1999, during the same period about 400 journalists of color a year left the industry.[8] The study showed that journalists of color were almost twice as likely as white journalists to leave the profession, with many citing as the primary reasons poor advancement and frustration over the inability to make a difference.[9]

But while the need for a viable alternative press is apparent, the diversity, however slight, of the mainstream media has contributed to the decline of the traditional black press. As mainstream newspapers and television began covering the civil rights movement, black readers became less reliant on the black press for news and information. So while circulation at the *Chicago Defender* reached 275,000 in 1945, it plummeted to 33,000 by 1970 and in the mid-1990s was around 25,000. Similarly, during the same period, the circulation at the legendary *Baltimore Afro-American* dropped from 137,000 in 1945 to 28,000 in 1970; and the *Pittsburgh Courier*'s from 202,000 to 20,000.[10] Still, the black press—including the more than 200 newspapers represented by the National Newspaper Publishers Association in 2004—Black Entertainment Television (BET)—which reaches some 74 million households—and numerous Web sites and radio stations, have continued to fill a void of news and information geared to black audiences, and newsmakers have taken notice. In 1996, on the heels of his acquittal in a high-profile murder case, O.J. Simpson granted an exclusive interview to BET, resulting in its highest ratings ever. When, in 2002, Senator Trent Lott faced pressure to resign as leader of the Senate Republicans for making inflammatory racial remarks, Lott appeared on BET to apologize. And in 2004 President Bush, Secretary of State Colin Powell, and Senator John Kerry, the Democratic presidential nominee, all addressed members of UNITY: Journalists of Color Inc., an alliance of the National Association of Black Journalists, the National Association of Hispanic Journalists, the Native American Journalists Association, and the Asian American Journalists Association. That year, the group, which was founded in 1994 and represents seven thousand media professionals of color, held its third joint convention in Washington, D.C.

Meanwhile, the Spanish-language media, like the Latino population, is exploding. Mirroring the dramatic growth of the Latino population (in the 2000 census Latinos surpassed African Americans as the largest minority group) is a wave of broadcasting and print outlets throughout the country. Since the *Miami Herald* in 1976 introduced a Spanish-language edition, many mainstream publishers have followed suit, including the *Los Angeles Times,* the *Chicago Sun-Times,* and the *Arizona Republic.* In 1981 the Gannett Corporation bought *El Diario/La Prensa,* New York's Spanish-language daily, which has since been purchased by California-based Clarity Partners. In 1999 the Tribune Company launched *Hoy,* which planned to expand to Chicago, where it would replace the free weekly Spanish-language *Exito.* In 2004 the *Dallas Morning News* launched *Al Día,* a six-day-a-week paper aimed at the city's 1 million Hispanic residents. In neighboring Fort Worth, the Knight Ridder–owned *Star-Telegram* expanded its free two-day-a-week *Diario La Estrella* to five days. And in May 2004 the Washington Post Company announced its plans to acquire *El Tiempo Latino,* the leading Spanish-language weekly in the Washington area, with a circulation of 34,000.

In 2004, Univision, the nation's largest Spanish-language broadcaster, had some fifty stations and forty-three affiliates and reached more than 80 percent of Spanish-speaking audiences in the cities where it broadcast. Its closest rival, Telemundo, had some fifteen stations and thirty-two affiliates. Among its stations was the top-rated NBC affiliate station in Los Angeles, whose core audience was the coveted eighteen-to-forty-two-year-old age group. Washington, D.C., alone had two Spanish-language television stations, eight AM and FM stations, a cable network, and two-dozen daily and weekly newspapers.

Among the estimated two hundred ethnic newspapers in New York City in 2000 were four daily Chinese-language newspapers and another dozen weeklies that provided information about China and, for new immigrants, information on jobs and apartments.[11] One of the largest was the *World Journal,* a division of the United Daily News Group of Taiwan, which also had newspapers in ten other cities, including San Francisco. The New York paper had some twenty-five reporters and twelve translators in New York.[12]

The Native American population has also benefited from the growing interest in media diversity and niche advertising. Among the 150 Native American papers published in 2000 was *Indian Country Today,* formerly the *Lakota Times,* the largest Native American weekly, with a circulation of about 13,000. A column published by the founder, Tim A. Giago Jr., is syndicated in some fourteen mainstream newspapers and earned the *Baltimore Sun's* H. L. Mencken Writing Award. In 2002 Dennis McAuliffe Jr., an associate professor at the University of Montana School of Journalism and cofounder of the Freedom Forum's American Indian Journalism Institute, launched Reznet, an Internet news site, to showcase the work of Native American student journalists. In 2004 there were also plans in the works to launch FACES, a Native American cable station, by 2007.[13]

While not all of these alternative media are overtly political and some deliver a steady diet of crime, wedding announcements, and social events, many tap into the legendary history of the early black press that cast a harsh and steady light on racial injustice and oppression.

Free Speech—At a Cost

While the independent spirit of the minority press is taken for granted today, it is difficult to fathom the kind of limitations on free speech that were, at the birth of the nation, imposed on African Americans and Native Americans and those who supported them. While freedom of speech is one of the cornerstones of American democracy, it did not extend to slaves, who could face the death penalty for planning a slave revolt.[14] In most states it was illegal to teach slaves how to read and write, and every Southern state except Kentucky passed laws restricting the advocacy of abolitionist causes. Virginia, in addition, passed a law requiring postmasters to intercept and report to a judge mail that encouraged rebellion or denied that slaves were the property of their owners. Attempts to pass a similar act in Congress failed.

Even without such legislation, the climate inhibiting abolitionist activism chilled free speech. In 1835 William Lloyd Garrison, a white abolitionist publisher, was beaten and dragged through the streets of Boston. That same year the Georgia Guard destroyed the Cherokee newspaper the *Phoenix,* whose lead type was dumped in a well. Prior to that, a number of state laws had been passed in Georgia to end Cherokee sovereignty and native resistance to removal from Cherokee land. One law required all non-Cherokees to take an oath of allegiance to the state or face prosecution. "This week we present to our readers but half a sheet," Boudinot, the *Phoenix* editor, wrote on February 19, 1831. "One of our printers has left us; and we expect another (who is a white man) to quit us very soon, either to be dragged to the Georgia penitentiary for a term not less than four years." He added: "Thus is liberty of the press guaranteed by the Constitution of Georgia."[15] In Illinois, the Reverend Elijah Lovejoy, publisher of the antislavery journal the *Observer,* saw his press destroyed three times. He was attacked and fatally shot when he attempted to operate a fourth press. Prior to the attack, Illinois lawmakers passed a resolution that insisted that the First Amendment did not extend to abolitionists. It would not be until 1868 that the Fourteenth Amendment extended constitutional rights to all American men in the United States, including African Americans and Native Americans. Women were denied the right to vote until 1920 when the Nineteenth Amendment enfranchised them.

Among the most famous of the early black newspapers was Frederick Douglass's *North Star,* launched in 1847 in Rochester, New York. By then Douglass had gained international fame due to the publication in 1845 of his autobiography, which chronicled his birth into slavery in 1817, his daring escape twenty-one years later, and his return in 1845 to buy his freedom from his Maryland owner. His riveting story coupled with his dynamic oratory skills catapulted him to worldwide renown as a leading abolitionist in demand as a lecturer throughout the United States and abroad.

Douglass's *North Star,* which had correspondents in Europe, in the West Indies, and in major cities throughout the United States, was widely read by blacks and whites alike. The newspaper's primary goal was explicitly stated in its first issue: "The object of The North Star will be to attack slavery in all its forms and aspects, advocate universal emancipation, exact the standard of the colored people; and to hasten the day of freedom to our three million enslaved countrymen."[16]

Douglass's activism did not go without consequence. His house was burned down and his newspaper press was destroyed, but he continued to publish, renaming the paper *Frederick Douglass's Paper* in 1851 to capitalize on his celebrity. He finally suspended publication in 1860, the year Abraham Lincoln was elected to the White House and the South seceded from the United States. Black newspapers proliferated following the Civil War, although the sobering realities of Emancipation tempered their militancy. Many former slaves were left destitute and forced to work as sharecroppers on the very plantations they had worked on as slaves. And the success of a relative handful of blacks during Reconstruction fueled a fierce backlash; blacks increasingly became the victims of lynching, segregation, and offensive character assassination in the mainstream press. In 1876 some forty-five black Republicans were killed in a series of attacks in South Carolina, resulting in the deployment of federal troops by President Rutherford Hayes. Some two decades later, South Carolina senator Benjamin Tillman bragged from the Senate floor about the reign of terror during which ballot boxes were stuffed and blacks were killed to maintain white domination.

"The people of South Carolina, in their Constitution, have done their level best to prevent the niggers from voting," Tillman was quoted in a *New York Press* article. Southerners, he continued, "rose in righteousness and might. We took the Government. We stuffed ballot boxes, we bulldozed the niggers and we shot 'em, And we are not ashamed of it."[17]

Fear of reprisal muted many in the black press, but not Ida B. Wells, the twenty-three-year-old editor and publisher of *Free Speech* in Memphis, Tennessee. Wells, a former teacher, challenged the pervasive myth that the widespread lynching of black men resulted from the rape of white women and suggested that the recent lynching of three black Memphis businessmen had been provoked by competing white businessmen.

"Nobody in this section of the country believes the old thread-bare lies that Negro men rape white women," she wrote in a May 21, 1892, editorial in her newspaper, brazenly suggesting that relations between black men and white women were consensual. "If Southern men are not careful they will over-reach themselves and public sentiment will have a reaction and a conclusion will be reached which will be very damaging to the moral reputation of their women."[18]

Wells's editorial provoked calls for retribution in the white press. The following Monday, the *Commercial Appeal* reprinted Wells's editorial accompanied by its own. "The black wretch who had written that foul lie should be tied to a stake at the corner of Main and Madison streets, a pair of tailor's shears used on him and he should then be burned at a stake."[19]

A mob destroyed the office and print shop of *Free Speech* and Wells, for fear of death, fled the South and took her antilynching crusade to the North. "Brave woman!" wrote Frederick Douglass in a letter dated October 25, 1892, and reprinted in Wells's antilynching pamphlet *Southern Horrors*. "You have done your people and mine a service which can neither be weighed nor measured."[20]

At the turn of the century, against a backdrop of black political disenfranchisement and widespread lynching, a handful of newspapers maintained their stridency, perhaps none more than the *Guardian,* published in Boston by William Monroe Trotter, a Harvard graduate. Trotter was among a handful of black journalists to publicly criticize Booker T. Washington, who emerged as the nation's most prominent African American following an 1895 speech in which he implored blacks to be patient in their quest for equality and to forsake higher education to instead earn the respect of whites through hard work in agriculture. His stature was cemented in 1901 with the publication of *Up from Slavery.*

"How long, O Booker, will you abuse our patience?" wrote Trotter in an editorial. "How long do you think your scheming will escape us? To what end will your vaulting ambition hurl itself? Does not the fear of future hate and execration, does not the sacred rights and hopes of a suffering race, in no ways move you?"[21]

In 1903, *The Souls of Black Folk,* a critically acclaimed book by W. E. B. Du Bois that chronicled the plight of African Americans, positioned Du Bois to rival Washington's prominence and influence. While Du Bois followed his success with the publication of two different publications, his greatest forum was as founding editor of the *Crisis,* the monthly organ of the National Association for the Advancement of Colored People. From its beginnings in 1910, the *Crisis* became the most influential journal of African American protest in the twentieth century. Du Bois edited the journal for twenty-four years, during which time he attacked white racism, but also the black clergy, public and elected officials, and members of the black and white press.

The Wartime Press

The hope for racial equality was never greater than during World War II, when thousands of black troops served valiantly, hoping to finally be seen as full-fledged Americans. But black soldiers, subjected to segregated regiments and mob attacks when they returned home, began demanding the same rights in the United States that they were fighting for on foreign soil. In 1946, as black veterans returned home, they were met by white mobs. In Atlanta, six black veterans were killed within a three-week period. It was Georgia's first multiple lynching since 1918. The discrimination against black veterans became a key issue of the black press, which realized increased circulation during the war. The *Pittsburgh Courier* launched its "Double V" campaign—which called for victory for black troops abroad and at home—and became a rallying cry for many blacks in and outside of the press. Largely due to the intense interest during World War II in the war and racial equality, circulation for black newspapers surged from 1 million in 1937 to 2 million in 1947.[22]

While more attention was focused on discrimination against African Americans, Asian Americans, whose numbers were far fewer, also continued to experience virulent discrimination. As Helen Zia notes in her book *Asian American Dreams,* some 23,000 Japanese Americans served in the U.S. Army during World War II, the majority in the segregated 442nd Nisei Regiment.[23] When the war ended, about forty-five thousand Japanese Americans were still interned. In 1947 a civil rights commission appointed by President Harry Truman issued the report *To Secure These Rights,* condemning the racial injustice suffered by blacks. That same year *A Free and Responsible Press,* a report commissioned by the publisher Henry Luce, contained the first major indictment of the press coverage of minorities by a mainstream panel. The report concluded that the press was more concerned with "scoops and sensations" than the social significance of news, and recommended a representative portrait of society. "Even if nothing is said about the Chinese in the dialogue of a film, if the Chinese appear in a succession of pictures as sinister drug addicts and militarists, an image of China is built which needs to be balanced by another. If the Negro appears in the stories published in magazines of national circulation only as a servant, if children figure constantly in radio dramas as impertinent and ungovernable brats—the image of the Negro and the American child is distorted."[24]

It added: "The truth about any social group, though it should not exclude its weaknesses and vices, includes also recognition of its values, its aspirations and its common humanity."[25] These ideals mirror those expressed by the editors of *Freedom's Journal* and foreshadowed by two decades a similar critique by a panel appointed by President Lyndon B. Johnson.

The Kerner Report

In 1967, as widespread poverty and disillusionment erupted in riots in black urban neighborhoods across the country, President Johnson assembled a panel to study the reasons for the unrest. A year later, the National Advisory Commission on Civil Disorders would draw attention to another facet of the media's social responsibility. In a blistering critique, the commission, chaired by Illinois governor Otto Kerner, warned that the nation was "moving toward two societies, one black, one white—separate and unequal."[26] The report faulted white racism and the media for distorted and inaccurate coverage of black America that it said contributed to black alienation and despair. While the panel was to look at the media's role in the racial unrest that rocked cities across the country, it reserved its harshest criticism for the daily coverage. "By failing to portray the Negro as a matter of routine and in the context of the total society, the news media have, we believe, contributed to the black-white schism in this country."[27]

It added: "Along with the community as a whole, the press has too long basked in a white world, looking out of it, if at all, with white men's eyes and a white perspective. That is no longer good enough. The painful process of readjustment that is required of the American news media must begin now. They must make a reality of integration—both their product and personnel."[28]

Media executives immediately vowed to diversify an overwhelmingly white press. In a decade a rigidly segregated industry made changes that, while numerically superficial, were nonetheless historic. Between 1968 and 1978, the percentage of minorities in the newspaper industry increased from less than 1 percent to 3.9 percent. During the same period, the percentage of minorities grew to 9.1 in the broadcast industry, largely as a result of a number of measures adopted by the Federal Communications Commission (FCC).[29] Federal policy adopted in 1969 stipulated that broadcast operating licenses would not be granted to stations that deliberately discriminated. In 1977 the FCC adopted a program that required licensees with more than fifty full-time employees to file detailed employment profiles to ensure that minorities were considered. While the National Association of Broadcasters called the program discriminatory, it survived a federal court challenge. Between 1977 and 2000, when the FCC profiling program was ultimately defeated as unconstitutional, the percentage of minorities in the broadcast industry rose to 20.6 percent (or 19 percent for English-language stations).[30]

At the dawn of the twenty-first century, the continuing desire for an alternative minority press reveals both the unmet promise of media diversity trumpeted in the 1960s, and the ever present yearning by distinct groups to assert their unfiltered voices in the marketplace of ideas. From the start, the ethnic media have been at the forefront of the battle not only for fair and inclusive media, but, more significantly, for a fair and representative democracy.

Notes

1. John Russwurm and Samuel Cornish, *Freedom's Journal* (New York) 1, no. 1, March 16, 1827.
2. Mark N. Trahant, *Pictures of Our Nobler Selves: A History of Native American Contributions to News Media* (Nashville, Tenn.: First Amendment Center, 1995), 3; available from the Freedom Forum, http://freedomforum.org.
3. Anti-Asian sentiment continued with the signing on February 19, 1942, of Executive Order 9066, which authorized the evacuation and internment of Japanese Americans.
4. The percentage of minority television journalists dropped for two years straight—from 20.6 percent in 2001 to 18.1 percent in 2003—following the elimination in 2000 of Equal Employment Opportunity Commission guidelines. The percentage of minority news directors during that same period dropped from 6.7 to 4.1 percent (RTNDA/Ball State University survey).
5. Mark Fitzgerald, "Black and White and Red All Over," *Editor & Publisher,* January 1, 2004.
6. Serafín Méndez-Méndez and Diane Alverio, *Network Brownout 2003: The Portrayal of Latinos in Network Television News, 2002* (Washington, D.C.: National Association of Hispanic Journalists, 2003), www.nahj.org/NAHJbrownoutreport03.pdf.
7. A yearlong content analysis of television news, newspapers, and magazines conducted by News Watch at San Francisco State University and released in 1994 concluded that the media's coverage of people of color "is riddled with old stereotypes, offensive terminology, biased reporting and a myopic interpretation of American society." "News Watch: A Critical Look at Coverage of People of Color," the Center for Integration and Improvement of Journalism, San Francisco State University,

www.newswatch.sfsu.edu. A study released in June 2004 by the Institute for Asian American Studies at the University of Massachusetts contended that despite the perception of Asian American affluence and the stereotype as the "model minority," the study found that the percentage of Asian American families in poverty was nearly double that of the total metropolitan Boston population. Paul Watanabe, Michael Liu, and Shauna Lo, *Asian Americans in Metro Boston: Growth, Diversity and Complexity,* http://www.iaas.umb.edu/research/Metro_Boston_PR.shtml.

8. Robert H. Giles, introduction to Lawrence T. McGill, *Newsroom Diversity: Meeting the Challenge* (Arlington, Va.: Freedom Forum, 1999), 3; http://www.freedomforum. org/publications/diversity/meetingthechallenge/meetingthechallenge.pdf.

9. McGill, *Newsroom Diversity,* 6.

10. Clint C. Wilson II, *Black Journalists in Paradox: Historical Perspectives and Current Dilemmas* (New York: Greenwood Press, 1991).

11. A survey released in 2000 by Independent Press Association counted 200 ethnic newspapers and magazines in New York City, a 33 percent increase since 1990. "Many Voices, One City," Independent Press Association–New York, http://www. indypress.org/programs/techassist.html.

12. Joseph Berger, "Newspaper War, Waged a Character at a Time: Chinese Language Dailies Battle Fiercely in New York," *New York Times,* November 10, 2003, B1.

13. The Reznet site is at www.reznetnews.org. For information on FACES see Jeff Commings, "Indian TV Channel Planned," *Albuquerque Tribune,* May 27, 2004, A1.

14. For slaves, not only was freedom of speech prohibited but so too were drums and horns. Dances, church services, and other social events were only permitted in the presence of a white person.

15. Trahant, *Picture of Our Nobler Selves,* 7.

16. *North Star,* November 1, 1847, 1.

17. "Shotgun Rule Defended by U.S. Senator Tillman," *New York Press,* February 27, 1900, p. 1.

18. Alfreda M. Duster, ed. *Crusade for Justice: The Autobiography of Ida B. Wells* (Chicago: University of Chicago Press, 1970), 65–66.

19. Ibid, 66.

20. Jacqueline Jones Roysler, ed., *Southern Horrors and Other Writings: The Anti-Lynching Campaign of Ida B. Wells, 1892–1900* (Boston: Bedford, 1997), 3.

21. *Guardian,* September 13, 1902.

22. Jannette L. Dates and William Barlow, eds., *Split Image: African Americans in the Mass Media* (Washington, D.C.: Howard University Press, 1990), 358.

23. Helen Zia, *Asian American Dreams: The Emergence of an American People* (New York: Farrar, Straus, and Giroux, 2000), 43.

24. Commission on Freedom of the Press, *A Free and Responsible Press: A General Report on Mass Communication,* edited by Robert D. Leigh (Chicago: University of Chicago Press, 1947; repr. 1974), 54.

25. Ibid., 26–27.

26. National Advisory Commission on Civil Disorders, *Report of the National Advisory Commission on Civil Disorders* (New York: Bantam Books, 1968), 1.

27. Ibid., 383.

28. Ibid., 389.
29. American Society of Newspaper Editors, annual survey, 1979.
30. Radio and Television News Directors Association/Ball State University annual survey, 2001.

Bibliography

Commission on Freedom of the Press, *A Free and Responsible Press: A General Report on Mass Communication,* edited by Robert D. Leigh. Chicago: University of Chicago Press, 1947; repr. 1974.

Dates, Jannette L., and William Barlow, eds., *Split Image: African Americans in the Mass Media.* Washington, D.C.: Howard University Press, 1990.

Duster, Alfreda M., ed. *Crusade for Justice: The Autobiography of Ida B. Wells.* Chicago: University of Chicago Press. 1970.

McGill, Lawrence T. *Newsroom Diversity: Meeting the Challenge.* Arlington, Va.: Freedom Forum, 1999.

National Advisory Commission on Civil Disorders. *Report of the National Commission on Civil Disorders.* New York: Bantam Books, 1968.

Newkirk, Pamela. *Within the Veil: Black Journalists, White Media.* New York: New York University Press, 2002.

Trahant, Mark N. *Pictures of Our Nobler Selves: A History of Native American Contributions to News Media.* Nashville, Tenn.: First Amendment Center, 1995.

Wilson, Clinton C. *Black Journalists in Paradox: Historical Perspectives and Current Dilemmas.* New York: Greenwood Press, 1991.

Zia, Helen. *Asian American Dreams: The Emergence of An American People.* New York: Farrar, Straus and Giroux, 2000.

6

JOURNALISM AND DEMOCRACY ACROSS BORDERS

John Keane

AFTER MORE THAN HALF A CENTURY FOLLOWING WORLD War II, fresh interpretations of the vital importance of journalism for democratic politics began to appear.[1] The new thinking began in the early 1990s, within a context that was abnormal: the forces of resurgent market liberalism, the decline of public service broadcasting, the global collapse of dictatorships, and the outbreak of the so-called catching-up or velvet revolutions of 1989–1991 all conspired to produce important, sometimes bitter policy controversies about the future of journalism and its role in stifling or fostering democratic institutions and ways of life. Especially in Europe, with its strong public broadcasting systems, some observers tried to defend the public service model against threats from both state authoritarianism and the forces of neoliberal politics,[2] but neoliberalism forcefully questioned the prevailing modes of state regulation. It quickly captured the high ground of public debate by using terms like *state censorship, individual choice, deregulation,* and *market competition* to criticize the prevailing mix of public and private communication systems operating within the boundaries of territorial states, whether democratic or not. Its partisans predicted an age of "democratic revolution" and multichannel communications structured by, in the words of Rupert Murdoch, "freedom and choice, rather than regulation and scarcity."[3] Such rhetoric prompted a third approach—a highly original defense of journalism as a tool for the public use and enjoyment of all citizens and not for the private gain or profit of political rulers or businesses.[4] This approach anticipated a genuine commonwealth of different forms of life, tastes, and opinions. It sounded utopian, but it saw itself as supported by real technological and social developments, such as multichannel cable television systems, global satellite communication, the Internet, and the renewal of cross-border relations of civil society. This third approach called for the empowerment of a plurality of citizens who would be governed neither by undemocratic states nor by undemocratic market forces but instead would take advantage of a rich plurality of nonstate and nonmarket media that functioned both as permanent thorns in the side of state power and served as the primary means of communication for citizens living within a diverse and horizontally organized civil society.

When assessing the impact of these three different reactions it seems obvious that everywhere, for the time being, market-liberal policies have gained the upper hand in political battles to redefine the field of journalism. This was by no means either guaranteed or inevitable. It has rather been determined by a combination of vast capital assets, persuasive rhetoric, skillful political maneuvering, and a shrewd grasp of the unfolding new communications revolution, whose main feature is the digital integration of text, sound, and image in mobile networks that are accessible through an affordable variety of media, from multiple points, on a global scale.[5] It has also been supported by nearsightedness in journalism scholarship, whose narrow definition of the journalistic profession has failed to grasp the key political, cultural, social, economic, and technological changes—especially the impact of globalization—that have beset journalism.[6] The combined effect has been to underestimate the world-transforming effects of the (potential) communicative abundance that results from such novel technical factors as electronic memory, tighter channel spacing, new frequency allocation, direct satellite broadcasting, digital tuning, and compression techniques. Chief among these factors is the invention and deployment of cable and satellite-linked computerized communication, which catalyzes both product and process innovations in virtually every field of media. When Diane Keaton's character told Tony Roberts, who played her workaholic husband in Woody Allen's *Play It Again, Sam,* that he should give his office the number of the pay phone they were passing in case they needed him, it was a big joke. What was farce in 1972 has become reality. In the space of a few minutes, we know well, an individual somewhere on the face of the earth can send a fax, be paged, access his or her e-mail on a mobile phone, send an e-mail from a personal computer, watch satellite/cable television, channel hop on radio, make a telephone call, read a newspaper, open the day's mail, even find time for a face-to-face conversation. Such trends have encouraged talk of universal abundance, which has begun to function as the ideology of computer-linked electronic communications networks. An early example was John Perry Barlow's "A Declaration of the Independence of Cyberspace," which claimed that computer-linked networks were creating a "global social space," a borderless "global conversation of bits," a new world "that all may enter without privilege or prejudice accorded by race, economic power, military force, or station of birth."[7]

Journalism and the End of Democracy?

The growth of a globe-girdling, time- and space-conquering galaxy of communication is arguably of epochal importance.[8] Communications media like the wheel and the press had distance-shrinking effects, but genuinely globalized communication only began (during the nineteenth century) with inventions like overland and underwater telegraphy and the early development of Reuters and other international news agencies. The process has culminated in the more recent development of wide-footprint geostationary satellites, computer-networked media, and the expanding and merging flows of international news, electronic data exchange, and entertainment and education materials controlled by giant firms such as Thorn EMI, Time Warner, News Corporation, the Walt Disney Company, Bertelsmann AG, Microsoft, Sony, and CNN. These global media linkages have helped to achieve something much more persuasively than the maps of Gerardus Mercator ever did: to deepen the visceral feelings among millions of people (somewhere between 5 and 25 percent of the world's population[9]) that our world is "one world," and that this worldly interdependence requires humans to share some responsibility for its fate.

What role can and should journalism play in this process? Contemporary journalism theory is often cocooned in assumptions about the primacy of territorial state institutions, yet it is worth noting that theories of how journalism should work have long supposed that interdependence and shared responsibility among citizens who are otherwise separated by geographic distance is an optimum goal. Think of earlier commentators as wide-ranging as Alexis de Tocqueville, Gabriel Tarde, Ferdinand Tönnies, John Dewey, and Walter Lippmann: all of them variously argued that journalism should serve "the public" and could best do so by molding socially disparate and geographically dispersed populations into publics united around shared concerns, or at the very least into publics that interacted with journalism in a predictive and patterned fashion.[10] In a similar vein, the 1947 Hutchins report, the findings of the Commission on Freedom of the Press, briefly mentioned the need for government to foster more worldly forms of journalism by using its influence in various ways: for instance, to reduce the costs of entry into communications markets, to break down barriers to the free and equal flow of information, and to collaborate with the United Nations in promoting the widest dissemination of cross-border news and discussion.[11] The leap from thinking that is attached to state-framed democracies to an understanding of the global role that can be played by journalism was also implicit in the classic textbook of the mid-twentieth century, *Four Theories of the Press*.[12] Adopting a cold war perspective on journalism, it looked to the free flow of information as a medicine for the world's ills. The approach sketched a set of optimum conditions for journalism to function in different geopolitical regions. It focused on patterns of ownership, licensing, regulation, and censorship in order to offer a typology for delineating different ways in which to connect journalism and government. The approach of *Four Theories of the Press* has subsequently been criticized heavily in various ways,[13] but what is striking is just how little attention has been paid to its deep normative presumptions about the desirability of a free flow of communication promoted by global markets, helped along by bodies such as the General Agreement on Tariffs and Trade (GATT), the UN Educational, Scientific, and Cultural Organization (UNESCO), and other agencies of the United Nations. The key question prompted by *Four Theories of the Press* consequently remains poorly addressed in journalism theory: Is there evidence that journalism and democracy can positively coexist in an age of global communication?

While it is today generally acknowledged that the accelerating growth of global media linkages has profound implications for journalism, it is much less certain that this process has an elective affinity with democratic institutions and ways of life. Although critics and commentators alike seem to agree that global media networks foster a common sense of worldly interdependence, some observers of the government/press linkage ask: What kind of worldly interdependence are we talking about? They note that today's global communications system is an integral—aggressive and oligopolistic—sector of the "turbo-capitalist" system that now operates as a global system.[14] Ten or so vertically integrated media conglomerates, most of them based in the United States, dominate the world market.[15] Pacesetters in a new species of private enterprise driven by the desire for emancipation from social custom, territorial state interference, taxation restrictions, trade union intransigence, and all other external restrictions upon the free movement of capital in search of profit, these global media conglomerates kick against the so-called "law" (formulated by the nineteenth-century economist Adolph Wagner[16]) of the expanding public sector. Their chief executives and shareholders push for a new global regulatory regime—for lighter and more flexible regulation, on a global scale.[17] Media business is no longer exclusively "homespun" (to use John Maynard Keynes's famous term for describing territorially bound, state-regulated markets). Bursting the bounds of time and space, language and custom, media business is instead transformed into complex global commodity chains, or global flows of information, staff, money, components, and products. Not surprisingly, the journalism associated with the global media conglomerates gives priority to advertising-driven commercial ventures: to salable music, videos, sports, shopping, and children's and adults' filmed entertainment. Program-making codes, in the field of satellite television news for instance, are consequently biased along turbo-capitalist lines. They are subject to specific rules of market *mise-en-scène*. Special emphasis is given to "news-breaking" and "blockbusting" stories that concentrate upon accidents, disasters, political crises, and the histrionics and cruelties of war. The material that is fed to editors by journalists reporting from or around trouble spots ("clusterfucks" as they are called in the trade) is meanwhile shortened, simplified, repackaged, and transmitted in commercial form. Staged sound-bites and "live" or lightly edited material are editors' favorites; so, too, are "flashy" presentational technologies, including the use of logos, rapid visual cuts, and "stars" who are placed center stage. News exchange arrangements—whereby subscribing news organizations exchange visual footage and other material—then complete the picture, ensuring a substantial homogenization of news stories in many parts of the globe, circulated at the speed of light.

These trends lead some observers to draw pessimistic conclusions. Far from nurturing democracy, they say, global journalism produces bland commercial pulp for audiences who are politically comatose. They warn of the *embourgeoisement* of the brain. They insist that American-style, turbo-capitalist culture is becoming universal because it is universally present. Algerian-desert dwellers smoke Marlboros. Nigerian tribespeople huddle around their televisions watching hand-me-down episodes of *Dallas.* Chinese peasants and workers meanwhile dream of owning and driving a Chrysler. Everybody who lives within global civil society is put under great pressure to adopt more or less unaffordable turbo-capitalist living standards that are adjusted to local conditions, many of them originally American, like automobility, Windows XP, Nike trainers, skateboards, MasterCards, shopping malls, and endless chatter about "choice." If during the eighteenth century a cosmopolitan was typically someone who thought *à la française,* who in other words identified Paris with cosmopolis, then three centuries later, thanks to turbo-capitalism, a cosmopolitan is turning out to be someone whose tastes are fixated on New York and Washington, Los Angeles and Seattle. Turbo-capitalism produces "McWorld": a universal tribe of consumers who dance to the music of logos, advertising slogans, sponsorship, brand names, trademarks, and jingles.[18] "The dictatorship of the single word and the single image, much more devastating than that of the single party," laments the social critic Eduardo Galeano, "imposes a life whose exemplary citizen is a docile consumer and passive spectator built on the assembly line following the North American model of commercial television."[19] Others express similar anxieties about the "monoculture of the mind" (the environmentalist Vandana Shiva) or "global cultural homogenization" in the form of "transnational corporate cultural domination": a world in which "private giant economic enterprises pursue—sometimes competitively, sometimes co-operatively—historical capitalist objectives of profit making and capital accumulation, in continuously changing market and geopolitical conditions."[20] The net effect is a silent takeover of the world, such that "consumerism is equated with economic policy, where corporate interests reign, where corporations spew their jargon on to the airwaves and stifle nations with their imperial rule. Corporations have become behemoths, huge global giants that wield immense political power."[21]

Such laments correctly warn of the dangers of "communication poverty" and "market censorship" that result from market-driven forms of media. Market forces serve as a structure of constraint in matters of communication in two ways. The first trouble with market competition is this: it necessarily produces losers. The cruel facts of communication poverty are common knowledge:

three-quarters of the world's population (now totaling 6 billion) are too poor to buy a book; a majority have never made a phone call in their lives; and only 1 or 2 percent currently have access to the Internet.[22] From their side, the excluded "participate" within the global communications industry in a derivative, minimal sense: thanks to aid programs, television, and Hollywood films, they know something about the lives of the rich and powerful of the world. Struggling to make ends meet, they are aware of how insubstantial is their share of the world's wealth and power and style. They sense that their lives are permanently under the shadow of "Westerners" and things "Western." They are subjected to crude and aggressive prejudices of those who shadow them. They feel scorned, as if they were the "wrongful" majority. They know that being marginal means being condemned to a much shorter life. They are made to feel like victims of a predatory mode of foreign intervention: they feel shut out from global civil society, or uprooted by its dynamism, or imprisoned within its discriminatory structures and policies, such as unpayable debt-service payments, or victimized by scores of uncivil wars.[23] Others—many Muslims, say—feel profound disappointment, tinged with anger. They reason that the enormous potential of global journalism to expand dialogue among civilizations, to "affirm differences through communication," is being choked to death by the combined forces of global markets and military might, manifested, for instance, in the repression of independent journalism throughout the Middle East and the dangerous and long-standing alliance between the United States and Israel.[24] Still others are gripped by feelings of humiliation: the sense of being crushed into the impotence that stems from the failure to be understood, the simple inability to make their voices heard, to be recognized as the potential makers of their own histories. Then, finally, there are the damned who curse quietly or express open hatred for this civil society—or who join Dostoyevsky's underground man by drawing the defiant conclusion, against all things "reasonable" and "Western," that two plus two indeed equals five. From there, it may be only a step or two to picking up a gun or detonating bombs—to fight for the cause of ridding the world of the hypocrisy and decadence of an immediate aggressor, or a pseudo-universal way of life.

Seen from this angle, the global journalism associated with such companies as Time Warner and News Corporation seems to give the upper hand to the wants and desires of certain groups, like those with large advertising budgets or those with enough capital to acquire and run a newspaper, a global television network, or mobile telephone system. This brings us to the second way in which, in matters of editorial and programming plans and decisions, media markets limit communication: they privilege certain criteria, such as profitability and allocative efficiency, at the expense of others, like experimental creativity or equality of representation. Pop videos, gardening programs, and reruns of *Bonanza* and *Hill Street Blues* may be low cost and high profit, but there is no necessary or even probabilistic relationship between them and the democratic principle of guaranteeing citizens equal chances of voicing concerns and affecting policy decisions. Corporate power can indeed pose as great a threat to democracy and freedom of communication as governmental power: communications markets can and do restrict freedom and equality of communication by generating barriers to entry, monopoly, and restrictions upon choice, and by shifting the prevailing definition of communication from that of a publicly useful and publicly meaningful good to that of commercial speech and the consumption of privately appropriable commodities.[25]

The case against straightforward accounts of market-driven journalism as the guarantor of democratic openness is strong. Yet there are problems lurking within broadsides against commodity production and exchange in the field of communication. In the American context, for instance, the organized filtering of text, sound, and images to and from local and planetary milieus through privately controlled but outward-looking newspaper media such as the *Los Angeles Times,* the *New York Times,* the *Financial Times,* and the *Washington Post* does not automatically or crudely work in favor of the turbo-capitalist system. Along with governments and social movements and civic initiatives, the global journalism associated with these media has helped lay the foundations of a global civil society that, although structured in part by large media conglomerates, is a basic precondition of nurturing democracy within and across borders, at the global level.[26] The general point is this: The rise of a global communications infrastructure does not straightforwardly result in "global cultural homogenization." It tends rather to have the effect of accentuating social diversity and visible social controversies within the emergent global civil society. Partly this is due to a fertile paradox: commercial journalism sometimes best serves its democratic obligations by following its mercenary instinct of outdoing competitors by being at the right place at the right time when a surprising revelation surfaces or an unanticipated event happens.[27] The accentuation of social differences is also due to the fact that profit-seeking media firms see the need to tailor their journalistic products to local conditions and tastes (hence the Coca-Cola advertisement: "We are not a multinational, we are a multi-local"). Local consumers of commercial journalism reciprocate: they display vigorous powers of reinterpreting these commodities, of giving them new and different meanings. True, globally marketed media culture is not the product of an equal contribution of all who are party to it, or exposed to it. Few are consulted in its manufacture—and yet, despite everything, that culture, disproportionately Atlantic in style and content, remains permanently vulnerable to the universal power of audiences to make and take meanings from it. The American golfer and media star Tiger Woods, who once described himself as "Cablinasian" (a blend of Caucasian, black, Indian, and Asian), is one symbol of this power.[28] Boundary-crossing cultural mixtures— "creolization" in the form of chop suey, Irish bagels, Hindi rap, Sri Lankan cricket, "queer jihad," veiled Muslim women logging on to the Internet, the

fusion of classical European, aboriginal, and Japanese themes in the scores of
Peter Sculthorpe—are consequently widespread. Examples of the survival and
flourishing of diasporic culture are also commonplace. So too are the examples
of "contra-flow," the commercial global successes of cultural products from
peripheral contexts—like Iranian and Chinese films, Brazilian *telenovelas*
(exported to more than eighty countries), and the Mexican soap opera *Los Ricos
Tambien Lloran (The Rich Also Cry)*, which was among the biggest television hits
in early post-Communist Russia. The consequence: in social terms, the global
civil society in which global journalism operates is a hodgepodge of nested
spaces marked by various blends and combinations, fusions and disjunctions.

The new global journalism, when it performs well, has similar characteristics. It includes all those forms of journalism that recognize that the borders
between "domestic" and "foreign" are negotiable and subject permanently to
osmosis. Global journalism is more or less aware of its dependence upon global
dynamics—and thus sees itself as contributing positively to citizens' understanding of the push-pull processes of global interdependence, conflict, and compromise that stretch from local milieus to the four corners of the earth and back
again. Within the United States, there are plenty of examples of the conscious
melding of global forms and themes with localized interests: CNN's *World
Report,* begun as five hours a week of material submitted by one hundred broadcast stations around the world, some professional and some amateur, and facilitated ironically by Ted Turner's now legendary prohibition of the word *foreign* on
air; the tailoring or "glocalization" of Spanish-language news magazines to
diverse regional areas elsewhere in the world; the growing diversification of
information supplied by tabloids, Internet chats, and Web logs;[29] and the journalistic outliers that cater to younger publics like the *Daily Show* and *MTV News.*
Such forms of global journalism are now deeply rooted within the American
context, but they suffer certain problems. The fusions they produce do not always
push toward journalism's more optimum forms, and there are those who argue
that the less endowed versions—local American news, for example—have
responded by *shrinking* the horizons of their audiences.[30] Exposed to or dependent upon local "content engine" newspapers like the *Desert Sun* in Palm Springs,
Cheyenne's *Wyoming Tribune-Eagle,* and Pensacola's *Gulf Herald,* citizens are fed a
starvation diet of global stories, which typically occupy no more than about 2
percent of column space. Reduced budgets for "foreign" news, an overloaded
dependence on English-language-dominated wire-service reporting or regional
news exchanges, and a reliance on field producers acting as journalists are all said
to contribute to this trend. The globalization of news is also restricted primarily
to the wire services, seen as the first global news agent,[31] and to broadcast or cable
news organizations; largely excluded from the global stretching of horizons are
the tabloids, the specialized press, and the journals of opinion, to name just a few.
Governments equipped with "flack packs" and dissimulation experts then handle

the rest: by cultivating links with trusted or "embedded" journalists and by organizing press briefings and advertising campaigns, they "frame"—or distort and censor—global events to suit current government policies.

Global Publics

The previous discussion provides a sober reminder of how global journalism looks from the bottom up—from the point of view of most citizens. Yet this is not the whole story. There are signs that the grip of parochialism upon citizens is not absolute, and that from roughly around the time of the worldwide protest of youth against the Vietnam War the globalization of journalism has had an unanticipated *political* effect: it has slowly but surely contributed to the growth of a plurality of differently sized public spheres, some of them genuinely global, in which many millions of people scattered across the earth witness mediated controversies about who gets what, when, and how on a world scale.[32]

How does global journalism work to produce such effects? Put simply, it creates global products for imagined global audiences: global journalism simultaneously supposes and nurtures a world stage or *theatrum mundi*. There is something necessary about this development, in that journalists, publishers, and broadcasters must always and everywhere presuppose the existence of "a public" that is listening, reading, watching, chatting, on- or offline. Journalists know that witnesses of media programs and outputs are required—that these outputs cannot play for long to an empty house. Of course, not all global media events—sporting fixtures, blockbuster movies, media awards, for instance—sustain global public spheres, which is to say that audiences are not publics and public spheres are not simply domains of entertainment or play. Strictly speaking, they are scenes of the political: within their imagined bounds, power conflicts and controversies erupt and unfold before millions of eyes and ears. These scenes are made possible by wide-bodied jet aircraft, computerized communications, and satellite broadcasting with large footprints, thanks to which the journalistic practice of nonviolently monitoring the exercise of governmental and nongovernmental power across borders has taken root. These global public spheres are sites within global civil society, where power struggles are visibly waged and witnessed by means other than violence and war: they are the narrated, imagined, nonviolent spaces within global civil society in which millions of people at various points on the earth witness the powers of governmental and nongovernmental organizations being publicly named, monitored, praised, challenged, and condemned by journalists, in defiance of the old tyrannies of time and space and publicly unaccountable power.

It is true that global public spheres are still rather issue-driven and better at presenting effects than probing the intentions of actors and the structural causes of events. Global public life is also highly vulnerable to implosion: especially vulnerable to state interference,[33] it is neither strongly institutionalized nor effectively linked to mechanisms of representative government. It is a voice without a coherent body politic. Yet in spite of everything, global public spheres have begun to affect the suit-and-tie worlds of diplomacy, global business, intergovernmental meetings, and independent nongovernmental organizations (INGOs). Helped along by initiatives like the Internet-based Earthwatch, the World Association of Community Radio Broadcasters (AMARC), the public-accountability initiative Transparency International, and by around-the-clock broadcasting organizations like CNN (available in over 800 million households and many thousands of hotels), the BBC World Service (which attracts 150 million viewers and listeners each week), and Al-Jazeera (with a weekly audience of 40 million people currently served by fifty-six correspondents in thirty-seven bureaus), global publics have begun to bite into various domestic settings. Few of the effects of global publics are reducible to the dynamics of rational-critical argumentation about matters of sober truth and calm agreement, although this sometimes happens.[34] Some of their effects are "meta-political," in the sense that the increased visibility of global publics works in favor of *creating* citizens of the new global order, in effect telling them that unless they find some means of showing that the wider world is not theirs, then it is. In this way, by calling citizens to pay attention to global dynamics, global public spheres function as temporary resting places or "cities of refuge" (in the words of Jacques Derrida) beyond familiar horizons; they give an entirely new meaning to the old watchword of Greek colonization, "Wherever you go, you will be a *polis.*" "Dwelling is the manner in which mortals are on the earth," wrote Martin Heidegger,[35] but the implication in that passage, that mortals are bound to geographic place, misses the new spatial polygamy that global publics make possible. Within global public spheres, thanks to global journalism, people rooted in local physical settings increasingly travel to distant places, without ever leaving home, to "second homes" within which their senses are stretched. They live locally, and think and act globally.

Thanks to journalistic narratives that address their audiences and probe the wider world in intimate (if ironic or hostile) tones, the participants of global civil society become a bit less parochial, a bit more cosmopolitan. This is no small achievement, especially considering that people do not "naturally" feel a sense of responsibility for faraway events. Ethical responsibility often stretches no farther than their noses. Yet when they are engaged by journalistic stories that originate in other contexts—when they are drawn into the dynamics of a global public sphere—their interest is not based simply on prurience, or idle curiosity, or schadenfreude. They rather align and assimilate these stories in terms of their own existential concerns, which are thereby altered. The world "out there"— whether it is some person or place in Iraq, or South Africa, or Brazil—becomes "their" world. Those who are caught up within global publics are taught lessons in the art of what can be called postnational citizenship: they learn that the boundaries between native and foreigner are blurred, that their commitments have become a touch more multiversal. They become footloose. They are here and there; they learn to distance themselves from themselves; they discover that there are different temporal rhythms, other places, other problems, other ways to live. They are invited to question their own dogmas, even to extend ordinary standards of civility—courtesy, politeness, respect—to others whom they will never meet.[36] Global public spheres centred on groundbreaking media events like Live Aid (in 1985 it attracted an estimated 1 billion viewers) can even be spaces of fun, in which millions taste something of the joy of acting publicly with and against others for some defined common purpose. Global publics, staged for instance in the form of televised world news of the suffering of distant strangers, conveyed in the photos that surfaced in 2004 of the abuse of Iraqi prisoners in Abu Ghraib prison, or of multimedia initiatives in campaigns of the kind that led to the UN Declaration for the Elimination of Violence Against Women,[37] can also highlight cruelty. Global publics can also function as a "gathering of the afraid" (in the words of Czech philospher and phenomenologist, Jan Patočka), as sites of disaster, spaces in which millions taste unjust outcomes, bitter defeat, and the tragedy of ruined lives. Whatever the case, the old motto that half the world does not know how the other half lives is no longer true. Media representation spreads awareness of others' damned fates. True, witnessing the pain of others often produces numbing effects, by which the act of seeing substitutes for other, more active modes of public response.[38] The portrayal of disasters through global journalism nevertheless does not (automatically, or on a large scale) produce ethically cleansed cynics, lovers of entertainment sitting on sofas, enjoying every second of the blood and tears. The publics that gather around the stages of cruelty and humiliation scrap the old rule that good and evil are typically local affairs. These publics make possible what Hannah Arendt once called the "politics of pity":[39] by witnessing others' terrible suffering, at a distance, millions are sometimes shaken and disturbed, sometimes to the point where they are prepared to exercise their sense of long-distance responsibility by speaking to others, donating money or time, or supporting the general principle that the right of humanitarian intervention—the obligation to assist someone in danger, as contemporary French law puts it—can and should override the old crocodilian formula that might equals right.

Global public spheres have other political effects. Especially during dramatic media events—like the meltdown at the Soviet Union's Chernobyl nuclear power plant in 1986, the Tiananmen Square massacre of pro-democracy students in China, the 1989 revolutions in central-eastern Europe, the overthrow and arrest of Yugoslav president Slobodan Milosevic, the September 11, 2001, terrorist attacks on New York, Pennsylvania, and Washington—public spheres intensify audiences' shared sense of living their lives contingently, on a knife edge, in the subjunctive tense. The witnesses of such events (contrary to the opinion of Marshall McLuhan and others) do not enter a "global village" dressed in the skins of humankind and thinking in the terms of a primordial "village or tribal outlook."[40] As members of a public sphere, audiences do not experience uninterrupted togetherness. They instead come to feel that the power relations of global civil society, far from being given, are better understood as "an arena of struggle, a fragmented and contested area,"[41] the resultant of moves and countermoves, controversy and consent, compromise and resistance, peace and war. Public spheres, backed by global journalism, not only tend to denature the power relations of global civil society and the conglomeration of variously sized and variously shaped governing institutions that straddle the earth. They most definitely increase their self-reflexivity, for instance by publicizing conflicting images of government and civil society. Publicity is given as well to the biased codes of global journalistic coverage—as can be seen, for instance, in the ongoing tit-for-tat conflicts between Al-Jazeera and American television news media coverage of the 2003 invasion of Iraq.

In these various ways, global journalism heightens the topsy-turvy feel of our world. Doubt is heaped upon loose talk that anthropomorphizes global civil society, as if it were a universal object/subject, the latest and most promising substitute for the proletariat, or for the wretched of the earth. Global public spheres make it clearer that "global civil society," like its more local counterparts, has no "collective voice"; that it is full of networks, flows, disjunctions, frictions; that it alone does nothing; that only its constituent individuals, group initiatives, organizations, and networks act and interact. Global publics consequently heighten the sense that the socioeconomic and political-legal institutions of our world are an unfinished—permanently threatened—project. They shake up its dogmas and inject it with energy. They enable citizens of the world to shrug off their insularity, to see that talk of global civil society is not simply Western turbo-capitalist ideology—even to appreciate that the task of painting a much clearer picture of the contours and dynamics of global civil society, a picture that is absent from most of the current literature on globalization, is today an urgent ethical imperative.

Cosmocracy

The contemporary growth of global journalism and global publics certainly points to the need to bring greater democracy to the global order. Not only are there vast numbers of nongovernmental organizations that know little or nothing of democratic procedures and manners. The world is structured as well by an agglomeration of governmental structures—a "cosmocracy" comprising bodies like the European Union, the United Nations, the World Bank—that defies the textbooks of traditional political science and political theory.[42] Its clumsy, dynamic, worldwide webs of more or less joined-up government and law interact, and have social and political effects, on a global scale. Many of the structures of the cosmocracy escape the constraining effects of electoral and parliamentary supervision—it is full of what the English call "rotten boroughs"—which is why the skeptics of extending democratic procedures and ways of life across territorial state borders raise strong objections. Consider the doubts of the doyen of democratic thought in the United States, Robert Dahl, who considers as utterly unrealistic the vision of democracy beyond state borders.[43] The growing complexity of decision making, for instance in the field of foreign affairs, renders impossible the "public enlightenment" so necessary for democracy. Meanwhile, legal and illegal immigration combined with a new politics of identity within and beyond territorial states lead to growing "cultural diversity and cleavages," which undermine "civil discourse and compromise," Dahl says. Worldwide threats of terrorist attacks make it even less likely that civil and political liberties could flourish within "international organizations."

Dahl's doubts about the potential to create democratic mechanisms that can monitor power exercised across borders are overdrawn, if only because they ignore a fundamental development of our times: the emergence of a global civil society and the birth of global journalism and global publics with power-monitoring potential.[44] Global publics have important implications for democratic theory and practice. By throwing light on power exercised by moonlight, or in the dark of night, global publics and the global journalism that supports them stretch citizens' horizons of responsibility for what goes on in the world.[45] They keep alive words like *freedom* and *justice* by publicizing manipulation, skulduggery, and brutality in other countries. Global publics, of the kind that in recent years have monitored the fates of Nelson Mandela, Aung San Suu Kyi, Yasser Arafat, and George W. Bush, muck with the messy business of exclusion, racketeering, ostentation, cruelty, and war. They chart cases of intrigue and double-crossing. They help audiences to spot the various figures of top-down power on the world scene: slick and suave managers and professionals who are well-practiced at the art of deceiving others through images; kingfishers who first dazzle others then stumble when more is required of them; fools who prey on their citizens' fears; quislings who willingly change sides under pressure; thugs who love violence; and vulgar rulers, with their taste for usurping crowns, and assembling and flattering crowds or beating and teargassing them into submission.

Global journalism and global public spheres can also probe the powers of key organizations of global civil society itself. While the multiple voices of this society function as vital checks and balances in the overall process of globalization, very few of the social organizations from which these voices emanate are democratic.[46] Publicity can serve as a reminder to the world that these organizations often violate the principle of public accountability. Reminders are served to those who read, listen, and watch that its empty spaces have been filled by powerful but publicly unaccountable organizations (such as the International Olympic Committee) or by profit-seeking corporate bodies (like Monsanto) that permanently aggravate global civil society by causing environmental damage, or swallowing up others by producing just for profit, rather than for sustainable social use. Global publics backed by global journalism can help to expose malfeasance—accounting and stock market frauds of the kind (in the United States, during 2002) that rocked the industrial conglomerate Tyco International, the energy trader Enron, the cable company Adelphia, and the telecommunications giant WorldCom. Global journalism can as well help question some of the more dubious practices of some nonprofit INGOs: for instance, their lingering colonialist habit of behaving like missionaries; their bureaucratic inflexibility and context-blindness; their spreading attachment to market values or to clichés of "project-speak"; or their mistaken belief in the supply-side, trickle-down model of social development.

Exactly because of their propensity to monitor the exercise of power from a variety of sites within and outside civil society, global journalism—when it functions well—puts matters like representation, accountability, and legitimacy on the political agenda. It poses questions like: Who benefits and who loses from global civil society? Who currently speaks for whom in the multiple and overlapping power structures of global civil society? Whose voices are heard, or half-heard, and whose interests and concerns are ignominiously shoved aside? How could there be greater equality among the voices that emerge from the nooks and crannies of this society? And through which institutional procedures could these voices be represented? By formulating such questions, sometimes succinctly, global journalism can help to ensure that nobody monopolizes power at the local and world levels. By exposing corrupt or risky dealings and naming them as such; by catching out decision makers and forcing their hands; by requiring them to rethink or reverse their decisions, global journalism helps remedy the problem—strongly evident in the volatile field of global financial markets, which on an average day turn over something like US$1.3 trillion, one hundred times the volume of world trade—that nobody seems to be in charge. And in uneven contests between decision makers and decision takers—corruption scandals within the International Olympic Committee or European Union controversies about American foreign policy are examples—global journalism and its publics can help to prevent the powerful from "owning" power privately. At its best, global journalism and its publics imply greater parity. They suggest that there are alternatives. They inch our little blue-and-white planet toward greater openness and humility, potentially to the point where power, whenever and wherever it is exercised across borders, is made to feel more "biodegradable," a bit more responsive to those whose lives it shapes and reshapes, secures or wrecks.

The Future?

Does democracy have a chance of taking root in the emerging global order? And can theories of journalism account for its capacity to do so? When considering these questions and the possible answers they prompt it is imperative to remember that democracy—a form of rule in which nobody privately owns the means of ruling—is neither a fixed set of institutions nor the monopoly of any people or country of the world. The history of democratic innovation since the middle of the eighteenth century has been a polymorphic and multicontinental process. The word *democracy* was first positively redefined under modern conditions in the Low Countries, in the 1580s. Swedish republicans and Philadelphian revolutionaries were responsible for kick-starting the trend toward written constitutions. Denmark abolished its slave trade well before the English did the same; and Haiti and newly independent Spanish American states abolished slavery well before the United States, some of whose states pioneered the abolition of property qualifications for voting. The uniform adoption of the secret ballot first happened in Australia; Pitcairn Islanders and New Zealanders and Finns witnessed the first national breakthrough for the women's suffrage movement; and so on.

Not only is it important to regard democracy as an open-ended political project—to grasp that the procedures for making power publicly accountable can take many different forms. It is also vital to remember that in matters of democracy absolutely nothing should be taken for granted. There are no historical laws working in its favor. Democratic institutions and democratic spirit can be made and—far more easily—unmade. That is why, in our times, the strange elusiveness of the democratic ideal should be kept in mind. Efforts to bring greater democracy into the world need to understand its uniqueness within the history of different types of earthly regimes. Exactly because it means, minimally, the self-government of equals—their freedom from bossing, injustice, and violence—it regularly demands more than humans seem willing to give or are capable of giving. What we call democracy is never "pure" or "authentic." Whether in the kitchen or the staff meeting, or in the boardroom or on the battlefield, it always seems to be in short supply. We are always chasing it around corners, through halls of mirrors, across uncharted landscapes and oceans, up into blue skies. And while improvement, perfectibility—and disappointment and failure—are inscribed within the very ideal of democracy, the role of journalism theory in such circumstances is to remind us of the practical requirements of the ideal—at the global level.

Theories of journalism have done an uneven job of addressing such issues. Work on globalization permeates the academy but it is not often found in journalism curricula, which mention globalization often as an aside or as a problem to be tackled, but rarely as a set of circumstances that require a rethinking of the premises through which journalism is supposed to work. Curricular developments in journalism—often themselves isolated in scholarly enclaves that separate efforts in international communication and international journalism from journalism history, democratic theory, and the like[47]—have not kept pace with the wide-ranging effects that result from the dynamic blending of the local, national, regional, and global domains. Although problems with defining "the global" and its asymmetries still linger—how different, we may ask, is globalization from Americanization or Europeanization?—its frequent absence from discussions of journalism urgently needs redress.

It is a truism that global journalism will only grow stronger when journalists themselves positively grasp the importance of local-global dynamics. Theories of journalism can help this development in modest ways by paying more attention to some of the consequent developments of globalization—and the role that journalism has played in making it possible. Some of these developments include: the growing power of hybrid identities and cultures; the multilinear flows of information; the tensions between fragmentation and homogenization; the proliferation of new forms of unaccountable governmental power and violence; the role of journalism in cultivating a politics of pity; and the often chaotic, contradictory, and unpredictable directionality of the global ebb and flow of media material. While each of these themes is beginning to rub against the territorial state biases of mainstream journalism theory, they have had the short-term effect—strangely—of reinforcing its bland presumption, originally set in place by early efforts like *Four Theories of the Press,* that globalization heralds the triumph of "democracy" through "freedom of information." The presumption that Western journalism has experienced a "triumph" of some sort should be questioned. Not only does it underestimate the vitality in the global environment of media organizations that operate from out-of-center locations, marginalized political viewpoints, and in conjunction with regional habits and peripheral customs. The failure of independent, freethinking journalism to take root across borders in various *undemocratic* environments, especially in the so-called "pariah" states of the Middle East and sub-Saharan Africa, also needs to be noted. Such developments cast doubt on simple-minded accounts of globalization and the benefits it brings to journalism. These developments should serve to complicate our understanding of the domestic role of journalism, to see that it is caught up in processes that were not predicted by existing theories of journalism, that the present growth spurt of globalization poses new challenges to journalism.

Theories of journalism certainly need to reflect upon the fate of democracy in a globalizing era. The normative question needs to be asked: What's so good about democracy, especially given that it consistently disappoints because in practice it never lives up to its promises? Why should we hang on to it and its corresponding forms of journalism? And why should we work to democratize institutions that straddle the earth? Part of our problem is that the standard answers of the past no longer seem plausible. The presumptions, for instance, that the Christian god blessed people with "liberty of the press" and the power or "natural right" to govern themselves, or that nations are naturally democratic, or that freedom of communication and self-government are requirements of a universal principle of happiness or the attainment of truth in human affairs, all seem and sound unconvincing, except perhaps to unembarrassed diehards with a poor sense of irony. The dogma that history or the market or the search for truth or happiness will deliver us into the arms of democracy and open communication is no less unconvincing.[48] Even the cherished notion that the "sovereign people" are the sacred first principle of democratic forms of government is questionable, and needs to be jettisoned on normative and empirical grounds. Especially under modern conditions, the sovereign people principle has repeatedly fraternized with the populist enemies of democracy, those who kick down against other citizens in the name of "the people." Its descriptive power has also been undermined by the invention of many different types of power-dividing and power-monitoring institutions—judicial review, second chambers, quota rules, citizenship rights legislation—that have the effect, among others, of highlighting the fictional and hubris-ridden character of the principle.[49] The upshot is that democracy nowadays resembles a drunk staggering in search of a lamppost, which is why new post-foundational justifications for the superiority of democracy as a way of organizing human affairs are badly needed. To note (in the form of empirical observation[50]) that thanks to the tragedies and the triumphs of the twentieth century, democracy has for the first time ever become a "universal commitment" is not enough (even if it were plausible as an observation). The question of why democracy is universally preferable is begged.

The presumption that American-style democracy is a good thing is evident in the aforementioned Hutchins report, authored by prominent public figures such as Zechariah Chafee, Harold Lasswell, Arthur Schlesinger, and Reinhold Niebuhr.[51] Its recommendations included constitutional guarantees of freedom of the press; government facilitation of new ventures and open competition in the communications industry; the legal enforcement of the view that agencies of mass communication should operate as common carriers of information and discussion; the encouragement of the press to use every means to increase the competence, independence, and effectiveness of its staff; and the establishment of a new and independent agency to appraise and report annually upon the performance of the press. Even if they need to be supplemented with new initiatives—like the Pew Global Attitudes Project[52]—these proposals certainly remain sensible. Yet nowhere in the Hutchins report is there a serious discussion of why democracy is a desirable goal—and why journalism should do all it can everywhere to defend, nurture, and extend both the spirit and institutions of democracy.

Even though the Hutchins report's support for democracy is admirable, the need to champion fresh claims appropriate to our times is pressing. Three interrelated lines of thinking seem especially worthwhile. The first is that democracy, far from being a first principle, is in fact the key condition of possibility of freedom from the compulsory adherence to all such principles, such as the nation or history or progress or the market or the state or the people. Seen in this way, as a set of institutions and as a way of life, a democracy is best considered as a nonviolent means of equally apportioning and (with the help of a rich diversity of communications media) publicly monitoring power within and among overlapping communities of people who live according to a wide variety of morals. A second line of justification highlights the ways in which democracy is an early-warning device, in that it can help to define and publicize risks, especially those generated by complex and tightly coupled organizations that have global effects. Still another argument for democracy was suggested by E. M. Forster: "So two cheers for democracy," the British novelist wrote. "One because it admits variety and two because it permits criticism. Two cheers are quite enough: there is no occasion to give three."[53] There is in fact a third, the cheer that should be given for democratic power-sharing as the best human weapon so far invented against the hubris that comes with concentrations of power.

The struggle against blind arrogance and stupidity caused by power is never ultimately winnable, yet it is among the struggles that we human beings abandon at our own peril. Democracy is a powerful remedy for hubris. It champions not the rule of the people—that definition of democracy belongs in more ways than one to the age of kings—but the rule that no single body should rule.[54] It refuses to accept that decision makers can draw their legitimacy from gods and goddesses, or tradition, or habit, or wealth. Democracy is a way of life and a way of governing in which power is publicly accountable, in which the use of violence and sitting on thrones and making decisions behind the backs of others—and the intrigues and ambitions that usually accompany arbitrary rule—are deeply problematic.

The history of democracy is replete with a weird and wonderful cast of figures who believed in democracy because they saw that it could humble blind arrogance. This history begins in the fifth century BC, with characters like the Cynics, who hurled javelins of fun and sarcasm—and farted and fornicated in public—for the purpose of democratically humbling arrogant authority. The history of democracy extends through to modern figures more familiar to us: God-fearing Christian and Republican opponents of slavery; atheist rebels who built street barricades, raised red flags, and aimed cobblestones at glass panes in the name of democratic liberty; workers who refused to be wage slaves; the suffragettes who read Ibsen and Pankhurst and Angelina Grimké, or chained themselves to railings, rented zeppelins to drop leaflets on parliament, and rallied in Trafalgar Square in defense of free speech, garbed in purple and green; the bearded dissidents of Moscow, Warsaw, and Prague, hunched over their typewriters and huddled together on sofas in smoke-filled apartments; and Buddhist monks in crimson robes, walking barefoot, keeping "the mind mindful" as they collected rice from the faithful for the cause of civil freedom against brutish dictatorship.

For all of these figures, democracy was a way of life, not a marketable commodity. They did not suffer fools gladly. They refused the temptations of aggrandizement and did not much like big clichés and smelly little orthodoxies. They trusted in simple decency. They did not believe that an unequal society was inevitable. They thought that human beings could and should govern themselves. They believed in the power of the powerless. That is why, in these testing times, their democratic spirit, helped along by global journalism, badly deserves to be nurtured—not only within but also beyond the borders of territorial states.

Notes

1. The early postwar years witnessed many initiatives and new lines of thinking about journalism and the future of democracy within a global context. See, for instance, Harold Laski et al., *The Future of Democracy* (London 1946); Albert Camus, *Neither Victims nor Executioners* (Berkeley, 1968 [first published in the autumn 1946 issues of *Combat*]); Pope Pius XII, *Democracy and Peace* (London 1945); A. D. Lindsay, *Democracy in the World Today* (London, 1945), which discusses the claim (first made by E. H. Carr) that it was Stalin who placed "democracy" in the forefront of Allied war aims by describing (in a radio broadcast of July 3, 1941) the Soviet war against Hitler as "merged with the struggle of the peoples of Europe and America for independence and democratic liberties."
2. Nicholas Garnham, "Public Service versus the Market," *Screen* 24, no. 1 (1986): 6–27.
3. See Rupert Murdoch, "Freedom in Broadcasting," James MacTaggart Memorial Lecture, Edinburgh International Television Festival, August 25, 1989.
4. John Keane, *The Media and Democracy* (Oxford, U.K., and Cambridge, Mass.: Polity Press, 1991).
5. Manuel Castells, *The Rise of the Network Society* (Malden, Mass.: Blackwell, 1996), especially chapter 5; and Manuel Castells, *The Internet Galaxy: Reflections on the Internet, Business, and Society* (Oxford, U.K., and New York: Oxford University Press, 2003).
6. Barbie Zelizer, *Taking Journalism Seriously: News and the Academy* (Thousand Oaks, Calif.: Sage, 2004).
7. John Perry Barlow, "A Declaration of the Independence of Cyberspace," Electronic Frontier Foundation, February 8, 1996, http://www.eff.org/~barlow/Declaration-Final.html.
8. Peter J. Hugill, *Global Communications since 1844: Geopolitics and Technology* (Baltimore, Md.: Johns Hopkins University Press, 1999).
9. John Keane, *Global Civil Society?* (Cambridge, U.K., and New York: Cambridge University Press, 2003), 16–17.
10. Gabriel Tarde, *L'opinion et la foule* (Paris: F. Alcan, 1901); Alexis de Tocqueville, *Democracy in America* (New York: Knopf, 1945), volume 1, chapter 11; Ferdinand

Tönnies, "The Power and Value of Public Opinion," in *Ferdinand Toennies on Sociology: Pure, Applied, and Empirical*, edited by Werner J. Cahnman and Rudolf Herberle, 251–65 (Chicago and London: University of Chicago Press, 1971); John Dewey, *The Public and Its Problems* (New York: Holt, 1927); Walter Lippmann, *Public Opinion* (New York: Harcourt, Brace, 1922).

11. Commission on Freedom of the Press, *A Free and Responsible Press; A General Report on Mass Communication: Newspapers, Radio, Motion Pictures, Magazines, and Books* (Chicago: University of Chicago Press, 1947), 90 and 4, where the duty of a "free press" is said to include the creation of "a world community by giving men everywhere knowledge of the world and of one another."

12. Fred S. Siebert, Theodore Peterson, and Wilbur Schramm, *Four Theories of the Press: The Authoritarian, Libertarian, Social Responsibility, and Soviet Communist Concepts of What the Press Should Be and Do* (Urbana: University of Illinois Press, 1956).

13. J. Herbert Altschull, *Agents of Power: The Role of the News Media in Human Affairs* (New York: Longman, 1984); James Curran and Jean Seaton, *Power without Responsibility: The Press and Broadcasting in Britain* (London and New York: Routledge, 1985); Denis McQuail, *Mass Communication Theory: An Introduction*, 2nd ed. (London: Sage, 1987); John Nerone, ed., *Last Rights: Revisiting Four Theories of the Press* (Urbana: University of Illinois Press, 1995); and John Merrill and John Nerone, "The Four Theories of the Press Four and a Half Decades Later: A Retrospective," *Journalism Studies* 3, no. 1 (February 2002): 133–36.

14. The term *turbo-capitalism* is drawn from Edward Luttwak, *Turbo-capitalism: Winners and Losers in the Global Economy* (New York: HarperCollins, 1999), and developed in different directions in Keane, *Global Civil Society?*, especially p. 65ff.

15. Robert Burnett, *The Global Jukebox: The International Music Industry* (London and New York: Routledge, 1996); Ali Mohammadie, ed., *International Communication and Globalization: A Critical Introduction* (London: Sage, 1997); and Edward S. Herman and Robert W. McChesney, *The Global Media: The New Missionaries of Corporate Capitalism* (London and Washington, D.C.: Cassell, 1997).

16. Adolph Wagner, *Die ordnung des österreichischen staatsshaushalts, mit besonderer rücksicht auf den ausgabe-etat die staatsschuld* (Vienna: C. Gerold's Son, 1863).

17. Miles Kahler, *International Institutions and the Political Economy of Integration* (Washington, D.C.: Brookings Institution, 1995), especially chapter 2.

18. Benjamin Barber, *Jihad vs. McWorld: How Globalism and Tribalism Are Reshaping the World* (New York: Times Books, 1995).

19. Eduardo Galeano, cited as the epigraph in Herman and McChesney, *The Global Media*, vi. More prudent assessments are presented in Aihwa Ong, *Flexible Citizenship: The Cultural Logics of Transnationality* (Durham, N.C.: Duke University Press, 1999); Richard Parker, *Mixed Signals: The Prospects for Global Television News* (New York: Twentieth Century Fund, 1995); Michael Schudson, "Is There a Global Cultural Memory?," unpublished paper (University of California at San Diego, 1997); and Mike Featherstone, "Localism, Globalism and Cultural Identity," in *Global-Local: Cultural Production and the Transnational Imaginary*, edited by Rob Wilson and Wimal Dissanayake (Durham, N.C.: Duke University Press, 1996).

20. Herbert Schiller, "Not Yet the Post-industrial Era," *Critical Studies in Mass Communication* 8 (1991): 20–21.

21. Noreena Hertz, *The Silent Takeover: Global Capitalism and the Death of Democracy* (New York: Free Press, 2001), 8.

22. John Keane, "Eleven Theses on Communicative Abundance," *CSD Bulletin* Vol. 5, No. 1 (Autumn 1997).

23. Fred R. Dallmayr, "Globalization from Below," *International Politics* 36 (September 1999): 321–34; Richard Falk, *Predatory Globalization. A Critique* (Oxford 1999), chapter 8; and Orhan Pamuk, "The Anger of the Damned," *New York Review of Books,* November 15, 2001, 12.

24. Interview with Professor Abou Yaareb al-Marzouki, Hammamet, Tunisia, April 18, 2001.

25. See Owen Fiss, "Why the State?," in *Democracy and the Mass Media* (Cambridge, U.K., and New York: Cambridge University Press, 1990), 136–54; and Keane, *The Media and Democracy,* especially 51–92.

26. Keane, *Global Civil Society?*

27. Michael Schudson, "For a Few Dollars More," *Financial Times Magazine,* July 31, 2004, 10.

28. *International Herald Tribune* (Paris), April 24, 1997, 3.

29. See the preliminary findings of the World Internet Project (UCLA Center for Communication Policy, 2004), http://ccp.ucla.edu/pages/internet-report.asp.

30. Phyllis Kaniss, *Making Local News* (Chicago: University of Chicago Press, 1991); Bob Franklin and David Murphy, eds., *Making the Local News: Local Journalism in Context* (London and New York: Routledge, 1998).

31. Oliver Boyd-Barrett and Terhi Rantanen, eds., *The Globalization of News* (London and Thousand Oaks, Calif.: Sage, 1998).

32. See John Keane, "Structural Transformations of the Public Sphere," *Communication Review* 1, no. 1 (1995): 1–22. Adam Michnik has suggested that the recent growth of global public opinion can be seen as the rebirth in different form of an earlier parallel trend, evident within nineteenth-century suffragette and socialist internationalism, that came to an end with World War I and its aftermath (interview, Washington, D.C., April 21, 2001).

33. Monroe E. Price, *Media and Sovereignty: The Global Information Revolution and Its Challenge to State Power* (Cambridge, Mass., and London: MIT Press, 2002); and Nancy Morris and Silvio Waisbord, eds., *Media and Globalization: Why the State Matters* (Lanham, Md.: Rowman & Littlefield, 2002).

34. Some limits of the rational communication model of the public sphere, originally outlined in the important work of Jürgen Habermas, *Strukturwandel der Öffentlichkeit: Untersuchungen zu einer Kategorie der bürgerlichen Gesellschaft* (Neuwied, Germany: H. Luchterhand, 1962), are sketched in John Durham Peters, "Distrust of Representation: Habermas on the Public Sphere," *Media, Culture and Society* 15 (1993): 541–71, and Keane, "Structural Transformations of the Public Sphere."

35. Martin Heidegger, "Building Dwelling Thinking," in his *The Question Concerning Technology and Other Essays,* translated by William Lovitt (New York: Harper and Row, 1982), 146.

36. See Stephen Toulmin's useful reflections on civility as the antidote to dogma in "The Belligerence of Dogma," in *Civility,* edited by Leroy S. Rounder (Notre Dame, Ind.: University of Notre Dame Press, 2000), 94–100.

37. Charlotte Bunch et al., "International Networking for Women's Human Rights," in *Global Citizen Action,* edited by Michael Edwards and John Gaventa, 217–29 (Boulder, Colo.: Lynne Rienner, 2001).

38. Barbie Zelizer, *Remembering to Forget: Holocaust Memory through the Camera's Eye* (Chicago and London: University of Chicago Press, 1998). See also Zelizer's "Journalism, Photography, and Trauma," in *Journalism after September 11,* edited by Barbie Zelizer and Stuart Allan (London and New York: Routledge, 2002), 48–68.

39. Hannah Arendt, *On Revolution* (London and New York: Penguin, 1990), 59–114; and the development of Arendt's idea by Luc Boltanski, *Distant Suffering: Morality, Media, and Politics,* translated by Graham Burchell (Cambridge, U.K., and New York: Cambridge University Press, 1999), and Clifford Christians and Kaarle Nordenstreng, "Social Responsibility Worldwide," *Journal of Mass Media Ethics* 19, no. 1 (2004): 3–28.

40. See the introduction to Edmund Carpenter and Marshall McLuhan, eds., *Explorations in Communication: An Anthology* (Boston: Beacon, 1966), xi: "Postliterate man's electronic media contract the world to a village or tribe where everything happens to everyone at the same time: everyone knows about, and therefore participates in, everything that is happening the minute it happens. . . . This simultaneous sharing of experiences as in a village or tribe creates a village or tribal outlook, and puts a premium on togetherness."

41. Margaret E. Keck and Kathryn Sikkink, *Activists beyond Borders: Advocacy Networks in International Politics* (Ithaca, N.Y., and London: Cornell University Press, 1998), 33.

42. See Keane, *Global Civil Society?* 175ff.

43. Robert A. Dahl, "The Past and Future of Democracy," revised manuscript version of a lecture delivered at the symposium Politics from the Twentieth to the Twenty-first Century (University of Siena, October 14–16, 1999); and Robert Dahl, *On Democracy* (New Haven and London: Yale University Press, 1998), 114–17.

44. The exclusion of the theme of public spheres from virtually all of the current literature on globalization is criticized by Tore Slaatta, "Media and Democracy in the Global Order," *Media, Culture and Society* 20 (1998): 335–44. A similar point is made implicitly by Arjun Appadurai, "Grassroots Globalization and the Research Imagination," *Public Culture* 12, no. 1 (2000): 1–19.

45. See the important introductory remarks by Michael Edwards in Edwards and Gaventa, eds., *Global Citizen Action,* especially 6–8.

46. Some of these undemocratic tendencies within nongovernmental organizations— satirized in the South African joke that those lucky to have an NGO job can "EN-J-OY" life—are discussed in Stephen N. Ndegwa, *The Two Faces of Civil Society: NGOs and Politics in Africa* (West Hartford, Conn.: Kumarian, 1996), especially chapter 6; Brian H. Smith, *More Than Altruism: The Politics of Private Foreign Aid* (Princeton, N.J.: Princeton University Press, 1990); and Steven Sampson, "The Social Life of Projects," in *Civil Society: Challenging Western Models,* edited by Chris Hann and Elizabeth Dunn (London and New York: Routledge, 1996).

47. For more on this, see Zelizer, *Taking Journalism Seriously*.
48. Keane, *The Media and Democracy*, 10–50.
49. See John Keane, *Whatever Happened to Democracy?* (London: Institute for Public Policy Research, 2002); and Pierre Rosanvallon, *Le people introuvable* (Paris: Gallimard, 1998).
50. Amartya Sen, "Democracy as a Universal Value," *Journal of Democracy* 10, no. 3 (1999): 3–17.
51. Commission on Freedom of the Press, *A Free and Responsible Press*.
52. For more information see Pew Global Attitudes Project, http://people-press.org/pgap.
53. E. M. Forster, *Two Cheers for Democracy* (New York: Harcourt, Brace, 1951), 70.
54. Further discussion of this point is to be found in John Keane, *Violence and Democracy* (Cambridge, U.K., and New York: Cambridge University Press, 2004), and Keane's "Democracy: The Rule of Nobody?" *B. N. Ganguly Memorial Lecture* (New Delhi, 2004).

Bibliography

Altschull, J. Herbert. *Agents of Power: The Role of the News Media in Human Affairs*. New York: Longman, 1984.

Boyd-Barrett, Oliver, and Terhi Rantanen, eds. *The Globalization of News*. London and Thousand Oaks, Calif.: Sage, 1998.

Camus, Albert. *Neither Victims nor Executioners*. Berkeley, Calif: World Without War Council, 1968.

Keane, John. *The Media and Democracy*. Oxford, U.K., and Cambridge, Mass.: Polity Press, 1991.

Keane, John. *Global Civil Society?* Cambridge, U.K., and New York: Cambridge University Press, 2003.

McChesney, Robert W. *The Global Media: The New Missionaries of Corporate Capitalism*. London and Washington, D.C.: Cassell, 1997.

Price, Monroe E. *Media and Sovereignty: The Global Information Revolution and Its Challenge to State Power*. Cambridge, Mass., and London: MIT Press, 2002.

Seibert, Fred S., Theodore Peterson, and Wilbur Schramm. *Four Theories of the Press: The Authoritarian, Libertarian, Social Responsibility, and Soviet Communist Concepts of What the Press Should Be and Do*. Urbana: University of Illinois Press, 1956.

Zelizer, Barbie. *Taking Journalism Seriously: News and the Academy*. Thousand Oaks, Calif.: Sage, 2004.

THE FUNCTIONS OF THE PRESS IN A DEMOCRACY

Timothy E. Cook

THE FIRST AMENDMENT TO THE U.S. CONSTITUTION declares, "Congress shall make no law . . . abridging the freedom of speech, or of the press." Political communication receives special treatment in the United States for a simple reason: it is vital to the consent of the governed. Elections require that candidates and parties defend their records and set forth their ideas and priorities so that citizens can cast votes in line with their own preferences and philosophies. Between elections, too, officials' communication with the public—and with one another—is crucial to the two central elements of representation: knowing how to act on behalf of the people and being responsive to their needs and concerns.

How well does the press live up to these requirements? This section addresses this seemingly straightforward question by looking at several functions that the press serves in a democratic political system. Political observers have posited divergent, not always compatible, functions for the press. We examine five of them here, concentrating on the ways in which American journalism can (and sometimes does) perform to advance the goals of democracy.

These essays do not focus on the long-revered standards of journalism, which often reflect the needs of news organizations and news workers at least as much as the requirements of politics. Our starting points are the requisites of democracy itself—and how the press contributes to them. Nor do we look at functions of the press in American society that have little to do with self-governance. For instance, the press undoubtedly fulfills functions of entertaining and reassuring the American public. But unless one endorses a notion that the people should be kept happy with "bread and circuses," in the style of ancient Roman rulers, it is hard to see how an entertained public is, in and of itself, pivotal for democracy. Likewise, the profit-minded news organizations of today act to generate income for investors. But moneymaking alone has little to do with encouraging or discouraging self-government.

A democracy, at base, is a political system where the people rule themselves. Americans rarely practice direct democracy—acting as a collectivity in the manner of, say, a New England town meeting. Instead, the United States is a representative democracy, where the people directly elect, or indirectly choose, officials to act on their behalf and where the officials are then accountable for their decisions and actions.

The Requisites of Democracy

We begin this section with an essay by James Curran that provides a fresh look at democracy's requirements for the press. Curran begins by noting the familiar job description captured in classic texts of the mid-twentieth century. As he points out, the prescription to "inform, scrutinize, debate, and represent" gives increasingly vague guidance. While he views these functions as vital, he urges that they be revisited and rethought. Most notably, Curran moves away from the usual prescription that all journalism and journalists should behave in similar ways. Instead, he astutely contends that the distinct functions of democracy may require different news outlets to act in varying ways—pushing individuals' attention to the workings of the news media system as a whole, not to the performance of specific news organizations.

To Curran, the typical "media-centered account" understates the significance of other connections between the people and their governments. And it obscures how the press facilitates communication among and between elites such as officials and political activists. By placing the press in the context of the overall political system, Curran observes how it can aid in several crucial requisites of a democracy:

Representation, by enabling groups to be heard

Deliberation, by providing a forum for discussion and presenting a wide range of voices in that forum

Conflict resolution, by working to promote norms and procedures of democracy and to resolve problems

Accountability, by monitoring diverse sources of power

Information dissemination, enabling citizens to enter into informed debate and decision making

The next five essays pick up where Curran leaves off. They turn from Curran's requisites in a democracy to assess a well-established function the press performs in American democracy in theory and practice. Each defines the function and its historical provenance. Each evaluates the evidence that measures the press's current performance of the function.

The Press as Marketplace of Ideas

Robert Schmuhl and Robert Picard address representation, deliberation, and conflict resolution by examining the metaphor of the "marketplace of ideas." A forum for the discussion and resolution of ideas and interests in a society may be the most venerable of these functions. It dates back to John Milton's 1644 suggestion that, in a free press, truth will vanquish falsehood. It has also been endorsed by many Supreme Court justices, starting with Oliver Wendell Holmes in the early twentieth century. However, Schmuhl and Picard note that the marketplace of ideas has numerous limitations in practice. They note the irony that the intellectual marketplace may be endangered by the accelerating commercialization of the news. Some voices have greater access to the news than others, the range of viewpoints is often constricted, and the competition is uneven. Nonetheless, individual news outlets and the news media often enable deliberation, debate, and decision making to occur. Schmuhl and Picard thus close by noting the continuing relevance—and abiding limits—of the metaphor.

The Press as Agenda Setter

There are many ways to assess how and whether the press helps to resolve conflicts in society. One has been uncovered by the empirical work of many scholars discussed by Maxwell McCombs: how the press serves to set the political agenda—that is, how it enunciates and ranks the most important problems to be addressed by the public and the political system as a whole.

Press coverage serves to concentrate the attention of the public, of political activists, and of officials on a short list of concerns, and encourages action to deal with these salient problems. As McCombs documents, scholarship now demonstrates clearly that the news media's agenda, revealed in the focus and prominence of coverage, has a substantial impact upon the agendas of the public (as shown by public opinion polls of "most important problems") and policy makers (as measured by the issues to which political institutions pay attention). Moreover, the explanatory frames that the news media apply to issues shape the public's and policy makers' interpretations of both problems and possible solutions. But as McCombs notes, the power that the press holds through agenda setting then raises a central question: Who sets the news media's agenda? Given that surveys of journalists suggest that they do not see agenda setting as an essential part of their jobs, figuring out which issues, interests, and actors are able to get covered becomes a crucial concern.

The Press as Watchdog

The news media address the requisite of accountability most fully through what is now called the watchdog function of the press. Here, the press acts on behalf of the public, which need not be involved for democratic processes to be served. In W. Lance Bennett's and William Serrin's definition, the press acts as a watchdog when it independently scrutinizes the workings of powerful institutions and provides an incentive for them to work for the public good. The news must document the activities of government, business, and other sources of power, ask tough and probing questions, and aim to advance the public interest.

Based on this definition, Bennett and Serrin trenchantly conclude that this function is the most unevenly performed of those we study here. As they document, reporters, more often than not, heavily rely upon the help of powerful institutions, go through the motions of acting adversarial without affecting substance, and are distracted from the public interest by profit-minded news organizations and the changing demands for advancing journalistic careers. They close their essay with a thought-provoking set of proposals to revive—and revise—the watchdog model for twenty-first century America.

The Press as Information Disseminator

The function of providing information for the public is perhaps the most familiar to journalists and scholars alike. By its logic, the press provides information to the public who can then come up with reasoned evaluations of contemporary conditions and decisions about politics and policies. On the basis of this information, citizens can then productively intervene in politics. As this function involves two stages—becoming informed and being mobilized—we consider it by means of two separate essays.

Thomas Patterson and Philip Seib assess the question of informing the public. They indicate how news coverage often fails to educate the public and lead them to more informed and discerning judgments. With respect to elections, voters sometimes understand less at their close than at their beginning! But just how fully informed must the public be in order to meet the requirements of democracy? Many political scientists document the relatively low interest, and even more limited knowledge, that average people have regarding government and politics. But other political scientists retort that much of life, including politics, consists of a collaboration of experts with people with less attention and knowledge. Patterson and Seib rightly note that, lacking a clear understanding of just how informed a citizen must be, the dispute is probably insoluble. Instead, they incisively suggest a substitute: not whether the news imparts bits and pieces of information but whether it instills in its readers, viewers, and listeners a curiosity about politics and a willingness and desire to become more informed.

The Press as Mobilizer

An additional problem with the criterion of an informed public is that being informed, in and of itself, may not be a requirement for democracy—at least until the public uses that information to choose whether and how to engage with and intervene in politics. Informing citizens is irrelevant to democracy unless that process leads to some political outcome. Thus we should address not just the information that the news media provide and that the public learns, but what citizens do with that information.

So one way of assessing whether the public is informed enough for democracy is to see if the news media provide citizens with what they need in order to intervene in ongoing political and social processes so as to pursue their own interests and their own understandings of the public interest. Such a function has a long heritage in the press, even if it has been identified historically with economic transactions, as when colonial newspapers notified readers about the arrival of ships carrying goods. More recently, it has found new life in the innovations since the mid-1990s known as public (or civic) journalism, where news organizations consciously seek to provide coverage that consults their readers, viewers, or listeners in addressing public concerns and facilitating solutions.

Esther Thorson assesses how well the press works to mobilize citizens in a democracy. She notes that doing so requires encouraging not just behavior, but also civic engagement and political interest, knowledge about politics, and attitudes conducive to participation. As she shows, a consistent finding across many studies is that the heaviest news consumers are those most engaged and active in the political system. However, the issue of causation is open to considerable question. Thus, Thorson turns to the impact of different news outlets, formats, and approaches (including civic journalism) upon civic engagement and mobilization. Finding considerable variation, Thorson is able to provide guidance on how best the news media may encourage citizens to act.

7

WHAT DEMOCRACY REQUIRES
OF THE MEDIA

James Curran

HOW THE MEDIA CAN BEST SERVE DEMOCRACY HAS BEEN the subject of broad agreement for over a century.[1] According to this consensus, the media should keep people informed about public affairs so that individuals are adequately briefed when they take part in the processes of self-government. The media should be fearless watchdogs, vigilantly examining the exercise of power and protecting the public from wrongdoing. The media should also provide a platform of open debate that facilitates the formation of public opinion. In addition, the media should be the voice of the people, representing to authority the citizenry's views and expressing the agreed aims of society. In short, the primary democratic tasks of the media are to inform, scrutinize, debate, and represent.

This litany is memorialized, with minor variations, in the celebrated public reports on the press of the mid-twentieth century—such as the 1947 Hutchins report in the United States and the first Royal Commission on the Press Report (1949) in Britain.[2] It is rehearsed time and again in standard media textbooks. It is reproduced in much theorizing about the media and the public sphere. Why, then, does it seem so platitudinous, so fossilized, so irritatingly pious?

The reason is not that this litany is fundamentally wrong. On the contrary, it conveys in a basic shorthand form the central contributions that the media should make to the workings of democracy. Yet, as we shall see, it does so in a way that obscures, simplifies, and ultimately distorts.[3]

Media-Centered Distortion

One limitation of the conventional approach is that it tends to cling to an antiquated notion of polity, conceived solely in terms of government and private citizens. In this otherwise unmediated world, the media empower citizens almost unaided.

The underlying simplicity of this approach is retained even in some revisionist accounts. These highlight the resources and time that governments devote to influencing the media in order to communicate official policies and concerns and win public approval. Rather than seeing the media as the champion of the people, these accounts argue, it is more realistic to view the media as a two-way channel of communication between government and governed. But while this reformulation reaches a different conclusion from that of the traditional approach, it often remains locked in the same media-centered framework. The media are still viewed as the central intermediary between government and people.

This media-centered approach has a long lineage. In the early eighteenth century two radical British pamphleteers, John Trenchard and Thomas Gordon, writing under the pseudonym Cato, portrayed the press as the principal means by which the government was rendered accountable to the people.[4] The distance between then and now is clear from the writers' frequent lapses into Latin (though not always very good Latin). Their argument was formulated in 1720s England, when most people did not have the vote, parliament was controlled by a landed elite, and even the legitimacy of organized, "loyal" opposition to government was questioned. It was then reasonable to make the claim that print was the principal agency of public accountability.

This claim seems more questionable almost three centuries later. The media are now merely one among a number of institutions, agencies, and actors mediating between government and governed. The most important of these intermediaries are independent judges, political parties, and the myriad organizations of civil society.

Furthermore, the media's relationship to politics is much more complex than traditional media-centered accounts allow. This is the implicit message of a number of important, debunking studies of investigative journalism. These studies point out that the conventional, romantic view of the investigative journalist as someone who pierces the veil of secrecy surrounding government, tirelessly tracks down evidence of abuse, and secures redress through public disclosure, usually downplays one key fact: The investigative journalist is often responding to an initiative from power holders, and reproducing pre-culled information. He or she is the outlet rather than prime mover of investigative stories, responding to processes within the state or political domain.[5]

The media thus need to be understood in relation to the wider political environment, rather than isolated by a spotlight, with the surrounding space cast in shadow. Even the revisionist view of the media as a two-way channel of communication between government and governed—though an advance on the traditional approach—needs to give way to something more complex. Some media, it is true, provide a vertical link between government and private citizens. However, the journalism of prestige dailies is often better viewed as a horizontal discourse between elites. Numerous political periodicals in Europe, and elsewhere, provide a bridge between state-funded intellectuals, politicians, civil servants, and activated publics. The media system, more generally, provides multiple links between state institutions, political parties, civil society, and citizens. It also articulates major social groups (such as social classes) and subgroups to the democratic system. To complicate things still further, the media system provides a channel of communication between different geographical spaces—global, continental, national, regional, and local—only some of which are coterminous with governmental and representative structures.

Media Representation

What, then, are the implications of rejecting a simplistic view of the media as the sole umbilical cord that links government and governed? Perhaps we should begin by questioning the traditional grandiose conception of the media as the "voice of the people." An alternative view is to conceive the media's representational role in terms of strengthening the already existing structures and processes of the democratic system. The media should enable organized groups to present their concerns and solutions to a wider public. If these concerns are viewed as legitimate and win support, the media system should mobilize public pressure for a response from government and the political system. In other words, the media are not a surrogate for the representative processes of society. While the media may speak on occasion for society, their more customary role is to enable the principal organizations and groups in society to be heard—and, where appropriate, to be heeded.

We should also reject the traditional view of the media as a unitary institution representing an indivisible public. In reality the media are constituted by different sectors (a recurring theme of this essay) that relate to different publics, sometimes in different ways. The representational role of these various media sectors within the democratic system is not the same.

Thus, one important sector for the functioning of democracy is "civic media." These have close links to the organizations of civil society, and are typified by political-campaign Web sites, party newspapers, public-interest-group newsletters, and some alternative media. These can promote a sense of purpose within organized groups, provide an internal channel of communication between their leadership and rank and file, connect organizations to useful ideas and information, and propagate their views to a wider audience. Their main democratic role is, thus, to assist civil society organizations to be responsive, representative, and effective.

One problem for the functioning of democracy is that this civic media sector is much weaker in the early twenty-first century than it used to be. The party press was a leading force in popular journalism in many early liberal democra-

cies, and played a key role in the development of political parties as mass movements. The decline of the party press (occurring very much later in Europe than
in the United States) is linked to the decline of political parties in numerous
countries where party membership and activism is falling, and where strong
party identification within the electorate is weakening. This is a source of growing concern especially in parliamentary democracies, where political parties have
a pivotal role as coordinating agencies: they aggregate interests, formulate programs that allocate costs and benefits within society, and define choices for the
electorate.

However, the Internet may provide a means of rejuvenating internal debate
and participation within political parties, and offer a way of involving more people in its processes. John McCain in the Republican Party, and even more dramatically Howard Dean in the Democratic Party, revealed the way in which
political outsiders could tap in to, and mobilize, new sources of activism and
financial support through the Net when they campaigned to be their party's candidate in, respectively, the 2000 and 2004 presidential elections.

If one sector of the media sustains democratic organizations, another sector
contributes to the political organization of social groups. This "social community" media sector can be locally based, national, or international. It can help to
constitute social groups by promoting a shared sense of identity, mediate
between their internal factions, assist in the definition of common concerns, and
present these to the wider world.

Susan Strohm's study of the black press in Los Angeles provides an illuminating insight into the functioning of this social community media sector.[6] Strohm
shows that the leading black local paper, the *Los Angeles Sentinel* (*LAS*), offered an
interpretation of the August 1965 riot in the LA district of Watts that was different from the much publicized views of the California state governor and the Los
Angeles mayor and police chief. While these white officeholders blamed the disorder on criminal elements, outside agitators, and general lawlessness, and called
for tougher law-and-order measures, the *LAS* attributed the riots to police
racism and deep-seated deprivation in housing, education, and employment
among black people, and called for the improvement of ghetto conditions. The
paper thus spoke up for its community, answered attacks on it, and defined an
alternative policy response to the riots. It also helped to ameliorate divisions
within the black community. The paper backed the community's traditional,
"respectable" leadership, and supported its peaceful strategy of struggle through
democratic institutions. However, it also gave space to the new generation of
young militants, and in this way exerted pressure on the traditional black leadership to accommodate to a new force within its community, and to pay more
attention to welfare issues. The paper thus played a constructive role in helping a
beleaguered community to construct a coherent political response to its predica-
ment—one that, for a time, proved effective.[7]

There is also a romantic, documentary and fictional tradition, represented not by a single media sector but by a recognizable genre, which seeks to represent the unorganized. In the words of Malcolm Maclean Jr., this tradition aims to "communicate what it means to be poor among the rich, to be hungry among the well-fed, to be sick among the healthy . . . to be unheard, unheard, unheard . . . in a society noisy with messages."[8] One of the greatest American exponents of this tradition is Studs Terkel.[9]

While peripheral media represent sectional groups, the "core" media sector—consisting of general, mass television channels and, in many countries, local monopoly dailies—has a different role. It provides the central meeting place of society where different social groups are brought into communion with one another. This core sector "holds the ring," enabling divergent viewpoints and interests to be aired in reciprocal debate. Their central democratic purpose is thus to mediate between social groups, rather than to champion exclusively one group and set of concerns.

However, this core sector does have a reserve representational function. By giving prominence to certain issues, concerns, and proposals, core media in effect privilege them and provide the opportunity for them to win wider support. Core media can also express an intergroup consensus on a particular topic, and even mobilize public pressure for this consensus to be acted on by those in authority. In such situations, the media can function as public tribunes.

A later episode in the politics of Los Angeles provides a concrete example of how core media representation works. In 1991 Rodney King, an African American motorist, was pulled over for speeding, fled, and was apprehended and then repeatedly beaten by three white Los Angeles police officers in front of a sergeant and seventeen other colleagues. The event, videotaped by an amateur cameraman, was broadcast numerous times in 1991–92 on American television, and was commented on by newspapers throughout the United States. In particular the dominant local daily, the *Los Angeles Times*, gave the incident extensive coverage. It also relayed black community complaints about racist policing, and gave these complaints credence by reporting that the city of Los Angeles had paid more than $20 million between 1986 and 1990 in judgments, settlements, and jury verdicts against local police officers in over three hundred lawsuits involving the excessive use of force. The paper pressed for reform, gave prominence to the findings of a commission of inquiry into the Los Angeles Police Department (LAPD), and inveighed against the racial slurs of Police Chief Daryl Gates. This did not prevent a Simi Valley jury from acquitting of most charges the police officers who were accused of beating Rodney King—a verdict that triggered a riot. However, the *Los Angeles Times* helped to mobilize elite and public pressure for more enlightened policing that resulted in the reform of the LAPD, and the forced resignation of Gates.[10]

Core media can also reinforce pressure for reform not only within local communities or nations but also on a continental or international scale. Thus, national television channels in European countries gave extensive publicity to the environmental-activism organization Greenpeace's protest against the Anglo-Dutch oil company Shell in the mid-1990s over its proposed dumping of the Brent Spar oil platform in the Atlantic Ocean, causing the corporation to reverse its decision.[11] Similarly, general newspapers and television channels in the United States, Portugal, Spain, and Japan publicized in the early 1990s the plight of Brazilian street children who were being murdered as part of an informal zero-tolerance policy against crime. This international publicity, mostly generated by Amnesty International, galvanized a stalled local campaign, won media attention in Brazil, and helped to secure increased official protection of street children in Rio de Janeiro and elsewhere.[12]

Media representation traverses geographical as well as "social" space, usually in response to cues from organized groups in the political domain. Indeed, the media are contributing to the development of a "new politics" that transcends national boundaries. This can be seen as a continuation of the democracy-building role of the media. The rise of the early press expanded the political community within the nation-state, contributing to the formation of public opinion as a democratizing force and the development of democratic structures within a national context.[13] The evolving media system is now contributing, it seems, to a comparable process in an international context. The Internet is facilitating the growth of global activism and international elite dialogue,[14] while television is promoting an increased sense of responsibility for distant others, and the development of a global agenda. More generally, internationalizing trends within the media system are contributing to the growth of multidirectional flows of communication between different peoples (though still in an unequal way). However, these changes are still at an early stage. The world's news media are predominantly national and local, rather than international, in terms of both audience and content. Global civil society is in its infancy: fragmented by linguistic divisions, distorted by global inequalities, segmented into single-issue-oriented constituencies, and insufficiently wired to structures of real decision making. Yet despite these qualifications, part of the media system is assuming a new representational role: that of bringing together peoples from different nations, promoting international dialogue and exchange, facilitating the coordination of international activism, and helping to develop an international political community to which global structures of power are potentially accountable.

Media Forum

If the media serve democracy by contributing to representative processes, they also serve by providing a forum for debate. The traditional approach is concerned primarily with the quality of ideas and interchange that takes place in the media. The objective of media debate, it argues, should be to advance public rationality and good government. The media is viewed as an autonomous space, detached from society, where ideas battle for supremacy on the basis of merit, and where a reason-based consensus emerges that guides the public direction of society. Indeed, some accounts portray the forum role of the media as the equivalent of a university seminar functioning as an engine of enlightenment within the democratic process. They betray no awareness that conflict, ideology, and the struggle for power provide the wider context in which the media operate, and that debates in the media are often an extension of this struggle.

By contrast, another orientation is more concerned with whether the media forum reflects the diversity of society. There are, in this view, real differences of interest between social groups over how opportunity, public resources, and rewards are distributed in society. There are also divergent understandings of what constitutes a good society based on different social values. These differences should find adequate expression in media debate in order to promote equitable outcomes.

The concern that elites tend to dominate public discourse typically informs this approach. Elites have unequal access to economic and symbolic resources. This can assist them to present their own special interests as being in the interests of all, and to win popular consent for the policies, social arrangements, and ideas they favor. Their dominance can cause other perspectives to be marginalized, and result in the media defining public debate largely in terms of differing elite positions. The conventions of "objective reporting" can reinforce this process— though this is of course not their intention. It can lead journalists to rely on established power holders and legitimated holders of knowledge as sources of news and comment, and unconsciously internalize assumptions that are "uncontroversial" within the prevailing framework of thought.

It is therefore healthy for the media system to include partisan and adversarial media. These are often more ready to voice maverick or dissenting opinion than mainstream media because they cater to minorities and are unconstrained by the "fair and balanced" norms of objective journalism. Adversarial media can potentially extend the diversity—and representative reach—of the media. They can also provide liberating access to alternative ideas and arguments. People do not instinctively know where their self-interest lies, because this knowledge does not spring preformed from social experience or class position. Exposure to dissent can help members of social groups to explore critically what best serves their interests.

There are also other compelling reasons why adversarial journalism enriches democracy. It can excite, involve, and mobilize people in the processes of democracy (though this depends partly on what form media partisanship takes[15]). It can lead to better outcomes, informed by an enhanced understanding of alternative claims and interests. It can assist society to adapt to necessary change. It can foster republican virtues: critical independence and distrust of authority. Above all, it comes out of a tradition of freedom very different from that prevailing in authoritarian societies, such as Saudi Arabia, where Article 39 of the Basic Law of Governance lays down that "publication of anything that might lead to rifts . . . is forbidden."[16]

The value of adversarial media can be illustrated by the way in which the rise of the "blogosphere" challenged "pack journalism"—the tendency of "big" media journalists to reach a group consensus. The blogosphere consists of online journals (Web logs) published by self-appointed pundits (bloggers) who tend in the United States to be right wing and whose numbers grew exponentially after free blogger software became available in 1999. Bloggers became a recognized force in 2002 when they drew attention to a birthday party speech by a senior Republican politician, Senator Trent Lott, in which Lott explicitly endorsed the racial-segregation politics of the past. Although numerous reporters heard the speech, they largely ignored it. This generated a growing volume of protest among bloggers (on both right and left), prompting the influential *New York Times* columnist Paul Krugman to criticize Senator Lott's speech five days after the event. Other media then focused belatedly on the story, and uncovered similar controversial statements made by Senator Lott in the past. In the ensuing public outcry, President George W. Bush felt obliged to dissociate himself, in a speech to a black audience, from Senator Lott's nostalgia for segregation. This increased political pressure on Lott, forcing him to stand down from his key position as the majority party leader in the Senate. In short, online independents successfully challenged the news values of journalists working for the big media, and in effect helped to redraw the boundaries of what was "acceptable" in contemporary, mainstream American politics.[17]

However, adversarial journalism can also have negative features. It can lead to the circulation of scurrilous information about public figures that has no foundation in truth. Media partisanship can become heavily skewed to the right or left, subverting the main democratic purpose of partisan journalism: to extend media diversity. Partisan values can also penetrate the workings of large media conglomerates and distort the functioning of democracy. This is exemplified by the way in which the Italian business tycoon Silvio Berlusconi's control of a large media empire provided the springboard for his elevation, without any prior experience of public office, to the premiership of Italy in 1994, and again in 2001.[18]

Division of Labor

While the media system should serve democracy by providing an open forum of debate that reflects the diversity of society, it should also assist the management of conflict. Ethnic, religious, and class-based animosities can turn into communal intimidation, sporadic acts of violence, even organized pogroms. Banal hatreds can become embedded within sectional communities and disable the political process, as has long been the case in Protestant-dominated Northern Ireland. One way of controlling group animosity is to impose limits on free speech through antihate law that prohibits communications liable to result in actual physical violence. However, a more positive approach is to entrench media structures and norms that promote conciliation.

This seems to pose a contradiction. How can the media system simultaneously promote conflict and conciliation, the expression of uncompromising views and the pursuit of compromise? The answer is that the media are not a single entity. There should be a division of labor in which different sectors of the media have different roles, practice different forms of journalism, and make different contributions to the functioning of the democratic system.

The core media of society—its mass television channels and monopoly local dailies—should be governed by the norm of "balanced" journalism, typified by the reporting of different viewpoints expressed by the spokespersons of opposing groups. More generally, these core media should seek to sustain a culture of "civic democracy" designed to promote conciliation and compromise. This civic culture can be best summarized in terms of seven values: *civility*, a way of expressing disagreement that does not seek to delegitimate or marginalize opponents through personal invective; *empathy*, a desire to comprehend other groups through sympathetic understanding; *mutuality*, a feeling of being connected to society and being concerned about the well-being of others; a commitment to the ideal of *objectivity*, that is, the shared pursuit of truth rather than cynical advocacy of positions favoring a prior conclusion; a *public interest* orientation that recognizes that "what's in it for me" is not the sole object of public discussion; a belief in *democratic efficacy*, acknowledging that the democratic state can achieve worthwhile ends that cannot be attained through individual action; and, lastly, a commitment to *social inclusion* through emphasizing a shared sense of humanity, common interests, and interdependence among peoples.

Core media should also promote conciliation by supporting the rituals and procedures of the democratic system. The most important of these are periodic elections, which not only determine the democratic leadership and broad policy direction of society, but also arbitrate between opposed groups and their followers on the basis of agreed rules. However, if elections are to function properly in these terms, they need to be involving and defining events. Core media should mobilize people to vote by giving prominence to election campaigns. They should also depict elections as significant moments in the collective determination of society by highlighting the political choices involved, rather than presenting them in the trivial terms of a horse race (or battle of wits between strategists) staged primarily for the entertainment of bemused bystanders. Elections that have low turnouts, and whose democratic significance is trivialized, weaken the legitimacy of democratic government and cease to function as pivotal events in the collective public life of society. It is also important that opposition representatives are adequately reported between elections, not only to sustain public dialogue and a democratic check on government, but also to ensure that "losers" among the electorate do not feel disenfranchised.

In brief, different media sectors have different functions, and legitimately employ different modes of journalism. While one sector should facilitate activism and conflict, another should promote dialogue and reciprocity. How the division of labor is organized between these different parts of the media system varies in different countries and at different times. For example, the growth in the number of television channels that occurred in many countries after 1980 caused a growing subdivision of the mass audience.[19] Mass television's integrative role in bringing people together and brokering a measure of agreement within the public sphere thus weakened. This made democratic government more difficult.

Media Watchdog

The traditional approach sees the watchdog role of the media as being confined to the state. This perspective is mired in a simplistic understanding of the state as the seat of power, and a blinkered view that sees state tyranny as the only potential threat to the welfare of society. Most commentators and journalists now conclude that this understanding of the media's watchdog role is too restrictive.

The implications of this revised consensus need to be explored further. In liberal democracies, the exercise of state authority is normally subject to numerous checks: the legislature's scrutiny of the executive; a written constitution upheld by the judiciary; the monitoring of state activity by opposition parties, nongovernmental organizations (NGOs), public audits, and think tanks; and so on. Information and critical comment about the functioning of the state are relayed to the media on a daily basis. The media's role as a watchdog of state power is thus enormously assisted—and, in a sense, subsidized—by public organizations.

By contrast, other sources of power are subject to less organized public scrutiny and criticism. The media's surveillance role outside the state is underassisted. This has prompted some to argue that the media should compensate by committing more of its resources to scrutinizing, and holding to account, nonstate forms of power such as that exercised in the boardroom.

Whatever view is taken, the media need to update their watchdog role by adjusting to the decline of the national state.[20] In particular, the power of governments over their economies has diminished as a consequence of the increasing influence of international regulatory agencies (such as the World Trade Organization); deregulated, global financial markets; large transnational corporations; and, in some contexts, new continental structures (such as the European

Union) and trading arrangements.[21] Most of these agencies are imperfectly accountable through democratic processes, and their activities are far from transparent.[22] They need to be subjected to more effective media scrutiny.

Informational Role

The media's watchdog role in monitoring power is of course merely one aspect of their wider informational role. There is general agreement that the media system should report important events and trends—"the news"—so that citizens are adequately informed. Beyond this, however, there are sharp disagreements.

One issue of contention has to do with reporting the "truth." According to one tradition, good government involves the practical application of knowledge in the interests of the wider community. The media should assist good government by transferring specialist knowledge to the public domain. For example, the media should alert people to medical evidence about the dangers of smoking. This not only informs people about the risks involved, but also helps to build consent for government action against smoking.

The implication here is that the media should signify, at least part of the time, what is "true" or at least reveal what is perceived to be true within the relevant knowledge community. This introduces a new element into the discussion. Partisan media are essentially propagandist, advancing at best partial truths. Balanced media report "multiple truths" advanced by rival spokespersons. Democracy, it can be argued, needs something more.

The contentious implications of the striving for balance are best illustrated by media reporting of global warming. There is now an international scientific consensus (reflected in an analysis of leading science journals)[23] that human use of fossil fuels (for example, petroleum) is a major cause of global warming. Yet a 2001 international survey found that Americans were less informed about the causes of global warming than the populations of most other advanced countries (and much less in favor of concerted international action to limit climate change). Indeed, Americans were, despite their higher level of education, only marginally better informed than Brazilians.[24]

While there are a number of possible explanations for this,[25] Jaclyn Dispensa and Robert J. Brulle attribute Americans' lack of knowledge about global warming to the influence of the powerful American fuel and related industries, which challenged the scientific consensus about global warming. This lobby's public intervention made global warming a contested issue in America, requiring from journalists balanced reporting of competing claims. Consequently, American newspapers gave in 2000 much greater prominence to arguments disputing the existence of global warming, and its human causation, than comparable papers in Finland and New Zealand, where the fuel industries had limited influence. In other words, the conventions of balanced journalism seem to have resulted in the American public being misinformed.[26]

A second key issue has to do with the volume and quality of news coverage. One tradition argues that news coverage should be extensive and intelligent. Important events and trends should be reported fully. News should be presented in a context that renders it meaningful. Causes, consequences, and implications—not just the bare facts of discrete events—should be part of the news diet. For example, a recent influential study in Britain argues that audiences often do not have the background knowledge of news events that journalists assume they have. Failure to provide contextual information leads to audience incomprehension, misconception, and baffled boredom.[27]

Another tradition champions the conventions of popular journalism. Personalization, simplification, and a focus on action make news stories accessible and involving. Stories should be brief because audiences have limited attention spans. News coverage has to be highly selective because people do not have an inexhaustible interest in public affairs. The real challenge facing journalists is to find ways of connecting people with little interest in politics to the democratic process. The answer is to offer news that is short, entertaining, and sounds a burglar alarm if something requires immediate public attention.

This debate appears to be solely about the public, its interests and capabilities. However, it is also informed by different implicit—and therefore undebated—understandings of democracy. These give rise to divergent views about what democracy requires from the media.

Rival Models of Democracy

One fashionable theory in "new media" literature is that new communications technology should lead to the introduction of "electronic democracy." Previously insoluble problems having to do with the scale of national communities, unequal access to knowledge, and the growing divorce between politicians and public, can now be solved, it is argued, through computer-aided, "direct" democracy. People can debate the pressing issues of the day through many-to-many, interactive Net technology, and then determine public policy through online voting.

This approach is a misguided chimera. Computer ownership is still very unequal, and online voting is liable to disenfranchise in particular low-income families. Direct democracy presupposes an intense level of political involvement that only a minority is willing to sustain for any length of time. It will result in people voting on numerous issues that they have not had time to debate and reflect upon. This will convert voting—and plebiscitary government—into the equivalent of online shopping. Its effect will probably be to move politics away from the formation of collective goals through public debate toward the aggregation of individual preferences with minimal deliberation: a recipe for me–centered politics.

A second model is deliberative, representative democracy. This favors a division of labor between the electorate and elected representatives on grounds of practicality and good administration. However, it also argues that the public should be alert, informed, and active in order to supervise the conduct of government. People need to be briefed fully if they are to be effective. They also need to assume responsibility for decisions taken in their name, and seek to change them if they are wrong. As Alexander Meiklejohn succinctly puts it, "Self-government is a nonsense unless the 'self' which governs is able and determined to make its will effective."[28] This tradition also stresses the central importance of public deliberation as an educative process for all those who take part. Through debate, people become aware of other viewpoints and interests, register complexity, explore common ground and differences, consider alternative options, and become willing to contemplate trade-offs. A democracy without vigorous debate, in this view, is a like a blindfolded person stumbling and groping in the dark. The implication of this tradition is that the media need to provide a full news service, and broad-based debate.

The third alternative is perhaps best called the "pragmatic democracy" model.[29] It argues that it is neither realistic nor desirable for everyone to become news junkies, striving to become experts in every department of public policy and seeking to have informed opinions on all major issues. Most people feel that they have better things to do with their lives. The investment of time involved in news "bingeing" is likely to be unproductive, on any realistic assessment of the likelihood of influencing public policy. Of course, people need to be sufficiently informed to choose between candidates running for office. They need also to be on standby, always ready to become democratically involved if the situation requires it. But the basic principle of the division of labor that encompasses all aspects of life—for example whether you do the repair yourself or call in a professional builder—applies also to democratic life. Many people feel that they can leave things to elected representatives, centers of policy expertise, and activist and other intermediary groups. So it makes sense in this view to scan rather than "study" the news in order to monitor whether there is anything that warrants attention. This approach implicitly endorses a basic news service for the majority, and a fuller news service for a self-selecting minority involved in government, political activism, and civil society.

Out of these three options, the deliberative democracy model has perhaps the best tunes. This is partly because the pragmatic model seems likely to result in elite domination of public life, subject at best to periodic checks when the general public is activated. It fails also to engage fully with the argument that democracies are devolved systems of power that entail responsibilities as well as rights and opportunities. This includes an obligation to be properly informed and concerned about major decisions taken by government. For example, members of a democracy that invades another country need to consider whether the invasion is justified, demand to know how many citizens are being killed in their name, and be briefed about what steps are being taken to serve the real interests of the country that is being occupied. Any democracy that is denied the opportunity to be fully informed about something so important, and that loses the habit of reflecting upon what is right, becomes a threat to the rest of the world.

This said, advocates of deliberative democracy sometimes propose news standards that seem impossibly high. They tend also to have a blind spot about media entertainment. The debate between adherents of deliberative and pragmatic democracy is far from over.

Self-Government

Self-rule is not only about legislation, public administration, and law enforcement. It does not simply involve elections and participation in the formal political life of society.

Self-rule, in any meaningful sense of the word, is also based on collective regulation through public norms. These are the tacit rules, conventions, and expectations that—through prescriptions and prohibitions—guide how individuals conduct themselves in everyday life (such as whether they stand in line or cut ahead of others, the way they respond to the frail, how they fulfill different social roles such as that of parent or child). These norms are, in a broad sense, collectively arrived at, maintained, and enforced. They are acquired through early socialization, and internalized and sustained through social interaction. But they can also be weakened, strengthened, or change over time in response to collective processes. Public norms—like laws—are one of the ways in which society governs itself.

The collective determination of public norms is conducted partly through the medium of so-called "soft" journalism and media entertainment. Thus, one genre of popular media content (often taking the form of crime reporting, human interest stories, and fictional melodrama) is concerned with "deviancy," and represents an important way in which public norms are reaffirmed. Typically this content arouses indignation against transgressors, and invites a shared sense of pleasure when they get their well-deserved comeuppance. Fictional variants of this genre tend to feature symbolic punishment in which the deviant is found out, suffers, and faces an uncertain or unhappy future. Journalistic versions more often relish real-life retribution when the wrongdoer is indicted and punished, or is subjected to public humiliation.

This last is the stock-in-trade of "tabloid" journalism in both television and newspapers. For example, the *Daily Mail* (Britain's second-biggest-selling daily, with over 2 million circulation), devoted a two-page article in 2003 to a hitherto unknown woman, Kim Marsham, under the banner headline "Is This Britain's Most Selfish Mother?"[30] Marsham, it was revealed, had gone on a one-week foreign holiday with her lover, leaving her five young children at home. She had casually left a note asking her neighbor to take care of her children. The neighbor proved to be away at the time, and Marsham's distraught children were taken into temporary care by the local council.

The *Daily Mail* news report condemned the mother for her "appalling moral and familial neglect." It also quoted comments about Kim Marsham from neighbors, former lovers, and so-called friends, which vividly conveyed an impression of an immoral, feckless woman. Marsham, it emerged, had had six children by four men. "Utterly lacking in any sense of self responsibility," according to the report, "she lives on benefits and takes handouts from the State as her due. She has repeatedly got herself pregnant in the most desperate circumstances." Readers' moral indignation was skillfully engendered through the contrast drawn between the children's tear-stained, "terrifying and bewildering ordeal" and Marsham's pleasure-seeking irresponsibility, captured by a large photograph of her looking relaxed and happy on holiday with her boyfriend on Grand Canary. This was heightened by the accumulation of telling detail (the holiday was on borrowed money, and the holiday couple were "dining on steak and chips every night").

Kim Marsham was placed in the symbolic equivalent of the stocks. Yet if some popular media enforce public norms through rituals of degradation, others engage in discussion. The more thoughtful television talk shows like *The Oprah Winfrey Show* in the United States or *Trisha* in Britain have made an impact partly because they allow "transgressors" to answer back, and enable the studio audience to join in. Their formats would have allowed Kim Marsham to defend herself, and this would have given rise to a discussion. Marsham might have tacitly upheld the norm of parental duty by pleading mitigating circumstance: she was a good mother, under stress, who had mistakenly assumed that her neighbor would help out. Alternatively, she might have contested the way in which she was being held solely responsible: don't absent fathers have a duty of care, too? Or, more improbably, she could have been defiant, saying that pleasure came first.

Progressive talk shows thus allow public norms to be evaluated through public debate. They make transparent, through condensed, choreographed moments of human revelation and confrontation a cumulative process of appraisal that involves television programs, films, newspaper and magazine articles, popular books, and Internet chat rooms, and the wider conversations that these stimulate and inform. This collective debate enables public norms to be modified over time.

This process is especially visible when it erupts into "culture wars." Such conflicts are fought in relation to high-octane topics such as gay marriage, teenage pregnancy, or in an earlier era "working mothers," that symbolize wider issues: the "validity" of sexual minority preferences, teenage morality, women's place in society. In these culture wars, rival normative groups (such as secular libertarians and Christian fundamentalists) seek wider support and public arbitration in their favor. Victory results in norms being upheld, revised, or reinterpreted. This is usually an incomplete and contested process because particular social groups can retain social norms that differ from those of society as a whole. Even so, most settlements that follow the ending of culture wars have significant outcomes in terms of influencing prevailing attitudes, social behavior, and sometimes legislation.

Media content that is often attacked as a diversion from the serious business of politics and the obligations of public life—"soft" journalism, "freak" talk shows, "formulaic" fiction—can thus be viewed as being part of the public conversation that guides an informal system of "self-government." It is part of the way in which society talks about its common social processes and the implicit rules that govern them. It is consequently an important aspect of the media's democratic functioning.

Similar arguments to those that were marshaled in relation to "serious" journalism apply here also. Entertainment and fiction in minority media should give full expression to the diversity of values and orientations within society in order to ensure that these are adequately represented in collective debate, and provide a potential source of emancipation. However, the central core of the media system should bring people together in reciprocal and conciliatory dialogue. A cardinal feature of this dialogue should be that "other" groups are portrayed with understanding rather than malignant contempt. The humanistic argument of the Hutchins report, written over half a century ago, is especially applicable in the contemporary context of the "war on terror" and growing tensions between Islam and Christianity:

> The truth about any social group, though it should not exclude its weaknesses and vices, includes also recognition of its values, its aspirations, and its common humanity. . . . If people are exposed to the inner truth of the life of a particular group, they will gradually build up respect for and understanding of it.[31]

Politics and Entertainment

There are also more general ways in which media entertainment is interwoven with the political process. First, important political issues, from crime to gender relations, are discussed—implicitly or explicitly—in media fiction. Second, ideological understandings of society and politically charged social values are also projected through entertainment. For instance, much western European television soap opera—typically located in working-class settings and evoking a strong sense of social solidarity, mutuality, and collectivism—gives expression to the social democratic values of the organized working class, and promotes these to a wider television audience.[32] Third, minorities constitute themselves partly through consumption of entertainment in ways that have political consequences. Thus, novels, films, music, and "soft" journalism played a significant part in the self-organization of gay communities and the mounting of a sustained public campaign against homophobia from the 1970s onward.[33] Fourth, how social groups are depicted in the media also influences their social standing and their political and other forms of leverage. For example, more progressive media representations of women in the period after 1980 was linked, in complex ways, to the advance of women in the workplace.[34] Fifth, people's sense of social identity (the extent to which they define themselves in terms of membership in a nation, local community, or religious, ethnic, class, gender, or generational grouping) is a key dynamo driving politics, influencing both political affiliation and belief. Yet social identity is significantly influenced by differentiated patterns of media consumption, which support some identities but not others—a key theme of the literature on subcultures.[35] In short, media entertainment and politics are so closely intertwined that it is difficult to understand why they should be viewed as distinct and separate.

The only legitimate justification for this has to do with where and how "politics" is conducted. The most important site of politics is the state. This is where laws are framed and enforced, and where peace or war is determined. The state is also the principal agency of social redress. The market system generates inequalities. These are mitigated in popular democracies through redistributions of wealth and resources from rich to poor. The nature and scale of these "transfers" is determined through politics.

Collective decisions made through the state should be influenced by relevant information and logical argument. Media entertainment does not provide an adequate way of being informed about what is happening in the world. Nor does it provide a suitable medium for evaluating alternative policy options. While it is an important arena for normative regulation, and is linked to the political process in numerous indirect ways, it is not the primary place where politics, centered on the state, should be mediated. If coverage and analysis of public affairs is eclipsed by entertainment, democracy becomes starved and anorexic.

Conclusion

The account presented above comes out of a mounting sense of dissatisfaction with the limitations of traditional understandings of the democratic role of the media.[36] These understandings mostly derive from the distant past. They downplay the role of social groups, political parties, civil society, ideology, and globalization, and therefore seem disconnected from how contemporary democracy works. They are also narrowly preoccupied with political journalism, and have little to say about the democratic significance of media fiction and entertainment—the content that accounts for most of what people consume in the media most of the time.

This essay begins the task of updating the relevant body of theory. However, it is mainly concerned with how the media *should* serve democracy—with the way it ought to be rather than the way it is. It has not discussed in any detail how the requirements of the market and the requirements of democracy conflict.[37] The market creates pressure for public affairs journalism to contract, for international affairs to be covered less extensively (unless it involves military action), for cuts to be made in investigative journalism, and for audiences to be entertained through being made indignant, and consequently for the weak and marginal to be bullied and denigrated.

Different countries have developed different approaches for reconciling the needs of the market and democracy. These boil down to four main strategies: public service broadcasting (through public regulation or ownership); social market policies (antimonopoly law and minority media subsidies); the strengthening of media staff rights and influence; and the fostering of a public service culture among journalists.

This last is sometimes called the "social responsibility" approach. Given a strong boost by the Hutchins report, this reform movement exerted a positive influence on the American media. However, its influence is now waning as a consequence of the strengthening of economic pressures within the American media system (especially television). This is causing the American media to fall short, at times, of what democracy requires—an argument made, at various points, in this book. What is the remedy? The answer to this question matters enormously not only to Americans but also to the rest of the world, because of the United States' position as the globe's sole superpower.

Notes

1. The author thanks Timothy Cook, John Keane, and Michael Schudson for their helpful comments on a draft version of this chapter.
2. Commission on Freedom of the Press, *A Free and Responsible Press* (Hutchins report); Great Britain, Royal Commission on the Press, *1947–1949 Report* (London: HMSO [Cmd. 7700], 1949).
3. This essay issues from a groundswell of dissatisfaction with traditional understandings of the role of the media in liberal democracy. Different, and sometimes opposed, reservations about the traditional approach appear in the following: Baker, *Media, Markets, and Democracy;* Bennett and Entman, eds., *Mediated Politics;* Cook, *Governing with the News;* Curran, *Media and Power;* Gans, *Democracy and the News;* Habermas, *Between Facts and Norms;* Robert Hackett and Yuezhi Zhao, *Sustaining Democracy?: Journalism and the Politics of Objectivity* (Toronto: Garamond, 1998);

Keane, *The Media and Democracy;* McChesney, *Rich Media, Poor Democracy;* Thomas Meyer, with Lew Hinchman, *Media Democracy: How the Media Colonize Politics* (Oxford, U.K., and Cambridge, Mass.: Polity, 2002); Schudson, *The Good Citizen;* Michael Schudson, *The Sociology of News* (New York: Norton, 2003); Street, *Mass Media, Politics, and Democracy;* and John Zaller, "A New Standard of News Quality: Burglar Alarms for the Monitorial Citizen," *Political Communication* 20 (2003): 109–30.

4. John Trenchard and Thomas Gordon, *Cato's Letters,* no. 15 (February 4, 1720); "Of Freedom of Speech: That the Same Is Inseparable from Publick Liberty," in Haig A. Bosmajian, ed., *The Principles and Practice of Freedom of Speech,* 2nd ed. (Washington, D.C.: University Press of America, 1983), 36.

5. Two good examples of this debunking tradition are Gladys Lang and Kurt Lang, *The Battle for Public Opinion: The President, the Press, and the Polls during Watergate* (New York: Columbia University Press, 1983), and Protess et al., *The Journalism of Outrage.*

6. Susan Strohm, "The Black Press and the Black Community: The *Los Angeles Sentinel's* Coverage of the Watts Riots," in *Framing Friction: Media and Social Conflict,* edited by Mary S. Mander (Urbana: University of Illinois Press, 1999).

7. This conclusion differs from that of Strohm, who emphasizes the role of the *Los Angeles Sentinel* as an agency of social control.

8. Cited in "Journalism, Advocacy and a Communication Model for Democracy," in *Communication for and against Democracy,* edited by Marc Raboy and Peter A. Bruck (Montreal and New York: Black Rose, 1989), 170.

9. For a good example of Studs Terkel's work, see his *Coming of Age: The Story of Our Century by Those Who've Lived It* (New York: New Press, 1995).

10. Ronald N. Jacobs, *Race, Media, and the Crisis of Civil Society: From Watts to Rodney King* (Cambridge, U.K., and New York: Cambridge University Press, 2000).

11. Paul Manning, *News and News Sources: A Critical Introduction* (London and Thousand Oaks, Calif.: Sage, 2001).

12. Sonia Serra, "Multinationals of Solidarity: International Civil Society and the Killing of Street Children in Brazil," in *Globalization, Communication, and Transnational Civil Society,* edited by Sandra Braman and Annabelle Sreberny-Mohammadi (Cresskill, N.J.: Hampton Press, 1996); and "The Killing of Street Children and the Rise of the International Public Sphere," in *Media Organisations in Society* (London: Edward Arnold; New York: Oxford University Press, 2000).

13. This is argued in numerous national press histories. For a rare example of comparative press history foregrounding this theme, see Bob Harris, *Politics and the Rise of the Press: Britain and France, 1620–1800* (London and New York: Routledge, 1996).

14. Wim Van de Donk et al., eds., *Cyberprotest: New Media, Citizens, and Social Movements* (London and New York: Routledge, 2004); James Curran, "Global Journalism: A Case Study of the Internet," in *Contesting Media Power: Alternative Media in a Networked World,* edited by Nick Couldry and James Curran (Lanham, Md.: Rowman and Littlefield, 2003).

15. Unremitting, mutual negativism can turn people off politics. See Thomas E. Patterson, *The Vanishing Voter: Public Involvement in an Age of Uncertainty* (New York: Knopf, 2003).

16. Cited in Street, *Mass Media, Politics, and Democracy,* 250.

17. Esther Scott, *"Big Media" Meets the "Bloggers": Coverage of Trent Lott's Remarks at Strom Thurmond's Birthday Party,* case study (Cambridge, Mass.: Kennedy School of Government Case Program, Harvard University, 2004), available from www.ksgcase.harvard.edu.

18. Paul Ginsborg, *Silvio Berlusconi: Television, Power and Patrimony* (London and New York: Verso, 2004).

19. This is happening more gradually than is widely thought. For data revealing the continuing hold of mass television in many countries, see Curran, *Media and Power,* table 7.2, 190.

20. The classic exposition of this argument is Susan Strange, *The Retreat of the State: The Diffusion of Power in the World Economy* (Cambridge, U.K., and New York: Cambridge University Press, 1996). For useful discussions of this new orthodoxy (which is in danger of becoming overstated), see David Held and Anthony McGrew, eds., *The Global Transformations Reader: An Introduction to the Globalization Debate,* 2nd ed. (Cambridge, U.K.: Polity, 2003), and Frank J. Lechner and John Boli, eds., *The Globalization Reader,* 2nd ed. (Malden, Mass.: Blackwell, 2003).

21. David Held et al., *Global Transformations: Politics, Economics, and Culture* (Cambridge, U.K.: Polity, 1999); Leslie Sklair, *Globalization: Capitalism and Its Alternative,* 3rd ed. (Oxford, U.K., and New York: Oxford University Press, 2002), among others.

22. A good, insider presentation of this case is provided by Joseph E. Stiglitz, *Globalization and Its Discontents* (New York: Norton, 2002).

23. Jaclyn Marisa Dispensa and Robert Brulle, "Media's Social Construction of Environmental Issues: Focus on Global Warming—A Comparative Study," *International Journal of Sociology and Social Policy* 23, no. 10 (2003): 74–105.

24. Steven Brechin, "Comparative Public Opinion and Knowledge on Global Climatic Change and the Kyoto Protocol: The U.S. versus the World?" *International Journal of Sociology and Social Policy* 23, no. 10 (2003): 106–34.

25. An earlier study, which also found that Americans knew less about international affairs than Europeans, attributed this to the failings of American television as "the least informative TV regarding international events." Michael Dimock and Samuel Popkin, "Political Knowledge in Comparative Perspective," in *Do the Media Govern?: Politicians, Voters, and Reporters in America,* edited by Shanto Iyengar and Richard Reeves (Thousand Oaks, Calif.: Sage, 1997), 223.

26. Dispensa and Brulle, "Media's Social Construction of Environmental Issues." While their study offers useful insights, it overstates the direct influence of advertising and corporate ownership on the U.S. media.

27. Greg Philo and Mike Berry, Glasgow University Media Group, *Bad News from Israel* (London: Pluto, 2004).

28. Alexander Meiklejohn, "The Rulers and the Ruled," in *The Principles and Practice of Freedom of Speech,* edited by Bosmajian, 276.

29. Two telling contributions to this tradition, strongly influenced by "rational choice" theory, are Schudson, *The Good Citizen,* and Zaller, "A New Standard of News Quality."

30. *Daily Mail,* March 8, 2003.

31. Commission on Freedom of the Press, *A Free and Responsible Press* (Hutchins report), 27.
32. Hugh O'Donnell, *Good Times, Bad Times: Soap Operas and Society in Western Europe* (London and New York: Leicester University Press, 1999).
33. Larry Gross, *Up from Invisibility: Lesbians, Gay Men, and the Media in America* (New York: Columbia University Press, 2002); Jeffrey Weeks, *Sex, Politics and Society: The Regulation of Sexuality since 1800,* 2nd ed. (London and New York: Longman, 1989).
34. Myra Macdonald, *Representing Women: Myths of Femininity in the Popular Media* (London: E. Arnold, 1995).
35. Ken Gelder and Sarah Thornton, eds., *The Subcultures Reader* (London and New York: Routledge, 1997).
36. See note 3.
37. This is the central theme of Curran, *Media and Power;* Bill Kovach and Tom Rosenstiel, *The Elements of Journalism: What Newspeople Should Know and the Public Should Expect* (New York: Crown, 2003); Colin Leys, *Market-Driven Politics: Neoliberal Democracy and the Public Interest* (London: Verso, 2001); and Donald R. Shanor, *News from Abroad* (New York: Columbia University Press, 2003), among numerous other books.

Bibliography

Baker, C. Edwin. *Media, Markets, and Democracy.* Cambridge, U.K., and New York: Cambridge University Press, 2002.

Bennett, W. Lance, and Robert M. Entman, eds. *Mediated Politics: Communication in the Future of Democracy.* Cambridge, U.K., and New York: Cambridge University Press, 2001.

Commission on Freedom of the Press. *A Free and Responsible Press; A General Report on Mass Communication: Newspapers, Radio, Motion Pictures, Magazines, and Books,* edited by Robert D. Leigh. (Hutchins report.) Chicago: University of Chicago Press, 1947.

Cook, Timothy E. *Governing with the News: The News Media as a Political Institution.* Chicago: Chicago University Press, 1998.

Curran, James. *Media and Power.* London and New York: Routledge, 2002.

Gans, Herbert J. *Democracy and the News.* Oxford, U.K., and New York: Oxford University Press, 2003.

Habermas, Jürgen. *Between Facts and Norms: Contributions to a Discourse Theory of Law and Democracy,* translated by William Rehg. Cambridge, Mass.: MIT Press, 1996.

Keane, John. *The Media and Democracy.* Cambridge, U.K.: Polity, 1991.

McChesney, Robert W. *Rich Media, Poor Democracy: Communication Politics in Dubious Times.* Urbana: University of Illinois Press, 1999.

Protess, David L., et al. *The Journalism of Outrage: Investigative Reporting and Agenda Building in America.* New York: Guilford Press, 1991.

Schudson, Michael. *The Good Citizen: A History of American Civic Life.* New York: Martin Kessler, 1998.

Street, John. *Mass Media, Politics, and Democracy.* Basingstoke, U.K., and New York: Palgrave, 2001.

8

THE MARKETPLACE OF IDEAS

Robert Schmuhl and Robert G. Picard

THE "MARKETPLACE OF IDEAS" IS AN OFTEN-USED YET imperfect metaphor that seeks to describe how the press and media operate in a democracy by providing distinct and frequently differing outlets for the discussion, debate, and resolution of ideas and issues. In the competition among various dimensions of political communication, the so-called marketplace becomes the principal forum for mass-mediated deliberation. How—and even whether—an idea or issue is perceived by the public is a consequence of what happens in the media marketplace, as messages gain acceptance, suffer rejection, or undergo modification in a continuing process of civic exchange.

History of the Metaphor

The concept of the marketplace originates in the agora, the place of congregation, in ancient Greece. The agora, typified by the heart of ancient Athens, was simultaneously the locus of commercial, political, administrative, social, religious, and cultural activity, and citizens freely participated in the range of activities. The modern conceptualization of the marketplace-of-ideas metaphor arose in the context of the democratic revolutions in Europe during the seventeenth and eighteenth centuries and followed development of fundamental economic ideas related to the effective workings of a marketplace for goods and services. The philosophical impetus for the marketplace concepts occurred when production and distribution of goods and services moved beyond the control of state authorities because of the decline of the feudal system and the development of economic systems that made the day-to-day commerce of mercantilism possible. These changes ultimately led to political, economic, and social developments that produced market economies and liberal democratic states.

A major tenet of market economies, explained by Adam Smith in his 1776 treatise *An Inquiry into the Nature and Causes of the Wealth of Nations*,[1] is that when producers and consumers engage in unrestrained competition among themselves, social and economic benefits will ensue. Thus constraints and controls on the market are generally undesirable because they preclude achievement of benefits. The development of the corollary concept of the marketplace for *ideas* grew from philosophers and others who challenged the continuation of the power of monarchies and the church to control political and social ideas and debates. They borrowed the idea of capitalist philosophers that there is an "unseen hand" of self-correcting elements in unfettered markets that ensures their effective operation, and transferred that concept to dissemination and discussion of ideas, arguing that broad social benefits are produced when information and expression of the independent ideas of citizens are permitted.

John Milton, who was actively seeking reform in the Church of England in the seventeenth century, wrote criticisms of the state-sanctioned church and its structures that were censored by the government. Subsequently he devised an impassioned plea for press freedom, *Areopagitica* (1644), which established the argument that truth will emerge in free and open discussions: "And though all the windes of doctrin were let loose to play upon the earth, so Truth be in the field, we do injuriously, by licencing and prohibiting to misdoubt her strength. Let her and Falshood grapple; who ever knew Truth put to the wors, in a free and open encounter."[2]

Milton's views were extended by the work of Jean-Jacques Rousseau, a major figure in the French Enlightenment, who argued that society was created by a social compact in which certain rights were surrendered to the general will in exchange for the protection and development of individuals. Rousseau argued that the institutions of government were not a party to the social compact but a creation of the compact, and that public opinion regarding government institutions should not be constrained, because they would lose the moral standing upon which they had been built.[3]

In the nineteenth century, the political economist and philosopher John Stuart Mill wrote extensively on governance and social and economic issues and articulated libertarian views toward free expression, arguing its centrality in democratic governance. Mill held that British laws on blasphemy and libel often inhibited expression in unwarranted fashion. Although Mill's views were similar to those of Milton on the struggle between truth and falsity, he did not believe that truth always triumphed. In *On Liberty*, Mill argued that the only legitimate reason for interfering in the liberty of others was to prevent harm to other persons, and that freedom of expression and disputes over ideas were helpful to society.[4] The nineteenth-century philosopher and economic historian Karl Marx extended the argument further by noting that social institutions under the control of the powerful—not merely government—could infringe on freedom of expression, and that a press free from all control over ideas was necessary.[5]

Since the democratic revolutions and the development of modern liberal democratic states, the primary efforts to free or preserve the marketplace of ideas have focused on halting governments from constraining information and dissemination of ideas necessary for individuals to play equal roles in determining the course of their lives and society. The concept of the marketplace of ideas as a means of protecting democracy and the public interest is now accepted as a major tenet of Western society.

Although the degree of protection against state control of the market in Western democratic societies has fluctuated at times, it is relatively well established, and the largest concerns in recent decades have resulted from economic controls over which only limited protections exist.

Although some observers attempt to make distinctions between the marketplace for goods and services and the marketplace of ideas, the Nobel Prize–winning economist Ronald H. Coase has argued that there is no valid distinction: "There is no fundamental difference between these two markets, and, in deciding on public policy with regard to them, we need to take into account the same considerations."[6] By marrying the different realms of the marketplace, it is easier to understand its workings and its functions—as well as its potential imperfections.

In the twenty-first century, the marketplace of ideas is generally seen to encompass those public spaces—including media—in which communication and discussion of ideas, public and social life, and developments in the larger world take place. Influences on the marketplace, specifically government and economic controls and internal, media-determined choices of information or ideas to amplify or exclude, affect the ability of the marketplace to connect political and social institutions and the public, and these can ultimately limit the effective functioning of the marketplace of ideas and knowledgeable participation in democratic society.

The American Marketplace

From the establishment of the United States, protections for the marketplace of ideas from political and legal interference have been provided. As the Constitution was debated, the lack of those protections led many citizens and colonies to seek its rejection until freedom of expression and religion were protected by the addition of the Bill of Rights. That provision has been the fundamental protection afforded to distribution and discussion of ideas, information, and broader array of expression throughout the history of the country.

"We live by symbols, and what shall be symbolized by any image of the sight depends upon the mind of him who sees it," Oliver Wendell Holmes Jr. observed in a 1901 speech honoring John Marshall.[7] Eighteen years later, in a dissent that proved more influential than the Supreme Court decision with which it took issue, Holmes created a symbol for the exchange of ideas that continues to shape the public's "image" and "mind" for determining the truth.

In *Abrams v. United States,* the court upheld the conviction of Jacob Abrams and other Russian immigrants for violating the Espionage Act of 1917 by printing and circulating leaflets in support of the Russian Revolution and the "workers of the world." The Espionage Act made it a crime to criticize the U.S. government; it issued from a post–World War I climate of fear in the United States spurred by the Communist takeover in Russia. After reviewing the facts of the case, Holmes in his dissent offered the logic of common sense: "Now nobody can suppose that the surreptitious publishing of a silly leaflet by an unknown man, without more, would present any immediate danger that its opinions would hinder the success of the Government arms or have any appreciable tendency to do so."[8] A few paragraphs later, Holmes criticized the punishment that Abrams and his codefendants received, but the argument became a more encompassing defense of the First Amendment: "In this case sentences of twenty years' imprisonment have been imposed for the publishing of two leaflets that I believe the defendants had as much right to publish as the Government has to publish the Constitution of the United States now vainly invoked by them."[9]

From the specifics of this particular case, with those sentenced described as "poor and puny anonymities," Holmes broadened his thinking in language that still echoes and with a symbol that endures:

> When men have realized that time has upset many fighting faiths, they may come to believe even more than they believe the very foundations of their own conduct that the ultimate good desired is better reached by free trade in ideas—that the best test of truth is the power of the thought to get itself accepted in the competition of the market, and that truth is the only ground upon which their wishes safely can be carried out. That, at any rate, is the theory of our Constitution. It is an experiment, as all life is an experiment.[10]

A ringing yet realistic endorsement of free speech in America, Holmes's dissent served a larger philosophical and practical purpose. Noting the "ultimate good" that derives from a "free trade in ideas," he used symbolism that participants in an economic system based on free enterprise would readily understand: "The best test of truth is the power of the thought to get itself accepted in the competition of the market."

Whereas John Milton in *Areopagitica* envisioned the emergence of "Truth" resulting from a constant battle with "Falsehood" during "free and open encounter," Holmes proposed a metaphor with indigenous American resonance—and ironic invocation, given the Bolshevik sympathies of Abrams and his fellow defendants. The image of a "marketplace of ideas," with endless testing to determine and yield the truth, took root in legal theory, practice, and scholarship as one way of approaching contesting viewpoints that offer radically different perspectives or types of information. Calling the dissent "one of the central organizing pronouncements for our contemporary vision of free speech," Lee C. Bollinger has noted: "If we may borrow a metaphor from the Enlightenment figure Adam Smith, Holmes may be read as suggesting the presence of an unseen hand that guides truth to victory over the challenge of falsity."[11]

The world of jurisprudence, however, was not the only audience for the Abrams dissent. In *The Mind and Faith of Justice Holmes,* Max Lerner called what Holmes wrote "the greatest utterance on intellectual freedom by an American, ranking in the English tongue with Milton and Mill."[12] Over the years, the symbol Holmes introduced has taken on a life of its own, with relevance and application outside the law. Most particularly, the media (broadly defined) are now considered the primary "marketplace of ideas" in the United States, the forum in which truth, falsehood, and every expression in between compete for acceptance and approval. Enduring as the symbol might be, it too is the subject of continuing debate, as "the competition of the market" becomes more intense in a rapidly changing communications environment. Whether Smith's "unseen hand" operates, let alone exists, in this ever fragmenting, content-multiplying, message-blurring world is a prime question in evaluating the merit of the marketplace metaphor.

To understand the historical context, the Abrams case revolved around two crudely printed leaflets, one in English and the other in Yiddish, haphazardly circulated in New York City in 1918. A year later, when the Supreme Court rendered its decision, there were 2,343 daily newspapers in the United States and 13,964 weeklies, according to the *American Newspaper Annual and Directory* assembled by N. W. Ayer & Son. To be sure, significant magazines—*Harper's,* the *Atlantic Monthly, McClure's, Collier's,* the *New Republic*—circulated at the time, but *Time, Newsweek,* and *U.S. News & World Report* did not begin publishing until years later. Primitive silent newsreels had started to play in movie houses in 1911; however, more immediate radio news would take its first halting steps in 1920 before its rapid development later in that decade. Television news, of course, was decades away.

Contrast the environment for information and ideas then with what exists at the beginning of the twenty-first century. The number of newspapers has decreased—down (in the statistics of *Editor & Publisher*) to 1,457 daily newspapers and 6,699 weeklies in 2002—but other (and newer) outlets grow, as each discovery in message transmission becomes technologically possible. Besides the wealth of ink-on-page publications—including 17,321 magazines in 2002 as counted by the *National Directory of Magazines*—all-news and discussion radio operations, 24-7 television news networks, Internet sites, and Web logs compete for a citizen's attention and time. Free speech is less of a concern than figuring out how to be heard above the din of rapidly circulating messages coming from every direction. A couple of pamphlets causing a stir and triggering a case that goes to the Supreme Court might strike some as ludicrously anachronistic today.

Modern Context

Information and ideas are now by and large the province of a modern communications system that is technologically tied together via computers, satellites, cable, and other wondrous inventions. As the means of circulation revolve around "the media" (in that catchall term), other factors come into play that affect and even shape the messages these media deliver. At about the same time Holmes was coining his metaphor, two related phenomena were starting to influence what the different forms of communication transmitted to their audiences.

Public relations and propaganda had existed as undefined, inchoate undertakings for centuries of human conduct; however, the second decade of the twentieth century brought both forms of publicity seeking to the fore. With public relations usually a force in the corporate world and propaganda principally associated with governmental information, both ways of gaining attention shared a similar point of view. In each case, a crafted, deliberate message sought what might be called opinion advantage. Stories that the public read in a newspaper or magazine were more likely to include information or ideas provided by someone other than the journalist, and the added material had a specific purpose that did not necessarily assist the people in determining truth from falsehood.[13]

As years passed and as sources of information proliferated, public relations and propaganda evolved in sophistication and style. The words *image* and *spin* entered daily parlance, and in both cases manipulated messages were involved. Communication sources had to contend with a steady stream of press releases or coverage-choreographed activities that emphasized what people outside of journalism wanted the public to perceive as news. By 1980 Sidney Blumenthal could survey the influence of political consultants and image-makers on American democracy and call what he saw (in the title of a book) *The Permanent Campaign*. From his reporting and analysis, Blumenthal made the case that traditional governing was no longer the consequence or purpose of electoral victory. The echo chamber of multiple communication outlets now placed a premium on the stagecraft of statecraft, and official business often resembled activities previously associated with running for office—rather than serving in office. In a small irony of history, Blumenthal left journalism in 1997 to become an advisor to then-president Bill Clinton. Blumenthal's White House memoirs, *The Clinton Wars* (2003), is an insider's look at "the permanent campaign" that helped keep Clinton president, despite impeachment and other efforts to weaken his authority.

The burgeoning volume of messages—many that originate to promote a person, cause, or organization—means that the marketplace of ideas includes patently biased information that a citizen must judge for its value in forming an opinion or making a decision. In this regard, Walter Lippmann's distinction between news and truth, articulated in *Public Opinion* (1922), remains pertinent: "News and truth are not the same thing, and must be clearly distinguished. The function of news is to signalize an event, the function of truth is to bring to light the hidden facts, to set them into relation with each other, and make a picture of reality on which men can act."[14]

Questions and Problems

A serious problem arises, however, when the news signalizing an event or initiative is itself at several removes from being remotely truthful. In this case, the marketplace of ideas is trading in misinformation that ultimately could be more influential and opinion shaping than what is subsequently revealed to be the accurate and authoritative accounting of an activity. These circumstances can draw into question the ultimate value of Holmes's metaphor and the logic of thinking that the media are the most appropriate place to look for truth—or even ideas that deserve scrutiny.

In a more limited marketplace, one with relatively few sources of ideas and information, trying to establish truth from falsehood is never simple, but the process of discovery is more manageable. However, when the metaphorical marketplace resembles something akin to the Mall of America, with its 4.2 million square feet of competing commerce, a person is forced to work harder to discover exactly what she or he wants.

Today the media marketplace is so cluttered with messages, and they circulate with such rapidity, that the belief of Milton or Holmes in a self-righting principle that yields truth is not only chancy but also doubtful. Exactly four decades after Holmes took his stand, Isaiah Berlin challenged the premise that falsehood is always vanquished in truth's struggle with opposing forces over enlightenment: "These are brave and optimistic judgments, but how good is the empirical evidence for them today? Are demagogues and liars, scoundrels and blind fanatics, always, in liberal societies, stopped in time, or refuted in the end? How high a price is it right to pay for the great boon of freedom of discussion?"[15]

These questions take on even greater meaning and pertinence today than when they were first posed in 1959, and they challenge whichever metaphor for a process to truth and understanding that might arise—marketplace, forum, or arena. The accelerated news cycle that now operates in a technological environment rich in communication options is far from deliberate in getting to the bottom of stories with conflicting information. Indeed, with political subjects of a highly partisan nature, charge and countercharge often compete for attention and acceptance. Reluctant to be perceived as taking sides, journalists leave such stories unresolved, and the public is never quite sure whose "spin"—if anyone's—is located in closest proximity to the truth. Another consequence of a constantly changing news cycle is that a story will receive some coverage, but then quickly vanish without the necessary follow-up reporting that the citizenry requires in order to gain an understanding of the larger implications of the original story.

Each metaphor—marketplace, forum, arena—evokes different realms of competition: economic, rhetorical, athletic. Although the concept of a forum is probably most appropriate to an environment of intellectual exchange, core concerns connect these three metaphors. Which messages receive the most circulation, attention, and acceptance? Why do certain messages stand out from the others? What impact do these messages have on opinion-shaping elites and the public at large? Who benefits the most as the process of competition plays out, and how fair (if not moral) is the contest? What are the results or final outcome as the interplay concludes, and to what extent were fairness and morality even factors in the ultimate resolution? Although parallel arguments could arise in discussing a forum or an arena, in terms of philosophical heritage and influence, the notion of the marketplace still commands the most scrutiny and inquiry, justifying such sustained probing.

The marketplace metaphor is somewhat dubious in the modern media environment because there is an implicit assumption that everyone constituting the public will be able to evaluate the competing messages in a discriminating way and that elements of the truth—leading to a more encompassing sense of "truth"—exist in those same competing messages. Today's reality, however, divides people into idea and information haves and have-nots, with such factors as economic status and educational background significant to whether a citizen has the wherewithal to participate fully in the marketplace of ideas. This reality is compounded by problems of information "wants" and "want nots." Society is increasingly witnessing large portions of the population choosing to avoid the marketplace of ideas and flee the flood of information that is increasingly rising in the modern communications environment. The phenomenon, however, does *not* mean that the marketplace ceases to function. Just as the economic marketplace follows its course without full public participation, the marketplace of ideas operates and resolves its concerns without the entire polity being closely engaged in all of its deliberations.

Media Ownership and the Marketplace

The diversity and variability in access to the media stand in stark juxtaposition to what some observers, with justification, see as message homogeneity that results from the concentration of ownership across commercial communications. Without competition from equivalent—or at least evenly matched—messengers, is it possible to examine all sides of a topic in a fair, discriminating way? Do the large, mainstream media tend to drown out the smaller tributaries of information? Needless to say, all ideas are not created equally, and they are not circulated with the same force or intensity.

For decades, Ben H. Bagdikian, former dean of the Graduate School of Journalism at the University of California at Berkeley, has persistently warned readers of his books and articles that fewer and fewer corporations are responsible for the content of more and more media outlets. His study *The Media Monopoly* was in its sixth edition in 2000, and with each revision, ownership concentration becomes more pronounced. In the preface to the fifth edition, published in 1997, he noted: "With each passing year . . . the number of controlling firms in all these media [newspapers, magazines, radio, television, books, and movies] has shrunk: from fifty corporations in 1984 to twenty-six in 1987, followed by twenty-three in 1990, and then, as the borders between the different media began to blur, to less than twenty in 1993. In 1996 the number of media corporations with dominant power in society is closer to ten."[16] The opening paragraph to the sixth edition is even more starkly threatening: "As the United States enters the twenty-first century, power over the American mass media is flowing to the top with such devouring speed that it exceeds even the accelerated consolidations of the last twenty years. For the first time in U.S. history, the country's most widespread news, commentary, and daily entertainment are controlled by six firms that are among the world's largest corporations, two of them foreign."[17]

Consolidation in newspapers and magazines continues apace, with such companies as Gannett operating one hundred papers and Knight Ridder over thirty. As the Federal Communications Commission eases restrictions on the purchase of television and radio stations, the number of owners is declining as the holdings of the largest, wealthiest companies increase. In recent years, Clear Channel Communications has acquired more than 1,200 U.S. radio stations, about 9 percent of all outlets. Numbers, of course, tell only part of the story. In an essay for the *Journal of Communication,* in a special section titled "The Marketplace of Ideas Revisited," Bagdikian argued: "The media marketplace of ideas cannot be measured by its size and technological virtuosity. Blandness and noise do not constitute ideas and information. When instruments of narrow ideas and triviality have sufficient power, they drown out lesser voices and discourage thought. The existence of lesser voices does not, by itself, relieve responsibility of the major media. Today the smaller voices have less access than ever to the major media: the usual saving remnant of small voices is less audible than ever."[18]

Although consolidation is significant, it alone is not the root of the problems with the marketplace of ideas. In the 1950s, 68 percent of homes in the United States received 3 or fewer television channels. By the late 1990s, 97 percent of homes received more than 30 channels. The number of national cable television channels available in the United States exploded from 27 in 1980 to 208 in 1995. The result of these changes and the rise of other terrestrial channels was that the three dominant national channels that received combined overall ratings of about 90 percent in the 1970s saw their combined ratings drop to 25 percent by 2001.

The examples of two firms that are often cited as poster children of the concentration problem, the Walt Disney Company and Viacom, reveal the limits of consolidation as the root of the problem. In the 1970s, American Broadcasting Company (ABC) had an average audience rating of between 25 and 30 percent each year. In 2004 ABC was owned by the Walt Disney Company, along with the Disney Channel, ESPN networks, ABC Family Network, SOAPnet, and Toon Disney, but the combined annual average television ratings for all of Disney's holdings had fallen to about 15 percent, about half what they were thirty years previous for ABC alone. Similarly, Columbia Broadcasting System (CBS) operated a single network in 1989 and achieved an annual average rating of 21 percent. By 1999, CBS was owned by Viacom along with seven other cable networks, including MTV, Nickelodeon, TV Land, TNN, and CMT, but the annual average ratings for all of the networks combined was just 21.2 percent.

One must also recognize that media companies really are not as big as people like to think them to be. If one considers the rankings of the top 2,000 companies in the world in 2002 (the overall rankings combine sales, profits, assets, and market value), one finds that there were no media companies among the top 50 firms. In fact, only 3 media firms (Viacom, Disney, and Clear Channel Communications) were in the top 250 firms in 2000 and only 1 percent of the top 2,000 firms were media companies.[19] Media firms are not monolithic organizations in terms of business size, and even the largest are ten to twenty times smaller than the world's leading firms from other industries.

The root of the marketplace-of-ideas problem, then, is not merely growth in the size of firms and consolidation into fewer firms, but how they approach content, opinion, and public needs when their primary motives are commercial and driven by financial-performance concerns.[20] It is their activities that overwhelm the communications marketplace with commercially viable and profitable entertaining content that are limiting the effectiveness of the marketplace of ideas.

New Technologies

To a certain extent, the Internet—with its capability for individual sites and Web logs—enlarges the marketplace, allowing people of limited means to post messages of their choosing to a potentially wide audience. In most cases, however, personal Web sites most closely parallel the pamphlets Abrams printed and distributed in 1918. Except in rare cases (the Drudge Report, Instapundit, the Kaus Files), singular, Internet-based communication is a modern form of free expression that often does more to satisfy the creator than to enlighten the citizenry.

Theoretically, however, the Internet does indeed offer a citizen greater access to ideas and information than the traditional outlets of what Bagdikian and others refer to as "the major media." Google and other search engines can target particular subjects for consideration, and a wealth of diverse material becomes available. At several Web sites maintained by mainstream, traditional journalistic outlets, it is possible to probe much more deeply into an issue by studying the entire transcripts of press conferences and interviews or the complete background documentation provided by a governmental agency or a research organization. To be sure, a considerable amount of unsubstantiated nonsense circulates in cyberspace, but a conscientious citizen—by analyzing a multitude of sources about what is presented concerning a particular subject—can usually distinguish between bona fide and bogus information.

Taking advantage of the availability of such detail, however, requires individual action and the explicit seeking of specific messages. The communications environment is now fragmented to the extent that it is much less possible to assume that the majority of the public shares a common body of information at any given time. Ensuring civic awareness of depth or seriousness demands a personal search of multiple sources, whether traditional or new, whether print, broadcast, electronic, or digital.

The media world of the twenty-first century is so vastly different from even a few decades ago—before CNN developed in the 1980s and the Internet flowered in the 1990s—that the relationship between the citizen and communication sources must be rethought. A passive connection is no longer possible, if someone desires a complete picture of a subject. Moreover, the symbol of the marketplace of ideas, with its idealistic appeal of eventually trading in truth, deserves reconsideration in light of current realities—and Holmes's own cautionary qualifications. In the *Abrams* dissent, Holmes noted that "all life is an experiment. Every year if not every day we have to wager our salvation upon some prophecy based upon imperfect knowledge." Suggesting the experimental and imperfect nature of the marketplace tempers the unrealistic fantasy that truth perforce will always emerge when ideas and information clash in the arena of contemporary communications. As Erik Åsard and W. Lance Bennett observe in *Democracy and the Marketplace of Ideas,* "Looking at how institutions shape and are shaped by ideas allows us to see the irony of a marketplace that is not moved by some hidden hand of rationality but, like the economic marketplace from which we derive our framework, can produce various unintended consequences, inefficiencies, and breakdowns despite efforts at rational institutional reform and regulation."[21]

Although we might "live by symbols," as Holmes thought, a symbol can endanger the public's understanding of a process or a subject if it exists untethered or removed from the reality it seeks to illuminate. For the marketplace of ideas to continue to have symbolic power and meaning in the modern communications environment of multiple media and messages without end, the lone, searching individual will need to discover, in a consciously deliberate way, the ideas and information that approximate the truth, from the perspective of a citizen-seeker.

That concept, in itself, might seem unrealistic—and almost as idealistic as the metaphor Holmes introduced—but it is what our experimental and imperfect times require.

Conclusion

The marketplace of ideas is endangered because its primary mediated locations are becoming dominated by the commercial marketplace for entertainment and by communications designed to support the marketplace for goods and services. As a result, contemporary arguments are on the rise that the Miltonian idea of truth ultimately triumphing in the marketplace of ideas may not be applicable if commercial media enterprises constrain the marketplace by their size and activities, by limiting who may introduce ideas and information, and by the range and scope of ideas, information, and discussion available.

Many social observers are no longer content with protections merely against governmental controls but are seeking legal and policy remedies for the economic constraints on the marketplace of ideas. It must be recognized, however, that many of the problems that critics associate with media consolidation and concentration—such as insipid programs, endless reruns, emphasis on fleeting celebrity, globalized content, and homogenization of ideas and opinions—result not from the structure of media and media firms, but rather from rampant commercialism and underlying changes in the economics of media that remove incentives for many firms to make expenditures for costly and less profitable content that serves the marketplace of ideas.

This is not to indicate that there are not significant concerns over consolidation and concentration. There clearly are media firms that use the advantages of multiple platforms created through consolidation to promote the political and social views of their owners, to engage in cross-promotion, to exclude competitors from access to systems of distribution, and to control price and output to the detriment of consumers. But the majority of constraints on the marketplace of ideas occur merely because that marketplace is ignored by commercial firms, or because these firms carry only those dominant ideas that will not harm their activities in the commercial marketplace. It has been noted that "even strong commercialized media companies fear the controversial. Stories that may offend audiences are ignored in favor of those that are more acceptable and entertaining. Stories that are costly to cover are generally ignored. When stories being covered created financial risks, even large firms may back away."[22]

If this unsatisfactory situation is to be overcome, media personnel and the public both must learn to behave in a manner that supports activities in the marketplace of ideas and the flow of information. Indeed, public policies in the twenty-first century will need to simultaneously control concentration, promote new competition, and counter commercialism to encourage and support the establishment of additional media, to ensure access for nonmainstream voices, and to promote alternative means of coverage of social and political issues.

Private media companies, like all corporations, exist primarily to serve the economic self-interest of their owners. Society must ensure that such self-interest does not continue to result in the types of harm that media consolidation and commercialism are producing. Unless we do more than merely halt additional consolidation and redress damage being done by concentration and commercialism, the situation will not improve and complaints about limits on the marketplace of ideas posed by the contemporary media system will continue.

Despite warranted and tough-minded reservations, it makes little intellectual sense to reject the metaphor outright. The process *can* work—as long as certain institutional and individual characteristics and properties exist. Near the end of *Who Deliberates?* Benjamin I. Page states:

> Classic liberals like John Stuart Mill and Oliver Wendell Holmes may have been correct: the marketplace of ideas actually works reasonably well, most of the time, so long as there is sufficient competition and diversity in the information system. Competition is a powerful force; true and useful ideas, once they are enunciated somewhere, have a way of spreading, willy-nilly, everywhere. Ideas that originate in relatively obscure places—in research organizations, tiny 'zines, or small-circulation journals—diffuse through word of mouth, the Internet, talk radio, and the like, and often leak into the mainstream media.[23]

"Competition" and "diversity," as they continuingly and conscientiously deal with political ideas and issues, are critical for the marketplace to operate effectively—and a citizen, too, must constantly wrestle with, in Page's recurring phrase, "mediated deliberation" to arrive at some proximity to the truth that a democracy requires for informed and purposeful self-governance.

Notes

1. Adam Smith, *An Inquiry into the Nature and Causes of the Wealth of Nations: A Selected Edition,* edited by Kathryn Sutherland (Oxford, U.K., and New York: Oxford University Press, 1998.)
2. John Milton, *Areopagitica: A Speech for the Liberty of Unlicensed Printing,* edited by H. B. Cotterill (New York: Macmillan, 1905; repr. 1959), 45.
3. Jean-Jacques Rousseau, *The Social Contract,* translated by Maurice Cranston (New York: Penguin, 1987).
4. John Stuart Mill, *On Liberty,* edited by Gertrude Himmelfarb (New York: Viking, 1982).
5. Karl Marx, *Rheinische Zeitung* 135 (May 15, 1842), supplement.
6. R. H. Coase, "The Economics of the First Amendment: The Market for Goods and the Market for Ideas," *American Economic Review* 64 (May 1974): 389.

7. Oliver Wendell Holmes, *Collected Legal Papers* (New York: Harcourt, Brace and Howe, 1920), 270.
8. "Two Leaflets and an Experiment," in *The Mind and Faith of Justice Holmes: His Speeches, Essays, Letters, and Judicial Opinions,* edited by Max Lerner (New York: Modern Library, 1954), 310.
9. Ibid., 311.
10. Ibid., 312.
11. Lee C. Bollinger, *The Tolerant Society: Freedom of Speech and Extremist Speech in America* (New York: Oxford University Press, 1986), 59.
12. Lerner, *The Mind and Faith of Justice Holmes,* 306.
13. For enlightening background about the development of public relations, see Stuart Ewen, *PR!: A Social History of Spin* (New York: Basic, 1996).
14. Walter Lippmann, *Public Opinion* (New York: Harcourt, Brace, 1922), 358.
15. Isaiah Berlin, "John Stuart Mill and the Ends of Life," in *Four Essays on Liberty* (London and New York: Oxford University Press, 1969), 187–88.
16. Ben H. Bagdikian, "Preface to the Fifth Edition: The New Communications Cartel," in *The Media Monopoly,* 5th ed. (Boston: Beacon, 1997); reprinted in *News: A Reader,* edited by Howard Tumber (Oxford, U.K., and New York: Oxford University Press, 1999), 150–51.
17. Ben H. Bagdikian, *The Media Monopoly,* 6th ed. (Boston: Beacon, 2000), viii.
18. Ben H. Bagdikian, "The U.S. Media: Supermarket or Assembly Line?" *Journal of Communication* (summer 1985): 109.
19. Forbes Global 2000 (2003), available at: http://www.forbes.com/2003/07/02/internationaland.html.
20. Robert G. Picard, "Delusions of Grandeur: The Real Problems of Concentration in Media," in *Global Media News Reader,* edited by David Demers, 33–48 (Spokane, Wash.: Marquette, 2002).
21. Erik Åsard and W. Lance Bennett, *Democracy and the Marketplace of Ideas: Communication and Government in Sweden and the United States* (Cambridge, U.K., and New York: Cambridge University Press, 1997), 46.
22. Robert G. Picard, "Media Concentration, Economics, and Regulation," in *The Politics of News: The News of Politics,* edited by Doris Graber, Denis McQuail, and Pippa Norris, 193–217 (Washington, D.C.: Congressional Quarterly Press, 1998).
23. Benjamin I. Page, *Who Deliberates?: Mass Media in Modern Democracy* (Chicago: University of Chicago Press, 1996), 123–24.

Bibliography

Altschull, J. Herbert. *From Milton to McLuhan: The Ideas behind American Journalism.* New York: Longman, 1990. An analysis of the concepts that shape news, including "the marketplace of ideas."

Auletta, Ken. *Backstory: Inside the Business of News.* New York: The Penguin Press, 2003. Probing reportage that helps explain the current journalistic landscape, its possibilities, and its problems.

Bagdikian, Ben H. *The New Media Monopoly*. Boston: Beacon, 2004. Inquiry into the consequences of corporate concentration on the media's messages.

Blumenthal, Sidney. *The Permanent Campaign*, rev. ed. New York: Simon and Schuster, 1982. How political communicators influence the media and public life.

Czitrom, Daniel J. *Media and the American Mind: From Morse to McLuhan*. Chapel Hill: University of North Carolina Press, 1982. A study of the development and significance of communications in the United States.

Emerson, Thomas I. *The System of Freedom of Expression*. New York: Random House, 1970.

Ewen, Stuart. *PR! A Social History of Spin*. New York: Basic Books, 1996. Detailed exposition on the growth of public relations and the role of "spin" in American journalism.

Fallows, James. *Breaking the News: How the Media Undermine American Democracy*. New York: Pantheon Books, 1996. Trenchant criticism of media performance and questioning of the contemporary marketplace.

Fraleigh, Douglas M., and Joseph S. Truman. *Freedom of Speech in the Marketplace of Ideas*. New York: St. Martin's Press, 1997.

Kovach, Bill, and Tom Rosenstiel. *Warp Speed: America in the Age of Mixed Media*. New York: The Century Foundation, 1999. An examination of the Clinton-Lewinsky story and how it was handled (and mishandled) by the ever-expanding media universe.

Lippmann, Walter. *Public Opinion*. New York: Harcourt, Brace and Company, 1922. Classic work about journalism, its role, and its effects.

Menand, Louis. *The Marketplace of Ideas*. New York: American Council of Learned Societies, 2001.

Schmuhl, Robert. *Statecraft and Stagecraft: American Political Life in the Age of Personality*, 2nd ed. Notre Dame, Ind.: University of Notre Dame Press, 1992. Analysis of the intertwining of governance, politics, and the media and what that means to the media marketplace and public understanding.

9

THE AGENDA-SETTING FUNCTION
OF THE PRESS

Maxwell McCombs

T HE PRESS PLAYS A MAJOR ROLE IN PUBLIC LIFE, INFLU-
encing citizens' focus of attention and providing many of the facts and
opinions that shape perspectives on the topics of the day. Beyond learning specific bits of information from the press, the public and policy makers in
government at all levels also receive subtle but powerful messages about what is
really important in the vast realm of public affairs. The result over time is that
those aspects of public affairs that are prominent in the press frequently become
prominent among the public and among government officials. This ability to
focus attention on a few public issues—as well as many other aspects of public
affairs—is the agenda–setting role of the press.

What Is an Agenda?

The term *agenda* is not used here in the pejorative sense of "having an agenda," a
premeditated set of priorities. The agenda-setting role of the press is the inadver-
tent outcome of the necessity of the news media, with their limited capacity, to
select a few topics for attention each day. *Agenda* is strictly a descriptive term for
a prioritized list of items, the major topics found in newspapers, television news
programs, and other mass media messages, for example, or those topics that the
public and policy makers regard as important. Reviewing the front pages of a
newspaper over a period of time will reveal that newspaper's agenda. Some issues
receive prominent play across many days. Others are there some of the time;
many appear only on occasion. Additional information about the position of
issues on the newspaper agenda is provided by such cues as the size of headlines
for individual articles, the length of articles, and the page numbers on which articles appear. There are similar patterns of coverage—and cues about the relative
importance of issues—in television news programs and other mass media. The

precise rank-order of public issues on these press agendas can be determined through systematic content analyses.

The public agenda is usually measured through survey research. Using a question developed by the Gallup Poll in the 1930s, public opinion pollsters ask, "What is the most important problem facing this country today?" The percentage of the public who nominate individual issues provides a succinct summary of the public agenda, and the issues can be ranked according to these percentages.

The agenda of policy makers in government can be measured by their activities and communications. The agenda of the president is revealed by the amount of attention devoted to various issues in his speeches. Congress's agenda can be measured by the number of committee hearings on various issues. And the Supreme Court's agenda is reflected in the docket of cases accepted for review.

Evolution of Agenda-Setting Theory

Hundreds of empirical studies worldwide on the agenda-setting influence of the press have compared the rank-order of issues on the press agenda with the rank-order of those same issues on the public agenda. There have been fewer comparisons of the press agenda with the agenda of policy makers. However, the vast majority of all these studies have found a high degree of correspondence between how issues are ranked on the press agenda and the agendas of the public and policy makers. These studies also report causal evidence that the pattern of emphasis on issues in the news is a major determinant of the subsequent importance accorded those issues by the public and by policy makers.

This idea of an agenda-setting role of the press has its origins in Walter Lippmann's *Public Opinion* (1922), which begins with a chapter titled "The World Outside and the Pictures in Our Heads." Lippmann argued that the press is a major contributor to those pictures in our heads, our mental conceptions of the larger world of public affairs that we never directly experience. Furthermore, Lippmann asserted that behavior is a response to these limited pictures of the world that we come to regard as the real world, rather than to the larger environment beyond our ken. He did not use the term "agenda setting" for this influence of the press, however, and many decades passed before his idea was subjected to empirical test.

During the 1968 U.S. presidential campaign, a seminal study of agenda setting in Chapel Hill, North Carolina, compared the agenda of issues in nine news media used by voters there to follow the election—a mix of local and elite national newspapers, network television news, and news magazines—with the agenda of issues subsequently regarded as important by those voters.[1] The authors of the study, Maxwell McCombs and Donald Shaw, found a nearly perfect correspondence between the ranking of major issues on the press and public agendas, and used the term *agenda setting* to describe this relationship.

The Chapel Hill study focused on undecided voters, because the prevailing view at the time was that media had only weak effects on voters, an outcome explained by the concept of selective perception, the idea that people primarily attend to political messages in the press that are supportive of their views and ignore those that are not in line with their opinions. McCombs and Shaw thought that whatever influence the media might have on voters, it would be strongest among undecided voters, persons interested in the election but not yet committed to a candidate.

To further test agenda setting's assertion of strong media effects, comparisons were made between the agenda-setting relationship—the correspondence between the public agenda and the agenda of issues found in the total news coverage—and the selective-perception relationship—the correspondence between the public agenda and the agenda of issues based on the news coverage of voters' preferred party. In the vast majority of cases, the agenda-setting relationship was stronger than the selective-perception relationship.

This initial evidence from Chapel Hill about the agenda-setting influence of the media among undecided voters was expanded by major panel studies in the next two presidential elections. During the summer and fall of 1972, three waves of interviewing measured the public agenda among a representative sample of voters in Charlotte, North Carolina. Shaw and McCombs's comparisons of this evolving public agenda with media agendas based on the local newspaper and network television news again documented significant agenda-setting effects. During the 1976 presidential election, panels of voters in three diverse communities—Lebanon, New Hampshire; Indianapolis, Indiana; and Evanston, Illinois—were interviewed nine times between February and December. Comparisons of these public agendas with the local newspapers and the national television networks by David Weaver and his colleagues also documented agenda-setting effects, especially during the spring primaries.[2]

In the years since these benchmark election studies, the agenda-setting influence of the press has been widely studied, both in election and nonelection settings, for a broad range of public issues, and beyond the United States, across Eurasia, Latin America, and Australia. As the press expanded to include online newspapers available on the Web, agenda-setting effects have been documented for these new media. In turn, the agenda-setting influence of traditional news media on Internet chat room discussions also has been documented.

This vast array of empirical evidence documents a powerful press influence on an initial step in the formation of public opinion, the focus of public attention. This influence is on the salience, the importance or prominence, of issues and other topics in the news, not on attitudes and opinions, which were the principal focus of media-effects research in the 1940s and 1950s. The core idea of agenda setting is the transfer of salience from one agenda to another agenda. As shown below, this core idea also can be applied in other settings—including the relationship between the press and policy makers—and does have significant implications for attitudes and opinions.

How Agenda Setting Works

The agenda-setting influence of the press results in large measure from the repetition of the major issues in the news day after day. The public learns about the issues on the press agenda with little effort on their part, and considering the incidental nature of this learning, issues move rather quickly from the press agenda to the public agenda. Harold Zucker found that public concern about three major issues across the 1960s and 1970s—pollution, drugs, and energy—reflected the network television agenda of the preceding month. An examination of civil rights coverage in the *New York Times* across a twenty-three-year period by James Winter and Chaim Eyal also found agenda-setting effects within a month.[3]

There are, of course, variations among individuals and across issues. Under conditions of high personal involvement, issue salience on the press agenda may transfer very quickly to the public agenda. During the 1996 presidential election, Marilyn Roberts and colleagues found that the salience of immigration, taxes, and health care on electronic bulletin boards reflected the press coverage of these issues within the past few days.[4] And sometimes the public ignores the press. Despite news coverage that has been described as "All Monica, all the time," the majority of Americans never accepted the Monica Lewinsky sex scandal that plagued the second term of President Bill Clinton as a major public issue.

Individual differences in responses to the press agenda are explained by the concept of need for orientation, the idea that individuals have an innate curiosity about the world around them. For a wide variety of public affairs topics, the news media provide this orientation. A person's level of need for orientation is defined by two components, relevance and uncertainty. The relevance to an individual of news coverage on public affairs depends on his or her level of interest in those topics. If a topic has low relevance, then that person's need for orientation is low. If the relevance is high, but uncertainty is low—the person knows as much as he or she wants to know about the topic—the need for orientation is moderate. If both relevance and uncertainty are high, the need for orientation is high. Both use of the press to follow public affairs as well as acceptance of the press agenda generally increase with rising levels of need for orientation.

Another way of thinking about how individuals respond to the press agenda is to locate public issues along a continuum ranging from obtrusive to unobtrusive. Obtrusive issues, such as inflation, are those that people encounter in their everyday lives. Unobtrusive issues, such as wars in distant places and abstract issues like budget deficits, are those beyond individuals' personal experience. For these unobtrusive issues, the press is the citizenry's principal source of information and enjoys considerable influence. Although for the public as a whole, most issues fall predominantly at one end of this continuum or the other, some issues that selectively affect individuals, such as unemployment, are in the middle of the continuum. Here the aggregate agenda-setting effects of the press are moderate.

Due to limited space in newspapers and limited time on television, agenda-setting effects center on five or fewer—usually fewer—issues at any moment. Moreover, there is a historical redundancy in the public agenda, such that a few issues have defined the major trends in American public opinion. In the 1940s and 1950s foreign affairs and economics dominated the public agenda. In the 1960s civil rights rose to prominence. Only in the final decades of the twentieth century did a handful of other issues gain positions on the public agenda because of the tendency of issues to move on and off the agenda faster than in previous times. This increased volatility of the public agenda is the result of a collision between limited agenda capacity and vastly increased levels of education, which expanded the number of issues with resonance for the American public.

For a wide variety of media effects, there has been long-standing curiosity about the comparative impact of newspapers and television. For agenda-setting effects, a rough rule of thumb is that about half the time, there is no difference in the influence of newspapers and television. For the other half of the time, newspapers have greater influence about twice as often as television. There are two ready explanations for this contradiction of the conventional wisdom about the power of television. First, television news is analogous to the opening pages of the newspapers, which means that newspaper readers frequently have a longer time to learn the emerging issue agenda. Second, citizens in many countries are aware that television is under a significant degree of influence from the government or a dominant political party. Under both of these circumstances, newspapers will exert a greater influence on the public agenda.

Levels of Agenda-Setting Influence

On balance, the press has a great ability to focus public attention, albeit not all media on all issues among all citizens. Moreover, the press is not only frequently successful in telling us *what* to think about, the press also is frequently successful in telling us *how* to think about it. The agenda-setting influence of the press operates at two sequential levels in the communication process: attention and comprehension.

At the level of attention, agendas are defined by a set of objects. Most frequently in the empirical research on agenda setting, these objects are public issues, but they can be public figures, institutions, or anything else that is the focus of attention. The term *object* is used here in the same way that social psychology uses the phrase *attitude object* to designate the thing that an individual has an attitude or opinion about.

In turn, these objects have attributes, a variety of characteristics and traits that describe them. When the press talks about an object—and when members of the public talk and think about an object—they also *characterize* the object. Some attributes are emphasized, others are mentioned only in passing. For each object on the agenda, there is an agenda of attributes. Analysis of how these objects are described in the press and by the public can establish a precise ranking of their attributes. In turn, these rankings on each agenda can be compared to determine the strength of the press's attribute-agenda-setting effects on the public.

This distinction between agendas of objects, the first level of agenda–setting effects, and agendas of attributes, the second level of agenda–setting effects, is intuitively clear in an election setting. The candidates seeking an office are the agenda of objects. The descriptions of each candidate in the press and the images of these candidates in voters' minds are the agendas of attributes. Attribute agenda setting is the influence of the descriptions in the press on the public's images of the candidates.

Evidence of attribute agenda setting was found by Lee Becker and McCombs during the 1976 presidential primaries, when eleven Democrats competed for their party's nomination. Comparison of New York Democrats' descriptions of these candidates with the press agenda of attributes found significant evidence of press influence. Moreover, the correspondence between the press agenda and voters' agendas of attributes increased from mid-February to late March as the New York primary approached. Voters not only learned the press agenda, but additional exposure to the press brought greater learning.[5]

Jimmy Carter emerged from the primaries to challenge the incumbent Republican president Gerald Ford, and Weaver and his colleagues found additional evidence of attribute agenda setting during the fall campaign. There was a high degree of correspondence between the agenda of candidate attributes in the *Chicago Tribune* and Illinois voters' descriptions of Carter and Ford. More recently, similar comparisons of voters' images of candidates with both news coverage and political advertising have found attribute-agenda-setting effects in settings as diverse as regional and national elections in Spain and mayoral elections in Taiwan and Texas.[6]

There also are attribute-agenda-setting effects for public issues. Some aspects of an issue are emphasized in news coverage, some receive secondary attention, and some are mentioned only in passing. At a time when the economy was frequently cited as the most important problem facing the country, Marc Benton and Jean Frazier examined which aspects of the economy Minneapolis citizens regarded as particularly troublesome. They found a high degree of correspondence with the economic coverage of the local newspaper, but not television news.[7]

Similar evidence of attribute-agenda-setting effects resulting from press coverage of the environment has been found in settings as diverse as Tokyo, Japan, and Bloomington, Indiana.[8] The prominence of an issue's attributes in the "pictures in our heads," to again quote Lippmann, is influenced by the pattern of attributes in the press coverage for that issue. Basic agenda-setting effects are what these pictures are about. Attribute-agenda-setting effects are literally what these pictures are. Both kinds of agenda-setting effects involve the transfer of salience from the press's pictures of the world to individuals' mental conceptions of the world. Elements that are prominent on the press agenda, both objects and their attributes, frequently become prominent on the public agenda. This is the agenda-setting role of the press.

Attribute Agenda Setting and Framing

Attribute agenda setting converges with another social science concept, framing. To paraphrase Lippmann, both ideas are concerned with how the press portrays the world outside and the effects of these portrayals on the pictures in our heads. In language very similar to that used to describe attribute agenda setting, Robert Entman's frequently cited definition of framing states: "To frame is to *select some aspects of a perceived reality and make them more salient in a communicating text, in such a way as to promote a particular problem definition, causal interpretation, moral evaluation and/or treatment recommendation* for the item described."[9]

However, there is little consensus regarding which aspects of reality or perceived reality are properly designated as frames. As previously noted, such aspects regarding candidates, public issues, and other objects also comprise an agenda of attributes. Many investigations of how the press frames various topics are essentially catalogs of the press's attribute agenda. An example is the lengthy agenda of attributes of three Republican contenders for their party's presidential nomination in 1996 as found on their Web sites and in the early press coverage.[10] In contrast to this wide-ranging catalog of frames, which is synonymous with an agenda of attributes, other investigations of framing in the press emphasize the dominant perspective(s) of the news coverage. Attribute agenda-setting effects during the 1993 Japanese general election were linked to the salience of systemic political reform, the aspect of reform emphasized in the press, but not to the salience of ethics-related aspects of reform, which received much less coverage.[11] In other words, reform was framed in systemic terms, and this dominant perspective—dominant attribute—in the press influenced the public. Framing and attribute agenda setting converge in their emphasis on how the press describes objects and the consequences of these descriptions for how the public comprehends these objects.

Consequences of Agenda Setting

Agenda-setting effects—the transmission of object and attribute salience from the press to the public about issues, political figures, and other topics—have significant consequences for people's attitudes and opinions. Altogether, there are three distinct consequences of agenda setting for attitudes and opinions: forming an opinion, priming opinions about public figures through an emphasis on particular issues, and shaping an opinion through an emphasis on particular attributes. There also are consequences of agenda setting for observable behavior.

In forming an opinion, there is a fundamental link between the prominence of an object and the existence of an opinion. With the increasing prominence of public figures in the news, more people form an opinion about these persons. In recent presidential elections there are wide variations in the proportion of the public expressing opinions about the Democratic and Republican candidates, variations strongly related to the volume of election coverage in the press. Years characterized by low attention in the press to the election campaign are years with a high proportion of the public who had no opinion. Years characterized by high attention to the election campaign in the press are years with a low proportion of the public with no opinion. Increased attention to a person or other object in the press results in more people forming an opinion about that object.

Turning to whether an opinion is positive, negative, or neutral, the influence of the press on the prominence of issues determines to a considerable degree the standards by which governments and political leaders are judged. This link between public opinion and the prominence of an object, a public issue, is called priming, a process whose psychological basis is the selective attention of the public. When asked their opinions about political topics of the day, such as the performance of the president, most citizens draw upon those bits of information that are particularly salient at the moment rather than assessing their total store of information.

These priming effects were demonstrated by Shanto Iyengar and Donald Kinder in a series of experiments that compared two groups, persons who saw no television news stories on a particular issue during the week versus persons who did see television news stories on that issue during the week.[12] Among those exposed to major news coverage on one or more of five different issues—defense, inflation, arms control, civil rights, and unemployment—their ratings of presidential performance on these issues influenced their overall opinion about the president's performance far more than among those for whom these issues were not particularly salient. In effect, the press sets the agenda of issues that citizens draw upon in making their overall judgments of presidential performance. This is a powerful extension of the press's role in the formation of public opinion.

Attribute agenda setting involves a third consequence of agenda-setting effects, the link between the prominence of particular attributes possessed by an object and opinions about that object. Obviously, the pictures in people's minds, which include both substantive attributes and the affective tone of these attributes, are related to people's opinions. Beyond the evidence that the press's agenda of attributes influences the images of public figures among the public, comparisons of Spanish citizens' attribute agendas for six major political figures with their opinions of those figures on a 10-point rating scale ranging from very negative to very positive found a high degree of correspondence.[13] Our opinions reflect the pictures in our heads.

Finally, the consequences of attribute-agenda-setting effects are not limited to expressed opinions. Negative newspaper headlines about the health of the economy influence the public's opinions, which in turn become self-fulfilling prophecies as people adjust their behavior to their beliefs. In sum, both traditional agenda setting and attribute agenda setting have major consequences with respect to opinions and attitudes and even observable behavior.

Origins of the Press Agenda

If the press sets the public agenda, who sets the press agenda? The pattern of news coverage that defines the press agenda results from the traditions of journalism, the daily interactions among news organizations, and the continuous interactions of news organizations with numerous sources and their agendas, especially including policy makers in government.

At the core of these layers of influence on the press agenda are the traditions and routines of journalism. The press itself is the final arbiter of what goes on the press agenda, of which events and topics will be reported and how they will be reported. The predilections of journalists for conflict, negative news, and political maneuvering, among other news values, are well documented. The result is a public affairs agenda sometimes at considerable variance with the reality of a situation and almost never a fully representative picture of the public arena.

Journalists routinely look over their shoulders to validate their sense of news by observing the work of their colleagues, especially the work of those at elite organizations such as the *New York Times, Washington Post,* and national television networks. The inaugural Chapel Hill study, which included these elite media in addition to local newspapers and news magazines, found a high degree of homogeneity among the agendas of all nine news media studied. This homogeneity is not limited to election years. The *New York Times* frequently functions as an agenda-setter for other members of the press, both print and electronic, especially in initiating new topics on the news agenda.

Prominent among the external sources of the press agenda are public officials, ranging from the president of the United States to local officeholders and administrators; a vast network of public relations activities; and especially during elections, political-campaign organizations. All of these are routine sources of news for journalists, far more influential than ordinary citizens and grassroots community organizations in determining which issues the press talks about and how it talks about them. To produce a newspaper or television broadcast each day requires an organized bureaucratic system, and these systems tend to center on key government officials and institutions as their major sources of news. In turn, these news sources typically have public information operations that facilitate press coverage of their activities. This does not mean that these sources fully determine the press agenda, but they can have considerable influence on what is covered and how it is covered.

Elections provide a special case of these activities, and during presidential elections political campaigns enjoy considerable success in setting the press agenda during the early months. However, this influence diminishes as the campaign moves toward Election Day and garners more and more attention from journalists. On the other hand, in state and local elections, settings where fewer journalistic resources are brought to bear, the candidates' influence on the press agenda is more consistent and tends to be stronger. Part of the explanation for the greater independence of the press in national elections is the influence that news media have on each other. In turn, this homogeneity of press coverage sometimes exerts an agenda-setting influence on the messages of the candidates.

More broadly, public relations activities in both the public and the private sector influence the press agenda. Over a twenty-year period, Leon Sigal found that nearly half of the front-page stories in the *New York Times* and *Washington Post* were based on press releases, press conferences, or other information subsidies provided by organized public relations efforts.[14] But to reiterate the point made previously, the press is the final arbiter of what goes on the press agenda, selecting from the welter of agendas presented by officials, political actors, and others those topics deemed most newsworthy.

News Coverage and Public Policy

At the national level, the president of the United States is not only the nation's number-one newsmaker, sometimes the president is the number-one agenda setter. Of course, not every issue emphasized by the president results in high salience on the press agenda nor is the president immune from press influence. Comparisons of the president's annual State of the Union address with the patterns of press coverage on those issues prior and subsequent to the speech reveal that sometimes the president sets the press agenda, while at other times the president's agenda is set by the press.[15] Although recent presidents have been particularly successful in influencing press coverage on those issues traditionally "owned" by their party, detailed analyses that sort out what causes what have found that the president's agenda is more responsive to the media's agenda than the other way around.

The ongoing symbiotic relationship between the press and a broad range of policy makers that is part of routine news coverage frequently has been described as a dance. In this dance, the partner who leads can change from issue to issue and moment to moment in time.[16] Instances where policy makers were key in setting the press agenda include such diverse issues as AIDS, drugs, and global warming. Instances where the press exerted influence on policy makers include a seminal article on child abuse in the *Journal of the American Medical Association* that stimulated considerable mass media attention and subsequent actions by the Congress and many state legislatures; and a community agenda on the editorial page of the *San Antonio Light*—supported by subsequent news reporting during the year—that resulted in vastly increased spending for children's programs by the city government.[17] Both of these children's issues are examples of sensational issues—unobtusive but concrete issues—where significant agenda-setting influence by the press on both the public and policy makers frequently occurs.

News coverage also can have significant, albeit more indirect, policy impacts through a shift in how an issue is framed, a change that may create a climate favorable to new policy approaches. It also is important to note that the influence of the press on the policy agenda frequently results from the personal interactions of journalists and policy makers, not the actual publication or broadcasting of news reports. This influence includes the detailed aspects of policy as well as the launching of new policy initiatives.

Coming to Public Judgment

The press exerts major influence on public opinion and on the formation of public policy. To a considerable degree, the press agenda directs the attention of the public and policy makers to particular topics and situations and to particular attributes and aspects of those situations. On the positive side, this contributes to the creation of consensus in society. However, the contribution can be negative. Although the press agenda is not immune to influence from real-world situations or from news sources, including policy makers, the press enjoys considerable freedom in the construction of its agenda, a freedom that sometimes results in pictures of the world that are poorly correlated with reality.

Fortunately, the public itself and policy makers—or at least significant portions of those groups—function as a check on the agenda-setting influence of the press. In particular, it is the public, the ultimate source of authority in a democracy, who determine the relevance of the objects and attributes on the press agenda. This underscores a final question about the extent to which the press agenda does contribute—and could contribute more—to the process of deliberation through which society sets its goals and its path toward those goals.

Notes

1. Maxwell McCombs and Donald Shaw, "The Agenda-Setting Function of Mass Media," *Public Opinion Quarterly* 36 (1972): 176–85.

2. Weaver et al., *Media Agenda-Setting in a Presidential Election*; Shaw and McCombs, *The Emergence of American Political Issues.*

3. See Zucker, "The Variable Nature of News Media Influence," and James Winter and Chaim Eyal, "Agenda Setting for the Civil Rights Issue," *Public Opinion Quarterly* 45, no. 3 (1981): 376–83.

4. Marilyn Roberts, Wayne Wanta, and Tzong-Horng (Dustin) Dzwo, "Agenda Setting and Issue Salience Online," *Communication Research* 29 (2002): 452–65.

5. Lee Becker and Maxwell McCombs, "The Role of the Press in Determining Voter Reactions to Presidential Primaries," *Human Communication Research* 4 (1978): 301–7.

6. Weaver, et al., *Media Agenda-Setting in a Presidential Election: Issues, Images, and Interest.*

7. Marc Benton and P. Jean Frazier, "The Agenda-Setting Function of the Mass Media at Three Levels of Information-Holding," *Communication Research* 3 (1976): 261–74.

8. Shunji Mikami, Toshio Takeshita, Makoto Nakada, and Miki Kawabata, "The Media Coverage and Public Awareness of Environmental Issues in Japan," Paper presented to the International Association for Mass Communication Research, Seoul, Korea, 1994; David Cohen, "A Report on a Non-Election Agenda Setting Study," Paper presented to the Association for Education in Journalism, Ottawa, Canada, 1975.

9. Robert M. Entman, "Framing: Toward Clarification of a Fractured Paradigm," *Journal of Communication* 43, no. 4 (1993): 52, italics in original.

10. Mark Milller, Julie Andsager, and Bonnie Riechert, "Framing the Candidates in Presidential Primaries," *Journalism & Mass Communication Quarterly* 75 (1998): 312–24.

11. Toshio Takeshita and Shunji Mikami, "How Did Mass Media Influence the Voters' Choice in the 1993 General Election in Japan?: A Study of Agenda-Setting," *Keio Communication Review* 17 (1995): 27–41.

12. See Iyengar and Kinder, *News That Matters.*

13. Esteban Lopez-Escobar and Maxwell McCombs with Antonio Tolsa, Marta Martin and Juan Pablo Llamas, "Measuring the Public Images of Political Leaders: A Methodological Contribution of Agenda-Setting Theory," Paper presented at the World Association for Public Opinion Research Conference, Sydney, Australia, 1999.

14. Sigal, *Reporters and Officials.*

15. Wayne Wanta et al., "How the President's State of the Union Talk Influenced News Media Agendas," *Journalism Quarterly* 66 (1989): 537–41.

16. George Edwards III and B. Dan Wood, "Who Influences Whom? The President, Congress, and the Media," *American Political Science Review* 93 (1999): 327–44.

17. Barbara Nelson, *Making an Issue of Child Abuse: Political Agenda Setting for Social Problems.* Chicago: University of Chicago Press, 1984; Marcus Brewer and Maxwell McCombs, "Setting the Community Agenda," *Journalism & Mass Communication Quarterly* 73 (1996): 7-16.

Bibliography

Gonzenbach, William J. *The Media, the President, and Public Opinion: A Longitudinal Analysis of the Drug Issue, 1984–1991.* Mahwah, N.J.: Lawrence Erlbaum, 1996.

Iyengar, Shanto, and Donald R. Kinder. *News That Matters: Television and American Opinion*. Chicago: University of Chicago Press, 1987.

Kingdon, John W. *Agendas, Alternatives, and Public Policies*. 2nd ed. New York: Longman, 1995.

Lippmann, Walter. *Public Opinion*. New York: Macmillan, 1922.

Protess, David L., et al. *The Journalism of Outrage: Investigative Reporting and Agenda Building in America*. New York: Guilford Press, 1991.

Semetko, Holli A., et al. *The Formation of Campaign Agendas: A Comparative Analysis of Party and Media Roles in Recent American and British Elections*. Hillsdale, N.J.: Lawrence Erlbaum, 1991.

Shaw, Donald L., and Maxwell E. McCombs, eds. *The Emergence of American Political Issues: The Agenda-Setting Function of the Press*. St. Paul, Minn.: West, 1977.

Sigal, Leon V. *Reporters and Officials: The Organization and Politics of Newsmaking*. Lexington, Mass.: D. C. Heath, 1973.

Weaver, David H., et al. *Media Agenda-Setting in a Presidential Election: Issues, Images, and Interest*. New York: Praeger, 1981.

Zucker, Harold. "The Variable Nature of News Media Influence." In *Communication Yearbook*. No. 2, edited by Brent Ruben. New Brunswick, N.J.: Transaction Books, 1978.

10

THE WATCHDOG ROLE

W. Lance Bennett and William Serrin

WATCHDOG, RECORD KEEPER, COAUTHOR OF HISTORY, citizen's guide to action, purveyor of daily social sensation: all of the above are part of the job description of the American press, and have been for some time.[1] But what is the proper role of the press in a democracy? Of all the established functions of the press in American public life, the watchdog role is among the most hallowed and, at the same time, the least securely institutionalized in the daily mission of the contemporary news organization. What is watchdog journalism, and why, despite its importance for democracy, is it so unevenly institutionalized within news organizations?

To begin with, *watchdog journalism* is defined here as: (1) independent scrutiny by the press of the activities of government, business, and other public institutions, with an aim toward (2) documenting, questioning, and investigating those activities, in order to (3) provide publics and officials with timely information on issues of public concern. Each of these elements—documenting, questioning, and investigating—can be found almost every day in reporting about some matters of importance for the working of American democracy. Yet there are also stunning gaps that, in retrospect, suggest the hesitancy or inability of news organizations to act systematically or routinely as watchdogs in covering other matters of high importance. In this chapter, we explore some of the factors contributing to the fragility of the watchdog role, by considering it in historical and contemporary context.

What Is Watchdog Journalism?

As noted in the above definition, the watchdog role of journalism may involve simply documenting the activities of government, business, and other public institutions in ways that expose little-publicized or hidden activities to public scrutiny. Much documentation of this sort does occur, yet journalists also often miss early-warning signs of important activities that later blow up as scandals that prove costly to the public. The energy crises and corporate accounting and fraud scandals of the early millennium come to mind here.

Another defining element of watchdog journalism involves clarifying the significance of documented activities by asking probing questions of public officials and authorities. Again, there are many cases of effective press interrogation of officials, as when high officers of the Catholic Church were challenged in the early 2000s about their knowledge of widespread child abuse at the hands of priests. Yet there are also puzzling lapses of critical questions, as when journalists initially reported administration claims about Iraqi links to the September 11 terror attacks and the presence of weapons of mass destruction in Iraq without giving similar space to the volume of challenging evidence to the contrary. When serious press challenges finally emerged, it was in response to questions raised by congressional leaders and public commissions. But those questions about the war came so late that the administration case for war was by then more a matter for historians to judge.

Also included in the above definition of watchdog journalism are the practices of enterprise or investigative reporting aimed at finding hidden evidence of social ills, official deception, and institutional corruption. Some instances of investigative reporting may point toward constructive reforms, or alert and mobilize publics to take action on pressing problems such as environmental hazards or health care abuses.[2] Other investigative reports may be aimed less at mobilizing broad publics than at finding failures that threaten the integrity of institutions themselves, such as the investigations of David Protess and Robert Warden that reversed the wrongful convictions of four black men accused in the brutal murder of a white couple in Illinois.[3]

Whether it involves merely documenting the behaviors of authorities and asking them challenging questions, or digging up evidence of corruption or deception, the idea of independent journalistic scrutiny of social, economic, and governmental institutions is commonly regarded as fundamental for keeping authorities in line with the values and norms that charter the institutions they manage. The watchdog function may also alert publics to issues that can affect their opinions and their modes of engagement in public life. Despite its prominence among the ideals that have come to define the press and its various professional responsibilities, the watchdog role has been rather weakly institutionalized in the daily routines and responsibilities of the press. In some instances, press performance provides exemplary service to the public interest, such as the disclosure of the My Lai massacre during the Vietnam War, coverage of the Watergate scandal in the 1970s, and the more recent widespread reporting on nursing home abuse and neglect of elderly patients. At the same time, there are examples of equally spectacular failures to challenge the claims of authorities, such as the gross imbalance between the high volume of reports and editorials publicizing Bush administration claims about links between the Iraq invasion and the war on terror, and the low volume of timely reports on available evidence that contradicted those claims.

An interesting journalistic retake on the Iraq War coverage was offered by the *New York Times,* which subsequently admitted that it had not been sufficiently independent or critical in evaluating or reporting many claims about the rationale for the Iraq War provided by administration officials and the often anonymous sources that the administration fed to reporters to construct "independent" verification of its claims. The *Times'* mea culpa stated that: "We have found a number of instances of coverage that was not as rigorous as it should have been. In some cases, information that was controversial then, and seems questionable now, was insufficiently qualified or allowed to stand unchallenged. Looking back, we wish we had been more aggressive in re-examining the claims as new evidence emerged—or failed to emerge."[4]

This introspective look at the lapse of watchdog journalism by the nation's leading news organization appeared just a few days ahead of an even more critical report by the paper's ombudsman, Daniel Okrent, who offered a list of reasons for the paper's loss of probity. Okrent did not blame individual journalists, but cited, instead, a set of common institutional practices found among even the best news organizations. Okrent's analysis suggests why watchdog journalism is often lost among the other considerations that drive news decisions: the "hunger for scoops" that lead news organizations to tolerate stories based on anonymous and often partisan sources; the "front-page syndrome" that leads reporters and editors to favor more dramatic and less qualified accounts; "hit-and-run journalism" that keeps news organizations from revisiting earlier headlines in light of later contradictory information; "coddling sources" to keep a story going at the price of granting them anonymity that disguises suspect motives and information; and "end-run editing" that leads editors to favor star reporter scoops, while discounting challenges by other reporters in the newsroom who may have different information from other sources.[5]

This essay explores how the gloried watchdog role has become an often-neglected element in such news decision-making processes. A look at the historical origins and contemporary practice of watchdog journalism indicates that neither the critics who condemn the press as the lapdog of the establishment, nor those idealists who see journalism as a tireless guardian of the public interest have got it quite right. Considerable evidence exists showing that contemporary journalism alternately raises impressive challenges and falls short of challenging public institutions and authorities that may have abused the public trust. This uneven performance of the press contains important insights for strengthening its democratic role.

Why Watchdog Journalism Matters

Journalism is the heart of democracy, the humorist Garrison Keillor once said. What he meant was that hard-edged reporting aimed at making the world a better place is central to democracy. "More crime, immorality and rascality is prevented by the fear of exposure in the newspapers than by all the laws, moral and statute, ever devised," said the publisher Joseph Pulitzer in 1878.[6] Without journalists acting as watchdogs, American democracy—at least in anything close to the form we know it today—would not exist. The watchdog role has been part of American newspapers from the very beginning—Benjamin Harris's first newspaper, *Publick Occurences,* was closed down in Boston after one issue, in 1690, because Harris criticized the colonial government. The founding fathers who insisted on the First Amendment did so in a time when there was almost no objective reporting, and the press was viciously and often unfairly partisan. Nonetheless, they understood that even with the faults of the press, a democratic nation cannot function without journalism acting as a watchdog. Whether operating in the partisan context of the early American press or in the generally nonpartisan climate of the modern press era, the watchdog role has been idealized as creating the independent popular forum required for citizens to discuss and evaluate their leaders and public institutions.

Communication scholars generally agree that democracy requires a public sphere where people can communicate about society and government at least somewhat independently of the authorities that convene and govern social institutions. In contemporary societies, the press and, more generally, the media make important contributions to the quality of this public sphere. Yet the mix of professional journalism norms, public tastes, political spin, and business imperatives that construct what we call news makes it difficult to imagine how to keep the public responsibilities of the press in step with a civic life that is also changing in terms of how citizens define their public roles and relations to government. In other words, it is not clear just how the press should facilitate the production of this public sphere. It is not even obvious how much scrutiny of public officials and their activities is the right amount. Too much press intrusion may become annoying and burdensome both to authorities and publics.[7] Too little critical reporting may produce poor-quality public policy debates and weaken the everyday accountability relations between authorities and publics.

Most writing about journalism is critical and therefore underemphasizes the fact that journalism, despite its many failings, is crucial to democracy and makes the United States a better place. Journalism deserves to be praised when praise is due. At the same time, it can be helpful to take a constructive look at current constraints on watchdog reporting from the standpoint of journalists, news organizations, and citizens.

Uneven Practice of the Watchdog Role

Michael Schudson has argued that the American press is not formally accountable to either government or to publics. Thus, while news organizations and journalists may claim considerable political autonomy, the existence of autonomy without accountability or clearly defined public or political responsibilities may not always produce the most desirable democratic outcomes.[8] Complicating the poorly defined public responsibilities of the press are the economic and competitive organizational pressures that often discourage the efforts of journalists and news organizations to think more seriously about their democratic responsibilities in covering particular stories. For these and other reasons, it is easier to say that journalists should be watchdogs than to find agreement on precisely what this entails or how it might be achieved consistently. Perhaps this is why the mythic status of the watchdog press looms larger than the evidence for its universally accepted practice. An initial keyword search on the Web site Google produced nearly 2.5 million hits on the term *freedom of the press*. By contrast, *watchdog journalism* produced a mere 18,900 hits. While hardly ignored, the idea of watchdog journalism clearly receives less regular exercise than its more developed companion, press freedom.

The veteran journalist Murray Marder argues that the problematic standing of watchdog journalism is revealed most clearly in how reporters praise the ideal without having a firm sense of how to put it into practice. In an address on the subject at Harvard's Nieman Center, Marder noted that, all too often, the press appear not as watchdogs, but as a snarling, barking pack, substituting the spectacle or the posture of adversarialism for the sort of journalism that might better serve the public interest. Marder's prescription for restoring the watchdog role involves a simple recommendation to his colleagues:

> Disassociate ourselves wherever we can from crude, discourteous behavior whether by packs of elbowing news people lying in wait for Monica Lewinsky, or by shouting, snarling participants in a television encounter posing as news commentators. . . . That will not come easy. For in my view, watchdog journalism is by no means just occasional selective, hard-hitting investigative reporting. It starts with a state of mind, accepting responsibility as a surrogate for the public, asking penetrating questions at every level, from the town council to the state house to the White House, in corporate offices, in union halls and in professional offices and all points in between.[9]

What Marder implies here is that the press sometimes gets it right and sometimes does not, but that there is great inconsistency in being able to predict when either result might happen. What accounts for this inconsistency and its accompanying lack of institutional grounding? The most obvious and frequently discussed factor is that most news organizations in the United States are driven by business formulas that exert various limits on defining and elevating democratic press functions above other considerations. In the case of public service organizations, news decisions are made in the context of politically sensitive governmental, foundation, or corporate funding constraints. What seems puzzling is that, for all the criticism of the press, there is surprisingly little formal discussion among journalists of just what the watchdog role might look like in practical terms, and how it might be promoted more effectively. Perhaps the illusion of press autonomy provides a false sense of confidence that if only journalists could be freed from corporate and organizational constraints, they would instinctively find the news formulas that serve citizen interests.

Just what would it mean in practical terms for journalists to define their relations with both their sources and their audiences in order to function consistently as instruments of democracy? Perhaps the last time that many working journalists engaged in serious debate about how to define and implement their daily democratic responsibilities occurred during the founding of the Newspaper Guild in the 1930s. Robert McChesney, in *The Problem of the Media,* describes how figures such as George Seldes and Heywood Broun argued that the press should serve as public advocate and voice for the less powerful in society. In the view of Seldes, this would require journalists to be given charge of managing news organizations, protected against pressures from corporate owners. Needless to say, this definition of the conditions required for making journalism a more consistent instrument of democracy did not carry the day, even in the Newspaper Guild. The politics required to institutionalize the watchdog role were regarded as unrealistic and not worth the struggle. Most journalists understood that media owners would never relinquish control of their newsrooms. As a result, journalists settled for something of a normative compromise with owners, and slowly institutionalized a professional press dedicated to objectivity. This has produced the now familiar symbiotic relationships between the press and the institutional authorities they cover. Some independent journalists such as I. F. Stone adopted the watchdog model, but were able to do so only outside of large news organizations.

With little elaboration of a clear set of democratic reporting responsibilities, the news that we witness today has evolved as a strange hybrid of deference to authorities, and ritualistic displays of antagonism and feeding frenzy against those same authorities, interspersed with occasional displays of watchdog reporting. While it is beyond the bounds of this essay to generalize about the daily results of this system, it is clear that reporters and news organizations are most drawn to stories that offer the greatest dramatic potential and hold the greatest promise of continuing plot development. Some of those stories end up being manufactured out of little more than spin, staging, and the efforts of the press pack to inject life into the political routine. Thus, election stories about candidates often explore character issues that arise from opposition research and are then passed on to journalists, who are under pressure that their competitors will break them first. Both Al Gore in 2000 (serial exaggeration problem), and Howard Dean in 2004 (anger-management problem) were tagged with story lines that dogged them through their campaigns, despite other available accounts that were perhaps more accurate frames for the incidents that provided the hooks for the stories. In other cases, well-staged events may win news-framing contests even when known details contradict the managed image behind the event. For example, when George W. Bush made his iconic aircraft carrier landing in May 2003 to declare the end of major combat operations in Iraq, there were plenty of critical questions that might have been raised about the origins and motives behind the event, including: Bush's own military record as a pilot, the messages embedded in the event (e.g., the declaration of an end to combat and victory in Iraq), and the relationship of those messages to the realities of the policy situation. Yet the press overwhelmingly celebrated the media moment out of context as the mother of all publicity coups for the president.[10] It was a well-staged drama that was simply too good to complicate with the facts. Thus, much of the time, the news covers itself, advertising its own production values as somehow transcendentally important.

When the Watchdog Barks

To return to the other side of the paradox, there are also many times when journalists raise challenges or discover hidden information that changes the thinking of publics or policy makers about important issues. Thomas Patterson has suggested that in its contemporary form, watchdog journalism may work best when in partnership with other institutions that are serving similar watchdog roles—parties and public-interest advocacy groups come to mind. Watchdog journalism may need these institutional partners in order to prosper—partners such as whistle-blowers (Deep Throat in the Watergate story), or political parties that are more concerned about principled opposition than strategic calculations. In this view of the watchdog, it is significant in evaluating the overwhelming Bush administration tilt in coverage leading up to the Iraq War to remember that the Democrats chose not to take a party position or to raise questions through hearings or other institutional means prior to the war. More probing voices are likely to be introduced into the news for more extended periods when journalists find sources with prominent institutional standing who are already raising critical questions.[11] Hence, the same concerns that existed before the invasion of Iraq (about lack of Bush administration evidence for linking Iraq to the war on terror) were only given sustained voice after the commission investigating September 11 invited witnesses to raise them. By the same explanation, when journalists are the lone voices raising concerns—even documentable concerns—it is far more difficult for them to perform the watchdog function. Ironically, the independent-press watchdog function may work least well when it is most needed.

A Brief History of Watchdog Journalism

In thinking about how watchdog journalism has evolved in such sporadic fashion, a historical overview suggests several insights:

> Whether referred to as adversarial or advocacy journalism, investigative reporting or muckraking, something like a watchdog role remains a defining part of the democratic press ideal in America.

> The prominence of watchdog reporting has ebbed and flowed in response to various historical conditions.

> Levels of watchdog journalism in the early twenty-first century are diminished but by no means absent.

> The watchdog function is practiced most often in partnership with other societal monitors (both government and public-interest agents), suggesting that a new model is needed that locates the watchdog in this larger practical context.

> Concerns expressed by both journalists and publics suggest that the times are ripe for a useful rethinking of the public responsibilities of the press.

The list of watchdog stories by the press over the years is long, and associated with important social and political changes. Journalists brought pressure to end slavery. They helped bring about women's rights. They helped end the color barrier in baseball, and strengthened the civil rights movement. Critical journalism helped end American involvement in Vietnam. And the pattern continues. Journalists helped expose the accounting abuses of Enron and other corporations. They showed the flaws in how host cities for the Olympic Games were chosen. They revealed PCBs in the Hudson River and dangers to workers in plutonium plants. They revealed abuses in how the New York Stock Exchange was run. They brought to public attention pedophilia in the Catholic Church.[12]

The time in history most associated with watchdog reporting was the turn of the twentieth century. Readers of a single issue of *McClure's Magazine* in 1903 were treated to one of Ida Tarbell's exposés on Standard Oil, a Lincoln Steffens investigation of government corruption, and a Ray Stannard Baker piece on labor racketeering. That edition of *McClure's* sold four hundred thousand copies. By 1912, according to an essay on the history of investigative reporting by Rosemary Aramao included in *The Big Chill: Investigative Reporting in the Current Media Environment,* there were "nearly 2,000 exposés about waste in local government, wrongdoing by insurance companies, poor conditions in tenements, job-related accidents, bank fraud, abuses in the meat-packing industry, mistreatment of minorities and other topics" (pp. 37–38). The public mobilization and political pressure surrounding these stories produced child labor protections, food and drug regulation, more inclusive election laws, and legal standards for policing government corruption and business practices, among other reforms. At its peak in 1916, according to Armao, the muckraking era of journalism was supported by nearly twenty-five hundred daily newspapers and hundreds of magazines. In addition to being buoyed by popular subscription, that grand era of investigative reporting was also sustained by social movements for business and government reform, labor and consumer protection, and women's rights, among others. Many of the investigative reporters in this era were also activists who brought sharp analytical, prosecutorial style to their journalism.

This intense period of reform and national dialogue concerning social ills receded in the wake of various factors. For example, advertiser pressures to shift the focus of journalism away from critical business and economic topics resulted in the economic collapse of many watchdog publications. The rise of objective reporting as a professional journalism standard exposed journalists to charges of partisanship and bias from all sides, attaching greater risk to asking challenging questions. A prolonged period of national crisis, spanning two world wars, a depression, and the beginning of the cold war, raised the level of government news management and active policing of radical politics. In addition, the successes of many of the muckrakers' reform movements may have reduced levels of institutional rot that inspired the muckraking enterprise.

Even at its zenith, muckraking was a controversial development in a national press system still searching for definition between the entertaining broadsheets of the Hearst and Pulitzer era and the dawn of the objective paper-of-record with the transformation of the *New York Times*. The very name associated with this iconic era of investigative journalism reflects ambivalence about investigative journalism carried to the extreme of a crusading press. The term *muckraking* originated in a widely reported speech by Theodore Roosevelt, who compared a press that crossed the line into pandering, sensation, and scandal with a character in John Bunyan's *Pilgrim's Progress* (1678): "The man who could look no way but downward with the muckrake in his hand." Roosevelt's concern was that a frenzy of imitative negative reporting came in on the tide of good investigative journalism and discouraged many citizens about politics and public life. For better or worse, this somewhat cautionary label of muckraking stuck, and has forever bracketed the grand era of investigative reporting.

The next period of widespread watchdog reporting would not come for more than a half century, during the 1960s and 1970s—another time of social protest, reform, and activism by citizens exploring new paths for political engagement. The image of journalism for a generation—both for publics and for journalists—was cast in reporting such as Seymour Hersh's My Lai investigations and the Watergate reports of Bob Woodward and Carl Bernstein for the *Washington Post*.

The end of this second golden era of investigation produced something of an effort by news organizations to institutionalize the watchdog role with the installation of investigative units that are now mostly gone in the wake of budget cuts and profit pressures. Investigative Reporters and Editors, Inc. (IRE), an association begun in 1975, continues to provide a national network and resource base for journalists, boasting some thirty-five hundred members and posting over nineteen thousand examples of investigative reports in its archives. Yet IRE also reports that in no year since its founding has it received more than five hundred submissions for its awards contest.[13]

Even by the late 1970s, the emerging institutional role of investigative reporting—particularly its advocacy tone and agenda-setting propensity—began to chafe within a profession still defined largely around an uneasy central norm of objectivity. The intrusion of business values in the newsroom further undermined the institutional place of investigative reporting in the mission of news organizations. One prominent book written by a former journalist, Doug Underwood, concluded that investigative work had become both marginalized and stylized—often undertaken with an eye to prize competitions to enhance corporate brands, or dressed as consumer and trend pieces of little consequence.[14]

As this brief overview of the watchdog role arrives at the present, several questions aimed at the future can be posed: What is the institutional status of investigative journalism today? What is the regard for this tradition among journalists and the public? What are the prospects for better integrating investigative and, more generally, watchdog reporting within the constraining matrix of corporate business imperatives, professional standards of the journalism profession, and the needs of citizens?

Status of the Watchdog Role

At the opening of the twenty-first century, there was still a good deal of watchdog reporting going on, but it was scattered unevenly across the media. In the case of investigative reporting—defined as enterprise reporting on important public issues involving the discovery and documentation of previously hidden information—far more of it could be said to emerge from the print press than from television news organizations. A five-year study of TV news at the turn of the millennium found investigative reporting on television, particularly at the local level, in continuing decline. By self-report of news directors in 2002, less than 1 percent of all news was station-initiated investigation. By the research team's judgment, the ratio was more on the order of 1 out of 150 stories, down from 1 in 60 in 1998. Most of the reports that qualified as station-initiated and as containing information not already on the public record dealt with government malfeasance, consumer fraud, and health care scandals.[15]

Whether the subject is investigative reporting, or the companion activities of documenting the claims and activities of institutional authorities and raising probing questions about them, most observers agree that the present period is not a time of rich watchdog reporting in any media. Perhaps this reflects the absence of large numbers of citizens mobilized in reform movements eager for a sense of common inclusion and good information about their causes. Perhaps it reflects a time in which political culture—or at least the parties in government and the corporate culture that supports them—is bent away from government regulation and progressive public legislation. History suggests that these conditions may change and kindle more investigative activity. However, as the run of corporate scandals, environmental deterioration, military adventures, and rising levels of inequality in the 1990s and 2000s indicate, there is no lack of material to investigate. Yet reporting on the epidemic of illegal corporate accounting, disclosure, and finance did not hit the front pages until government investigations and whistle-blower reports had already begun. And the timidity with which mainstream journalism handled early evidence of Bush administration distortions in the campaign to go to war against Iraq suggests that news organizations are not eager to reframe heavily spun stories in the absence of voiced outrage from credible political-opposition voices.[16] In light of these patterns, two concerns seem to highlight the watchdog role of the press in the present era:

1. *The watchdog role has become overly stylized or ritualized.* The press has adopted a tone of cynicism and negativity often without offering original documentary material or constructive solutions to accompany that tone.[17] Television news magazines have appropriated a pseudo-investigative style, emphasizing consumer rip-offs and celebrity confessionals of little broad social consequence.

2. *When potentially significant investigative reports do surface, they are often not pursued or even echoed by other organizations cautiously following the collective lead.* Recent years have witnessed early-but-isolated news warnings about Enron, timely and disturbing information about electricity deregulation, and Seymour Hersh's reports challenging Bush administration framing of the link between Iraq and al Qaeda. Even though such reports were surely read by many journalists, there was little concerted effort to follow them up or to shift general press coverage in a timely fashion—that is, before situations had grown so serious that officials inside government finally began formal investigations.[18]

Perhaps the good news is that neither publics nor journalists seem particularly happy with this state of affairs. Not surprisingly, the public has been less happy with the negative tone of journalism than reporters, who understandably perceive themselves as doing the best they can, often triumphing under challenging organizational conditions. Andrew Kohut summarized polling on the watchdog role by the Pew Research Center for the People and the Press in these terms:

The biggest gap between the people and the press is over the way news media play their watchdog role. Almost all journalists are sure that media scrutiny of politicians is worth the effort because it prevents wrongdoing. But the percentage of Americans thinking that press criticism impedes political leaders from doing their jobs has increased . . . while the number saying they value the press's watchdog role has fallen. . . . Many Americans see an ill-mannered watchdog that barks too often—one that is driven by its own interests rather than by a desire to protect the public interest.[19]

Kohut goes on to elaborate these findings, noting that only 24 percent of those polled at century's end felt that the news media concentrated on the facts of stories, while 72 percent believed that news organizations actively drive stories in the direction of sensationalism and scandal. Many members of the press are coming to share these popular perceptions. A majority of reporters surveyed in local news organizations in 1999 agreed that news organizations often drive stories in sensational directions, rather than reporting them with attention to detail and relevance. The national press are not as strongly in agreement, but show a trend toward these concerns.[20] The larger question here is whether "just reporting the facts" is really what watchdog journalism needs in order to prosper. In fact, the watchdog ideal may require journalists to drive stories, but to be guided by more independent considerations of social and political relevance and source credibility than by the current mix of scoops, frenzies, ratings, spin, and sensationalism.

The good news here is that both journalists and publics seem to recognize that the watchdog role has somehow gone off course, and that it may be time to think more seriously about how to bring it back in line with contemporary public values and concerns. Encouraging poll trends suggest strong public support for the watchdog ideal, if not for the way if is often bent in practice. For example, a review of five national polls from the 1980s through the 1990s showed increases in public support for investigative reporting to a peak of 84 percent in 1997. However, there was also considerable objection to the practices often employed in what passes for investigative journalism today, and the emphasis on pseudo investigation and sensationalism.[21] All of this leads to the question of why watchdog journalism seems to have lost its bearing, and what can be done about it.

The Sleeping Watchdog?

Newsrooms are often organized in an old-fashioned way that dates to the founding of modern journalism in the 1840s. Because of this, many areas that should be important receive little or no watchdog coverage—advertising, the military (except for coverage of war), farming and food policy, taxes, and government regulatory and other so-called alphabet agencies. At the same time, many beats in journalism that should be important essentially are backwaters, among them religion, environment, education, labor, urban affairs, state governments, and road and sewer construction. It is sometimes said that mankind's greatest needs are food, clothing, and shelter: none of these areas are covered well. Beats that came out of the 1960s and 1970s, such as consumer beats, urban affairs beats, and coverage of the environment, had virtually disappeared by 2000.

Generally, rocking boats is not a way to get ahead in newsrooms. Publishers and editors often distrust reporters who they think have a point of view. It is OK to say you want to be a reporter covering sports, politics, or business, say, but it you want to cover the poor or labor or the environment, you are often regarded as a person with an agenda. You often won't be promoted, and you'll be watched with great suspicion.

Journalists have sold their souls for access to public officials: Will Congressman Smith return my call? Senator X took my call. The White House called on me at the news conference. So-and-so agreed to be on my show this week. I got the "get." This is not an attitude that makes for good journalism. As the onetime *Newsweek* correspondent Karl Fleming once said, he had spent his life cozying up to people in power and position and finally realized that they had never told him anything important anyway. Fleming went off to run a bed and breakfast in California. William Safire wrote in the *New York Times* in 2003 about being at a holiday party at the home of Defense Secretary Donald Rumsfeld, where he had spoken with Rumsfeld and CIA director George Tenet. Saddam Hussein had been captured several hours before the party, but no one told Safire. So much for access, Safire wrote.[22]

This is a particular problem in Washington, D.C. Reporters there want to cover the White House or Congress or the Pentagon, but most people do not want to cover the regulatory agencies, where things that affect people happen. Journalistic careers seldom flourish by covering the latter; star journalists are drawn to the glitter of the Georgetown social circuit and the White House. As a result, in the nation's capital, the press is often not the "fourth estate," it is part of government. And the same tendencies apply in the state house, at city hall, and at corporate headquarters.

It is also important to ask the question of who goes into journalism today. As Russell Baker has pointed out, as the news business has become more professionalized, many reporters and editors now come from upper-class and middle-class backgrounds. They are well bred, they have impressive educations, but the average American reporter has little or no knowledge of how people beyond his or her class think or act. "They belong to the culture for which the American political system works exceedingly well," Baker said, adding, "This is not a background likely to produce angry reporters and aggressive editors."[23] Instead, reporters have a feeling of identification with the ruling classes. Courage has been bred out of them. They are afraid to confront power. And they think that their own lives are the ones everyone else leads. These tendencies are all reinforced by editors who hire and promote people like themselves. Often those people who become editors or news directors are viewed as being "safe." They are hired because they will be gatekeepers, keeping the newsroom out of trouble, rather than being the kind of boss who has the reporters seek out and engage trouble.

When attention is turned away from digging for new and perhaps disturbing angles, it is not surprising that much of the news begins to sound formulaic and repetitive. Generally in American newsrooms there exists what some people call the "master narrative" that constrains the news by resorting to familiar formulas (the campaign horserace, the war room election, the legislative victory of the president) over fresh looks at developing situations. As Jay Harris, the publisher of *Mother Jones,* said in 2000, "The master narrative is part ignorance, part arrogance, part bias, part laziness, and part the economic self-interest of media owners, publishers, editors, and aspiring reporters."[24] When this master narrative exists, reporters and editors come to know, without anything being written down, what kind of stories can be done, how they must be done, and what kind of stories can't be done. For all the seeming competition, newsrooms become reluctant to do a story in a way different from the way other organizations do the story.

Journalism education plays a role in all this, and often a negative one. Journalism schools provide a largely mainstream, middle-of-the-road education for future journalists. Schools and departments send out few students who are infused with the idea of righting wrongs. Rather, they are energized by the desire to build a career. This is especially true of broadcast students. In a given year, one of the authors (William Serrin) comes in close contact with more than a hundred journalism students: it is a remarkable year when more than ten—and typically it is more like four or five—are interested in going out and doing battle. Journalism schools are producing students more interested in their careers than in the greater purpose of journalism. Indeed, it is important that students come out of school with this mission, because once they are employed in newsrooms, they will quickly realize how most newsrooms judge advancement—it is by doing stories that please the editors, that are splashy, that are clever—not by being watchdogs—that journalists generally advance. Students are being sent out without having been given any idea how to, first, survive, and then to prosper in the newsroom. Surviving in the newsroom—doing watchdog stories—takes a great deal of personal and political skill. Reporters must have a sense of guerilla warfare tactics to do well in the newsroom.

Linked to this is the matter of ambition. As the American newsroom has become more professionalized and better paid and largely white collar, there is a lot of money to be made, both on the print and broadcast sides. Generally one starts out in a small paper or market, stays there the shortest time possible, then moves up to a medium-size organization, then jumps to a national paper or to a network. Doing watchdog stories can help on this path, but usually doesn't. What is rewarded are flashy stories on national topics, stories that get reporters inter-viewed by other reporters, that bring book contracts or promotions to top net-work jobs.

With conglomeration, and Wall Street's definition of what constitutes proper profits, media corporations are often run as if they were nothing more than any other kind of business. Newsrooms are deliberately kept understaffed to save money. Reporters are pressured to do more stories in less time—again, to save money. Expense budgets for travel are cut. Increasing conglomeration means that news organizations are often part of a larger parent company, such as ABC and Disney, that constrains the organizations' reporting on these companies. And with increasing conglomeration, there are fewer media voices.

The business of journalism has also been rocked in recent years by advances in newsroom technology. This has, ironically, made it easier for reporters to be lazy. Pat and Tom Gish, who have published a small-town paper, the *Mountain Eagle,* in Whitesburg, Kentucky, since 1957, explain "It is now possible for a small daily paper to be essentially a one-person news operation." Nowadays a reporter can sit in a newsroom and pull information from the Web, from fax machines, from C-Span and CNN, from electronic databases, and not leave the newsroom. Jimmy Breslin has observed that what makes good reporting is shoe-leather. But in many newsrooms the shoe-leather reporters are often regarded as throwbacks or has-beens.

In all this, it must be remembered that watchdog reporting is particularly challenging. In the case of investigative reporting, the journalist is looking for things that people want to keep hidden. It is time-consuming and expensive. Simply documenting the background details of public activities and official claims takes time and work. Rarely can a reporter drop all other responsibilities to concentrate on one investigative story. Moreover, asking challenging ques-tions of sources that must be covered on a regular basis may strain journalists' future relations with those sources. Reporters, beware the watchdog role: You will make enemies doing it.

Strengthening Watchdog Journalism

It is unhelpful to designate some journalists as investigative reporters and others simply as reporters. All reporters should be investigative—watchdog—reporters and develop the necessary habits of vigilance and scrutiny in their journalistic practice. As Murray Marder has noted, the single most important element of watchdog journalism is the mindset of the reporter, the way he or she thinks about a story and formulates questions. It is imperative that this mindset be fos-tered in journalism education and news organizations alike.[25]

Reporters and editors must make a deliberate effort to seek out and talk to and represent in the media ordinary people, to focus on their problems. Few government agencies or corporations or people of power abuse the wealthy. Unless journalists seek out those without wealth, power, and access, they will miss potential stories requiring a watchdog stance.

News organizations must be more creative in establishing new beats. Beats that lend themselves to the watchdog role include gambling, immigration, transportation, farm and food policy, prisons, land use, and government contracts—at the local, state, and national level—and youth. Traditional beats need to be turned upside down: all too often in American journalism, such subjects as automobiles, food, home construction, real estate, and travel are served by special sections, the primary objective of which is obtaining advertising revenue. These sections rarely if ever rock any boats.

Small papers and broadcast outlets may simply lack sufficient funds to adequately perform a watchdog role. Nonprofit and foundation grants could be used to help augment reporters' salaries, perhaps on condition that reporters who benefit from the grants remain on staff for a designated time period. (Reporter transience makes it particularly difficult for small news outlets to sustain an investigatory role in the community.) Such grants could also support workshops on investigative techniques.

Ways must be found to strengthen the relationships between American newsrooms and journalism education. Programs in which professional investigative journalists participate in established journalism programs for a semester or year, perhaps teaching a class but primarily associating with students and professors, with the goal of helping build more productive relations between students and newsrooms, are beneficial. Journalism organizations have been parsimonious about helping fund journalism education. Law schools, medical schools, and business schools generally have larger endowments and better respect from their fields than journalism schools do. There must be more programs to bring in lower-income, minority, and working-class students, whose work would be informed by their life experience and who could raise the awareness of their more privileged classmates. Above all, the idea of journalism education must be reformed. There remains in American newsrooms and even in some journalism schools the notion that journalism education is not necessary, that an individual can learn to be a journalist by hanging around a newsroom, in the same way that in the 1800s an individual could learn to be a veterinarian by hanging around horses.

There ought to be in every newsroom a motto or creed emphasizing the watchdog role—raise hell and sell papers; comfort the afflicted and afflict the comfortable. But the understanding should also involve a positive component. The image of investigative reporting should conjure up more than a hardnosed reporter seeking out negative, one-dimensional stories. Investigative journalism should also be understood to include stories on what works, and how it worked, rather than just on corruption and programs and individuals gone bad.

Journalists should be less concerned about status and their own celebrity, and news organizations should be aware of the perils of "brand building" through the seeking out of journalism prizes. A prize mentality swept through the journalism profession beginning in the 1970s. As a result papers began to pay more attention to the look and format of stories and the length of their reports than to how the information would be received by the readers. The goal became the prize, not the journalism. Journalists should end their involvement with press clubs and follies with government and business officials whom it is their job to cover, and eliminate the Gridiron Club, correspondents' association dinners, and activities that encourage them to socialize with the very people they should be covering. Journalists should stop accepting speakers' fees, sometimes in the thousands of dollars, from organizations and institutions that they should be covering. Reporters should not be in the position to vote on awards given to the people they cover, be this in sports or entertainment or anything else. It goes without saying that press junkets compromise journalistic integrity and should be discouraged.

Finally, journalists must report on themselves. The media reporters who exist at most papers generally do average work at best. They don't make it a practice to visit other newsrooms and they don't write about their own newspapers. Stories in many areas should mention the relevance to the newspaper, magazine, or broadcast station: stories about downtown development (for example, Times Square in New York, where the *New York Times* may benefit from particular projects), about use of immigrant labor, about the lack of coverage of the Federal Communications Commission proposal to loosen ownership rules. This is a responsibility for all newsroom editors, not just media reporters. News organization ombudsmen, introduced in the 1980s, have not produced a substantial body of good work. Many are hired because their editors think that they will be team players. Many take on this duty after long careers at the organizations in which they are given an ombudsman role. For three years Sydney Schanberg, one of the nation's most distinguished reporters and writers, approached top news organizations about securing a position as a media writer who would give journalism the same scrutiny that journalism is supposed to give other areas of American life. He was unsuccessful in securing such a role.

Conclusion

In this essay several factors have been identified that affect when the watchdog role of the press is likely to work well, and when it is not. Not surprisingly, watchdog journalism functions best when reporters understand it and news organizations and their audiences support it. The business climate of many news organizations today is not fully supportive; nor is the curriculum in most journalism schools; nor are publics who, perhaps rightly, see too much negativity and insider posturing in place of reporters simply asking hard questions about important subjects.

In addition, it may be time to rethink the curious professional norms of the objective or politically neutral press that remains a legacy of the Progressive Era. Such norms often seem to pit the journalistic commitment to balance and objectivity against the values of advocacy or probity. What the public receives as a result are confusing debates that seem impossible to resolve or make much sense of. What, for example, is the point of the construction of a two-sided debate about global warming when one side consists overwhelmingly of scientists who have little scholarly doubt or disagreement, and the other side consists primarily of politicians and business interests who have quite another agenda fueling their skepticism? What was the point of "balancing" the findings of the National Commission on Terrorist Attacks upon the United States (the 9/11 Commission), which stated that there was no evidence of Iraqi involvement, with continued face-value reporting of unsupported claims to the contrary from the president and vice president? How can journalists moderate such debates when their own current practices compel them to report them in ways that may create more confusion than clarity? The flip side of this normative dilemma is the problem of what watchdogs should do when one side of an issue is dominated by spin from a media-savvy source with high social standing, and opponents have failed for whatever reasons to mount an equally effective press relations campaign. All too often, the watchdog retreats, and what is reported as the public record goes unchallenged in the news.

In the current era, the press is buffeted by a "perfect storm" of sorts: adverse business contexts, an unsupportive public, and little clear consensus on what its democratic role is, or even what the basis for legitimate claims to such a role really is. When today's press watchdog serves the public interest, it is generally in a partnership with other public watchdogs such as public interest or consumer advocacy organizations, courts, interest groups, and government itself.

During an era of a conservative turn away from public life and institutions, this somewhat limited watchdog function may be the best that can be hoped for from an embattled press. Yet there is also a prescription here for strengthening the watchdog role in these times:

1. Find new ways to define the democratic responsibilities of the press through journalism education, foundation support, and public discussion.
2. Strike a better balance between currently embattled professional norms and some broad and well-crafted notion of the public interest.
3. Expand beats and sources to give more voice to those who are currently left out of democratic debate, and who might subscribe to papers and watch the news if they saw themselves represented more frequently and more fairly there.

4. Stimulate debate in the profession about steering a clearer course between fear and favor in relations with the powerful sources who continue to dominate the news.
5. Explore new institutional means—including government support and regulation, public commissions, and new business models for news—to create better accountability relations between journalists and other democratic stakeholders.

Mythology aside, perhaps it is the lack of clear democratic standing for the press as expressed in daily reporting practices that best explains why the watchdog sometimes barks when it should, sometimes sleeps when it should bark, and too often barks at nothing.

Notes

1. The authors wish to thank Tim Jones, Carolyn Lee, and Sophia Wilson for their help with research on this chapter. We also acknowledge the helpful comments of Tim Cook, Robert McChesney, Thomas Patterson, and Michael Schudson.
2. See Protess et al., *The Journalism of Outrage.*
3. David Protess and Robert Warden, *A Promise of Justice: The 14 Year Fight to Save Four Innocent Men* (New York: Hyperion, 1998).
4. *New York Times,* May 26, 2004.
5. *New York Times,* May 30, 2004.
6. As cited in Serrin and Serrin, eds., *Muckraking!*
7. See John Zaller, "A New Standard of News Quality: Burglar Alarms for the Monitorial Citizen," *Political Communication* 20, no. 2 (2003): 109–30.
8. Michael Schudson, "Autonomy from What?" Unpublished manuscript. University of California, San Diego, 2004.
9. Murray Marder, "This Is Watchdog Journalism" (2 parts), *Nieman Reports* 53, no. 4 (winter 1999), and 54, no. 1 (spring 2000), http://www.nieman.harvard.edu/reports/99-4_00-1NR/Marder_ThisIs.html.
10. See Bennett, *News: The Politics of Illusion.*
11. W. Lance Bennett, "Toward a Theory of Press-State Relations in the United States," *Journal of Communication* 40 (spring 1990): 103–27.
12. See Serrin and Serrin, eds., *Muckraking!*
13. More on Investigative Reporters and Editors can be found at www.ire.org.
14. Doug Underwood, *When MBAs Rule the Newsroom.* See also Michael Schudson, *Discovering the News;* and Bill Kovach and Tom Rosenstiel, *Warp Speed.*
15. Marion Just, Rosalind Levine, and Kathleen Regan, "Investigative Reporting Despite the Odds: Watchdog Reporting Continues to Decline," Local TV News Project, http://www.journalism.org/resources/research/reports/localTV/2002/investigative.asp.
16. W. Lance Bennett, "Toward a Theory of Press-State Relations" and "The Perfect Storm? The American Media and Iraq," OpenDemocracy, August 28, 2003, http://www.opendemocracy.net/debates/article-8-92-1457.jsp.

17. Cappella and Jamieson, *The Spiral of Cynicism;* Thomas Patterson, "Doing Well and Doing Good: How Soft News and Critical Journalism Are Shrinking the News and Weakening Democracy—And What News Outlets Can Do about It" (working paper, Joan Shorenstein Center on Press, Politics and Public Policy, Kennedy School of Government, Harvard University, Cambridge, Mass., 2000).
18. See Entman, *Projections of Power.*
19. Andrew Kohut, "Public Support for the Watchdog Role Is Fading," *Columbia Journalism Review* (May/June 2001): 46.
20. Ibid.
21. Lars Willnat and David H. Weaver, "Public Opinion on Investigative Reporting in the 1990s: Has Anything Changed since the 1980s?" *Journalism and Mass Communication Quarterly* 75 (autumn 1998): 449–63.
22. William Safire, "From the 'Spider Hole,'" *New York Times,* op-ed, December 15, 2003.
23. *New York Review of Books,* December 18, 2003, http://www.nybooks.com/articles/16863.
24. *The Business of Journalism: Ten Leading Reporters and Editors on the Perils and Pitfalls of the Press,* edited by William Serrin (New York: New Press, 2000).
25. Marder, "This Is Watchdog Journalism."

Bibliography

Aramao, Rosemary. "The History of Investigative Reporting." In *The Big Chill: Investigative Reporting in the Current Media Environment,* edited by Marilyn Greenwald and Joseph Bernt, pp. 37–38. Ames: Iowa State University Press, 2000.

Bennett, W. Lance. *News: The Politics of Illusion.* 6th ed. New York: Pearson/Longman, 2005.

Cappella, Joseph N., and Kathleen Hall Jamieson. *Spiral of Cynicism: The Press and the Public Good.* New York: Oxford University Press, 1997.

Entman, Robert M. *Projections of Power: Framing News, Public Opinion, and U.S. Foreign Policy.* Chicago: University of Chicago Press, 2004.

Kovach, Bill, and Tom Rosenstiel. *Warp Speed: America in the Age of Mixed Media.* New York: Century Foundation, 1999.

McChesney, Robert W. *The Problem of the Media: U.S. Communication Politics in the Twenty-first Century.* New York: Monthly Review, 2004.

Protess, David L., et al. *The Journalism of Outrage: Investigative Reporting and Agenda Building in America.* New York: Guilford, 1992.

Schudson, Michael. *Discovering the News: A Social History of American Newspapers.* New York: Basic, 1978.

Serrin, Judith, and William Serrin, eds. *Muckraking!: The Journalism That Changed America.* New York: New Press, 2002.

Underwood, Doug. *When MBAs Rule the Newsroom: How the Marketers and Managers Are Reshaping Today's Media.* New York: Columbia University Press, 1993.

11

INFORMING THE PUBLIC

Thomas Patterson and Philip Seib

THEORISTS HAVE LONG ARGUED THAT THE FOUNDATION of informed opinion is widespread public discussion and debate.[1] It is through this deliberative process that "unwashed" public opinion is refined and transformed into "informed" opinion. Although this conception is appealing, it does not mesh well with reality. Most citizens do not talk very much about politics, and when they do they tend to speak with others of like mind. When disagreement is likely, many citizens fall silent, preferring harmony to social discord.[2]

The notion that informed citizenship emerges from a deliberative process also poses analytical problems.[3] The unit of analysis is not the individual citizen but the public as a whole. The test of an informed "public," as opposed to the informed "citizen," is the level of public debate and discussion. But how is this level to be measured and evaluated in any particular case, and how does it relate to the decisions of elected officials, or even to the quality of an individual's opinions?

On the individual level, informed opinion has usually been judged by whether citizens possess a substantial amount of factual information about relevant political issues, problems, and personalities. Most citizens fail this test. Most citizens are unaware of or confused about even the simplest "facts" of public life, including the names of their representatives, the issue stands of political candidates, and the geographical location of nations.[4] Clearly, most citizens are not very adept at gathering and storing political facts. Some, as a result of education or cast of mind, are good at it. Most are not.

There is an argument to be made for sticking with the possession of facts as the identifying characteristic of the informed citizen. The equating of "informed" with "information" has an obvious logic. But although citizen information is important, we believe there is a better standard, one that also allows clearer thinking about the role that the media does and should play in fostering an informed citizenry.

The Inquiring Mind

The mark of an informed citizen ought to be an inquiring habit of mind—a tendency to "think about" leaders, issues, and developments. Is the citizen curious enough about items of public affairs to think actively about them? And does the citizen do so regularly? An isolated act of inquiry would not by itself constitute informed citizenship. The question is whether the citizen engages the issues on a more or less regular basis.

We do not assume that the citizen will think about everything under the sun. Many citizens conserve their attention, concentrating on areas of special interest. Nor do we assume that the purpose of inquiry is the formation of new opinions. It can also buttress old views or serve a social purpose. Inquiry could originate in anything from curiosity—"What are the Mars rovers finding?"—to need—"How will the new legislation affect my medical coverage?" And inquiry can occur with or without discussion. Although a tendency to "give voice" to politics in the home or at work is a manifestation of this type of informed citizenship, a solitary retiree holed up in an apartment could also meet the standard.[5]

We do not consider any and all inquiry about objects of public affairs—even if habitual—as constituting informed citizenship. Although we reject the idea that informed judgment can be reached only in the context of substantial amounts of accurate information, we do impose a standard: critical thinking occurs in the context of interests, values, beliefs, understandings, or principles. New information is weighed against existing positions, perceptions, or biases. Thoughts that are not of this type are regarded as uncritical.

As we see it, information is as much a consequence of inquiry as a cause of it. Although new information can trigger critical inquiry, the probability that it will do so is small. Citizens are bombarded every day with hundreds of items of information, nearly all of which go unattended. The larger problem in a media-saturated society is not the supply of information, but the demand for information, which rises only as the citizen demonstrates interest. The process of inquiry is normally what leads the citizen to attend to information. Interest and involvement spark the search for information. In their absence, very little information acquisition takes place.

Information is a byproduct of inquiry in a second way as well. Once a judgment is reached, much of the information that contributes to it is disgorged. The judgment is retained but most of the raw material that went into it is not. From studies of "learning without involvement," we know that the half-life of undigested information is measured in minutes, sometimes seconds.[6] The half-life of digested information is measurably longer, but much of this is nonetheless soon lost to memory.

Thus, our conception of informed citizenship emphasizes "information in use." Citizens are not required to have large amounts of public affairs information in their heads or to activate all that they know. They are "cognitive misers,"[7] who operate largely by short-term memory. Information is thus less like the automobile that travels from place to place than it is like the gasoline that is burned in the process of getting somewhere.

Our conception is not a novel one. Although it differs from the conventional approach, it bears a resemblance to those advanced by Daniel Yankelovich, Samuel Popkin, and others.[8] Like our notion, their conceptions also highlight values, inquiry, and the applied use of information. For our purpose here, it is not important to explore the differences between these conceptions. We have sought only to provide a baseline for evaluating the news media's contribution to informed citizenship.

The News Media's Contribution to Informed Citizenship

The conventional standard for judging informed citizenship places a heavy burden on the news media. If the test of an informed citizen is the amount of current-affairs information in that citizen's head, then it is the media's job to put it there. There is no other source that can routinely provide it.

This line of reasoning has led scholars to conclude that the media fail in their responsibility to inform the public. Although the possession of "facts" is related to citizens' media exposure, the correlation is weak, particularly in the case of television news. And once one controls for education level, the correlation nearly disappears.[9]

These findings, in turn, have led scholars to conclude that the news media should devote more coverage "to the issues." Nearly all of the proposals put forth by scholars to strengthen the media as an instrument of democracy are premised on the notion that the cure for the problem of the uninformed citizen is more and better information. Although it is impossible to watch television news or read the typical newspaper without concluding that the quality of information could be higher, it is less certain that raising the level would produce a markedly better-informed public. Such a claim would have to address any number of inconvenient facts. What should we make, for example, of the fact that, though most Americans cannot recall the names of their two U.S. senators, they have seen or heard the names many times over in the news?

Our conception of the informed citizen places a smaller burden on the press. If informed citizenship is a habit of mind, we would first emphasize the contribution of families and schools.[10] Do they foster a habit of inquiry, or blunt it? The media might not even be third in this instructional process, since the practical puzzles of everyday life are themselves an education in problem solving, which is why bricklayers are sometimes better at it than are college students.

Nevertheless, the news media play an important role in the process of citizen inquiry. For citizens, politics is a secondhand experience, lived through the stories of journalists. Citizens do not directly observe most of the political actors, problems, or developments they think about. The news media are their window onto the world of politics, and what they see through it will affect not only what they think about but how they think about it.

In terms of our conception, the question of media performance, in the first instance, is less a question of information than of stimulation. Does the news lead citizens to take note of political developments? Does it spark their interest? Does it trigger thought about public matters? Does it bring their political values and interests to the surface?

As we will attempt to show in the following sections, research studies suggest that news content sometimes has these effects. Yet the studies also suggest that the media's ability to inform citizens is weakened by particular journalistic norms and imperatives.

Signaling and Agenda Setting

As Walter Lippmann saw it, the primary role of the press is to act as a signaler, alerting the public to important developments as soon as possible after they happen.[11] And in fact, the American press is largely organized around this role. Breaking developments—what has happened in the past twenty-four hours—are the focus of journalists' work and the subject of most of their top stories.

In this capacity, the press clearly affects what is in people's thoughts and on their lips. A longitudinal study of the 2000 campaign found, for example, that as the amount of election coverage rose and fell, so, almost in lockstep, did the level of conversations and thought about the campaign.[12] As Bernard Cohen noted in 1963, the press "may not be successful much of the time in telling people what to think, but it is stunningly successful in telling them what to think about."[13]

This is a critical first step in the process of citizen inquiry, but also an under-appreciated one because it is commonplace. Just as the weather is a topic of thought and discussion in virtually every community, so too are the top stories in the day's news. But the sheer ordinariness of this effect should not be reason to discount its importance. Arguably, the most significant fact about the news is that it allows the public to track the flow of daily events.

But what are people thinking about as a result of their exposure to these events? What do the media cover? Increasingly, the news has contained "soft" subjects, including celebrity profiles, lifestyle scenes, hard-luck tales, good-luck tales, and other human-interest stories. Soft news has been displacing traditional hard news (events involving top leaders, major issues, or significant disruptions to daily routines). Since the 1980s, hard news has declined from 70 percent of the news content to 50 percent. In the 1970s, national and international leaders were three times more likely than show-business celebrities to grace the covers of *Time* and *Newsweek*. In 2000, they were three times less likely.[14]

By the traditional standard for informed citizenship, soft news has little redeeming value, since it contains few political facts and displaces content that does. By our standard, however, the judgment is less severe. Soft news content attracts some citizens who would otherwise pay less attention to traditional news and thereby would give less thought to political matters.[15] Soft news can also contribute directly to citizen inquiry. Jacked-up stories about crime, exotic places, celebrities, and medical breakthroughs—real and fancied—may not offer much in the way of facts but they sometimes touch on topics in ways that provoke thought about public affairs. A study conducted by Matthew Baum, for example, found that soft news coverage of war encourages otherwise politically disengaged citizens to think about foreign policy issues. Soft news coverage of science and health, such as the spate of stories in the early 2000s about the risks of obesity, can have the same effect.[16]

At the same time, there is a question, as yet unanswered, as to how much soft news is too much. Nearly all would agree that a modicum of soft news is harmless. Even the most ardent hard-news consumer enjoys the occasional entertaining or heartrending news item. But as Neil Postman noted in *Amusing Ourselves to Death*, there is a point where entertainment content so overwhelms hard news that it drives citizens to distraction and dumbs down thought and discourse.

There is also the issue of whether soft news, when it sparks inquiry, channels it in sensible directions. There was, for example, the "if it bleeds it leads" period in the 1990s when crime news skyrocketed and people came to believe that the crime rate was rising even though it was actually falling.[17] Of course, traditional hard news itself is not always reliable. One study found that hard news is a poor guide to actual economic conditions.[18] Nonetheless, soft news has a greater likelihood than does hard news of sending citizens' thoughts into fanciful or deadend worlds.

Framing

The power of the press to a large degree issues from its ability to frame events. Framing is the process by which journalists give interpretation or definition to an event or development in order to provide an explanation or judgment about it, as when a rise in the stock market is attributed to a change in interest rates. A news story would be a buzzing jumble of facts if journalists did not impose meaning on it. At the same time, it is the frame, as much as the event or development itself, which affects how the citizen will interpret and respond to news events. As *New York Times* executive editor Bill Keller observes, a principle responsibility of journalism is "applying judgment to information."[19]

Ideally, the press would apply frames that help people to understand what is at stake in public affairs. However, Shanto Iyengar, in *Is Anyone Responsible?: How Television Frames Political Issues,* found that most news stories employ episodic frames that focus on particular events, cases, or individuals. Episodic framing leads viewers to concentrate on the individuals directly involved, to make few connections to larger forces in society ("the big picture"), and to deny accountability to anyone but those directly involved. A general effect is to turn potentially public and enduring stories into essentially private and momentary ones.

Less often, news events are framed thematically—that is, within a context larger than the event itself. Iyengar found that viewers exposed to thematic frames tend to raise large issues of cause and effect, to consider how public policy and social conditions might be related, and to take a longer-range view of policy problems and solutions. In other words, thematic framing stimulates the kind of inquiry characteristic of informed citizenship. Again, however, it is applied with much less frequency than is episodic framing.

Although Iyengar was studying television, the press's narrow perspective on news events is not something that originated in the television age. In 1947 the Commission on Freedom of the Press concluded that a major defect of newspaper coverage was its consistent failure to place events in a meaningful context. This tendency works against almost any conceivable notion of informed citizenship, but is particularly detrimental when informed citizenship is defined as thoughtful inquiry. As Iyengar notes: "The portrayal of recurring issues as unrelated events prevents the public from cumulating the evidence toward any logical, ultimate consequence" (p. 143).

Objectivity

Modern conceptions of public opinion and citizenship took shape during the Progressive Era, which also had a substantial impact on American journalism. Until then, journalism was steeped in partisan debate and values. The Progressives believed that the news should convey information rather than argument.[20] The result was objective journalism, which was based on the reporting of facts rather than opinions and was "fair" in that it presented both sides of partisan debate. Ever since, American journalists, unlike some of their European counterparts, have underplayed the values at conflict in politics. Facts can be reported and evaluated; values can be reported but not evaluated.

The distinction is not always maintained in practice and, through its political coverage, the press to some degree does bring values into view. Nevertheless, the wall that separates facts from values in American news coverage—what the British journalist Martin Walker calls "this intellectual apartheid"—is a substantial constraint on the news media's ability to stimulate and guide value-based inquiry.[21] Of course, the media do cover political debate. However, the presentation is highly stylized—"he said, she said"—and seldom goes beyond position taking.

Rather than reporting politics as a struggle over values and beliefs, American journalists tend to depict it as a conflict between top leaders for competitive advantage.[22] This frame allows journalists to play at politics without venturing into partisanship. Yet the effect is to turn partisan conflict into a political game rather than a struggle over issues of public policy. Indeed, Doris Graber found that when news stories "discussed serious social problems," people were inclined to think about ways of addressing them, but when stories discussed strategic maneuvering, people had less involved reactions, including "feelings of resignation about politicians' behavior."[23]

However, as John Zaller argues, political conflict and gamesmanship can enliven the news, thus widening its appeal. A "good fight" draws people to politics, creating a higher level of interest and provoking more thought than would occur in its absence. Thomas Patterson's study of the 2000 presidential election found that news of controversial issues and sensational revelations produced higher levels of audience involvement than news of the candidates' policy positions.[24] There is clearly a trade-off between political substance and gamesmanship, and the question again is one of balance.

The balance has shifted sharply toward the framing of political conflict in a game context. According to one study,[25] the "game" frame and the "policy" frame were applied about equally in political coverage during the 1960s but, three decades later, the game frame fully dominated. Although the values and policies at stake in political conflict still get some attention in the news, political coverage is dominated by the conflict itself—the pursuit of ambition and the struggle for partisan advantage.

The shift is largely attributable to a change in the style of journalism from a descriptive form that centered on the actions and words of political leaders to an interpretive form that features the journalists and highlights their explanation of events. Telling why things happened, rather than simply what has occurred, can—if well done—increase interest in the news.[26] But the shift toward an interpretive style of journalism has brought the wrong voices and a narrow take on politics to center stage. Whereas political leaders once received nearly as much airtime on the evening newscasts as the journalists who were covering them, in 2002 they got a sixth as much time.[27] As political leaders' voices have diminished, so has their way of talking about politics, which is through reference to policy problems and proposals. And as journalists' voices have risen to the fore, so too has their game-centered rendition of politics.

Overall, the effect on citizen inquiry has been an adverse one. Research indicates that news stories framed fully in the context of strategy are substantially less likely than those framed also in policy terms to draw a response from viewers and readers.[28]

Surveillance

In 1948 Harold Lasswell argued that a basic function of the press is that of surveillance or, as Philip Seib expressed it in 2002, to serve as an advance warning system about problems before they become full-blown crises.[29]

In general terms, the press is usually no better at this task than the institutions of record enable it to be. In the period before September 11, 2001, even citizens who followed the news closely would have had little reason to worry about global terrorism. Although there was news coverage of the first bombing of the World Trade Center in 1993, the embassy bombings in Kenya and Tanzania in 1998, and the attack on the USS *Cole* in Yemen harbor in 2001, the press made no real attempt to connect these developments and gave almost no coverage to analysts and policy makers who were trying to sound the alarm.[30] Nevertheless, there is one area where the press has taken the lead—alerting the public to the failures and foibles of their leaders. The watchdog role and its attendant skepticism date to the Progressive Era, but took on added weight with Vietnam and Watergate, which led many in the press to conclude that politicians were an untrustworthy bunch. The press was unable, however, to sustain the exacting scrutiny that had characterized their Vietnam and Watergate coverage. For one thing, politicians' statements are often expressions of value rather than fact, and thus not subject to truth tests. Second, investigative reporting requires a level of time and information that journalists do not routinely possess. (See Bennett and Serrin in this volume.)

By the late 1970s, reporters had settled upon a substitute. They began to use opponents as a means of undermining a politician's actions or claims. When a politician made a statement, journalists turned to his or her adversaries to attack it. By the 1980s, journalists had themselves joined the chorus of criticism; they routinely dismissed what politicians were saying.[31] This reporting had the look of watchdog journalism, but it exalted controversy and was premised on the assumption that politicians could not be taken at their word.

Although attack journalism is circumscribed in that it excludes criticism of the values that underlie political conflict, journalists routinely question politicians' motives and competence. In the tone of news coverage, cynicism seems frequently to supercede skepticism. All of the major presidential nominees since 1988, for example, have received more negative than positive coverage in the national press.[32] Negative coverage of the Congress, the bureaucracy, and the presidency is also dramatically higher than it was a few decades ago.

Studies indicate that negative information—emanating from the news media or from politicians themselves—gets closer attention than positive information.[33] People are more alert to threats than to positive developments. But when the news is relentlessly negative, the effect is quite different. Persistent charges of wrongdoing in high places reduce people's sensitivity to such charges and thus their willingness to ponder them. Joseph Cappella and Kathleen Hall Jamieson found that negative news generates "cynical responses to politicians, politics, governance, campaigns, and policy formation."[34] Negative news also appears to reduce interest in politics. Americans of all education levels who have a low opinion of politicians are significantly less likely to talk and think about politics.

The News Media and the Citizen

When the news media are assessed on their ability to stimulate thought about politics, they appear to fare at least as well as when evaluated by the traditional information standard, although that by itself is faint praise.

Why do the media struggle as an instrument of informed citizenship? The problem is partly rooted in the Progressive Era notion that sound information supplied by the media is the path to good citizenship. In a 1920 article, Walter Lippmann and Charles Merz, two of the foremost advocates of objective journalism, commented: "All that the sharpest critics of democracy have alleged is true if there is no steady supply of trustworthy and relevant news."[35] Although sensible enough by itself, the coupling of this idea with a distrust of partisan argument weakened the capacity of the news to inform. The Progressives' faith in reason and scientific management led them to see partisan debate as an inferior form of politics—one unsuited to resolving the complex policy problems spawned by industrialization.

Thus the print journalism that emerged from Progressive ideas squeezed out political values and argument.[36] They were dispatched to the editorial page, just as the advertising department was walled off from the news department. The news would convey "truth" within the limits of public knowledge and the fast pace of the news cycle. Of course, "fairness"—the principle that both sides of partisan debate would be voiced through the news—meant that argument would not be completely shut out. But it would be argument without judgment. As the CBS News executive Richard Salant expressed it in the 1960s journalists cover politics from "nobody's point of view."[37]

This is not altogether a bad thing, but it does mean that the language of the journalist will differ from the language of the citizen. The language of the journalist is fact-laden and fact-driven and therefore descriptive and analytical. The language of the citizen is value-laden and value-driven and therefore evaluative and opinionated. As a result, unlike the case in some European news systems, the burden of translating the raw material of news falls largely on the citizens themselves.

We should not be surprised, therefore, when mind and matter fail to come together in a tidy way. It is no small task for citizens to convert raw facts into value-based judgments. Citizens regularly try to apply their values to new information. But often the effect is uncertainty, not about their values, but about how those values might apply in a particular case.[38] The American media are not designed to assist citizens with this process in a large way. Of course, the media do provide some cues. Paul Kellstedt found, for example, that equalitarian cues in the media rise and fall over time, affecting attitudes—pro and con—toward issues impacting minorities.[39] Nevertheless, aside from a few outlets, such as FOX News, the media are not cue givers in any large way—except in the signaling of events—and they have set themselves up in opposition to partisan politics, thereby indicating that the words and actions of the cue givers—those who are part of the partisan fray—should be discounted.

So what should we expect from the American press, and what might we ask of it? Its primary contribution to informed citizenship is what it does best, which is not the provision of information but is instead the coverage of new developments and events. Novelty—what's new about today as compared with yesterday—is ultimately the reason why millions of citizens return each day for another dose of news. They are not there to pack their heads with information. They are there to find out what's new in the world. In the process, they gather raw material that encourages them to think and talk about recent developments in the world of public affairs.

We should therefore worry less about the press's ability to inject factual information and the public's ability to store it, and worry more about what the press thrusts into public view and whether this material provokes thought and discussion relevant to public matters.

The Internet and the Informed Citizen

Because of the Internet, the range of information sources available to citizens has literally exploded beginning in the 1990s. Competition among media is nothing new; the printed page has faced challenges from radio and television for the better part of a century. But information delivered through the newest player—the Internet—originates from remarkably diverse sources, including many that have no grounding in journalism. Governments, corporations, advocacy groups, and other entities have long relied on the news media as the delivery mechanism for influencing a mass audience, but now they also go directly to the public through the Web.

Unmediated media enable citizens to acquire information independently rather than depending on journalists to find, filter, and package news for them. Why turn to the *Washington Post* to tell you what is going on in the Israeli-Palestinian conflict when you can get your information directly from the U.S. State Department, the Israeli Ministry of Foreign Affairs, the Palestinian Ministry of Information, think tanks, advocacy groups, and other interested parties, such as Hezbollah?

While the Internet delivers traditional news organizations' products, it is changing news-consumption habits. In ways similar to those established by cable television's news channels, "news on demand" is replacing scheduled delivery of news. News is also becoming more pervasive as people receive streams of headlines on their computer screens, cell phones, and other electronic paraphernalia. As the din of media voices grows ever louder, people might be inclined to tune it out. A more optimistic view is that they may instead think more carefully about the news and become more engaged with the larger world around them.

What is beyond dispute is that the Internet fosters self-reliance in the public's search for information. Individual news consumers take on more responsibility for determining what is worth paying attention to. The Internet has virtually an infinite capacity, so its users must discriminate as they sift through the contents of the Web. In this sense, the Internet fosters informed citizenship. Use of the Web as an information source requires the user to weigh the information that is being sought and selected. Compared with news consumption, information consumption through the Internet is a more active process.

Politics will remain a secondhand experience for most citizens, but the Web will bring it closer. People will plunge into the vast reservoir of online information to find out more about political items that they may have picked up from traditional news sources or in casual conversation. People will increasingly expect that they can find answers to political questions online and they will turn to the Internet as a matter of intellectual habit.[40] Connections between politicians and voters will also change as the Internet becomes a more significant campaign venue. The 2004 presidential campaign proved that the Internet is an increasingly valuable—although still evolving—tool for mobilizing supporters, raising money, and winning votes.

As candidates and other political players take advantage of the Internet, the relationship between press and public may be altered. But that kind of change will probably be limited. The new communications technologies do best at delivering information, not news, and the distinction between the two will remain the ultimate reason for the existence of journalism. The case for journalism rests on the premise that news is more than information and that it can open the citizen's mind to unexpected developments and unfamiliar perspectives. The case for other trusted information sources is that citizens choose them on the basis of shared interests or values and look to them for guidance in making value-based judgments.

Thus the problem is not that citizens might use other information sources, but that they might rely exclusively on them. These sources might supply or withhold information according to agendas that are grounded in self-interest. The good news, at least at this point in history, is that Americans still turn to the press to satisfy their thirst for novelty—their desire to find out what's new about today. No institution but the press is designed specifically for the purpose of providing that kind of information. The challenge is to get the press to present news in ways that will encourage citizens to think about what they are seeing and hearing.

Notes

1. James Bryce, *The American Commonwealth* (London and New York: Macmillan, 1888); Jürgen Habermas, *The Structural Transformation of the Public Sphere: An Inquiry*

into a Category of Bourgois Society, translated by Thomas Burger, with Frederick Lawrence (Cambridge, Mass.: MIT Press, 1989).

2. See Noelle-Neumann, *The Spiral of Silence.*

3. See Dietram A. Scheufele, "Deliberation or Dispute? An Exploratory Study Examining Dimensions of Public Opinion Expression," *International Journal of Public Opinion Research* 11 (1999): 25–58.

4. See Neuman, *The Politics of Mass Politics,* and Delli Carpini and Keeter, *What Americans Know about Politics and Why It Matters.*

5. Pomper and Lederman, *Elections in America;* Jenkins et al., "Is Civic Behavior Political?: Exploring the Multidimensional Nature of Political Participation," paper presented at the Midwest Political Science Association, Chicago, April 2003.

6. Herbert E. Krugman, "The Impact of Television Advertising: Learning without Involvement," *Public Opinion Quarterly* 29 (1965): 349–56.

7. S. E. Taylor, "The Interface of Cognitive and Social Psychology," in *Cognition, Social Behavior, and the Environment,* edited by John H. Harvey (Hillsdale, N.J.: Lawrence Erlbaum, 1981), 189–211.

8. Yankelovich, *Coming to Public Judgment;* Popkin, *The Reasoning Voter.*

9. See Patterson, *The Mass Media Election.*

10. Richard G. Niemi and Julia Smith, "Enrollments in High School Government Classes: Are We Short-Changing Both Citizenship and Political Science Training?" *PS: Political Science & Politics* 34 (2001): 281–87.

11. Lippmann, *Public Opinion.*

12. Patterson, *The Vanishing Voter.*

13. Bernard Cohen, *The Press and Foreign Policy* (Princeton, N.J: Princeton University Press, 1963), 13.

14. Committee of Concerned Journalists, News Magazine Cover Appeal, Web release, May 1998.

15. Thomas E. Patterson, "Doing Well and Doing Good: How Soft News and Critical Journalism Are Shrinking the News Audience and Weakening Democracy—And What News Outlets Can Do About It" (working paper, Joan Shorenstein Center on the Press, Politics and Public Policy, Harvard University, Cambridge, Mass., 2000).

16. Baum, *Soft News Goes to War;* Regina Lawrence, "Framing Obesity: The Evolution of Public Discourse on a Public Health Issue" (working paper, Joan Shorenstein Center on the Press, Politics and Public Policy, Harvard University, Cambridge, Mass., 2003).

17. Thomas E. Patterson, "Time and News: The Media's Limitations as an Instrument of Democracy," *International Political Science Review* 19 (1998): 55–67.

18. S. Robert Lichter and Richard E. Noyes, "Bad News Bears," *Media Critic* (1994): Vol. 6, 81–87.

19. Quoted in Reeves, *What the People Know,* 9.

20. Christopher Lasch, "Journalism, Publicity, and the Lost Art of Argument," *Kettering Review* (spring 1995): 44–50.

21. Quoted in Patterson, *Out of Order.*

22. Seymour-Üre, *The Political Impact of Mass Media;* Patterson, *Out of Order.*

23. Graber, *Processing the News,* 203–6.

24. See Patterson, *The Vanishing Voter.*
25. Patterson, *Out of Order.*
26. Seib, *Campaigns and Conscience.*
27. Stephen J. Farnsworth and S. Robert Lichter, *The Nightly News Nightmare: Network Television's Coverage of U.S. Presidential Elections, 1988–2000.* Lanham, Md.: Rowman and Littlefield, 2003.
28. See Patterson, *The Mass Media Election,* 86–89.
29. Harold D. Lasswell, "The Structure and Function of Communication in Society," in *The Communication of Ideas: A Series of Addresses,* edited by Lyman Bryson, repr. (New York: Cooper Square, 1964); Philip Seib, *The Global Journalist.*
30. Matthew V. Storin, "While America Slept: Coverage of Terrorism from 1993 to September 11, 2001" (working paper, Joan Shorenstein Center on the Press, Politics and Public Policy, Harvard University, Cambridge, Mass., 2002).
31. See Sabato, *Feeding Frenzy.*
32. Patterson, *The Vanishing Voter.*
33. Pamela J. Shoemaker, "Hardwired for News: Using Biological and Cultural Evolution to Explain the Surveillance Function," *Journal of Communication* 46, no. 3 (1996): 32–47
34. Cappella and Jamieson, *Spiral of Cynicism.* See also Patterson, *The Vanishing Voter.*
35. Cited in Lasch, "Journalism, Publicity, and the Lost Art of Argument," 47.
36. Kaplan, *Politics and the American Press.*
37. Quoted in Edward J. Epstein, *News from Nowhere: Television and the News* (New York: Random House, 1973), ix.
38. See Alvarez and Brehm, *Hard Choices, Easy Answers.*
39. Kellstedt, *The Mass Media and the Dynamics of American Racial Attitudes.*
40. See Cornfield, *Politics Moves Online.*

Bibliography

Alvarez, R. Michael, and John Brehm. *Hard Choices, Easy Answers: Values, Information, and American Public Opinion.* Princeton, N.J.: Princeton University Press, 2002.

Baum, Matthew A. *Soft News Goes to War: Public Opinion and American Foreign Policy in the New Media Age.* Princeton, N.J.: Princeton University Press, 2003.

Cappella, Joseph N., and Kathleen Hall Jamieson. *Spiral of Cynicism: The Press and the Public Good.* New York: Oxford University Press, 1997.

Cornfield, Michael. *Politics Moves Online: Campaigning and the Internet.* New York: Century Foundation, 2004.

Delli Carpini, Michael X., and Scott Keeter. *What Americans Know about Politics and Why It Matters.* New Haven, Conn.: Yale University Press, 1996.

Gans, Herbert J. *Democracy and the News.* Oxford, U.K., and New York: Oxford University Press, 2003.

Graber, Doris A. *Processing the News: How People Tame the Information Tide.* 2nd ed. Lanham, Md.: University Press of America, 1993.

Iyengar, Shanto. *Is Anyone Responsible?: How Television Frames Political Issues.* Chicago: University of Chicago Press, 1991.

Kaplan, Richard L. *Politics and the American Press: The Rise of Objectivity, 1865–1920*. Cambridge, U.K., and New York: Cambridge University Press, 2002.

Kellstedt, Paul M. *The Mass Media and the Dynamics of American Racial Attitudes*. Cambridge, U.K., and New York: Cambridge University Press, 2003.

Lippmann, Walter. *Public Opinion*. Repr. New York: Free Press, 1965.

Lodge, Milton, and Kathleen M. McGraw, eds. *Political Judgment: Structure and Process*. Ann Arbor: University of Michigan Press, 1995.

Neuman, W. Russell. *The Paradox of Mass Politics: Knowledge and Opinion in the American Electorate*. Cambridge, Mass.: Harvard University Press, 1986.

Noelle-Neumann, Elisabeth. *The Spiral of Silence: Public Opinion, Our Social Skin*. Chicago: University of Chicago Press, 1993.

Patterson, Thomas E. *The Mass Media Election: How Americans Choose Their President*. New York: Praeger, 1980.

Patterson, Thomas E. *Out of Order: How the Decline of the Political Parties and the Growing Power of the News Media Undermine the American Way of Electing Presidents*. New York: Knopf, 1993.

Patterson, Thomas E. *The Vanishing Voter: Public Involvement in an Age of Uncertainty*. New York: Knopf, 2002.

Patterson, Thomas E., and Robert D. McClure. *The Unseeing Eye: The Myth of Television Power in National Politics*. New York: Putnam, 1976.

Pomper, Gerald M., and Susan S. Lederman. *Elections in America: Control and Influence in Democratic Politics*. 2nd ed. New York: Longman, 1980.

Popkin, Samuel L. *The Reasoning Voter: Communication and Persuasion in Presidential Campaigns*. 2nd ed. Chicago: University of Chicago Press, 1994.

Postman, Neil. *Amusing Ourselves to Death: Public Discourse in the Age of Show Business*. New York: Viking, 1985.

Reeves, Richard. *What the People Know: Freedom and the Press*. Cambridge, Mass.: Harvard University Press, 1998.

Sabato, Larry J. *Feeding Frenzy: How Attack Journalism Has Transformed American Politics*. New York: Free Press, 1991.

Seib, Philip. *Campaigns and Conscience: The Ethics of Political Journalism*. Westport, Conn.: Praeger, 1994.

Seib, Philip. *The Global Journalist: News and Conscience in a World of Conflict*. Lanham, Md.: Rowman and Littlefield, 2002.

Seymour-Üre, Colin. *The Political Impact of Mass Media*. Beverly Hills, Calif.: Sage, 1974.

Yankelovich, Daniel. *Coming to Public Judgment: Making Democracy Work in a Complex World*. Syracuse, N.Y.: Syracuse University Press, 1991.

Zaller, John, "A New Standard of News Quality: Burglar Alarms for the Monitorial Citizen," *Political Communication*, Vol. 20, No. 2, April–June 2003.

12

MOBILIZING CITIZEN PARTICIPATION

Esther Thorson

IS THE UNITED STATES' PRESS SERVING TO ENCOURAGE Americans to be knowledgeable about their government and communities, to believe that they can make a difference in political decision making, that their vote counts, and to be active in community organizations that benefit their community? Or have alleged press shortcomings—that its content has gone "soft," that it treats politics in terms of election strategies to the exclusion of issues, that it overemphasizes all things negative, that it sensationalizes, gives short shrift to serious topics, and squanders its time on celebrities, scandal, and the most hair-raising instances of crime—created citizen apathy or "malaise" that threatens the successful operation of American democracy? Does the press cause citizen mobilization or citizen malaise? Or is the press simply not particularly relevant? This essay addresses these complex and controversial questions.

A democracy is like a party. It won't work if nobody knows about it, nobody cares, and nobody comes. In their seminal book on political participation, Sidney Verba, Kay Scholzman, and Henry Brady observe that

> citizen participation is at the heart of democracy. Indeed, democracy is unthinkable without the ability of citizens to participate freely in the governing process. . . . Political participation provides the mechanism by which citizens can communicate information about their interests, preferences, and needs and generate pressure to respond.[1]

American political thought has long suggested that citizen participation is guided and stimulated by the press. The media researcher Michael Schudson quotes the editor of one of Philadelphia's earliest newspapers, the *Federal Gazette,* as saying in 1791 that newspapers help people "feel, in solitude, a sympathy with mankind. . . . Men stick to their business, and yet the public is addressed as a town meeting."[2]

And the famous French observer of the workings of early American democracy, Alexis de Tocqueville, wrote in 1835 in *Democracy in America*:

A newspaper is an advisor who . . . talks to you briefly every day of the common weal. . . . Newspapers therefore become more necessary in proportion as men become more equal, and individualism more to be feared. To suppose that they only serve to protect freedom would be to diminish their importance: they maintain civilization.[3]

News is a critical channel through which people link with their civic environment. But that proposition has been controversial from the very beginnings of the United States' establishment. George Washington said in 1792 that "if the government and Officers of it are to be the constant theme for newspaper abuse, and this too without condescending to investigate the motives or the facts, it will be impossible, I conceive, for any man living to manage the helm or to keep the machine together."[4] And Thomas Jefferson, who was in many ways an advocate of newspapers, nevertheless said that "the man who never looks into a newspaper is better informed than he who reads them, inasmuch as he who knows nothing is nearer the truth than he whose mind is filled with falsehoods and errors."[5]

Critiques of the Press and Civic Disengagement

Critics have argued since at least the mid-twentieth century that the quality of American civic life is diminishing,[6] and that perhaps puts today's critiques in perspective. Nevertheless, there is no shortage of claims that civic engagement and the news media's performance as a foundation and stimulator of citizenship are on the skids. There has been a flood of criticism of the press's role in "citizen malaise" since the 1980s.[7] Neil Postman, in an influential critique of television, argued that Americans were "amusing themselves to death" in front of their TVs. Another media critic, Thomas Patterson, contended that journalism has sold out to soft news that ignores public affairs and emphasizes celebrities, lifestyles, and sensationalized stories. And the former journalist David Krajicek outlined the case that news coverage of crime and its threat to American communities has spiraled down into "sex, sleaze, and celebrities."[8]

The tabloidization of news (think FOX News, *Crossfire,* or the *National Enquirer*) has been identified as another major culprit by a variety of observers of today's press.[9] And critics have argued that the conglomeration and corporatization of the American press, with its attendant profit pressure, is rapidly degrading newspapers, network, and local and cable television news to a point that they will be unable to perform any of the classic functions of the press in a democracy.[10]

Superimposed on these perceptions are some impressively negative statistics about citizen performance. From the 1960s to 2000, voter turnout declined by 25 percent. The percentage of Americans who said they had little or no trust in government rose from 30 percent in 1966 to 75 percent in 1992.[11] Participation in civic groups has decreased by 25 percent or more.[12] National Opinion

Research Center surveys from 1973 and 1993 suggest significant decreases in people's confidence in religion (from 35 percent to 23 percent), education (from 37 percent to 23 percent), the executive branch of government (from 29 percent to 12 percent), the press (from 23 percent to 11 percent), and Congress (from 24 percent to 7 percent).[13]

Furthermore, news use is down for all media. Newspapers have been losing audience since 1970, first as a percentage of the population and then in absolute terms. In 1970 newspaper reading in the United States peaked at 62 million newspapers per day. Between 1990 and 2002, however, newspaper circulation dropped at the rate of 1 percent per year. From 1990 to 2003 newspaper circulation declined 11 percent.[14] Network news audiences have shrunk from a high of 90 percent ratings to around 50 percent. Even cable news, which between 1997 and 2001 saw its ratings soar (audiences for CNN, FOX, and MSNBC nearly quadrupled according to Nielsen Media Research), have since November 2001 lost eight hundred thousand viewers.[15]

What does this tsunami of criticism and bad news about media consumption mean? Is the press guilty of approaches that not only fail to mobilize citizens, but actually help to "demobilize" them? The political scientist Timothy Cook asks whether the loss of audience and the increased criticism of audiences of their news media creates a "legitimacy crisis" for media institutions.[16] If the news media lose credibility, it is unlikely that they will be effective in encouraging citizens to participate in the polity. People are generally more positive about their own local news outlets. But even if audiences for news continue to diminish, the media may create their activating role by influencing political players and citizen activists. We look further at these possibilities below. But first it is necessary to define important terms and concepts, and look at the evidence with an eye toward evaluating the press function of mobilization.

Some Basic Definitions

"Mobilization" of citizens essentially means motivating people to engage with their governance systems or, more broadly, their civic environment or "public sphere." A public sphere in its broadest definition is anywhere people come together to communicate about public or civic affairs. It is this communication that enables citizens to define and pursue common goals.[17]

In this essay the word *civic* is used as a substitute for *political*, because we are concerned with the entire social environment in which people find themselves located, not just what is narrowly thought of as "political." Democratic citizenship, then, involves all kinds of aspects of behavioral encounters with others where discussion, deliberation, and decision making occur. It also involves interest in public affairs, knowledge about public affairs, and attitudes toward the public sphere. Thus the question of press mobilization must take into account at least four kinds of human response: civic interest, knowledge, attitudes, and behavior.

Some observers of democracy point out that there are different levels at which citizens might participate.[18] In a limited citizenship, people would simply choose, periodically, officials to represent them. In contrast, other democratic theories suggest a stronger role for citizens. These theories include feminist theory, communitarian democratic theory, and social movement theory. Here we take the position that democracy requires some level of citizen participation beyond just voting, but that there are variations in how actively different citizens relate to their polity.

A third important concept is that of "cause." *Mobilize,* as defined here, focuses on the press's role in causing citizen responses to their public sphere. Demonstrating causation is difficult and controversial in science, and even more so in social science. It may be that the use of news by individuals causes mobilization (and/or malaise). Or it may be that when citizens are active, that process causes them to use the press. Or both may be true. Most research on this issue has tested causal flow from the news media to citizen performance, but in reality it is most likely that the relationship between news and people is a feedback loop in which those wanting to participate turn to the media for information and ideas, and that this exposure leads to increased participation.[19]

A fourth important concept is *citizen.* The meaning of that term in the American democracy has changed significantly over time. It is important to ask whether the press mobilizes citizenship in the context of various competing notions of what citizenship has meant in the past and may mean at the beginning of the twenty-first century.

Michael Schudson, in *The Good Citizen,* suggests that citizenship in the American democracy has transitioned through four distinct models. In colonial times, the citizen was a white male landowner who deferred to those higher in his social hierarchy. He was expected to support consensus and to vote. There was controversy about just how much information he did or did not need to vote. And perhaps most interestingly, in spite of the likelihood of being fined for failing to vote, voting turnouts were rarely above 50 percent.

Beginning in the nineteenth century the concept of citizenship shifted to a focus on political parties and party membership as forming the central aspect of American democracy. During this period voting was at its highest level in American history.

But right after the turn of the twentieth century, during the Progressive Era, the ideal citizen came to be seen as an independent individual who was "informed"—that is, knowledgeable about his or her government, political issues, and all other information relevant for political decision making. From that time and continuing today, there is much discussion of just what information is important to have, and whether the average person is capable of learning, understanding, and applying that information.[20] This question has continued to drive a significant portion of modern research on the impact of the press on civic learning (see Patterson and Seib, "Informing the Public," in this volume).

Although lip service continues to be paid to the value of "informed citizens," Schudson argues that today the ideal citizen is the "rights-conscious" man or woman. In this model, citizens understand their rights and want them respected. They (usually) respect the rights of others. They are willing to expend energy to protect these rights. Although they do not have the time to learn everything about their democracy, they "monitor" what is going on enough to know when their rights are threatened or when there is something in the polity that needs to be addressed.

Schudson's overview of what it has meant to be a citizen in the American democracy is important to the question of mobilizing citizens because it suggests a wider conception of just what citizen acts need to be mobilized. As noted above, four categories of citizen performance need to be mobilized in order to create an "ideal" citizen: (1) civic interest; (2) civic learning; (3) civic attitudes toward government, politicians, political institutions, and the relationship of self to these entities; and (4) civic behaviors such as voting, talking to others about public affairs, and participation in organizations the help shape the face of democratic communities. Again, civic learning and its relationship to the press are extensively examined elsewhere in this volume and therefore less will be said about it here.

News Use and Community Participation

When we look at the social scientific study of how news use relates to citizenship, it is quickly apparent that such use—modified by structural variables that describe who people are and the environment in which they live (length of residence, density of the community, age, gender, income, education, and so on)—and civic responses are highly interrelated. (It should be noted that "highly interrelated" does not necessitate one specific direction of causal flow.)

In an early example of this interconnectedness, Morris Janowitz, in his classic text *The Community Press in an Urban Setting* (1952), showed that newspaper readers were more involved in church, community groups, and even local sports. Many other researchers have shown that "community commitment"—that is, a person's relationships with others involved in his or her daily life[21]—is correlated with reading metropolitan newspapers and reading neighborhood newspapers.[22] This research tradition demonstrates strongly that news use broadly defined is closely linked to patterns of people being active in their public sphere.

But just what role does the press play in this linked network? To answer this, we have to look at research that focuses on the relationship of the press and civic interest, civic learning, civic attitudes, and civic behavior. The model that has emerged suggests that news mediates the relationship between citizens and their public sphere through generation of the four crucial components: interest, learning, attitudes, and behavior.[23]

Mobilization of Civic Interest

It would be difficult to find a study that failed to show a strong correlation between news consumption and civic interest. In many of the studies, civic interest is treated as a driver of news use.[24] In other studies, civic interest is a response to news use.[25] In a handful of studies that examine the same people over time, there is strong evidence that both newspaper and TV news use increases political interest.[26] In any case, it is hard to imagine that people interested in civic issues would be willing to forgo their use of news to find out the latest information and opinions of others about those issues. Unfortunately, there are not many studies that ask whether people who are not interested in the civic sphere would become so if exposed to news.

Mobilization of Civic Learning

As has been argued elsewhere in this volume, a critical component in democratic philosophy is the idea of the citizen as a knowledgeable actor in decisions that involve collective action. As previously noted, Tocqueville wrote in the early days of America that the best-functioning citizen was the one who kept up with the news as it appeared in print. Certainly modern social and political science has operated on the assumption that to perform his or her duties, a citizen must be knowledgeable.

The link between news use and civic knowledge is a strong one and has been tested for many kinds of people, many kinds of civic information, and a variety of news sources. It has been pointed out that politics includes not only "facts" such as the stands that parties and candidates take on issues but also promises, hopes, personal characteristics of candidates, and even denials of reality.[27]

It is generally agreed that Americans are not and perhaps never have been very good with the factual aspects of politics. But it turns out that newspaper and television news use is one of the best predictors of "civic knowledge," measured in terms of knowing specific information about candidates and parties and their stands on issues.[28] This was also true for immigrants who had just become U.S. citizens.[29] As is the case for political interest, we have to ask whether the press could do a better job of imparting information to citizens, but we virtually never find informed citizens who are not news users.

Mobilization of Civic Attitudes

Many researchers argue that it is important that a citizen hold certain basic beliefs along the lines of what the communication researcher Maxwell McCombs, the father of agenda setting, labeled "civic attitudes."[30] For McCombs these attitudes are measured in terms of agreement with the following kinds of statements: (1) We all have a duty to keep ourselves informed about news and current events; and (2) It is important to be informed about news and current events. Heavy news users are far more likely to hold these attitudes, and they are also more likely to be active in their communities in a variety of ways.

Other researchers measure civic attitudes in terms of agreement with statements such as, "I am usually interested in local elections" and, "People like me have much to say about government."[31] Newspaper use is usually highly positively related to such agreement.

Many researchers have suggested that attitudes about whether a person can actually make a difference or not in the public sphere are critical. This notion is often termed political or social efficacy and is characterized by statements such as, "My vote can make a difference," "I have no real say in government," and "I can't make politicians listen." News use is almost always related positively to efficacy.[32]

Another important civic attitude is trust. There are a number of different kinds of trust. Two of the most important appear to be trust in government and other social institutions like religion, education, and so on, and trust in others (social or interpersonal trust). Institutional trust is measured with questions such as, "How much do you trust the government?"; "How much tax money does government waste?"; "Is government run by a few big interests or does it work for the benefit of all?"; and "How many people in government are crooked?"[33] Social trust is measured with respect to whether "most of the time other people can be trusted" or "most of the time other people try to be helpful." Newspaper use is nearly always associated with higher levels of interpersonal and institutional trust.

Other important research identifies some additional critical citizen beliefs and behaviors, including (1) fundamental decency and respect enacted toward others daily; (2) recognition that one is a member of a greater social-political entity; (3) recognition of the value of sometimes subordinating personal or group interests to perpetuate the existence of a larger organization of people; and (4) perception of inequalities and injustices in the community and concern that these be rectified.[34] These attitudes are also positively related to news use.

Social Capital and Civic Attitudes

Attitudes like those identified above can be thought of as forming a related cluster of beliefs or values that guide people's behavior toward participating in their public sphere.[35] Since its beginnings in what sociologists call social network theory, to newer articulations by the well-known sociologist John Coleman and popularization by Robert Putnam, a concept called "social capital" made attitudes like these a centerpiece.

Sociologists who studied the role of networks in society were interested in the attitudes that lead people to connect with one another and, as a result, expand their own power, rights, and possibilities. These connections create social capital. A helpful specific definition of social capital calls it "the aggregate of the actual or potential resources which are linked to the possession of a durable network of more or less institutionalized relationships of mutual acquaintance and recognition."[36] Robert Putnam defined social capital as "features of social life—networks, norms, and trust—that enable participants to act together more effectively to pursue shared objectives."[37] Norms and trust are measured in terms of the kinds of attitudes discussed above. And the bottom line in social science research on these attitudes is that they are almost always highly associated with news use.

Mobilization of Civic Behaviors

In a representative democracy, voting is a primary behavior. Whether news use has a positive or negative impact on voting is controversial, with considerable evidence on both sides. Many studies show a positive impact.[38] But a great deal of research argues that negativity and horse-race political coverage turns citizens into cynical, passive spectators.[39] Examination of recent studies that look explicitly at the relationship between news use and voting, however, suggests that the majority opinion is that there is a positive relationship between news use and voting.

In addition to voting there are other important formal forms of participation in electoral politics. Some of these behaviors are: belonging to a political party, contributing to candidates or parties, wearing a campaign button, or placing a political sign in one's yard. Again, there is controversy here. Nevertheless, social science evidence shows that these behaviors are positively related to both newspaper reading and watching local or network television news.[40]

As noted above, another category of behavior that is argued to be critical to the functioning of democracy is social capital. Social capital creates energy and behaviors to get work done. Social capital is often indexed in terms of the organizations in which people participate. The more citizens participate in their communities, the more they build up trust and learn about cooperation, compromise, and the sanctions that occur when these norms are broken. Most of the recent research from mass communication and sociology, as well as the older literature referred to above, provides strong evidence that there is a positive link between news use and participation in organizations.

Because of the importance of deliberation in democracy, another relevant citizen behavior is attendance and speaking at public forums.[41] Forums allow citizens to exchange information with one another, and in many cases to directly influence the decision making by policy makers. Attentive use of local news media has been shown to increase the likelihood that people would participate in local forums about community issues.[42]

From Interest to Learning to Attitudes to Behavior: Models of the Mobilizing Process

A significant number of researchers have been attempting to link all the mobilization impacts into a single theory about how the press affects people. One of the best known of these models, developed at the University of Wisconsin,[43] suggests that the impacts are linked in a causal chain. The more people read newspaper hard news (politics, the economy, and social issues in the city where people were tested), the more knowledgeable they were and the more they felt that they could make a difference in their community. And these people were more likely to participate in civic behaviors such as attending a neighborhood meeting, voting, and contacting a local public official. They also found that newspaper use predicted whether people would be willing to attend a public forum and speak up about their views at such a forum

This is not to say that there are not many types of news available to Americans that are damaging to their behavioral activation in the public arena. Again, negativity and overemphasis on who is winning and who is losing in campaigns and more recently the decreased amount of attention in the press to public affairs lead many to associate steadily increasing civic distrust and decreasing voting levels to poor news quality.[44]

Michael Schudson has observed that "most of the time, news coverage moves few to reflection and fewer still to action."[45] But after that very negative statement Schudson moves to consideration of what specific news features have positive effect and what ones have negative impact. For example, he is concerned with how news is framed, its role in legitimizing issues and how they're talked about, and how news constructs "social reality" for people—that is, how it influences how they think about themselves, their community, and their nation.[46] So, clearly, we have to ask not just the general question about the press and citizen mobilization; we have to look at specific kinds of news and mobilization.

What Kinds of News Are There?

There is no homogenized entity that represents "news." News is first differentiated in terms of sources. In the early days of American democracy, there was only one source of news, namely newspapers. Since then, of course, we have added magazines, radio, and television, and recently the Internet. And within each of these media channels, there are a variety of genres. There are national and regional daily newspapers. There is the alternative press, and there are local weeklies. On television, there is local and network news, and there are the 24-7 cable news channels CNN, MSNBC, and FOX News. There are morning and evening news shows such as *20/20, Nightline,* and *The Today Show.* On radio, there is local news, call-in news shows, and National Public Radio. There are the three national newsmagazines, *Time, Newsweek,* and *U.S. News & World Report,* and specialty newsmagazines like the *Economist* and the *New Yorker.* There are televised political debates, and there are many varieties of political sites on the Internet. Thus when we consider the "press" and mobilizing impact, we need to consider a variety of different forms of the press, for it is clear that these provide very different kinds of content and styles of "news."

And even within news channels and genres, there is variation in how news is "told." There is relatively descriptive reporting of events. There is opinion about events. There is highly perspectival reporting of events. And even within these features of news, there are frames within which events are reported. All of these features of how news is told have been shown to make a difference in impact on people. A review of all of these effects is beyond the scope of this essay. Instead we will look at just a few examples. As noted before, in political reporting there is evidence that overemphasis on horse-race reporting and extremely negative coverage of candidates and their motivations creates cynical citizens and reduces political trust and interest.[47]

Examination of the details of impact of news channels, news genres, and how news content is structured is also beyond the scope of this essay. What we have tried to do is look broadly over the various literatures that ask what impact news in all its many variations has on the creation of citizens and see what generalizations can be drawn. We would characterize that examination as demonstrating four major points. First, certain channels, genres, and news contents are clearly more effective than others. Newspapers virtually always have positive impacts. Television news, both local and network, often but not as consistently has a positive impact. The budding electronic research area also indicates that use of the Internet for "surveillance" or "monitoring of the environment" is associated with positive impacts on interest, learning, attitudes, and behavior.[48]

Second, as noted above, some channels, genres, and news contents actually seem to have negative effects on making citizens of individuals. Third, as we have also seen, the press does not operate in a vacuum, but rather interacts with a variety of other important variables in affecting citizenship. And fourth, given where social science is today in creating a science of political impact of the news, it is often not clear just where news operates in the causal chain. In fact, it is often argued that being a good citizen makes someone a better news consumer. At the least, it is clear that certain kinds of news use is a critical component in a feedback loop in which citizen interest, knowledge, attitudes, and behavior, and the environments in which they must operate, are all predictably linked.[49]

News Content Relevant to Democratic Citizenship

In the earliest days of the American press, content of the news was primarily a description of events. A ship would arrive carrying products for sale. A meeting would be held to air community complaints. As the press became more sophisticated, most newspapers took a point of view, and there was free intermingling of opinion in the "description" of events. Michael Schudson has observed that the concept of "objective" reporting got started only later in the nineteenth century. Newspaper owners came to believe that expression of opinion, while attracting those who agreed, drove away other potential customers who disagreed. Schudson also suggested that the shortening form of messages demanded by the telegraph led to a "just the facts" orientation to reporting, as did the wire services, which provided information to all the newspapers.

Just how much interpretation there is in the relating of events is a matter of disagreement, although there is now general recognition that in spite of adherence to the ideal of "objective" reporting, there is plenty of interpretation not only in the telling of stories, but also in the selection of which stories and whose stories to tell. And there are many stereotyped frames in which news telling typically occurs.

One of the most common examples of such a frame is "conflict." Side 1 wants this; side 2 wants something very different. And the fewer the number of conflicting sides there are, the better. Another common frame is the representation of events from the point of view of a power elite—rich people, men, white people, executives, and officials. And with the rise of public relations in the last half of the twentieth century, there was more news whose sources desired representation of events from a point of view that would be most profitable to their and their employer's interests.

Since the 1980s, there has been much critique of these news frames, both from practitioners and from scholars. One of the most high-impact practitioner-initiated critiques has been of civic journalism. Davis Merritt and Jay Rosen argue that news should not just issue from elite information sources but represent a diversity of voices that contribute to the perpetuation of a democratic way of life.[50] They also argue that news should stress the interconnectedness of decision making and people's individual lives. Others have suggested that news, certainly political news, should be told from citizen perspectives rather than just that of the power elite,[51] and that the conflict frame should be replaced by explanatory news, problem-solving frames, and emphasis on possible solutions.

There is widespread use of civic-journalism approaches in the American news media.[52] Specifically, as many as one-fifth of American dailies (322 out of 1,500) have experimented with or are experimenting with concepts of civic journalism, or are employing new ways of telling stories through technologies such as civic mapping and interactive Internet use. Importantly, 96 percent of the projects examined used an explanatory story frame to cover public affairs, eschewing the conflict frame. Eighty-five percent of the stories included citizen perspectives, and 78 percent reported not just on problems, but on possible solutions. Further, 53 percent of the civic-journalism projects provided evidence that the community's public discussion was increased by citizen events associated with projects. And 37 percent of the projects provided evidence that public policy was directly affected.

Furthermore, there is an intriguing social science literature that examines the changes civic journalism can or sometimes does make to news content, and the impact of the revised news content on citizens. In fact, recent studies have shown consistently positive impact of exposure to civic-journalism-shaped news on civic learning and attitudes and on behavior.[53]

While some specific activities by civic journalists are problematic, the increased attention to its responsibility to citizens and their participation has been an important step forward.

Conclusion

An overview of the social science literature on media impact on civic interest, learning, attitudes, and behavior is encouragingly positive. There is a tremendous range and amount of news available to Americans and strong empirical support for the linkage of both television and newspaper news with the four kinds of citizen response that most agree must be mobilized.[54]

News use, at least of newspaper and television local and network types, is virtually always a significant component in a pattern of positive citizen responses to their civic sphere: interest in public affairs, evidence of learning about public affairs, positive attitudes toward public affairs in their community and their relationship to those affairs, and civic behaviors such as voting, participating in the community, and other indicators of political energy including talking with others about public affairs, contacting public officials, putting political signs in their yard, and the like.

However, there are threats to the future of the press's mobilizing function. Patterns of corporate ownership and the demand for profits threatens the quality of news and the size of the news hole, that is, the amount of space in a newspaper for news content as opposed to space for advertising.[55] News use is down, and certainly news use is not keeping up with population growth. Worse yet, the greatest loss is among the young, which means the downward trend will only accelerate if conditions remain as they are.

Are there things that can be done? Civic journalism has certainly provided focus for news professionals on their role as mobilizers of citizens, and the results of many experiments are encouraging. If efforts to cover public affairs with civic-journalism techniques become part of the normal news process, that would likely increase the impact of news use on mobilization. The likelihood of this embedding of civic journalism into the journalism of the future is increased by the fact that so many journalism schools now teach this approach.

With regard to economic threats to journalistic integrity, there is a great deal of national attention being paid to just what profit pressures are doing. For example, Leonard Downie and Robert Kaiser focus much of their book *The News about the News* on the issue. A special issue of *Newspaper Research Journal* brings together scholars, news professionals, and news observers to focus on the threats and what can be done to protect news quality from their encroachment.[56]

Perhaps most significant, however, is the role of education, particularly elementary and high school education. Certainly one of the best predictors of news use is education. But it is clear that too little time is spent in teaching youth to become news consumers.[57] There is a national program administered by the National Association of Newspapers that focuses on teaching youth to use newspapers. In 2004 there were 950 newspapers that provided schools with free newspapers for teachers who wanted to incorporate the content of those papers into their curriculum.[58] The Newspapers in Education program claims some minor victories here, but in truth, there is no evidence that the efforts have been at all effective. A few strategies aimed toward examining ways to involve young people early and intensely in news use are encouraging, but much work remains.

The Internet is often recommended as being a potential stimulus to both news use and improved news quality.[59] Certainly the most disaffected citizens are youth, and youth are also the heaviest users of the Internet. Organizations such as Project Vote Smart suggest that Internet-based public affairs information can be effective for youth.[60] Further, the Internet, with its variety of content, holds many other potentials for citizen participation.[61] This possibility, however, must be weighed against arguments that the Internet is bad for democracy, in order to engage a variety of viewpoints on this issue.[62]

Notes

1. Sidney Verba, Kay Lehman Scholzman, and Henry E. Brady, *Voice and Equality: Civic Voluntarism in American Politics* (Cambridge, Mass.: Harvard University Press, 1995), 1.
2 Schudson, *The Good Citizen*, 66.
3. Alexis de Tocqueville, *Democracy in America*. Abridged, edited and with an introduction by Andrew Hacker. Translated by Henry Reeve; revised by Francis Bowen. New York: Washington Square Press. 1976.
4. Schudson, *The Good Citizen*, 70.
5. Ibid., 76.
6. Ibid., 295.
7. Pippa Norris, "The Impact of Television on Civic Malaise," in *Disaffected Democracies: What's Troubling the Trilateral Countries?*, edited by Susan J. Pharr and Robert D. Putnam, 231–51 (Princeton, N.J.: Princeton University Press, 2000); W. Lance Bennett and Robert M. Entman, eds., *Mediated Politics: Communication in the Future of Democracy* (Cambridge, U.K., and New York: Cambridge University Press, 2001).
8. Neil Postman, *Amusing Ourselves to Death: Public Discourse in the Age of Show Business*

(New York: Viking, 1985); Thomas E. Patterson, *Out of Order* (New York: Knopf, 1993); David J. Krajicek, *Scooped!: Media Miss Real Story on Crime while Chasing Sex, Sleaze, and Celebrities* (New York: Columbia University Press, 1998).

9. Downie and Kaiser, *The News about the News.*

10. Leo Bogart, *Commercial Culture: The Media System and the Public Interest* (New York: Oxford University Press, 1995); Gilbert Cranberg, Randall Bezanson, and John Soloski, *Taking Stock: Journalism and the Publicly Traded Newspaper Company* (Ames: Iowa State University Press, 2001); McChesney, *Rich Media, Poor Democracy.*

11. Lee, Gang Heong, Joseph N. Cappella, and Brian Southwell, "The Effects of News and Entertainment on Interpersonal Trust: Political Talk Radio, Newspapers and Television. *Mass Communication and Society,* 6, no. 4 (2003): 413–34.

12. Robert D. Putnam, "Bowling Alone: America's Declining Social Capital," *Journal of Democracy* 6 (1995): 65–78.

13. Joseph N. Cappella and Kathleen Hall Jamieson, *Spiral of Cynicism: The Press and the Public Good* (New York: Oxford University Press, 1997).

14. Project for Excellence in Journalism, Annual Report on the Media, 2004, www.stateofthenewsmedia.org.

15. Ibid.

16. Timothy Cook, "The Future of the Institutional Media," in *Mediated Politics,* edited by Bennett and Entman, 182–200.

17. Jürgen Habermas, *The Structural Transformation of the Public Sphere: An Inquiry into a Category of Bourgeois Society,* translated by Thomas Burger, with Frederick Lawrence (Cambridge, Mass.: MIT Press, 1989); Schudson, *The Good Citizen,* 12; Bellah et al., *Habits of the Heart;* James S. Coleman, *Foundations of Social Theory* (Cambridge, Mass.: Harvard University Press, 1990).

18. William Gamson, "Promoting Political Engagement," in *Mediated Politics,* edited by Bennett and Entman, 56–74.

19. Norris, "The Impact of Television on Civic Malaise," 232.

20. John Dewey, *The Public and Its Problems* (New York: Henry Holt, 1927); Walter Lippmann, *Public Opinion* (New York: Harcourt, Brace, 1922).

21. Ann H. Hawley, "Sociological Human Ecology: Past, Present and Future," in *Sociological Human Ecology: Contemporary Issues and Applications,* edited by Michael Micklin and Harvey M. Choldin, 1–19 (Boulder, Colo.: Westview, 1984).

22. Keith R. Stamm and Lisa Fortini-Campbell, "The Relationship of Community Ties to Newspaper Use," *Journalism Monographs* 84 (1983); Leo W. Jeffres, Jean Dobos, and Mary Sweeney, "Communication and Commitment to Community," *Communication Research* 14, no. 6 (1987): 619–43.

23. Jack McLeod et al., "Understanding Deliberation: The Effects of Discussion Networks on Participation in a Public Forum," *Communication Research* 26, no. 6 (1999): 743–74.

24. Ibid.

25. Jack McLeod et al., "The Impact of Traditional and Nontraditional Media Forms in the 1992 Presidential Election," *Journalism and Mass Communication Quarterly* 73, no. 2 (1996): 401–16.

26. Norris, "The Impact of Television on Civic Malaise."

27. Steven H. Chaffee, Xinshu Zhao, and Glenn Leshner, "Political Knowledge and the Campaign Media of 1992," *Communication Research* 21, no. 3 (1994): 305–24.

28. William P. Eveland, "The Cognitive Mediation Model," *Communication Research* 28, no. 5 (2001): 571–601.

29. Martinelli, Kathleen A., and Steven H. Chaffee, "Measuring new-voter learning via three channels of political information." *Journalism and Mass Communication Quarterly*, 74 (Spring 1995): 18–32.

30. McCombs, Maxwell, and P. Poindexter, "The Duty to Keep Informed: News Exposure and Civic Obligation." *Journal of Communication*, 33 (1983): 88–96.

31. Leo W. Jeffres, David Atkin, and Kimberly Neuendorf, "A Model Linking Community Activity and Communication with Political Attitudes and Involvement in Neighborhoods," *Political Communication* 19 (2002): 387–421.

32. Bruce E. Pinkleton, Erica Austin, and K. J. Fortman, "Relationships of Media Use and Political Disaffection to Political Efficacy and Voting Behavior," *Journal of Broadcasting & Electronic Media* 42 (1998): 34–49; M. K. Jennings and R. G. Niemi, "The Persistence of Political Orientations: An Overtime Analysis of Two Generations," *British Journal of Political Science* 8 (1978): 333–63; Steven H. Chaffee and Lee B. Becker, "Young Voters' Reactions to Early Watergate Issues," *American Politics Quarterly* 3 (1975): 360–85.

33. Patricia Moy and Dietram A. Scheufele, "Media Effects on Political and Social Trust," *Journalism and Mass Communication Quarterly* 77 (2000): 744–59.

34. Christopher J. Schroll, "Theorizing the Flip Side of Civic Journalism: Democratic Citizenship and Ethical Readership," *Communication Theory* 9, no. 3 (1999): 321–45.

35. Mark S. Granovetter, "The Strength of Weak Ties," *American Journal of Sociology* 78, no. 6 (1973): 1360–80; John P. Burke, "Democracy and Citizenship," in *Critical Perspectives on Democracy,* edited by Lyman H. Legters, John P. Burke, and Arthur DiQuattro, 157–89 (Lanham, Md.: Rowman and Littlefield, 1994); Peter V. Marsden, "Network Diversity, Substructures, and Opportunities for Contact," in *Structures of Power and Constraint: Papers in Honor of Peter M. Blau,* edited by Craig Calhoun, Marshall W. Meyer, and W. Richard Scott (Cambridge, U.K., and New York: Cambridge University Press, 1990).

36. Pierre Bourdieu, "The Forms of Capital," in *Handbook of Theory and Research for the Sociology of Education,* edited by John G. Richardson, 241–58 (New York: Greenwood, 1986).

37. Putnam, 664–65.

38. Steven H. Chaffee, Y. M. Moon, and Michael McDevitt, "Immediate and Delayed Effects of an Intervention in Political Socialization: A Disequilibration-Restabilization Model," paper presented at the annual meeting of the International Communication Association, Chicago, May 1996; Naewon Kang and Nojin Kwak, "A Multilevel Approach to Civic Participation: Individual Length of Residence, Neighborhood Residential Stability, and Their Interaction with Media Use," *Communication Research* 30, no. 1 (2003): 80–106; Glenn Leshner and Esther Thorson, "Overreporting Voting: Campaign Media, Public Mood, and the Vote," *Political Communication* 17 (2000): 263–78; Garrett O'Keefe, "Political Malaise and Reliance on Media," *Journalism Quarterly* 57 (1980): 122–28.

39. Cappella and Jamieson, *Spiral of Cynicism*; Thomas E. Patterson, "Doing Well and Doing Good: How Soft News and Critical Journalism Are Shrinking the News Audience and Weakening Democracy—And What News Outlets Can Do about It" (working paper, Joan Shorenstein Center on the Press, Politics and Public Policy, Harvard University, Cambridge, Mass., 2000); Larry J. Sabato, *Feeding Frenzy: How Attack Journalism Has Transformed American Politics* (New York: Free Press, 1991).

40. Karin Wilkins, "The Role of Media in Public Disengagement from Political Life," *Journal of Broadcasting & Electronic Media* 44, no. 4 (2000): 569–80.

41. James S. Fishkin, *The Voice of the People: Public Opinion and Democracy* (New Haven, Conn.: Yale University Press, 1995); Yankelovich, *Coming to Public Judgment*.

42. McLeod et al., "Understanding Deliberation."

43. Ibid.

44. Cappella and Jamieson, *Spiral of Cynicism*; Downie and Kaiser, *The News about the News*.

45. Schudson, *The Good Citizen*, 482.

46. Tuchman, *Making News*.

47. Cappella and Jamieson, *Spiral of Cynicism*; Patterson, "Doing Well and Doing Good."

48. Patterson, "Doing Well and Doing Good."

49. Barbara Kaye and Thomas J. Johnson, "Online and in the Know: Uses and Gratifications of the Web for Political Information," *Journal of Broadcasting & Electronic Media* 46, no. 1 (2002): 54–71.

50. Davis Merritt and Jay Rosen, "Imagining Public Journalism," in *Assessing Public Journalism*, edited by Edward B. Lambeth, Philip E. Meyer, and Esther Thorson, 36–56 (Columbia: University of Missouri Press, 1998).

51. James Carey, "Community, Public, and Journalism," in *Mixed News: The Public/Civic/Communitarian Journalism Debate*, edited by Jay Black, 1–15 (Mahwah, N.J.: Lawrence Erlbaum, 1997).

52. Lewis Friedland and Sandy Nichols, "Measuring Civic Journalism's Progress," as cited on the Pew Center for Civic Journalism Web site, 2002, http://www.pewcenter. org/doingcj/spotlight/index.php.

53. Frank Denton and Esther Thorson, "Effects of a Multimedia Public Journalism Project on Political Knowledge and Attitudes," in *Assessing Public Journalism*, edited by Lambeth, Meyer, and Thorson, 143–57 (Columbia: University of Missouri Press, 1998); Esther Thorson et al., "Audience Impact of a Multimedia Civic Journalism Project in a Small Midwestern Community," in *Assessing Public Journalism*, edited by Lambeth, Meyer, and Thorson, 158–77 (Columbia: University of Missouri Press, 1998); Friedland and Nichols, "Measuring Civic Journalism's Progress."

54. Doris Graber, "The Rocky Road to New Paradigms: Modernizing News and Citizenship Standards," *Political Communication* 20 (2003): 145–48.

55. Downie and Kaiser, *The News about the News*.

56. Stephen Lacy, Esther Thorson, and John Russial, eds., *Newspaper Research Journal* 25 (2004), special issue, "Good Journalism, Good Business."

57. Kevin G. Barnhurst and Ellen Wartella, "Newspapers and Citizenship: Young Adults' Subjective Experience of Newspapers," *Critical Studies in Mass Communication* 8 (1991): 195–209.

58. Newspaper Association of America, http://www.naa.org.
59. Michael X. Della Carpini, "Gen.com: Youth, Civic Engagement, and the New Information Environment," *Political Communication* 17, no. 4 (2000): 341–49.
60. Project Vote Smart is a non-partisan information-based organization established in 1992 that provides detailed information about candidates and issues to American voters. Available at http://www.vote-smart.org.
61. See the articles on the Internet and civic engagement in *Political Communication* 17, no. 4 (2000).
62. See "New Democracy Forum: Is the Internet Bad for Democracy?" in the *Boston Review* (summer 2001).

Bibliography

Bellah, Robert N., et al., *Habits of the Heart: Individualism and Commitment in American Life*. Berkeley: University of California Press, 1985.

Corrigan, Don H. *The Public Journalism Movement in America: Evangelists in the Newsroom*. Westport, Conn.: Praeger, 1999.

Downie, Leonard, Jr., and Robert G. Kaiser. *The News about the News: American Journalism in Peril*. New York: Knopf, 2002.

Janowitz, Morris. *The Community Press in an Urban Setting: The Social Elements of Urbanism*. 2nd ed. Chicago: University of Chicago Press, 1967.

McChesney, Robert W. *Rich Media, Poor Democracy: Communication Politics in Dubious Times*. Urbana: University of Illinois Press, 1999.

Schudson, Michael. *The Good Citizen: A History of American Civic Life*. New York: Martin Kessler, 1998.

Tuchman, Gaye. *Making News: A Study in the Construction of Reality*. New York: Free Press, 1978.

Yankelovich, Daniel. *Coming to Public Judgment: Making Democracy Work in a Complex World*. Syracuse, N.Y.: Syracuse University Press, 1991.

GOVERNMENT AND THE PRESS: AN AMBIVALENT RELATIONSHIP

Martha Joynt Kumar

THE GOVERNMENT-PRESS RELATIONSHIP IS A MIX OF cooperation and conflict as well as dependence and independence. Despite the ambivalence of the relationship, both government officials and news organizations have the same client base: the public. Citizens depend on news organizations to inform them about the actions of government and problems faced by communities and the nation. The information provided by news organizations is equally useful to those who govern and to the governed. On the other hand, governmental action is important to the healthy maintenance of news organizations. Reporters and media organizations depend upon the government to provide them with information and protect their position as an essential element of a representative government.

The essays in this section focus on three aspects of the government-press relationship. First, the nature of the relationship is examined in terms of the ways in which the partners interact with each other. The modes of interaction are discussed, as well as the mutual benefits of the partnership. Government is the object of press coverage, but government also supports and protects news organizations. Second, the essays explore the importance of the relationship to the effective operation of the American political system. From the perspective of the First Amendment and public-interest theorists, news organizations have a special place in a democratic political system. In viewing the place of the press in the U.S. system, important changes have taken place in the ways in which news organizations operate today as compared with their organizational characteristics in the mid-twentieth century. Third, these essays explore particular aspects of the relationship, most importantly press coverage of war.

Nature of the Relationship

While the public face of the relationship is one of conflict, the everyday reality is that government and the press typically work together to each other's advantage.

As Martha Joynt Kumar and Alex Jones observe in "Government and the Press: Issues and Trends," public officials regularly complain about their press coverage, but in fact the relationship is characterized by cooperation. Whether it is the president and his staff or members of Congress and their aides, all work with news organizations to provide them with information they seek and do so on a schedule consistent with reporters' needs. News organizations are both a resource for officials and a source of pressure. They are a resource because officials need to communicate with their constituents and must go through news organizations and their reporters to do so. At the same time, news organizations are a source of pressure on government officials because reporters want information on terms favorable to them. Rather than simply accept selected information that officials decide to provide them, reporters want information specific to their requests, and they want to acquire it promptly. Therein lies a basic ever-present conflict in the relationship. If officials do not provide reporters with the information they ask for, reporters look elsewhere for it, which often results in a tougher story than if officials provided the requested material at the outset. Because each partner in the relationship has an ongoing need of the other, the relationship is a continuous one. Reporters practice the same sort of information gathering no matter what branch of government they cover or in what time period they are doing their work. They want accurate information, responsive to their needs, provided in a timely manner.

Professor Timothy Cook, in "Public Policy toward the Press: What Government Does *for* the News Media," explains the close connections between government and the news media. News organizations are dependent on government as well as operating as independent actors in the political system. Cook demonstrates the degree to which all three branches of government provide support for news organizations. In the earliest days of the partisan press, government provided direct sponsorship of newspapers, including awarding them printing contracts. Gradually government ended its sponsorship relationship, yet continued to support news organizations in significant ways. Later in the nineteenth century and up until the present, the federal government provided subsidies for news organizations in a broad range of ways, including postal subsidies, supporting the development of new technologies, creating regulations to protect intellectual property rights, and developing regulation of electronic media in a manner responsive to profitability concerns of the corporations owning such media. Government also has created an information staff structure in all branches of government tasked with providing information to news organizations.

While there is continuity in the government-press relationship in terms of the mutual need of the partners, there has been change as well. In 1947 the Commission on Freedom of the Press, chaired by University of Chicago president Robert M. Hutchins and composed of prominent academics and former government officials, measured the health of the government-press relationship.

In applying the observations of the Hutchins Commission to the current status of the relationship, Professor Jane Kirtley finds societal and legal changes influencing both partners, such as the development of the Internet and the growing concentration of news organizations. In the decades since the Hutchins Commission report, the press has found added protections through the development of case law relating to the government-press relationship, such as the body of cases allowing news organizations the right of access to criminal court proceedings. At the same time, with the creation of C-SPAN, Congress has become more open to public view through the coverage of its floor proceedings and committee hearings. The executive branch, too, has become more transparent since the Hutchins Commission, especially through the creation of the Freedom of Information Act (FOIA) in 1966, which calls for government records to be opened unless there is clear justification for their remaining closed. While FOIA has not been as timely an information tool as Congress might have anticipated, it has been vital in giving journalists access to important records. Kirtley also addresses the Hutchins Commission's concern for what its members saw as a growing concentration of media ownership, a trend that has continued despite a climate of economic deregulation.

Importance of the Relationship

The Supreme Court has recognized the importance of the press to the functioning of the American representative political system. In "The First Amendment Tradition and Its Critics," Bruce Sanford and Jane Kirtley trace two centuries of the First Amendment experience. Their conclusion is that the First Amendment "remains the heart of American democracy." The importance of the press to the effective operation of government was recognized in the John Peter Zenger case in 1741, well before the U.S. Constitution was adopted. Declaring truth to be a defense in a case of libel, the courts acknowledged the value of accurate information. The crucial role of the press is acknowledged in the First Amendment in the brief statement: "Congress shall make no law . . . abridging the freedom of speech, or of the press." As Sanford and Kirtley observe, its brevity "belies its complexity." Over the years, there have been five basic approaches toward the First Amendment, all of which acknowledge the important role of the press in the operation of government. The absolutists "maintain that no government interest can justify abridging or punishing the exercise of press or speech freedoms." The marketplace model was advanced by Justice Oliver Wendell Holmes, who said that "the best test of truth is the power of the thought to get itself accepted in the competition of the market, and that truth is the only ground upon which [men's] wishes safely can be carried out." As Sanford and Kirtley point out, in this theory "First Amendment freedoms are valuable because they help society find truth in the 'market' of ideas." A third approach, the personal-autonomy paradigm, emphasizes the importance of the First Amendment as a vehicle to allow individual citizens to develop and express their beliefs. Press freedoms are also at the heart of the "self-government" theory calling on the press to distribute information to a public requiring accurate information in order to make electoral decisions. Others argue as well that the press has a "preferred position" in American society due to its importance in addressing the public's right to know about the operations of government. In spite of their differences, these five approaches are united in the importance of the press to the effective functioning of American government.

In "The Role of Communications Regulation in Protecting the Public Interest," Professor Robert Horwitz views the communications system as an outgrowth of liberal democracy in the United States, where private capital and the state operate in an environment of creative tension. "At the heart of that tension is the concept of the public interest, a concept that legitimates state intervention in particular kinds of private property and subjects that property to government regulation," he comments. Horwitz describes the United States communications system as one with a history of state intervention. In the early years, government fostered technological developments, such as the telegraph. Later it regulated an important public resource, the airwaves, by licensing radio and television stations. Horwitz points out that the "public-trustee status of broadcast licensees meant that broadcasters were to serve a public rather than a purely private function, and were expected to orient programming to their local communities." Diverse programming and the airing of different points of view were important parts of the regulatory culture surrounding the electronic media prior to the creation of a new system in the 1980s and 1990s, with the divestiture of AT&T and the signing into law of the Telecommunications Act of 1996. The new communications environment emphasizes deregulation and competition. Some traditional regulations, such as the fairness doctrine, have been phased out, but others remain. In his article, "Journalism and the Public Interest," veteran journalist Daniel Schorr provides information on the struggle between secrecy and disclosure, a struggle carried out throughout our history by the federal government and the news media.

The Relationship in Wartime

In "The Military and the Media," William Prochnau tracks the importance of the press to the information American citizens receive about wars undertaken by their government. The history of the government-press relationship during wartime mirrors that found in peacetime in terms of the pressure exerted by news organizations for access to information and the attempt by government officials to control what is released. Prochnau demonstrates that there is no one model of government-press relations during wartime. In the post-Vietnam era many in the military erroneously believed that the war was lost because of negative press coverage, and consequently military leaders adopted restrictive press policies. Government tried a no-press-access military incursion into Grenada, and gave reporters very limited battlefield access in the Gulf War of 1991, practices that met with heavy criticism from news organizations. Another model, embedding reporters with military units where they could observe the actions of war, was adopted in the Iraq War of 2003. While not without its critics, the Iraq model satisfied the press's demands for access and for reporting with limited censorship. Prochnau sees the basic paradigm this way: "The packaging of wars is a natural function of governments, the unpackaging of them a natural function of the media." This packaging and unpackaging of information extends also to the peacetime practices of government officials and reporters, as the battlefield gives way to the White House, Congress, the courts, and the bureaucracy.

13

GOVERNMENT AND THE PRESS: ISSUES AND TRENDS

Martha Joynt Kumar and Alex Jones

THE RELATIONSHIP BETWEEN GOVERNMENT AND THE press is crucial with respect to what citizens learn about the individuals and institutions that operate on their behalf. In a more direct way, the relationship influences how both reporters and government officials do their jobs. Elected officials need the press in order to reach the publics upon whom they depend for electoral support, and to gain knowledge of the public's policy interests. Facilitating the connection between government and citizens is essential to good journalism.

This discussion explores five aspects of the government-press relationship. First, the nature of the connection is examined, and second, the impact of the press on those who govern is discussed. This is followed by a look at the influence that the government exerts on the operations of news organizations. Fourth, the historical relationship is reviewed by means of an examination of three developmental periods. Fifth, the people who cover government, and how reporters have changed in terms of their professional background and work processes, are analyzed.

News organizations with an impact on national government operations include a broad range of media, including broadcast, cable, print, and Internet operations that deliver opinion as well as hard news and pictures. All of these types of media influence, in various ways and to various extents, both officials holding posts in the federal government and citizens. What was in the mid-nineteenth century an untidy handful of newspaper reporters covering the government in Washington has become in the early twenty-first century a large and varied group of media professionals focused on particular beats.

Nature of the Relationship

On the surface, the press-government relationship appears to be an acrimonious one, in which cooperation is far from the operating mode. President George W.

Bush complained about the press standing as a "filter" between him and the public. "I know we've got a construction plan [in Iraq], and we'll continue to explain it," President Bush told a group of regional reporters in 2003.[1] "Sometimes it's hard to get through the filter." Reporters can be just as unhappy with their treatment by the president and his staff. "Too often they treat us with contempt," commented Elisabeth Bumiller of the *New York Times*.[2] Yet beneath the tension is a relationship in which reporters do find the information they seek, even if they have to go elsewhere to get it and it takes longer than they wish.

The relationship is multilayered. First, government officials and news organizations spend a great deal of time and resources making use of the presence of the other, even if there is mutual mistrust of motives and actions. Second, there are personal and institutional layers shaping the manner in which each side approaches and considers the other. While the personal relationship appears combative, with reporters and officials sometimes openly critical of one another, the institutional relationship is a continuing one wherein the two sides cooperate with one another in ways intended to maximize their own advantages. That leads to a surface tension in the relationship, but in the main the news and information demands of each of the partners forces both sides to cooperate. Third, the continuing character of the relationship is based on the consistent nature of the information needs, and the institutional responses, of both partners. News organizations assign reporters to cover a president in much the same way no matter who is serving as chief executive, and White House officials, regardless of party, retain the basic White House staff units handling the information requests of reporters and designing strategies for making full use of the presence of news organizations. The same is true of the media practices of the Congress and the various government departments and agencies, as well as the news organizations covering them.

News Organizations as a Resource and Source of Pressure

The press serves both as a resource for those who govern and as a source of pressure on officials, who must respond to press demands for information, information that government might not want to provide. Whether they are in the Congress or the White House, officials and their staffs spend a great deal of time designing strategies to make use of news organizations to get to the public and, secondarily, to respond to the media's information requests. In the White House, the Congress, and the government departments and agencies, sophisticated press and communications operations are designed to meet both of those needs. The amount of time presidents spend responding to reporters' questions can serve as a measure of the importance to chief executives of their relationship with news organizations. In his eight years in office, President Bill Clinton had 1,603 interchanges with reporters.[3] The numbers break down in the following way: 193 press conferences; 368 interviews in which the president sat down with one or more reporters for an exclusive session; and 1,042 short question–and–answer sessions with reporters. Taken together, President Clinton met with reporters an average of 3.85 times a week and 16.7 occasions a month during his two terms in office. In his first term, President George W. Bush had fewer sessions with reporters, an average of 2 a week and 8.66 a month through 2003.

For their part, news organizations spend a great deal of their own resources covering the president. The five major television networks (ABC, CBS, NBC, CNN, and FOX) have rotating groups of reporters, and regularly put two reporters, a producer, and a camera crew of three at the White House each day. The major news organizations assign two to three reporters to watch the president and his White House. When the president travels, regardless of the purpose, news organizations assign a pool of reporters, and a camera crew for broadcast organizations, to go along. On especially important trips, many reporters travel with the president. A 2004 journey to Asia by President George W. Bush cost news organizations approximately $25,000 for each accompanying journalist for airfare, hotel, and workspace.[4]

While presidents spend a great deal of time responding to queries from reporters, they also make full use of the presence of news organizations at the White House. Since the time when CNN began covering the White House in 1981, presidents and their staffs have capitalized on cable television's interest in providing continuing coverage of presidential speeches and events. In 1996 FOX News and MSNBC joined the cable ranks at the White House, providing additional opportunities for the president to speak directly to the public through news organizations. Presidents and their staffs have responded to this publicity opportunity by scheduling frequent presidential appearances. In President Clinton's eight years in office, he gave 30 addresses to the nation, 410 weekly radio addresses, and 4,037 addresses and remarks, for a total of 4,477 presidential appearances.[5] Although while in his first three years President Bush's numbers were less than President Clinton's in his first three years, the difference is only marginal.

Personal and Institutional Aspects

The government-press relationship has both personal and institutional layers. The personal relationship between officials and reporters is sometimes a strained one, but the institutional tie is basically cooperative. The tension arises because each side approaches the other trying to establish the terms of the relationship, and fights for what it considers to be its turf and rights. Reporters emphasize the public's right to know what government is doing and the media's role as surrogates for the public. For their part, elected officials believe that they are the representatives of the people and have the right to determine what the public should know about the workings of government and government officials. Officials would like reporters to be their partners in delivering what they see as appropriate information to the public, while reporters want access to information they regard as important for the public to have. That difference in perspective has led to many a conflict between reporters and elected officials, most especially between presidents and the press.

While it may seem that the relationship in action is a personal one, in reality it is more an institutional one.[6] The relationship is based less on who the reporters are and who the elected president or member of Congress is than on the needs of reporters' and officeholders' respective institutions. That leads to a continuing relationship no matter who is in office or who is doing the reporting. As officials have become more public in what they do and their words and actions are increasingly on the record, the response of the institutions in which they serve is to create ongoing units handling and maintaining that relationship. While at one time presidents and their senior staffs frequently dealt directly with reporters, today there are established White House staff organizations that handle press relations.

Demands for Accurate and Timely Information

The continuity of the relationship can be seen in what reporters demand from government. No matter whether elected officials are Democrats or Republicans or what branch of government they are in, reporters want similar information and on terms consistent with their news routines. Presidents and members of Congress as well respond to reporters' demands by establishing institutions and positions responsive to the needs of news organizations.

No matter what the time period, information lies at the core of the relationship. Consistently, reporters present three basic demands to elected officials and those who work for them. The demands are: accurate information provided on a timely basis and responsive to the news needs of reporters; a policy of equal access to information; and guarantees of an open information policy. While officials in the executive branch rarely meet those demands wholeheartedly, the president and his staff find that if they don't comply with these demands they will often face continuing, clamorous complaints from the press. When President George W. Bush claimed in his 2003 State of the Union address that Iraqi president Saddam Hussein had made overtures to acquire uranium from Niger, reporters asked for the documentation. At first White House staff did not respond, but once knowledgeable people outside of government, such as former Ambassador James Wilson, provided information challenging the president's set of facts, staff found they had to admit their error and discuss where the speech vetting process went wrong.[7]

The demands for accurate and timely information have led to strains in the relationship between reporters and officials, especially in the presidential press relationship beginning in the mid-twentieth century. For much of early American history, presidents were able to choose what information they released and on what terms. In the twentieth century, as the executive branch was required to provide increasing amounts of information on the record, conflicts increased over the release of specific information reporters wanted and the accuracy of what they were given. Beginning in the late 1950s with inaccurate accounts of a U.S. spy plane shot down over the Soviet Union, reporters complained loudly about being given false information.[8] In this case, the White House had first indicated that the plane was a weather plane, not the reconnaissance plane it actually was. The administrations of Presidents Lyndon Johnson and Richard Nixon repeatedly lied to reporters, which created continuing conflict between the presidents and news organizations.

A routine type of conflict between reporters and officials occurs over what constitutes news. Officials and those running for office regard their agenda as newsworthy, while reporters often consider it otherwise. Dan Balz of the *Washington Post* explained the difference between tracking down information that a news organization believes to be important for the public, and serving the interests of public officials. "We should recognize that political campaigns and elections at their heart belong to the voters and not to the candidates," Balz said.[9] "It is often easy to organize the coverage of a campaign around candidates as opposed to voters. Candidates have their own agenda, but it is not necessarily the same as what the voter's agenda is. It's important for the press from the outset of a campaign to try to get a fix on what the voter's agenda is and not simply what the candidates have decided they want to talk about." The same conflict over what is newsworthy repeats itself in coverage of government policy and decision making.

Impact of the Press on Governing

In a government in which the citizens elect officials who set government policy, there are generally three sets of linkage institutions affecting the relationship between those governing and the public in whose interest decisions are made. In the United States, those three institutions are the political parties that organize elections, interest groups that serve as intermediaries in the policy-making process, and the news media, which carries information between government officials and the public. News organizations have a crucial role in informing the public of their government's actions, even in those circumstances in which the government would prefer to hold information close within its ranks.

There are four central ways in which the combined and singular media impact both those who govern and the governing process. First, news organizations inform the public of the actions of their national government officials. Second, the information provided by news organizations influences the conduct of those in government. Third, through their published work, reporters inform people within government of the actions of other governmental institutions.

Often people working in Congress discover what is going on at the White House through reading newspaper accounts. Fourth, information provided by news organizations serves as an early warning system for government officials of problems they may not have recognized or issues coming to the surface that they did not see coming.

Informing the Public

The basic responsibility of reporters covering governmental institutions is to inform the public of what officials are doing and about official policies and goals. White House reporters, for example, provide information about actions taken and statements made by the president and the president's senior-level advisers. While the president and the president's staff would perhaps like the media to limit their coverage to statements made by them, there is more to the task of covering the White House than serving as a direct transmission line. White House reporters blend information from the president and presidential staff members with that received from other sources, including officials who work in Congress, the bureaucracy, and the institutions outside of government interested in governmental policies and actions.

Governmental institutions vary greatly in the degree to which their operations are visible to the public. One of the most significant developments of the twentieth century was the trend to put government on the record. For most of its history, the Congress did a great deal of its business behind closed doors, though floor debates were open sessions. Committee hearings were held outside public view until congressional reforms adopted in 1970 required a recorded vote by committee members to close hearings and meetings. Governmental departments and agencies did not open their records to public view until the 1966 Freedom of Information Act required that documents be made available unless officials could present an acceptable legal argument for why they should remain closed. News organizations have used the law as an important lever to pry out information that officials seek to keep hidden. In 1991, during the administration of George H.W. Bush, when reporters for the *Washington Post* could not get information from the White House staff on the finances involved in the personal travels of Chief of Staff John Sununu, they used the Freedom of Information Act to get the information. The released records revealed that Sununu used public funds to pay for travel to his dentist and to a stamp auction in New York.[10] He resigned within the year.

Influencing Behavior

With television pictures aired worldwide in the summer and fall of 1992 showing people suffering from extreme malnourishment in Somalia, President George H. W. Bush responded to the calls for help from the United States by sending troops there. Prior to that point, complained at least one official in the

State Department, those calling for action had little effect on administration officials. "A State Department official said the Bureau of African Affairs tried in vain
to obtain the priority attention of Secretary of State James A. Baker III, his top
echelon of senior advisers and the White House," reported Don Oberdorfer in
the *Washington Post*.[11] The State Department staff member complained he could
not get the attention of senior administration people because they only "react to
headlines and television pictures."

Particularly with the rise of television, governments respond to humanitarian crises around the world even though, as in the Somalia case, the situation
turned out to be far more complicated than the president and his staff anticipated
when entering the country. President Clinton met and responded to similar
demands for action with the coverage of ethnic violence in Bosnia.

News organizations have an impact on what happens to legislation through
the assessments they make of the prospects of a proposed bill becoming law.
When the second Strategic Arms Limitation Treaty (SALT II) was before the
Senate in 1979, the bleak assessment in the press about its chances for ratification
influenced the thinking of senators. "When we say it won't win, it makes it easier for a senator to say no," commented the *Wall Street Journal* correspondent
Dennis Farney, who was then covering Capitol Hill.[12] Sometimes an assessment
of poor prospects for a bill can aid a president in shaping strategic dealings with
members of Congress. The president can claim in personal discussions with
members that their support is needed. Based on their internal assessment of the
poor prospects for the legislation as contained in press reports, President Reagan
and his staff developed a strategy to get Senate approval for the sale of sophisticated AWACS surveillance planes to Saudi Arabia. Instead of dealing with the
importance of the sale itself, the president appealed to senators based on a president's need for congressional support of him as a world leader. The opening up
of congressional proceedings influenced the decision-making process in yet
another way. Once meetings were open to the public, those interested in legislation under discussion could learn a great deal about what was going on by reading press accounts of the sessions. Interest groups and individuals could then craft
strategies to advance their cases.

Knowing that news organizations are seeking the unofficial as well as the
official version of a situation also influences individuals' behavior. Conflict-of-
interest situations, for example, provide ready-made copy for news organizations.
Whether the conflicts involve close relationships between government officials
and corporations or campaign contributors, those issues get close attention from
media organizations of all types, electronic and print. In George W. Bush's first
term in office, for example, news organizations gave close attention to the
appointments made by the president to track those who gave large amounts of
money to the president's 2000 campaign. In addition, they also followed the government contracts awarded to the Halliburton Corporation and its subsidiaries,

because Vice President Richard Cheney formerly headed the company. Elected officials are aware of how they can draw the attention of news organizations and the ways in which they can avoid doing so. There is a familiar strategy for releasing bad news: To minimize coverage, release the information on a Friday, around 4:00 PM, because it will appear in the Saturday papers, which have a lower readership than other days, and come out at a time when the public is less likely to watch television.

Informing Government Officials

News reporting informs government officials of events and issues of which they were unaware. Members of Congress often learn of issues from news organizations, and use news vehicles to keep themselves current on foreign and domestic policy developments. Representative Thomas Carper of Delaware commented that when he served in the House, the press was an important source of information for him. "Part of my job in Congress is a learning process—to learn about issues," he remarked.[13] The same can be said for those in the White House, though the extensive staff support enjoyed by the chief executive makes it less likely that the president will learn something first from a newspaper or television broadcast.

There are stories that bring about governmental responses. In 2004 the *Washington Post* ran a series of articles on the Nature Conservancy, a nonprofit organization, detailing questionable financial practices.[14] It was not long before the Senate Finance Committee began looking into the organization's financial practices, followed by notification by the Internal Revenue Service that it planned to do an on-site audit. An earlier *Post* series on the United Way of America led to federal government prosecution, and ultimately conviction, of organization head William Aramony for misuse of funds.[15]

One of the information-dissemination activities among news organizations is the release of polling results. Beginning in the 1970s, news organizations went into partnership with one another, and often associated with an established polling organization, to produce public-opinion polls related to the popularity of government officials, with a focus on the president, and public thoughts on individual policy initiatives. Some of the polling combinations include the *Washington Post* and ABC News; CNN, *USA Today,* and the Gallup organization; CNN and *Time;* and NBC News and the *Wall Street Journal.* Polls also plumb the effectiveness of institutions, such as the Congress and the news media. Results are closely watched by those inside government as well as those in the Washington community. A hint of softness in the support of a president can influence what elected officials and others do. The consistent public support for President Clinton during his impeachment trial in 1999, as seen through public-opinion polls, made it difficult for those pressing the case to get a conviction.

Early Warning System

The press serves as an early warning system for government officials on emerging problems. The questions reporters raise in their regular meetings with officials and their staffs can alert officials as to what's making news. An important function of the press secretary's morning information session with reporters, popularly known as the "gaggle," is to give White House aides the opportunity to discover what is on reporters' minds. That way, staff members can better prepare for their day, as they want to make certain that when the televised briefing occurs, they will be well prepared.

Government Influence on News Organizations

All three branches of government consistently serve as an influence on the organization, operations, and actions of news outlets. Government actions run the gamut from measures taken to regulate news organizations to procedures used to protect the routines and products of news media. There are times when news organizations use one part of government to protect themselves from another. The *Washington Post* and the *New York Times*, for example, sought the protection of the courts to publish segments of a Rand Corporation study of Vietnam War decision-making, publication of which the Nixon administration tried to prevent. The Rand Corporation study became known as the Pentagon Papers as the study was contracted by the Defense Department.

With respect to the impact of the government on the press, there are four areas of inquiry. First, governmental branches and units take actions to protect news organizations as an essential part of a republican form of government. Recognizing that news organizations have a vital role in public understanding of government, governmental organizations have taken action to protect the place of news organizations in American society. Second, through facilitators paid by public funds, government provides information to news organizations about the operations of government. Information that these governmental officials provide and what they hold back makes a difference with respect to what the public knows about government operations. Third, news organizations have historically been a beneficiary of government support. Congress has enacted legislation protecting faltering newspapers from antitrust legislation and presidents have chosen newspapers to act as their official organ for printing administration information.

Fourth, government regulates news organizations, most especially radio and television. In the case of the Internet, government agencies developed a new medium and then chose to provide little regulation of it. Finally, officials have used informal means to influence the actions of news organizations, including intimidation. During the Nixon years, the president and his staff leaned on news organizations to adopt behaviors more in line with what the administration considered acceptable.

A robust press is important to the proper functioning of a republican government. "In a political democracy, the media are a vital force in keeping the concerns of the many in the field of vision of the governing few," observed Michael Schudson.[16] "When the audience for news is expanded, the shape of politics changes." Once people are aware of problems, from reading or listening to news media accounts of issues and actions, government officials receive demands for responses. Recognizing the important place of news organizations in finding out about and dealing with societal problems, government sometimes provides protection for those who do the reporting. Many states, for example, have shield laws, which provide that reporters do not need to reveal their sources. Shield laws are a recognition by government that the society prospers when there is an active press.

The courts at the state and national levels have been important in protecting reporters and interpreting the Constitution where it relates to news organizations and their role in society. So, too, has the Congress, through a variety of laws, including ones protecting the ability of the news media to be profitable. Newspapers and magazines "benefit from policies that help to protect profitability and to restrict new competition," the media scholar Timothy Cook has observed.[17] Sometimes governmental efforts to protect news organizations have resulted in creating exemptions for them from certain laws. The Newspaper Preservation Act of 1970, for example, allowed newspapers facing financial difficulties to combine publishing operations with other newspapers in the same cities in spite of existing antitrust laws. Cook concludes, "Both the legislative intent *and* the policy outcome are to protect the ability of news organizations to make a profit, by removing regulation that they would otherwise have to undergo if they were just any other business."[18]

In their effort to make certain that reporters and their news organizations are aware of their intentions and actions, government officials have staff whose role it is to facilitate the process of getting information to the media. While members of Congress did their own press work until the mid-twentieth century, presidents hired staff knowledgeable in the ways of the press in the period after the Civil War. Routinely, the president's secretary, a person analogous to a chief of staff today, had a background in newspaper reporting. In the twentieth century, a senior aide with tasks dedicated to press matters was first hired in the Hoover administration. Later administrations augmented the staff to include a communications director. In the early twentieth century, governmental departments routinely hired public affairs officers to handle their press relations. In the 1960s and 1970s, members of Congress hired press secretaries to deal with the daily news needs of reporters, and then a decade later they recruited communications directors to plan out their publicity strategies.

In addition to providing select governmental information to news organizations, some laws serve as tools for news organizations to unearth information they are seeking from government officials. The strongest of those tools is the Freedom of Information Act, enacted in 1966 and strengthened several times afterward. Reporters have used the law to pry loose information and even to retrieve photographs, as was the case in 2004 when reporters used the act to get photos of the coffins of military personnel killed in Iraq as they returned to the United States.

As mentioned previously, news organizations have been the beneficiaries of government support. In the early years of the United States, an administration coming into office bestowed printing contracts on one newspaper, which was also granted the privilege of publishing government information. Congress, too, chose newspapers to publish its record of floor activity. Because of the perceived importance of the press, newspapers and magazines receive favored postal rates in order to disseminate information at reasonable costs, by dint of legislation beginning with the Postal Act of 1792. The Internet receives favored treatment by having a tax-free status.

While newspapers do not work under regulations established by government, electronic media do. Whether it is radio or television, the airwaves are viewed as belonging to the public and therefore subject to regulation to protect citizens' interests. Government has validated the stake of the public in the news media by enacting legislation such as the Radio Act of 1927, in which the Congress declared the airwaves to be public and created a system of licensing. The Federal Radio Commission and then later the Federal Communications Commission established a process for granting licenses to stations and then reviewing their renewal. The FCC has within its scope of duties the tasks of monitoring what specific media air and determining in rare cases when there are breaches of rules calling for fines. At the same time, other government agencies are involved in decisions relating to media operations, including the Justice Department, which brings actions in cases of antitrust violations. Congressional committees follow trends in the news industry to look for restraint of trade and conduct issues as oversight procedures.

Also important are the informal ways in which government officials influence the conduct of news organizations and those who report for them. As mentioned above, during the administration of President Nixon, the White House staff kept a list of their detractors, regularly complained to and threatened news organizations, engineered contests over license renewals, and had administration spokesmen, including Vice President Spiro Agnew, sharply criticize news organizations for their reporting.[19] While news organizations felt intimidated by some of the administration's actions, critical reporting continued apace. The *New York*

Times and the *Washington Post* went to court when the administration sought to stop publication of the Pentagon Papers, and the *Post* strongly backed up its reporters Bob Woodward and Carl Bernstein when they were developing information on Watergate.[20]

Development of the Relationship

While there are a variety of ways to chart developments in the government-press relationship, three illustrative elements include the development of press routines and rules in covering government, the change of focus in press reporting from the Congress to the president, and the growing professionalization of the press as well as its independence from the political parties of the time. Taking these three elements as our guide, one can chart at least three general periods in the development of the press-government relationship. What was at first a situation where officials in government determined when they talked to reporters and to whom they spoke has evolved into a relationship where elected officials regularly undergo questioning by reporters. Theirs is a relationship in which rules of conduct gradually developed, controlled by government officials and, to a lesser extent, professional organizations protecting the interests of reporters. In the early twenty-first century, for example, reporters operate under a different set of rules in their relationship with the president than they did a hundred years before, when a corps of reporters first covered the White House on a regular basis. At that time, the rules favored the president to a degree that they do not today. It was the president's decision to call in reporters, and the president who decided on what was talked about and what could become public. Today reporters expect the president to respond to reporters' questions in limited and open settings several times a month. All of those sessions are made publicly available.

During the first period, from 1789 to 1860, a Washington press corps developed and the relationship between government officials and the press was characterized by partisanship, a state that lasted well into the second period. The media had an important role in meshing together the electorate and national political institutions. From 1860 to 1932 news organizations set up specific governmental beats, with rules governing their operations. For most of this period, Congress was the central location for coverage of government, with the presidency gradually winning an important share of news attention during the administrations of Presidents Theodore Roosevelt and Woodrow Wilson. The period 1932–2004 saw the president becoming the focus of government coverage, and more transparency in governmental actions due to freedom-of-information legislation. In addition, publicity organizations were created in most national governmental units, including government departments and agencies as well as the Congress, the White House, and the federal courts.

The Partisan Years: 1789–1860

U.S. newspapers initially developed as organizations with links to particular political parties that provided the news organizations with printing contracts. The partisan nature of the relationship resulted in the deepening of the two-party system. "More effectively than substantive issues alone, the extensiveness of the press's political coverage, the penetrating partisanship of its new journalistic style, and the press's tight organizational links to the parties, all helped make possible a new and tumultuous era of American politics—the politics of mass mobilization in a firmly entrenched two-party system," commented the political scientist Richard Rubin.[21]

In those early years, news organizations did not cover the capital city by a beat system, in which reporters were assigned to particular government institutions. Instead the Congress drew the attention of most reporters. Crosby S. Noyes, who became publisher of the *Washington Evening Star,* described reporting in the capital city when he came to Washington in January 1848. "The corps of correspondents was small then—less than a dozen in all. The Senate chamber was the center of interest."[22] Journalistic practice was more a matter of gathering tidbits from each of the institutions of government than questioning its officials. Franklin Howe spoke of how *Star* reporters worked. After putting together clippings, the person assigned to gather news would "then go up to the White House, the War and Navy Departments and the treasury, gleaning from them such news as was obtainable; stop at the office and leave his copy, and then, when Congress was in session, get up to the Capitol by about half-past 12 o'clock, and send from there such matter as was of particular interest to Washington readers, as late as he could get anything in for that issue."

With the crowd of reporters a small one, there were tacit understandings, but few rules governing the manner in which reporters operated. There were no limits on who could cover the Congress or the other institutions. Reporters talked with presidents and other officials when both perceived the need.

Development of Accreditation and News Beats: 1860–1933

In 1860 the Government Printing Office took over the printing of government documents, which was one factor leading to an unraveling of the close relationship between administrations, political parties, and the press. "The establishment of the GPO signals an important change—but it is a signal, not a fact of a forthcoming independence," commented the journalism professor Michael Schudson.[23] "Lincoln rewarded just as many editors with ambassadorships in1864 as in 1860. He still relied on a party press. The press was intensely partisan for decades to come."

Reporters came to Washington as the center of action for the national government and, as their numbers proliferated, began focusing their attention on covering specific institutions of government. Nationwide, the number of daily newspapers grew from 387 in 1860 to 2,044 in 1931.[24] Government began regulating its relationship with reporters through credentialing of those who covered the actions of the Congress, the institution consistently drawing the largest number of reporters. But that focus gradually shifted as the twentieth century progressed, to a preponderance of attention paid to the presidency. The press followed the actions of government, and once the United States became a great world power, the president was perceived to have awesome authority.

One of the most important continuing contacts between presidents and journalists was established during the early part of the twentieth century. The first president to regularly meet directly with reporters was Theodore Roosevelt, who agreed to be interviewed in the morning, while he was being shaved by his barber. Reporters could ask him questions, but nothing was to be used in their reporting. While President William Howard Taft met with reporters from time to time, he chose those whom he felt comfortable with and did not have an established routine. It was President Woodrow Wilson who established the press conference as a basic forum in which the president met with reporters to answer questions posed by them. Wilson's press conferences were the first regular meetings in which Washington correspondents were granted equal access to the president. President Wilson met regularly with reporters his first two years in office and then essentially stopped the practice, except for an occasional session. President Warren Harding met with the press on a regular basis during his two and a half years in office, but no transcripts have been found to authenticate the regularity of the sessions. President Calvin Coolidge conducted 521 press conferences in five and a half years, establishing the press conference as a regular session. President Hoover followed his practice, though he had fewer press conferences and was less forthcoming in responding to policy questions.

Transparency and Presidential Dominance: 1933–2004

As the twentieth century progressed, reporters gained ground in their relationship with the government through the gradual opening to public view of the workings of governmental institutions and through routines established for getting information from government officials. In the executive branch, reporters grew to expect meeting with the president for sessions in which the president was questioned first on an off-the-record basis and then, beginning in the Eisenhower administration, on the record in sessions aired on television. President Franklin Roosevelt met with reporters twice a week, and he and his press secretary, Stephen Early, decided what parts of the sessions reporters could use in their stories. President Harry Truman reduced the frequency of these meetings to once a week, but retained the off-the-record nature of the sessions. Once the sessions became on the record, and televised at that, their frequency diminished. When remarks made at press conferences were off the record, the risk of error was relatively low. The president con-trolled what was released.

As the presidency has become a more public institution, so too has the Congress. In both institutions, the growth in on-the-record sessions with reporters has resulted in the development of communications operations. Today members of both houses of Congress have press secretaries who handle daily press operations, as well as a communications staff involved in publicity planning. At the White House, the publicity staff developed at an earlier point than it did on Capitol Hill. The publicity staff went from a dozen people during the Eisenhower administration to fifty-two in the administration of President George W. Bush. In addition, the units dealing with the press have grown and become specialized. All daily contacts and long-range planning in the Eisenhower years was done in the Press Office by Eisenhower's press secretary, James Hagerty. In George W. Bush's first term, five institutions handled publicity: the Press Office, the Office of Communications, Media Affairs, Speechwriting, and Global Communications.

While in the 1970s members of Congress began to hire a staff person dedi-cated to dealing with the press, in 2004 all House members and senators had press secretaries who handled daily relations with reporters and communications directors to plan publicity strategy. But members of Congress are generally more accessible to the press than is the president. Reporters can talk directly with members of Congress, whose doors are typically open to the press and who gen-erally welcome publicity for their initiatives and for themselves. In addition, the leaders of both houses meet with reporters before legislative business begins for the day. Typically, in the House all of the majority party leaders are accessible to the press following the Speaker's session.

Information coming from other parts of government has been adapted to routine as well. Even the courts and agencies and departments have hired public-ity staffs that are responsible for handling dealings with news organizations. Each of the departments and agencies has a public affairs office of some kind. The Supreme Court has an official handling media contacts and a room reserved for news organizations to report on court decisions and activities. Supreme Court justices, traditionally reluctant to deal with news organizations, have become somewhat more public, and occasionally grant interviews, including on-camera interviews, to reporters.

Coverage of Government and Evolution of Government Reporting

Once Washington became the federal city in the early nineteenth century, reporters staked out their territory to follow its operations. News from Washington, however, was not of much interest to the elite New York newspa-pers. Writing about his early days as a newspaper reporter in Washington,

Lawrence Gobright, the first Washington bureau chief for Associated Press, commented: "The New York papers, which were regarded, even at that time, as enterprising, rarely contained more than half a column of Washington news, Congressional proceedings included; and this was the complexion of all journals outside of Washington."[25] When Gobright came to Washington in 1834, the press corps was small and "poorly paid," he noted. For six weeks of the year Gobright was the only correspondent in town. "It was the fashion for almost every newspaper man to follow the example of the members of Congress, and leave the city at the same time they did."[26]

Gradually a Washington press corps developed. The first correspondents were letter writers, such as Matthew Davis, who submitted items to several publications under different names. He sent his letters to the *New York Courier and Enquirer* under the name of "The Spy in Washington" and to the *London Times* as "The Genevese Traveler."[27] James Gordon Bennett became a Washington correspondent in 1828 for the *New York Enquirer*. A description of his coverage by a contemporary, Benjamin Perley Poore, suggests he viewed his assignment as providing not only a roundup of political information, but social tidbits as well. All his reporting was delivered as a personal observation. "These letters were lively, they abounded in personal allusions, and they described freely, not only Senators, but the wives and daughters of Senators, and they established Mr. Bennett's reputation as a light lance among the hosts of writers," wrote Poore.[28] Letter writers did have substance in their pieces as well as accounts of the atmosphere of the institutions. In 1857 a committee was appointed in the House of Representatives to follow up on charges of corruption relating to the passage of legislation. The action resulted from information contained in a letter written by James Simonton appearing in the *New York Times*.[29] Three House members resigned as a result of the investigation.

While partisanship in the press remained for some while, there were trends toward a more objective press. Beginning in 1865 the Associated Press provided via telegraph the texts of speeches and documents as well as presidential messages and congressional proceedings.[30] The development of the telegraph in 1844 and subsequently the rise of Associated Press led to reporting with a timeliness and a more objective style than had previously been the norm. "The heads of the Associated Press were troubled by warped opinions and the twisted reports in news columns, which had helped stir sectional antipathies before the [Civil] war," noted Douglass Cater.[31] "They started to lay down rules about 'straight' reporting which would avoid all bias and alienate none of their numerous member papers." The number of reporters in Washington increased during the Civil War years, with forty-nine listed in the 1867 Congressional Directory for the press galleries, which was up from the handful there when L. A. Gobright came to town in 1834.[32] The press corps covering Washington was without rules and represented a diverse group. The first woman to cover the Congress was Jane

Swisshelm, who came to Washington in 1850 to write a column for the cele-brated *New York Tribune*. Women were not a large group of reporters in the nine-teenth century, but they did represent 12 percent of the 167 correspondents accredited to the press galleries of the two houses of Congress prior to 1880.[33]

O. O. Stealey, who was the Washington correspondent for the *Louisville Courier-Journal* for almost a quarter century, described the close relationship of reporters and officials during the late 1800s from the vantage point of the early twentieth century. "Then, as now, the Washington correspondents enjoyed the close companionship of the men who run the Government," he said. "There was not a night, twenty years ago, that the offices of the boys on 'Newspaper Row,' then extending along Fourteenth Street from the Ebbitt House to the avenue, were not crowded with Senators, Representatives, and cabinet officers."[34] In the 1870s the close relationship between officials and reporters led to problems for both. Reporters were caught up in the Credit Mobilier scandal. Credit Mobilier was a single-purpose board created by the Union Pacific Railroad, designed to receive funds coming from government contacts. Stock in Credit Mobilier went to government officials, many of whom lost their positions. In 1875 the House of Representatives expelled all reporters who acted on behalf of legislation. Shortly thereafter the Congress adopted rules of accreditation for congressional correspondents. Donald Ritchie's description of the rules suggests the incestuous environment that had existed. "These rules defined an accreditable correspon-dent as one whose primary salary came from sending telegraphic dispatches to daily newspapers. The rules also barred lobbying by any member of the press gallery; and prohibited all clerks from executive agencies (although not from congressional committees)."[35] While bringing some regulation to the reporting process, the effect of the rules was to bar from the galleries those who reported for weeklies and who did not send their copy by telegraph, a relatively expensive way of transmission. Women in particular were harmed, as many worked for news organizations with limited funds. Only one woman, Emily Briggs, was able to continue reporting from the congressional galleries.

As the Congress developed processes for accreditation, the White House created space for the reporters who were coming daily to cover the president. By 1896 reporters had space at the White House on the second floor and a small group of reporters, including William Price and Robert Hazard, were regularly there.[36] When reporters were allowed to follow presidents at close range and meet with them regularly, the two sides sometimes worked together in ways later thought to be too close. A correspondent with forty years in Washington explained the close relationship presidents sometimes had with reporters. "Mr. [Teddy] Roosevelt did not hesitate, indeed, to suggest news articles and news paragraphs to the reporters, and even went so far on more than one occasion as to write out with his own hand what he wanted sent over the wires," David Barry noted in the early 1920s.[37] Barry recounted one example relating to railroad rate legislation in 1905, where President Roosevelt wrote out for the news wires a response to an action by Standard Oil Company. While reporters were sometimes willing to let the president take the initiative in writing copy, they also gave the president advice. Oscar King Davis, the Washington bureau chief of the *New York Times,* advised President Taft on how he could improve his speechmaking.[38]

Reporters had close relationships with their colleagues as well as with some chief executives and their staffs. With so many of them working out of Newspaper Row and in offices close to one another, they sometimes shared information or even their copy. Leo Rosten, who chronicled the habits of the Washington press corps in the 1930s, indicated correspondents worked together sharing information in several ways. "Information is shared, advice given freely, the fruits of individual labor pooled," he commented.[39] "The National Press Club serves primarily as a clearing house for the exchanges of facts, tips, leads, and gossip. After any press conference, for instance, correspondents compare notes, consult colleagues on the 'angle' to be followed in interpretation, and seek the opinion of reporters more expert in certain fields of news." A second way reporters worked together was through a practice known as "blacksheeting," which referred to the carbon copy of a journalist's typewritten story. "The correspondent receiving the blacksheet from a colleague is free to treat it as he sees fit," Rosten wrote after talking with reporters who observed the practice.[40] "Generally he uses it as a guide and a source, incorporating only its substance into his own news-story." Reporters generally did not use blacksheet copy as their own, but there were instances of plagiarism. After Herbert Hoover accepted the Republican presidential nomination, the stories reporting the event in the *New York Herald Tribune* and the *Baltimore Sun* were almost identical.[41]

By the 1930s, reporters worked in a more independent and straightforward way, rather than being directed by headquarters as to which officials they were to feature and which to avoid mentioning. "The policy of a newspaper is maintained through less conscious and more subtle channels: through a choice of personnel, through subjective adjustments on the part of reporters, and through the institutionalization of a scale of values within the organization." News organizations could be selective in the hiring of Washington correspondents. Rosten's survey found 65 percent of his sample of Washington correspondents had college degrees and another 28 percent had attended college without receiving a degree.[42] Only 23 percent had no college work at all. Those figures contrast with the education level Stephen Hess found in his 1981 survey of members of the Washington press corps. Hess's respondents not only had college degrees, but those on the high-prestige and specialty beats had graduate degrees as well. Of those reporters on the White House and covering Congress, 41 percent and 29 percent, respectively, had graduate degrees.[43] Richard Strout, who first began reporting from Washington in the 1920s, commented to Hess that, comparing

the press when he first began in the 1920s with correspondents in the early
1980s, "The press is more sophisticated and less partisan than fifty years ago."[44]
His view was shared by the other older journalists with whom Hess spoke.

In addition to the changes that have taken place in how the press corps
works and their relationships with officials and their colleagues, the size and the
variety of media in the Washington press corps has developed since the time the
press corps was formed. At the end of the Civil War, when the corps began to
take its shape, there were 49 correspondents in the congressional galleries who
worked for wires or newspapers.[45] In the early twenty-first century, the group of
correspondents numbered approximately 8,000 accredited reporters in the four
divisions of the congressional galleries.[46] There are 2,000 newspapers; 1,835 periodicals; 2,527 radio and television; and 354 photographers. While in the early
years of the Washington press corps only newspaper correspondents covered the
political scene, in the latter part of the nineteenth century those working for
services, magazines, and photographers for print publications were gradually
added to the numbers. In the twentieth century, electronic media joined the
corps, first with radio and then television. With the addition of each new
medium, the configuration of Washington press coverage has changed. Once television came to the capital city, elected officials and their staffs favored broadcast
journalists. What has remained the same is the interest reporters have in digging
out the story of how governmental institutions operate, and in acquiring accurate information on a timely basis.

Notes

1. Quoted in Mike Allen, "What the $87 Billion Speech Cost Bush: Polls May Indicate
   That TV Address Eroded President's Support on Iraq," *Washington Post,* September
   20, 2003.
2. Quoted in Ken Auletta, "Fortress Bush," *New Yorker,* January 19, 2004, 55.
3. Martha Joynt Kumar, "The White House and the Press: News Organizations as a
   Presidential Resource and as a Source of Pressure," *Presidential Studies Quarterly* 33,
   no. 3 (September 2003): 672.
4. Background interview with a White House correspondent who frequently travels
   with the president.
5. Kumar, "The White House and the Press," 676.
6. See Grossman and Kumar, *Portraying the President,* 17–35.
7. See Dana Milbank and Walter Pincus, "Bush Aides Disclose Warnings from CIA;
   Oct. Memos Raised Doubts on Iraq Bid," *Washington Post,* July 23, 2003.
8. For a thorough discussion of government efforts to mislead reporters, see Wise, *The
   Politics of Lying.*
9. Remarks made during "Election 2004: Advancing Our Domestic Agenda," seminar
   sponsored by the Manship School of Mass Communication, Reilly Center for
   Media and Public Affairs, Louisiana State University, November 4, 2003, Washington, D.C.

10. For coverage of then chief of staff John Sununu's trip to New York to attend a stamp auction, see Ann Devroy and Bill McAllister, "Sununu's Trip Lawful, White House Aides Say" and "'Doing Official Business' When in the Car," *Washington Post*, both June 18, 1991, A1. For news articles on his use of military aircraft, see Ann Devroy and Charles R. Babcock, "Sununu: Frequent Flier on Military Aircraft; Trips to Ski Resorts, Home, Fund-Raisers," *Washington Post*, April 21, 1991, A1.

11. Don Oberdorfer, "U.S. Took Slow Approach to Somali Crisis; Delay in Action Attributed to Civil War, Other Global Problems, Lack of Media Attention," *Washington Post*, August 24, 1992, A13.

12. Interview with Dennis Farney by Martha Joynt Kumar, Washington, D.C., June 25, 1979.

13. Interview with Representative Thomas Carper by Martha Joynt Kumar, Washington, D.C., January 19, 1984.

14. Joe Stephens and David B. Ottaway, "IRS to Audit Nature Conservancy from Inside," *Washington Post*, January 17, 2004, A1.

15. Bill Miller, "Ex-United Way Chief Found Guilty"; "Aramony, Two Others Convicted of Scheme to Cheat Charity," *Washington Post*, both April 4, 1995, A1. The original *Washington Post* article detailing William Aramony's misdeeds is Charles E. Shepard, "Perks, Privileges and Power in a Nonprofit World; Head of United Way of America Praised, Criticized for Running It Like a Fortune 500 Company," February 16, 1992, A1.

16. Schudson, *The Power of News,* 20.

17. Cook, *Governing with the News,* 58.

18. Ibid., 59.

19. For a thorough treatment of the attacks upon the press by Nixon White House officials, see Porter, *Assault on the Media*. 20. *New York Times Co. v. United States,* 403 U.S. 713 (1971).

21. Rubin, *Press, Party, and Presidency,* 52.

22. Crosby S. Noyes, "Washington Journalism, Past and Present," *Washington (D.C.) Evening Star,* December 16, 1902.

23. Comments to the authors, February 10, 2004.

24. Harold W. Stanley and Richard G. Niemi, *Vital Statistics on American Politics,* 5th ed. (Washington, D.C.: CQ Press, 1995), 50.

25. L.A. Gobright, *Recollection of Men and Things at Washington during the Third of a Century* (Philadelphia: Claxton, Remsen, & Haffelfinger, 1869), 400.

26. Ibid.

27. Ben[jamin] Perley Poore, *Perley's Reminiscences of Sixty Years in the National Metropolis* (Philadelphia: Hubbard Brothers, 1886), vol. 1, 57.

28. Ibid., 58.

29. Gobright, *Recollection of Men and Things at Washington,* 402–7.

30. Marbut, *News from the Capital,* 134.

31. Cater, *The Fourth Branch of Government,* 85.

32. N. O. Messenger, "Reporting and Publishing the News of Congress Then and Now," *Washington (D.C.) Evening Star,* December 16, 1902.

33. Poore, *Perley's Reminiscences,* 77–78.

34. O[rlando] O. Stealey, *Twenty Years in the Press Gallery* (New York: Publishers Printing Company, 1906), 1–2.
35. Ritchie, *Press Gallery,* 109
36. See Martha Joynt Kumar, "The White House Beat at the Century Mark," *Harvard International Journal of Press/ Politics* 2, no. 3 (summer 1997): 10–30.
37. David S. Barry, *Forty Years in Washington* (Boston, MA: Little, Brown, 1924), 271.
38. Oscar King Davis, *Released for Publication: Some Inside Political History of Theodore Roosevelt and His Times, 1898–1918* (Boston: Houghton Mifflin, 1925), 102–3.
39. Rosten, *The Washington Correspondents,* 88.
40. Ibid., 89.
41. Ibid.
42. Ibid., 159, 221.
43. Hess, *The Washington Reporters,* 53.
44. Ibid., 82.
45. Since most working reporters covering national governmental issues deal with the Congress, they become members of the congressional galleries. Even for those covering the White House, the congressional galleries are important, as almost all reporters are first a member of a gallery before receiving White House accreditation through their respective news organizations.
46. These figures come from Senate and House employees responsible for the individual congressional galleries. The figures are as of December 2003.

Bibliography

Cater, Douglass. *The Fourth Branch of Government.* Boston: Houghton Mifflin, 1959.

Cook, Timothy E. *Making Laws and Making News: Media Strategies in the U.S. House of Representatives.* Washington, D.C.: Brookings Institution, 1989.

Cook, Timothy E. *Governing with the News: The News Media as a Political Institution.* Chicago: University of Chicago Press, 1998.

Cornwell, Elmer E. *Presidential Leadership of Public Opinion.* Bloomington: Indiana University Press, 1965.

Davis, Richard. *Decisions and Images: The Supreme Court and the Press.* Englewood Cliffs, N.J.: Prentice-Hall, 1994.

Grossman, Michael Baruch, and Martha Joynt Kumar. *Portraying the President: The White House and the News Media.* Baltimore: Johns Hopkins University Press, 1981.

Hess, Stephen. *The Washington Reporters: Newswork.* Washington, D.C.: Brookings Institution, 1981.

Hess, Stephen. *The Government/Press Connection: Press Officers and Their Offices.* Washington, D.C.: Brookings Institution, 1984.

Linsky, Martin. *Impact: How the Press Affects Federal Policymaking.* New York: Norton, 1986.

Marbut, F. B. *News from the Capital: The Story of Washington Reporting.* Carbondale: Southern Illinois University Press, 1971.

Ritchie, Donald A. *Press Gallery: Congress and the Washington Correspondents.* Cambridge, Mass.: Harvard University Press, 1991.

Rosten, Leo. *The Washington Correspondents.* New York. Harcourt, Brace, 1937.

Rubin, Richard. *Press, Party, and Presidency.* New York: Norton, 1981.

Schudson, Michael. *Discovering the News: A Social History of American Newspapers.* New York: Basic Books, 1978.

Schudson, Michael. *The Power of News.* Cambridge, Mass.: Harvard University Press, 1995.

Sigal, Leon V. *Reporters and Officials: The Organization and Politics of Newsmaking.* Lexington, Mass.: D. C. Heath, 1973.

Summers, Mark Whalgren. *The Press Gang: Newspapers and Politics, 1865–1878.* Chapel Hill: University of North Carolina Press, 1994.

Wise, David. *The Politics of Lying: Government Deception, Secrecy, and Power.* New York: Vintage, 1973.

14

PUBLIC POLICY TOWARD THE PRESS: WHAT GOVERNMENT DOES *FOR* THE NEWS MEDIA

Timothy E. Cook

THE UNITED STATES HAS A WELL-DEVELOPED, IF NOT ALTO-gether coherent, public policy toward the press. Beyond the rights that the Supreme Court has established as deriving from the Constitution's guarantee of freedom of the press, the day-to-day conduct of news workers and the substance of the news are deeply influenced by legislation passed by Congress and by officials through their interactions with the news media. A depiction of these policies and practices is not simply one of government restrictions on the press. Instead, government subsidizes the news by limiting risks and cutting costs of gathering, publishing, and disseminating it; indeed, such subsidies may make news possible.

These conclusions may well be a bit startling. After all, the language of the First Amendment is bracingly direct: "Congress shall make no law . . . abridging the freedom of speech, or of the press." To some, this suggests that government should keep its hands off—and enable the news media to develop autonomously as journalists apply professional standards of their profession in response to their readers, viewers, and listeners. Governmental action toward the press is then viewed with suspicion, presuming that the best policies toward the news amount to the least policies.

Such absolutism has found a powerful voice among First Amendment lawyers, who posit unique responsibilities and privileges accruing to the press. Their touchstone is a 1975 speech by the late Supreme Court justice Potter Stewart.[1] Stewart began by noting that the media's revelations of the Watergate scandal, which helped push Richard Nixon from the presidency, made many citizens "deeply disturbed by what they consider to be the illegitimate power of the organized press in the political structure of our society." He retorted that the First

Amendment envisioned precisely such an adversarial relationship, "to create a fourth institution outside the Government as an additional check on the three official branches." To provide "organized, expert scrutiny of government," the Constitution must seek the "institutional autonomy of the press." In his oft-quoted words, "The publishing business is . . . the only organized private business that is given explicit constitutional protection."

However, Stewart's views did not prevail in the Supreme Court. Contrary to his claim, the news media receive no rights broader than those accruing to members of the public. Instead, the Court pointedly declined to recognize a number of constitutional rights: for news organizations to be free of economic regulation that applied to them as businesses, for reporters to refuse to disclose names of confidential sources, for journalists to have access to government proceedings barred to the public, for newsrooms to be free of legal police searches, or for an "editorial privilege" around the newsgathering process comparable to the "executive privilege" the Court found for decision making in the presidency.[2]

This outcome may well be correct. For one, Stewart's historical account is flawed. The historian Charles Clark, assessing what he calls "the press the founders knew," suggests that the newspapers of the early republic were highly dependent on partisan help and government largesse.[3] While they then scrutinized in an organized way, they were neither expert nor independent of political power.

Of equal importance, American government has, since its inception, enacted and enforced public policies that apply to the press. These policies contradict absolutists' suggestions that government power is inimical to a free press. This essay looks beyond the celebrated court cases on freedom of expression. The full range of public policy toward the press shows that it is characterized as much by what government does *for* the press as the absolutists' concern with what government does *to* the press.

From Sponsorship to Subsidies

Why do we usually presume that freedom of the press means a hands-off approach to public policy?

First, public policy toward the press does not always appear to be "about" the news. For example, the media scholar Leo Bogart has written of "the crazy quilt of regulations that constitute our ad hoc national media policy, one that even its most dedicated interpreters find hard to make sense of, much less apply in any rational way."[4]

Second, most considerations of freedom of the press are by students of constitutional law, who gravitate quickly to judicial decisions, especially by the Supreme Court. Such a list is incomplete. Congress and the executive are also centrally involved in applying the Constitution.[5] More specifically, the Supreme Court was all but silent about the First Amendment until the twentieth century.

The scholar David Rabban has remarked, "No group of Americans was more hostile to free speech claims before World War I than the judiciary, and no judges were more hostile than the justices on the United States Supreme Court."[6] The key developments in freedom of the press, such as the demise of the Sedition Act in 1800 or the debate over the policy prohibiting abolitionist publications from being mailed, came instead from Congress and the president, often after widespread public debate.[7]

Federal and state officials outside the judiciary continue to create their own understandings of freedom of the press, which are sometimes more generous than that of the Court. For example, the Supreme Court, in 1969, found that two Arizona newspapers violated antitrust laws when they shared a physical plant but maintained separate editorial operations. Congress and the president promptly (in 1970) enacted the Newspaper Preservation Act, exempting such newspapers from antitrust laws. Similarly, after the Supreme Court declined to find a constitutional right for reporters to protect identities of confidential sources, many states enacted shield laws that granted journalists this right.

Finally, journalists themselves have had less of an interest in depicting the advantages given to them than in claiming constitutional rights. As W. Lance Bennett and William Serrin make clear in their essay in this volume, news workers gain much of their legitimacy by claiming to be acting on behalf of the people as independent watchdogs over power. The classic textbooks of journalism history depict the emergence of such professionalism as the news media moved away from a reliance upon partisan sponsors to become a more independent and objective institution.[8]

Decline of Sponsorship

History does reveal a shift away from what can be called "the sponsored press."[9] In the early years of the American republic, newspapers were usually financed by factions or were extensions of party machines. Each president designated a Washington newspaper as "official," thereby giving it lucrative printing contracts that would keep it afloat. The secretary of state selected a newspaper in each state to publish the laws, facilitating a national system of administration newspapers. If Congress allowed reporters to have access to congressional proceedings, it used such power on a case-by-case basis to admit friendly reporters and keep others out. Such sponsorship created the vibrant (if vituperative) news media system that Alexis de Tocqueville encountered in his American travels in the 1830s, with competing partisan newspapers being found in almost every far-flung city, town, and hamlet.[10]

Beginning in the 1830s, with relatively inexpensive mass-circulation "penny papers," a commercial journalism developed that began to displace the party press. The new use of steam power, more powerful presses, and less expensive paper enabled increasingly large numbers of issues aimed at the growing urban population. Partisanship, as well as politics as an issue, was downplayed in order to attract a mass audience that would interest advertisers—who, by the 1890s, provided the main economic support for the news.

At the turn of the twentieth century, newspapers, especially in cities, were enormous enterprises, free of political and financial sponsorship by government. From there, newspapers developed many of the central practices and norms of today's news media: a focus on fact above opinion, the rise of reporters rather than editors as central figures of journalism, a professional ethic of objectivity, and the taking on of a watchdog role on behalf of the public.

As newspapers became more financially independent of government and decreased their attention to politics, the onetime sponsorship did not matter so much. Officials began to conclude that offering advantages to news outlets on a case-by-case basis was sometimes not worth the resultant headaches. Thus, in 1841, the Senate got out of the business of ruling on reporters' credentials but admitted all who were "bona fide Reporters, to be so certified by the Editors of the papers for which they report."[11] When the current Capitol was constructed in the 1850s, separate press galleries for reporters were built to accommodate their continuing presence. With the creation of the Standing Committee of Correspondents in the 1870s, reporters themselves were delegated the task of deciding who should be admitted to the congressional press galleries. And after years of turmoil in designating official newspapers, the federal government got out of the business of awarding printing contracts, with the establishment of the Government Printing Office in 1860 and the *Congressional Record* in 1873.[12]

Rise of Subsidies

While sponsorship thus declined over the nineteenth century, subsidies available to news publications and reporters grew.[13] These subsidies were further supplemented by Congress's power under the Constitution (Article I, Section 8, Clause 8) to safeguard intellectual property rights.[14] Copyright enables authors (and media organizations) to make money from their publications. Individuals holding intellectual property do not, unlike physical property, own it in perpetuity, but the length of copyright protection has been dramatically extended over the years. Copyright also now applies in domains where it was once excluded, notably the news.

Subsidies, strictly speaking, are grants from government to private organizations. But media organizations can also be subsidized by exemption from regulation, by tax deductions, and by reduced government charges, all of which allow news outlets to keep more of their money, or put funds back into media operations. More broadly, subsidies encompass all government practices that reduce the cost of gathering, assembling, and disseminating the news. Thus, subsidies include government spending to provide reporters with information: by opening up government documents and processes for public scrutiny; and by establishing and staffing public information offices throughout government that provide facts, produce press releases, generate media events, and respond to reporters' inquiries.

Subsidies of continuing importance to the press include, in chronological order of adoption: (1) below-cost postal rates for sending periodicals through the mail; (2) government underwriting of new technologies that benefit the news media; (3) regulation, especially of broadcast and cable media, in ways that stabilize the prospect for profit; and (4) a public relations apparatus that permeates all branches and all levels of government to serve the needs of reporters and the news.

Development of the Media System

A national news media system in what would become the United States predates a national political system. At first, each of the thirteen British colonies was governed separately, and most commerce and news traveled back and forth to London. The first regularly produced newspapers in the colonies, starting in Boston in 1704, were officially sanctioned. Their printers tended to be postmasters who sent their products for free through the mail.

Printers' Exchanges

Newspapers proliferated to include all of the colonies. Some printers, such as Philadelphia's Benjamin Franklin, created networks of newspapers by sending coworkers to new locales. But the growing number of newspapers that printers sent free of charge weighted down the post, and printers had trouble collecting on subscriptions from those who were mailed newspapers. In 1754 Franklin—now deputy postmaster general for America with fellow printer William Hunter—set forth a policy on carrying newspapers in the mail. Delivery of newspapers would be restricted to paying subscribers, and postmasters would enforce the collection. The policy forbade postmaster-printers from mailing their products without charge, with one key exception, "the single Papers exchang'd between Printer and Printer." And more regular service would be instituted across an increasingly extensive network of publicly built "post roads."[15] These policies facilitated the news, as printers readily found a variety of timely newsworthy items in other newspapers and borrowed them for use in their own.

As a result of these exchanges, the number of newspapers grew again, and their content shifted away from a focus on distant Europe to matters on the American side of the Atlantic.[16] The resultant wide circulation of news throughout the colonies made the American Revolution possible. Newspapers carried word of local problems and built consensus on collective grievances against the British. After the Revolution, too, advocates of a stronger federal government who had drafted a new Constitution were able to benefit from the flow of newspaper content from one state to the next to skillfully build support for its ratification.

Postal Act of 1792

The post office was by far the biggest part of a then-small federal bureau-cracy. Among the first decisions made in the new political system was the Postal Act of 1792, which preserved printers' exchanges and added new sub-sidies, while enlisting postmasters to be subscription agents. Congress rejected proposals to target benefits to only certain (presumably official) newspapers. It extended privileges to all newspapers—thereby recognizing the press as a collective entity in its own right. Those who favored free mail delivery for newspapers did not prevail, but the Postal Act instituted low rates below the cost of delivery. That approach persists today, with artificially low second-class postage for periodicals.

Printers had already shown that they could influence government action when they successfully campaigned against the reinstatement of newspaper taxes after the Revolution.[17] From 1792 on, they lobbied to preserve newspaper subsi-dies against postmasters general who complained of the losses of revenue from newspapers, which filled up the mailbags and brought in little income. Congress's support of the subsidies—and indeed for many later public policies that benefited local news outlets—is easily explained: there were well-connected printers in every state and district. By 1843, one writer would gripe, "There does not appear to have been a man in Congress who suspected that newspapers had not a divine right to some exclusive privilege at the post-office."[18]

The post office served newspaper printers more than it did everyday corre-spondents. Costly postage for letters made up losses incurred by delivering the news. Starting in 1792, the post office allowed printers to hire private post riders to use post roads, but barred a similar privilege for the delivery of letters. The post office also introduced quicker methods of delivering the mail: by sea in 1798 and, from 1825, by versions of the pony express, which mostly carried newspa-pers and brief bulletins, known as "slips," sent for free under the printers' exchange policy.

The Persistence of Postal Subsidies

All these ways that government absorbed the expenses of the press proved difficult to eradicate. The only privileges that vanished had outlived their utility. For example, free printers' exchanges were abolished in 1873, long after tele-graphic news and the Associated Press made them obsolete. If policies did pres-ent new restrictions, they were sweetened with new benefits. Thus, when Congress required publishers to prepay postage in 1875, it cut their costs by charging by the pound rather than by the issue.

Sometimes Congress has been more generous with certain publications, such as by allowing free in-county delivery of newspapers until 1962. But it has rarely tried to attach conditions to these subsidies. The one exception in 1912 required periodicals seeking second-class postage to identify their owners, disclose their circulation, and label as advertisements commercial content that mimicked the format of news—something that publishers soon found boosted the legitimacy of their editorial content; in the 1940s, weekly newspapers requested and got the same regulation.[19]

Beneficial second-class rates for periodicals exist today, even while the mail is now handled by a government corporation, the U.S. Postal Service (USPS), which is expected to balance costs and benefits. Today's postmasters general, like their predecessors, are sometimes stymied in their efforts to cut the expenses of delivering the news. For instance, in 1995 the USPS sought a new pricing structure, to subsidize only those periodicals that were presorted for automated processing by zip code into bundles of no less than twenty-four pieces, and increase the charges to others, mostly small-circulation periodicals. Groups representing newspapers, such as the American Newspaper Publishers Association (ANPA), lobbied to save the benefit, and the ultimate compromise produced far less divergence in cost between high- and low-circulation news outlets.

Underwriting Costs of New Technologies

Another historical continuity with respect to the American press is that the federal government has underwritten the costs of developing and implementing new technologies that benefit the news media, something that can be seen in the histories of the telegraph, radio, and Internet.[20] The inventor of the telegraph, Samuel Morse, received $20,000 from Congress for his early efforts in developing the technology—once successful, Morse suggested that the post office take control of the telegraph industry. Reginald Fessenden's pathbreaking radio broadcast experiments were underwritten by the U.S. Weather Bureau, which sought a way to quickly inform people of approaching storms. The Internet was developed as a national defense initiative in partnership with public universities.[21] In each case, the government declined to continue supervising the medium, even if it assisted its spread. For instance, private industry took over the telegraph business, helped by the federal government policy allowing for wires to be erected free of charge, alongside railroad rights-of-way. News organizations rapidly benefited from this government largesse by having easy access to quick information following the establishment of the Associated Press, a cooperative venture to send news bulletins across the wires, in the 1840s.

Regulation on the Media's Own Terms

First Amendment absolutists sometimes suggest that any form of regulation threatens the guarantee of freedom of the press. They ask, for instance, why broadcast and cable should be subject to greater regulation than print and, more recently, the Internet. But media organizations (including those for print and the

Internet) are not uniformly opposed to regulation, only to regulatory policies that do not reinforce their profitability.

Most media regulation is beneficial to news outlets. It stabilizes a market-place and reinforces the status quo against new competitors. The freewheeling development of the Internet has taken place largely without regulation, but those who wish to exploit its possibilities for profit are beginning to turn to government to figure out ways to deal with scourges like spam, viruses, and worms.

It is little wonder, then, that the communication industry has long organized into lobbies not to keep government at bay, but to protect and receive government benefits. For example, state press associations first appeared in the 1850s to defend the lucrative practice of legal printing. On the federal level, the ANPA was founded in 1887 for a common front on policies such as postal subsidies and copyright. The influence of industry can most clearly be seen with respect to radio and television regulation.

Broadcast Regulation

In 1912 Congress heard rumors that radio amateurs had interfered with the sinking *Titanic*'s broadcast pleas for help. In response, it obliged each radio operator to be licensed on a given broadcast frequency.[22] Since then, while assuming that the airwaves are publicly owned, the government has meted out frequencies to broadcasters (whether individuals, institutions, or corporations), who hold them as property.

The commercial possibilities of radio had gone virtually unexplored until the National Association of Broadcasters (NAB) was launched in 1923. This trade association of commercial broadcasters lobbied for government protection by establishing an independent commission to regulate radio. Commerce Secretary Herbert Hoover happily exclaimed, "This is probably the only industry in the United States that is unanimously in favor of having itself regulated."[23]

Opposition to a commission came from small nonprofit broadcasters who feared that such a commission might be held hostage by what they called "the radio trust." But NAB got its way. The Federal Radio Commission (FRC)—instituted in 1927 and succeeded in 1934 by the Federal Communications Commission (FCC)—implemented Congress's charge to protect "the public interest, convenience, or necessity." Applicants for licenses were favored if they were well financed, had sophisticated equipment, and aimed at a mass public. Such criteria played to the advantage of large commercial broadcasters.

Licenses, once granted to commercial broadcasters, have almost always been renewed. Regulation ended up working toward an oligopoly of a handful of large radio (and then television) broadcast networks. Efforts to expand the number of broadcasters by adding the ultrahigh frequency (UHF) dial or FM broadcasting or by fostering pay television and cable television were slow, and when successful, included protection of already existing stations from new competition.[24] For instance, the Supreme Court case that held that cable television could be constitutionally regulated focused on the "must-carry" requirements in a 1992 act of Congress, requiring cable systems to set aside several channels for local television stations, then among the most profitable of media operations.[25]

Regulation of radio and television permitted the industry to reap consistent high profits. It subsidized news operations, which were easy ways to meet the government's policy that stations must operate in "the public interest" for licenses to be renewed. If news programs lost money, such a loss was outweighed by the guaranteed market and impressive overall profit margins.

Broadcast Deregulation

Starting in the mid-1970s and accelerating with the election of Ronald Reagan to the presidency in 1980, public policy shifted away from economic regulation in many fields. But such deregulation has been selective.

Take the example of radio, where many restrictions have been lifted. In 1987 the FCC repealed the fairness doctrine, which required radio and television stations to accord equal news coverage to both sides of controversial issues, and streamlined the license-renewal process, downplaying the "public interest" criterion. The net result was to foster stations devoted to partisan commentary on the radio, exemplified by that of conservative talk-show host Rush Limbaugh, and to reduce the devotion to news as a recurring feature of most other radio stations' fare. In 1996 Congress passed the most sweeping telecommunication act since the FCC was set up in the 1930s, which removed most limits on the ownership of radio stations and directly led to a frenzy of buying and selling that produced consolidated empires of radio stations providing homogenized coverage that often had little to do with the local listenership.

But despite these reforms, radio still operates via the allocation of a small number of broadcast frequencies in a given locale, usually to commercial broadcasters. Attempts to change, even democratize, this system have been frustrated. In 2000 the FCC created a new policy to provide additional frequencies, wedged in between more powerful ones, for low-wattage community radio. The radio industry (including public radio) was united in its opposition and successfully urged Congress to repeal the policy.

And regulation still has its advocates, notably in lobbies such as NAB. For instance, when the FCC adopted rules in 2003 relaxing the cap on networks' ownership of local television stations, the NAB went to Congress and found allies from rural, predominantly Republican states like Alaska and Mississippi. Congress succeeded in lowering the number of network-owned stations and would have reduced it still further had President George W. Bush not threatened a veto of such legislation.

Newspapers and Regulation

Print media are less regulated by federal and state policies. However, like their broadcast counterparts, they benefit from policies that reinforce their profits and restrict competition. In particular, news organizations have asked for, and received, exemptions from numerous regulations required of other industries.[26] Notably, these exemptions stem from legislative discretion rather than judicially enforced rights.

For instance, news deliverers are excluded from federal minimum wage, overtime, social security, and child labor laws.[27] Newspapers and magazines receive federal tax breaks for certain activities, notably the broad category of "establishing, maintaining or increasing circulation." Many states exempt periodicals from sales taxes. Certain low-circulation newspapers are not covered by federal minimum-wage and unemployment rules. And, as mentioned previously, the Newspaper Preservation Act gives newspapers immunity from antitrust prosecutions when an "economically distressed" newspaper shares a physical plant with but has separate editorial functions from another newspaper.

Provision of Public Information

The crucial "information subsidy" is a matter of practice more than of law. Stated most bluntly, government spends public funds to staff offices and employ workers and in turn to generate the news. News workers require such assistance because they face a vexing dilemma: much news is emerging and unexpected, yet reporters must also generate news on a routine day-in-day-out (or, today, hour-in-hour-out) basis. The news thus relies on a steady stream of authoritative information, and on events involving newsworthy players, that government institutions can provide. Government, in short, dramatically cuts the cost of news-gathering.

Freedom of Information

Government subsidizes the news without directly intending to do so. Bureaucracies have their own internal "reporting systems"—documents, records, and reports upon which journalists can rely. Thus, crime reporters can turn to the police blotter rather than the invariably fruitless task of going out and looking for crimes that are occurring. As the sociologist Mark Fishman notes, "In routine newswork the detection, interpretation, investigation, and a good deal of the formulation of the written story have already been done by police, city clerks, insurance adjusters, morticians, and the like. . . . The work of these outsiders costs the news organization nothing other than the reporter's time to collect what is available."[28]

News workers can also gain information in ways provided to the public as a whole. For instance, sunshine laws enacted in the 1970s and intended to open up governmental processes to the public have actually been employed most heavily by professional observers including lobbyists and reporters. The Freedom of Information Act, enacted by Congress in 1966 to make the executive branch more accountable,[29] makes it a right for any person to seek access to the records of any federal agency, but business and journalism have been the most regular requesters of such information.

Public Information and Press Offices

News organizations divide the world up into beats—locales, institutions, or subject areas a reporter is assigned to cover that have been productive sources of news in the past. Reporters, to cover their beat, go on predictable rounds. They check with official sources and observe unfolding governmental processes. When the news beat is institutional, such as the White House, the Congress, the Supreme Court, or the police station, reporters are physically housed at the beat, along with counterparts from other news outlets, and repeatedly interact with the same officials and spokespersons. The process is self-perpetuating: reporters go where news is expected to happen, and officials then have an incentive to supply them with information, which continues to attract reporters, and so forth.

An oft-stated maxim is that reporters and officials are in tension, since reporters are interested in dissemination of information and officials in secrecy. But this argument is misleading. Officials are, in fact, highly interested in using the news as a way to communicate their views and priorities to a larger audience. But in the executive branch, they are legally prohibited from doing so directly, since Congress routinely bars federal funds from being used "for publicity or propaganda purposes." Others who are not legally barred find that going through the news enhances the credibility and reach of their messages.[30]

Officials find news useful for several purposes: setting concerns on the agenda, influencing the interpretation of issues, pressuring others to act, and, in general, winning public support for themselves and their institutions. As Martin Linsky points out, "When policymakers talk about time with the press, they do not see the press as an intrusion into their lives, but as a resource for them in doing their job."[31]

Thus, in each branch and at every level of government, reporters encounter many designated spokespersons, sometimes occupying full-time positions as press officers, press secretaries, or public information officers. It is a truism that wherever one goes in government, one finds more staffers and more activity geared toward the news than was the case when the classic accounts of American politics were published in the 1960s. Press officers are organized and ready to respond to reporters' inquiries, which means that they must often anticipate what reporters are likely to inquire about and find information accordingly. Of course, they are also eager to present their own versions of the news, for example through press releases. As part of press officers' tasks of getting news that reflects favorably on their institutions, they try to anticipate what reporters want and find ways to meet those needs. They consider it their job to deal with any and all reporters who request information.

We need not investigate here the effect that this system has on the content of the news. Suffice it to say that the growing commitment by officials of time, energy, and resources to dealing with the news absorbs many of the costs news organizations would otherwise incur. Indeed, without the routine involvement of government and of officials, it is hard to see how the newsmaking process could function at all.

Conclusion

Public policy in the United States works to facilitate, possibly enable, the work of the press. Government policies subsidize the expenses incurred in making the news. And government practices, especially the burgeoning public relations apparatus found in every branch and at every level of government, make the production of the news possible on a day-to-day basis.

Why does all of this matter? Simply put: if the news media's actions and contents are centrally influenced by public policy, and if we as citizens do not find that the news fits our needs or those of democracy, there are alternative ways to reform and improve the news beyond appealing to journalists and journalism—all the while preserving, perhaps enhancing, freedom of the press.

Notes

1. Potter Stewart, "Or of the Press," *Hastings Law Journal* 26 (1975): 631–37.
2. See *Associated Press v. National Labor Relations Board,* 301 U.S. 103 (1937); *Associated Press v. United States,* 326 U.S. 1 (1945); *Branzburg v. Hayes,* 408 U.S. 665 (1972); *Pell v. Procunier,* 417 U.S. 817 (1974); *Zurcher v. Stanford Daily,* 436 U.S. 547 (1978); *Herbert v. Lando,* 441 U.S. 153 (1979).
3. Clark, "The Press the Founders Knew."
4. Leo Bogart, "Shaping a New Media Policy," *Nation* (July 12, 1993): 58.
5. See Whittington, *Constitutional Construction.*
6. Rabban, *Free Speech in Its Forgotten Years,* 15.
7. See Curtis, *Free Speech, "The People's Darling Privilege."*
8. See, for example, Michael Emery, Edwin Emery, and Nancy L. Roberts, *The Press and America: An Interpretative History of the Mass Media,* 9th ed. (Boston: Allyn and Bacon, 2000).
9. See Cook, *Governing with the News,* chapter 2.
10. See Smith, *The Press, Politics, and Patronage.*
11. Quoted in Marbut, *News from the Capital,* 62. See also Ritchie, *Press Gallery.*

12. Frederick B. Marbut, "Decline of the Official Press in Washington," *Journalism Quarterly* 33 (1956): 335–41.
13. See Cook, *Governing with the News,* chapter 3, and Starr, *The Creation of the Media.*
14. See Sunstein, *Democracy and the Problem of Free Speech.*
15. See Kielbowicz, *News in the Mail.*
16. Charles E. Clark and Charles Wetherell, "The Measure of Maturity: The *Pennsylvania Gazette,* 1728–1765," *William and Mary Quarterly* 46, 3rd series (1989): 279–303.
17. John B. Hench, "Massachusetts Printers and the Commonwealth's Newspaper Advertisement Tax of 1785," *Proceedings of the American Antiquarian Society* 87 (1977): 199–211.
18. Quoted in John, *Spreading the News,* 30.
19. See Linda Lawson, "When Publishers Invited Federal Regulation to Curb Circulation Abuses," *Journalism Quarterly* 71 (1994): 110–20; and Lawson, *Truth in Publishing.*
20. See Richard B. Du Boff, "The Rise of Communication Regulation: The Telegraph Industry, 1844–1880," *Journal of Communication* 34, no. 2 (1984): 52–66; and Robert W. McChesney, "The Internet and U.S. Communication Policy-Making in Historical and Critical Perspective," *Journal of Communication* 46, no. 1 (1996): 98–124.
21. Thompson, *Wiring a Continent,* chapter 1; Douglas, *Inventing American Broadcasting;* and Hafner and Lyon, *When Wizards Stay Up Late.*
22. See Douglas, *Inventing American Broadcasting,* chapter 7.
23. Quoted in Rosen, *The Modern Stentors,* 49.
24. See Krasnow, Longley, and Herbert, *The Politics of Broadcast Regulation.*
25. *Turner Broadcasting System, Inc., v. FCC,* 512 U.S. 622 (1994).
26. See Lacy and Simon, *The Economics and Regulation of United States Newspapers.*
27. Marc Linder, "From Street Urchins to Little Merchants: The Juridical Transvaluation of Child Newspaper Carriers," *Temple Law Review* 63 (1990): 829–64.
28. Fishman, *Manufacturing the News,* 151.
29. See Foerstel, *Freedom of Information and the Right to Know.*
30. Cook, *Governing with the News.*
31. Linsky, *Impact,* 82.

Bibliography

Baldasty, Gerald J. *The Commercialization of News in the Nineteenth Century.* Madison: University of Wisconsin Press, 1992.

Busterna, John C., and Robert G. Picard. *Joint Operating Agreements: The Newspaper Preservation Act and Its Application.* Norwood, N.J.: Ablex, 1993.

Chermak, Steven M. *Victims in the News: Crime and the American News Media.* Boulder, Colo.: Westview, 1995.

Clark, Charles E. "The Press the Founders Knew." In *Freeing the Presses: The First Amendment in Action,* edited by Timothy E. Cook. Baton Rouge: Louisiana State University Press, 2005.

Cook, Timothy E. *Making Laws and Making News: Media Strategies in the U.S. House of Representatives.* Washington, D.C.: Brookings Institution, 1989.

Cook, Timothy E. *Governing with the News: The News Media as a Political Institution.* Chicago: University of Chicago Press, 1998.

Curtis, Michael Kent. *Free Speech, "The People's Darling Privilege": Struggles for Freedom of Expression in American History.* Durham, N.C.: Duke University Press, 2000.

Davis, Richard. *Decisions and Images: The Supreme Court and the Press.* Englewood Cliffs, N.J.: Prentice-Hall, 1994.

Douglas, Susan J. *Inventing American Broadcasting, 1899–1922.* Baltimore: Johns Hopkins University Press, 1987.

Fishman, Mark. *Manufacturing the News.* Austin: University of Texas Press, 1980.

Foerstel, Herbert N. *Freedom of Information and the Right to Know: The Origins and Applications of the Freedom of Information Act.* Westport, Conn.: Greenwood, 1999.

Gandy, Oscar H., Jr. *Beyond Agenda Setting: Information Subsidies and Public Policy.* Norwood, N.J.: Ablex, 1982.

Grossman, Michael Baruch, and Martha Joynt Kumar. *Portraying the President: The White House and the News Media.* Baltimore: Johns Hopkins University Press, 1981.

Hafner, Katie, and Matthew Lyon. *Where Wizards Stay Up Late: The Origins of the Internet.* New York: Simon & Schuster, 1996.

Hess, Stephen. *The Government/Press Connection: Press Officers and Their Offices.* Washington, D.C.: Brookings Institution, 1984.

John, Richard R. *Spreading the News: The American Postal System from Franklin to Morse.* Cambridge, Mass.: Harvard University Press, 1995.

Kaplan, Richard L. *Politics and the American Press: The Rise of Objectivity, 1865–1920.* Cambridge, U.K., and New York: Cambridge University Press, 2002.

Kielbowicz, Richard B. *News in the Mail: The Press, Post Office, and Public Information, 1700–1860s.* New York: Greenwood, 1989.

Krasnow, Erwin G., Lawrence D. Longley, and Herbert A. Terry. *The Politics of Broadcast Regulation.* 3rd ed. New York: St. Martin's, 1982.

Lacy, Stephen, and Todd F. Simon. *The Economics and Regulation of United States Newspapers.* Norwood, N.J.: Ablex, 1993.

Lawson, Linda. *Truth in Publishing: Federal Regulation of the Press's Business Practices, 1880–1920.* Carbondale: Southern Illinois University Press, 1993.

Linsky, Martin. *Impact: How the Press Affects Federal Policymaking.* New York: Norton, 1986.

Marbut, F. B. *News from the Capital: The Story of Washington Reporting.* Carbondale: Southern Illinois University Press, 1971.

McChesney, Robert W. *Telecommunications, Mass Media, and Democracy: The Battle for the Control of U.S. Broadcasting, 1928–1935.* New York: Oxford University Press, 1993.

Mindich, David T. Z. *Just the Facts: How "Objectivity" Came to Define American Journalism.* New York: New York University Press, 1998.

Rabban, David M., *Free Speech in Its Forgotten Years.* Cambridge, U.K., and New York: Cambridge University Press, 1997.

Riker, William H. *The Strategy of Rhetoric: Campaigning for the American Constitution.* New Haven, Conn.: Yale University Press, 1996.

Ritchie, Donald A. *Press Gallery: Congress and the Washington Correspondents.* Cambridge, Mass.: Harvard University Press, 1991.

Rosen, Philip T. *The Modern Stentors: Radio Broadcasters and the Federal Government, 1920–1934.* Westport, Conn.: Greenwood, 1980.

Schudson, Michael. *Discovering the News: A Social History of American Newspapers.* New York: Basic Books, 1978.

Smith, Culver H. *The Press, Politics, and Patronage: The American Government's Use of Newspapers, 1789–1875.* Athens: University of Georgia Press, 1977.

Starr, Paul. *The Creation of the Media: Political Origins of Modern Communications.* New York: Basic Books, 2004.

Streeter, Thomas. *Selling the Air: A Critique of the Policy of Commercial Broadcasting in the United States.* Chicago: University of Chicago Press, 1996.

Sunstein, Cass R. *Democracy and the Problem of Free Speech.* New York: Free Press, 1993.

Thompson, Robert Luther. *Wiring a Continent: The History of the Telegraph Industry in the United States, 1832–1866.* Princeton, N.J.: Princeton University Press, 1947.

Tuchman, Gaye. *Making News: A Study in the Construction of Reality.* New York: Free Press, 1978.

Whittington, Keith E. *Constitutional Construction: Divided Powers and Constitutional Meaning.* Cambridge, Mass.: Harvard University Press, 1999.

15

THE FIRST AMENDMENT TRADITION AND ITS CRITICS

Bruce W. Sanford and Jane E. Kirtley

VIRTUALLY ALL OF THE LAW DEFINING PRESS FREEDOM IN the United States grows from the First Amendment to the U.S. Constitution: "Congress shall make no law ... abridging the freedom of speech, or of the press." The protections of the First Amendment, which on its face only constrains the federal government, have applied to state governments since the 1920s through the Fourteenth Amendment. Those who have not studied the history of free speech in the United States in any detail may still recognize the rough outlines of what makes the tradition unique: the early rejection of seditious libel (libel against the government); the revulsion for licensing of the press and for prior restraint; the deep reluctance to punish speakers based on their viewpoints. The power of core beliefs from colonial times goes a long way toward explaining why the First Amendment experience in the United States has adapted to an unpredictable array of challenges since the eighteenth century and remains the heart of American democracy.

The brevity of the First Amendment belies its complexity. The words themselves seem unambiguously to prohibit Congress from censoring or controlling newsgathering activities and media content. But the development of the robust protections enjoyed by the press in the United States is of course a much more interesting story.

We look first at the history of the First Amendment and the various theoretical justifications behind the growth of First Amendment freedoms, an evolution that has dramatically accelerated since the 1970s. We then consider how these free-press principles have been applied in specific types of cases before the U.S. Supreme Court, such as those involving prior restraint, libel, privacy, and access to government information. Finally, we discuss the criticism that this expansion has generated, particularly among members of the Supreme Court itself.

History of the First Amendment

The enactment of the First Amendment in 1791 did not mark the beginning of free-speech protections in America. Nearly fifty years earlier, the trial of John Peter Zenger dramatically shaped colonial views on free speech and revealed a prerevolutionary desire for self-governance long before the first musket shots cracked on Lexington Green. Zenger, publisher of the *New York Weekly Journal,* had printed a series of harsh criticisms of the colonial governor of New York and, at the governor's demand, was charged with seditious libel. Although under British law, truth was not a defense to a seditious libel claim, the New York jury essentially rewrote the law, finding Zenger not guilty. Other courts were not bound to follow the jury's interpretation, but the truth defense was widely recognized throughout the colonies, and it largely put an end to seditious libel prosecutions as a method of British oppression.

In addition to the ever growing defiance of British rule, the influences of the Enlightenment had a significant impact on the development of free-speech theory in eighteenth-century America. Thomas Jefferson, James Madison, and other founding fathers subscribed to the tenets of the Enlightenment—the search for truth, the power of reason, the perfectability of society—and viewed freedom of expression as an essential tool for the ambitious democratic project that the new nation was about to launch.

Thus, when the Constitution was written in 1787 without explicit protection for free speech, it was not because no such protection existed as a matter of practice or belief, but rather because the founders feared that in enunciating such protections, they would inadvertently place restrictions on them. Likewise, when the First Amendment was added four years later as part of the Bill of Rights, it was not so much a declaration of new liberties as it was a reflection of political horse-trading—a restriction on the powers of the new federal government to make the Constitution more palatable to states' rights advocates.

It is impossible to know exactly what the founders intended by the press protections of the First Amendment. At the very least, the First Amendment was designed to prohibit the conditioning of speech on the securing of a license. However, many framers likely saw the protections as prohibiting a much broader array of efforts to inhibit press freedoms. This uncertainty has led to the development of various conceptions of the press clause of the First Amendment, each of which emphasizes different values and goals.

Conceptions of the First Amendment

No Law Means No Law

Those who believe that the First Amendment must be read literally—that is, to prohibit *any* regulation of speech or the press—are called First Amendment "absolutists." They maintain that no government interest can justify abridging or punishing the exercise of press or speech freedoms. Thus, they do not believe that it is within the legitimate role of legislatures or courts to balance First Amendment rights with competing concerns such as national security, reputation, privacy, and the administration of justice. Absolutists still have important lines to draw—between expression that merits complete protection as a "speech" or "press" activity, for example, and "conduct" that does not. Thus, although First Amendment absolutists may argue that laws punishing obscene magazines are unconstitutional, they are likely to find that putting an obscene image on a T-shirt and wearing it to a demonstration is punishable because it amounts to conduct, not speech.

Among the most well-known proponents of the absolutist theory were two long-serving justices on the United States Supreme Court—Hugo Black, who sat from 1937 to 1971, and William O. Douglas, whose term stretched from 1939 to 1975. When the Supreme Court in the 1960s moved to constitutionalize the law of libel—a body of law that previously had been in the hands of the states and their own common-law traditions—Black and Douglas voted with the majorities to expand protection for the press but indicated that they would have taken more drastic steps toward abolishing recovery for defamation. Informative examples of their views can be found in Justice Black's concurring opinion in *New York Times Co. v. Sullivan* and Douglas's concurring opinion in *Garrison v. Louisiana* (both 1964).[1] Although First Amendment absolutism offered the appeal of textual support in the Constitution and bright-line rules for deciding cases, it never enjoyed majority support on the Supreme Court and no longer can count among its followers leading jurists comparable to Black and Douglas. The absolutist view proved to be too one-dimensional for a world in which speech and press rights were bumping up against other societal interests and in which constitutional guarantees such as "due process" and "equal protection" were also subject to balancing.

Marketplace Model

For absolutists, the source of strong speech and press freedoms is the language of the First Amendment itself. One could theoretically be a First Amendment absolutist, in other words, without necessarily believing that these rights benefited a democratic society. Other thinkers who played major roles in the development of First Amendment freedoms in the twentieth century believed that it was necessary to identify the values or interests that these freedoms would advance. One of the first of these interpretations to gain currency was the idea that First Amendment rights were essential in guiding society in its search for truth.

This notion found its initial judicial voice in Justice Oliver Wendell Holmes's dissenting opinion in *Abrams v. New York* (1919), a case involving the criminal prosecution of socialist pamphleteers opposed to U.S. policy in Soviet Russia. The convictions were upheld, but Holmes's dissent endures: "When men have realized that time has upset many fighting faiths, they may come to believe ... that the ultimate good desired is better reached by free trade in ideas—that the best test of truth is the power of the thought to get itself accepted in the competition of the market, and that truth is the only ground upon which their wishes safely can be carried out."[2] Reflecting his nation's traditions of capitalism, Holmes wrapped his theory in the metaphor of the marketplace—First Amendment freedoms are valuable because they help society find truth in the "market" of ideas (see Schmuhl and Picard in this volume).

Echoes of Holmes's marketplace model can be heard in Justice William Brennan's opinions for the Supreme Court in the libel cases of *Sullivan* and *Garrison*. Marketplace concepts have also informed court decisions in a wide variety of areas—from cases protecting academic freedom on university campuses to those applying antitrust laws to media companies. As the law professor Lucas Powe has observed, "It is difficult to avoid Holmes' marketplace metaphor because it captures so much. It recognizes change; it resonates with an adversarial and competitive system that lawyers and economists find congenial; and it offers a more neutral arbiter of truth than the appraisal of a single individual or government."[3] But Powe is also quick to note that among the limitations of the marketplace model are "a belief in objective truth and in the predominance of rational thought, and an almost religious faith that truth will prevail, all of which beliefs have suffered greatly in [the twentieth] century."[4]

Personal Autonomy Paradigm

Another model for speech and press freedoms that flows from the writings of the Holmes era is the notion that First Amendment rights exist in order to enable citizens to pursue their intellectual desires and to develop as individuals through the expression of their views and beliefs. This approach has historical roots in the concurrence of Supreme Court Justice Louis Brandeis—who joined Justice Holmes's opinion in *Abrams*—in *Whitney v. California* (1927), a case involving the speech rights of union members. As Brandeis famously wrote, "Those who won our independence believed that the final end of the State was to make men free to develop their faculties. . . . They valued liberty as both an end and as a means."[5] The Supreme Court would decades later refer to the importance of this "intellectual individualism" in upholding the First Amendment right of citizens *not* to speak, in *West Virginia State Board of Education v. Barnette*, (1943), which struck down a state law requiring schoolchildren to recite the pledge of allegiance.[6]

Justifications for First Amendment freedoms that emphasize the intellectual and moral pleasures they provide to the individuals exercising these rights are probably more evident in cases focusing on "speech" as opposed to "press" protections. Even then, most theorists today look beyond this individual ful-fillment model to a more societal or communal role for the First Amendment. As Harvard University's Frederick Schauer explains, "We do not think of free speech primarily as an interest of the speaker. True, it is speakers that we are protecting, and it is speakers who 'create' or 'produce' the ideas and informa-tion that . . . we take to be so important. But . . . it is society's interest in knowledge and information that is important. The interest of the speaker is recognized not primarily as an end but only instrumentally to the public inter-est in the ideas presented."[7] Such structural considerations have probably been most responsible for driving First Amendment law since the mid-twentieth century.

Self-Government and the Rights of Listeners

The philosopher Alexander Meiklejohn was the architect of much mod-ern First Amendment theory. In *Free Speech and Its Relation to Self-Government,* published just after World War II, Meiklejohn laid out a vision of democracy in which the most important "public official" may well be the ordinary citi-zen. Meiklejohn argued that democracy earned its legitimacy from constant scrutiny and supervision of the governors by the governed. Citizens in this framework have something akin to a duty to criticize their elected officials in order to check state power and make government run honestly. To fulfill this duty, they must be well informed on public affairs. The key role that First Amendment freedoms—particularly press freedoms—play in this system is pro-viding citizens with the knowledge they need in order to govern themselves and to use their votes wisely. The press is vital in this scheme because of its ability to disseminate information widely and rapidly to the public. Thus, con-trary to an "absolutist" First Amendment based on the text of the Constitution, or a model of free speech based on individual fulfillment or a search for truth, Meiklejohn privileged press freedoms because of the structural glue they pro-vided to a self-governing people.

The ultimate expression of this conception of the First Amendment was the Supreme Court's opinion in *New York Times Co. v. Sullivan,* where Justice Brennan rejected the rules of common law libel for deterring "would-be crit-ics of official conduct" from "voicing their criticism."[8] Brennan reasoned that the "citizen-critic of government" should at the very least have the same pro-tection from defamation suits as government officials themselves enjoy.[9] "It would give public servants an unjustified preference over the public they serve, if critics of official conduct did not have a fair equivalent of the immunity granted to the officials themselves," he wrote.[10] Brennan supplied the First Amendment tradition with its most celebrated words since Holmes when he spoke of a "profound national commitment to the principle that debate on public issues should be uninhibited, robust, and wide-open."[11] In the

Meiklejohn–Brennan universe, speech on political and governmental matters takes on special importance because of its vital role in rejuvenating democracy and checking abuse of power.[12]

Once the Supreme Court accepted an instrumental view of the First Amendment, new questions arose regarding the extent to which newspapers and media companies could be regulated by the government in order to improve or enhance the quality of public debate. Supporters of regulation turned their focus on not the concerns of the speaker but the interests of the audience, thus giving birth to the "listeners' rights" model of the First Amendment or the "right to receive information." Advocates of listeners' rights argued that infringing the autonomy of publishers was necessary to ensure that the public was exposed to a variety of viewpoints on matters of public concern. Those who rejected the listeners'-rights approach believed that editorial independence was a bedrock principal of First Amendment freedoms that could not be disregarded, even in the name of attempting to improve public discourse.

These two approaches collided in a pair of Supreme Court decisions. In *Red Lion Broadcasting Co. v. Federal Communications Commission* (1969), the listeners'-rights model prevailed. The Supreme Court upheld the power of the FCC to compel broadcasters, as a condition of receiving and retaining a license, to air programming addressing controversial issues of public importance and to require them to carry replies by political candidates who had been criticized on air. The high court based its decision in part on the notion that the broadcast spectrum was a scarce public resource subject to limitations of space, time, and frequency. Some method of equitably allocating those frequencies had to be devised.

By contrast, in *Miami Herald Publishing Co. v. Tornillo* (1974),[13] the Court struck down a Florida statute that forced newspapers to publish candidates' replies under comparable circumstances. The Court opined that compulsory publication impermissibly intrudes on the function of newspaper editors, who, under the First Amendment, have the absolute right to exercise their own judgment about what they will publish. Although acknowledging the merit of Florida's intention of encouraging the press to provide a forum for a variety of viewpoints, the Court observed that "a responsible press is an undoubtedly desirable goal, but press responsibility is not mandated by the Constitution, and like many other virtues it cannot be legislated."[14]

Even though *Red Lion* was not technically overruled, a listeners'-rights conception of press freedoms that would trump the editorial autonomy of publishers did not recover from the loss in *Tornillo. Red Lion* thus remains an aberration in the First Amendment tradition, a precedent that is confined to its particular facts and to the perceived scarcity rationale involving the broadcast spectrum.

A Privileged Position and the Right to Know

At the same time that the tradition of editorial independence was being challenged in *Red Lion* and *Tornillo,* the press went on the offensive to test a theory of its own: that due to its instrumental position in keeping the American public informed and government accountable to the people, it should be vested with special privileges to carry out its job. Under this model—whose appeal may have peaked during the Nixon years, when the investigative journalists Bob Woodward and Carl Bernstein captivated the country with coverage of Watergate—reporters were to be permitted access to people and institutions denied to the public at large and granted special dispensation from laws of general applicability when such laws would harm newsgathering or publishing activities. As Justice Douglas wrote, "The press has a preferred position in our constitutional scheme, not to enable it to make money, not to set newsmen apart as a favored class, but to bring fulfillment of the public's right to know."[15]

Douglas's invocation of the "right to know," as this theory came to be known, appeared, however, in a *dissent* in *Branzburg v. Hayes* (1972), where the Supreme Court rejected the argument that reporters have a special testimonial privilege when questioned by grand juries. After *Branzburg,* media litigants lost other cases attempting to establish particularized rules for the press in a variety of circumstances, such as access to prisons and protection from search warrants. (In a dissent in one of the prison cases, *Houchins v. KQED, Inc.* [1978], Justice John Paul Stevens linked special access privileges for reporters to the "right to receive information" belonging to the public.)[16] Although a federal reporter's privilege was eventually recognized in many appellate circuits and by statute in many states, the "right to know" imperative met with little success in significantly extending press freedoms.

One Supreme Court justice who fought for the press in some of these battles, Potter Stewart, advised his friends in the media to give up on the notion of special favors. Stewart believed that the best perch for the press was as a "Fourth Estate"—a "fourth institution outside the government to check the potential excesses of the other three branches." He distilled the First Amendment tradition to these memorable words in a speech at Yale Law School:

So far as the Constitution goes, the autonomous press may publish what it knows, and may seek to learn what it can. But this autonomy cuts both ways. The press is free to do battle against secrecy and deception in government. But the press cannot expect from the Constitution any guarantee that it will succeed. There is no constitutional right to have access to particular government information, or to require openness from the bureaucracy. The public's interest in knowing about its government is protected by the guarantee of a Free Press, but the protection is indirect. ... The Constitution ... establishes the contest, not its resolution.[17]

Key U.S. Supreme Court First Amendment Rulings

Prior Restraint

A unique characteristic of First Amendment law is its strong aversion to prior restraint on expression, derived from an antipathy, dating back to the nation's colonial days, to government suppression of controversial ideas. In the seminal case of *Near v. Minnesota* (1931),[18] the Supreme Court struck down a state statute permitting government officials to prohibit the publication of newspapers that were found to be "malicious, scandalous, and defamatory" and requiring publishers who had been enjoined to obtain court approval before publication could resume. The high court ruled that prior restraint—government censorship—would be presumed to violate the First Amendment. However, the prohibition was not "absolutely unlimited." Chief Justice Charles Evans Hughes suggested that, for example, publication of the details of troop movements in wartime, obscenity, or incitement to violence might be restrained under certain circumstances.

Subsequent cases, most notably the Pentagon Papers case in 1971,[19] expanded and cemented the fundamental principle that, even when national security is at stake, the presumption against prior restraint holds, with the government bearing the burden of justifying any attempt to silence the press. That strong presumption has been explicitly extended to include speech advocating the violent overthrow of the government, as long as no imminent lawless action is likely to occur.[20] Even obscenity, a type of speech not protected by the First Amendment and therefore subject to government regulation and even criminal penalties,[21] is carefully defined through common law and by statute to provide adequate notice to speakers and to ensure that expression with serious literary, artistic, political, or scientific value is not restricted.

The need to protect reputations and personal privacy rights has been recognized by the high court. But *postpublication* lawsuits for civil damages, as opposed to *prior restraints* to prevent the speech in the first place, are considered to be the appropriate remedy in virtually every instance. Similarly, although the publication of details concerning criminal investigations arguably poses a potential threat to fair trial rights and the administration of justice, the Supreme Court generally has struck down "gag orders" imposed on the press, directing trial judges to first consider other solutions and to impose restrictions on the news media only when no viable alternative exists.[22]

An exception to the general presumption against prior restraints, however, is intellectual property. Under Article I, Section 8 of the U.S. Constitution, copyright holders enjoy "the exclusive right to their respective writings and discoveries," and federal copyright statutes provide them with various remedies, including the right to obtain injunctions against unauthorized infringement of their works. Although "fair use" of copyrighted materials for scholarship, criticism, and news reporting is permitted, even the news media can be sanctioned if their use exceeds reasonable limits.[23] A second exception concerns advertising, or speech that does nothing more than propose a commercial transaction. Although as recently as 1942, the Supreme Court considered advertising to fall outside the scope of the First Amendment, since the 1980s, the high court has expanded the protection for commercial speech to an extent that rivals that of political speech.[24]

A third exception arises with the regulation of the broadcast and cable media. Although the Supreme Court rejected prior review, and therefore de facto licensing, of the print media in *Near*, in *Red Lion* it upheld the power of government to license those who wished to utilize the electromagnetic spectrum for mass communication. The advent of new technologies, such as satellites and the Internet, has prompted courts and legislatures to reexamine whether this type of content regulation is ever justifiable. Some argue that with the introduction of new forms of media, reconsideration of the fundamental principles of freedom of expression characterizing U.S. jurisprudence is necessary. Others counter that technological advances have always provided governments with a pretext to exert control over the media, and that these attempts must be resisted at all costs. So far, the latter argument has had the upper hand; communications over the Internet enjoy the same degree of First Amendment protection as print media.[25]

Libel

Until 1964, the publication of false and defamatory statements about an individual enjoyed no constitutional protection. But in *Sullivan,* the Supreme Court recognized that, in order to promote robust debate about issues of public importance, news organizations must be given some leeway to make mistakes in good faith without facing liability. This landmark decision, decided in the midst of the civil rights movement, resulted in what some might regard as a paradoxical rule of law: The First Amendment must protect some falsity in order to encourage truthful speech. Thus, despite the fact that false speech remains an unprotected category of expression, the rules governing defamation are among the most complex in American law.

In *Sullivan,* the high court, much as it would later do in regard to the Pentagon Papers, shifted the burden of proof to government officials who wished to bring a civil action for libel. They would be required not only to prove that the statements complained of were false, but that the publisher either knew them to be false, or acted with reckless disregard of whether or not they were true. This so-called "actual malice" standard of fault, which is distinguishable and distinct from common-law malice or ill will, was subsequently extended to include libel suits brought by public figures as well. As a matter of constitutional law, the fifty states must adhere to this standard, although in suits brought by private figures, they may establish their own fault requirements, ranging from negligence to actual malice, as long as some degree of fault is required to be demonstrated.

In order to be actionable as libel, the statement complained of must be a statement of fact, not of opinion. This means that the statement must be capable of being proven true or false.[26] Truth is considered to be an absolute defense to a civil libel action, and, in the same term that it decided *Sullivan* (1964), the Supreme Court struck down the Louisiana criminal libel statute (in *Garrison*) because it did not permit defendants to assert a defense of truth. Today, private-figure libel plaintiffs also have the burden of proving falsity.[27] In *Hustler Magazine v. Falwell* (1988),[28] the Supreme Court declared that even "outrageous" and deliberate attacks on public figures could not be the basis of a lawsuit claiming libel or infliction of emotional distress, unless the plaintiff could demonstrate both falsity and actual malice.

Privacy

Privacy is not explicitly protected under the U.S. Constitution. Although the Supreme Court has interpreted the Fourth Amendment's prohibition of unreasonable searches and seizures by the government to include privacy rights, "the right to be let alone" by other individuals was not articulated until 1890, in "Right to Privacy," a *Harvard Law Review* article by Brandeis, before he ascended to the Supreme Court bench, and his law partner, Samuel Warren.[29] Subsequently, most states have recognized some or all of four distinct types of invasion of privacy: intrusion on seclusion, publication of private facts, portrayal in a false (not necessarily defamatory) light, and misappropriation of an individual's name or image for commercial use.

The attempt to balance privacy interests against the rights of a free press presents profound challenges for the courts and for society. Although the Supreme Court has recognized the importance of the individual's right to autonomy and to a private life, it has weighed those interests against the rights of the press to publish truthful information, even against the wishes of the news subject, provided that the information is a matter of legitimate public concern. On the other hand, although the Court recognized in *Branzburg* that "without some protection for seeking out the news, freedom of the press would be eviscerated," it has never defined the parameters of that protection with precision. Laws of general applicability, such as trespass or wiretap laws, apply to the press unless enforcement would impermissibly abridge the exercise of First Amendment rights.[30]

The "false light" tort of privacy, which is based on a claim that a publication is an untrue, but not necessarily defamatory, portrayal of an individual, has been discredited by some courts as constituting little more than an amorphous, watered-down version of libel, although others have considered it an essential remedy against distortion, embellishment, or fictionalization.[31] The tort of misappropriation, stemming from a "right to publicity" that is akin to a property right to control the exploitation of one's image, raises constitutional issues, at least in the news reporting context, similar to those posed by copyright.[32] Privacy law remains, unsurprisingly, one of the most volatile and controversial subjects in American jurisprudence.

Access to Government Information and Proceedings

In *Richmond Newspapers, Inc. v. Virginia* (1980),[33] the Supreme Court recognized that the First Amendment guarantees both the press and the public the right to attend criminal trials. Although the rights established in *Richmond Newspapers* plainly belong equally to both public and press, with technically no "preferred position" for the latter, Chief Justice Warren Burger's opinion for the Court expressly notes the distinctive structural role of the media as a surrogate for the general public in a democracy. In subsequent cases, the high court has extended this right to other proceedings as well, such as voir dire (selection of jurors) and preliminary hearings, although the right is not absolute. Portions of proceedings may be conducted in secret when the interests of justice demand, but closure should be as limited in scope and duration as possible.

Press and public access to the executive branch is primarily guaranteed through specific legislation, such as the federal Freedom of Information Act, although common-law and even constitutional rights of access to certain types of records have been recognized by some courts. The Freedom of Information Act creates a presumption of openness in records held by federal agencies, but includes nine specific exemptions, which are supposed to be narrowly construed. All fifty states have similar statutes in place governing public access to state and local records. In the post–September 11 era, perceived threats to national security have resulted in increasing restrictions on access to information, posing profound challenges to the press and its ability to keep the public informed on matters of concern to the nation.

The Critics

The free speech traditions that developed in the latter half of the twentieth century are not without their critics, of course. Some of these detractors, in fact, had a ringside seat in the development of this law. Justice Byron White, for example, who served on the Supreme Court from 1962 to 1993, the very period in which libel law was constitutionalized, resisted the Court's continued expansion of the *Sullivan* doctrine. Despite authoring one of the early press-friendly, post-*Sullivan* rulings clarifying the scope of the actual malice rule,[34] by the mid-1970s he had had enough and wrote a sharply worded dissent in *Gertz v. Robert Welch, Inc.* (1974). White stated that the limitations on libel suits by private figures established by the Court in that case were unjustified, and accused the majority of "deprecating the reputation interest of ordinary citizens and rendering them powerless to protect themselves."[35]

White's frustration with the high barriers to libel lawsuits in the United States does not make him an isolated figure on the bench. Defamation is for the most part a settled area of the law today, but even when ruling for press litigants, some judges cannot resist taking a gratuitous shot at perceived media excesses. Although the "actual malice" rules of *Sullivan* and later cases are well entrenched in American law, these protections and the theories behind them have not traveled well beyond U.S. borders. In *Hill v. Church of Scientology of Toronto* (1995), for example, the Supreme Court of Canada expressly rejected incorporating *Sullivan*-style protections into Canadian law.[36] The Canadian court laid out a number of criticisms of the actual malice rule, ranging from its responsibility for shifting focus away from what some perceive as the purpose of libel litigation—determining the truth of a challenged statement—to its role in driving up the costs of litigation.

English courts have also declined to adopt *Sullivan*. As Lord Nicholls of Birkenhead, speaking of the tension between free press and reputational interests, explained in his opinion in *Albert Reynolds v. Times Newspapers Limited* (1999), "No answer is perfect. Every solution has its own advantages and disadvantages. Depending upon local conditions, such as legal procedures and the traditions and power of the press, the solution preferred in one country may not be the best suited to another country."[37] Rejection of the actual malice standard is just one way in which the British have resisted the free-press ideals of their former colonists. Libel in Britain remains a strict liability offense—*no* degree of fault, whether recklessness or negligence, must be shown. In addition, libel defendants in England shoulder many of the evidentiary burdens that have been transferred to plaintiffs in the United States. A libel defendant in England, for example, must prove the truth of published statements. The press in the United Kingdom also can be subjected to prior restraint far more easily than their counterparts in the United States.

In short, courts in England and the commonwealth are far more likely to privilege reputational concerns and view curbs on media activity as necessary to protect other societal interests, such as the right to a fair trial. Although press freedoms in the United States are enviable, to be sure, First Amendment litigation has also stalled since the 1980s. The Supreme Court, for example, has not heard a libel case since 1991. The *Richmond Newspapers* line of decisions has been quiet since 1986. For First Amendment protections to remain strong, the law must continue to evolve and innovate.

Notes

1. *New York Times Co. v. Sullivan,* 376 U.S. 254 (1964); *Garrison v. Louisiana,* 379 U.S. 64 (1964).
2. *Abrams v. New York*, 250 U.S. 616, 630 (1919) (Holmes, J., dissenting).
3. Lucas A. Powe, Jr., *The Fourth Estate and the Constitution* (Berkeley: University of California Press, 1991), 237–38.

4. Ibid., 239.
5. *Whitney v. California,* 274 U.S. 357 (1927), 375 (Brandeis, J., concurring).
6. *West Virginia State Board of Education v. Barnette,* 319 U.S. 624 (1943).
7. Frederick Schauer, *Free Speech: A Philosophical Enquiry* (Cambridge: Cambridge University Press, 1982), 159.
8. *New York Times Co. v. Sullivan,* 279.
9. Ibid., 282.
10. Ibid., 282–83.
11. Ibid., 270.
12. See Brennan, William J., Jr. "The Supreme Court and the Meiklejohn Interpretation of the First Amendment." 79 *Harvard Law Review* 1 (1965).
13. *Red Lion Broadcasting Co. v. Federal Communications Commission,* 395 U.S. 367 (1969); *Miami Herald Publishing Co. v. Tornillo,* 418 U.S. 241 (1974).
14. *Miami Herald Publishing Co. v. Tornillo,* 256.
15. *Branzburg v. Hayes,* 408 U.S. 665 (1972), 721 (Douglas, J., dissenting).
16. *Houchins v. KQED, Inc.,* 438 U.S. 1 (1978).
17. Potter Stewart, "Or of the Press," *Hastings Law Journal* 26 (1975): 636.
18. *Near v. Minnesota,* 283 U.S. 697 (1931).
19. *New York Times Co. v. United States,* 403 U.S. 713 (1971).
20. *Brandenburg v. Ohio,* 395 U.S. 444 (1969).
21. *Miller v. California,* 413 U.S. 15 (1973).
22. *Nebraska Press Association v. Stuart,* 427 U.S. 539 (1976).
23. *Harper & Row Publishers, Inc. v. Nation Enterprises,* 417 U.S. 539 (1985).
24. *Central Hudson Gas & Electric Corp. v. Public Service Commission,* 447 U.S. 557 (1980); *McConnell v. Federal Election Commission,* no. 02–1674 (December 10, 2003).
25. *Reno v. American Civil Liberties Union,* 521 U.S. 844 (1997).
26. *Gertz v. Robert Welch, Inc.,* 418 U.S. 323 (1974).
27. *Philadelphia Newspapers v. Hepps,* 475 U.S. 767 (1986).
28. *Hustler Magazine v. Falwell,* 485 U.S. 46 (1988).
29. Samuel Warren and Louis D. Brandeis, "The Right to Privacy," *Harvard Law Review* 4 (1890): 193.
30. *Bartnicki v. Vopper,* 532 U.S. 514 (2001).
31. *Time, Inc. v. Hill,* 385 U.S. 374 (1967); *Cantrell v. Forest City Publishing Co.,* 419 U.S. 245 (1974).
32. *Hoffman v. Capital Cities/ABC, Inc.,* 255 F.3d 1180 (9th Cir. 2001).
33. *Richmond Newspapers, Inc., v. Virginia,* 448 U.S. 555 (1980).
34. *St. Amant v. Thompson,* 390 U.S. 727 (1968).
35. *Gertz v. Robert Welch, Inc.,* 418 U.S. 323, 370 (White, J., dissenting).
36. *Hill v. Church of Scientology of Toronto, 2 SCR 1130 (1995).*
37. *Albert Reynolds v. Times Newspapers Limited,* 3 WRL 1010 (1999).

Bibliography

Bezanson, Randall P. *How Free Can the Press Be?* Urbana: University of Illinois Press, 2003.
Bollinger, Lee C. *Images of a Free Press.* Chicago: University of Chicago Press, 1991.

Etzioni, Amitai. *The Limits of Privacy.* New York: Basic Books, 1999.

Friendly, Fred W. *Minnesota Rag: The Dramatic Story of the Landmark Supreme Court Case That Gave New Meaning to Freedom of the Press.* New York: Random House, 1981.

Kalven, Harry, Jr. *A Worthy Tradition: Freedom of Speech in America.* New York: Harper & Row, 1988.

LaMay, Craig L., ed. *Journalism and the Debate over Privacy.* Mahwah, N.J.: Lawrence Erlbaum, 2003.

Lessig, Lawrence. *Code and Other Laws of Cyberspace.* New York: Basic Books, 1999.

Lewis, Anthony. *Make No Law: The Sullivan Case and the First Amendment.* New York: Random House, 1991.

Meiklejohn, Alexander. *Free Speech and Its Relation to Self-Government.* New York: Harper, 1948.

Powe, Lucas A., Jr. *The Fourth Estate and the Constitution: Freedom of the Press in America.* Berkeley: University of California Press, 1991.

Smolla, Rodney A. *Free Speech in an Open Society.* New York: Knopf, 1992.

Sunstein, Cass R. *Democracy and the Problem of Free Speech.* New York: Free Press, 1993.

Ungar, Sanford J. *The Papers and the Papers: An Account of the Legal and Political Battle over the Pentagon Papers.* New York: Columbia University Press, 1989.

16

LEGAL EVOLUTION OF THE GOVERNMENT– NEWS MEDIA RELATIONSHIP

Jane E. Kirtley

The primary protector of freedom of expression . . . is government. . . . But any power capable of protecting freedom is also capable of endangering it.
Hutchins Commission, *A Free and Responsible Press,* 1947

THE PARADOX SET FORTH IN THE HUTCHINS COMMIS-sion report continues to resonate with contemporary readers: How can the government be expected to "protect" the press when the government's instinct is to control it? Given that tension, what is the appropriate role for a free press in a democracy? Watchdog or lapdog? Adversary, "loyal opposition," or cheerleader?

Has the government–news media relationship changed since the publication of the report of the Commission on Freedom of the Press in the 1940s? In the decades since the Hutchins Commission met and drafted its report, a variety of political events have challenged and radically altered assumptions about the government-media relationship. Some selected examples, not intended to be exhaustive, would include the following:

Korean War
Army–McCarthy hearings
Civil rights movement
Vietnam War
Watergate
Iran-Contra
Clinton impeachment
September 11, 2001
War on terrorism

Coupled with legal and social changes, such as the women's rights movement, and shifts in concentrations of media economic power, the relationship between the media and the government has been altered inexorably. In addition, the advent of the Internet has broken the media monopoly on news, changing forever the press's relationship with its readers and viewers, particularly as broker and filter of information.

On the other hand, the tension between the government's desire to regulate and control the news media and the media's desire to remain unfettered is essentially unchanged. The public remains ambivalent about the value of a free press, and what curbs, if any, should be imposed by the government.[1] Concentration of media ownership, with its attendant impact on the public's ability to receive information representing diverse sources and viewpoints, is even more troubling today than in the 1940s, as the media are increasingly associated with the institutions of power and perceived as part of the establishment rather than as an advocate for the powerless.

The years since the Hutchins Commission report have brought the most significant developments in First Amendment jurisprudence in the history of the United States. Coupled with statutory guarantees of access to government information and technological advances undreamed of in 1947, the press has more practical ability to gather and disseminate news today than ever before. Yet accusations of partisanship, sensationalism, and ethical breaches threaten to undermine public confidence in the institution of the press as a source of information.

Constitutionalization of the Media-Government Relationship

In 1931, long before the Hutchins Commission began its deliberations, the Supreme Court's seminal decision in *Near v. Minnesota* established the strong presumption against the constitutionality of prior restraint on the press.[2] "Prior restraint" refers to any attempt by the government, including the judiciary, to censor or otherwise prevent the publication or dissemination of information. But in the tumultuous years of the 1960s and 1970s, the high court presided over a variety of battles that were to define the limits of the power of government to rein in the press.

Prior Restraint and National Security

The Hutchins report devoted many pages to concerns about the government's power to restrict or punish expression advocating the overthrow of the government. Although the commission's concerns may seem justified in light of the Red Scare of the 1950s, in fact, as early as 1951, in *Dennis v. United States*, the high court recognized that the formulation by Justices Oliver Wendell Holmes and Louis Brandeis of a "clear and present danger" test had been embraced by a majority of the justices, even though a plurality chose not to apply it in that particular case.[3] In 1957, in *Yates v. United States*, the Supreme Court reversed convictions under the Smith Act of 1940, which made it a crime to advocate, or form or belong to an association that would advocate, the violent overthrow of the government. Twelve years later, in *Brandenburg v. Ohio*, it was made clear that criminal syndicalism statutes may not be used to forbid advocacy of the use of force or of the violation of law, except when such advocacy is directed to inciting imminent lawless action.[4]

But what about government censorship in the name of protecting national security? *Near* and its progeny[5] had not involved classified information. It took the Pentagon Papers case,[6] a raw collision of power between the Nixon administration and the twin bastions of American journalism, the *New York Times* and the *Washington Post,* to prompt the Supreme Court to establish the principle that, if the government wishes to prohibit publication of its secrets, it must bear the burden of justifying the need for that prior restraint. Although the high court did not rule out the possibility that the press could be subjected to postpublication sanctions for breaches of national security based on laws of general applicability, it set the bar against prior restraint so high as to make it virtually insurmountable.

Despite a handful of cases involving injunctions, civil lawsuits, and prosecutions of government employees who attempted to disclose or leak classified information,[7] no prosecutions of the press have occurred. The *Progressive* case, involving a court order enjoining a magazine from publishing an article describing how to build a hydrogen bomb, an order that was subsequently rendered moot by another newspaper's decision to publish a letter containing the same information, illustrated the futility, even in the pre-Internet era, of attempting to control the release of information by gagging media outlets one at a time.[8]

Criticism of the Government

Against the backdrop of the civil rights movement, the Supreme Court enshrined the First Amendment "right to be wrong" in its 1964 ruling in *New York Times v. Sullivan*. Recognizing for the first time constitutional protection for false and defamatory speech about government officials by requiring proof of actual malice (knowledge of falsity or reckless disregard for the truth), the Court, in *Sullivan* and the same term's *Garrison v. Louisiana*, dealt a death blow to statutes punishing seditious libel.[9]

The legacy of *Sullivan* and its progeny, of course, is hardly lacking in controversy. Many have argued that these cases provide the press with nothing less than a license to lie about officials and have discouraged qualified individuals from pursuing public service careers.[10] For their part, journalists have argued that *Sullivan* is a two-edged sword, inviting litigants to probe journalistic standards and reporters' motivations to an unacceptable degree, in ways that would have been irrelevant but for adoption of the *Sullivan* actual-malice standard.[11] Criminal libel statutes still exist, and have been enforced, in several states. But the practical impact of the Supreme Court's decisions has been to provide the press in the United States with virtually unlimited discretion to report on and to criticize the government.

Rights of Access to Government Information

In a series of decisions beginning in 1980, the Supreme Court identified a presumptive First Amendment right of access to criminal court proceedings.[12] The Court also ruled that the imposition of restraining orders on the press is almost always an unconstitutional (and ineffective) means of ensuring a fair trial.[13] These decisions have left the news media free to gather and report information about arrests, investigations, and prosecutions, from virtually any source at their disposal. In practical terms, however, in large part because of ethical restrictions on defense attorneys, what this often means is that the press relies heavily on law enforcement officials for leads and tips, inevitably skewing coverage in favor of the prosecution.

It is probably impossible to overestimate the significance of these rulings on the coverage of the judicial branch, especially when coupled with the Court's decision in *Chandler v. Florida* in 1981.[14] *Chandler* made clear that, despite perceived media "excesses" in the electronic coverage of high-profile trials, televising a criminal trial over the objections of the defendant did not necessarily violate the Sixth Amendment right to a fair trial. Despite the Supreme Court's continued resistance to electronic coverage of its own oral arguments, cameras in the courtroom have become a fixture in most jurisdictions. The impact of their presence on the administration of justice remains a source of continual debate.

The media's relationship with the legislative branch, traditionally the most accessible branch, also has been changed by technology, culminating in C-SPAN's cameras providing the public with "unfiltered" access to congressional proceedings. News reporters and pundits have not been eliminated, but their roles have altered.

The right of access to the executive branch, by contrast, has been almost exclusively the province of legislation. The Administrative Procedure Act was passed in 1946, during the deliberations of the Hutchins Commission, but it took another twenty years for Congress to enact the federal Freedom of Information Act (FOIA) granting an affirmative right of access to executive branch agency records.[15] The FOIA is broad in scope and powerful in its presumption of openness, including only nine narrowly tailored exemptions and placing the burden for justifying nondisclosure on the government. From its inception, the FOIA has been a political football and legislative orphan, subject to periodic, and sometimes ruthless, amendment by Congress, and to the vagaries of each administration's interpretation. This has been particularly true during the post–September 11 era.

Many journalists declare that they never use FOIA, relying on traditional newsgathering techniques such as the cultivation of knowledgeable sources to pry loose government information, rather than a statutory scheme that they find cumbersome, unwieldy, and slow. Nevertheless, the existence of FOIA has forced government agencies to affirmatively disclose records that, if the agencies were left to their own devices, would probably have remained under wraps.

The right of access to other government institutions, including prisons, has also been considered by the Supreme Court. However, the resolution of these issues has been less than satisfactory from the media's standpoint. In cases such as *Houchins v. KQED, Inc.,* a divided Court held that despite the importance of oversight of the operation of jails and prisons, the press has no greater right of access to them than the general public does.[16] This principle has been embraced by the military, which has used it to, for example, justify excluding the press from Dover Air Force Base in Delaware, site of the return of soldiers' remains to the United States.[17] The media's attempts to assert a constitutional right of access to military operations have resulted in inconclusive rulings, with judges dodging the First Amendment issue by asserting impediments based on "mootness" or "ripeness."[18]

A legacy of the Vietnam period, with its open coverage of the war, was a powerful resentment of the news media among senior military officials. This led to the exclusion of the press from the invasion of Grenada in 1983 (see Prochnau in this volume). Subsequent attempts to reconcile the military's need for secrecy with the media's desire for information led to the formation of the Sidle Commission in November 1983, which proposed the concept of the Pentagon press pool. Supposedly designed to guarantee minimal media access to military operations, the press pool, at least initially, was considered a fiasco. Problems with accreditation and conflicts over "security review" of copy underscored an adversarial relationship, based on a fundamental distrust on both sides contrasting sharply with the cooperation that typified military–press relations during World War II. The press pool system underwent multiple reinventions and variations, culminating most recently in the "embedding" program in the Iraq War. Although the embedding program has been praised by the government and by some journalists as providing the public with eyewitness accounts of military operations, others have suggested that reporters operate as little more than a public relations branch of the armed forces.

Government Regulation of the Media

The Hutchins report devoted considerable space to the issue of regulation of the media. It focused on concentration of media ownership, as well as the disparate treatment (and second-class status, from a First Amendment perspective) of the electronic media.

Despite extensive deregulation of the electronic media during the Reagan administration, the broadcast media, and, to a lesser extent, cable, remain subject to greater government control over content than would be permissible for the print media. The disparity is even more remarkable given the Supreme Court's ringing affirmation that the Internet, despite being a new, electronic, and intrusive medium, is nevertheless entitled to the fullest First Amendment protection.[19] Attempts by the Bush administration in 2003 to lift caps on media cross-ownership have met with a public and judicial backlash suggesting that concentration of media outlets in a few hands is still regarded as problematic, even with the advent of new, more accessible forms of mass communication.[20]

Nevertheless, government content regulation of the electronic media is still alive and well. The fairness doctrine may be gone,[21] but the McCain-Feingold campaign finance reform law, enacted in 2002, can control political messages in the electronic media in ways that would be constitutionally suspect for print.[22] The contretemps following the pop singer Janet Jackson's breast-baring performance at the 2004 Super Bowl halftime show in Houston led to Federal Communications Commission chairman Michael Powell's vow to investigate, and presumably enforce, the commission's broadcast indecency rules, which could include the imposition of fines and license revocation. Thus, the Hutchins Commission's recommendation that the constitutional guarantees of freedom of the press should be recognized to include the broadcast media remains unrealized.

Notes

1. *State of the First Amendment 2004* (Washington, D.C.: Freedom Forum, 2004), http://www.firstamendmentcenter.org/about.aspx?item=state_of_First_Amendment _2004. Also, http://www.firstamendmentcenter.org/PDF/SOFA2004results. pdf.
2. *Near v. Minnesota,* 283 U.S. 697 (1931).
3. *Dennis v. United States,* 341 U.S. 494 (1951). Holmes-Brandeis doctrine promulgated in *Whitney v. California,* 274 U.S. 357 (1927).
4. *Yates v. United States,* 354 U.S. 298 (1957); Alien Registration Act of 1940 (Smith Act), *U.S. Code* 18 § 2385 (2004). *Brandenburg v. Ohio,* 395 U.S. 444 (1969). See also *Hess v. Indiana,* 414 U.S. 105 (1973), in which the Supreme Court clarified that "lawless action" must also be "imminent."
5. *Bantam Books, Inc. v. Sullivan,* 372 U.S. 58 (1968); *Organization for a Better Austin v. Keefe,* 402 U.S. 415 (1971).
6. *New York Times Co. v. United States,* 403 U.S. 713 (1971).
7. See, for example, *United States v. Marchetti,* 466 F.2d 1309 (4th Cir.), *cert. denied,* 409 U.S. 1063 (1972); *Snepp v. United States,* 444 U.S. 507 (1980); *United States v. Morison,* 844 F.2d 1057 (4th Cir.), *cert. denied,* 488 U.S. 908 (1988).
8. *United States v. Progressive, Inc.,* 467 F. Supp. 990 (W.D.Wis. 1979), dismissed as moot, 610 F.2d 819 (7th Cir. 1979).

9. *New York Times v. Sullivan,* 376 U.S. 254 (1964); *Garrison v. Louisiana,* 379 U.S. 64 (1964).
10. *Hustler Magazine v. Falwell,* 485 U.S. 46 (1988). The Supreme Court ruled that public officials and public figures may not successfully sue for the intentional infliction of emotional distress arising from a publication (in this case, a cartoon parody lampooning the Reverend Jerry Falwell) without also demonstrating both falsity and actual malice.
11. *Herbert v. Lando,* 441 U.S. 153 (1979). The Supreme Court refused to recognize a constitutionally based reporter's privilege to protect the "editorial process" from scrutiny in libel cases, under the theory that a plaintiff who was required to prove actual malice in order to prevail would need to explore the reporter's newsgathering methods and sources.
12. See, for example, *Richmond Newspapers, Inc. v. Virginia,* 448 U.S. 555 (1980); *Press-Enterprise Co. v. Superior Court,* 464 U.S. 501 (1984); *Press-Enterprise Co. v. Superior Court,* 478 U.S. 1 (1986).
13. *Nebraska Press Ass'n v. Stuart,* 427 U.S. 539 (1976).
14. *Chandler v. Florida,* 449 U.S. 560 (1981).
15. *Administrative Procedure Act, U.S. Code* 5 §§ 553 et seq. (2004); *Freedom of Information Act, U.S. Code* 5 § 552 (2004).
16. *Houchins v. KQED, Inc.,* 438 U.S. 1 (1978).
17. *JB Pictures, Inc. v. Dep't of Defense,* 86 F.3d 236 (D.C. Cir. 1996).
18. *Flynt v. Weinberger,* 762 F.2d 12 (D.C. Cir. 1985); *Nation Magazine v. Dep't of Defense,* 762 F.Supp. 1558 (S.D.N.Y. 1991); *Flynt v. Rumsfeld,* 355 F.3d 697 (D.C. Cir. 2004).
19. *Reno v. American Civil Liberties Union,* 521 U.S. 844 (1997), *Miami Herald Pub. Co. v. Tornillo,* 418 U.S. 241 (1974), *Red Lion Broadcasting Co. v. FCC,* 294 U.S. 367 (1969).
20. *Prometheus Radio Project v. Federal Communications Commission,* 373 F.3d 372 (3rd Cir. 2004).
21. The so-called 1985 Fairness Report, *Inquiry into Section 73,1910 of the Commission's Rules and Regulations Concerning the General Fairness Obligations of Broadcast Licensees,* 102 F.C.C.2d 143 (1985).
22. *Bipartisan Campaign Reform Act of 2002,* Public Law 107-155.

Bibliography

Lewis, Anthony. *Make No Law: The Sullivan Case and the First Amendment.* New York: Random House, 1991.

Snepp, Frank. *Irreparable Harm: A Firsthand Account of How One Agent Took on the CIA in an Epic Battle over Secrecy and Free Speech.* New York: Random House, 1999.

Stewart, Potter. "Or of the Press." In *Cases and Materials: Mass Media Law,* edited by Marc A. Franklin, David A. Anderson, and Fred H. Cate, pp. 85–90. 6th ed. New York: Foundation Press, 2000.

Ungar, Sanford J. *The Papers and the Papers: An Account of the Legal and Political Battle over the Pentagon Papers.* New York: Columbia University Press, 1989.

17

COMMUNICATIONS REGULATION IN PROTECTING THE PUBLIC INTEREST

Robert B. Horwitz

THE DEVELOPMENT OF THE AMERICAN COMMUNICA-
tions system reflects the nature of the United States as a liberal democracy, in which private capital and the state interact in creative tension. At
the heart of that tension is the concept of the public interest, a concept that legitimates state intervention in particular kinds of private property and subjects that
property to government regulation. The concept of the public interest is best
understood by analyzing its embodiment in regulatory practice. This essay offers
a broad overview of the traditional regulatory regime in communications, how
and why the character of the public interest and regulation changed beginning
in the 1980s, and the nature of the regulatory mechanisms in place at the beginning of the twenty-first century.

The communications system in the United States is the upshot of the
American configuration of the relation between state and private power,
between capitalism and democracy. Although largely privately owned and operated within a profit-oriented market system, communication infrastructure and
services in the United States have been subject to an unusually high degree of
state intervention. Early on, this intervention consisted of direct construction.
The fledgling federal government created the first national communication network—the mail—through the considerable efforts of the U.S. Post Office.[1] By
the mid-nineteenth century, state involvement shifted from direct development
to promotion and subsidy of private companies that would build networks and
provide communication services, establishing a "path dependent" model
whereby these early policy choices strongly shaped later ones.[2] The growth of
telegraphy gained enormously from government grants of land, timber, and
rights of way, and the fact that Western Union became the de facto telegraph system of the Union army during the Civil War.[3] Telephony benefited from patent
law and government determination that the service, dominated by AT&T, con-

stituted a natural monopoly.[4] Radio came to be because the U.S. Navy required feuding manufacturing companies to pool patents during World War I and acted as midwife to the establishment of RCA following the war.[5] Satellite communications and the Internet were made possible, in part, through the military Keynesianism of the cold war.[6] Whereas the First Amendment to the Constitution forbade the federal government from controlling the press, it did not preclude government from aiding the press and facilitating the circulation of information by means of high-quality mail service, second-class postage subsidies for newspapers, and the protections that copyright law accorded publishers and authors. That assistance in part underlay Alexis de Tocqueville's observation on the wealth of communication and information that even the rural American received in the 1830s.[7] In this respect, the establishment of an arena in which citizens in principle had access to information and the ability to converse about matters of the commonweal—what has come to be called the public sphere—was not just a matter of government forbearance, but of active government policy to aid in its formation and expansion.[8]

The apparent paradox of a liberal state intervening extensively in the private economy can be explained by the special nature of communications as an essential form of infrastructure that abets trade, discourse, and military capability.[9] Such industries are very often the focus of direct state intervention. This has been true in the Anglo-American context since thirteenth-century English common law courts declared certain kinds of occupations to be possessed of a particular status—the so-called common callings.[10] This status of common calling conveys the sense that certain kinds of industry or services are special in some way, imbued with something larger, something more general than private interest. Because the parties that provide these services possess unusual power, they historically have been subject to special obligations. In the words of the famous 1877 railroad case of *Munn v. Illinois,* they stand "in the very gateway of commerce," and hence they may be subject to government oversight.[11] The *communications* infrastructure contains within it the added feature of facilitating the practice of democracy and the administrative authority of the state. The concept of the public interest in communications thus embodies a mix of imperatives within a liberal democracy: the promotion of networks and services, maintenance of a free flow of commerce on and among privately operated networks, and the preservation—even, in principle, the enhancement—of a free and diverse marketplace of ideas. Hence issues of access, equity, and diversity and the political struggle over them are as much part of the development of American communications as are wires, transmitters, receivers, and profits. Even as government promoted communications, to protect against too much private power in communications commerce and the circulation of information and opinion, government policies often came with various quid pro quos. The key public-interest policies of the obligation to serve all comers, nondiscriminatory access, and universal service in telephony and public trusteeship in broadcasting were rooted in the concern to protect commerce and the public sphere from domination by too-powerful private entities. Government itself was constrained by the First Amendment.[12]

Traditional Communications Regulatory Regime

By the early-to-mid-twentieth century, the key state intervention in communications was regulation by a congressionally created independent regulatory agency—the Federal Communications Commission (FCC). Established originally as the Federal Radio Commission in 1927, the agency came into being to sort out the interference mess in which early wireless broadcasters found themselves. With the passage of the Communications Act of 1934, the FCC was charged with the oversight of wired and wireless communications. U.S. communications traditionally fell under three distinct regulatory schemes, in large part dictated by medium and mode of delivery: print, broadcast, and common carrier. Although the print press had the explicit protection of the language of the First Amendment, publishers were still subject to the antitrust laws with regard to ownership and business practices. The Supreme Court's reasoning in the 1945 case of *Associated Press v. United States* put forward the Court's thinking about free speech, corporate power, and the public interest to maintain a robust information environment. In language that has since assumed a kind of talismanic status in First Amendment jurisprudence and scholarship, the Court stated that

> [The First] Amendment rests on the assumption that the widest possible dissemination of information from diverse and antagonistic sources is essential to the welfare of the public, that a free press is a condition of a free society. Surely a command that the government itself shall not impede the free flow of ideas does not afford non-governmental combinations a refuge if they impose restraints upon that constitutionally guaranteed freedom. Freedom to publish means freedom for all and not for some. Freedom to publish is guaranteed by the Constitution, but freedom to combine to keep others from publishing is not. Freedom of the press from governmental interference under the First Amendment does not sanction repression by private interests.[13]

Because the press could itself stifle freedom of speech through its business practices (in this case by the use of restrictive membership rules), the First Amendment did not bar government from applying the antitrust laws to that medium.

Broadcasting presented a somewhat different set of issues. The FCC regulated broadcasting through its oversight of the electromagnetic spectrum, understood to be a scarce natural resource held in common by the people of the

United States. Radio and television operators had to obtain licenses from the FCC and, because of the perceived scarcity of the spectrum and its palpable proclivity toward disruptive interference, broadcast licensees were given time-bound permission to operate on designated frequencies to serve local communities. Broadcasters thus were considered trustees of the spectrum, charged with public-interest obligations that were not imposed on newspapers or magazines. As the Supreme Court put it in *Red Lion Broadcasting Co. v. FCC,* because of the scarcity of the spectrum and the necessity of government licensing for the medium to function, "It is the right of the viewers and listeners, not the right of the broadcasters, which is paramount. . . . It is the purpose of the First Amendment to preserve an uninhibited market-place of ideas in which truth will ultimately prevail, rather than to countenance monopolization of that market, whether it be by the Government itself or a private licensee."[14]

The courts came to see the telegraph and telephone companies, which held themselves out to the public for hire to provide communications transmission services, as infrastructure networks. As infrastructure networks they stood, as we have seen, in the gateway of commerce. Their pivotal effect on commerce underlay their eventual treatment as common carriers, subject to price and entry regulation and guaranteed a fair rate of return, and in due course enfolded into the New Deal commitment toward nondiscriminatory and universal service.

In the Communications Act of 1934 Congress gave the FCC a mandate to make available a rapid, efficient, affordable nationwide radio service to all the people of the United States. In the effort to fulfill that broad but vague mandate, the FCC enacted a series of substantive structural, content, and behavioral regulations in order to foster the more specific, but still general, goals of diversity, competition, and localism in broadcasting and electronic media. The commission based its regulatory policy on the theory that the diversification of mass media ownership serves the public interest by preventing undue concentration of economic power and by promoting a variety of viewpoints. Historically, regulation was devoted to the separation of elements of the communications industry, defined for the most part according to medium and technology. Among the more important of these separations was that between content and conduit. The Communications Act established at the outset a structural rule that a broadcaster could not be a communications carrier and vice versa. Congressional fear of radio's potentially dangerous concentration of political power in part underlay the act's prohibition against any joint ownership of radio and wired systems.[15] This early separations policy had the added consequence of largely restricting the ability of wired carriers to generate communication content, at the time believed important in the containment of AT&T's massive presence in the industry. Similar separations or cross-ownership rules came to be applied to prevent a player in one part of the industry from dominating another part, and to limit broadcast-station ownership at national and local levels. As the FCC argued in a

1953 multiple-ownership rulemaking, the "fundamental purpose" of these structural rules was "to promote diversification of ownership in order to maximize diversification of program and service viewpoints."[16] "The greater the diversity of ownership in a particular area," the commission wrote in a related, later rulemaking, "the less chance there is that a single person or group can have an inordinate effect in a . . . programming sense, on public opinion at the regional level."[17]

The main ownership rules in the history of electronic mass media are:

- Dual-network rule: Prohibited broadcast stations from affiliating with any entity that maintained more than a single network.[18]
- One-to-a-market rule: Prohibited the ownership or control of more than one station in the same broadcast service (AM radio, FM radio, or television) in the same community.[19]
- Television duopoly rule: Established that a broadcaster could own or control only one television station in a market.[20]
- National multiple-ownership rule: Limited the total number of television and radio stations an entity could own nationally, irrespective of location. (Between 1953 and 1985 the number was seven AM radio, seven FM radio, and seven television stations, with a maximum of five in the more desirable VHF television band).[21]
- Broadcast/newspaper cross-ownership rule: Prohibited the same company from owning a newspaper and a broadcast station in the same market.[22]
- Broadcast network/cable system cross-ownership rule: Prohibited the same company from owning a broadcasting network and a cable system.[23]
- Broadcast station/cable rule: Prohibited the same company from owning a cable system and a broadcast television station in the same market.[24]
- Telephone/cable cross-ownership rule: Prohibited the same company from owning a cable system and a telephone system in the same market.[25]

Nearly all of these regulations were challenged in the federal appellate courts and upheld under the rationale that the FCC had acted within its jurisdiction. The courts consistently ruled that the FCC's ownership regulations maintained, in the oft-quoted words of *New York Times v. Sullivan,* the nation's "profound national commitment to the principle that debate on public issues should be uninhibited, robust, and wide-open."[26]

Indeed, it was the courts that forced the FCC to expand its diversity policy to encompass preferences in ownership for racial minorities and women. Whereas the diversification of ownership was one factor of several in the mix of elements considered by the FCC in comparative hearings for broadcast license applications before 1973, minority ownership was not. Arguing that the Communications Act was "colorblind," the FCC would take an applicant's race into account only to the extent that the applicant could show that his or her race would likely lead to better, more diverse programming in the particular instance. Accordingly, the D.C. Circuit Court of Appeals ruled in a 1973 case that the racial identity of an African American applicant for a radio license *was* a relevant consideration in choosing between and among applicants. There was no justification of minority preference to remedy past discrimination; the court reasoned instead that minority ownership could result in diverse programming.[27] In the wake of this decision, the FCC formulated a policy that gave evaluation enhancement in comparative hearings to minority ownership and participation in station management by members of minority groups.[28] The FCC's review board subsequently extended this enhancement to women.[29] Included in the 1978 policy statement were a minority tax certificate program (which provided incentives to owners of existing broadcast properties to sell their properties to minorities) and a distress-sale program (which allowed a broadcaster whose license had been designated for a revocation hearing to sell his station to a minority-controlled entity at 75 percent or less of the station's fair-market value).[30]

The public-trustee status of broadcast licensees meant that broadcasters were to serve a public rather than a purely private function, and were expected to orient programming to their local communities. This, in turn, meant that broadcasters were in principle obliged, within reason, to air a varied and balanced set of programs to a range of audiences. The local program orientation entailed, again in principle, a preference for local ownership and control of broadcast stations. Who better to be aware of local issues than an owner rooted in the community? The instruction to offer "a well-rounded program" was couched in the requirement that broadcast service "must be without discrimination as between its listeners" and that stations were not to be used as "propaganda stations." As the commission put it in a 1929 statement of policy, the "public interest requires ample play for the free and fair competition of opposing views, and the commission believes that the principle applies . . . to all discussions of importance to the public."[31] After a period of time in the 1940s when the FCC implemented that expectation by prohibiting advocacy or editorializing, the commission returned to its "balanced program" and evenhandedness position with the 1949 report on editorializing—the basis of the fairness doctrine.[32] The fairness doctrine emerged as a seemingly neutral way for the FCC to ensure that a scarce frequency be used for public rather than private purposes, without the commission itself dictating the content of programming. The doctrine declared that the right of the public to be informed was paramount, and, as a corollary, required the broadcaster to present a balanced treatment of controversial issues of public importance. But it left the choice of time and subjects of such treatment to the discretion of the broadcast licensee. The doctrine mandated a reasonable opportunity for opposing viewpoints, but entrusted the presentation of such with the licensee as a matter of editorial discretion. Thus the fairness doctrine placed an abstract obligation on the broadcaster without stipulating specific speech or requiring access. The related personal-attack rule held that when, during the presentation of views on a controversial issue of public importance, an attack is made on the honesty, character, integrity, or similar personal qualities of an identified person or group, the licensee must notify the person or group attacked by providing a script or summary, and an offer of a reasonable opportunity to respond over the licensee's facilities.[33]

The equal-opportunities rule provides access and fairness in the electoral process. If a broadcaster permits a legally qualified candidate for any public office to use the station, the licensee must afford equal opportunities to all others who are qualified. In 1971 Congress expanded political access by giving the FCC the right to revoke a license "for willful or repeated failure to allow reasonable access to or to permit purchase of reasonable amounts of time for the use of a broadcasting station by a legally qualified candidate for Federal office on behalf of his candidacy," and by stipulating that candidates be charged rates not to exceed "the lowest unit charge of the station for the same class and amount of time for the same period" during the forty-five days before a primary and the sixty days before a general election.[34]

The public interest in broadcasting was translated to mean the preservation of diverse viewpoints, some degree of local control and local program orientation, the provision of news and information, a general balance of programming (what we now call format diversity, understood vertically; that is, within each broadcast outlet), and equitable treatment of political candidates. This regulatory effort was undertaken within the context of an advertiser-supported broadcast system and in a political environment that largely favored the granting of broadcast licenses to corporate applicants. The vast majority of licenses, issued to commercial/corporate broadcasters in the critical early years, established a powerful economic and political pattern privileging commercial broadcasting.[35] Later, when the FCC wasn't giving away frequencies to favored constituents, subsequent commissions struggled, contrarily and with limited success, to formulate policies that would encourage broadcasting in the public interest against the powerful constraints established by a broadcasting system in which centralized networks created commercially attractive programs for affiliated individual broadcast stations. As the consequences of broadcasting's commercial structure and the commission's largely corporate license grants became clear, the FCC initiated some structural policies to deal with network domination and the dearth of local production.[36] It also fashioned behavioral policies to induce broadcast licensees to air, among other things, more public affairs, educational, and locally oriented programming.[37]

Commercial broadcasting did some things tremendously well. It created certain kinds of programming, largely entertainment in orientation, that appealed, sometimes quite strongly, to large numbers of consumers. Whether it produced programming that appealed to minority tastes or satisfied the other expectations of public-interest programming is another matter. Most scholars have concluded that the policies to control network domination could not overcome the economic incentives inherent to a commercial broadcast system. The behavioral policies, which might have had an impact if applied vigorously in the license-renewal process, were largely defanged via industry and congressional pressure. The 1946 *Public Service Responsibility of Broadcast Licensees* (the "Blue Book") articulated four factors relevant to broadcast service in the public interest ("sustaining," or nonsponsored, programs, local live programs, programs devoted to the discussion of public issues, and limits on advertising excesses), and advised that the commission would consider how well a licensee fulfilled these when evaluating renewal of the license. After the successful attacks on the Blue Book, the FCC changed course in 1960 and withdrew the heavy regulatory scrutiny in favor of a policy wherein broadcast licensees were obliged to fulfill the public interest by discovering and satisfying the tastes, needs, and desires of the audience in the broadcast service area.[38] The FCC's 1971 *Primer on Ascertainment of Community Problems by Broadcast Applicants* standardized this obligation.[39] Licensees and applicants for a broadcast license were to determine the economic, ethnic, and social composition of the communities they served, consult with leaders from each significant community group, and design programs to meet the community interests and problems identified. The ascertainment policy substituted identified community interests for regulators' ideas of what constituted "good" programming. Although the ascertainment obligation represented an effort to respond to pressure from minority groups and the broadcast reform movement, it functioned mainly as window-dressing. One FCC rule from the era that did have impact, if minor, on the racial and gender composition of station workforces prohibited broadcast licensees from engaging in discrimination in employment and required them to adopt an equal-employment-opportunity program to attract minority employees. This resulted in "employment profile screening guidelines," which required stations to employ women and minorities according to a numerical formula.[40]

The New Regime

At the risk of oversimplification, the old communications system could be said to have been limited but universally available, predominantly privately owned and commercially viable though regulated, and dominated by particular corporations confined to providing particular communication services. In broadcasting, one could say that there was a vague commitment to liberal pluralism within a mainly private system of provision. The traditional communications regulatory regime was predicated on the stability of broadcast and wired technologies.

When new technologies came along, such as cable television, satellite, microwaves, and computers, the FCC typically tried to squeeze them into the existing regulatory formulas governing broadcast and common carrier. This strategy had the short-term result of lending economic protection to the traditional service providers and technologies, whether AT&T or FM radio or VHF broadcasting, while it also served to preserve the conceptions of the public interest that attached to those technologies. Over time, however, a combination of the growth of new technologies, administrative irrationalities, and tough corporate lobbying and legal challenges from large users and would-be entrants prompted the FCC to relax some regulations and permit new, if limited, communications services to blossom. In the beginning, these relaxations of rules were not undertaken as part of an ideological shift away from regulation and toward market solutions. But the emergence of new services and delivery options, in turn, highlighted policy contradictions and eventually underscored the inadequacy of existing communication law, policies, and regulation. These factors made communications an industry open to the ideology and practice of deregulation.[41] Although the FCC's many small deregulatory efforts beginning in the late 1970s set the stage, it was the 1982 consent decree compelling the divestiture of AT&T that constituted the first major break in the traditional regime. The 1996 Telecommunications Act was the second.

The AT&T divestiture, which emanated from the courts, not from the FCC or Congress, reconfigured certain industry separations and hastened some technological convergences. The old regulatory separations between content and conduit providers, between telephony and cable television, between local and long-distance telecommunications, between computers and telecommunications, finally seemed outmoded, especially with the technological developments of digitalization and compression. Regulating the old separations, especially as technology was making them untenable, was increasingly difficult. Attempts to rewrite the 1934 Communications Act had been before Congress for well over twenty years, but were always thwarted by various industry groups unwilling to give up existing policy protections. By the mid-1990s, things had changed. What would it take for the various big industry players to relinquish existing policy protections and face competition in their own turfs in order to expand into someone else's territory and invest in new areas? The widespread assumption was that constructing competitive communications networks would be high-risk, capital-intensive endeavors. It would require the resources of large and flexible corporations (whose needs and failures would also spur small businesses and entrepreneurs in budding and niche markets). The brokered compromises among major industry players and their congressional champions that constituted the Telecommunications Act of 1996 redrew the policy map. The act articulated a bold shift in the goals and mechanisms of policy and regulation: The public interest would be secured not by regulation but by competition. A key concept was regulatory forbearance: Regulation would be deployed only to the degree that it encouraged a competitive telecommunications marketplace. The act eliminated the legal basis for protected monopoly in telecommunications and encouraged mergers and vertical integration as ways to facilitate what was termed "cross-platform" competition, that is, competition between previously separated industries providing the same service. Ownership ceilings were lifted entirely for radio and raised for television, and the regulatory oversight over broadcast stations, already limited from earlier deregulatory moves was, for all intents and purposes, eradicated. The act thus created—by design—unprecedented conditions for competition *and* for the concentration of ownership. Passage of the act unleashed a frenzy of mergers and acquisitions as corporations positioned themselves to expand into new services and protect their home turf.[42]

The Telecommunications Act of 1996 reflected the growth of media (as well as the rise of political conservatism). The long period of limited media, characterized by few players and government regulation to limit their market power, had given way to a period of multichannel communications that greatly expanded the overall media market. The relevant institutional authorities—FCC, Justice Department, and federal courts—largely accepted the concept of "substitutes," that the product offered by, say, cable television, broadcast television, satellite television, and video rentals is essentially the same. Thus, companies previously understood as individual media segments operating in separate product markets are now seen as competing with one another and therefore included in the same product market, for purposes of antitrust analysis.[43] The overall growth of media (and the particular growth of the Internet) and the acceptance of the concept of substitutes convinced many that diversity and regulation needed to be reconceptualized. In a limited media system, such as the old broadcast one, went the argument, it might make sense to regulate vertically; that is, require that any individual outlet air a broad and diverse mix of programming. But in an extensive media system, doesn't it make sense to look at the diversity question horizontally—that is, across all substitutable outlets? If so, and that market shows no troublesome concentration, government intervention is not needed and is, in fact, pernicious. Simple vigilance on the antitrust front would safeguard diversity and economic power.[44] With the Telecommunications Act, many of the old rules governing broadcasting and cable, already relaxed, were eliminated or relaxed further. These included:

- The dual-network rule. The rule was eliminated with regard to radio in 1977. The Telecommunications Act of 1996 revised the rule for television to prohibit a party from affiliating with an entity if that entity controlled more than one of the four largest networks—ABC, CBS, FOX, and NBC—or with an entity that controlled one of these four networks and either of two emerging networks (UPN and WB). In 2001 the FCC amended the rule to permit one of the four major television networks to own, operate, maintain, or control the UPN and/or the WB network.

- The one-to-a-market rule. Since 1989 the FCC generally waived the rule in the top twenty-five markets if, after the combination, there remained at least thirty separately owned independent voices (including radio and TV stations and certain local newspapers and cable stations) in the market.

- The television duopoly rule. The rule was replaced in 1999 so that a company may own two television stations in the same Nielsen-designated market area if one of the stations is not among the four highest-ranked stations in the market, and so long as eight independently owned, full-power, operational television stations remain in the market after the merger.

- The national multiple-ownership rules. In 1984 the FCC increased the ceiling to twelve AM, twelve FM, and twelve television, and in 1992 raised the national radio ownership limits to thirty AM and thirty FM. The Telecommunications Act of 1996 repealed all national ownership limits for radio; locally a company may now own five to eight radio stations in a single market, depending on the size of the market. The act also repealed the twelve-station national cap for television, replaced by a rule stipulating that a single company may not own stations that reach more than 35 percent of the nationwide television audience.

- The cable horizontal-ownership rule. Pursuant to the requirements of the Telecommunications Act of 1996, the FCC adopted rules prohibiting any one entity from having an attributable interest in cable systems reaching more than 30 percent of cable homes passed nationwide. The FCC changed the method by which the horizontal-ownership cap was to be calculated in 1999, effectively raising it from 30 percent to 36.7 percent.

- The cable vertical-ownership rule. Pursuant to the requirements of the Telecommunications Act of 1996, a cable company could not have any ownership affiliation with more than 40 percent of the programming that it carried on any of its cable systems with up to seventy-five channels. On systems with more than seventy-five channels, forty-five channels were required to be reserved for nonaffiliated programming.

- The cross-ownership rule, broadcast networks/cable systems. Relaxed in 1992, the rule was eliminated by the 1996 Telecommunications Act.

- The cross-ownership rule, broadcast/cable. Adopted in 1970, the FCC prohibited the same company from owning a cable system and a broadcast television station in the same local market. Congress codified the policy in 1984. The 1996 Telecommunications Act eliminated the statutory cross-ownership restriction, but the FCC has retained the rule.

- The cross-ownership rule, cable/telephone. The rule was eliminated by the 1996 Telecommunications Act.

A final factor in the new regulatory regime is the role of the federal appellate courts. Increasingly skeptical of congressional or regulatory assertions of media concentration and the defense of old ownership rules, the courts began insisting on a new concentration metric based on "nonconjectural" empirical evidence of anticompetitive behavior and verification of the efficacy of regulatory remedies. In a series of cases beginning in the 1990s, the courts expressed irritation at what the judges saw as the FCC's unreflective, ritualistic invocation of diversity in defense of many of its long-standing structural rules on ownership.[45] This change reflects not only a changed communications environment, but a changed legal environment, to wit, the rise of a conservative formalism in equal-protection law largely as a result of the appointment to federal judgeships by Republican presidents since the 1980s. The jurisprudential change highlights the change in what diversity is taken to mean. Diversity analysis in mass media had always been a part of the regulatory mandate of the FCC, albeit in a general way. Diversity analysis attained significantly more bite when, in the late 1960s, civil rights litigation provided diversity a much more specific definition. In the media ownership arena, diversity's star, as it were, was hitched to the success of the legal logic of civil rights and affirmative action. After the 1960s the FCC assessed diversity in broadcasting and other communications industries essentially by how accessible media were to minority, particularly racial minority, participation. In general, the diversity rationale received strong support in both judicial and congressional forums for the roughly twenty years between 1970 and 1990. The link between the diversity of viewpoints and a diversity of owners was assumed. In fact, the empirical evidence of the relationship between the diversity of ownership and the diversity of content is weak, and an increasingly conservative, formalistic judiciary in effect called the FCC's bluff.[46] In *Time Warner v. FCC,* for example, the D.C. Circuit Court of Appeals struck down the FCC's horizontal and vertical cable-ownership rules as unsupported by evidence and thus a violation of cable companies' First Amendment rights to reach new audiences and to control their programming.[47]

In response both to court challenges to some existing rules and to the requirement of the 1996 Telecommunications Act that the FCC assess its ownership rules on a triennial basis, in 2003 the FCC voted to change:

1. The local TV multiple-ownership limit. In markets with five or more TV stations, a company may own two stations, but only one of these can be among the top four in ratings. In markets with eighteen or more TV stations, a company can own three TV stations. The FCC has a waiver process for markets with eleven or fewer stations in which two of the top four stations wish to merge.
2. The national TV ownership limit. A company can own TV stations reaching no more than a 45 percent share of U.S. TV households, up

from the previous 35 percent. (The FCC maintains the historical ultrahigh frequency [UHF] "discount": stations in the UHF band count only 50 percent for calculating the national television reach.)

3. The cross-media limits. In markets with three or fewer TV stations, no cross-ownership is permitted among TV, radio, and newspapers. In markets with between four and eight TV stations, combinations are limited to one of the following:

   • a daily newspaper, one TV station, and up to half of the radio station limit for that market
   • a daily newspaper and up to the radio station limit for that market (no TV)
   • two TV stations and up to the radio station limit for that market (no newspapers)[48]

These forces reveal the context that underscores the FCC's ownership-rule changes of 2003. The George W. Bush administration FCC, under the chairmanship of Michael Powell, entered into a kind of alliance, even one-upmanship, with the Court of Appeals in paying obeisance to corporations' First Amendment rights and removing remaining traditional ownership limitations. Because the social science data on the nexus between ownership policies and programming are weak, the appellate courts tended to read most ownership or structural regulations as violations of the speech rights of corporations. Although the FCC's new rules elicited public and congressional tumult and a court decision remanding the rules back to the commission, the 1996 Telecommunications Act and the new judicially required standards of social scientific proof in the long run favor the continued relaxation of ownership limitations.[49] The new version of the public interest is predicated on presumptions of media abundance and regulatory forbearance.

Paradoxically, FCC and congressional revulsion at media excess ignited by the televised baring of the pop singer Janet Jackson's breast during the halftime show of the 2004 Superbowl has, at least for the moment, created the worst of worlds with regard to regulation. In the old regulatory regime, the FCC tried to regulate broadcasting at the structural level but largely stayed out of content; the new regime retreats from structural regulation but has begun to regulate content through the imposition of heavy fines on offending licensees.

Conclusion

Historically, the regulation of electronic media was a principal means by which the liberal democratic state took advantage of the dynamism of private enterprise to supervise the construction of a nationwide communications system while guarding against the accumulation of private power over the marketplace of ideas and over the communication networks themselves. The liberal tradition generally and the First Amendment specifically prevented government domination of media and constrained the scope of regulation. Traditional regulation invoked the concept of the public interest to legitimize and guide state intervention in the communication industry. The traditional regulatory regime kept different parts of the industry separated to prevent the restraint of trade and to maintain a diversity of voices. Wired networks were governed by common-carrier law; the key quid pro quo of regulated monopoly was an obligation to serve and nondiscrimination in access and pricing. Broadcasting, understood to be characterized by scarcity of spectrum, required a license, and broadcasters were obliged to operate as trustees of the spectrum. The growth of media, digitalization, and technical convergence and the rise of deregulation as political ideology hastened a change in the concept of the public interest from one of regulatory intervention and oversight to one of government forbearance in favor of competition. Many of the traditional regulations have been dismantled, and political and legal dynamics are in place to countenance further deregulation and media mergers. However, the regulation of communications has not by any means disappeared, and public outcry over the FCC's 2003 efforts to relax its ownership limits indicates that a significant portion of the American public is anxious about the decline of the old regulatory model and the seeming triumph of deregulation and ever more consolidated mass media.

Notes

1. John, *Spreading the News.*
2. Goodrich, *Government Promotion of American Canals and Railroads;* and Carter Goodrich, "The Revulsion against Internal Improvements," *Journal of Economic History* 10 (November 1950): 145–69.
3. Thompson, *Wiring a Continent.*
4. Horwitz, *The Irony of Regulatory Reform;* Stone, *Public Service Liberalism.*
5. Barnouw, *A History of Broadcasting in the United States.*
6. Donald C. Beelar, "Cables in the Sky and the Struggle for Their Control," *Federal Communications Bar Journal* 21, no. 1 (1967): 26–41; Schiller, *Mass Communications and American Empire;* Abbate, *Inventing the Internet.*
7. Tocqueville, *Democracy in America.*
8. Habermas, *Structural Transformation of the Public Sphere;* Dewey, *The Public and Its Problems;* Garnham, "The Media and the Public Sphere."
9. See Headrick, *The Invisible Weapon.*
10. See Angell, *A Treatise on the Law of Carriers;* Irwin S. Rosenbaum, "The Common Carrier-Public Utility Concept: A Legal-Industrial View," *Journal of Land and Public Utility Economics* 7 no. 2 (May 1931): 155–68.
11. *Munn v. Illinois,* 94 U.S. 113 (1877), 132.
12. Robert B. Horwitz, "The First Amendment Meets Some New Technologies:

Broadcasting, Common Carriers, and Free Speech in the 1990s," *Theory and Society* 20 (1991): 21–72; Baker, *Media, Markets, and Democracy;* Starr, *The Creation of the Media.*

13. *Associated Press v. United States,* 326 U.S. 1 (1945), 20

14. *Red Lion Broadcasting Co. v. FCC,* 395 U.S. 367 (1969), 390.

15. *Communications Act of 1934,* Public Law 416, 73rd Cong., secs. 3(h) (1934), 313, 314.

16. *Amendment of Sections 3.35, 3.240, and 3.636 of Rules and Regulations Relating to Multiple Ownership of AM, FM, and Television Broadcast Stations, Report and Order,* 18 FCC 288 (1953), 291.

17. *Amendment of Sections 73.35, 73.240, and 73.636 of Commission's Rules Relating to Multiple Ownership of AM, FM, and Television Broadcast Stations, Report and Order,* 45 FCC 1476, 1477, 1482 (1964).

18. See *National Broadcasting Co. v. United States,* 319 U.S. 190 (1943).

19. *Multiple Ownership of Standard Broadcast Stations (AM Radio),* 8 Fed. Reg. 16065 (1943); *Rules and Regulations Governing Commercial Television* § 4.226, 6 Fed. Reg. 2284–2285 (1941); *Rules Governing Standard and High Frequency Broadcast Stations (FM Radio)* § 3.228(a), 5 Fed. Reg. 2382, 2384 (1940).

20. *Amendment of Sections 73.35, 73.240, and 73.636 of Commission's Rules Relating to Multiple Ownership of AM, FM, and Television Broadcast Stations, Report and Order,* 45 FCC 1476, 1477, 1482 (1964).

21. *Amendment of Sections 3.35, 3.240, and 3.636 of Rules and Regulations Relating to Multiple Ownership of AM, FM, and Television Broadcast Stations, Report and Order,* 18 FCC 288, 291 (1953).

22. *Rules Relating to Multiple Ownership of Standard, FM, and Television Broadcast Stations, Second Report and Order,* 50 FCC 2d 1046 (1975) (hereinafter cited as Order), as amended upon reconsideration, 53 FCC 2d 589 (1975). The FCC "grandfathered" combinations established before 1970.

23. *Second Report and Order in Docket 18397,* 19 R. Reg. 2d 1775 (FCC, 1970).

24. *Second Report and Order in Docket 18397,* 19 R. Reg. 2d 1775 (FCC, 1970).

25. *Associated Bell Systems, Inc.,* 5 FCC 2d 357 (1966); *Applications of Telephone Companies for Section 214 Certificates,* 21 FCC 2d 307, reconsideration granted in part 22 FCC 2d 746 (1970).

26. *New York Times v. Sullivan,* 376 U.S. 254 (1964), 270.

27. *TV9, Inc. v. FCC,* 495 F.2d 929 (D.C. Cir. 1973).

28. If and when a broadcast license came available, there were often several applicants for it. The FCC would conduct a comparative hearing to determine which applicant should be awarded the license. Evaluative criteria in comparative license applications traditionally included local ownership, the integration of ownership and management, past performance, broadcast experience, proposed programming, and diversification of control of media. With the 1978 minority ownership policy, minority applicants in comparative license hearings would receive "extra points," as it were, in the evaluation process. *FCC, Statement of Policy on Minority Ownership of Broadcasting Facilities,* 68 FCC 2d 979 (1978).

29. *Gainesville Media, Inc.* 70 FCC 2d 143, Rev. Bd. (1978). However, women's enhancement was less than that of racial minorities, because women, in the commission's

view, have "not been excluded from the mainstream of society" due to prior discrimination. *Mid-Florida Television Corp.*, 69 FCC 2d 607 (1978), 652.

30. The Supreme Court upheld these policies in *Metro Broadcasting v. FCC,* 497 U.S. 547 (1990).

31. *Great Lakes Broadcasting Co.*, 3 FRC Ann.Rep. 32,33 (1929), aff'd in part and rev'd in part, *Great Lakes Broadcasting Co. v. FRC 37 F.2d 993* (D.C. Cir. 1930), cert. dismissed 281 U.S. 706 (1930).

32. *In the Matter of the Mayflower Broadcasting Corporation and the Yankee Network, Inc.*, 8 FCC 333 (1941); *In the Matter of Editorializing by Broadcast Licensees,* 13 FCC 1246 (1949). Congress amended the Communications Act in 1959, giving statutory recognition to the fairness doctrine. Public Law 274, 86th Congress (1959).

33. 47 U.S.C. § 73.123.

34. 47 U.S.C. § 312(a)(7) and 315(b). However, broadcasters often increase the lowest unit charge weekly during peak election season because of increased demand (FCC, 1988 Public Notice, 3).

35. See, among others, Bernard Schwartz, "Comparative Television and the Chancellor's Foot," *Georgetown Law Journal* 47 (1959): 655; Rosen, *The Modern Stentors*; and McChesney, *Telecommunications, Mass Media, and Democracy.*

36. The *Report on Chain Broadcasting,* an investigation of network domination of programming, led to rules that limited the exclusive affiliation of stations, regulated terms of affiliation, and protected the ability of affiliates to reject network programs (*Report on Chain Broadcasting,* pursuant to Commission Order No. 37, Docket No. 5060, May 1941). The 1970 Prime Time Access Rule was designed to prevent network-affiliated television stations in the top fifty television markets from broadcasting more than three hours of network or "off-network" (i.e., rerun) programs during the four prime-time viewing hours (47 C.F.R. § 73.658[k]). The Financial Interest and Syndication Rules, also dating from 1970, limited broadcast networks' ability to integrate vertically into the sale and distribution of syndicated programming (*Report and Order,* 23 FCC 2d 382 [1970]).

37. *Public Service Responsibility of Broadcast Licensees* (March 7, 1946); *Network Programming Inquiry, Report and Statement of Policy,* 25 Fed. Reg. 7295 (1960).

38. A separate course of action in response to the limited efficacy of regulation, pursued by President Lyndon Johnson and Congress, was the passage of the Public Broadcasting Act in 1967. Public Law 90-129, 90th Congress, November 7, 1967.

39. *Primer on Ascertainment of Community Problems by Broadcast Applicants,* 27 FCC 2d 650 (1971).

40. 47 C.F.R. § 73.2080(a), 73.2080(c)(2); *Report and Order in MM Docket No. 85-350,* 2 FCC Rcd 3967 (1987).

41. It is important to see deregulation in the United States as a general *political* phenomenon, not confined to communications and not the particular consequence either of the technological revolution in communications or of some abstract notion of economic necessity. Deregulation in the United States affected particular kinds of industries under particular kinds of regulatory controls: infrastructure industries, such as airlines, trucking, telecommunications, banking, natural gas, electricity, to some degree broadcasting, all of which had been under price-and-entry regulation,

where government determined the number of firms to provide service and set the prices the regulated firms could charge consumers for the services rendered. The success of price-and-entry regulation was dialectically the reason for its downfall. On the one side, the tightly regulated system became subject to criticism in the 1960s by liberals and a thriving public-interest movement as evidence of the "capture" of regulatory agencies by the industries under regulation. Regulators and large regulated industries were thought to be in bed with each other. On another side were academic economists who had been criticizing the efficiency of regulated industries for several years. They concluded that regulation was sometimes irrational, that monopolies thought to be "natural" were in fact maintained only through regulation, that regulation stifled innovation, and that regulation often was used as a means of cartel management. By the mid- to late 1970s these criticisms found an audience in business, now suffering under the regulatory consequences of 1960s politics. This resulted in the clarion call to "get the government off the backs of the people." In short, these agencies and these regulated industries had earned the wrath of *both* liberals and conservatives. Each wing of a curious, heterodox political alliance of liberals and conservatives, of public-interest-movement leftists and free-market ideologues, operating wholly within their own internal ideological logics of participatory democracy and free-market economics, respectively, believed that the reform of price-and-entry regulation was in the public interest. These politics of deregulation affected some, largely the economic, aspects of broadcasting. But other aspects of the deregulation of broadcasting, such as the rescinding of the fairness doctrine in 1987, provoked the heated politics between liberals who strongly advocated the maintenance of the doctrine against conservatives allied with broadcasters and backed by Reagan appointees to the FCC and federal judiciary, who successfully eliminated it. See Horwitz, *The Irony of Regulatory Reform; Syracuse Peace Council v. FCC,* 867 F.2d 654 (D.C. Cir. 1989).

42. See Aufderheide, *Communications Policy and the Public Interest.* A map of the new media ownership patterns is at http://www.mediachannel.org/ownership/chart.shtml.

43. *Cable Holdings of Georgia v. Home Video, Inc.,* 712 F. Supp. 1389 (N.D. Cal. 1989), aff'd, 903 F.2d 659 (9th Cir 1990). See also H. Peter Nesvold, "Communications Breakdown: Developing an Antitrust Model for Multimedia Mergers and Acquisitions," Virtual Institute of Information, http://www.vii.org/papers/peter.htm.

44. See Eli M. Noam, "Media Concentration in the United States: Industry Trends and Regulatory Responses," Virtual Institute of Information, www.vii.org/papers/medconc.htm; and Compaine, "Distinguishing between Concentration and Competition."

45. See, among others, Justice O'Connor's dissenting opinion in *Metro Broadcasting v. FCC,* 497 U.S. 547 (1990); *Lamprecht v. FCC,* 958 F.2d 382 (D.C. Cir. 1992); *Lutheran Church-Missouri Synod v. FCC,* 141 F.3d 344 (D.C. Cir. 1998); *Time Warner v. FCC,* 240 F.3d 1126 (D.C. Cir. 2001); *Fox Television Stations v. FCC,* 280 F.3d 1027 (D.C. Cir. 2002).

46. See Robert B. Horwitz, "On Media Concentration and the Diversity Question" (working paper, Department of Communication, University of California at San Diego, La

Jolla, 2004), http://communication.ucsd.edu/people/ConcentrationpaperICA. htm.

47. *Time Warner v. FCC*, 240 F.3d 1126 (D.C. Cir. 2001).

48. FCC, *Report and Order and Notice of Proposed Rulemaking, 2002 Biennial Regulatory Review—Review of the Commission's Broadcast Ownership Rules and Other Rules Adopted Pursuant to Section 202 of the Telecommunications Act of 1996 (MB Docket 02-277),* adopted June 2, 2003; released July 2, 2003.

49. *Prometheus Radio Project v. FCC,* Nos. 03-3388 et al. U.S. Court of Appeals, Third Circuit, decided August 24, 2004.

Bibliography

Abbate, Janet. *Inventing the Internet.* Cambridge, Mass.: MIT Press, 1999.

Angell, Joseph K. *A Treatise on the Law of Carriers of Goods and Passengers, by Land and Water.* 5th ed. Boston: Little, Brown, 1877.

Aufderheide, Patricia. *Communications Policy and the Public Interest: The Telecommunications Act of 1996.* New York: Guilford Press, 1999.

Baker, C. Edwin. *Media, Markets, and Democracy.* Cambridge, U.K., and New York: Cambridge University Press, 2002.

Barnouw, Erik. *A History of Broadcasting in the United States.* 3 vols. New York: Oxford University Press, 1966–70.

Compaine, Benjamin. "Distinguishing between Concentration and Competition." In Benjamin M. Compaine and Douglas Gomery, *Who Owns the Media?: Competition and Concentration in the Mass Media Industry.* 3rd ed. Mahwah, N.J.: Lawrence Erlbaum, 2000.

Dewey, John. *The Public and Its Problems.* Denver: Swallow, 1954.

Garnham, Nicholas. "The Media and the Public Sphere." In *Habermas and the Public Sphere,* edited by Craig Calhoun, 359–76. Cambridge, Mass.: MIT Press, 1992.

Goodrich, Carter. *Government Promotion of American Canals and Railroads, 1800–1890.* New York: Columbia University Press, 1960.

Habermas, Jürgen. *Structural Transformation of the Public Sphere: An Inquiry into a Category of Bourgeois Society.* Translated by Thomas Burger, with Frederick Lawrence. Cambridge, Mass.: MIT Press, 1989.

Headrick, Daniel R. *The Invisible Weapon: Telecommunications and International Politics, 1851–1945.* New York: Oxford University Press, 1991.

Horwitz, Robert B. *The Irony of Regulatory Reform: The Deregulation of American Telecommunications.* New York: Oxford University Press, 1989.

John, Richard R. *Spreading the News: The American Postal System from Franklin to Morse.* Cambridge, Mass.: Harvard University Press, 1995.

McChesney, Robert W. *Telecommunications, Mass Media, and Democracy: The Battle for the Control of US Broadcasting, 1928–1935.* Oxford, U.K., and New York: Oxford University Press, 1993.

Rosen, Philip T. *The Modern Stentors: Radio Broadcasters and the Federal Government, 1920–1934.* Westport, Conn: Greenwood, 1980.

Schiller, Herbert I. *Mass Communications and American Empire*. Boston: Beacon Press, 1971.

Starr, Paul. *The Creation of the Media: Political Origins of Modern Communications*. New York: Basic Books, 2004.

Stone, Alan. *Public Service Liberalism: Telecommunications and Transitions in Public Policy*. Princeton, N.J.: Princeton University Press, 1991.

Thompson, Robert Luther. *Wiring a Continent: The History of the Telegraph Industry in the United States, 1832–1866*. Princeton, N.J.: Princeton University Press, 1947.

Tocqueville, Alexis de. *Democracy in America*, Translated by Henry Reeve. 4 vols. London: Saunders and Otley, 1835–40.

18

JOURNALISM AND
THE PUBLIC INTEREST

Daniel Schorr

Congress shall make no law respecting an establishment of religion, or prohibiting the free exercise thereof; or abridging the freedom of speech, or of the press; or the right of the people peaceably to assemble, and to petition the government for a redress of grievances.

THE FIRST AMENDMENT, RATIFIED IN 1791, ITS REACH extended to the states by the Fourteenth Amendment in 1868, makes the press the only private industry afforded specific constitutional protection. It was intended to protect printers and pamphleteers like Benjamin Franklin and Thomas Paine against censorship imposed by the politicians they criticized. The framers of the Constitution, who regarded a free press as vital to a democracy, could not have conceived that one day this cloak would embrace vast empires of newspaper chains, radio and television conglomerates, and Internet outlets that stretched the very meaning of journalism.

The press (now more commonly called the news media) continues to insist on constitutional shelter in the public interest while primarily serving substantial private interests, and sometimes being accused of acting against the public interest.

The guarantee of press freedom has, since the eighteenth century, been subject to attacks, legal and otherwise. The first major test was the controversy set off by passage of the Sedition Act of 1798. Signed into law by President John Adams on July 14, 1798, the act made it a crime for any person "to write, print, utter[,] or publish . . . any false, scandalous and malicious writing or writings against the government of the United States, or either house of the Congress or President . . . with intent to defame . . . or to bring them, or either of them, into contempt or disrepute; or to excite against them . . . the hatred of the good people of the United States." Violation of the statute was punishable by a $5,000 fine and five years in prison.

James Madison and Thomas Jefferson were among those who condemned the act as unconstitutional, and they coauthored resolutions against it. In the Virginia Resolutions of 1798, the General Assembly protested that the act "exercises . . . a power not delegated by the Constitution, but, on the contrary, expressly and positively forbidden by one of the amendments thereto—a power which, more than any other, ought to produce universal alarm, because it is leveled against the right of freely examining public characters and measures, and of free communication among the people thereon, which has ever been justly deemed the only effectual guardian of every other right." Opposition to the act fueled the publication and circulation of Republican newspapers and became a major issue in the presidential election of 1800. The newly elected president, Jefferson, pardoned those who had been convicted under the act and remitted their fines, saying: "I considered, and now consider, that law to be a nullity, as absolute and as palpable as if Congress had ordered us to fall down and worship a golden image." The act expired in 1801.

More than a century later, during World War I, the Espionage Act of 1917 prohibited antigovernment speech that interfered with the success of the military. In 1919 the Supreme Court upheld the espionage conviction of Charles Schenck, secretary of the Socialist Party, for circulating leaflets opposing the draft to men who had already been drafted. In upholding his conviction, the justices said that Schenck's actions created "a clear and present danger." According to majority opinion: "When a nation is at war many things that might be said in a time of peace are such a hindrance to its effort that their utterance will not be endured so long as men fight and that no Court could regard them as protected by any constitutional right."[1]

In *Near v. Minnesota* in 1931, the court struck down a state law that authorized censorship of scurrilous material published by a local newspaper. While Justice Pierce Butler, in his dissenting opinion, wrote that the Constitution was not intended to "protect malice, scandal, and other defamation when untrue or published with bad motives or without justifiable ends," the majority ruled that even outlandish material was protected. "Charges of reprehensible conduct, and, in particular, of official malfeasance, unquestionably create a public scandal," went the majority opinion, "but the theory of the constitutional guaranty is that even a more serious public evil would be caused by authority to prevent publication."[2]

A truly landmark case in terms of undergirding freedom of the press was *New York Times Co. v. Sullivan* in 1964. In a 6–3 decision, the Supreme Court struck down a lower court decision that Alabama police commissioner L. B. Sullivan had been libeled in a full-page advertisement in the *New York Times* taken out by civil rights activists. The Court majority held that a public official enjoyed less legal protection than an ordinary citizen. Further, it held that a claim of defamation had to be backed not only with proof that a statement was false, but that it was intentionally false. The "actual malice" doctrine has served to protect unnumbered defendants in libel suits ever since.[3]

The Pentagon Papers case of 1971 raised in stark terms the issue of press freedom versus national security. A former government employee, Daniel Ellsberg, had conveyed to the *New York Times* and *Washington Post* copies of a classified seven-thousand-page history of the United States' involvement in the Vietnam War. As soon as the first excerpts appeared in the *Times,* the Nixon administration, in the person of Attorney General John Mitchell, sought from the federal district court an injunction against further publication. Mitchell claimed that further excerpts would cause "irreparable injury" to the national security.

In the end, the Supreme Court held that the restraining order on the *Times* and the *Post* be lifted. Justice Hugo Black said, for the majority, that it was the intention of the framers of the Constitution that the press should be free "so that it could bare the secrets of government to inform the people."[4]

Justices William Douglas and William Brennan were alone in their contention that the First Amendment banned *all* prior restraint. Four justices—Douglas, Potter Stewart, Byron White, and Thurgood Marshall—raised the possibility of criminal prosecution *after* publication. Since then government officials have, on occasion, threatened prosecution under the espionage statute to keep a newspaper from publishing sensitive information.

In 1985 Central Intelligence Agency director William Casey made such a threat to Ben Bradlee, editor of the *Washington Post,* over a story that the *Post* was planning to run about the tapping of underwater Soviet cables. Bradlee quoted Casey as saying, "There's no way you can run that story without endangering national security. I'm not threatening you, but you've got to know that if you publish this I would recommend that you be prosecuted."[5] President Richard Nixon then had *Post* publisher Katharine Graham called out of her shower to warn against publication.

In the end, the *Post* printed the story—and no one from the newspaper went to jail. The issue is a tricky one—the national interest in keeping the citizenry informed versus the national security interest in keeping secrets. In this case, as it turned out, the Soviet authorities knew that their undersea communications had been compromised and no harm was done by publication.

So, the government could threaten prosecution, but it could not forbid publication as the British government might have done under its Official Secrets Act. This is due to what may be the key provision of the Pentagon Papers decision dealing with prior restraint. The decision made clear that the right of publication was not absolute. It held that in this case, the government had not met the "heavy burden" of establishing a threat to the national security so great as to warrant advance censorship. Nor had that heavy burden been met by 2004. What the

Court left open was the possibility of subsequent (postpublication) prosecution or libel action.

Yet the high court had generally heeded the advice of James Madison that "a popular government without popular information or the means to acquiring it is but the prologue to a farce or tragedy." And the advice of Woodrow Wilson, "Everybody knows that corruption thrives in secret places and avoids public places and we believe it a fair assumption that secrecy means impropriety."

Since the terrorist attacks of September 11, 2001, the government has found other ways of influencing the press. One way is to appeal to patriotism at a time when the nation is engaged in a war against terrorism. In October 2001, Condoleezza Rice, then President George W. Bush's national security advisor, arranged a telephone conference call with six television news executives, urging them to limit the use of videotaped addresses by al Qaeda leader Osama bin Laden, which might have a negative effect on the American public and might even contain coded messages to al Qaeda followers. Never mind that bin Laden's statements are available to anyone with a satellite receiver. Most of the news executives agreed to cut back on the use of such tapes.

The tension between press and government about keeping secrets is heightened by the knowledge that classification goes far beyond real need, activated more by fear of personal embarrassment than a threat to national security. J. William Leonard, a National Archives official, testified before a House committee, "It is no secret that the government classifies too much information."

Pressures on the media are enormous. Walter Isaacson, the former president of Cable News Network (CNN), has commented on the media's constant whipsawing between "the Patriotism Police," demanding support of the government, and "the Lapdog Police," complaining of a too-compliant attitude toward the government.

"In this war we need to return to our nation's tradition of cooperation and self-defense," said Attorney General John Ashcroft in a speech in June 2003.

The battle between secrecy and disclosure has generated periodic clashes over leaks and confidential sources. For the news media, freedom of press implies freedom to use information from confidential sources. The Supreme Court, in a 1972 decision, recognized a limited reporters' "privilege" but said that it had to yield to the needs of grand juries for information that they could not acquire any other way.[6]

In the early 2000s, two major "sources" issues were being fought out before the courts. In Washington, five reporters representing the Associated Press, CNN, the *Los Angeles Times,* and the *New York Times* had been cited for contempt by a federal judge. They refused to answer questions about confidential sources in a civil defamation suit brought by Wen Ho Lee, a Los Alamos Nuclear Laboratory scientist who claimed he was wrongly accused of espionage. In another such controversy, reporters for the *New York Times,* the *Washington Post,* and NBC were subpoenaed by a special prosecutor investigating the leak in 2003 of the identity of Valerie Plame, a CIA undercover employee.

Hostility to the press often emanates from the Oval Office itself, and sometimes with good reason. At least three recent presidents could attribute their greatest woes to journalists and journalism.

Richard M. Nixon was embarked on the road to disgrace in June 1972, because of reports in the *Washington Post* followed by those of other media organizations. The *Post* linked a break-in into Democratic headquarters in the Watergate office building to the Nixon campaign committee. There followed disclosures about disbursement of campaign money for illicit purposes, and, in the end, a draft bill of impeachment in the House forced Nixon to resign. William Safire, a Nixon speechwriter then, quoted Nixon as saying, "The press is the enemy."

Ronald Reagan, who once said, "I'm up to my keister in leaks," was damaged by the Iran-Contra scandal that started, oddly, with a story in a little weekly magazine in Beirut, Lebanon, called *al-Shiraa*. Obviously planted by the Iranian authorities to embarrass the Reagan administration, the story revealed that former national security advisor Robert McFarlane had flown to Tehran with a planeload of antitank missiles, which he hoped to barter for the release of American hostages held by pro-Iranian terrorists in Lebanon. Subsequently it emerged that the proceeds of the arms sale were to be used to arm the Contra rebels in Nicaragua, something that Congress had specifically forbidden. The prestige of a popular president was shaken by the revelations that started with a little Beirut weekly.

Bill Clinton was started down the road to impeachment by the news media—in this case, the Internet. On the night of January 17, 1998, gossipmonger Matt Drudge posted word on his Web site that *Newsweek* magazine was working on a story of the president's relationship with a White House intern. Drudge was quoted the next morning on ABC television, and within days the story was all over the print and electronic media and the ordeal of President Clinton had begun.

In making presidents accountable for their misdeeds, the press clearly served the public interest. Yet an old-time journalist finds it a matter of sorrow that the press, at the height of its influence, is at a depth of its public approval. Protected by the Constitution as the guardian of the public interest, the news media are not regarded by most Americans as dedicated to the public interest as they strive for circulation, ratings, and profits.

One Roper–Freedom Forum poll found that fewer than 20 percent of respondents rated journalistic ethics as high. Sixty-five percent thought that there are times when publication or broadcast should be "prevented" in the public interest. Did we win the fight over prior restraint in the Supreme Court only to lose it in the court of public opinion?

In the television world of today news has come to occupy a corner of a vast entertainment stage, sharing the techniques and values of entertainment. It is perhaps because of the blurring of the line between reality and fantasy that several journalists have tried to build careers on invented stories.

In 1980 the *Washington Post* had to return a Pulitzer Prize awarded to Janet Cooke for a made-up story about an eight-year-old child hooked on drugs. Two-thirds of the stories written by Stephen Glass for the *New Republic* between 1995 and 1998 turned out to be fabricated. The champion liar was Jayson Blair, who filed many stories for the *New York Times* using false datelines naming places Blair had never been. In 2004 Jack Kelley resigned from *USA Today* after a series of dramatic but untrue stories, such as witnessing a suicide bombing in Jerusalem.

Opinion polls beginning in the late 1990s have registered growing public distrust of the increasingly concentrated, profit-driven news media. In 2002, forty-six corporations controlled more than 50 percent of the news media—an array that included some 1,800 daily newspapers, 11,000 magazines, 2,000 television stations, and 11,000 radio stations. All of the principal television networks are extensions of large corporations—ABC's parent company is the Walt Disney Company, NBC's is General Electric, Viacom owns CBS, and Time Warner, CNN.

On February 22, 1971, more than a year before Watergate, President Nixon, his words recorded on Oval Office tape, remarked to his counsel, John Dean, "Well, one helluva lot of people don't give one damn about the issue of the suppression of the press, etc."

Cynical, but perceptive. Yet no one demonstrated better than Nixon that, for all its faults and failings, the press, at crucial moments, is there to defend the public interest.

Notes

1. *Schenck v. United States,* 249 U.S. 247 (1919).
2. *Near v. Minnesota,* 283 U.S. 697 (1931).
3. *New York Times Co. v. Sullivan,* 376 U.S. 254 (1964).
4. *New York Times Co. v. United States,* 403 U.S. 713 (1971).
5. See Bradlee, *A Good Life,* 473.
6. *Branzburg v. Hayes,* 408 U.S. 665 (1972). The author admits to a personal interest in this issue. In 1976 the House Ethics Committee threatened me with a citation for contempt of Congress and a possible jail sentence if I did not disclose where I had gotten a House Intelligence Committee report, which the House had voted to suppress for revealing too much classified information. I held my ground behind a First Amendment privilege that Congress did not recognize. The Ethics Committee eventually voted 6 to 5 to let me off with a rebuke but, happily, without a jail sentence.

Bibliography

Anderson, Bonnie M. *News Flash: Journalism, Infotainment and the Bottom-Line Business of Broadcast News.* San Francisco: Jossey-Bass, 2004.

Bradlee, Ben. *A Good Life: Newspapering and Other Adventures.* New York: Simon and Schuster, 1995.

Entman, Robert M. *Projections of Power: Framing News, Public Opinion, and U.S. Foreign Policy.* Chicago: University of Chicago Press, 2004.

Hentoff, Nat. *The First Freedom: The Tumultuous History of Free Speech in America.* New York: Delacorte, 1980.

Kurtz, Howard. *Hot Air: All Talk, All the Time.* New York: Times Books, 1996.

Mayer, Martin. *Making News.* Garden City, N.Y.: Doubleday, 1987.

Mindich, David T. Z. *Tuned Out: Why Americans under 40 Don't Follow the News.* New York: Oxford University Press, 2005.

Mitroff, Ian I., and Warren Bennis. *The Unreality Industry: The Deliberate Manufacturing of Falsehood and What It Is Doing to Our Lives.* New York: Carol, 1989.

Rudenstine, David. *The Day the Presses Stopped: A History of the Pentagon Papers Case.* Berkeley: University of California Press, 1996.

Schorr, Daniel. *Staying Tuned: A Life in Journalism.* New York: Pocket Books, 2001.

Schwartz, Tony. *Media, the Second God.* New York: Random House, 1981.

Serrin, William. *The Business of Journalism: Ten Leading Reporters and Editors on the Perils and Pitfalls of the Press.* New York: New Press, 2000.

Starr, Paul. *The Creation of the Media: Political Origins of Modern Communications.* New York: Basic Books, 2004.

Twentieth Century Fund Task Force on Justice, Publicity, and the First Amendment. *Rights in Conflict.* Background paper by Alan Barth. New York: McGraw Hill, 1976.

19

THE MILITARY AND THE MEDIA

William Prochnau

O N A CHOPPY MORNING IN THE CARIBBEAN IN LATE
October 1983, a United States naval aircraft made one pass and then
another over a small boat bearing several American reporters from
Barbados toward the tiny island of Grenada, where American troops were
engaged in the U.S. military's first combat mission in ten years. On both passes, the
plane fired shots across the bow, a universal warning signal, and the reporters
reluctantly decided to take their country's navy seriously. Wisely, they returned to
Barbados, where hundreds of their colleagues were chafing at being contained
170 miles away from the fighting, as the press was prohibited from the theater of
operations for the first time in a modern American war. One of the reporters later
confronted the invasion commander, Vice Admiral Joseph Metcalf III, and asked
what he would have done if the media boat had continued. Metcalf's answer was
a sign of the post-Vietnam times: "I'd have blown your ass right out of the water."[1]

This riposte has set Metcalf among the dark legends of quotable military
leaders in the endless battle between the media and the military. (The favorite
remains General William Tecumseh Sherman, who, upon hearing of the death of
several Civil War correspondents, said: "That's good. We'll have dispatches now
from hell before breakfast.")[2]

Still, Sherman and Metcalf can be forgiven on several counts—and surely by
journalists who relish pungent quotes. Sherman's words came in the midst of a
terrible internecine war, and the beginning of a large-scale American war correspondence that sent five hundred of "those buzzards of the press," as he called
them, onto Civil War battlegrounds. In Grenada, Metcalf's moment came ten
years into an angry thirty-year post-Vietnam battle between the military and the
media unlike any in American history. Tangled in the legacy of Vietnam, and a
new, younger military's certainty that the press had contributed to the United
States' loss in that war, besmirching the military's honor in the process, the animosity became laced with rare vitriol. Words like *hatred, enemy,* and worse
resounded.

310

The conflict between the military and the media, however, is both normal and inevitable. The institutions invariably collide at moments of highest possible stress, with the highest possible stakes for the country. One of the great paradoxes of their constitutional roles is that the institution most unfettered by the Constitution, the press, is invariably restrained in wartime, and the one that was fettered, the military, seems unloosed, although that is mostly illusion, and properly so, as the civilian architects of the confrontation hold the military on a taut string.

Moving through the history of press-military relations chronologically makes it possible to show how the struggle of the press for access and the government for control has produced different types of reporting over time. Media access to American battlefields, which was denied throughout most of the post-Vietnam era, is a far more crucial issue to both the media and the American people than reasonable restrictions through censorship (although such censorship all too often becomes unreasonable). But even in the warp speed of modern life, a story told late is better than a story never told, the latter akin to the proverbial tree that falls in the wilderness. This chronology will demarcate as well how changes in technology have increased the impact of reporters' accounts of wars and, with that impact, increased the military's attempts to shape reporting and constrain reporters, or use them to their own ends.

From the Mexican War to the Civil War: The Journalist as Unreliable Witness

Formal American war reporting dates back to 1846, when the *New Orleans Picayune* stampeded the U.S. government into invading Mexico and then sent its reporters, led by George Wilkins Kendall, riding, eating, drinking—and often fighting—alongside the U.S. forces. Before Kendall and his colleagues, generals often were the chroniclers of their own wars, a perquisite the loss of which many have rued since. Wilkins set a nineteenth-century standard for the new craft. His dispatches dripped with glory and heroism, sent the *Picayune*'s penny-paper circulation soaring, and provided early editors with a lesson quickly learned: War news sold papers.[3]

By the time the Civil War began little more than a decade later, editors had learned their lessons well. They sent hordes—some serious, dedicated journalists and many not—onto the battlefields. A latter-day kinsman, the historian-journalist James M. Perry, described the rowdy band as "mostly rough, sometimes ready," who "lied . . . cheated . . . spied on one another . . . made up battles they had never seen . . . drank too much . . . and did a lot of things reporters are still doing today."[4] The military responded to the interlopers with distaste and occasionally more—punishments that ranged from imprisonment to humiliation to banishment. One reporter was court-martialed as a spy, then reprieved by

President Abraham Lincoln; in one of the military's most degrading punishments, another was ridden through the ranks seated backward on a woeful mule and wearing a sign that read, "Libeler of the press."[5]

Before the invention of the telegraph in 1844, news moved so slowly—by ship, horseback, and pigeon—that thousands were killed in the Battle of New Orleans after the War of 1812 had ended.[6] By the time the Civil War began in 1860, technology had completed as profound a leap forward as television would make in the next century. At the outset of the war, fifty thousand miles of wire had been strung and a significant part of military strategy was devoted to stringing up more for its own use and tearing it down to block others, including the press. News moved at astonishing speed—the "lightning," editors called it.

The technology of media changed war as much as the technology of weaponry. Newspapers ran war stories the day after battles were staged, and for the first time generals faced a phenomenon that irritated them ever after: micromanagement of tactics and strategy by civilian leaders based on information (not always reliable information) that often reached Washington through the press before the official battle reports.

American journalism of the nineteenth century operated under different standards from the journalism of the late twentieth century. Bias, opinion, and political positions were as expected as that unattainable goal of objectivity is today. There were Democratic papers, Whig papers, and, with the arrival of the new party of John Frémont and Lincoln, Republican papers. A newspaper's politics did not stop at the editorial pages.

With the end of the Civil War, it was time, regardless of the improbability of a code of standards among the rabble rousers, for some general sense of obligation and professionalism among correspondents. It would not come until much later—and at a time when journalists were attacked the most passionately—in Vietnam.

The Spanish American War: Newspapers as Instigators of War

As the army subdued the last of the Indian tribes in 1890, newspapers were dreaming up the next war, a low point in the history of the American press. Two New York tabloid publishers, one whose name will forever be attached to rabble-rousing yellow journalism and the other, ironically, to the most prestigious award for exemplary journalism, set their eyes on circulation, sensationalism, and, coincidentally, Spanish Cuba. William Randolph Hearst, publisher of the *New York Journal,* and Joseph Pulitzer, publisher of the *New York World,* locked into a circulation battle of historic proportions. Hearst became the provocateur, hiring the artist Frederic Remington for $3,000 a month, a huge sum at the time, to produce drawings of Spanish atrocities that existed only in Hearst's mind. He paid the same amount to the most famous war correspondent of the day, Richard

Harding Davis. After months, Remington asked to come home, wiring Hearst that he had found no war to illustrate. Hearst reportedly wired back: YOU FURNISH THE PICTURES. I'LL FURNISH THE WAR.

The *Journal* began printing stories so outrageous about atrocities so phony and appalling that the *New York Times* called them "freak journalism" and, briefly forgetting the First Amendment, suggested that such a practice should be banned by law. Hearst's biographer, W. A. Swanberg, described the *Journal's* reporting as "the most disgraceful example of journalistic falsehood ever seen." Circulation, however, soared; Pulitzer matched fictional piece with fictional piece and reaped a five-million-copy increase in sales for the *World* in one week. The newspapers helped drive the United States into war. Pulitzer became somewhat shamefaced; Hearst gloried in it, advertising: "How do you like the *Journal's* War?" One of the legacies of the event more than a century later is the number of Americans who believe that the news media use sensationalism to boost profits. Forgotten is that the heightened costs of the coverage caused the *World* to lose money that year.[7]

The World Wars: Censorship and Access

World War I began with the sternest censorship possible, which was perhaps necessary to continue the inhumanity of trench warfare without public revulsion. The war became one of the most crippling in history—England, a victor, losing most of a generation of its brightest young men and never again returning to its full international glories. German losses were so thoroughly hidden from the German people that, after four years, the populace went into shock when their forces surrendered. That shock helped set the stage for another, wider world war to come.

The Americans did not enter the war until its third year. To keep the horror of the trenches from reaching home, the U.S. government followed suit with the sternest censorship and press regulation in its history. For the first (and only) time in its history the U.S. government charged a fee to the journalists or their employers of $1,000 for accreditation, severely limiting access. It then required correspondents and their employers to sign pledges that they would refrain from publishing news that might abet the enemy, and post a $10,000 bond ($150,000 in today's dollars[8]) as a guarantee against violations.

Access was further limited when the correspondents reached Europe. Few were allowed anywhere near the front lines—a boon to their mortality but not to the public's need to know in a war in which more than a million men were killed and wounded in a single battle that ended, like most, in a draw.[9] No correspondents viewed the battle; no casualty figures emerged until after the war.

Still, even with access virtually closed, censorship became so total, the censors so powerful, that the results became ludicrous. One correspondent's cabled expense account was censored, apparently because it revealed that he had bought an expensive lunch for an American general. In another case references to good-will gifts of wine from French villagers to American troops were deleted on the grounds that they suggested "bibulous indulgence by American soldiers which might offend temperance forces in the United States." In frustration, one correspondent left the war zone and sailed back to New York to get his story printed. He was fined $10,000. World War I became a story that simply wasn't told until long after it was too late.[10] It left a haunting message about what denial of access, censorship, and claims of protecting "national security" can wreak.

World War II was brutal in a different fashion, new inhumanities such as the firebombing and total destruction of cities and massive civilian casualties accepted far too nonchalantly. Decisions to attempt to destroy the German and Japanese will to fight by destroying their people and cities merited public debate. But, with millions of civilians killed, World War II nevertheless became, in the view of many strategists, soldiers, journalists, and historians, "the good war."

The Uniformed Reporter

For the first time since the Civil War, the fate of the nation was at stake, and good, old-fashioned, simple patriotism—as well as a liberal dose of jingoistic propaganda, an inevitable by-product of war—reigned. Correspondents wore the uniform of their country, took on a mock rank of major, and settled relatively comfortably into censorship as a necessity about which they would occasionally gripe—what news person doesn't?—but nonetheless accept. A sense of trust built up between war makers and correspondents, a relationship that would, with the exception of the long cold war with the Soviets, be tested greatly in the less fundamental wars that followed.

But a key to this was access. Stunning as it may be even in concept in today's world of anti-terrorism activities and routine "black ops" that are totally off limits to the media, a reporter for the *New York Times* was invited to observe the first test of the preeminent secret of World War II: the atomic bomb. The reporter, William L. Laurence, not only watched the top-secret test of the bomb in the desert of New Mexico and kept it secret, but he accompanied the first two bombs to the Pacific and flew in an observer plane the second time the bomb was used against Japan, at Nagasaki.[11] General George S. Patton thought nothing of inviting a half-dozen reporters into his tent at night to chew over plans and strategy for coming actions. No correspondent ever leaked a word.[12] The reporters dug in with the troops for lengths of time and horrors of combat undreamed of by their grandchildren who "embedded" in Iraq.

Was the war better covered, the public better served? Surely better than during World War I. But secrets often were kept to protect public morale rather than to keep information out of enemy hands. The American public was given no idea of the magnitude of the damage to the U.S. fleet at Pearl Harbor in 1941 until halfway through the war, although the Japanese knew. Grotesque photographs of dead enemy troops were shown from the outset, but the public was protected from the vision of dead Americans until almost two years into the war. Even the GIs began to complain that people at home were fighting one war, while they were fighting another. *Life* magazine showed one of the first casualty photos, in September 1943. The bodies of three soldiers, two facedown, one whose face was obscured, lay in the ebbing waters of Buna beach in New Guinea. It was a strong photo but its impact was mainly emotional.[13]

Korea: Press Requests for Censorship

Korea followed World War II almost like an asterisk, the first hot war of the cold war, the first United Nations war, although it was fought primarily by Americans and was a horrendous experience for the troops as well as the correspondents. In June 1950 North Korea launched a massive invasion of South Korea. Although the UN quickly voted to defend the South and the United States almost immediately began shipping troops and weaponry in from nearby Japan, chaos reigned, and one loss followed another throughout most of the summer. Green and ill-equipped, American soldiers often dropped their carbines, the only weapons they had to defend against invading tanks, and ran in tears. Soldiers and reporters, who also quickly moved in from Japan, were caught behind enemy lines.

The war began so suddenly and with such surprise that censorship was not installed and as a result the words sent home were as tough and realistic as any from a war front, partly because the soldiers themselves begged the correspondents to tell the people the real story. "Are you telling the people back home the truth?" a young lieutenant begged Marguerite Higgins, a *New York Herald Tribune* correspondent who became famous in the war. "Are you telling them that out of a platoon of twenty we have three left . . . that it is an utterly useless war?"[14] She and others did, writing, as Philip Knightley described it, of "whipped and frightened GIs and desperation, horror and, and lack of purpose." The generals panicked, not only at the losses but the descriptions of it. Communications were so wrecked by the invasion that the reporters had to fly to Tokyo to file their stories. Several were berated as traitors and briefly denied the right to return. General Douglas MacArthur relented, but not before lecturing several correspondents that they had "an important responsibility in the matter of psychological warfare."[15]

The Journalist's Responsibility in Time of War

As the United States moved into an era of less certainty about the wars it fought, MacArthur's reaction had posited the basic question for American journalism, one that would grow more complicated through the next fifty years of little wars and wars less clearly tied, in some minds, at least, to the nation's security. In time of war, is the press to be flag waver or watchdog? What is the jour-nalist's responsibility when the shooting starts—and indeed, in modern wars, just before? Do reporters have the same idealistic responsibility they routinely assume in covering daily political affairs, relaying to the public both civic progress and corruption? Does the public have a right to know that its young soldiers are sent into war to fire at tanks with rifles, that they are being slaugh-tered, that they are turning and running not out of cowardice but out a lack of preparedness? Or should the media take on a role in national "psychological warfare" that might enable the government to rally and march fresh troops back over the stacks of bodies toward victory—or in Korea's case, a draw—in a war that might not be worth it? What does "psychological warfare" really mean: get-ting the nation's citizenry psyched to fight (morale building) or psyching out the enemy (morale degrading)? Can the two be separated and, if so, should a free press be a witting participant in misleading the public? The questions go to the very essence of a free press in a free country, but in time of war they are freighted with complexity.

There are too many different kinds of wars for easy answers. The solution, as it does in so much of life, lies in judgment calls. Journalists are citizens and human beings. In Korea they worried about what they were doing and finally did what many considered the journalistically unthinkable: They asked for guid-ance and censorship, with the Overseas Press Club petitioning the government to bring in the blue pencil. For the government, it didn't take much encourage-ment. With censorship installed, General MacArthur added his own caveat: All mention critical of him would be banned, too.[16] National security can cast a large and heavy blanket.

Vietnam: The Living Room War

And so came Vietnam, uncensored (except for one three-week period of dark comedy in 1963),[17] and with a freedom of movement and expression rarely accorded to war correspondents. No sign of benevolence or new thinking, the decision on censorship grew out of the trap of a diplomatic Rubik's Cube built by the Kennedy administration. At the beginning it tried to create the illusion (untrue) that American soldiers were not fighting, but simply advising. Later administrations entrapped themselves in the rationale that they couldn't censor because it wasn't their war—it belonged to the South Vietnamese government. In both cases, there was no American war, no censorship.

The myths about the media and Vietnam are many. This essay focuses on three: that the early reporters in Vietnam were the war's first antiwar activists and negativists, setting a standard that continued throughout; that the on-the-ground relationship between the media and the military was unusually rancorous; and that biased or downbeat media coverage was responsible for the loss of the war.

Myth One: The First Correspondents Set an Antiwar Tone

The earliest reporters to cover Vietnam—correspondents such as Malcolm Browne of the Associated Press, Neil Sheehan of United Press, and David Halberstam, a brassy, indefatigable reporter from the *New York Times*—indeed were regularly attacked by the government as biased, unpatriotic, and unmanly. Out of these characterizations grew the first myth: that these correspondents were the first of the Vietnam antiwar activists. Ironically, they wished later that the myth had been true, because they came to believe that the seemingly endless war was without reason. Instead, they were establishment-educated—Harvard for Sheehan and Halberstam, Swarthmore for Browne—children of the cold war who believed to the man that the war was a proper extension of American foreign policy against Communist expansion. Halberstam, who became the bête noir of generations of military men, once thumped his fist on a Saigon barroom table and announced for all to hear: "My God! We *can't* let this go over to the Communists."[18]

But what these reporters did discover and report was a campaign of pervasive lies about the war, its conduct and its successes. Those lies would become the foundation of more than a decade of lies about Vietnam. Body counts? The brass were demanding results so out of line with reality that the joke among the military "advisers" in the field was that after counting a chicken here, a child or grandmother there, and every blood droplet leading into the jungle, you doubled the number and sent it to Saigon. There, the military men in the field knew, the system would require at least another doubling to satisfy the war makers back home. These numbers then were announced to correspondents, some of whom had been at the battles, at daily press briefings soon known as "The Five O'Clock Follies." Halberstam said later, "There were 30,000 Vietcong rebels there when I arrived. There were 30,000 killed while I was there. And there were 30,000 there when I left."[19]

The brass and the civilian leadership simply stopped talking to the renegade correspondents. Ambassador Frederick Nolting threw Halberstam out of his Saigon office. Inadvertently, these actions did the reporters a favor and undermined the leadership further. "We couldn't get anything out of official sources," Sheehan said. "It was a very good thing for us." In such a situation good reporters do what good reporters do: They found other sources—young military men, captains, majors, and bird colonels fighting in the field and closest to the action. Paradoxically these men were the predecessors of the same younger military officers who became so certain of the mythology of the postwar period.[20] What the correspondents found is what they reported: that the brass was saying one thing but the young officers in the field were saying another. The American military men in the field said the war was being fought foolishly and being lost, and that the American public was being misled by cooked numbers and inappropriate optimism.

Myth Two: The Media-Military Relationship Was Rancorous

Most reporters and young military officers from Vietnam remember little serious hostility between them at the time. A Vietnam correspondent, and as good a daily newsman as the late twentieth century produced, R. W. ("Johnny") Apple of the *New York Times,* scoffs at the postwar mythology: "Whatever the military may say now about the problems they encountered with us in Vietnam, they didn't say then."[21] The author made two combat tours as a correspondent and never heard anything other than the blunt lectures of the commanders whose troops he was joining: "For my sake, don't get yourself killed and, for your sake, don't get any of my men killed."

Myth Three: Negative Media Coverage Lost the War

The largest and most pervasive myth, held widely in some circles and later within the military, is that negative press coverage was responsible for losing the war. A central part of this myth springs from coverage of the 1968 Tet Offensive, a surprise attack by the North Vietnamese on South Vietnamese cities, including a brief intrusion into the American Embassy. Whatever the military outcome of the offensive, the attacks inflicted a major psychological blow to the United States in its contentions that it was winning the war. Later evidence indicated that the invading forces virtually depleted themselves in the attack and, in effect, lost the offensive militarily. But for months in 1968, an American election year, television news and front-page stories showed a war campaign in chaos and rising casualties. At home, President Lyndon Johnson, whose administration had been trumpeting success in Vietnam, withdrew from reelection. His eventual successor, Richard Nixon, implied that he had a "secret plan" to end the war. In this kind of environment—turmoil in Vietnam, political unraveling at the very top of the U.S. government—it seems naive to deduce that loss of public support was a product of media negativism.

Contemporary polls also show clearly that public support for the war in Vietnam had turned long before the press delivered up the "hot" pictures and words of the Tet Offensive. In wars involving less than national survival, it is a maxim that public support declines as body bags increase (in 2003 President George W. Bush banned the media from filming the return to U.S. military bases of soldiers killed in the Iraq War). In 1973, John E. Mueller used contemporary Gallup Polls to show two substantial points: (1) As casualties rose, public support for the war declined, and (2) public support for the war dropped below 50 percent when the American death toll passed ten thousand in the summer of 1967—more than six months before the Tet Offensive—and never rose to a majority again.[22]

Scholars are not the only ones who find the American loss in Vietnam rooted in far more serious matters than media coverage. Anthony C. Zinni, a young second lieutenant blooded in Vietnam, took a square look at the blame and did not see the media. "I wondered at the time just what in hell our generals—my heroes who fought in World War II—thought they were doing," Zinni said twenty-five years later when he retired as a general of the Marine Corps. "We [young officers] lost faith in our senior leadership." But Zinni also knew that the generals were taking their orders from civilian war makers in the White House and Pentagon whom he despised for their late-life contriteness, "as though saying mea culpa often enough will absolve them of the terrible responsibility they still bear."[23]

Vietnam's Bitter Aftermath

Still, nowhere did the mythology set deeper roots than among the new officers coming into the ranks after Vietnam. Another young Marine veteran of Vietnam who rose to the rank of general before retiring in the 1990s, Bernard E. Trainor, listened to decades of junior officers come out of the academies so full of anger he concluded: "The credo of the military seems to have become: 'Duty, honor, country, and hate the media.'"[24] The architects of the failure, the civilian leaders, were even quicker to pass blame.

"There are no more Ernie Pyles" became a favored antimedia catchphrase, one voiced by former secretary of defense James Schlesinger in 1984.[25] Ironies abounded. More than fifty journalists, correspondents, and the greatest risk-takers of all, the photographers, had been killed in action in Vietnam. The ratio of journalists killed was higher than that of soldiers, simply because the average correspondent saw more combat than the average soldier. Most died with the grunts they were covering, just as Ernie Pyle died next to his GIs. But, post–Vietnam, with the government denying access to battlefields, how could a reporter become an Ernie Pyle? The complaint seemed, at best, arrogant, and, at worst, ignorant.

With Vietnam over, the military, particularly the army, faced daunting problems of rebuilding. Morale had sunk to a perilous low. The country was drained, unsympathetic, and wanted to forget. With the draft ended, force replenishments had to be lured into a new all-professional service with large and costly inducements. It was clear that the country would not go lightly into another war in the near future. Career advancement is slow without combat experience. What future was there in it? With all those woes, plus the first losing war in American history, it was not unnatural to seek a scapegoat. Since Homer, the messenger has been the favored candidate—and became the choice once again.

Over the next years the military produced volumes of research studies on how to cope with the media. In one nine-year period after Vietnam, *Parameters,* the U.S. Army War College quarterly, published no fewer than fifteen articles studying the media problem.[26] In 1982 a Naval War College publication offered up the opinion from one of its public relations officers that the best approach would be to "sanitize the visual images of war, control media access to theaters [of war], censor information that could upset readers and viewers, and exclude journalists who would not write favorable stories."[27] The military never quite went this far, but it came close. The study in the naval journal was worrisome in other ways as well:

1. It was written shortly after the British almost completely shut down press coverage of the 1982 Falklands War, which the *Guardian* called "the worst covered war since the Crimean," and Julian Barnes, in the same newspaper, complained that news was sent back to England by the "swiftest carrier turtle" the Royal Navy could find, so heavily doctored that even lines saying the stories were censored were censored.[28]

2. That the U.S. Navy, or the American government, might pick up on these British tactics showed how negated the Constitution and the Bill of Rights can become in time of war. The First Amendment was written, at least in part, to counteract the crown's control of the media, which still exists to some extent in Britain.

3. A year later, almost identical tactics were used in Grenada. The simplest way to control war coverage is to prevent access—and that appeared to be the U.S. government's choice.

Grenada: A New Beginning for Control of Media Access

A tiny Caribbean island with a landmass less than twice that of the District of Columbia, Grenada, despite a small Cuban presence and a handful of American medical students in potential duress, did not rank high as a major threat to U.S. security. But it was a big story—the first armed foray by the American military since the withdrawal from Vietnam a decade earlier, one of the longest periods of military inactivity in U.S. history. For the first two days of the operation, the only crucial time, the navy kept the media bottled up and fuming 170 miles away, on the island of Barbados. This was a sea change of major proportions and a complete about-face from Vietnam. But the angry barbs fired by the media at the navy and the military were launched at the wrong target. The military may implement media policy, but it doesn't make it.

"Don't blame [the media ban in] Grenada on the Pentagon," Lawrence Eagleburger, undersecretary of state at the time, said later. "It was a political decision. As far as I can recall it came out of the White House."[29] It did. Michael Deaver, President Ronald Reagan's deputy chief of staff, later wrote that the White House was surprised that "we got away with it," but the plan worked "by not letting the press in and justifying it later."[30]

One variation or another of that policy would hold through the rest of the century despite "a long and mostly losing struggle" to resolve the access problem, wrote Maud S. Beelman of the International Consortium of Investigative Journalists.[31] Named for its chairman, Lieutenant General Winant Sidle, a former chief of the Office of Information in Vietnam, the Sidle Commission became what most thought the weightiest and most promising of the efforts to resolve the problem. In the wake of the Grenada fiasco, it created a Department of Defense National Media Pool, which the Pentagon agreed to take in with the first wave of troops in future wars, much as General Dwight D. Eisenhower, during World War II, had allowed reporters and photographers to accompany the military on the first amphibious landings at Normandy. (In the late twentieth century the very size of the media—more than fourteen hundred would show up for the Gulf War in 1991—had become a serious logistical problem.) The media has traditionally voiced its disregard for the obligated sharing inherent in pool arrangements. The *New York Times* doesn't want to collaborate with the *Washington Post;* CBS doesn't want to contribute to CNN. Agreement came largely out of desperation. But it was to no avail. In its first test, during the invasion of Panama in 1989, the pool reporters were flown to the scene but buttoned up in an air force base as the action unfolded. They not only missed early combat but, as in Grenada, some very messy early mistakes. The decision to corral the reporters despite the government's agreement once again came at the "highest levels"[32]—which in Washington parlance means the president and his closest advisers.

The Gulf War and Spinning the Media

The Gulf War, or first Iraq War, of 1991 began after Iraq invaded and captured the little oil-rich country of Kuwait. In response, the United States and a coalition of thirty-four nations amassed 660,000 troops (almost 500,000 were American, approaching the high point of the troop commitment in Vietnam) and pushed the Iraqis back out of Kuwait in a devastating assault lasting less than a week. Media pools were formed again but with little to show for it, partly in this case because of confusion, logistics, inability to find communications, and the very speed of the war. Few of the pool stories made it into the public domain before the fighting ended. Once again, the idea of pools aggravated much of the media, leading to a lawsuit by nine news organizations questioning the constitutionality of limiting access to the battleground. The major media generally have avoided going to the courts, fearing that a loss is possible if not probable and that a loss would be irrecoverable.[33] In the 1991 case the court ruled the question moot because the war was over before the case could be decided. Later such cases have also been mooted by time or yielded a ruling unfavorable to the media, although none has gone to the U.S. Supreme Court.

Then secretary of defense Richard Cheney called the war "the best-covered war in history," admitting, however, that he could find few journalists to agree with him. Little wonder: A prewar decision had been made by those "highest sources" to largely deliver the news directly to the public through television, bypassing the filter of the news media. In effect, the secretary of defense became the nation's war correspondent.[34]

That old adage about the camera, however, is not necessarily true. The camera can lie. Unfiltered "news" and pictures of the war were heavily loaded with spin. Unchallenged at the time, the Pentagon claimed an 80 percent success rate for Patriot missiles attacking incoming Iraqi Scuds. The only evidence was night pictures of explosions in the sky. After the war, the success claims dropped off to 40 percent and, still later, congressional and other investigations indicated it may have been far lower than that, perhaps as few as one interception.[35] Videos were shown nightly of laser-guided smart bombs striking targets as small as trucks and command centers, gaining the conflict the nickname the "video-game war" and leaving the impression of a "clean" bombing assault on Iraq. Afterward, however, the Pentagon reported that 98 percent of the explosives dropped in the war were old-fashioned "dumb" bombs that destroyed unselectively.

Three years after the Gulf War and more than twenty after Vietnam, Frank J. Stech, a reserve army colonel, wrote that the military was still trying to find ways to spin the press, like politicians in an election campaign.[36] "A recent Air University thesis argues that 'media spin' has become a new principle of war," Stech wrote. He found such efforts to be "a zero-sum game, where the military wins by keeping secrets, and the media wins by revealing them."[37]

The CNN Effect

In the 1990s military concerns with the media were dominated by the arrival of 24-7 cable television and the so-called CNN effect. At first the military and civilian policy-makers feared that the inherent emotionalism of the effect— the ability of, first, CNN and then other cable news networks to focus on highly dramatic humanitarian problems and bloody local wars the United States might be better off ignoring—would drive American foreign policy by public outcry. The regularly repeated example became Somalia, where televised images of starving children ostensibly drove President George H. W. Bush into an unwise commitment of American troops on a humanitarian mission, and the ubiquitous pictures of a dead American soldier dragged through the streets of Mogadishu drove President Bill Clinton to a precipitous decision to withdraw them. Stech observed acerbically that, if American foreign policy had been driven by either example, it might be time for the country's leaders to listen to Winston Churchill's warning: "Nothing is more dangerous in wartime than to live in the temperamental atmosphere of a Gallup Poll, always feeling one's pulse and taking one's temperature."[38]

Television journalists reveled in the new technology and imputed power. Ted Koppel used ABC's *Nightline,* which had become by 2005 sadly old-fashioned in the crossfire world of know-nothing "shout TV," to conduct one-on-one televised foreign-policy discussions with world leaders. So successful did Koppel become in attracting world leaders to his TV "summits," the Washington rumor mill speculated that his next career step would be secretary of state. At CNN, Christiane Amanpour could penetrate the facade of the most hardened official with her imploring, when-are-we-going-to-do-something-about-it CNN reports from isolated redoubts of misery and strife. One of the State Department reporters at the *Washington Post* told the author at the time that daily meetings focused on Amanpour and her schedule to ascertain where to deploy the diplomatic forces next.

The flurry over the CNN effect rapidly altered the texture of the post-Vietnam battle between the military and the media and would eventually resolve part of the access problem, if not wholly satisfactorily and with no certainty of permanence. In 1984 General William C. Westmoreland, commander in chief of the U.S. forces in Vietnam from 1964 to 1968 and the first general to be faced with televised war, remarked that the new realism of blood on the rug in snug, far-off homes might have a beneficial effect for mankind. "Television might end all wars," he said.[39] The general was wrong. But if his thought was naive, it was at least in part so because no war-fighter could imagine that the public would long tolerate a war in which live television brought the flying limbs and spattering blood into their living rooms every night. One can only imagine what live television from the trenches of World War I would have done to public support. But Westmoreland, the first to deal with television, failed to appreciate just how much American television would censor itself. Televised war would be adrenaline pumping, perhaps, but it would be sterile, as it proved to be as the tanks rolled toward Baghdad in the Iraq war of early 2003. It would show neither the near-total destruction of Iraqi cities like Fallujah nor the beheading of captives by enemy insurgents, although most of the world saw those events on non-American television. Responsible? Irresponsible? These are questions to be answered elsewhere. But it would take far more than television to end war. It would take a way of thinking.

Just the titles of the evolving war-college studies at the beginning of the twenty-first century indicated where the military would be going next. Stech's paper was called "Winning CNN Wars." The emphasis moved from blocking the media, particularly television, to using it. The most quoted widely circulated of these reports was written on the eve of the Iraq War. Provocatively entitled "The CNN Effect: Strategic Enabler or Operational Risk?" the report was written by an army lieutenant colonel, Margaret H. Belknap, and appeared as part of an Army War College "strategic research project" in the autumn 2002 edition of *Parameters.* Belknap's message was straightforward: "Stop hating and start using."

Belknap is no Dr. Strangelove–like figure whipped out of the right wing of the military-industrial complex. She stated what she, if few members of the media, considered a quandary: "The debate on whether the military will be able to control the media or should be able to control the media continues." She acknowledged difficult cultural differences: "The military depends on people who respect authority while a chief role of the media is to question authority." She quoted an unexpectedly reassuring poll after decades of anger. Almost one thousand military officers were asked to respond to this statement: "The news media are just as necessary to maintaining the freedom of the United States as the military." Eighty-three percent agreed.[40]

Belknap did not report the results of another question in the same poll: "Military leaders should be allowed to use the news media to deceive the enemy (thereby deceiving the American public)." To that, 60 percent of the officers agreed.[41] She reported how Colin Powell, as a general, instructed his officers on the new realities: "Once you've got all the forces moving . . . turn your attention to television because you can win the battle or lose the war if you don't handle the story right."[42]

Media as Strategic Enabler

Belknap's paper, and the military thinking it apparently reflected, could hardly reassure the media and it should not reassure the public. Hers was a variety of the Cheney statement: In time of war, the military (i.e., government) should usurp the power of the media, or, at least, put the power to its own uses. If the post-Vietnam anger was beginning to dissipate, was the media now to become a hand-in-glove "strategic enabler" for the American military? "Strategic enabler" is one of those technocratic phrases not too difficult to understand, but she broke it down clearly into its various elements.

"The satellite television age offers strategic leaders and war-fighters exceptional opportunities to leverage the vast resources of the fourth estate. The media *offers itself* as a strategic enabler in a number of ways—to communicate the objective and endstate to a global audience, to execute effective psychological operations (PSYOPS), to play a major role in deception of the enemy, and to supplement intelligence collection efforts." Belknap went on to argue that the military had a large popularity and trust advantage over the media in the public mind and "must leverage" this advantage.[43] She surely was right about the public's feelings. A Pew Research Center survey, while taken only a month after the September 11 attacks in 2001, asked whether the military should exert more control over news coverage of war. Fifty-nine percent said yes, with 28 percent saying they would leave it to the news organizations and 13 percent not sure.[44]

Richard Halloran, a former military correspondent for the *New York Times,* immediately rebutted Belknap, urging the Pentagon and "particularly the nation's uniformed leaders" to "resolutely resist" her recommendations. "Lying to the press is not so important in itself," Halloran wrote, "but lying through the press to the citizens is the surest way to destroy the already fragile trust the people have in their government," and such action "means lying to our own soldiers, to the Congress that controls the military budget, and to America's allies and friends around the world."[45]

The idea of the press as a strategic enabler and partner of the military is antithetical to media purists on all levels, even if reality is often, if not usually, different. It can be particularly dangerous to frontline correspondents. Perhaps a century or two of genocide has nullified any meaning in the Geneva Conventions, but an unarmed correspondent is a civilian and theoretically accorded legal protections in a war. Maintaining their status as noncombatants is the reason most war correspondents don't carry weapons, although with thuggery, tribalism, and terrorism dominating recent wars, many are beginning to weigh the risks differently. Still, can a strategic enabler, a participant in psychological warfare, and a partner in intelligence gathering be an unarmed civilian or is such a correspondent a powerfully armed combatant?

The war on terrorism and the two fighting wars that quickly followed the September 11 terrorist attacks on New York and Washington have changed so much in American society that they merit separate study at a more detached date. The immediate events did not bode well for a watchdog press, perhaps even a free press. Just two weeks after the World Trade Center and Pentagon attacks, David Talbot, the editor of the online magazine *Salon,* wrote: "Truth is not the only early casualty of war. So is rational thought."[46] The media itself was hardly above irrational thought. A handful of reporters and columnists were fired or humiliated by their own publications for merely criticizing President George W. Bush in the wake of the attack.[47]

Afghanistan and Iraq: From "No Reporters Wanted" to Open Arms for "Embeds"

The attack on U.S. soil led to an almost immediate retaliatory war in late 2001 against Afghanistan and its Taliban government, which openly supported and gave refuge to al Qaeda terrorists and their leader, Osama bin Laden. The war began with some of the strongest public support and least media coverage of any war in American history. As the war on terrorism and then the war in Afghanistan unfolded, it was unclear what kind of role the media would play, if any, in future battle coverage. In the early months of the Afghan War, the media was barred from American military bases and actions, many of which were black, covert, or commando operations and unrealistic hosts for any outsiders. Few argued that the media should be taken on clandestine operations by the military or CIA, which took on a clear military function in the "new war" and became known in the field as the OGA, or Other Government Agency.

When dealing with the question of access it is important to understand that the media were not barred from entering Afghanistan but were denied the protection and frontline view of American troops. This made coverage not only unproductive but dangerous. For months, journalists entered the war-torn country unescorted. They often were repulsed, even threatened at gunpoint, by American soldiers. The danger caused some of the country's most prestigious news organizations to question whether the limited view was worth the risk. For journalists, unescorted and unprotected in a land of warlords, bandits, and a government under siege, the war became as deadly as war coverage can get. In one sixteen-day period, eight members of the media were killed. War is not a comfortable place for unescorted journalists, and year after year the number killed in the small, obscure wars of the time is counted in the dozens. Not counting Afghanistan, twenty-eight journalists were killed in twenty-five other countries in the year 2001, according to records kept by the Committee to Protect Journalists.

Seventeen months later, when the United States invaded Iraq in March 2003, the rules for journalists changed radically, with the thirty-year post-Vietnam struggle over access apparently resolved by a Pentagon willing to "embed" 662 journalists in military units with the invading force. The invasion was a relatively conventional mechanized ground and air assault, the kind of warfare that could easily accommodate journalists, and the embedding was largely a return to the practices in Vietnam, Korea, and World War II. Still, the news media—and particularly television, with its live videophones and other technological paraphernalia instantly projecting images of gunfire and dusty troops, if few images of raw combat—quite properly embraced the end of a thirty-year blackout.

Still, the Pentagon's cooperation on access in the Iraq War did not leave the media without questions to ask themselves and serious thoughts to ponder. The celebratory attitude of government leaders over the embedding arrangement was less than reassuring about how well the media had played its watchdog role. The wartime director of public affairs for the Marine Corps, Brigadier General Andrew B. Davis, viewed the results in a way that should at least give the media pause: "I knew that embedding worked *for us* when journalists' reports from Iraqi combat fields ceased the use of 'they' and started saying 'we.' "[48] Davis's statement inadvertently cut to the quick of the media's never-ending dilemma. Did the use of the terms *we* and *they* project a proper perspective for a patriotic but hopefully questioning press? Cranked back into the action after so long, had the media paid the price already by becoming strategic enablers?

These were not easy questions. Variations of them have been asked in every war. Nor will the answers be found here any more than the answer to the even more difficult issue: Did the establishment media ask the right questions about the U.S. government's justifications for invading Iraq in the first place?

But merely asking the questions makes a key point: For the media, and the service it can provide in a democracy, the granting of access is far more important than the burden of censorship, no matter how onerous. Far more trees fell soundless in Afghanistan than in Iraq. As the situation unfolds, and memoirs and investigative reporting reveal something of the full story of the Iraq War, it is helpful to listen to the after-battle thoughts of the American commander of forces in the 1991 conflict, Army General H. Norman Schwarzkopf. During the Gulf War, Schwarzkopf took a lot of heat from the media for keeping correspondents penned up in press conferences as he delivered rambunctious answers and "video game" presentations of those multimillion-dollar "smart bombs" taking out $2,000 trucks. But, like Admiral Metcalf, he too was following orders, which is *his* constitutional responsibility.

The media cameras finally did get out and show massive destruction of Iraqi tank columns and what appeared to be an equally massive slaughter of Iraqi soldiers (although most had apparently fled, affirming again that the camera can lie). The White House quickly became nervous about the images arriving in American living rooms. It looks like "wanton slaughter," came one radiotelephone warning to Schwarzkopf. Not long after that came the call that the White House wanted to end the war in just six and a half hours. Two powerful benefits would accrue to the war makers: It would end the images of "slaughter" and give the war the ring of rapid success: "The Five-Day War." President George H. W. Bush would be announcing the end at precisely that time, Schwarzkopf was told. As a general, Schwarzkopf would have cleaned up a few loose ends. But he knew that "there wasn't enough left of Iraq's army for it to be a regional military threat," a footnote seemingly forgotten a decade later. He had been around the army long enough to recall the subtitle of Phillip Knightley's book and know full well that the "propagandists" and "myth makers" were not only the war correspondents. He also knew who was boss. "I know how to salute," he wrote, a sentence that appears in almost every military officer's biography, no matter how high he or she rises.

So Schwarzkopf bowed to higher authority, his proper role, and made preparations to wrap it up on Washington's new schedule, tidy or not. For the first time in months Stormin' Norman had a moment to think. "I had to hand it to them," he mused about the White House decision. "They really knew how to package an historic event."[49]

Conclusion

The packaging of wars is a natural function of governments, the unpackaging of them a natural function of the media. Winston Churchill, a war correspondent early in his life and a war maker later, wrote the words so often quoted as the great propaganda machines of war begin rolling: "In wartime truth is so precious that she should always be attended by a bodyguard of lies." Few journalists would disagree about World War II secrets such as the invasion of Normandy, the atomic bomb, or the breaking of the Nazi code. However, the bodyguard should never be immune to assault when it covers, as it almost always does, wartime mistakes, career embarrassments, and inhumanities. For government officials, constantly falling back on Sir Winston's words, and journalists, sometimes too quick to accept them, putting Churchill's words in context and continuing to his rarely quoted next sentence enlarges on them and perhaps on their risk, too. Churchill wrote the words in recalling a wartime meeting in Potsdam with the Soviet dictator Joseph Stalin, who had no problem placing the bodyguard around the murder of millions of his own people. The unremembered next sentence? "Stalin and his comrades greatly appreciated this remark when it was translated, and upon this note our formal conference ended gaily."[50]

The conflict between the military and the media will pervade the future just as it has the past. Because the institutions collide at moments of such high stress for themselves, and usually danger for their nation, the conflicts seem more abrasive than they do in the natural camaraderie of citizens of the same nation under fire on the battlefield.

Again, the Constitution produces one of the great paradoxes in the relationship. The founding fathers, their experience rooted in the recent history of Europe, went out of their way to ensure civilian protections against a runaway military just as they guaranteed freedom of the press to protect the new nation from the tyranny of its own leaders. As noted at the beginning, this produces an aberration each time America goes to war. Struggling to deal with each other anew, the most constitutionally fettered institution, the military, appears to become unfettered (the catch being civilian control), while the most constitutionally unfettered, the media, becomes fettered.

This produces a little war within each new American war. Richard Reeves, a distinguished journalist and critic, laments that the media is forced to go "hat in hand" to the government to redefine its constitutional rights in each new war.[51] But no easy solution is at hand and perhaps never will be. "I don't think there is a *right* balance," commented William S. Hammond, an army historian and longtime student of military-media relations. "The media has to do what it has to do and so does the military."[52]

The little war has to be fought and fought again, tenaciously, even at the risk of antagonizing the media's lifeblood, an American public growing increasingly hostile to the supplier of a dangerous world's discomfiting news. Even the media has a tendency to set war apart as a special part of journalism, an irregular part of daily life in America. Even to the most serious journalists, politics and public affairs and government are the meat and potatoes of their life—the regular "beats" to be covered. War is an unusual event with unusual rules. But as much as Americans like to think of themselves as a peace-loving people, war is not an unusual event in the life of their nation. Of 225 years of its history, the United States had been at war or had troops in action in all but thirty-seven. It had sent military forces overseas two hundred times.[53]

That simple reality alone raises to the very highest levels of national importance the responsibility of the American media not only to cover wars thoroughly, but, as the nature of these wars change, to probe the war makers'—the civilian leadership's—reasons for waging them. And to go into the "little war" for its rights not with hat in hand but with all possible vigor.

Notes

1. Quoted in H. Norman Schwarzkopf, with Peter Petre, *It Doesn't Take a Hero: General H. Norman Schwarzkopf, the Autobiography* (New York: Bantam Books, 1992), 258.

2. Quoted in James M. Perry, *A Bohemian Brigade: The Civil War Correspondents, Mostly Rough, Sometimes Ready* (New York: Wiley, 2000), 159.

3. John Hohenberg, *Foreign Correspondence: The Great Reporters and Their Times* (New York: Columbia University Press, 1964).

4. James M. Perry, *A Bohemian Brigade*, x–xi, title page.

5. Perry, *A Bohemian Brigade*, 251; Louis M. Starr, *Bohemian Brigade: Civil War Newsmen in Action*, repr. (Madison: University of Wisconsin Press, 1987), 278.

6. Bob Sullivan, "From Telegraph to Videophone, Journalists at the Front Have Always Relied on Latest Gadgets," MSNBC Interactive, April 2003, http://www.wsnbc.msn.com/id/3078676.

7. W. A. Swanberg, *Citizen Hearst: A Biography of William Randolph Hearst* (New York: Scribner, 1961); W. A. Swanberg, *Pulitzer* (New York: Scribner, 1967).

8. Inflation calculation, Federal Reserve Bank of Minneapolis.

9. John Keegan, *The First World War* (New York: Random House and Knopf, 1999), 298–99.

10. Philip Knightley, *The First Casualty; From the Crimea to Vietnam: The War Correspondent as Hero, Propagandist, and Myth Maker* (New York: Harcourt Brace Jovanovich, 1975), 124, 130–31.

11. Susan E. Tift and Alex S. Jones, *The Trust: The Private and Powerful Family behind The New York Times* (Boston: Little, Brown, 1999) p. 232–33.

12. Jason DeParle, interview of Colin Powell in "Long Series of Military Decisions Led to Gulf War News Censorship," *New York Times,* May 5, 1991, A1.

13. Susan D. Moeller, *Shooting War: Photography and the American Experience of Combat* (New York: Basic Books, 1989), 205–6.

14. Marguerite Higgins, *War in Korea: The Report of a Woman Combat Correspondent* (New York: Doubleday, 1951), 83; Knightley, *The First Casualty*, 337.

15. Knightley, *The First Casualty*, 337.

16. Douglas Porch, "'No Bad Stories': The American Media-Military Relationship," *Naval War College Review* 55 (winter 2002): 5.

17. William Prochnau, *Once upon a Distant War* (New York: Times Books, 1995), 336–99.

18. Ibid., 142.

19. Interview with author, 1987.

20. William Prochnau, *Once upon a Distant War*. For Sheehan quote, Deborah Susan Kalb, "The Uncontrollable Element: American Reporters in Vietnam, 1961–1963," honors thesis (Harvard University, 1985).

21. Frank Aukofer and William P. Lawrence, *America's Team. The Odd Couple, a Report on the Relationship between the Media and the Military* (Nashville, Tenn.; Freedom Forum First Amendment Center, 1995), p. 89.

22. John E. Mueller, *War, Presidents, and Public Opinion* (New York: Wiley, 1973).

23. General Anthony C. Zinni, USMC, "A Commander Reflects," *Proceedings*, Naval Institute Press, (Annapolis, MD) July 2000, 34–36.

24. Bernard E. Trainor, "The Military and the Media: A Troubled Embrace," in *Newsmen and National Defense: Is Conflict Inevitable?* edited by Lloyd J. Matthews (Washington, D.C.: Brassey's, 1991), 122.

25. *The Military and the Media* "A Question of Access," (Fred Friendly Seminars), taped at Princeton University and aired on PBS, 1984.

26. "Cumulative Index of *Parameters* Articles and Review Essays," *Parameters* 33 (winter 2003). The quarterly, while an official publication of the U.S. Army War College, makes it clear that articles are meant to provoke thought but do not represent official army policy.

27. Richard Reeves, "Truth in the Packaging of War News," Universal Press Syndicate, October 18, 2001, available from http://richardreeves.com/columns/archive. html#2001; Jeffery A. Smith, *War and Press Freedom: The Problem of Prerogative Power* (New York: Oxford University Press, 1999), 202.

28. Julian Barnes, "The Worst Covered War since the Crimean," *Guardian*, February 25, 2002.

29. Frank Aukofer and William P. Lawrence, *America's Team, The Odd Couple: A Report on the Relationship between the Media and the Military* (Nashville, Tenn.: Freedom Forum First Amendment Center, 1995), 105.

30. Michael K. Deaver, with Mickey Herskowitz, *Behind the Scenes: In Which the Author Talks about Ronald and Nancy Reagan . . . and Himself* (New York: Morrow, 1987).

31. Maud S. Beelman, "The Dangers of Disinformation in the War on Terrorism," *Nieman Reports* 55 (winter 2001): 16.

32. Bob Woodward, *The Commanders* (New York: Simon & Schuster, 1991), 178.

33. Homefronts Confidential "Covering the War," report of The Reporters Committee for Freedom of the Press, 2004, http://www.rcfp.org/homefrontconfidential/covering.html.

34. Frank Aukofer and William P. Lawrence, America's Team, *The Odd Couple: A Report on the Relationship between the Media and the Military* (Nashville, Tenn.: Freedom Forum First Amendment Center, 1995), 102.

35. Jennifer Weeks, "Patriot Games: What Did We See on Desert Storm TV?" *Columbia Journalism Review* (July/August 1992), 13–14.

36. Frank J. Stech, "Winning CNN Wars," *Parameters* 24 (autumn 1994): 37–56.

37. Stech, "Winning CNN Wars," 48; Stech referred to a thesis by an Air Force officer/student, Marc D. Feldman, "The Military/Media Clash and the New Principle of War Media Spin" (Maxwell AFB, Ala.: Air University Press, 1993).

38. Winston Churchill, speech, House of Commons, September 30, 1941.
39. Extended conversations between the author and General William C. Westmoreland, Charleston, South Carolina, May 1984.
40. Margaret H. Belknap, "The CNN Effect: Strategic Enabler or Operational Risk?" *Parameters* 32 (autumn 2002): 100–14.
41. Aukofer and Lawrence, *America's Team, The Odd Couple,* 29.
42. Woodward, *The Commanders,* 155.
43. Margaret H. Belknap, US Army. "The CNN Effect: Strategic Enabler or Operational Risk?" (original), Strategy Research Project, US Army War College, March 30, 2001, 15, www.iwar.org.uk/psyops/resources/cnn-effect/Belknap_M_H_01.pdf. (This article was also published in a different version under the same title by "Parameters," Autumn 2002, 109.)
44. Pew Research Center for the People and the Press, "Public Remains Steady in Face of Anthrax Scare," survey report of 891 adults polled October 10–14, 2001.
45. Richard Halloran, "The Military, the Media and Deception," letter to *Parameters* (spring 2003).
46. David Talbot, "Democracy Held Hostage," *Salon.com*, September 29, 2001.
47. Ibid.
48. Andrew B. Davis, "Strange Bedfellows," *Medillian*, Medill School of Journalism, Northwestern University (summer 2003); emphasis added.
49. Schwarzkopf, *It Doesn't Take a Hero,* 470–72.
50. Winston Churchill, *The Second World War,* vol. 5, *Closing the Ring* (New York: Houghton Mifflin, 1952), 383.
51. Richard Reeves, "Truth in the Packaging of News," syndicated Internet column, Yahoo.com, December 19, 2001.
52. William S. Hammond to media critic Mark Jurkowitz, *Boston Globe,* October 10, 2001.
53. Jeffery A. Smith, *War and Press Freedom,* 192.

Bibliography

Hallin, Daniel C. *The "Uncensored War": The Media and Vietnam.* New York and Oxford: Oxford University Press, 1986.

Hersh, Seymour M. *Chain of Command: The Road from 9/11 to Abu Ghraib.* New York: HarperCollins, 2004.

Knightley, Phillip. *The War Correspondent as Hero and Myth-Maker from the Crimea to Kosovo.* New York: Harcourt Brace Jovanovich, 1975

Prochnau, William. *Once Upon a Distant War.* New York: Random House/Times Books, 1995.

Sheehan, Neil. *A Bright Shining Lie.* New York: Random House, 1988.

Stone, Geoffrey R. *Perilous Times: Free Speech in Wartime from the Sedition Act of 1798 to the War on Terrorism.* New York: W. W. Norton & Company, 2004.

STRUCTURE AND NATURE
OF THE AMERICAN PRESS

Theodore L. Glasser

THE CHAPTERS IN THIS SECTION DEAL WITH THE CUL-
tural and institutional norms of American journalism. They focus, critically but mostly optimistically, on the premises and assumptions that
have come to define the distinctive character and charter of the press in the
United States. Taken separately, these chapters examine different aspects of the
newsmaking enterprise, from its attention to audiences of a certain quality to its
commitment to keeping citizens informed and engaged. Taken together, they
offer a number of key claims about the relationship between the practice of journalism and the performance of the press.

Beyond various ideas about how journalism works and what the press
accomplishes, three related but broadly distinguishable themes account for much
of the discussion in this section. The first concerns the market-driven nature of
American journalism and the inevitable—and arguably unfortunate—treatment
of news as a commodity. The second concerns newsroom ideals and the role they
play in positioning the press as a democratic institution. The third involves mainstream journalism's grossly inadequate coverage of minority communities and
the demand this creates for alternative forms of journalism. While these themes
do not, obviously, add up to an exhaustive response to questions about the
"structure and nature" of the press in the United States, they do provide fertile
ground for a fairly broad assessment of the quality and value of contemporary
American journalism.

The Commodification of News

Both Robert Picard and James Hamilton take on the topic of newsroom economics and the tensions that journalism endures as it tries to serve both private
and public interests. With a few notable exceptions—public broadcasting, for

example, and a handful of publications like *Consumer Reports*—American news media are privately owned, privately controlled, and designed to make a profit. Liberal democracies of the kind that prosper in the United States generally equate a free press with free enterprise, and for good reason: Private ownership insulates the press from the state and prevents direct and overt control of the news by government officials. But market forces, Picard and Hamilton remind us, create their own forms of coercion; they put pressure on journalists to pay attention to interests that may or may not coincide with the public's interests. Gaining the "benefits of a free and independent media system," Picard writes, requires "careful balancing" between that which is genuinely the "public interest" and the "financial self-interests" of owners.

Appropriately enough, Picard regards money, media, and the public interest, a phrase that makes up the title of his chapter, as an alliance rooted in the history of American journalism: "Media firms in the United States operate primarily as commercial firms and have since the eighteenth century." Picard traces the development of this alliance as it responds to the expansion of markets and the diffusion of new communication technologies. He makes the point that financially secure firms can best cope with shifts in markets and changes in technology; that profitability provides the "resources that allow commercial media to provide breadth of service, invest in quality, and withstand pressures that might otherwise harm their ability to serve social goals"; that a strong and vibrant press depends, in short, on economically viable media firms. But Picard worries that the marketplace alone fails to hold media firms accountable for the quality of the news they produce. Trustworthiness, prestige, influence, and other "intangible incentives" may or may not induce media firms to look beyond the bottom line. Notwithstanding a tradition of First Amendment jurisprudence that looks askance at a heavy-handed state, Picard believes that serious consideration must be given to policies that encourage the creation of opportunities for the quality and range of media content on which a democratic society depends.

Hamilton shares Picard's concerns about the consequences of economics playing such a major role in transforming the way news is defined and delivered. Without discounting the significance of recent changes in news markets that "have brought new media, generated diverse offerings, and added opportunities to find both hard and soft news," Hamilton finds that news coverage today "has shifted to an increasing emphasis on what people want to know and away from information that they may need as voters." As a case study of how economic factors shape news coverage, Hamilton offers a sobering account of changes in network television news since the 1970s. In 1969, Hamilton reports, network news executives debated over which stories about domestic politics and foreign policy ought to go on the air. In 2000, by contrast, light features about health and entertainment supplanted stories about foreign policy; except for instances of military action, foreign policy coverage disappeared. Hamilton explains this shift in news content with reference to changes in technology, including the advent of the Internet and the escalating competition for inexpensive news; changes in patterns of media ownership, especially the growth of publicly traded media conglomerates; and changes in "product definition and differentiation," particularly the drive to find novel ways of pleasing and thus keeping viewers. These and other changes in how news is "defined, distributed, and consumed" underscore Hamilton's point about what the industrialization of journalism boils down to: "News is a commercial product."

The Values of American Journalism

Like Picard and Hamilton, Carolyn Marvin and Philip Meyer wonder what happens when there is no "happy convergence" between the needs of advertisers who support the press and the needs of citizens who consume it. They also are interested in what happens when the "digital revolution" so vastly enlarges the "reach, volume, and speed of gathering and delivering information" that journalists lose the capacity to render the world intelligible and distinct. Commerce, "which distracts mortal minds from higher things," and technology, "the most powerful expression of human pride," are among the most important threats to journalism.

Marvin and Meyer take some comfort in the values of good journalism, which they locate in the "serviceable traditions of Western rationalism and journalistic practice." Their chapter celebrates the prospects for a new and better journalism. New opportunities, the authors believe, can emerge in response to the material changes the press faces. As technologies of communication shatter the "centuries of scaffolding designed to shore up accounts of the world proposed and mostly ratified by elites," for example, journalists might finally escape the "privilege gap," which keeps them in a "closed circuit of conversation" with leaders and officials whose interests seldom coincide with the interests of the larger public; journalists might thereby deepen their commitment to news as a public good. Other changes, however, will be more difficult to reconcile with enduring values. Thus, while journalists need to remain wary of genres of journalism that seek to gain the public's attention with "sensationalism and gimmicks," they also need to find ways of engaging forms and sources of news that defy traditional conceptions of journalism: "Not all news and political intelligence," Marvin and Meyer point out, "need come in distinct, clearly labeled packages in order to contribute to public information."

The tension between enduring values and current newsroom conditions animates the discussion in "The Legacy of Autonomy in American Journalism." Theodore Glasser and Marc Gunther challenge conventional views of journalistic autonomy by inviting journalists to look carefully at what autonomy means, how it works, and why at times it undermines what journalists often say they value most: a free and responsible press. Glasser and Gunther point to three areas where the legacy of autonomy in journalism deserves scrutiny: "When autonomy trumps accountability; when autonomy *in* the newsroom threatens autonomy *for* the newsroom; and when autonomy, under the guise of competition, undermines the independence of judgment that good journalism demands." Alternatively, by looking at autonomy as a positive achievement rather than what "naturally" or "normally" exists in the absence of conditions that prevent it, Glasser and Gunther invite journalists to imagine for themselves and for the press a broader conception of press freedom than traditional readings of the First Amendment usually permit. In this broader view of press freedom, the press embraces "an overtly political and an expressly democratic justification for constitutionally protected expression," one that understands freedom of communication as protection for the content of expression rather than individual expression; in this broader view of press freedom, paradoxically, limiting individual autonomy can at times enrich and even expand freedom of communication in and for the larger community.

Democracy and Exclusion

In "The Press and the Politics of Representation," Mitchell Stephens and David Mindich focus on the "distortions and exclusions" that litter the history of American journalism. They use the African American press to illustrate "the inherent blind spots and prejudices" of the mainstream press.

African Americans were more or less excluded from most newsrooms, and thus subject to coverage over which they retained no control, until the years following the 1968 Report of the National Advisory Commission on Civil Disorder, popularly known as the Kerner Commission, which warned that the "press too long basked in a white world, looking out, if at all, with white men's eyes and a white perspective." The commission called on the press to begin "the painful process of readjustment" that will "make a reality of integration . . . in both their product and personnel." Of course, African Americans did not wait for the Kerner Commission to create for themselves a press that took their community seriously. *Freedom's Journal*, the first African American newspaper, began publication in 1827 with the observation that "too long have others spoken for us"; now, the paper explained, "we wish to plead our own cause." Still, Stephens and Mindich point out, if "it is fair to say that behind most successful African American publications is a failure by the mainstream press," it is also fair to say that "African Americans would have created their own newspapers even if the mainstream press had been more responsive to them." That is to say, coverage *by and for* a community will probably always distinguish itself from coverage *of* a community.

20

MONEY, MEDIA,
AND THE PUBLIC INTEREST

Robert G. Picard

MEDIA COMPANIES SERVE THE PUBLIC INTEREST BY supplying information, opinion, and diversion, and by facilitating the social interactions that are vital to the functioning of society and democratic institutions. Simultaneously, media companies in the United States are economic actors that create, produce, market, and distribute their products in a commercial marketplace. These different roles create tensions within media companies and among media policy-makers that require careful balancing if society is to gain the benefits of a free and independent media system.

The performance of media firms in maintaining a balance between the public interest and their own financial self-interests has been increasingly criticized by observers across social and political spectrums and from within media companies themselves. Strengthening this performance by changing media policy or behavior is difficult, however, because many of the factors that have produced the current situation are the result of fundamental changes in technology, economics, policy, and society.

Commercial versus Democratic Goals

Media firms in the United States operate primarily as commercial firms and have since the eighteenth century. In colonial times privately owned newspapers struggled to gain the right to publish and to carry information and opinion independent of the government. After the American Revolution, the importance of a free press was recognized and the rights of individuals to operate print media were protected by the Bill of Rights. When broadcasting developed in the early twentieth century, policy choices extended the notion of private, commercial operation to radio and then to television stations.

Although many nations decided that broadcasting should be provided by the government or public-service organizations and operated via not-for-profit firms, American policy-makers decided that broadcasting should be commercial. This occurred partly because broadcasting had been developed by commercial firms, partly because of the strength of arguments for media to be independent of government, and partly because the federal government was small and did not have the financial resources to operate a nationwide broadcasting system when radio first appeared.

Today, media in the United States and other liberal democracies are expected to serve a variety of social goals regardless of their ownership and commercial status. Media are normatively expected to provide diverse and pluralistic content that includes a wide range of information, opinions, and perspectives on developments that affect the lives of citizens. Media are expected to mobilize the public to participate in and carry out their responsibilities in society. Media are expected to help citizens identify with and participate in the lives of their community, their state, and the nation. Media are expected to serve the needs and represent the interests of widely differing social groups and to ensure that information and ideas are not narrowed by governmental, economic, or social constraints. Simultaneously, they are expected to serve their economic self-interests to produce profits, to grow, and to contribute to national economies.

These conflicts create a paradox, because it is recognized that commercially funded media require financial resources and strength to sustain and nurture their activities, but they cannot fully pursue their economic self-interests without harming optimal public service. Optimal service can thus be achieved only if firms temper their self-interests or if legal and regulatory actions require them to do so.

Because commercial media are guided by economic principles that obligate them to pursue profit and maximize company value, privately owned commercial media entities can only be expected to voluntarily temper their self-interests if there are incentives to do so. These may be intangible incentives such as the accumulation of trustworthiness, prestige, and influence, or economic incentives such as profitability and increases in company value. If legal and regulatory requirements are used to ensure that media serve public interests, media independence must also be guaranteed. Many regulations cannot be placed on media in the United States because of the broad protections granted by the First Amendment and because the ability of government to regulate television, cable, and satellite is also limited by a long series of policy considerations and legal rulings.

The challenge of inducing media entities to provide content that serves social functions is compounded in the commercialized environment because most of the activities that support public interests and democratic processes—news, political discussions, public-affairs information, social commentary, and so on—do not attract large audiences, are often costly, and are typically less profitable than producing other content. Conversely, entertaining content that violates social norms or is deemed by many observers to be vulgar, insipid, and harmful sometimes generates large audiences and advertising revenue for commercial media and thus supports their economic interests.

Complaints about the effects of economic choices and the pursuit of monetary interests by commercial media have grown as media firms have grown in size. Historically, media firms tended to be small- and medium-size enterprises that produced steady incomes for their owners and provided regular returns beyond the costs of their operation. During the second half of the twentieth century, the progressive growth of advertising expenditures in the United States increased those returns significantly, turning media companies into investment vehicles and increasing the economic and commercial pressures on media firms.

Changes in technologies produced additional types of media and many media firms began developing strategies of growth and expansion. The availability of capital through equity markets helped finance expansion, and large media conglomerates developed in the 1980s and 1990s. In the early years of the twenty-first century, dozens of media companies were among the leading companies in America. Many critics believe that the financial pressures on and economic self-interests of media firms are conflicting with the social roles and functions of media in modern democracies and that there is a growing disparity between the behavior desired from media firms and that which is observed.

Competition, Financial Strength, and Independence

The question on the minds of most media observers is how to ensure that democratic functions are served by commercial enterprises. An underlying difficulty in answering the question results from the reality that financially successful media companies have the resources to serve social needs and be more independent of outside pressures over time than less financially secure firms.

A number of economic and financial factors have been identified as requirements if media are to be able to facilitate and conduct activities that support public interests and democratic processes. These include a competitive marketplace, effective business models, and financial strength. Competing sources of news, opinion, and entertainment increase the possibilities for variety and diversity in content. Steady income produced by effective business models and financial strength achieved through profitability are seen as providing resources that allow commercial media to provide breadth of service, invest in quality, and withstand pressures that might otherwise harm their ability to serve social goals.

Competition among media outlets has long been considered a requirement for an effective system of expression and debate. It is seen as providing sufficient opportunities for multiple information, idea, and mobilization functions to be carried out simultaneously; as promoting increases in information quality, quantity, and service; as protecting against private constraints on information, ideas, and voices conveyed; as serving the varying information and expression needs of differing social groups; and as providing service at multiple market levels so that information and debate needs in different geographic levels and locations are served.

Effective business models are necessary to sustain media operations and ensure sufficient revenue streams, to avoid dependencies that can limit diffusion of information and ideas and constrain debate, and to provide reasonable stability in incomes so that fluctuations do not unduly constrain activities.

In order to be effective as conveyers of information, media entities require financial strength so that they can support information gathering and dissemination activities and produce quality entertainment. Without a strong financial base, media do not have the resources necessary to adequately explore issues and developments in communities, states, the nation, or the world. Financial strength is also important if media are to subsidize content and programming that serves public needs. Financial strength allows media to maintain their independence and engage in activities designed to hold government and other institutions in society accountable, even if the actions cause financial sources to withdraw their support. Such strength creates conditions in which companies can act with integrity, provide quality content, and behave in ways that go beyond basic economic self-interests.

These factors, however, do not in themselves guarantee better performance regarding social needs, because there are tensions between these economic and financial elements and social goals for media. Firms with highly effective business models and financial strength tend to have greater success in the media marketplace. They are able to offer better content, which garners larger or more attractive audiences and a higher proportion of advertising expenditures. A reality of market economies is that when there is success there is also failure. As a result, media firms that are not as successful lose the resources to produce quality content and lose financial strength. Some will wither or fail and some will be acquired by successful competitors. The end result is a reduction in the competition that is seen as beneficial in terms of diversity, plurality, and democratic debate.

Newspapers, for example, rely upon large advertisers for the bulk of their income, and this has created a systemic economic problem that makes it nearly impossible for competing general-circulation papers to survive in the same locality. When more than one paper exists in a market, the secondary paper is disadvantaged because a disproportionate amount of advertising is given to the leading paper, regardless of how closely the second paper approximates its circulation.[1] The paper with the largest circulation in a market gains financial and economic advantages that enable it to improve content and increase advertising and circulation income by attracting customers from the smaller paper. As the leading paper attracts more circulation, it attracts more advertising, which in turn attracts more circulation, trapping the secondary paper in a circulation spiral that ultimately leads to its demise.[2]

Financial success and stability is also a two-edged sword. Because financial stability can lead to improved content and strengthen the independence of media, it is seen as important for commercial firms to return profit that can be reinvested in the enterprise to further improve content, provide better service, and adequately compensate owners. However, high levels of profit can lead to funds being funneled away to provide high returns for owners or to expansion through acquisition of other media properties. It can lead to media behaving just like any other commercial company and moving away from costly activities that may serve the community but adversely affect profits.

"Appropriate" profit levels for media companies have been debated since media profitability began rising significantly during the last quarter of the twentieth century. In recent decades media companies have typically returned double-digit profits, often five to ten times higher than profits for department stores, banks, pharmaceutical companies, and automobile manufacturers. This profitability has changed perceptions of the media, turned media firms into highly successful vehicles for investments, and produced demands for even higher profits.

The debate inside and outside media over what profit is reasonable is difficult because it is impossible to put a single number on what "reasonable profit" is. At a basic level, a reasonable profit for any firm must allow appropriate resources for continuing operations, create funds for adequate reinvestment, and provide a good return on invested capital. In principle, it needs to be above income that would be received from capital preservation investments because of the higher economic risks of operating the media enterprise. Reasonable profit differs among media and media units because investment risk varies depending upon the market and the unique situation of each media operation.

The desire for media to have effective business models with steady revenue streams also creates difficulties in the ability of contemporary media to meet democratic objectives. Advertisers provide the primary revenue stream for most media operations, and they exhibit little interest in ensuring that social and democratic goals for media are fulfilled.

Newspapers, for example, receive income from advertisers and readers, but they became increasingly dependent on advertising throughout the twentieth century. U.S. newspaper publishers received 2.6 times as much total advertising income in real terms in 2000 than they received in 1950, one of the factors that has made them so profitable and desirable as investments. The growth of that revenue, however, has made newspapers highly dependent upon advertisers. In 2000, 82 percent of newspaper revenue came from advertisers.[3]

It has long been recognized that dependence on limited sources of critical resources weakens the position of a firm or industry, because any shifts in availability of the resource can rapidly harm the firm or industry. In the case of newspapers, the high dependence on advertising revenue makes the industry highly vulnerable to downturns in the economy. Research has shown that newspaper advertising income is now dramatically affected by recessions and that economic downturns lead to large layoffs and significant reductions in news coverage.[4] A major cause of this is that newspapers are so dependent upon retail advertising and some categories of classified advertising that are highly affected by downturns in the economy. Newspapers are affected more than other media and lose about four times as much advertising income as television during recessions.[5]

The high dependence on advertising also creates vulnerability to pressure from advertisers. Most newspapers, for example, receive about three-fourths of their advertising income from two-dozen advertisers; in many cases, five or six advertisers provide about half the advertising income received by the paper. Should the paper's content somehow offend one of these advertisers and they decide to withdraw or reduce their advertisements, significant financial damage and weakening of the paper can occur. Because the level of dependence is so high, close contacts and coordination with major advertisers is increasingly evident. Boards of directors of most large media companies, for example, now include directors from major retail advertisers to help stabilize relations and permit easier exchange of information for mutual benefit.[6]

The Changing Ownership of Media

The increasingly profitable and commercial nature of media in the second half of the twentieth century led to dramatic changes in types and extent of media ownership. Media, especially newspapers and local broadcasting stations, were traditionally family-owned companies or privately held corporations. After the middle of the twentieth century, as advertising revenues grew and media companies became more valuable, it became difficult to maintain family ownership because of inheritance-tax issues and insufficient capital in family companies, which made acquisitions and expansion difficult.[7] As a result, media ownership in 2005 is markedly different from what it was at the end of World War II. At that time, few newspaper chains existed and more than 80 percent of all newspapers in the United States were independently owned; large media groups and media conglomerates did not exist. In the last decades of the century, however, social, economic, technical, and regulatory changes promoted new types of ownership and created new operational goals for media firms.

Today, ownership is dominated by large firms, many of which have specific strategies for growth and expansion through acquisitions of smaller media companies. Newspapers that were built and owned by individual proprietors, families, and partnerships were first purchased by other firms, creating newspaper chains that owned large numbers of newspapers. As a result, more than 80 percent of daily newspapers are now owned by groups. The number of stations that broadcasting companies are allowed to own increased over time and the companies began purchasing cable systems, networks, newspapers, and other media, thus creating large media groups. Conglomerates that operated outside the media field also began to purchase media companies and groups.

Major media firms are billion-dollar enterprises that are among the leading American companies today. Included in this list are firms such as Viacom, Clear Channel Communications, the Walt Disney Company, Comcast, Time Warner, the Tribune Company, and Gannett. Major firms from other industries, such as General Electric and Sony, also own large media entities. Large foreign companies such as Bertelsmann AG (the world's largest book publisher), Hachette Filipacchi (the world's largest magazine company), Reed Elsevier and Wolters Kluwer (the world's leading professional and scientific publishers), and Pearson (the world's leading textbook publisher) also have enormous U.S. holdings.

The growth of these media and communication firms has required large amounts of financing and made them dependent upon stock markets as capital sources. Today the primary holders of stock in media companies are banks, investment houses, and pension funds,[8] and these investors are primarily interested in the financial performance of the firms, rather than content quality and the meeting of social and democratic goals.[9]

The growth of these companies has led to industry consolidation; large numbers of media outlets are now held by single firms. Clear Channel Communications, for example, owns more than twelve hundred of the nation's radio stations, Gannett owns one hundred of the country's newspapers, and Viacom owns not only the CBS television network but seven cable networks. Growth has also led to highly diversified media conglomerates. Time Warner, for example, owns cable and television networks, magazines, movie and television studios, record companies, and online firms. The Tribune Company owns a range of media holdings including newspapers, television stations, television production companies, and cable operations.

The change to public ownership has increased pressures on large media companies and focused managerial concern on short-term financial goals and the pursuit of higher returns than in smaller media companies with other forms of ownership.[10] The increasing commercialization has led to financial pressures playing the dominant role in decisions about what type of news and entertainment is presented to the public in print and broadcasts.[11]

Many of the complaints about media operations result not from there being fewer owners of few media, but from the fact that there are more and more commercial firms operating for profit that are willing to overtly act in their own self-interest. Among media that produce the largest audiences, commercial pressures dominate content decisions. This has occurred concurrently with media being subject to fewer and fewer regulatory requirements and less oversight. Consequently, media firms are generally free to behave in ways designed to generate large audiences, with little regard to social or cultural effects.

The Changing Media Environment

Despite the fact that media companies are larger than in the past and generate significant revenue, most media companies today are in substantially weaker competitive and financial positions than they were in the mid- to late twentieth century. Media companies today are struggling to adjust to wide-ranging changes that are increasing competition and eroding their audience and advertiser bases. These changes are affecting the economics and financing of media, altering the structures of media industries, and changing the types of content that are provided.

Fundamental changes are occurring because of the integration of information and communication technologies and changes in the potential and perception of the role of media. The most important change is the convergence of the three underlying communications industries: content creation and packaging, computers and software, and telephony. This development is changing how communication takes place, what is communicated, who can communicate, and the speed of communication. It is creating flexibility in the use of content, making it possible for a wide range of players to produce and use content.

The development of new communication capabilities in postindustrial society has been supported by changes in governmental approaches that emerged first in telecommunications policy and then in media policy. Changes in public policies have radically altered the regulatory environment, creating a largely deregulated realm for media and information-related industries. These changes have brought large amounts of capital into telecommunications and media, leading to the creation of new firms and media industries and affecting the structure of traditional media industries. These new competitors and disruptive technologies are eroding the customer and financial bases of existing media.

Increases in the types of media and communications systems and concurrent increases in the number of units of media have increased the levels of competition experienced in media markets. The number of direct and indirect competitors has risen, spreading audience and advertiser expenditures across a greater number of firms and reducing the financial strength of previously dominant firms.

New types of media and communications systems based on the Internet and mobile communications are challenging print, audio, and audiovisual media. The availability of motion pictures, television programming, and other content in the form of videotapes and DVDs, and through cable and satellite channels and video-on-demand systems is increasing competition. The effects of these developments are more competition for consumer spending, declining profits per title, channel, or product, and declining profits for many firms in most established media industries.

The increasing number of communication channels has concurrently broadened choices available to audiences. However, media use competes with a variety of activities, including commutes to and from work or school, family and home-life requirements, and a host of alternative leisure activities. Technological changes in the media environment are permitting individuals greater choice to determine what communication and information they will receive and use, to decide when they will receive it, and to filter communication in ways unimaginable in the past. These factors are creating individual use patterns for media, and thus audiences are fragmenting significantly, and the individual media outlets to which large groups of the public attend are simultaneously diminishing.

The increase in media and communication types and the rising number of individual units of media has led advertisers to alter their expenditures and placement of advertising in different media. As audiences have accepted new types of media, advertisers have shifted some of their expenditures to those media. Because audiences have fragmented and declined for established media and channels, advertisers are unwilling to pay the same prices previously paid.

The changes in the market are placing additional pressure on media companies, reducing the availability of critical advertising resources and the stability and profitability of their business activities. These changes, as well as the general commercialization of the industry, are fundamental forces that have led many media managers to pursue economic self-interest at the expense of public interests.

Content Effects

Changes in the media environment have altered the resources available for content and changed the content that is provided. In television, for example, financial pressures force most broadcasters to find ways to reduce programming costs. Typical methods of cost reduction include broadcasting more syndicated programs, using fewer expensive personalities in in-house productions, making inexpensive reality programs, game shows, and talk shows, and increasing the number of times a program is rebroadcast. In a desperate search for audiences, television programs are crafted to attract viewers with content that is salacious and titillating, voyeuristic, shocking, violent, or insipid. Content that explores the human condition, provides more wholesome diversion, or serves broader purposes tends to be minimized.

Likewise, the majority of content in newspapers today is not anything that can be considered "news." About two-thirds of most newspapers is advertising, and of the remaining editorial matter only about 15 percent is news; the remainder is lifestyle material devoted to topics such as fashion, automobiles, entertainment, homes, sports, and so on.

Content choices being made in media obviously have consequences on the overall diversity and quality of material offered and, thus, their desirability to audiences. They also have significant social and cultural implications because they tend to work counter to achievement of the social and democratic goals that are ascribed to media.

One of the major alterations in media content as contemporary changes have occurred has been the loss of localism. Radio and television stations, for example, had traditionally operated as local media with large amounts of locally produced entertainment, news, and public affairs programming. Today, little programming is locally produced and the majority of what is offered is obtained from national networks or programming syndicates. In radio today, it is not uncommon for the program choices and on-air personalities to be thousands of miles away from the station that carries them.

In newspapers, the growth of newspaper groups has led to more shared content—and cost savings for the owners. This means that more content is produced outside the community, that fewer local employees are needed, that the local community is covered less, that local issues appear less often in editorial and opinion columns, and that the hopes, dreams, and issues of local citizens have diminished opportunity to be publicly acknowledged.

Because the larger cities in the United States are also where the primary entertainment and information content providers are located and where the heaviest media competition occurs, content that is designed to appeal in those environments is created and distributed nationwide.

The end result of such factors is that media pay less attention and give lower credence to the interests, tastes, and values of local communities nationwide. Instead, the interests, tastes, and values of residents in locations such as New York, Los Angeles, Chicago, and Washington, D.C., dominate media content. Entertainment, information, and lifestyles that reflect the largest communities and those with less-traditional lifestyles become the norms reflected in media.

In the heavily commercialized environment of media, content increasingly marginalizes information and discussion of community, national, and world issues in the pursuit of entertainment and diversion that may attract audiences and advertisers that can produce higher income. Instead of serious drama we get reality shows; instead of documentaries we receive talk shows; instead of family programming we are broadcast violent action shows. Admittedly, we all need some diversion in our lives, and modern mass media have always provided it. However, such mindless entertainment is now becoming the dominant function of media, and media companies are making fewer attempts to balance it with other necessary content.

Implications

The economic changes and financial pressures on media have significant implications for citizens' understanding of the world, for public discourse, and for the development and maintenance of social communities.

Although technology and the increase in media outlets create great possibilities for more information to become available, they also reduce information because financial necessities, operational choices, and consolidation are increasingly leading to large portions of news and information coming from the same sources and merely being repackaged and reused by various media outlets. This reduces the number of independent observers and voices and creates a homogenization of information available across media.

Similarly, much of the programming in television comes from networks, syndicators, and programming libraries and is broadcast nationwide and rerun endlessly. This also creates a homogenization of content available and reduces the number of sources that produce news, feature, and entertainment programming.

Even when major commercialized media produce their own information, they tend to do so with similar ideologies of news and information and the same general perspectives, so that the ideas presented and breadth of coverage offered are limited. This tends to promote one model or frame of society by focusing on visible occurrences and debates among easily accessible political figures and dominant organizations while generally ignoring concerns outside those parameters. The range of debate is thus not representative of the diversity of opinion throughout society.[12] A similar restriction takes place in production of entertainment programming.

Commercialization of the media has also been problematic because even financially strong media companies have come to fear the controversial. Entertainment, news stories, and presentations that may offend even small portions of the audiences are increasingly being dropped or ignored in favor of those that are generally acceptable. When programs and stories that create audience or financial risks are rejected, the range of perspectives on life and the continuum of ideas in society are diminished.

An increasing concern is that the loss of localism through the nationalization and globalization of content, and the fragmentation of audiences across the wider array of media outlets, is reducing opportunities for readers, viewers, and listeners to gather together and share similar experiences and develop similar values. This change has enormous social implications, because it is the sharing of experience and commonality of values that allows for development of community and a flourishing democracy.

How society responds to the performance of the media in the coming years is crucial. Private media companies, like all corporations, exist primarily to serve the economic self-interests of their owners. When that self-interest is at stake, it is difficult to expect that companies will remain guardians of social interests. If society desires that media firms serve public interests by supplying necessary information, wide-ranging opinion, and a broad range of entertainment, and that they facilitate social interactions needed for society and democracy to thrive, concerted action will be needed.

Significant consideration must be given to policy, particularly in broadcasting and telecommunications, to respond to the challenges of commercial ownership and consolidation. Until policies address the range of content provided, ensure a broader spectrum of producers and voices, and reflect the spectrum of values and communities in society, little change will occur and complaints about the contemporary media system will continue.

Media personnel themselves need to carefully reconsider their actions and the parts they play in creation and maintenance of the current environment and to respond even before policy changes intended to alter behavior are fashioned. If their credibility and integrity are lost or they are seen as behaving responsibly only through coercion, their influence and importance to society will be significantly reduced.

Finally, we as audiences and consumers of media need to look inside ourselves, at our choices, and at our patterns of media use. As in nutrition, we need to choose among various options to ensure that we have a healthy diet of content that serves our different needs for news, information, and entertainment so that we can fully participate in democratic society and enrich our lives.

The media environment in the twenty-first century is faced with significant challenges to ensure the continuation of democratic society. Everyone with an interest in media—audiences, advertisers, media personnel, owners and investors, community groups, and policy makers—has an obligation to help nurture an environment that goes beyond narrow and self-serving interests to ensure that the broader interests of society are served.

Notes

1. See Robert G. Picard, "Pricing Behavior of Newspapers," in *Press Concentration and Monopoly: New Perspectives on Newspaper Ownership and Operation,* edited by Robert. G. Picard et al., 55–69, esp. 60–61 (Norwood, N.J.: Ablex, 1988), and Jon G. Udell, *The Economics of the American Newspaper* (New York: Hastings House, 1978), 109.

2. Lars Furhoff, "Some Reflections on Newspaper Concentration," *Scandinavian Economic History Review* 21 (1973): 1–27; Karl Erik Gustafsson, "The Circulation Spiral and the Principle of Household Coverage," *Scandinavian Economic History Review* 28 (1978): 1–14; Lars Engwall, "Newspaper Competition: A Case for Theories of Oligopoly," *Scandinavian Economic History Review* 29 (1981): 145–54.

3. Robert G. Picard, "U.S. Newspaper Ad Revenue Shows Consistent Growth," *Newspaper Research Journal* 23, no. 4 (2002): 21–33.

4. Robert G. Picard and Tony Rimmer, "Weathering a Recession: Effects of Size and Diversification on Newspaper Companies," *Journal of Media Economics* 12, no. 1 (1999): 1–18.

5. Robert G. Picard, "The Effects of Recessions on Advertising Expenditures: An Exploratory Study of Economic Downturns in Nine Developed Nations," *Journal of Media Economics* 14, no. 1 (2001): 1–14.

6. Kyun-Tae Han, "Composition of Boards of Directors of Major Media Corporations," *Journal of Media Economics* 1, no. 2 (1988): 85–100.
7. James N. Dertouzos and Kenneth E. Thorpe, *Newspaper Groups: Economies of Scale, Tax Laws, and Merger Incentives* (Santa Monica, Calif.: Rand, 1982); Loran Ghiglione, ed., *The Buying and Selling of America's Newspapers* (Indianapolis: R. J. Berg, 1984); Picard et al., eds., *Press Concentration and Monopoly*; Elizabeth MacIver Neiva, "Chain Building: The Consolidation of the American Newspaper Industry, 1953–1980," *Business History Review* 70 (spring 1996): 1–42; Patricia Aufderheide et al., *Conglomerates and the Media* (New York: New Press, 1997); Ben H. Bagdikian, *The Media Monopoly*, 6th ed. (Boston: Beacon Press, 2000).
8. Robert G. Picard, "Institutional Ownership of Publicly Traded U.S. Newspaper Companies," *Journal of Media Economics* 7, no. 4 (1994): 49–64.
9. Cranberg, Bezanson, and Soloski, *Taking Stock*.
10. William B. Blankenburg and Gary W. Ozanich, "The Effects of Public Ownership on the Financial Performance of Newspaper Corporations," *Journalism Quarterly* 70 (spring 1993): 68–75; Stephen Lacy, Mary Alice Shaver, and Charles St. Cyr, "The Effects of Public Ownership and Newspaper Competition on the Financial Performance of Newspaper Corporations: A Replication and Extension," *Journalism and Mass Communication Quarterly* 73, no. 2 (1996): 332–41; Kuang Kuo Chang and Geri Alumit Zeldes, "How Ownership, Competition Affect Papers' Financial Performance," *Newspaper Research Journal* 23, no. 4 (2002): 101–7.
11. John H. McManus, *Market-Driven Journalism: Let the Citizen Beware?* (Thousand Oaks, Calif.: Sage, 1993); Bagdikian, *The Media Monopoly*; Croteau and Hoynes, *The Business of Media;* James T. Hamilton, *All the News That's Fit to Sell: How the Market Transforms Information into News* (Princeton, N.J.: Princeton University Press, 2004); Ken Auletta, *Backstory: Inside the Business of News* (New York: Penguin, 2003).
12. Doris Graber, Denis McQuail, and Pippa Norris, eds. *The Politics of News: The News of Politics* (Washington, D.C.: Congressional Quarterly Press, 1998); Robert M. Entman, *Democracy without Citizens: Media and the Decay of American Politics* (New York: Oxford University Press, 1989); W. Lance Bennett, "Toward a Theory of Press-State Relations in the United States," *Journal of Communication* 4 (spring 1990): 103–25.

Bibliography

Bagdikian, Ben H. *The New Media Monopoly*. Boston: Beacon Press, 2004.

Compaine, Benjamin M., and Douglas Gomery. *Who Owns the Media?: Competition and Concentration in the Mass Media Industry*. 3rd ed. Mahwah, N.J.: Lawrence Erlbaum, 2000.

Cranberg, Gilbert, Randall Bezanson, and John Soloski. *Taking Stock: Journalism and the Publicly Traded Newspaper Company*. Ames: Iowa State University Press, 2001.

Croteau, David, and William Hoynes. *The Business of Media: Corporate Media and the Public Interest*. Thousand Oaks, Calif.: Pine Forge, 2001.

Doyle, Gillian. *Media Ownership: The Economics and Politics of Convergence and Concentration in the UK and European Media*. London and Thousand Oaks, Calif.: Sage, 2002.

McChesney, Robert W. *The Problem of the Media: U.S. Communication Politics in the Twenty-first Century.* New York: Monthly Review, 2004.

Napoli, Philip M. *Audience Economics: Media Institutions and the Audience Marketplace.* New York: Columbia University Press, 2003.

Picard, Robert G. *The Economics and Financing of Media Companies.* New York: Fordham University Press, 2002.

21

THE MARKET AND THE MEDIA

James T. Hamilton

SINCE MARKET FORCES HAVE PLAYED THE MOST DECISIVE role in transforming the delivery of news, the history of the American press from the 1970s to the present is economic history. Although journalists may not explicitly consider economics as they cover the day's events, the stories, reporters, firms, and media that ultimately survive in the marketplace depend on economic factors. The decisions of producers and editors are driven by supply and demand: Who cares about a particular piece of information? What is an audience willing to pay for the news, or what are advertisers willing to pay for the attention of readers, listeners, or viewers? How many consumers share particular interests in a topic? How many competitors are vying for readers' or viewers' attention, and what are these competitors offering as news? What are the costs of generating and transmitting a story? Who owns the outlet? What are the owners' goals? What are the property rights that govern how news is produced, distributed, and sold? News is a commercial product.

News outlets that cover public affairs have always struggled with the tension between giving people what they want to know and giving them what they need to know. The low probability that any reader has of influencing the outcome of a policy debate leaves many readers "rationally ignorant" about the details of governing.[1] From an investment perspective, why learn about global warming if your actions have little chance of affecting policy? News outlets do face strong demand for entertaining news, or information that helps people in their role as consumers or workers. Some people may also express a demand for news about politics, though the set of viewers that prefers politics covered as a sport or drama may exceed that which prefers detailed analysis.

In this essay I argue that since the 1970s news coverage has shifted to an increasing emphasis on what people want to know and away from information that they may need as voters. I identify three economic factors that help account for this shift: changes in technology, product definition and differentiation, and media ownership. I will examine in detail how each has affected news content

351

over time. I then focus on network evening news programs in a case study that demonstrates how these economic factors have shaped news coverage. After providing a snapshot of current media coverage, I conclude with a section analyzing the implications of these alterations in the ways in which news is defined, distributed, and consumed.

What's Different: Technology, Products, and Owners

Three technological changes have affected the way in which images and information have entered households since 1970: the growth of cable television; the advent of the Internet; and the increased use of satellite technology to transmit news across continents and into homes. The spread of cable television in the 1980s and 1990s and introduction of direct-broadcast satellite delivery meant that by 2003 at least 85 percent of television households subscribed to multichannel delivery systems. The average number of channels per home went from 7.1 in 1970 to 71.2 in 2001. The average number of channels viewed weekly for at least ten minutes went from 4.5 to 13.5 channels per television household.[2] This proliferation of channels meant that news on cable could focus on specific niches. Rather than attempting to garner 10 million viewers (the audience attracted by the *NBC Nightly News* in 2003), a cable news program could be successful by attracting less than 1 million viewers. The result is that cable channels can focus their products on particular types of news: sports stories on ESPN; business news on CNBC; storm data on the Weather Channel; and news that appeals to a conservative audience on FOX News Channel. Both the network evening news programs and daily newspapers have broader audiences than cable channels. If survey respondents are asked to rate themselves on an ideological scale of liberalism and conservatism, the average rating for consumers of the network evening news programs and daily newspapers is the same as the national sample average. The regular consumers of the FOX News Channel, however, have the most conservative ideological rating in the survey. Cable political shows such as *Crossfire* and *Hardball,* in contrast, attract audiences more likely to rate themselves as liberal.[3]

The relatively small audiences of some cable news programs yield profits because of low production budgets. Since talk can be cheap, cable news programs often feature journalists acting as political pundits. Political pundits, who offer a mixture of fact and opinion, face many market constraints. Since readers have the freedom to sample and ignore stories across the portfolio of topics covered in a paper, those writing for newspapers can aim for a relatively educated audience and afford to write about topics that may not be of interest to many. Television pundits, in contrast, operate in a medium where viewers of a particular program all consume the same story. If these pundits pick topics of little interest, they risk losing viewers, who may be less educated (than newspaper readers) and more likely to search for entertainment than enlightenment from television. The result is that pundits choose different languages to talk about politics, depending on the avenue of expression.

To see these differences, consider the case of George Will, who writes a syndicated column and appears as a commentator on ABC News programming.[4] As I demonstrate in my book *All the News That's Fit to Sell,* the print George Will uses a greater variety of terms and longer words than the television George Will. When composing for a print audience, Will uses more abstract terms such as those relating to inspiration, as well as more numeric terms. He writes about groups rather than individuals, as reflected in a greater focus on core values and institutions. In television appearances, Will changes expression to comply with the greater demands for entertainment. He uses more human-interest language. He makes more self-references. He simplifies and summarizes, and at the same time hedges his bets through qualifications (higher use of ambivalent language). His statements on television focus more on the present and emphasize motion. On television, Will offers opinions that are marked by greater activity and realism. Although George Will has developed a brand name for expression, he changes the delivery of his product to suit the audience demands and cost constraints of the medium.

The push for entertainment and simplicity on television also affects the differences in language used by liberal and conservative pundits. Relative to their statements in print, there are more differences in the language that liberals and conservatives use to talk about politics on television. Overall, liberal pundits on television use language that is more optimistic and focuses on groups, while conservatives are more likely to express ambivalence (about government) and focus on distinctions among individuals.

A second technological change affecting news markets is the spread of the Internet. Competition for attention across sites has driven the price of news on nearly all Internet sites to zero (the marginal delivery cost of the information). This explosion of free information has many ramifications. Consumption of high-quality newspapers, for example, is now possible around the world. If one looks at the top one hundred newspapers in the United States, the circulation of the top five (the *Wall Street Journal, USA Today,* the *New York Times, Los Angeles Times,* and *Washington Post*) accounted for 21.5 percent of the total newspaper circulation in 1999.[5] If you look at the links generated on the Internet by these top one hundred newspapers, however, the top five papers in terms of links (which included *USA Today,* the *New York Times,* and the *Washington Post*) accounted for 41.4 percent of the total links. In part this reflects the advantages of established brands on the Internet, since familiarity with a product's existence and reputation can lead to its consumption. The use of links can operate like an information cascade, with Internet users spreading links via emails to friends. Network effects also exist, since the value to an individual of a news site can increase as the use by others raises the quality of interactive discussion on a site.

The low cost of entry to placing information on the Internet has had many effects on news. The ability of news outlets, and columnists such as Matt Drudge, to post instantly during any time of the day has extended news cycles and created additional pressure on traditional news outlets to run with breaking news.[6] The lack of large investment in sites means that news provided may not be heavily edited or screened, which can give rise to a spread of rumor and gossip. The archiving of data on the Internet and easy accessibility make it easier for errors in reporting to propagate, as journalists access information collected by others and incorporate it into stories. The widespread existence of government and non-profit Web sites lowers the cost of information generation and analysis for reporters. Journalists writing about campaign finance, for example, can readily locate data at the individual contributor level at the Federal Election Commission Web site or at Opensecrets.org. Similarly, reporters writing about the environment can use government data aggregated by the nonprofit Environmental Defense, which posts detailed pollution data by the zip code level at Scorecard.org.

Widespread use of satellite technology to beam images across the country and the world marks a third change in news reporting. During the 1970s the three evening network news programs had an "oligopoly of image," where viewers tuned in the programs in part to see the first pictures of the day's breaking stories. The deployment of satellite technology across the country, however, soon meant that local television stations had the ability to import stories quickly from other parts of the country and to go live to events in their own city. The ability of local stations to share in network feeds or tap into other sources of pictures meant that local news programs began to offer viewers images of national or international stories, which in turn put pressure on the evening news to offer a differentiated product (including more interpretative or contextual material). The existence of satellite technology also meant that international coverage could take place in real time, including the coverage of the Iraq War by embedded reporters.[7]

These technological changes have put increased pressures on traditional news outlets to compete for readers and viewers. The growth in cable channels and cable/direct broadcast satellite subscription has eroded the market share of the network evening news programs and focused attention on retaining viewers. The network evening news programs have a core audience of faithful viewers and a set of marginal viewers, those who may tune in to the news or choose another program depending on what has happened in the world or what types of news the networks choose to focus on. News directors will select a mix of stories aimed at capturing the marginal viewers while not alienating the average or regular viewers. The result of competition from cable is a mix of stories that leaves average viewers somewhat frustrated and marginal viewers somewhat placated.

Survey data from the Pew Center for the People and the Press in 2000 show the tension between the interests of the average (i.e., regularly view) and marginal (i.e., sometimes view) consumers of the network nightly news programs.[8] A majority of the regular viewers are over fifty (54.8 percent) and female (53.9 percent). The marginal viewers are much younger. Females aged eighteen to thirty-four account for 20.6 percent of those who sometimes view the national news, and males aged eighteen to thirty-four account for 17.5 percent of these sometime viewers. In contrast, eighteen-to-thirty-four-year-old females are only 9.1 percent of the regular audience, and males of that age group only 9.2 percent of the regular viewers. These demographic differences translate into predictable and sharp differences between the interests of marginal and average viewers. Marginal viewers are not as attached to the news. When asked whether they enjoyed keeping up with the news, 68.1 percent of average viewers responded that they did "a lot" versus only 37.0 percent for the marginal viewers. A majority of marginal viewers said that they followed national or international news closely "only when something important or interesting is happening." Marginal viewers also were more likely to report that they watched the news with "my remote in hand" and switched channels when they were not interested in a topic.

What captures the interests of occasional viewers differs from the type of news favored by loyal viewers. The marginal and average viewers have the same top two news interests, crime and health, which may explain the prevalence of these news categories on the network evening news. The two sets of viewers differ markedly, however, in their interest in politics. For the average viewer of network news, news about political figures and events in Washington ranked fifth out of thirteen news types. This same category of news ranked tenth among marginal viewers. Political news about Washington was followed very closely by 28.4 percent of the average viewers, versus 12.3 percent of the marginals. Sports ranked sixth and entertainment news ranked twelfth among the regular viewers. These topics ranked much more highly among marginal viewers, who ranked them third and eighth among the thirteen news topics.

Viewers who are younger than fifty may also merit attention for another reason—they are more highly valued by advertisers. Reasons offered for why advertisers pay more for viewers under fifty include a belief that their brand preferences are not as fixed and the fact that they watch less television and hence are harder to reach. The rewards for capturing relatively younger viewers offer another reason for news directors to pay less attention to the (older) loyal watchers. One way to forge a compromise between the interests of average and marginal viewers is to cover the political issues of interest to younger viewers. The January 2000 Pew survey asked respondents to indicate the priority they attached to twenty political issues. When I examined the number of minutes or number of stories devoted on each network to these issues in 2000, I found that the higher the priority attached to an issue at the start of the year by the eighteen-to-thirty-four set, the more attention devoted over the year by the network news. The priorities of older viewers had no impact or a negative effect on coverage devoted by the networks. The survey data indicate that females in the age range care relatively more about issues such as dealing with the problems of families with children and strengthening gun control laws. Searching for marginal viewers and those valued by advertisers may thus lead the networks to talk about issues often associated with the Democratic Party. The competition generated by technology, and the influence of advertiser values, thus generate pressure to provide network stories that may give rise to perceptions of media bias. Among those identifying themselves as very conservative, 37.4 percent reported in 2000 that they viewed the national nightly network news as very biased. Among survey respondents who labeled themselves as very liberal, only 16.6 percent saw network news programs the same way.

Product Changes

In print and broadcast, there has been a substantial change in the content and style of news coverage since 1970. These product changes are numerous: a decrease in hard news (e.g., public-affairs coverage) and an increase in soft news (e.g., entertainment, human-interest stories); an increase in negative tone to cover elections; less focus on watchdog stories (e.g., those dealing with the operation of government); and an increase in the mix of opinion and interpretation in news coverage. These product changes also have many origins. Emphasis on cost cutting and profits has led to declines in international coverage. Competition across media and the pressure for product differentiation within a market have led some outlets to specialize in soft news. The drive to entertain can transform political coverage into horse-race coverage, with a focus on who is ahead in the polls and a tone that is often critical of candidates and events. In publicly traded companies, pressures to meet market earnings expectations can mean more focus on pleasing readers and viewers and less room for journalists to exercise their own news judgment. Changes in rules by the Federal Communications Commission (FCC) have reduced station worries about whether views expressed on air are "fair" and removed specific requirements that broadcasters provide a minimum amount of public-affairs coverage. In this section I describe the dimensions of news product changes since 1970. These changes in product attributes result from an interplay of demand and supply factors, though I do not attempt here to specify which factors generate particular product alterations.

Content analysis by the Committee of Concerned Journalists (CCJ) in 1998 captured broad changes in the media by examining for 1977, 1987, and 1997 one month of coverage on the three network evening news programs, each cover story during the year for *Time* and *Newsweek,* and each front-page story for the *New York Times* and *Los Angeles Times.* For this sample of 3,760 stories, the CCJ found that straight news accounts (e.g., what happened yesterday) went from 52 percent of stories in 1977 to only 32 percent in 1997. Story topics in traditional hard-news areas (i.e., government, military, and domestic and foreign affairs) went from 66.3 percent of all reports to 48.9 percent. Feature stories such as those about entertainment, celebrities, lifestyle, and celebrity crime grew from 5.1 percent in 1977 to 11.1 percent in 1997. Crime stories went from 8.4 percent to 11.4 percent and personal health from 0.7 percent to 3.5 percent. Attention also grew for stories about science (2.7 percent to 5.9 percent) and religion (0.5 percent to 3.7 percent).[9]

Analyzing a random sample of 5,331 news stories from 1980 to 1999 from two networks, two weekly news magazines, three large daily newspapers, and twenty-six local daily papers, Thomas Patterson found a similar pattern. Stories without a clear connection to policy grew from about 35 percent of the stories in 1980 to close to 50 percent in 1999. Reports with a sensational focus went from nearly a quarter of all stories in the early 1980s to almost 40 percent in 1999. Human-interest stories, a staple of soft-news coverage, went from 11 percent in 1980 to 26 percent in 1999. Crime and disaster coverage climbed from 8 to 13 percent. These trends held across media. Patterson found that the likelihood that a person would encounter a soft-news story increased between 1994 and 1998 for consumers of news magazines, network news, and newspapers.[10]

As hard-news coverage declined, the tone of many stories about elections grew more critical. Assessing coverage of major-party presidential nominees in *Time* and *Newsweek* from 1960 to 1992, Patterson found that unfavorable references to the candidates grew from approximately 25 percent in 1960 to 60 percent in 1992. Studying front-page election stories in the *New York Times,* he found that in the 1960s the candidates and other partisan sources set the tone of nearly 70 percent of the articles. By 1992, journalists set the tone for the reports about 80 percent of the time. Kiku Adatto documented similar patterns of a shrinking role for the candidate and increasing role for the reporter on network television coverage of presidential campaigns. She found that in 1968 the average sound bite for a presidential candidate on the network evening news was 42.3 seconds. By the 1988 campaign this figure dropped to 9.8 seconds (and decreased further to 8.4 seconds in the 1992 general election). What replaced the words of the candidates was strategy coverage provided by reporters, who gave viewers their assessment of why the candidate was engaged in a particular strategy and how the candidate was faring in the horse race. Critical coverage also greeted the eventual winners. A study for the Council for Excellence in

Government found that in the first year of the presidencies of Ronald Reagan (1981), Bill Clinton (1993), and George W. Bush (2001), coverage of the administration on network television news was negative in tone by a ratio of nearly two to one. The critical eye reporters used in covering government emerged in part from journalists' experience with government deception during both the Vietnam War and Watergate.[11]

Further evidence on changes in the news comes from surveys of those who produce it. David Weaver and G. Cleveland Wilhoit compared surveys of journalists taken in 1971, 1982, and 1992. They estimate that during this period the number of full-time journalists in the United States increased from 69,500 to 122,015. Although more people were engaged in covering the news in the 1990s, the journalists working then reported heightened frustration with their work. Relative to reporters surveyed in 1971, reporters in 1992 were much less likely to say that they had the freedom to select their own stories or the freedom to decide what aspects of a story to emphasize. They pointed to an emphasis on profit over quality as a constraint on their reporting. Those working for smaller media outlets (e.g., weekly newspapers or radio stations) or for group-owned, privately held outlets were more likely to say they enjoyed autonomy in their work. Compared with 1982, reporters in 1992 were less likely to say their operation was doing an outstanding job; a lower percentage were also willing to say their organization did a very good or outstanding job. Those reporters who indicated their news organization did only a poor or fair job linked this to insufficient resources, staff, and news space, or indicated that their outlets failed to provide enough in-depth coverage.

Product changes are evident too in the percentage of journalists saying that a particular media role was extremely important. In 1971 76 percent of journalists said investigating government claims was an extremely important mass media role, 61 percent said the same for providing analysis of complex problems, and 55 percent for discussing national policy. These figures dropped in 1992 to 67 percent for investigating government, 48 percent for analysis of complex problems, and 39 percent for national problems. Journalists in 1992 were much more likely (69 percent) to say that getting information to the public quickly was an extremely important role, versus 56 percent in 1971.[12]

In extended interviews with journalists, Howard Gardner, Mihaly Csikszentmihalyi, and William Damon also found that journalists were frustrated: 51 percent said changes in the media were negative, versus 24 percent indicating that the changes were positive. Sixty-four percent of the journalists they interviewed said the demands to comply with business goals in journalism were increasing, and 63 percent said there was a perceived drop in ethics and values in the media. Many of those interviewed pointed to the drive for market share as a prime force undercutting the performance of journalists.[13]

Changes in government regulation also affected the extent and kind of information provided. Prior to 1987, the FCC's fairness doctrine required broadcasters to provide free and equal time to parties that dissented from controversial views that stations chose to air. While the policy may have promoted perceptions of fairness, empirical evidence indicates that the policy may have chilled speech by discouraging stations from presenting viewpoints that might trigger demands for free response time on air.[14] Once the fairness doctrine was abolished by the FCC, the genre of informational programming immediately expanded on radio. This radio genre, which includes news programming and the talk-radio format made famous by Rush Limbaugh, became both a popular and controversial force in public-affairs debates in the 1990s.

Ownership

Change in ownership of news media outlets is a third factor affecting content. There are many theories about why ownership matters: publicly traded firms could be more likely to focus on profits than journalism properties (e.g., newspapers) owned by individuals or families; outlets owned by groups, whether a newspaper in a chain or a broadcast station owned by a network may be less likely to identify with the problems of a specific city; and the concentration of ownership in a small number of firms may crowd out a diverse set of views.

Calculating how ownership has changed over time requires defining a medium and a market. Between 1970 and 1998, the number of daily newspapers declined from 1,748 to 1,489 and average circulation dropped from 62,202 to 56,183. The number of weekly newspapers, however, grew from 7,612 to 8,193 and average circulation jumped from 3,660 to 9,067. The number of cities with two or more fully competing dailies with different ownership declined from 37 in 1973 to 19 in 1996. The number of newspaper groups dropped from 157 in 1970 to 129 in 1996. In the same period, the percentage of dailies owned by chains grew from 50.3 percent to 76.2 percent and the percentage of daily circulation accounted for by these group-owned papers increased from 63.0 percent to 81.5 percent. The fifteen largest newspaper chains generated slightly more than half of the daily circulation of newspapers in the United States in 1998.[15]

At a broad level, the media have not become significantly more concentrated (in terms of the concentration of sales in a specific number of firms) over this time period. It is estimated that in terms of revenues, the top fifty media firms (which include newspaper, broadcast, cable, publishing, music, and film companies) accounted for 79.7 percent of all media industry revenues in 1986 and 81.8 percent in 1997; the share of the top four firms grew from 18.8 percent to 24.1 percent.[16] As measured by the Herfindahl-Hirschmann Index, an index based on the sum of the squared market shares, the media industry went from an HHI of 206 in 1986 to 268 in 1997.[17] The Department of Justice generally considers industries with an HHI of less than 1,000 to be unconcentrated. One study looked at how ownership had changed between 1960 and 2000 for ten local media markets in the United States. After counting for each local market the number of broadcast outlets, cable systems, direct-broadcast satellite systems, and daily newspapers available, the study found that the percentage growth in the total number of media outlets available averaged more than 200 percent between 1960 and 2000. The percentage increase in the number of owners in the market averaged 140 percent.[18]

The actual impact of group or chain ownership in media outlets is a topic of spirited empirical debate. Reviewing the social science evidence on the impact of chain ownership on newspaper operation in 1994, Edwin Baker concluded, "Chain ownership's primary documented effects are negative. However, the findings seem tepid, hardly motivating any strong critique of chain ownership or prompting any significant policy interventions." Lisa George found that as the number of owners in a local newspaper market goes down, product differentiation between newspapers increases and the number of topical reporting beats covered in the market overall goes up. The Project for Excellence in Journalism found that in local television markets, stations affiliated with networks produced higher-quality news programs than those actually owned and operated by the networks, that stations owned by a company also operating a newspaper in the market generated higher-quality local television news programs, and that locally owned stations were not obviously superior to other stations in news production.[19]

The Changing Nature of Network News

The transformation of the network evening news programs since 1970 offers a case study of the impact of changes in technology, news definitions, and ownership.[20] In 1969 the daily debates among network news executives and reporters about what stories to include in the evening news broadcasts centered around which domestic politics and foreign policy stories to cover. Each television network was part of a media company. For each of the three networks, the founder or an early leader was still involved and identified with the operation of the organization. Network news operations were expected to generate prestige, part of which reflected back on the owners and broadcasters. The FCC routinely examined the number of hours of public-affairs programming provided when stations had their licenses renewed. A reputation for covering public affairs well in the news provided added security when licenses were up for renewal. If viewers did not enjoy the hard-news stories provided in the evening news programs, they had few other options on the dial. The average television household received seven channels. At the dinner hour more than one-third of all television households watched the network evening news. The stories they saw were news to most viewers. National news programs were not on earlier in the afternoon, and local news programs lacked the technology and time to cover national events on their own. Decision makers on network news programs felt a responsibility to provide viewers with information they needed as citizens. The large audience share and focus on politics attracted significant scrutiny of the programs, which were a frequent target of criticism from the White House.[21]

In 2000 the daily debates in network story conferences centered on whether to include domestic political stories or softer news items about health and entertainment topics. Foreign coverage was not often on the agenda, except in cases of military action. Each network was part of a publicly traded conglomerate. Network news operations were expected by corporate managers and Wall Street analysts to generate profits. The FCC no longer scrutinized public affairs coverage and license renewals were virtually assured. Television households received an average of sixty-three channels. Viewers at the dinner hour could watch sitcoms, entertainment news, sports news, and news on PBS. The three major network news programs combined captured only 23 percent of all television households. Viewers often came to the network news programs with a sense of the day's headline stories, after watching news on cable channels or local television programs containing stories and footage from around the nation. Network decision-makers felt pressure to gain ratings, which translated into a competition to discover and serve viewers' interests. Anchors and reporters were promoted as celebrities. Political criticisms of news coverage focused more on the content of cable news programs, though press critics faulted the network evening news shows for an increasing shift to soft-news stories.

To see the shift in news content, consider how the network evening news treated a consistent set of stories over time. Each year, *People* magazine selects its "25 Most Intriguing People" of the year, which consist of a set of soft-news personalities (i.e., television stars, movie actors, sports figures, persons involved in famous crimes, and royalty) and a set of famous figures from business and politics. In 1974–78, 40 percent of the soft-news personalities on the *People* list were covered in stories on at least one of the three major network evening news programs. In 1994–98, this figure rose to 52 percent. For those soft-news personalities that generated coverage over the course of the year they were listed by *People,* on ABC the "Intriguing" person averaged 9.9 stories and 1,275 seconds in coverage per year in 1974–78. This grew to 17.2 stories and 2,141 seconds of annual average coverage by 1994–98. NBC's reputation of providing more soft news than the other two networks is confirmed by its average of 25.6 stories and 3,238 seconds of coverage in 1994–98.

By many measures hard-news coverage dropped over this period. Each year, *Congressional Quarterly* identifies the key votes that take place in the U.S. Senate and House. In 1969–73, 82 percent of these major votes were covered on at least one of the network evening news programs on the day of or day after the congressional action. Yet for the period 1994–98, only 62 percent of the *CQ* votes generated network stories. A similar pattern holds for the key legislative votes identified each year by two ideological interest groups, the Americans for Democratic Action (ADA) and the American Conservative Union (ACU). The percentage of key interest-group votes in Congress that generated stories on the nightly news dropped from 64 percent in 1969–73 to 44 percent in 1994–98. The shift on the network news away from a headline service toward more background reporting is evident in the fact that those bills that were covered got more time on the evening news programs. On ABC, for example, the mean coverage length for *CQ* bills went from 117 seconds in 1969–73 to 211 seconds in 1994–98.

Statistical analysis shows that many factors contributed to these changes in coverage. *People*'s intriguing personalities were more likely to be covered over the course of a year on the network evening news in the era (i.e., 1984 or later) when the FCC had deregulated much of broadcast television. Coverage of *CQ* votes declined in election years (when they were probably crowded out by campaign stories) and dropped as cost cutting became more prominent in network news operations. Interest-group vote coverage declined on each network as the percentage of households with cable increased, indicating how broadcast television shifted away from some forms of hard news as competition increased from cable. In the period 1969 to 1999, the number of network evening news stories mentioning soft-news terms such as *actor, sex,* or *movie* increased along with the percentage of households with cable. In the post-deregulation era, stories about hard-news topics such as education or Medicaid or NATO declined.

Network evening news anchors not only covered celebrities, they became them. News products have always been what economists call experience goods, which means that companies have always sought ways to signal to potential customers what today's version of events will look like in their papers or programs. The pressure for journalists to become part of the news product, however, is increasing as the number of news outlets expands. In a world of four broadcast television channels, a consumer can easily switch among viewing options to sample content. In a world where channels can number in the hundreds, sampling becomes more time-consuming.[22] If viewers recognize and enjoy watching a particular journalist on television, they may be more likely to watch a given channel because of this familiarity. The personalities of those who present the information become shortcuts for viewers to find their news niche. The changing salary rewards in network evening news programs provide evidence of how journalists have become part of the product in news.

Although network anchors deliver the news, they are rewarded in the marketplace for delivering viewers to advertisers. The salary patterns for network evening news anchors suggest that the value attached to the personal ability of these stars to deliver viewers increased markedly during the 1990s. The pay trends at first appear counterintuitive. The share of television viewers who watch the evening news has declined dramatically from 72 percent in 1980 to 44 percent in 2000.[23] In terms of viewing households for one of the network evening news programs, an average of 9.8 million watched in 1975 versus 8.1 million in 1999.[24] Yet the real dollar amounts paid for ads on the shows and the cost per thousand viewing households reached actually increased during this time period. Expressed in 1999 dollars, advertisers paid $3.93 to reach one thousand households in 1975 and $5.78 in 1999. Although the absolute size of the network evening news audience has shrunk with the increased viewing options available on cable, ratings for network programs overall have declined. Between 1985 and 1997, the share of the viewing audience watching network stations in prime time declined from 74 percent to 57 percent. Network news still attracts a relatively large program audience, which advertisers value since it means lower transaction costs in getting a viewer and less duplication of effort to reach a given audience size. So even though the absolute number of households tuned to a network evening news program has declined, advertisers are now willing to pay more per thousand viewers reached. This may reflect higher ad rates overall, and a premium attached to reaching a relatively larger audience in an era marked by highly fractured viewing.

Although expansion of viewing options and diminishment of audience sizes may raise the value of advertising on network news programs, it may also raise the value of network anchors. When consumers have many more choices, the value of a known commodity can increase. Network anchors become a way for channels to create a brand image in viewers' minds. If anchors become more important in drawing viewers to programs, this may translate into higher returns for anchors in salary negotiations. The pattern in salaries from 1970 to 1999 confirms this story. The amount in salary that an anchor received for attracting a thousand viewing households increased from a range of $0.13 to $0.31 (in 1999 dollars) in 1976 to a range of $0.86 to $1.07 in 1999. Another way to view this is to look at the ratio of the anchor's salary to the ad price on the evening news programs. In 1976 anchors such as Walter Cronkite and John Chancellor were paid the equivalent of 28 ads per year, while in 1999 this had grown to 149 ads for Dan Rather and Tom Brokaw. The marked increase in the amount paid per viewing household, salary expressed in ad revenues, and the absolute magnitude of the salary took place in the 1990s. This was a time of declining absolute audiences, but rising importance of anchors in attracting viewers. The increased value placed on anchors is consistent with these personalities playing a growing role in attracting viewers in a multichannel universe.

Current News Markets

The expanding opportunities for individuals to consume media products has meant declining market shares for most traditional news media outlets.[25] The percentage of survey respondents saying that they were regular consumers of a specific news outlet dropped substantially between May 1993 and April 2002 in Pew surveys: from 77 percent to 57 percent for local television news; 60 percent to 32 percent for nightly network news; and 52 percent to 24 percent for network television news magazines. Between 1994 and 2002, Pew surveys indicated drops in regular consumption from 47 percent to 41 percent for radio and 58 percent to 41 percent for newspapers. Respondents reporting regular consumption of online news grew from 2 percent in April 1996 to 25 percent in April 2002; NPR's figures also increased during that period, from 13 percent to 16 percent. In April 2002, 33 percent of survey respondents reported that they were regular consumers of cable television news.

Market forces influenced the content and consumption of news on nearly all these media. Local television programs in areas with higher viewer interest in hard news carried a higher number of national hard-news stories and local political stories.[26] In areas where viewers demonstrated a greater taste for entertainment news (through higher subscription rates to *People* magazine), news directors added more soft-news stories to local broadcasts. Stations owned by group owners carried fewer hard-news stories and fewer stories about a state's U.S. senators. Network affiliation also influenced which celebrities and television programs were discussed on local television news. FOX stations were more likely to carry stories about the FOX program *Greed*. ABC stations were more likely to talk about Monica Lewinsky during the time when that network's star Barbara Walters became the first person to interview in-depth the former intern about her relationship with President Clinton.

Local newspaper content also reveals an attempt to serve reader interests. In markets with higher interest in hard news, newspapers provide more stories about poverty, Medicaid, and campaign finance reform. For topics likely to be of interest to the paper's target readers, such as computers or soft-money contributions in politics, the greater the real-world incidence of these topics in the community, the larger the number of stories about the topic in the paper. As the number of papers held by the parent company of a paper grew, the percentage of soft-news figures covered in the paper increased. An area where local interest does not appear to affect coverage is the tone used in political articles about presidential candidates. The language used by papers to cover the convention speeches in 2000 for Al Gore and George W. Bush did not differ based on the editorial endorsements the papers made.

At first glance, Internet economics might appear to offer a solution to the lack of policy content in traditional media outlets. The low costs of providing information on the Internet, coupled with the willingness of nonprofits and government agencies to provide extensive information there, means that hard-news topics are discussed on a greater number of Web sites than topics in soft news or consumer/producer information.[27] In terms of information demanded by individuals, however, the dominance of entertaining and personally useful information is clear. People are much more likely to search the Net for information about entertainment figures than political issues. Decisions about purchasing a consumer item or making a business purchase attract more attention (and advertiser support) than voting decisions.

From the perspective of a person interested in public affairs, the variety of readily available news sources that cover politics was much greater in 2004 than in 1970. A person in search of hard news could watch the *NewsHour with Jim Lehrer* on PBS (as did 2.7 million people each weeknight), read the *New York Times* (or the *Washington Times*) on the Internet, and listen to National Public Radio. Raw data about the performance of government programs was available on the Web sites of nonprofits and government agencies. Interest groups and think tanks lowered the costs of learning about politics for reporters and citizens. A question about campaign finance could be investigated at Opensecrets.org, which takes federal data from the Federal Election Commission on political campaign contributions and makes it searchable by donor, candidate, or industry. The increasing use of information provision by the government as a regulatory tool has expanded the data available about private-sector activity. Environmental reporters, for example, have made significant use of the Toxics Release Inventory (TRI), an Environmental Protection Agency database that reports yearly pollution totals for more than 650 chemicals at the plant level. The TRI data have generated coverage that draws local scrutiny on local polluters, moved the stock market when it was released, and spurred actions by companies to reduce their reported pollution emissions.[28]

The multiplication of news outlets on cable and the Internet means that an individual is more likely today than in the 1970s or 1980s to find a news outlet closer to his or her ideal news source. The creation of niche programming and content means that individuals may be more likely to find what they want. But the division of the audience into smaller groups also means that any one channel may be less likely to attract viewers, less likely to amass advertiser revenue, and hence less able to devote resources to programming. There may be a trade-off between cable channels' catering to individual topical interests and the quality of programming that can be supported by the audience size. On the Internet, the drive of competition means that price eventually equals marginal costs (zero), so sites are searching for ways to generate revenue. This means that breaking news becomes a commodity essentially offered for free. The lack of revenue may mean that sites simply repeat readily available information rather than generate their own coverage. In a study of Internet content during the 2000 presidential primaries, the Committee of Concerned Journalists found that one-quarter of the political front pages on Internet sites they studied had no original reporting.[29] The time pressure to provide news generated by the Internet and the lack of resources to do original reporting may increase the likelihood that information cascades occur. When initial news reports get facts wrong, the tendency of reporters to rely on the work of others and the quick multiplication effects can mean that bad information propagates. Chip Heath and Jonathan Bendor traced out, for example, how the media came to repeat statements falsely attributed to Al Gore during the 2000 campaign.[30]

An additional dilemma for hard-news consumers is the economic pressures that may push some outlets away from offering the type of news they prefer. If advertisers value younger viewers and younger viewers demonstrate a higher willingness to switch channels, then broadcast programs may end up at the margins, putting more soft-news topics into previously hard-news programs. This explains in part the increased emphasis on entertainment and human-interest stories on the network news broadcasts. Media bias can also emerge as a commercial product, in at least two forms. If networks are targeting relatively younger female viewers, and these viewers express more interest in issues such as gun control and the problems of families with children, the network news programs may focus on traditionally Democratic (liberal) issues out of economic necessity. The development of niche programs on cable can also generate programs targeted at viewers with a particular ideology. The FOX News Channel, for example, attracts a relatively conservative audience and offers the cable news program with the largest audience—*The O'Reilly Factor*. The added variety arising from the expansion of cable programming means that viewers uninterested in politics can more readily avoid it. In 1996 viewers with cable who had low levels of political interest (i.e., had low levels of political information) were much less likely to watch presidential debates than viewers who had broadcast channels.[31] Those who were not interested in politics but had only broadcast television did end up watching these debates, since their options were limited. The greater entertainment options provided by cable television also appear to affect who votes. Among viewers with high interest in entertainment programming, those with cable are much less likely to vote (perhaps because they are able to avoid political programming by watching the many entertainment channels offered on cable).[32]

How individuals react to current media content depends in part on whether it is targeted at them. Assessing the statement, "People who decide what to put on TV news or in the newspapers are out of touch with people like me," 10.7 percent of females aged eighteen to thirty-four agreed versus 23.9 percent of males fifty and over in a Pew survey conducted in 2000.[33] This is consistent with older viewers, who are less likely to be the marginal viewers sought by broadcasters, being frustrated by content aimed at keeping younger eyeballs watching. Perceptions of media bias depend in part on product positioning and tastes. Conservatives are much more likely to say that news programs that attract liberal audiences are biased, while perceptions of a news program's bias among liberals declines as the average audience for a show becomes more liberal. The younger viewers valued by advertisers are more likely to see trends in news as positive, even as they are bemoaned by older viewers. When asked whether they thought hosts on news programs expressing strong political opinions was a good thing, 58 percent of those aged eighteen to twenty-nine agreed versus 33 percent of those sixty-five or older.[34] Asked to assess the growth of political news talk programs on cable, 53 percent of those eighteen-to-twenty-nine-year-olds saw this as a good thing versus 35 percent of those sixty-five or older. Faced with the choice between hard and soft news, the audience clearly segments by age and gender. The majority of the viewers of the *NewsHour with Jim Lehrer* are age fifty or over; the majority of the readers of personality magazines such as *People* are female; the largest audience for shows such as *Entertainment Tonight* or *Access Hollywood* comes from eighteen-to-twenty-four-year-olds; and the vast majority of viewers of sports news on ESPN are male.

Changes in news markets from 1970 to today have brought new media, generated more diverse offerings, and added opportunities to find both hard and soft news. In pushing for the deregulation of broadcast television in the 1980s, FCC chairman Mark Fowler declared famously, "The public's interest . . . defines the public interest."[35] The competition for interested audiences has clearly driven many of the recent changes in journalism. Whether the aggregation of individuals pursuing the stories they want to know about yields the type of information they need to know about as citizens and voters is a question pursued further in other chapters in this volume.

Notes

1. Anthony Downs, *An Economic Theory of Democracy* (New York: Harper Books, 1957). Downs coined the term *rational ignorance* to refer to the fact that the small probability that an individual has of influencing public policy decisions means that it may be rational to remain ignorant of current affairs, if one views information only as an instrument in making decisions and calculates the personal payoffs from keeping up with public affairs. There may still be a demand expressed for political coverage, from those who feel a duty to be informed, people who find the details of politics and policies inherently interesting, or people who derive entertainment from politics as drama, horse race, or scandal. The logic of rational ignorance may help explain why Delli Carpini and Keeter find that "despite the numerous political, economic, and social changes that have occurred since World War II, overall political knowledge levels in the United States are about the same today as they were forty to fifty years ago" (*What Americans Know about Politics and Why It Matters*, 270).
2. For data on channel availability and consumption, see Ed Papazian, ed., *TV Dimensions 2002* (New York: Media Dynamics, 2002).
3. For an analysis of media audience composition, see Hamilton, *All the News That's Fit to Sell*, 107–11.

4. To study the market for pundits, I analyzed a sample of the print offerings and broadcast transcripts of fifty-six pundits in 1999 using the text analysis software DICTION. See chapter 8 in Hamilton, *All the News That's Fit to Sell*.

5. For analysis of news markets on the Internet, see chapter 7 in Hamilton, *All the News That's Fit to Sell*.

6. See Kovach and Rosensteil, *Warp Speed*, and Kalb, *One Scandalous Story*, for discussions of the time pressures on journalists created by the speed of information transmission and the Internet.

7. Hamilton, *Channeling Violence*, examines how audience interest in violent content influences the decisions of local-news directors in determining whether to include stories about crimes outside their areas or cover stories involving military action. Hess and Kalb, *The Media and the War on Terrorism*, present discussions of how technology affects coverage of war, including the U.S. war on terrorism.

8. See chapter 3 in Hamilton, *All the News That's Fit to Sell*, for an analysis of the network news audience.

9. Committee of Concerned Journalists, *Changing Definitions of News* (Washington, D.C.: Committee of Concerned Journalists, 1998), available from www.journalism. org.

10. Thomas E. Patterson, "Doing Well and Doing Good: How Soft News and Critical Journalism Are Shrinking the News Audience and Weakening Democracy—And What News Outlets Can Do about It" (working paper, Joan Shorenstein Center on Press, Politics and Public Policy, Kennedy School of Government, Harvard University, Cambridge, Mass., 2000).

11. Patterson, *Out of Order*; Addatto, *Picture Perfect*; Council for Excellence in Government, *Government: In and Out of the News*, study by the Center for Media and Public Affairs, 2003, available at http://www.excelgov.org/displaycontent. asp?keyword=prnHomePage. Patterson's *Out of Order* also includes a discussion of distrust between reporters and politicians.

12. Weaver and Wilhoit, *The American Journalist in the 1990s*.

13. Gardner, Csikszentmihalyi, and Damon, *Good Work*.

14. Thomas W. Hazlett and David W. Sosa, "Was the Fairness Doctrine a 'Chilling Effect'?: Evidence from the Post-Deregulation Radio Market," *Journal of Legal Studies* 26, no. 1 (1997): 279–301.

15. For data on newspaper markets, see Compaine and Gomery, *Who Owns the Media?*

16. Ibid.

17. Ben Compaine, "Domination Fantasies: Does Rupert Murdoch Control the Media? Does Anyone?" *Reason*, January 2004, http://www.reason.com/0401/fe. bc.domination.shtml.

18. Scott Roberts, Jane Frenette, and Dione Stearns, "A Comparison of Media Outlets and Owners for Ten Selected Markets: 1960, 1980, 2000" (working paper, Media Ownership Working Group, Federal Communications Commission, Washington, D.C., 2002).

19. For discussion of the impact of media ownership and concentration on content, see Peter O. Steiner, "Program Patterns and Preferences, and the Workability of Competition in Radio Broadcasting," *Quarterly Journal of Economics* 66 (1952):

194–223; Demers, *The Menace of the Corporate Newspaper;* Bagdikian, *The Media Monopoly;* McChesney, *Rich Man, Poor Democracy;* Jeff Chester, "Strict Scrutiny: Why Journalists Should Be Concerned about New Federal and Industry Media Deregulation Proposals," *Harvard International Journal of Press/Politics* 7, no. 2 (2002): 105–15; and Roberts and Kunkel, eds., *Breach of Faith.* The quotation on ownership studies comes from C. Edwin Baker, "Ownership of Newspapers: The View from Positivist Social Science" (research paper, Joan Shorenstein Center on the Press, Politics and Public Policy, Kennedy School of Government, Harvard University, Cambridge, Mass, 1994), 19. See also Lisa George, "What's Fit to Print: The Effect of Ownership Concentration on Product Variety in Daily Newspaper Markets" (working paper, Michigan State University, East Lansing, Mich., 2001), and Project for Excellence in Journalism, *Does Ownership Matter in Local Television News? A Five-Year Study of Ownership and Quality,* updated April 29, 2003, http://www.journalism.org/resources/research/reports/ownership/default.asp.

20. This section excerpts and summarizes analysis from chapters 6 and 8 of Hamilton, *All the News That's Fit to Sell.*

21. In 1969 the founders or early leaders of each network still served as the chairman of the board: William S. Paley (CBS); David Sarnoff (RCA, which owned NBC); and Leonard Goldenson (ABC). For an overview of the networks that focuses on the 1980s, see Auletta, *Three Blind Mice.* Data on channels per television household come from Ed Papazian, ed., *TV Dimensions 2001* (New York: Media Dynamics, 2001), which indicates (on p. 22) that averages were 7.1 for 1970 and 63.4 for 2000. Larry M. Bartels and Wendy M. Rahn, in "Political Attitudes in the Post-Network Era" (paper prepared for the Annual Meeting of the American Political Science Association, Washington, D.C., September, 2000), report that the sum of the Nielsen ratings for the three network evening news programs was close to 36 in 1970–71 and 23 in 1999–2000. For the text of Vice President Spiro Agnew's speech attacking network television news on November 13, 1969, see James Keogh, *President Nixon and the Press* (New York: Funk & Wagnalls, 1972).

22. In summer 2001 DirecTV, a digital satellite service, offered subscribers more than 225 channels (see www.directv.com). The average number of channels received in U.S. television households grew from 28 in 1988 to 49 in 1997. Households clearly have favorites among these channels. The average number of channels viewed per household, where viewing is defined as "10 or more continuous minutes per channel," was 12 in 1997. See Nielsen Media Research, *1998 Report on Television* (New York: Nielsen Media Research, 1998), 19.

23. For historical ratings and share information, see Nielsen Media Research, *1998 Report on Television,* 25. The estimate of a combined 44 percent share for 2000 viewing comes from Terence Smith, "Evening News Evolution," *NewsHour with Jim Lehrer,* aired March 9, 2001, available at http://www.pbs.org/newshour/media/evening_news/index.html.

24. Data on average households viewing network evening news programs, advertising rates, and cost per thousand viewing households used in this chapter come from Television Bureau of Advertising, "Network Television Cost and CPM Trends," July 3, 2001, http://www.tvb.org.

25. See Pew Research Center for the People and the Press, *Public's News Habits Little Changed by September 11: Americans Lack Background to Follow International News* (survey report, Washington, D.C.: Pew Research Center for the People and the Press, June 9, 2002), available from http://people-press.org.

26. For statistical analysis of the content in 1999 of local television stations and newspapers, see chapter 5 in Hamilton, *All the News That's Fit to Sell.*

27. Hamilton, *All the News That's Fit to Sell,* contains research on the market for hard and soft news on the Internet.

28. For evidence on how journalists used the TRI data when it was first released see James T. Hamilton, "Pollution as News: Media and Stock Market Reactions to the Toxics Release Inventory Data," *Journal of Environmental Economics and Management* 28 (January 1995): 98–113.

29. Committee of Concerned Journalists, *ePolitics: A Study of the 2000 Presidential Campaign on the Internet* (Washington, D.C.: Committee of Concerned Journalists, 2000), available from www.journalism.org.

30. Chip Heath and Jonathan Bendor, "When Truth Doesn't Win in the Marketplace of Ideas: Entrapping Schemas, Gore, and the Internet" (working paper, Institute of Governmental Studies, University of California at Berkeley, 2003), http://www.igs.berkeley.edu/research_programs/ppt/papers/Gore412.pdf.

31. See Matthew A. Baum and Sam Kernell, "Has Cable Ended the Golden Age of Presidential Television?" *American Political Science Review* 93, no. 1 (1999): 99–114.

32. Markus Prior, "Avoiding Politics: The Relation of Entertainment Preference and Partisan Feelings" (paper prepared for the Annual Meeting of the American Political Science Association, San Francisco, September 2001). Prior finds that for viewers with high preferences for entertainment programming, those with cable are less likely to vote than those who only watch broadcast television. This provides evidence that cable offers more opportunity to watch entertainment programming, which reduces the consumption of political information and thereby leads to a lower probability of voting by those with strong interest in entertainment fare. See Baum, *Soft News Goes to War,* for an analysis of how the consumption of soft news may affect viewers' political opinions about American foreign policy.

33. For analysis of Pew survey results on media consumption and media bias, see chapter 3 in Hamilton, *All the News That's Fit to Sell.*

34. See Pew Research Center for the People and the Press, *Strong Opposition to Media Cross-Ownership Emerges* (survey report, Pew Research Center for the People and the Press, July 13, 2003), available from http://people-press.org.

35. See Hamilton, *All the News That's Fit to Sell,* 1.

Bibliography

Adatto, Kiku. *Picture Perfect: The Art and Artifice of Public Image Making.* New York: Basic Books, 1993.

Auletta, Ken. *Three Blind Mice: How the TV Networks Lost Their Way.* New York: Random House, 1992.

Bagdikian, Ben H. *The Media Monopoly.* Boston: Beacon Press, 1997.

Baum, Matthew A. *Soft News Goes to War: Public Opinion and American Foreign Policy in the New Media Age*. Princeton, N.J.: Princeton University Press, 2003.

Compaine, Benjamin M., and Douglas Gomery. *Who Owns the Media?: Competition and Concentration in the Mass Media Industry*. 3rd ed. Mahwah, N.J.: Lawrence Erlbaum, 2000.

Delli Carpini, Michael X., and Scott Keeter. *What Americans Know about Politics and Why It Matters*. New Haven, Conn.: Yale University Press, 1996.

Demers, David P. *The Menace of the Corporate Newspaper: Fact or Fiction?* Ames: Iowa State University Press, 1996.

Downie Jr., Leonard, and Robert G. Kaiser. *The News about the News: American Journalism in Peril*. New York: Knopf, 2002.

Gardner, Howard, Mihaly Csikszentmihalyi, and William Damon. *Good Work: When Excellence and Ethics Meet*. New York: Basic Books, 2001.

Hamilton, James T. *Channeling Violence: The Economic Market for Violent Television Programming*. Princeton, N.J.: Princeton University Press, 1998.

Hamilton, James T. *All the News That's Fit to Sell: How the Market Transforms Information into News*. Princeton, N.J.: Princeton University Press, 2004.

Hess, Stephen, and Martin Kalb, eds. *The Media and the War on Terrorism*. Washington, D.C.: Brookings Institution Press, 2003.

Kalb, Marvin. *One Scandalous Story: Clinton, Lewinsky, and Thirteen Days That Tarnished American Journalism*. New York: Free Press, 2001.

Kovach, Bill, and Tom Rosenstiel. *Warp Speed: America in the Age of Mixed Media*. New York: Century Foundation Press, 1999.

McChesney, Robert W. *Rich Media, Poor Democracy: Communication Politics in Dubious Times*. Urbana: University of Illinois Press, 2000.

Patterson, Thomas E. *Out of Order*. New York: Knopf, 1993.

Roberts, Gene, and Thomas Kunkel, eds., *Breach of Faith: A Crisis of Coverage in the Age of Corporate Newspapering*. Fayetteville: University of Arkansas Press, 2002.

Weaver, David H., and G. Cleveland Wilhoit. *The American Journalist in the 1990s: U.S. News People at the End of an Era*. Mahwah, N.J.: Lawrence Erlbaum, 1996.

22

THE PRESS AND THE POLITICS
OF REPRESENTATION

Mitchell Stephens and David T. Z. Mindich

"WE WISH TO PLEAD OUR OWN CAUSE," THE FIRST African American newspaper, *Freedom's Journal,* famously announced in the third paragraph of its first issue, on March 16, 1827. "Too long have others spoken for us."

Many, probably most, who have found their affairs subject to news coverage have undoubtedly wished—given the limitations of such coverage—for a similar opportunity. Perhaps no group in the United States has so needed and deserved such an opportunity as African Americans. "Too long has the public been deceived by misrepresentations in things which concern us dearly," the editors John B. Russwurm and Samuel Cornish went on to say in that first issue of *Freedom's Journal.*

If democracy requires a press that provides a true account of a nation's doings, then it must be said that the American press has failed. Some of its failings are, perhaps, inevitable; some are not and are, therefore, more disturbing. This essay begins with a general account of the tendency of the press to misrepresent, before considering, as an example of the political consequences of such misrepresentation, some of its failures with regard to African Americans.

The Mirror and Its Distortions

Charles Dickens, in his book *American Notes,* written after a visit to the United States in 1842, succumbs upon occasion to outrage. Some of his anger is directed toward minor targets, such as a shoemaker who fails to remove his hat in the author's presence. A large portion is aimed, appropriately, at "the upholders of slavery."

Since Dickens failed to descend below Fredericksburg, Virginia, during his four-month journey, this observer nonpareil is forced to depend on the press for most of his observations on slavery. He contradicts the assertion that slavery "is not so bad as you in England take it to be" by reproducing forty-four newspaper advertisements for runaway slaves; they mention injuries and scars inflicted on slaves from the wearing of irons, dog bites, brandings, whippings, beatings, stabbings, shootings, mutilations, and amputations. And Dickens supports his argument that white Americans are excessively violent, a trait he attributes to the "the deformity and ugliness of slavery," by reprinting a dozen short newspaper accounts of revenge murders (or attempted murders) and duels.[1]

This latter use of news stories as sociological evidence raises interesting questions, however. For Dickens is relying here upon an American institution at which he will, seven pages later, direct a burst of outrage less extended but no less intense than that which he levels at slavery.

American news organs have inspired more than their share of critics. Few have been harsher than this novelist and reporter. The press on this side of the Atlantic—most of it—is, for Dickens, "foul," "licentious," "abject," "vicious," "a disgrace," a spreader of "moral poison," a "frightful engine," and a "monster of depravity"; it "has its evil eye in every house"; it is guilty of "rampant ignorance and base dishonesty."[2]

Dickens is perfectly capable of deploying irony ("how perfectly contented the slaves are") and of pointing out ironies. (He makes sure that those grand American terms *Republican* and *Liberty* find themselves in the same sentences as *slavery* and *slaves*.) However, Dickens fails to acknowledge the irony in his own reliance upon the work of those he accuses of "ignorance and base dishonesty." Indeed, his use of scattered news accounts to characterize an entire society demonstrates that his antipathy toward the American press is not accompanied by insight into the congenital blind spots of the press.

This is understandable. Such insights into the biases and limitations of forms of representation would be, for the most part, a product—perhaps the primary intellectual product—of the next century.

Much twentieth-century philosophy was devoted to mulling over the primary mechanism humans have for presenting, or re-presenting, the world to themselves: language. "Philosophy is a battle against the bewitchment of our intelligence by means of language," the influential philosopher Ludwig Wittgenstein suggested.[3]

Late-twentieth-century literary theory was largely devoted to understanding limitations in the human effort to share meanings through writing. "Meaning is context bound and context is boundless" is how Jonathan Culler, a literary theorist, expressed one of the problems. Stuart Hall, a major theorist in the cultural-studies movement, argues that representation "doesn't capture meaning," because meaning is never "fixed" and cannot exist outside of discourse, outside of some form of communication. "Representation," Hall maintains, "doesn't occur *after* the event; representation is constitutive of the event."[4]

Media studies began in the twentieth century with the understanding that the medium itself—the form of representation—even more than its content is, as Marshall McLuhan, one of the field's founders, frequently put it, "the message," that which changes, or "massages" us.

All of these lines of thought pose challenges to the traditional view of representation: that forms of communication are transparent, or are "mirrors," merely reflecting what happens to be in front of them; that language merely expresses our thoughts, writers merely say what they mean, communication merely describes events, media merely transmit different kinds of programming. These lines of thought would also challenge, of course, a basic assumption about journalism: that the press merely reports what is happening. But before getting to that challenge, it is necessary to acknowledge that that basic assumption does not go back particularly far. In journalism the mirror metaphor, which assumes that forms of communication should and can present accurate reflections of reality, arrived relatively late.

Dickens brooks no doubt in his *American Notes* about the importance and (malign) influence of the press: "While the newspaper press of America is in, or near, its present abject state, high moral improvement in that country is hopeless." He sees the "odium" of that press "upon the country's head and . . . the evil it works . . . plainly visible in the Republic." But that "odium" and "evil," for Dickens, do not arise from failures in accurately *reflecting* what is going on in society; they arise from what he sees as depraved, base, and vicious *comment* upon society. The American press, in his view, is ignorant and dishonest not in what it reports but in what it, incessantly, attacks.

However, in aiming his bright searchlight upon the undersides of English society—"the sallow cheeks, the brutal eyes, the matted hair, the infected, vermin-haunted heaps of rags"[5]—Dickens himself, in his nonfiction and fiction, would help direct our understanding of the purpose of journalism toward reportage. Indeed, journalism came to play a leading role in the fact-obsessed, Dickens-like sport of reality hunting that came to dominate literature and the arts, as well as science, in the second half of the nineteenth century.

Partisans of a journalism devoted to the earnest mirroring of reality soon learn to scorn those who smear that mirror with the filth of sensationalism and those who tint it with their biases. This is what passes for odious and evil, for ignorant and dishonest, in the positivist world of "objective"—"just the facts"— journalism. We still live, to a large extent, in that world. We still reserve most of our scorn for those who sensationalize and those who impose political biases or, better, those, like William Randolph Hearst or Rupert Murdoch, who seem to do both. Journalism has remained the last redoubt of the nineteenth-century faith in realism. Consequently, the hold of the mirror metaphor upon journalism, once most journalists began seeing themselves as mirrors more than commentators, has been particularly tenacious.

But, of course, cracks developed in that (hopelessly problematic) metaphor.[6] The journalist Lincoln Steffens explains in his autobiography, published in 1931, that, by happening to cover a burglary that would normally have been ignored, he once inspired a competition among his colleagues in New York City to cover more burglaries. The original idea wasn't to sell more newspapers (though competitive pressures did quickly kick in). Steffens did not do it in the service of any political cause. (In fact the reformers, whom he supported, were in power at the time.) Still, Steffens, as he words it, "made" a "crime wave." Mirrors aren't supposed to be so creative.[7]

And if cities can suddenly be subject to apparent crime waves just because of changes in the operating procedures of journalists, the reflection of reality their work provides can hardly be termed faithful. We have to begin to ask—the more academically inclined journalism critics did begin to ask—what other apparent trends in society come or go because of changes in such practices?

Walter Lippmann—an academically inclined journalism critic who didn't work in academia—also asked a couple of other crucial questions: First, how good a job do journalists actually do of reporting what happens in the world? In 1920 in the *New Republic*, Lippmann, together with Charles Merz, published a detailed analysis of coverage in the *New York Times* of the Russian Revolution. How did the *Times* do? "On the essential questions the net effect was almost always misleading," Lippmann and Merz concluded. "A great people in a supreme crisis could not secure the minimum of necessary information on a supremely important event."[8]

The second question they asked was, Why? And here Lippmann and Merz dismiss the usual villain according to subscribers to the mirror metaphor: some conscious effort to bias the news, "a conspiracy." Instead, they find a more subtle but no less disturbing explanation: "The news as a whole is dominated by the hopes of the men who composed the news organization." The staff of the *New York Times* wanted the Bolsheviks to lose; they thereby overplayed their defeats and underplayed their victories. What kind of mirror bends and twists with hopes and fears? Journalism here, if not actually constitutive of the event, was certainly constitutive of understanding of the event.

Those who have studied journalism from this perspective—a very twentieth-century perspective—have found numerous other exclusions and distortions in its representations of reality. Consider, for example, what other thoughts in the heads of journalists besides hopes and fears—thoughts that journalists may not even know they have—can do to the news. What if, for example, they, and almost all of their colleagues, simply consider some opinions wacky, too "extreme," beyond the pale, impossible to take seriously? Will those opinions get a place in the on-the-one-hand-this on-the-other-hand-that balancing act with which "objective" journalists usually cover controversy?

Daniel Hallin has come up with a simple representation of this: He draws an interior circle called the "Sphere of Consensus"; these ideas are so accepted, they are not even challenged—not even seen as possible to challenge—in mainstream news organs. Hallin draws an exterior circle called the "Sphere of Legitimate Controversy"; these ideas are allowed places in the "objective" balancing act. Then Hallin wonders about all the ideas that are outside of both these circles, in a shapeless, borderless "Sphere of Deviance"; these are ideas that don't generally find their way into the news at all.[9]

The mirror provided by journalism (to switch back to the original metaphor) is limited in size—encompassing only the inner two of Hallin's spheres. Some unconventional opinions, some groups of people who hold unconventional opinions, do not find themselves reflected in it.

This problem can be eased by making the mirror (or the circles, if you will) larger. But the press, alas, rarely widens the Sphere of Legitimate Controversy on its own. When Edward R. Murrow dared criticize Senator Joseph McCarthy on the CBS television program *See It Now* in 1954 (to choose what many believe to be one of the more noble examples of twenti-eth-century American journalism), it was *after* many other influential Americans had already begun to lose patience with McCarthy's anti-Communist crusade. Similarly, when Walter Cronkite, the leading newscaster of his day, made his much-remarked-upon statement in 1968 (after the Tet Offensive) that Vietnam was "mired in stalemate," many influential Americans, including some leading politicians, had already reached that conclusion.

Even if we had braver, more original journalists, we would never entirely succeed in making the mirror large enough: someone with a still weirder, less seemingly legitimate, take on things would still, inevitably, be excluded. Journalism, the point is, is mindset bound, and mindsets are boundless.

Some of the limitations in journalism have to do with the nature of news itself. Events become news in large part because they are exceptional: an unusu-ally devastating drought, an unusually corrupt corporation, an unusually famous defendant. This taste for the exceptional appears to be built into the definition of news. Yet, we and our opinion leaders are often busy using news items as evi-dence of what is usual, evidence upon which we base political conclusions. We try, in other words, to find rules in these exceptions.[10]

A society supported by the sale of human beings and by the whipping and beating of those human beings must indeed have spread its violence and ugliness beyond the racial group being sold and beaten, but a dozen news items about revenge murders, such as those cited by Dickens, do not provide sufficient evi-dence of that, any more than a news report on the assassination of a Swedish prime minister provides evidence that Sweden is a violent and ugly place.

This mirror often behaves like a funhouse mirror. Violence, tragedies, crime, loom large; their actual prevalence in a society can easily be exagger-ated. Some groups may appear in the news predominantly as perpetrators or as victims; some groups may not behave sufficiently unusually to be noticed at all. Sometimes entire sections of society, even whole nations, find themselves in the position of vampires, who, legend has it, can never be caught in a mirror's reflection. While a people gaze into this mirror, believing what it sees to be "reality," numerous specters drift by unnoticed. And their invisibility is sometimes enforced by another human interest that seems to have been enshrined in the definition of news: an enthrallment with the close, the familiar.

In the early twentieth century, a sign in the office of a London tabloid read, "One Englishman is a story. Ten Frenchmen is a story. One hundred Germans is a story. And nothing ever happens in Chile." Although the calculus, we would hope, is less crass today, journalists do continue to make news judgments, consciously or not, that take into account proximity and national affinity. Occasionally in those judgments these journalists may also consider their or their presumed audience's familiarity with certain areas or neighborhoods. Even more discreditably, they may include in their calculus cultural or racial familiarity or proximity.

It is an invidious calculus—leading to frightening distortions and exclusions—but a pervasive one. In 1999, when the Newseum (a Washington, D.C., museum devoted to news) asked American journalists and critics to pick the top one hundred news stories of the century, their choices reflected their cultural and nationalistic biases. True, their top stories included indisputably important subjects (1: U.S. drops atomic bomb; 2: Men first walk on the moon; 3: Japan bombs Pearl Harbor). But while the list makes room for the Beatles' tour of the United States (58) and Babe Ruth's sixtieth home run (89), the entire African continent gets just one mention: the end of Apartheid (49). Nowhere else on the list do we see anything about the end of colonialism and the rise of independence on that continent. Latin America fared only a bit better than Africa: the Newseum's list noted the Cuban missile crisis (35) and the construction of the Panama Canal (81), two stories that were arguably as much about the United States as about its southern neighbors. Nothing south of the canal was mentioned. (South America must have had a dull century.) From the perspective of American news organizations, it still sometimes appears as if "nothing ever happens in Chile."

The inherent blind spots and prejudices of journalism, along with the often unrecognized blind spots and prejudices of its practitioners, are themselves, in many instances, the "message," the factor that changes our view of the political world. We have to battle, the point is, against the bewitchment of our politics by means of journalism.

This is much more than an academic exercise. When misrepresentations in the news affect "things" that "concern" certain groups "dearly," these groups often suffer dearly. We now turn, by way of example, to a closer consideration of the sufferings of one such group at the hands of American journalism.

African Americans in the Mirror

African Americans would have created their own newspapers even if the mainstream press had been more responsive to them. Their press has had no shortage of justifications for its existence: Until segregation ended in the 1960s, the African American press catered to autonomous and often vibrant African American enclaves, profited from advertisement by African American businesses, and addressed issues relating to the African American community with a depth that even the most responsive mainstream publications could not match. Still, it is fair to say that behind most successful African American publications is a failure by the mainstream press.

At the time of the publication of *Freedom's Journal* in 1827, the need to "plead"—already so intense because of slavery and discrimination—may have been made even more pressing: both political parties were trying to limit the potential competition offered by black labor and offering policies that would send ("repatriate") free blacks abroad, mainly to Africa and the Caribbean. Because mainstream American newspapers—emphasizing commentary more than reportage—were essentially mouthpieces for political parties, the failure of either national party to protect free blacks and call for abolition meant that that perspective was shut out of Hallin's Sphere of Legitimate Controversy. Given this omission, it is not surprising that one of the nineteenth century's most outspoken critics of slavery, William Lloyd Garrison, a white man, would also feel called upon to start his own newspaper, the *Liberator* a few years later, in 1831.

Garrison, like Russwurm and Cornish, demanded inclusion in the debate. "Urge me not to use moderation in a cause like the present. I am in earnest—I will not equivocate—I will not retreat a single inch—AND I WILL BE HEARD," he wrote in an editorial in the paper's first issue. Although edited by a white man, the *Liberator* was, for most of its existence, the leading showcase of black writers, speakers, and correspondents. And the *Liberator's* subscribers were mainly free blacks.

Even after larger audiences and more efficient advertising policies made it possible for the press to prosper independent of political parties, the rights of African Americans were still only rarely discussed in the mainstream press. In 1846, when African Americans and their supporters tried to overturn discriminatory voting requirements in the New York Constitution, almost every local newspaper was against the change.

The *New York Sun,* which had a wonderfully inclusive motto, "It shines for all," apparently did not consider blacks to be worthy of its rays. When a black man, William Hodges, sent a letter to the editor, the *Sun* published it as an advertisement and charged the man fifteen dollars. The editor explained, "The *Sun* shines for all white men, and not for colored men."[11]

Within a year, Hodges founded a newspaper, the *Ram's Horn;* Frederick Douglass, an ex-slave who was lecturing against slavery, became its editor; later Douglass would found his own newspaper, the *North Star.* Douglass's opening editorials in the *North Star* asserted his desire to force his way into the Sphere of Legitimate Controversy: "The truth must be told. . . . I will not be silent."[12]

That many blacks felt that their causes were not addressed in the antebellum era is not surprising when we remember that blacks were not even considered to have the protections of the United States Constitution as late as 1857. That was the year the Supreme Court decided the *Dred Scott* case, codifying the idea that blacks, whether slaves or free, were not citizens. Although the mainstream press was increasingly nonpartisan and independent during the 1840s and 1850s, it showed its habitual reluctance to expand the mirror; it rarely (Horace Greeley of the *New York Tribune* and a few others being exceptions) broke new ground on racial issues.[13]

Aside from the abolitionist press, which generally warmed to the notion of black citizenship beginning in the 1830s, the mainstream press was aggressively excluding African American points of view or distorting African American lives, or both. In news copy and illustrations, blacks were depicted in gross caricatures, even in newspapers and magazines that tended to be progressive, such as *Harper's Weekly*, in which a black mother tells her son, "Now den Julius! If yer ain't a good litte nigger, mudder'l call de big ole Bobolitionist and let um run away wid yer."[14] This flagrant and exaggerated stereotype (combined with a swipe at abolitionists) appeared in 1860, nearly a year before the start of the Civil War.

While misrepresentations would persist throughout the nineteenth century (and, indeed, the twentieth century), the mainstream image of blacks did begin to evolve and improve during the course of the Civil War. Frederick Douglass had predicted that as soon as blacks became soldiers and wore the U.S. emblem on their uniforms, their basic right to citizenship would be irrevocably decided. Indeed, Northerners (and the Northern mainstream press) did begin to change their perceptions of blacks when they became soldiers.

This can be seen in a perusal of Northern papers during the Civil War. In illustrations from *Harper's Weekly,* for example, African Americans were now presented less as caricatures and more as humans, humans who deserve rights. In one, two soldiers, white and black, stand symmetrically in a pose of wounded-but-proud brotherhood. In another, a black soldier, third in line with other African Americans, is waiting to exercise his right to vote.[15] These two cartoons—which appeared between the proposal of the Thirteenth Amendment, barring slavery (1865) and the passage of Fourteenth Amendment granting blacks full citizenship (1868)—both reflected and may have helped to transform the political realities of the day. This new sensibility came late, nearly forty years after Russwurm and Cornish pled their own cause, but it helped to make African American citizenship, at least in the North, a legal and conceptual verity.

After Reconstruction, and its failure in 1876, a period of intense instability swept across the South. Whites lynched blacks in record numbers; from 1889 to 1901, more than one hundred people were lynched every year in the southern states, the vast majority being African American men. In the 1890s Americans widely believed the myth that African Americans were lynched in the South because they raped white women. As the *New York Times* declaimed on August 2, 1894, "The crime [rape] for which negroes have frequently been lynched, and occasionally been put to death with frightful tortures, is a crime to which negroes are particularly prone." Ida B. Wells, a journalist working for the *Memphis Free Speech,* an African American paper, railed against lynching, exposed the myths about black "lawlessness," and was run out of town. It was a classic battle between a minority journalist and those who would keep the minority voice out of the Sphere of Legitimate Controversy. The extent to which that sphere was closed to Wells and the handful of other antilynching advocates around the country is apparent when we consider that even Frederick Douglass, by now the elder statesman of the black-rights movement, believed the myths about black rape; he told Wells that until he read her evidence to the contrary, he too was troubled by "lasciviousness on the part of Negroes."[16]

Wells moved to the North. With the aid of northern African American organizations, she presented clear evidence that (1) despite the *belief* that most lynchings were a response to African Americans raping whites, the fact was that rape was not even the stated cause in most cases; (2) African American victims were often charged with rape only *after* the lynchings became public; and (3) charges of "rape" were often made in cases involving an African American man and a white woman "caught" in a consensual relationship. These facts took more than a decade to overwhelm even the stereotypical views about lynching and rape held by progressives and more than two decades to find their way into the mainstream press.

Other stereotypes about African Americans, of course, have lingered much longer. Some have been furthered by the funhouse-mirror tendency of the press to exaggerate the incidence of crime. The same tendency that Charles Dickens exploited in an attempt to prove the depravity of slave society contributed, throughout the twentieth century, to an exaggeration of the percentage of African Americans who commit crimes. Too often African American criminals were the only identifiable African Americans on television news or in the newspaper. And African American victims of crime were regularly slighted.

Racism—in the form of the fears and prejudices of journalists and their sources—certainly contributed here. The historian Robert Darnton, who has analyzed some of his experiences during an earlier career as a journalist, remembers, as a cub reporter for the *Newark Star Ledger* in 1959, coming upon an especially engaging police report, which would have made great copy. When Darnton showed the "squeal sheet" to a policeman, the officer pointed to the

"B" designating the race of the victim. "Can't you see that's a black, kid?" asked the disgusted officer. "That's no story."[17]

Just as the Negro League waned after Jackie Robinson broke the color line in major league baseball, the African American press has waned as the sometimes more subtle color lines in the mainstream press have been broken—by desegregation; by the civil rights movement; after the report of the Kerner Commission, which investigated the causes of the urban riots of the late 1960s and pinned some of the blame on unrepresentative newsrooms; by affirmative action.[18] The film *All the President's Men,* about the Watergate investigation at the *Washington Post* in the early 1970s, depicts a world in which a group of white male editors decide what goes into a newspaper in a city with an African American majority. That world is no more. And yet, while the situation has certainly improved, problems—exclusions and distortions in news coverage of African Americans—certainly remain.

Don Heider, a former television journalist, recalls in his book *White News: Why Local News Programs Don't Cover People of Color,* his own days in a newsroom in the1980s: "I knew that journalists didn't generally sit around the table and say: 'how do we exclude — (insert Blacks, Latinos, Asians, or Native Americans) today?' Yet if you watched our 5 P.M. show, it was as if that's *exactly* what we had done."[19] Minorities, writes Heider, were systematically shut out of the news mix. Disturbed by these recollections, Heider went back into newsrooms in the late 1990s and found that the practice persists.

There are other fairly recent examples of the persistence of what appears to be a racial double standard in American journalism. In August 1986, a white teenager, Jennifer Levin, was murdered in New York City's Central Park. In the week following her death, the *New York Times* ran four front-page stories about what the tabloids were calling the "preppy murder." During the same night Levin was killed, a young woman was found dead, half naked, on a Harlem rooftop; the Harlem "DOA" was practically ignored by the media. Why was the white woman covered and the black woman ignored? In 2003 two female U.S. soldiers, both working in the same unit in Iraq, were injured and held prisoner in Iraq. Shoshanna Johnson was black and Jessica Lynch was white. Why was it that only the white woman became the subject of magazine cover stories and major newspaper articles, as well as a made-for-TV movie?

Of course, the news media's distortions and exclusions hardly affect only African Americans—the example, a crucial example, we have been using here. Consider, for another example, coverage of the AIDS epidemic of the 1980s. In the early years of the epidemic, the mainstream media viewed the disease as affecting mainly gays and drug users—two rather unpopular groups at the time. Groups advocating more spending on AIDS research spent a considerable amount of time lobbying the *New York Times* and other news organizations for greater coverage. But the devastation wrought by this then-fatal disease wasn't much reflected on the news media's mirror until a well-known actor, Rock Hudson, contracted AIDS.[20] And it took much more time, and much more advocacy, for worldwide AIDS to get significant coverage. It was only in the first years of the twenty-first century that magazines such as *Newsweek* put the AIDS crisis in Africa (by far the worst-hit continent) on their covers.

Responding to Distortions and Exclusions

The examples used here of flawed press coverage are, alas, mostly the easy examples. We have grown more alert, most of us, to the treatment of African Americans. We are growing more sensitive to gays and AIDS (if not to drug users or Africa). We have the benefit of decades or at least years of hindsight in spotting these limitations in news coverage. It is, of course, much harder to sense the newer swirls and currents—racial, sexual, economic, cultural, political, journalistic—that undoubtedly cloud and disturb news coverage today.

Good journalists and good news organizations have and must struggle to locate and reduce such distortions and exclusions. They have and must find more reliable and precise ways of examining society, locating trends, and evaluating policies. They have and must search wider, look longer. They have and must struggle to expand the range of groups and opinions to which attention is paid in their reports.

It is also crucial that their readers or viewers grow more alert to potential distortions and exclusions; for, even if journalists become more conscientious, such lacunae will never be entirely eliminated. We have to remember that no form of representation, certainly not journalism, is clear, comprehensive, and unbiased. We have to remember that journalism, to the extent that it can even be called a mirror, is a mirror of limited size, a distorting mirror—turned and swiveled, often erratically, by fallible, subjective individuals. Democracy requires not only a continual struggle to improve journalism but a continual struggle to see beyond the limitations of journalism.

Certainly we can understand why some groups believe the public has been so "deceived by misrepresentations" that they have no choice but to start their own news organ, to "plead" their "own cause." We might benefit from more such efforts.

Notes

1. Charles Dickens, *American Notes and Pic-Nic Papers* (Philadelphia: T. B. Peterson & Brothers, 1842), 52, 96, 101.
2. Charles Dickens, *American Notes and Pic-Nic Papers,* 102–3.
3. Ludwig Wittgenstein, Remark 109, *Philosophical Investigations* (New York: Macmillan, 1964), 47.
4. Culler, *On Deconstruction,* 123; Stuart Hall, *Representation and the Media* (lecture on

video), produced and directed by Sut Jhally (Northampton, Mass.: Media Education Foundation, 1997).

5. Charles Dickens, *American Notes and Pic-Nic Papers,* 102–3.

6. For a discussion of some of the problems, see Theodore L. Glasser, "Journalism's Glassy Essence," *Journalism and Mass Communication Quarterly* 73 (winter 1996): 784–86.

7. Lincoln Steffens, *The Autobiography of Lincoln Steffens* (New York: Harcourt, Brace, 1931).

8. Walter Lippman and Charles Merz, "A Test of the News," *New Republic,* August 4, 1920, reprinted in Tom Goldstein, ed., *Killing the Messenger: 100 Years of Media Criticism* (New York: Columbia University Press, 1989).

9. Hallin, *The "Uncensored War,"* 117.

10. See Stephens, *A History of News,* 119–31.

11. Carter R. Bryan, "Negro Journalism in America before Emancipation," *Journalism Monographs* (September 1969): 19.

12. McFeely, *Frederick Douglass,* 123.

13. See Mindich, *Just the Facts,* 40–63.

14. "At the South," *Harper's Weekly,* January 28, 1860, 64, http://blackhistory.harpweek.com/7Illustrations/!ListOfIllusLevelOne.htm.

15. "A Man Knows Best," *Harper's Weekly,* April 22, 1865, 265; "The First Vote," *Harper's Weekly,* November 16, 1867, 721, http://blackhistory.harpweek.com/7Illustrations/!ListOfIllusLevelOne.htm.

16. Ida B. Wells, *Crusade for Justice: The Autobiography of Ida B. Wells,* edited by Alfreda M. Duster (Chicago: University of Chicago Press, 1970), 72.

17. Robert Darnton, "Writing News and Telling Stories," *Daedalus* 104, no. 2 (spring 1975): 175–94.

18. For a thoughtful discussion of the successes and failures of efforts to integrate American newsrooms, see Newkirk, *Within the Veil.*

19. Heider, *White News.*

20. Randy Shilts, *And the Band Played On: Politics, People, and the AIDS Epidemic.* (New York: Penguin, 1988).

Bibliography

Culler, Jonathan. *On Deconstruction: Theory and Criticism after Structuralism.* Ithaca, N.Y.: Cornell University Press, 1982.

Hallin, Daniel C. *The "Uncensored War": The Media and Vietnam.* New York: Oxford University Press, 1986.

Heider, Don. *White News: Why Local News Programs Don't Cover People of Color.* Mahway, N.J.: Lawrence Erlbaum, 2000.

McFeely, William S. *Frederick Douglass.* New York: Norton, 1991, 123.

Mindich, David T. Z. *Just the Facts: How "Objectivity" Came to Define American Journalism.* New York: New York University Press, 1998.

Newkirk, Pamela. *Within the Veil: Black Journalists, White Media.* New York: New York University Press, 2000.

Stephens, Mitchell. *A History of News.* Fort Worth, Tex.: Harcourt Brace College, 1996.

23

THE LEGACY OF AUTONOMY IN AMERICAN JOURNALISM

Theodore L. Glasser and Marc Gunther

IN A SLIM BUT SIGNIFICANT BOOK CALLED *THE IRONY OF Free Speech*, Owen Fiss, a member of the Yale Law School faculty, works to unravel a paradox that usually escapes the American imagination, especially the imagination of American journalists: limiting autonomy can at times enrich and even expand freedom. Fiss's thesis, which he develops through a critique of recent Supreme Court cases, rests on the premise that freedom of expression, particularly freedom of the press, deserves constitutional protection not as an end in itself but as a means to a larger end, namely, the creation and preservation of the conditions for free and full participation in the very processes of "collective self-determination" that self-governance demands. The First Amendment, Fiss argues, exists to safeguard popular sovereignty, not individual self-expression; it serves as an instrument of democracy, not as a tool that individuals can use to promote themselves and their personal interests.

We begin where Fiss concludes: with the complicated and contradictory truth that "the state can be both an enemy and a friend of speech; that it can do terrible things to undermine democracy but some wonderful things to enhance it as well."[1]

We briefly develop this theme, following Fiss, as an opportunity to introduce the important role that individual autonomy plays in the principles and practices of the press in the United States, which, framed as a discussion of competing views of press freedom, lays the foundation for an examination of three areas where, in our judgment, the legacy of autonomy in American journalism invites scrutiny: when autonomy trumps accountability; when autonomy *in* the newsroom threatens autonomy *for* the newsroom; and when autonomy, under the guise of competition, undermines the independence of judgment that good journalism demands. In each of these areas we want to look at conventional views of autonomy by focusing on the unquestioned newsroom assumptions about what autonomy means and how it works. Our goal is not to challenge the importance of autonomy in journalism, however, but to call attention to an aspect of autonomy that journalists too often ignore: the tension between its ascription and its achievement.

Fiss and others make a point of distinguishing between ascribing autonomy and achieving it, between preserving what presumably already exists and attaining what arguably could exist. Most accounts of American democracy, especially ones tied to Enlightenment ideals, ascribe autonomy by viewing it as what "normally" or "naturally" exists in the absence of conditions, usually associated with an overbearing state, that diminish or prevent it. Robert Post, for example, views autonomy this way when he observes that citizenship "presupposes the attribution of freedom," that the "ascription of autonomy is . . . the transcendental precondition for the possibility of democratic self-determination."[2] But other accounts of democracy, like Fiss's, regard autonomy as a positive accomplishment that often requires conditions only the state can create and sustain. Thus Cass Sunstein, with Fiss, rejects the notion of autonomy as a *pre*condition of citizenship; he argues instead that citizens remain "unfree and nonautonomous" until they overcome circumstances, well beyond a coercive state, that in any way impair or inhibit the judgments individuals make: "autonomy should refer . . . to decisions reached with a full and vivid awareness of available opportunities, with reference to all relevant information, and without illegitimate or excessive constraints on the process of preference formation."[3]

By questioning the ascription of autonomy, Fiss and others cast doubt on the well-worn dichotomy between a laissez-faire state that lets individuals act on their own and a state that provides some collective assistance for the actions individuals want to take. Of course, Sunstein writes, through private-property rights and other means, any "democratic state should attempt to give citizens a sense of independence from the state itself."[4] But, significantly, this sense of independence—this freedom *from* the state—seldom secures the complementary freedom *to* participate in the life we live with others. Hannah Arendt puts it another way but makes much the same point when she cautions against confusing "being liberated" from something and "being free" to do something else: "Liberation may be a condition of freedom but by no means leads automatically to it."[5]

Contested Meaning of Freedom of the Press

With an acknowledging nod to Alexander Meiklejohn, an important First Amendment theorist who in the mid-twentieth century developed the basic framework for the proposition that the First Amendment protects speech but not speakers, Fiss distinguishes between "freedom of speech" and the "freedom to speak," arguing in effect that the Constitution protects the latter only as it contributes in some substantive way to the former. Put a little differently, Fiss makes a case for protecting the *content* of expression, even if that protection requires limits on *individual* expression. When Meiklejohn said, "What is essential is not that everyone shall speak, but that everything worth saying shall be said," he meant that the First Amendment, properly conceived, provides for "the common needs of all members of the body politic" and has, comparatively, "no concern" for the needs of individuals to express themselves.[6]

This provocative reading of the First Amendment rejects the standard libertarian view of freedom of expression, which regards individual autonomy as sacrosanct, and substitutes for it a rationale for free speech and a free press that honors what champions of the First Amendment seldom take seriously: the importance of the opportunity to benefit from open and genuinely public exchanges of ideas. To be sure, by shifting First Amendment jurisprudence away from what individuals want to say and toward what citizens need to hear, Fiss embraces an overtly political and an expressly democratic justification for constitutionally protected expression; the whole point of having freedom of speech and freedom of the press, he says, "is to broaden the terms of public discussion as a way of enabling common citizens to become aware of the issues before them and of the arguments on all sides and thus to pursue their ends fully and freely."[7]

As an advocate for what the Supreme Court justice William Brennan famously described as "uninhibited, robust, and wide-open" debate,[8] Fiss, logically, positions himself as a First Amendment absolutist; like Meiklejohn, he calls for unqualified protection for any and all forms of political expression. But, significantly, to secure this protection, to achieve this freedom, to affirm the vitality of the relationship between freedom of expression and democratic participation, Fiss asks precisely the question that absolutists typically shun: "Might the state have a role in furthering the democratic mission of the press?" And he answers his question with a celebration of one of the few Supreme Court decisions to uphold one of the state's occasional efforts, as Fiss summarizes the essence of the *Red Lion* case, "to limit autonomy in the name of freedom."[9]

In 1969 in *Red Lion Broadcasting Co. v. FCC*, the Supreme Court upheld the constitutionality of a federal policy, the Federal Communications Commission's fairness doctrine, which required radio and television stations to treat controversial issues in a fair and balanced manner and to provide individuals with an opportunity to respond when someone in a broadcast personally attacks them or when a station editorializes against them. Basically, the court found that broadcasters do not enjoy unlimited discretion in the programming choices they make; that the state has a legitimate interest in assuring that radio and television operators provide a certain quality of public debate and discussion; that the fairness doctrine enhances rather than abridges freedom of expression; and that, in short, the right to hear trumps the right to be heard. Specifically, the Court made note of the "ends and purposes of the First Amendment," which in the case of broadcasting include the "right of the public to receive suitable access to social, political, esthetic, moral and other ideas and experiences,"[10] and found the fairness doctrine to be consistent with them. In light of the absence of a constitutional right to receive a broadcast license, and given the history of constitutionally permissible obligations that Congress and the FCC have imposed on individuals who benefit from the privilege of broadcasting, the Court saw no First Amendment barrier to regulations that protect the public's interest in the uses to which its own airwaves are put. In the sentence most frequently quoted from *Red Lion*—a sentence that caused considerable consternation among journalists of all kinds, print and broadcast alike—the Court endorsed a hierarchy of First Amendment values that assigned in stark terms a higher priority to consumers of communication than producers of communication: "It is the right of the viewers and listeners, not the right of the broadcasters, which is paramount."[11]

Print journalists, at least, had little to worry about, as the Court made clear a few years later, in 1974, when it confronted a roughly analogous set of circumstances in the form of a Florida right-of-reply law that required Florida's newspapers to provide political candidates with free and equal space to respond to published attacks on their record or character. In *Miami Herald Publishing Co. v. Tornillo*, the Court dismissed Florida's claims for an enforceable right of access to newspapers; it ruled that the First Amendment does not allow the state to implicate itself in the "exercise of editorial control and judgment."[12] As praiseworthy as it might be for the press to commit itself to what Justice Byron White described in his concurring opinion as "full and fair debate on important public issues,"[13] the Court concluded that "press responsibility is not mandated by the Constitution."[14] While acknowledging the deteriorating marketplace for newspapers—less competition, fewer newspapers, and "almost impossible" barriers to entry—the Court nonetheless rejected the very contention it had earlier found so compelling: that the "government has an obligation to ensure that a wide variety of views reach the public."[15] That there exists in any given market a greater scarcity of newspapers than radio or television stations made no apparent difference to the Court, which declined an invitation to protect the audience for newspapers in ways it protected the audience for radio and television—and did so, remarkably, without a single reference to *Red Lion*. Whatever "access rights" might be appropriate for newspapers and other print media, a question *Tornillo* left unanswered,[16] the Court clearly accepted a division, though not a very well articulated one, between the rights of readers and the rights of viewers and listeners.

The differences between *Red Lion* and *Tornillo* sparked considerable debate among legal scholars and others, but not among journalists, who as a rule viewed *Red Lion* as a dangerous departure from conventional readings of the First Amendment and *Tornillo* as vindication of the importance of their independence and autonomy. Unsurprisingly, no one in the journalism establishment viewed *Tornillo* as an opportunity to extend the First Amendment to readers as *Red Lion* had extended it to viewers and listeners. In fact, fearing passage of similar right-of-reply laws in other states, the press stood united behind the *Miami Herald* in its rejection of a statutory right of access to the pages of a newspaper; "a dozen major news organizations," *Newsweek* reported at the time, "filed friend-of-the-court briefs arguing that the government has no place in the nation's newsrooms."[17] But probably no one in the press went quite as far as the *Washington Post*, which editorialized in support of *Tornillo* by arguing, basically, that the First Amendment was so important and so special that the state should step aside and let others enforce it: Officials of the press, not officials of the state, "must guarantee the people's First Amendment right by seeing to it as best they can that all sides of public issues are heard and make certain that public officials who are attacked have the opportunity to tell their side."[18] The *Post* editorial made no mention of what would happen to "the people's First Amendment right" if, as *Tornillo* permits, the press decides to ignore it.

Triumph of Autonomy over Accountability

Journalism's response to *Red Lion* and especially *Tornillo* underscores a view of press freedom that places a premium on individual and institutional autonomy, a reading of the First Amendment that defines the integrity of the press principally, though not exclusively, in terms of journalists' willingness to wage—and their ability to finally succeed in—battles against the state. Freedom of the press means freedom from the state, a form of independence built on a distrust of—indeed, a disdain for—any role governments might play in structuring or facilitating a community's commitment to public communication. More so in the United States than elsewhere, and probably more so today than ever before, journalists measure themselves and their independence against the Kantian ideal of wholly autonomous agents whose legitimacy and authority require complete isolation—or at least effective insulation—from any pressure or influence that might compromise the presumably "pure" judgments they can and should make.

The reigning "model of journalistic autonomy," as Lee Bollinger, the president of Columbia University and a widely known First Amendment scholar, characterizes the conception of journalism that both contributes to and benefits from "the central image of the American ideal of press freedom," confers on journalists an unfettered "freedom to make mistakes" and an unconditional "power to err"; it promotes "a posture toward the world that says, in effect, no one will tell you what to do."[19] From this perspective, the First Amendment serves not only as a shield journalists can use to deflect meddlesome agents of the state but as a rhetorical device that journalists can deploy to ward off critics who pose no constitutional challenge to a free press. The First Amendment works this way as journalists conflate their rights, properly the domain of law, with what is right, properly the domain of ethics, as though the law somehow affirms the propriety of conduct not expressly proscribed by it. Through this amalgamation of law and ethics, journalists position themselves as adversaries of accountability in just the way James Carey describes: "To raise any ethical question with journalists is to invite the response that the First Amendment is being violated in even considering the issue."[20]

Whereas the *Tornillo* Court ruled that the state cannot mandate a responsible press, most journalists define *any* demand for accountability, especially when accountability implies liability, as a violation of the sanctity of the newsroom. Even journalists who stress the importance of the connection between news and democracy, between journalism and citizenship, prefer to diffuse the accountability issue by confining ethics and responsibility to questions that individual practitioners can answer for themselves and by themselves. Ethics and responsibility in this tradition require only a heavy dose of self-awareness, as Bill Kovach and Tom Rosenstiel, two former journalists who have devoted themselves to press reform, illustrate with the title, which fairly summarizes the content, of the concluding chapter of their influential account of the values of good journalism: "Journalists Have a Responsibility to Conscience."[21]

Journalists' self-image, buttressed by "the individualistic ethos that so dominates our popular and political culture," as Fiss describes the larger landscape in which journalism needs to be understood,[22] transforms autonomy into something more (or less) than an argument about the independence of the press: an attribute of a lifestyle. Journalists like to think of themselves as loners and skeptics whose detachment and disinterestedness—even their irreverence—enable them to practice their craft without the entanglements that they and others might view as real or potential conflicts of interest. Journalists today, like journalists before them, work hard to make good on a promise made by James Gordon Bennett, the legendary editor of the *New York Herald*, who in the 1830s claimed that his newspaper, sold for a penny and written for "the great masses of the community," would serve the "public interest" by disassociating itself from all other interests.[23] Free from the partisan interests of the party press, free from the commercial interests of the mercantile press, and free even from the interests of advertisers, who would not play a major role in the economics of journalism for at least another couple of decades, the new "penny press," arguably the beginning of the era of modern American journalism, presented itself as independent in much the same way journalists today present themselves as independent: untainted by special interests.

However routine and mundane their everyday work might be, journalists revel in certain styles and forms of journalism, to return to Bollinger's assessment of journalists' visceral attachment to autonomy, that "breathes life" into "a press conceived in the image of the artist . . . who lives (figuratively) outside of society, beyond normal conventions, and who is therefore better able to see and expose its shortcomings."[24] Historian Thomas Leonard paints a similar portrait of journalists who "often fancied themselves as bohemians: detached, mocking critics of respectable society." While acknowledging the difficulty of measuring the "wildness of this occupational group," Leonard concludes that the press stands alone in its displays of defiance: "There was no other profession whose most visible elite (Washington Gridiron Club) organized for the purpose of scoffing at authority. Surely no other budding profession celebrated Jack the Ripper (as reporters in Chicago did in their Whitechaple Club) or convened in 'the bucket of blood' (a lair for the Denver press cops)."[25]

In this romanticized view of journalism—popularized on television and in scores of movies, plays, and books—journalists assert their independence and autonomy by establishing, sometimes literally but usually metaphorically, certain boundaries for the profession. To vivify journalism's division of authority, which reminds everyone of their proper place in and around the newsroom, journalists build "walls"—walls between news and advertising, between the news pages and the opinion pages, between the business of journalism and the practice of journalism, between publishers and editors. And to establish the credibility of the day's news, journalists draw "lines"—lines between facts and opinions, between description and promotion, between analysis and advocacy, between news judgments and moral judgments, between a journalist's private beliefs and the public expression of them. Through the walls they build and lines they draw, journalists accentuate forms of control that place power precisely where journalists want it: at the level of the individual journalist.

But the strongest of walls and the boldest of lines bring journalists no closer to the levels of control where forces beyond the newsroom and even beyond journalism define the limits of journalistic autonomy. On the contrary, by focusing their attention on crumbling walls and blurring lines, journalists distract themselves from a diffusion of power that forestalls their participation in many of the more important decisions that shape the future of American journalism. Paradoxically, the boundaries designed to secure autonomy *in* journalism work just as effectively to undermine autonomy *for* journalism.

Power and Control in American Journalism

The distinction between "operational" and "allocative" control[26] helps explain the resistance journalists face as they seek to influence or change the conditions under which they work. In terms of the day-to-day operation of the newsroom, journalists retain a remarkable degree of control and autonomy; they and they alone decide how to write their stories, which sources to contact, what quotes to use, and so on. But power at this level differs in kind, and pales in comparison to, the power associated with the allocative decisions that determine basic policies, long-term goals, and the general disposition of resources. Journalists usually find themselves excluded—or they exclude themselves through the walls they build and the lines they draw—from decisions about, say, the allocation of corporate funds, the deployment of personnel, strategies for growth or containment, and a host of matters concerning corporate "synergies" and other economies-of-scale issues. Journalists seldom participate in the hiring of key newsroom mangers, who in turn establish, usually unilaterally, standards of quality and other newsroom norms. Journalists lead newsroom meetings that make obviously important choices about the composition of the next newspaper or newscast, but they seldom sit on corporate boards where they might influence "colleagues" whose interests extend far beyond—and at times run counter to—the welfare, as rank-and-file editors and reporters might define it, of any particular newsroom.

The segregation of journalists from many of the centers of power in journalism points to one of the unintended consequences of the press's preoccupation with individualism and individual autonomy: the lack of a tradition of organized, collective action on behalf of the interests of the working journalist. Although all professions experience some tension between preserving the autonomy of the individual practitioner and cultivating associations that advance the collective interests of the profession, journalism faces a particular dilemma: How to gain the authority to organize itself? Other professions normally acquire this authority through their relationship with the state, which creates a bureaucratic infrastructure that includes the formal recognition of a hierarchy of professional associations, but journalists do not view this as an option insofar as they prefer to steer clear of any relationship with the state. Unlike physicians and lawyers but similar in some ways to clergy, journalists view what they do as more of a right than a privilege; they therefore loathe any role the state might play in promulgating a definition of journalism that would inevitably exclude some, perhaps many, from their ranks.

In the absence of any authority or oversight from the state, journalism endures a hodgepodge of professional associations that attract very few members and exist in no discernible relation to each other. The percentage of journalists with membership in professional journalism organizations dropped significantly between 1971 and 1992, even as the number of organizations increased, up from thirty-five in 1982 to fifty-five in 1992. Fewer than 7 percent of practicing journalists belong to the largest of these groups, the Society of Professional Journalists; a much smaller percentage belong to niche groups like the Religion Newswriters Association or the Society for Newspaper Design.[27] While the leaders of these groups get together occasionally under the auspices of the Council of National Journalism Organizations to exchange ideas and information, they do not take up such substantive questions as whether, as one study recently concluded, the "splintering rolls of the major national groups" and the steady decline in membership across all groups "almost certainly signaled the erosion of an already weak institutional fabric."[28]

The benefits of a variety of groups serving a single profession presuppose a formal hierarchy among them. No stably organized profession, as studies of the sociology of the professions remind us, can exist with competing or equally credible professional associations. It always needs to be clear, to take the example of medicine, who credentials physicians and who, in turn, credentials specialists among physicians; it needs to be clear, too, which credentials come first.[29] Journalism, however, not only rejects the very premise of credentialing, except when access to events requires it, but shows no interest in coordinating the roles and responsibilities of its various professional associations for the purpose of bringing some order and logic to the organization of the profession writ large. Thus disconnected from each other and from the vast majority of working journalists, these groups remain mostly small, weak, and inconsequential.

What further weakens these groups are their failure to confront the widening gap between the autonomy journalists enjoy and the power and control journalists need to make genuinely independent judgments about how to best define and present the day's news. In other words, with or without a mandate from the state or from the profession itself, journalism organizations marginalize themselves to the extent that they ignore the larger and arguably more important issues in journalism and focus instead, as they often do, on uncontested standards of professionalism and the most egregious violations of them. Their codes of ethics, to take one handy marker, provide little guidance or inspiration for the growing cohort of journalists that views the problems of journalism, as a number of recent studies and commentaries suggest, as having less to do with individual misconduct and more to do with a division of labor that fails to place journalists in control of journalism. If most codes in most professions belabor the obvious by articulating "what most professionals do by habit and personal conviction,"[30] belaboring the obvious in journalism means conserving a status quo that already leaves many journalists feeling disenfranchised and disheartened. In comparison to most professions, journalists leave their profession sooner and at an earlier age.[31]

Indeed, codes of ethics in journalism, as compelling as they may be as evidence of journalists' commitment to honesty and integrity, do not—and probably cannot—address the most insidious manifestation of the influence of allocative decisions on operational autonomy: self-censorship. Given the nature of self-censorship, and the consequences of acknowledging it, little literature exists that documents in any systematic way instances of it. But a recent survey of journalists by *Columbia Journalism Review* and the Pew Research Center for the People and the Press concluded, without citing examples, that self-censorship "is commonplace in the news media today."[32] When asked about avoiding stories that could damage the news organization or parent company, only 25 percent of the respondents reported that it never happens or that they are unaware that it happens; 29 percent reported that it happens "sometimes" and 40 percent said that it happens but only rarely. A similar distribution of responses came in response to a question about avoiding stories that could adversely affect advertisers.

Competition and the Conditions for Independent Journalism

Self-censorship in the service of owners and advertisers illustrates the quandary journalists find themselves in when they face private rather than public sources of coercion. Because most American journalists, like most Americans, equate a free press with free enterprise, it is almost unimaginable to think in terms of alternatives to privately owned and privately controlled newsrooms. Public broadcasting exists, but barely; the logic of a system of publicly subsidized journalism enjoys about as much cultural and political currency as the Supreme Court's decision in Red Lion, which has been fairly termed "illiberal" and "contrary to the nation's traditions."[33] When the nation's top editors, publishers, news producers, and media executives gather to discuss the future of the quality and independence of journalism, as they did in August 2000 at the invitation of the Aspen Institute, no one takes seriously the proposition that a truly free press ought to be as free from the interests of the marketplace as it is free from the demands of the state; no one considers privately organized alternatives to private enterprise, like the system of subvention cable operators used in the 1970s when they created C-SPAN; and no one looks outside the United States, where many forms of "illiberal" journalism prosper, for ideas and inspiration.[34] Instead, journalism's leaders resign themselves to the "realities" of what they readily recognize as a deteriorating climate for good journalism; they regard the "changes roiling the journalism business" as "inexorable" and "inescapable," an "evolving business environment" to which they can at best "*adapt*." As Richard Smith, chairman and editor in chief of *Newsweek*, put it, "We can't shout back the tide of business change."[35]

Journalists will now and then call on the state to curb abuses of the marketplace (e.g., predatory pricing) or to correct its flaws (e.g., the Newspaper Preservation Act), but in newsrooms and boardrooms alike there remains an unquestioned, though usually unstated, faith in the value and values of market-driven journalism—and, to return to Fiss's view of the problem, a "marked hostility toward the state and a refusal to acknowledge the role the state can play in fostering freedom of speech."[36] Even prominent and persistent critics of the escalating concentration of control in American journalism, like Ben Bagdikian, take for granted the prevailing economic order and define independent journalism accordingly. Reminiscent of the "big is bad" theme of the Progressive Era of the early 1900s, Bagdikian's plans to "undo excess," from a tax on advertising to a cap on the number of newspapers any one company can own, leave intact the basic structure of the U. S. press: "The threat does not lie in the commercial operation of the mass media," Bagdikian concludes. "It is the best method there is and, with all its faults, it is not inherently bad."[37]

Of course, leaving intact the basic structure of the American press does not turn American journalists into lap dogs of capitalism or slaves to the bottom line. Most newsrooms tolerate, and the better ones encourage, the kind of watchdog journalism that invariably conflicts with, even challenges, the property interests of owners, advertisers, and others (see Bennett and Serrin in this volume). Journalists regularly make judgments about what the community "needs," even at the expense of what demographically attractive individuals in the community might "want" (see Meyer and Marvin in this volume). And more than a few news organizations invest enormous resources in projects that no one really wants or needs but which must be published or broadcast in order to gain the attention of policy makers and political leaders.[38] These are but some of the contradictions that characterize the role of the mainstream press in the United States, a role that in certain instances openly disregards what it discreetly upholds.

To be precise, these are the characteristics of the widely discussed but not easily understood "hegemonic" role of the press, a role that positions the press not as a political institution that provides news and information but as a cultural institution that contributes to the "maintenance of consent" for the existing "system of power" in society;[39] a role that exhibits itself not through a CEO's memoranda, a publisher's editorials, an editor's policies, or other forms of rigid or overt control but through a quiet acceptance of the unexamined assumptions that make up "common sense"; and a role that depends on journalism's credibility and authority—as well as journalists' self-esteem—and that depends, therefore, on evidence of support for the widely shared value of a free and autonomous press. Hegemony works, then, not as it bludgeons anyone into ideological submission but as it subtly sustains—legitimizes—the prevailing norms of power and control. Even the most aggressive reporting will conserve, not challenge, the status quo to the extent that journalists uncritically accept the existing political and economic order and focus their attention on abuses or violations of it.[40]

Among the norms of power and control that pervade American culture, few capture the spirit of individualism and individual autonomy as well as the ideal of *competition*. From economics to politics, in science and in the arts, competition is taken to be self-evidently good. Its virtues are legion: Competition combats conformity; through it, individuals assert their individuality. Being competitive means doing well; it provides a benchmark for success. Understood as a process, competition enables individuals to improve over time; it refines and polishes their performance. As an antidote for lethargy or complacency, competition motivates people; win or lose, succeed or fail, it gets them to do their best work. It comes as no surprise that Herbert Gans found that in the several major newsrooms he studied, "competitive considerations function largely as a form of quality control."[41]

Business motives alone do not explain the drive to compete. Journalists cherish *individual* competition, which may or may not translate into higher profits; they enjoy the camaraderie that comes from being competitive, a sense of "community in competition," as one study has described the phenomenon.[42]

Quite aside from economic calculations and corporate incentives, this study of televison journalism suggests, journalists embrace an ethos of competition "which holds that it is right and inevitable to measure one's performance consistently against that of others." This ethos, firmly planted in the American "ethic of competitive individualism," helps journalists understand themselves and their place in the enterprise of journalism; it "is at the heart of the way in which journalist view their work."[43] The very idea of competition, especially at the level of the working journalist, commemorates individual initiative and reinforces the notion that journalists control their own work.

Journalists view competition in much the same way their managers view the marketplace: susceptible to individual abuse but fundamentally sound. While the practice of competition, the unindicted co-conspirator in any number of recent newsroom scandals, receives some criticism, its principle stands unscathed. Accepted on faith and transformed over time into a conception of journalism in which individuals rule themselves, the ideal of competition in journalism, like the ideal of competition elsewhere in society, conveys a reassuring image of individuals, not some bureaucracy, in control. But competition also conveys a cramped view of community. A community of competitors values conflict over cooperation, a community in which it is presumptively better for an individual to be pitted against others than to work in concert with them. The implication is that when individuals win or succeed, so does the community: what is good for journalists is ipso facto good for journalism.

Even in the absence of abuse and under the best of circumstances, competition promises more than it delivers. For example, competition promises choice but delivers little of it. Highly competitive newsrooms tend to produce similar, not dissimilar, accounts of the day's news; coverage differs in usually the most banal ways: The greater the competition, the greater the incentives for homogeneity. Viewers of local television news know this better than anyone: In markets where newscasts compete for the same audience at the same time of the day or evening, the choice of consequence is typically between the personality and appearance of teams of news anchors, which literally reduces choice to the mere appearance of differences. The genuinely different newscast, the one that covers the community differently and offers viewers a substantive choice, is most likely to come from the station that decided not to compete, the station that, say, airs its newscast at ten when all of the other stations air theirs at eleven.

Neither bizarre nor cynical, this view of the relationship between competition and choice comes from any standard economics text and corresponds to the everyday meaning of these terms. A sports afficionado regards athletes or teams as competitive, for instance, only when they are of roughly similar quality; a fan might prefer one athlete or team over another, but not because they are qualitatively different. Choice of this kind implies variety, not diversity; it means a range of essentially fungible "products" that appeal to individuals on the basis of purely personal and idiosyncratic preferences. Markets generally respond to the most profitable aggregation of these preferences, which accounts for the claim, to which even the most ardent laissez-faire economists accede, that market forces discriminate against minority tastes and interests.[44] Diversity of content exists in journalism in spite of, not because of, competition among news organizations.

The more a newsroom becomes preoccupied with market dynamics and consumer preferences, the more it risks focusing on content that attracts a large and lucrative audience but that leaves journalists unprepared to defend, except with reference to "the competition," the judgments they make. With this in mind, the newspaper publisher John Cowles once argued, in a 1951 essay with the remarkable title "Fewer Papers Mean Better Papers," that less competition, not more, might improve the quality of journalism by safeguarding a newsroom's independence of judgment:

> those newspapers that are not in hotly competitive fields are better able to resist the constant pressure to oversensationalize the news, to play up the cheap crime and sex story, to headline the story that will sell the most copies instead of another story that is actually far more important. The daily that is alone in its field can be as free as it wants to be from the urge to magnify the tawdry and salacious out of its importance in the news of the day. The newspaper that is alone in its field can present the news in better perspective and can free the news of details which pander rather than inform.[45]

Whether or not competition yields content that devolves into the "tawdry and salacious" details of the "cheap crime and sex story," it promotes a "scoop or shun" mentality that clouds journalists' judgments, diminishes their autonomy, and ultimately limits the public's freedom of choice. The pressure to be fast and first shifts the journalist's attention away from judgments about what the public needs or wants and toward a calculation of what the competition might do, an intramural contest of some significance to newsroom insiders but of little or no interest to most readers, viewers, and listeners. Shunning the competition is the other side of the same coin. Competition in this case results in a very peculiar form of self-censorship: a refusal to cover a story only because it appeared first in another publication. Daniel Okrent, the new "public editor" at the *New York Times*," recently complained about three stories "launched elsewhere" that the *Times* either "diminished or disregarded," stories that were, in his mind, of obvious importance and interest to readers:

"If the goal of newspapering is to inform readers and create a historical record, shouldn't editors be telling us about everything they think is important, no matter where they find it?"[46]

Notes

1. Fiss, *The Irony of Free Speech*, 83.
2. Robert Post, "Managing Deliberation: The Quandary of Democratic Dialogue," *Ethics* 103 (July 1993): 672
3. Sunstein, *Free Markets and Social Justice*, 19.
4. Ibid., 208.
5. Hannah Arendt, *On Revolution* (New York: Viking, 1963), 22.
6. Meiklejohn, *Political Freedom*, 26, 55.
7. Fiss, *The Irony of Free Speech*, 3.
8. *New York Times Co. v. Sullivan*, 376 U.S. 254, 270 (1964). See also William J. Brennan Jr., "The Supreme Court and the Meiklejohn Interpretation of the First Amendment," *Harvard Law Review* 79 (1965): 1–20.
9. Fiss, *The Irony of Free Speech*, 51, 69.
10. *Red Lion Broadcasting Co. v. FCC*, 395 U.S. 367 (1969); quoted in Douglas H. Ginsberg, *Regulation of Broadcasting: Law and Policy towards Radio, Television, and Cable Communications* (Saint Paul, Minn: West, 1979), 506–7.
11. Quoted in Ginsberg, *Regulation of Broadcasting*, 506.
12. *Miami Herald Publishing Co. v. Tornillo*, 418 U.S. 241 (1974); quoted in Ginsberg, *Regulation of Broadcasting*, 497.
13. Quoted in Ginsberg, *Regulation of Broadcasting*, 497.
14. Ibid., 496.
15. Ibid., 494.
16. For an early recognition of the likelihood that *Tornillo* does not stand for absolute First Amendment protection of newsroom autonomy, see Schmidt, *Freedom of the Press vs. Public Access*. For a useful comparison of *Red Lion* and *Tornillo*, see Friendly, *The Good Guys, the Bad Guys, and the First Amendment*.
17. *Newsweek*, July 8, 1974.
18. *Washington Post*, June 27, 1974.
19. Bollinger, *Images of a Free Press*, 57.
20. James W. Carey, "The Press and Public Discourse," *Center Magazine* (March–April 1987): 10.
21. Bill Kovach and Tom Rosenstiel, *The Elements of Journalism: What Newspeople Should Know and the Public Should Expect* (New York: Crown: 2001).
22. Fiss, *The Irony of Free Speech*, 3.
23. James Melvin Lee, *History of American Journalism*, rev. ed. (Boston: Houghton Mifflin, 1923), 95. See generally Michael Schudson, *Discovering the News: A Social History of American Newspapers* (New York: Basic Books, 1978).
24. Bollinger, *Images of a Free Press*, 55.
25. Leonard, *News for All*, 207.
26. The distinction is developed by Graham Murdock, "Large Corporations and the

Control of Communications Industries," in *Culture, Society, and the Media,* edited by Michael Gurevitch et al. (London and New York: Methune, 1982), 118–50.

27. David H. Weaver and G. Cleveland Wilhoit, *The American Journalist in the 1990s: U.S. News People at the End of an Era* (Mahwah, N.J.: Erlbaum, 1996), 129.

28. Weaver and Wilhoit, *The American Journalist in the 1990s,* 129.

29. See Magali Sarfatti Larson, *The Rise of Professionalism: A Sociological Analysis* (Berkeley: University of California Press, 1977), 70.

30. John Kultgen, "The Ideological Uses of Professional Codes," in *Ethical Issues in Professional Life,* edited by Joan C. Callahan (New York: Oxford University Press, 1988), 417.

31. Weaver and Wilhoit, *The American Journalist in the 1990s,* 115–18.

32. Andrew Kohut, "Self-Censorship: Counting the Ways," *Columbia Journalism Review,* (May/June 2000), 43

33. Ithiel de Sola Pool, *Technologies of Freedom* (Cambridge, Mass.: Belknap Press, 1983), 146.

34. For a report of the Fourth Annual Aspen Institute Conference on Journalism and Society, see David Bollier, "The Evolution of Journalism in a Changing Market Ecology," in *Old Values, New World: Harnessing Independent Journalism for the Future,* edited by Peter C. Goldmark Jr. (Washington, D.C.: Aspen Institute, 2001), 27–49.

35. Bollier, "The Evolution of Journalism in a Changing Market Ecology," 37.

36. Fiss, *The Irony of Free Speech,* 79.

37. Ben H. Bagdikian, *The Media Monopoly,* 6th ed. (Boston: Beacon, 2000), 223.

38. On this last point—the idea that news content might be aimed at a very small but influential audience but needs the appearance of wide dissemination—see David L. Protess et al., *The Journalism of Outrage: Investigative Reporting and Agenda Bulding in America* (New York: Guilford, 1991).

39. Daniel C. Hallin, *We Keep America on Top of the World: Television Journalism and the Public Sphere* (London: Routledge, 1994), 12, 75. At several points in his book Hallin offers brief but masterful accounts of what hegemony means and how it works.

40. For an illustration of how investigative reporting works this way, see James S. Ettema and Theodore L. Glasser, *Custodians of Conscience: Investigative Journalism and Public Virtue* (New York: Columbia University Press, 1998).

41. Gans, *Deciding What's News,* 50.

42. Matthew C. Ehrlich, "The Competitive Ethos in Television Newswork," *Critical Studies in Mass Communication* 12 (1995): 207.

43. Ehrlich, "The Competitive Ethos in Television Newswork," 207, 196.

44. See for example Bruce M. Owen, *Economics and Freedom of Expression: Media Structure and the First Amendment* (Cambridge, Mass.: Ballinger, 1975), 114.

45. John Cowles, "Fewer Newspapers Means Better Newspapers," in *Reporting the News: Selections from Nieman Reports,* edited by Louis M. Lyons, ed. (Cambridge, Mass.: Belknap Press, 1965), 162.

46 Daniel Okrent, "All the News That's Fit to Print? Or Just Our News?" *New York Times,* February 1, 2004, sec. 4, 2.

Bibliography

Baker, C. Edwin. *Media, Markets, and Democracy.* Cambridge, U.K., and New York: Cambridge University Press, 2002.

Barron, Jerome A. *Freedom of the Press for Whom?: The Right of Access to Mass Media.* Bloomington: Indiana University Press, 1973.

Bollinger, Lee C. *Images of a Free Press.* Chicago: University of Chicago Press, 1991.

Chafee, Zachariah, Jr. *Government and Mass Communications: A Report from the Commission on Freedom of the Press.* Vol. 2. Chicago: University of Chicago Press, 1947.

Fiss, Owen. *The Irony of Free Speech.* Cambridge, Mass.: Harvard University Press, 1996.

Friendly, Fred W. *The Good Guys, the Bad Guys, and the First Amendment: Free Speech vs. Fairness in Broadcasting.* New York: Random House, 1976.

Gans, Herbert J. *Deciding What's News: A Study of* CBS Evening News, NBC Nightly News, Newsweek *and* Time. New York: Pantheon, 1979.

Isaacs, Norman E. *Untended Gates: The Mismanaged Press.* New York: Columbia University Press, 1986.

Leonard, Thomas C. *News for All: America's Coming-of-Age with the Press.* New York: Oxford University Press, 1995.

Meiklejohn, Alexander. *Political Freedom: The Constitutional Powers of the People.* New York: Harper, 1960.

Schmidt, Benno C., Jr. *Freedom of the Press vs. Public Access.* New York: Prager, 1976.

Sunstein, Cass R. *Free Markets and Social Justice.* Oxford, U.K., and New York: Oxford University Press, 1997.

24

WHAT KIND OF JOURNALISM DOES THE PUBLIC NEED?

Carolyn Marvin and Philip Meyer

THE DISTINCTIVE SHAPE OF THE TWENTIETH-CENTURY press emerged from the high value of journalistic credibility to advertisers and audiences. Advertisers wanted a trustworthy platform for their messages, the public sought reliable information, and journalists needed a loyal audience and a faithful source of economic support.

In the twenty-first century, technology is threatening to break that connection. New ways of directing commercial messages to smaller and more specific audiences are undermining support for mass media that speak to the public as a whole. This development threatens to undermine journalism's moral foundation as well.

American journalism has been conceived as a spiritual vocation with the task of combating worldly evils that threaten the democratic spirit. "A newspaper is like a church," says author-journalist David Ignatius in one of his novels. "It is built by ordinary sinners, people who in their individual lives are often petty and corrupt, but who collectively create an institution that transcends themselves."[1]

The metaphor that takes secular journalism to spiritual heights appeals to Western moral sentiments. Hegel noted that the press provided a kind of daily morning prayer. And during the twentieth century, the standards of objectivity and detachment, the press version of divine truth, were as uncompromising as any religious doctrine, and defended with the same faith in their power to transform the world.

Like the clergy, journalists often work for low wages and respond to the same call to rise above the corruption of material concerns to minister to a congregation of believers seeking an authoritative narrative of truth and a vision of the common good.

The important threats to journalism have thus been material ones. They include technology, that most powerful expression of human pride, and commerce, which distracts mortal minds from higher things. Since technology and commerce were also the material foundations of the American nation, the battle for the American soul has been unending.

Two landmark expressions of concern for the spiritual welfare of journalism marked both halves of the twentieth century. They were *Public Opinion* by Walter Lippmann, and *A Free and Responsible Press* by the Commission on the Freedom of the Press (also known as the Hutchins Commission), both efforts to set the world right with the journalistic ideals of their respective postwar periods.[2] Writing in 1922 about media transformed by the telegraph, the telephone, and the high-speed rotary press, with the changes to be wrought by radio still only a glimmer, Lippmann worried about democracy adrift in a technologically expanding universe too much out of reach, out of sight, out of mind for citizens to comprehend.

The world was always too large for direct comprehension, of course. But in Lippmann's eyes new technologies of communication were dangerous agents of deceptive appearance. Technological pride without wisdom portrayed the world as transparent and manageable when it was treacherously complex. It thus presented a false picture of the world.

After a quarter of a century and another world war, the Hutchins Commission, on the brink of the introduction of television and sobered by the power of radio, weighed in on the commercial threat to journalistic integrity. The commission feared an increasingly monopolistic press, feeding on a commercially driven popular culture that tempted citizens to superficial pleasures at the expense of democratic responsibilities. Commercialism was a distraction from civic virtue.

Truth

In the twenty-first century commerce and technology continue to raise many of the same concerns in addition to some new ones. Technology is more powerful and seductive than ever. All sides acknowledge that the digital revolution has not only vastly enlarged the reach, volume, and speed of gathering and delivering information but has transformed the character of its presentation. With the addition of the Internet to broadcast media, printed books and periodicals, network and cable television, newsstands and libraries, some version of full access to the day's intelligence, the hope of the Hutchins Commission, has been achieved for most Americans.

One might expect that opening up technical capacity would deliver a more comprehensible reality. But as communications technology expands to capture the world, visions of journalistically mastering it recede. Just as printing destroyed the illusion of an authoritative biblical text and challenged a Catholic hierarchy, conflicting journalistic accounts cast doubt on the press's ability to present the world with authority.

In response to such uncertainties, Lippmann still hoped for a best-possible truth assembled by extrajournalistic wise men. Today popular opinion is morally ambivalent toward elites of any kind. Without public confidence in the moral authority of knowledge elites, there is less reason to hope that the public will trust the final truth to come from journalism.

The good news is that giving up on final truth still leaves intact some of the most serviceable traditions of Western rationalism and journalistic practice. Central to both is the principle that knowledge is always provisional and open to testing. What technology has shattered is not truth, which never existed in the form Lippmann and other guardians hoped for, but centuries of scaffolding designed to shore up an account of the world proposed and mostly ratified by elites.

The journalism that the public needs and deserves is trustworthy and aware of its own limitations. It strives to deploy the full available range of information-gathering and -validating techniques. This is because trustworthiness in journalism belongs not to a doctrine of salvation through grace but through works that are compatible with the best professional standards. In keeping with this goal, journalists must strive relentlessly to acquire new information-retrieving and interpreting skills, and must submit to a ruthless self-imposed transparency.

Wire and broadcast communication created the pressures of the twenty-four-hour news cycle. Now that digital communications put so many in touch so much of the time, journalists face a deadline every minute. These new challenges must be met without sacrificing those sturdy workhorses of professionalism—skepticism, multiple sourcing, firsthand investigation, and contextual explanation. But journalists must also acquire the skills to assemble and frame information with techniques that can meet more demanding standards of validity.

These include the use of statistical models to search for correlations and causal models that account for patterns and structures in the political and social worlds. An example is the way in which the *Miami Herald* reporter Stephen Doig correlated Hurricane Andrew's devastation of Miami homes with their year of construction, to provide evidence of time-related corruption in enforcement of the building code.[3] Good analytical journalism also requires subject-matter specialization. The media have been slow to recognize the value of grounding familiar journalistic skills in specialist intellectual training, including extrajournalistic certification. There are some isolated exceptions. Television weather reporters are often certified by the American Meteorological Society. Thomas Friedman, the Pulitzer Prize–winning columnist for the *New York Times,* holds an advanced degree in modern Middle East studies from Oxford University, while the *Times'* Supreme Court reporter Linda Greenhouse holds a master of studies in law from Yale Law School. (NPR's legal correspondent Nina Totenberg, on the other hand, is the exception that proves the rule, having dropped out of college and never attended either journalism or law school.) A number of print and broadcast medical reporters have medical degrees. Combining substantive knowledge with the ability to present and interpret facts in a compelling way points to the kind of journalism informed citizens need.

Still another aspect of trustworthiness is replicability. Journalists need to provide the transparency that permits colleagues and competitors to build on their investigative efforts and allows audiences to judge the quality of their conclusions. The journalism of *Time* magazine's Donald L. Barlett and James B. Steele, who follow paper trails and reveal their sources so that other investigators can check their results, is a good example. A trustworthy journalism must identify its sources, protecting them as a last rather than first resort so that information is accountable.

The journalism we need should not squander its credibility by fronting questionable sources nor failing in a timely way to disclose its biases, both editorial perspectives and economic interests that may arise from financial holdings, secondary employment, or involvement in political, civic, and other organizations. This accountability is an emergent aspect of professionalism, and calls for journalists to commit to forthright self-examination and public acknowledgment of mistakes. It takes courage and honesty worthy of the best journalistic traditions to submit one's own performance to the inspection of ombudsmen, public editors, professional societies, and other agents of internal and public criticism, to say how stories went wrong or how internal processes may have broken down.

A transparent journalism respects the public enough to take it behind the scenes and explain everything from how letters to the editor are selected to how stories are chosen for the front page. A welcome but still far too rare development has been the willingness of national media, including the *New York Times* and *USA Today*, to air the events by which errors come to be made, and to institute visible steps to minimize their reoccurrence

Sometimes the spotlight on journalistic procedures must shine from outside. The Minnesota News Council offers a model that stood alone for years before other venues started to experiment with it. Organizations of journalists have found it easier to write codes of ethics than to enforce them, even when enforcement consists solely of inviting public attention to the infractions. But there is some movement in this direction.

In 2000, the board of the Minnesota professional chapter of the Society of Professional Journalists (SPJ) publicly criticized a television reporter who obtained evidence of a crime by committing one himself, namely, removing an incriminating videotape from its owner's car. "Professional journalists cannot and will not condone these types of actions in pursuit of this story," the board said, citing four broad violations of the SPJ code.[4] More recently, the national board of the ten-thousand-member society invoked the code to denounce incidents of blending news and advertising by broadcasters, though it stopped short of naming the perpetrators.[5]

Public Good

Just as new technology calls into question the relationship of journalism to accuracy and truth, the new commercial developments it facilitates challenge traditional notions of journalism and the public good. By this we mean the tradition in which courageous resistance by the press to commercial pressures was long thought to confer special insight into the public good on journalists and special responsibility for offering it to their audiences. It must be said that this notion of the public good included a somewhat ambivalent regard for a public not always as politically attentive as elites might have hoped, and inclined to live out many of their hopes and dreams as consumers.

Looking back, for example, on the serious and thoughtful efforts of Lippmann and the Hutchins Commission, it is striking how blinkered and suspicious was their estimation of the public. Lippmann's view of the ordinary citizen was often just short of contemptuous. To assemble a picture of the circuit of public information in American society, the Hutchins Commission never directly consulted the readers and listeners whose interests it invoked, apparently concluding that ordinary citizens lacked the capacity to contribute significantly to that circuit. They believed that a democratic public needed to be coddled and shaped into fragile existence by journalists able to convey perspectives validated by cultural elites. Exhorting journalists to identify common goals and aspirations of the citizenry, these reformers were reluctant to legitimize many of the most popular expressions of these aspirations.

Americans are not generally opposed to a commercial press in principle. They respect its resources. An advertiser-supported journalism was morally justified by the belief that a financially independent journalism can best perform the most basic obligation of a free press: to help keep the government honest. In an era of big government, perhaps only big media have the sustained resources to challenge official malfeasance, or even to keep track of what government is doing. A market model of quasi-monopoly has been legitimized by owners who use social responsibility to gain trust and strengthen market position. But the business models being developed to exploit new communications technologies too rarely take the public interest into account.

So long as successful mass media were coveted by advertisers because they garnered the largest audiences, this monopolistic model made sense. But like today's cadres of independent specialized journalists, advertisers are finding that technology makes it cost-effective to send many more messages to smaller and smaller groups of people. Operating independently of traditional mass media, advertisers can use the Internet to precisely target ads to consumers most likely to buy, and strike quickly to make a sale when targeted consumers respond within seconds of exposure. The result threatens to undermine advertiser-supported media.

These new realities push journalism increasingly toward sources of noncommercial funding. National Public Radio offers one model for direct subscriber support. Information subsidies from government and charitable organizations are also filling some of the gap. The American Press Institute, the Poynter Institute, and the National Institute for Computer-Assisted Reporting are among the federally recognized nonprofits the newspaper industry relies on for midcareer training functions.

There are also examples of direct entry by nonprofits into the field of investigative journalism. Charles Lewis left broadcast journalism to found the Center for Public Integrity, which has won awards for its journalistic efforts. Having bankrolled much of the experimentation in civic journalism, the Pew Charitable Trusts has begun to subsidize traditional reporting through the Pew Center on the States, which generates stories and reference material for statehouse reporters.

Some journalists express reservations about taking information subsidies from foundations, fearing to open breaches through which interest groups might gain undue influence. A variety of arrangements between media outlets and commercial and noncommercial sources of support is thus likely to be most beneficial for citizen audiences.

As financial pressures on media threaten the quality of information the public receives, we must ask whether journalism can be a beacon for the public good. The answer must address our changed imagination of relations between cultural elites and citizens in the public arena. In a postmodern, multicultural country ever more aware of its religiously, ethnically, and sexually diverse communities, where democratic publics overlap but never completely coalesce, it may no longer be possible to speak comfortably of the presentation of a single unified set of goals for society.

In their response to an imagined public with no unifying value center, even the most professionally prestigious outlets have often been halting and uncertain. How the press might implement a more complex vision of the public and the public good is not always clear or practicable.

One result has been the development of a privilege gap, a vigorous but closed circuit of conversation between journalists and their elite sources from which the larger public is distanced, as striking a feature of modern journalism as the amplification of its volume, reach, and speed. This development raises challenging questions not only about journalists' distance from their audiences, but about their social and professional relationships to those they cover. Al Neuharth, who founded *USA Today* for "down-home" appeal, lamented years after his retirement that his paper was changing in ways favored more by those who live "east of the Potomac and east of the Hudson."[6]

If some celebrity journalists have become worrisomely interchangeable with the elites they cover, stakeholder elites and the public relations experts, lobbyists, and political consultants who serve them have become adept at journalistic techniques for manipulating public information to their advantage.

Attention

The privilege gap plays out in other ways. Lacking the resources and the disciplined culture of the best professional reporting, lower rungs of the information ladder ape elite style with a celebrity journalism that does not deliver much critical information and covers what is cheap and attractive. Flying in and out of hotspots for thirty seconds of smartly attired visuals is not conducive to a journalism of understanding. The veneer of false intimacy that is characteristic of such journalism ultimately reinforces the cultural and demographic remoteness of celebrity journalists from their audiences and those they cover.

Such developments reinforce the status quo from two different directions. Elite journalism becomes a remote narrative of clashes among the powerful rather than a larger story that faithfully integrates the lives and interests of nonelites. Failing to see themselves treated as participants, nonelites become willing to yawn without engaging as the elite parade passes by. The hope that the movement of minorities and women into elite status would close this gap has not been fulfilled, although it has created a more diverse elite.

A press that is not read is, of all presses, the most useless. A press may not be read if audiences believe the discussion does not concern them. It may also go unread if an impenetrable forest of apparently infinite information choices overwhelms those without the cash, the technological literacy, or the time to process them. As Herbert A. Simon noted long ago, a surplus of information creates a scarcity of whatever information consumes. Just as a surplus of rabbits creates a scarcity of lettuce, a surplus of information creates a scarcity of audience attention. Thus frustrated, the public may fail even to seek access to information. Anthony Downs developed the idea that citizens may consider their chances of affecting policy outcomes so slim as to render pointless learning about issues and candidates, or even voting. He called this response "rational ignorance." Recent work by economist James T. Hamilton suggests a set of policies to address this.[7]

Fighting the attention barrier with sensationalism and gimmicks is an arms race that serious journalism will lose. The challenge is to bring nonelite publics into the circuit of public information as active audiences and contributors. A journalism that engages its audience does not require undiscriminating surrender to commercial formulas. Both elite and popular journalism have distinctive and legitimate content and styles of appeal. We need no Lippmanesque overseers, though anyone who wants to set up shop as a critic of the press should be welcome to do so.

The public needs a press able to communicate on more than one level. Popular media are often more allusive, fluid, and inventive than traditional news sources. What popular media can offer to debates about the public good needs to be recognized, taken seriously, and engaged in larger discussions about participation and democratic ideals. Popular culture has always been a special domain of the public sphere where dreams and nightmares are acted out and alternatives presented against the grim determinism of fate.

When young people report that a substantial portion of their political information is filtered through late-night television comedy, adults should perceive this posture, whatever they may see as its generation-going-to-hell shortcomings, as the embryo of a politically critical sensibility. Political satire has an honored place in civic discourse. Zesty gossip and broad, puncturing portraits telegraph that something is going on, offer more or less explicit criticism, and model a shrewd distance that deflates arrogance and moralistic self-righteousness.

The public needs a journalism sophisticated and generous enough to relinquish the patronizing notion of a passive citizenry. Granted, to be informed requires sustained attentiveness, which gradually cultivates sophistication. The price of achieving sophistication remains high, and there is no way around this.

Popular or vernacular media—local news media outlets and entertainment media at both national and local levels—must be engaged by journalists and citizens to think through their responsibilities as participants in public discussion. Not every interweaving of entertainment and news is dangerous. The presentation of entertaining environments from which all news interest is excluded is nevertheless a problem. Not all news and political intelligence need come in distinct, clearly labeled packages in order to contribute to public information. Human culture has never been so neat. The best condition is the most varied condition, and demonstrates a respect for the capacity and interest of all.

The New Journalists

What the public needs from journalism in the early twenty-first century is improved information gathering and analyzing skills from the established press, and new means for hungry, critical, dogged information seekers, assemblers, and distributors who lie outside the circle of information elites to join the circuit of public information and debate. Toward this latter goal, a particularly hopeful development is new forms of journalism that are reflecting and sometimes leading conversations about critical problems that confront American democracy.

An amorphous and changing collection of Web-based information producers and consumers has emerged from the same technological crucible that presents new challenges and opportunities to traditional media. These producers and consumers are independent journalists, bloggers, and occasional authors of individual pastiches of information and commentary in Web logs that are posted to the Internet and distributed to like-minded audiences of other bloggers, journalists, and citizens in dense, cross-cutting networks of participants, observers, and partisans.

Since independent journalists and bloggers generally lack the institutional infrastructure that makes serious resources available for journalistic inquiry and an institutional culture of safeguards against error and distortion, their contributions often lack the reliable accuracy and honed polish that characterize professional journalism, though these may be some of the most vital discussions taking place right now in America. Fearing to be confused with amateurs who lack professional standing and whose standards they deplore, some established journalists and critics are predictably alarmed. But as a stimulus to public debate, the scrappy, rasping journalism for which blogs are known stacks up well against an established journalism that too often takes cover under a bland civility that reflects cowardice and indifference rather than professionalism.

The technological narrative of this development is a familiar one. Impertinent media horrify established media that are forced to define and sharpen their own standards in response, and impertinent media gradually adopt an increasingly professional manner until they spawn the next generation of information challengers. *USA Today* was first denounced, then imitated, by established journalists. Now, closing the loop, *USA Today* has become more mainstream, with longer stories and periodic investigative efforts.

When early radio and television practitioners challenged print media, they were just as furiously denounced for lowering journalistic sights. Although the rigor of newspaper journalism was never as great as its defenders insisted, these challengers brought their own unique gifts to the information arena and gradually absorbed the best lessons of professionalism.

Few would now turn back the clock to a time before radio and television journalism. Fair observers must acknowledge that the disclosure of serious journalistic errors by national media is a sign of higher, not failing, standards. The increased velocity of information makes errors easier to catch, and competition makes managers more eager to fix them.

The path to improved public information is not to eliminate independent, noninstitutional news efforts, but to support them with greater resources and attention. This will improve their product and pave the way for increasing self-criticism and competence. One promising site, the Campaign Desk, is a venture of the *Columbia Journalism Review* and the Columbia University Graduate School of Journalism and reviewed the coverage of the 2004 presidential campaign in traditional media outlets. Other blogs have taken on the coverage of the Iraq War.[8] Meanwhile, established media are rapidly incorporating the special capacities of Web sites to enhance their own information distribution and audience convenience.

There's more to the current ferment that is also hopeful. What's important about blogs, Listservs, and chat rooms is that they make participation and response so easy. The Internet provides technically facilitated opportunities for nonelites to enter the fray, not only with innovative sources and compilations, but as civic commentators, where "civic" refers to a level of passionate and energetic engagement in public affairs and a greater willingness to exchange views and options than can be had in relation to the established press.

This is not to ignore the well-documented skew of even popular computer-based resources toward white middle-class males, though the vast majority of these folks are not culturally powerful elites. These upstart bloggers remind us of the challenge that the now idealized bourgeois public sphere emerging from eighteenth-century mercantile culture posed to monarchical absolutism. Pamphleteers, journalists, and essayists were interested and energetic, full of gossip, rumor, and partisanship and not evenly distributed in the population. But their imperfect and engaged efforts attracted the participation of the larger public with a developing range of opinions and interests.

Today's larger public is not a blank slate, a child, or a neurotic. The people are not retarded, or emotionally or intellectually stunted. The multiple publics of the United States need journalists who take them seriously as citizens. They deserve a journalism that shares the stage with different levels of information and different perspectives, that tells the truth about where information comes from, that corrects itself publicly, that offers what well-trained and experienced fact-finders and observers believe these publics ought to know, that expects from these same publics the resources needed to get the job done.

Civic responsibility is a two-way street. To expect journalists to assume the sole responsibility for producing and managing the information environment is democratically unworkable. Citizens must support a press that does not let them off the hook of civic judgment by pretending to pronounce authoritatively on the world. To do its work successfully, journalism will always need the help of other institutions including schools, families, professional and cross-class membership associations, and all the complex infrastructure of civil society. Most of all, the press needs a public willing to take the time to inform itself, that will engage and talk to journalists and one another, that is willing to invest resources for quality information.

Journalism needs to accelerate its tentative moves to professionalize itself. This effort will have to come from the ground up. Journalism as a business is under such pressure to lower standards that its owners and managers alone cannot be counted on to maintain quality.[9] For journalism to maintain its identity against all the commercial forces trying to co-opt it, working journalists must organize to set and maintain standards of both morality and craftsmanship.

Part of the definition of professionalism is access to an arcane body of knowledge.[10] When journalists were hunters and gatherers of information, the existence of such a body of knowledge was questionable. But in an age of information surplus, they have become processors of information. Instead of merely delivering it, they organize it, digest it, make it attractive and palatable, and guide users to understanding of the little subsets of the total that they need. Such work requires special skills. Add the need for procedural skill to the need for substantive understanding, and the education requirements are suddenly intense. Journalism schools that offer midcareer certification programs in such fields as medical and business reporting are a sign that the marketplace recognizes this need.

The other significant piece of professionalism is the moral component. The halting, sometimes uncertain, efforts of rank-and-file journalists to articulate and implement moral standards should be encouraged. Without these efforts, the public might get a journalism that can no longer be distinguished from entertainment, public relations, and advertising. Technical competence and morality must become more explicit parts of journalism's self-definition lest it lose its identity altogether.

In the crisis of faith that bedevils journalism in the twenty-first century, we may not be able to depend on a journalism animated by grace to set out the true and the good. But we can hope for work undertaken with humility and virtuous devotion by journalists, and received realistically and with a readiness for public discussion on the part of citizens. Such developments can take us beyond cynicism or resignation to a more vigorous public sphere.

Notes

1. David Ignatius, *A Firing Offense* (New York: Random House, 1997), 300.
2. Walter Lippman, *Public Opinion* (New York: Harcourt, Brace, 1922); Committee on Freedom of the Press, *A Free and Responsible Press: A General Report on Mass Communication; Newspapers, Radio, Motion Pictures, Magazines, and Books*, edited by Robert D. Leigh (Chicago, University of Chicago Press, 1947).
3. "What Went Wrong," The *Miami Herald*, Special Report, December 20, 1992.
4. David Chanen, "Journalists' Group Criticizes Reporter's Actions," *Minneapolis Star Tribune*, May 13, 2000, 3B.
5. Society of Professional Journalists, "SPJ Calls on News Media to Maintain Clear Separation of News and Advertising," press release, November 11, 2003, http://www.spj.org/news.asp?ref=351.
6. Al Neuharth, "Plain Talk," *USA Today*, April 16, 2004, 13A.
7. James T. Hamilton, *All the News That's Fit to Sell: How the Market Transforms Information into News* (Princeton, N.J.: Princeton University Press, 2004), 31–34.
8. Campaign Desk is located at http://campaigndesk.org. For an example of Iraq War blogging, see http://rantingprofs.typepad.com.
9. Philip Meyer, *The Vanishing Newspaper: Saving Journalism in the Information Age* (Columbia: University of Missouri Press, 2004).
10. Wilbert E. Moore, *The Professions: Roles and Rules* (New York: Russell Sage Foundation, 1970), 6.

Bibliography

Bogart, Leo, *Preserving the Press.* New York: Columbia University Press, 1991.

Delli Carpini, Michael X., and Scott Keeter, *What Americans Know About Politics and Why it Matters.* New Haven: Yale University Press, 1996.

Downie, Leonard, Jr., and Robert G. Kaiser, *The News about the News: American Journalism in Peril.* New York: Alfred A. Knopf, 2002.

Fukuyama, Francis, *Trust: Social Virtues and the Creation of Prosperity.* New York: The Free Press, 1995.

Gans, Herbert, *Democracy and the News.* New York: Oxford University Press, 2003.

Greenburger, Martin, ed., *Computers, Communications, and the Public Interest.* Baltimore: The Johns Hopkins University Press, 1971.

Habermas, Jurgen, *The Structural Transformation of the Public Sphere*, translated by Thomas Burger. Cambridge: MIT Press, 1991.

Kovach, Bill, and Tom Rosensteil, *The Elements of Journalism: What News People Should Know and the Public Should Expect.* New York: Three Rivers Press, 2001.

Lyons, Louis M., *Reporting the News.* Cambridge, Mass.: The Belknap Press of Harvard University Press, 1965.

Merrill, John, and Ralph Lowenstein, *Media, Message, and Man.* New York: David McKay, 1971.

Merritt, W. Davis "Buzz," *Public Journalism and Public Life: Why Telling the News Is Not Enough.* 2d edition. Mahwah, N.J.: Lawrence Erlbaum Associates, 1998.

Meyer, Philip, *Ethical Journalism: A Guide for Students, Practitioners, and Consumers.* White Plains, N.Y.: Longman Inc., 1987.

Meyer, Philip, *The Vanishing Newspaper: Saving Journalism in the Information Age.* Columbia, Missouri: The University of Missouri Press, 2004.

Mitchell, Lawrence E., *Corporate Irresponsibility: America's Newest Export.* New Haven: Yale University Press, 2001.

Moore, Wilbert, *The Professions: Roles and Rules.* New York: Russell Sage Foundation, 1970.

Neuman, W. Russell, *The Future of the Mass Audience.* New York: Cambridge University Press, 1991.

Popkin, Samuel L., *The Reasoning Voter: Communication and Persuasion in Political Campaigns.* Chicago: University of Chicago Press, 2d ed. 1994.

Roberts, Gene, and Thomas Kunkel, *Breach of Faith: A Crisis of Coverage in the Age of Corporate Newspapers.* Fayetteville, Arkansas: The University of Arkansas Press, 2002.

Schudson, Michael, *The Good Citizen: A History of American Civic Life.* Cambridge, Mass: Harvard University Press, 1998.

Stamm, Keith, *Newspaper Use and Community Ties: Toward a Dynamic Theory.* Norwood, N.J.: Ablex, 1985.

Udell, Jon G., *The Economics of the American Newspaper.* New York: Hastings House, 1978.

Zaller, John R., *The Nature and Origins of Mass Opinion.* Cambridge: Cambridge University Press, 1992.

THE FUTURE OF NEWS, THE FUTURE OF JOURNALISM

25

THE FUTURE OF NEWS, THE FUTURE OF JOURNALISM

John Carey and Nancy Hicks Maynard

WHAT DO WE KNOW, REALLY, AND HOW DO WE KNOW it? This play on words from the Watergate era captures a vexing problem we face today. A virtual feast of information explodes all around us in twenty-four-hour television on hundreds of TV channels, on talk radio, in publications, and of course on the Internet. But reading and viewing even the best news and journalism is about more than consuming large quantities of information. In its constitutionally protected role, the press is assumed to build an informed citizenry that can engage in vibrant civic dialogue. The goal was always more aspirational than attainable, mostly because of the natural tension between passionate practitioners and practical proprietors of news organizations. Yet in the opening years of the twenty-first century, so many new economic, technological, and demographic trends are in play that the very nature and purpose of news is called into question.

Consider these issues:

The World Wide Web provides copious information, but how do consumers determine its veracity? Does the source matter?

If individuals can create personal information agendas through technology that filters stories and tunes out a collective understanding of events, what happens to public dialogue?

How will individuals' "picture of the world" change when they can control the news they receive without benefit of an editor or other "gatekeeper"?

What is the impact of industry consolidation on the gathering and dissemination of news that citizens need as well as want—the vaunted public purpose of journalism?

Digital technology improves photography but also facilitates manipulation of visual images. What is the impact on our perception of reality?

And the list goes on: new and changing sources of revenue; new technologies in the journalist's toolbox; changing demographics that drive the news habits of younger Americans; a growing population of immigrant and second-language ethnic groups who are developing their own robust news media; and government regulation. There is no telling how it will all settle down, but the major forces for change are in place. This chapter will assess a number of these trends and consider their implications for journalism and public policy in the future.

Changes in Lifestyles, Changes in News as a Business

One of the key factors in understanding the changes in news over the last century—from the penny press to the Internet—has been the changing lifestyle of the American family and the nature of work. Newspapers were the sole form of information for much of the early twentieth century, and each city had many, most published in the afternoon, when factory shifts ended and men returned home to relax with the newspaper and a beer or cocktail before dinner. The growth of radio news accompanied the beginning of print consolidation, especially post–World War II, when workers began commuting to work from the suburbs, listening to news en route in their cars. In a pattern that would repeat itself, the new technology brought competition to an existing medium, fracturing its audience and reducing the number of companies that could stay in business profitably. Television provided another big leap. Those commuting workers consumed their cocktails with broadcast TV news, and newspapers began converting to morning publication in earnest.

The census of 2000 indicated that the nuclear family—comprised of a father, mother, and children—the organizing assumption of news production, makes up only about one-quarter of American households.[1] With the change in household composition has come a parallel change in news consumption. Few eat a full breakfast anymore; nor do they consume a full breakfast of news. Dinner can be a serial activity, with each household member eating what they want when they want it. What's more, we have become a highly mobile society with one in six households moving each year, half in the same county and half outside, spreading families across the country.[2]

The rhythm of news consumption has always been tied to demographics and lifestyle. There were afternoon newspapers when a large portion of the workforce had early shifts at factory jobs. In the post–World War II environment of more white-collar work and suburban living, newspaper publishing moved to morning, when there was more time to read, especially on a train commuting to work. The change also accommodated, in part, growing competition from television news, broadcast as the family gathered at day's end.

As the family became more mobile and fractured, the Internet arrived just in time to free news consumers from the publishing and broadcast cycles that drove the news business over so many years and that were tuned to earlier lifestyles. Indeed, Internet news can be updated continuously, fitting into the hectic schedules of modern families, whereas print and network news adheres to fixed publication schedules.

The role of the computer and the Internet in today's information revolution has widespread implications for news gathering and consumption. Before the Web came into general use around 1995, people consumed news in much the same way as they did food in prerefrigeration days. Families bought what was fresh because they had a limited ability to preserve it. Buy and eat fresh fish on Friday, or lose it. The news business ran the same way. Stories might not have been vital to most people on a given day, but unless consumed or saved when presented, they would be lost to a new news cycle; only scholars or commercial interests willing to pay search firms large sums could retrieve them.

The twentieth century began with almost daily food shopping for city folks. The twenty-first century and the new millennium began with mostly weekly shopping trips that haul in large amounts of food. Families use refrigeration to store and preserve provisions. Digitization of the news is like food refrigeration: presumptions about freshness, perishability, and delivery times are changing. Search engines "defrost" information when we want it. The public largely controls what it knows and when it knows it.

This is a simple proposition on its face but one with seismic consequences for news as we have known it. It promises to change everything about the way journalists identify, organize, package, and produce the news, twenty-four-hour news cycles notwithstanding. A morning newspaper when no one is home to read it? Evening television news when household members are working or otherwise engaged? An advertising base tied to these changing habits and pleased to pay higher prices for whatever audience is left? Breaking news covered extensively on television, cable, or the Internet, hours before a newspaper goes to press?

The implications of these trends are critical for the news business. Because news industries are mostly advertising-supported, economists have traditionally calculated the value of news media in two ways: the number of people reading or watching, and the time they spend with the "product." Advertisers consider consumer time to be a proxy for paying television news and entertainment companies—the same is true for print advertisers, since publication subscription prices are modest compared with the cost of producing and distributing publications.

Technology and the shift of audience behavior have made a huge impact on the economics of the industry, driven by more than $200 billion in U.S. advertising sales. Newspapers historically commanded the largest share, but broadcast TV and cable ad spending have taken over in the twenty-first century.[3] The Internet has not yet threatened the advertising base of newspapers or television but this may change.

Historically, classified advertising for jobs has been the growth engine of newspapers, the seminal economic medium for news and information. But in this season of global and technological life, two trends are working against conventional wisdom. First of all, much employment advertising is migrating to the Internet at profit rates much lower than those that supported newspapers. Also, the "jobless recovery," which sees work migrating abroad, means that ads for those jobs are not making their way into U.S. media outlets. The implications for the future of the newspaper ad base and, therefore, the size and robust nature of news, are significant.

One answer has been a quickened pace of consolidation among media, in an effort to lower operating costs and keep financial returns among the highest of any industry—well over 20 percent annually, on average. Consolidation is not new for media. Throughout the twentieth century, companies swallowed each other in efforts to grow audience share. Samuel Newhouse, for example, bought rival newspapers in New York and shut them down to eliminate competition.[4] Most consolidation was in local markets, because the media were mostly local. The news industry in the information economy can sustain a few national brands. But advertising's function is to sell goods. Traditionally that function has been local, although the Internet is slowly changing this distribution chain in ways that will become clear only in the future.

What is different about this wave of consolidation is that it is both horizontal and vertical. Like media merge, but so do all news, information, and entertainment entities. Journalism is becoming a smaller and smaller piece of behemoth corporations, many not beholden to the traditions of truth telling and transparency that have been the espoused values of these enterprises in the past. For journalists, the most potentially dangerous aspect of these practices is the trend toward cross-media synergy, in which stories appear in multiple forms and lines between entertainment and journalism or news and business get blurred in a clash of cultures, one contentious—the principles of journalism and the business interests of corporate parents, one cooperative— the entertainment side of journalism and the revenue requirements of those same corporate parents, as the media critic Ken Auletta reminds readers regularly in his "Annals of Communications" articles for the *New Yorker.* In 2004 the country was split in half politically, and the largest, wealthiest, and most robust news media in history had not been able to put business and mission together.

Technology Trends

Several important technology trends under way in the early twenty-first century have affected the distribution of and control over news content as well as how journalists gather and report the news.

The Digital Era

The Web, digital cable services, satellite TV, video camcorders, still cameras, television sets, and computer monitors have been or are in the process of becoming digital. This has a number of implications. It means that more information can be transmitted or stored in the same channel or storage system, higher-resolution images on larger screens can be supported, and, in many cases, two-way transmission lets users interact with content. Such developments will provide a richer media environment such as sound and video on a news Web site that previously had only text and graphics, or much better sound and video on television news. Further, digital technology makes it easier to store text or video news content for on-demand retrieval. However, it also opens a door to greater manipulation of images and the potential to mislead. There have been several notable examples, some of which involved poor judgment by photo editors or news producers, while others have been intended to deceive the public.

In one case, *National Geographic* digitally manipulated a picture of two of the great pyramids in Egypt in order to fit both images on the cover. In a second case, *CBS Evening News* was broadcasting live from Times Square on December 31, 1999, the eve of the new millennium. In the background behind Dan Rather, there was a large electronic sign with a promotion for NBC, but CBS digitally superimposed its own logo over the sign. Both of these examples could be ascribed to poor judgment. However, there was also a photo that circulated broadly on the Web following September 11, 2001, that purported to show a tourist on the observation deck of the World Trade Center with the American Airlines plane in the background a few hundred feet away, just before it crashed into the building. In another case, a photograph was widely circulated on the Web showing 2004 presidential candidate John Kerry and Jane Fonda sharing a speaker's platform at a 1971 antiwar rally, though the two never were on the same speaker's platform. These latter two cases were digital forgeries that combined two separate and unrelated photos. Similarly, there have been a number of cases where hackers copied Web sites then superimposed content of their own to embarrass, deceive, or show off their ability to break into a legitimate Web site. These examples belie the myth that photos never lie.[5] In addition, the speed at which the Web can transmit photos around the world can help to spread the lie very quickly.

Changing Distribution Technologies

New technologies are changing the distribution patterns of news for both consumers and news organizations. For the consumer, news will be available just about anywhere. Pervasive access will be made available by wireless networks in public places, advanced cell phones, wireless personal digital assistants, satellite radio to cars, and even electronic signs on highways that display headlines, traffic information, and weather. In addition, people will have many more news services at their disposal: The Web carries thousands of news services, satellite TV and cable bring multiple news services into homes twenty-four hours a day, and satellite radio provides a dozen news services for cars anywhere in the country.

For news organizations, satellite transmission has dramatically transformed distribution and will continue to do so. This includes distribution of national newspapers to local printing plants, where the electronic signals are turned into locally printed newspapers. This practice has enabled *USA Today,* the *Wall Street Journal,* and the *New York Times* to compete with local newspapers that have increasingly relied on national wire services for news at the expense of local reporting.[6] Satellites have also allowed local television stations to feed their stories to other markets and to receive the same feeds as national news services. This has enabled them to offer the same national stories on the local six o'clock news as is carried later on national network news. Some argue that this has diminished the value of network news since viewers have already seen many of the stories the networks cover on local news programs.

Control over Content

Technologies such as video-on-demand (VOD) and personal video recorders (PVRs) will provide people with more control over content. Some of this is control over time: getting news stories whenever a person wants, or storing them, to be retrieved at an individual's convenience. Some analysts argue that with the exception of announcements for live programming, the television schedule may be becoming obsolete. Greater control also means choosing news stories from menus and watching or reading only those stories of personal interest. Such choice has been a feature of newspaper, magazine, and Web use for some time; it is now an option for digital cable subscribers and will likely extend generally to consumers of television and radio news in the future.

Smart Systems

Smart systems are an extension of segmented news content. For many years, news magazines such as *Time* and *Newsweek* have offered specialized versions of the magazine for doctors or other professional groups and provided unique content for those groups. Similarly, newspapers have offered zoned editions that provide additional content about a geographic region. Computers and electronic distribution of content can extend this process in many new ways. A few of these have been implemented; many more are likely to follow in the future. For example, a news site can ask a person to enter his or her zip code, then provide pertinent weather or news stories. Similarly, a news Web site can place ads next to a story that are specifically related to the story content. Some of these placement decisions are made by people, for example the placing of an ad for a bookstore next to a review of a book; other sites have automated the process with sometimes bizarre results. One example was the *New York Post* online, which used a system called AdSense to place advertising near related content. However, next to a story about a murder in which the victim was dismembered and stuffed in a suitcase, the automated system placed an ad for a luggage store.[7] The prevailing assessment of these early smart systems is that they are not so smart. However, as the technology develops, this may change.

The software that supports some of these smart systems also poses a threat to privacy. Many Web sites install "spyware" on a person's computer without permission, which then reports back to the Web site about what content a person has viewed. This information can be used to send specialized content based upon a person's interests, but more typically it is used to send targeted ads.

Another form of smart system is the automated aggregator of news, such as that provided by Google. This is a fully automated system that searches through a few thousand news sources and, using keywords, displays a brief summary of what the system interprets to be important stories and a link to the full story. There are no people in the loop making these decisions, except for the programmers who originally set up the algorithms by which "hits" are delivered. This may be viewed as a positive development, in that users are presented with stories from a wide variety of sources, or a negative one, in that the information is unfiltered; no judgment is included that might inform users of the value or reliability of sources.

Expanding Sources of News

Technology is greatly expanding the sources of news content. One benefit is lower costs that put technologies such as digital camcorders in the hands of many more people. As a result, amateurs are frequently on hand when a story breaks (capturing the terrorist planes as they flew into the World Trade Center, for example, or the Concorde crashing as it took off from Paris in 2000). But the same technology has allowed fugitives and terrorists to create video and offer it to the press.[8] In a more organized way, many corporations create video press releases and package them as news stories, then offer them to news organizations. Sometimes the sources for these stories are identified and sometimes they are not.

Another important trend is for organizations outside the traditional news media to offer news. Some of these are search engines such as Google (noted above) or Yahoo! Others are service organizations such as financial firms or banks that offer information related to their services. Some of these stories are from traditional news sources but others are not. In addition, Internet service providers such as AOL offer news, and many shopping services provide content that has traditionally been part of a news service, such as product reviews. It is unclear how this trend will evolve in the future or if these alternative information providers pose a threat to traditional news organizations.

New Tools for Journalists

Technology is providing a broad range of new tools for journalists and news organizations. Some of these are extensions of trends that have been under way for some time. One example is greater mobility in gathering and transmitting news. It began with the telegraph in the nineteenth century, which allowed journalists to report stories electronically from great distances. In the last half of the twentieth century, microwave and later satellite trucks allowed journalists to send video back to a news station without transporting a tape or film physically.[9] This has allowed more on-the-scene reporting and "floating anchors" who host news programs from the scene of breaking stories. More recently, the cost and size of this equipment has been reduced dramatically, allowing embedded reporters to transmit live pictures and sound while riding on a tank in the Iraq War, for example, or reporting from an isolated mountain range in Afghanistan. Similarly, embedded reporters in the 2004 presidential election were given privileged access to behind-the-scenes activities of the candidates where they recorded, edited, and transmitted stories from the field.[10] The mobility of reporters has been further enhanced by Wi-Fi hotspots in public locations that allow reporters to send back stories from wireless laptops, personal digital assistants (PDAs) that store information for reporters in the field, ultralight laptop computers, and global positioning systems (GPS) that aid in identifying locations. Professor John Pavlik of Rutgers University has envisioned a "mobile journalist workstation" in the future that would feature these and other enhanced reporting tools, such as being able to access databases with background information about a story while in the field.[11]

New software tools also enable investigative reporters to search large public databases and report on trends that might have required months of field work in the past or simply have been inaccessible to a reporter.[12] The miniaturization and reduced cost of field equipment will enable individual journalists to become multimedia reporters, capturing stories for print, the Web, radio, and television, or allow journalists to cross over from one medium to another, for example from still photography to video. There have been some examples of this to date, such as *Nightline* using video documentaries created by still photographers who moonlighted as broadcast journalists.[13] And there are many economic incentives for news organizations to encourage more reporters to practice media crossover in the future. Further, news in the future might be packaged similar to special-edition DVDs of movies, providing extra content such as photographs that never appeared in the original published story, accompanied by a narrative from the photographer who was on the scene. However, media crossover by journalists is also a controversial trend that is resisted by unions, which fear the practice will lead to job losses since one reporter will be asked to do work previously accomplished by multiple reporters, and by some journalists, who feel it will lead to less professional reporting and more treatment of news as entertainment.

Consumer Behavior and the Web

Changes in the business environment for news organizations and advances in technology are two of the forces shaping the future of news and the future of journalism. A third important indicator of the future news environment is how people use media. Here, we concentrate on use of the Web as a harbinger of future practices, drawing from our own research and other sources.

The Web Environment

The Web environment in homes, offices, schools, and public locations is very different in 2005 as compared with 1995 when the technology first emerged, and Web usage will continue to evolve. It is becoming pervasive, surrounding people in multiple locations and even in many homes, where there are multiple units. Wireless networks in the home have and will bring the Web throughout the household, even into many kitchens.[14] Broadband connections to the Web are likely to be commonplace in the future, providing faster access to content and a bigger "pipeline" to transmit multimedia images and sound, including video. However, the most important characteristic of broadband is the way it encourages Web users to keep their computer on whenever they are home. The Web then becomes more a constant source of news and information, absorbed in short and long sessions, rather than a work tool that is turned on when a person wants to search for specific content. In addition, the household computer monitor is being absorbed into the social fabric of homes and treated like a member of the family, often decorated with family photographs, stuffed animals, and mementos.[15] This environment resembles the way television became a core part of households in the 1950s and 1960s.

Web Usage Patterns

News usage on the Web is changing as the environment in which people use the Web changes and as people's relationship to computers in the household becomes more casual and constant. In the future, as people gain more experience on the Web and as a young generation that grew up online enters adulthood, Web usage of news and entertainment is likely to become a seamless component of everyday life. This may erode the readership for newspapers and magazines and lead media outlets to develop a different style of presenting the news, one that more closely mimics the style of Web usage. For example, some news organizations have developed shorter tabloid newspapers that emphasize brevity and are free, in order to appeal to younger readers accustomed to getting their information online.[16]

The patterns of future Web usage at news sites are now being set in many homes, especially those with a broadband connection. They include habitual use of favorite sites that in some ways accommodate newspaper reading and television viewing habits.[17] There is also a great deal of simultaneous media use, especially by younger Web users, such as watching TV and using the Web at the same time or sending instant messages to friends while reading a news story. Many people customize news sites so that local or special-interest content, specific to their stated interests, is presented to them when they go to the news site, or they customize the news themselves by, for example, bookmarking one news site for international news, another for sports stories, and another for the weather. Navigation patterns are evolving rapidly. Many people come to news sites from newsletter or e-mail hyperlinks and read only the linked story. These patterns are likely to lead to very different designs for news sites in the future. In the near term, many traditional news organizations with a Web presence have been reluctant to accommodate the preferences of many Web users when doing so would include providing hyperlinks that send people away from the news site.[18] However, some nonnews organizations such as Google and Yahoo have built their businesses on sending people to other sites.

The Reader as Writer

One of the most significant trends in Web usage and a potential harbinger of the future direction of news sites on the Web as well as news programming in other media is the emergence of the reader as a writer. Traditionally, newspapers and magazines have published reader feedback in the form of letters to the editor; more recently, readers could submit columns for op-ed pages. In the online world, the reader has emerged as a major force in discussing the news as well as reading it. The process started with bulletin boards on home computers in the 1980s and 1990s with a dial-up modem. At one point, over sixty thousand households hosted bulletin boards on topics from religion to sports and invited people to post an opinion or comment.[19] Later, the Web became a fertile medium for discussion forums, Usenet newsgroups, live chat rooms, and reader reviews on a broad variety of topics, hosted by news organizations and many other groups. More recently, hundreds of thousands of people have created Web journals, or blogs, for anyone who wants to read them. Blogs vary in style and format. They resemble traditional newsletters, newspaper columns, special-interest magazines, and personal diaries. Many present partisan political views; others are devoted to gossip, humor, and unearthing scandals. It is unclear whether blogs are a fad or an important new medium of expression. Further, they have earlier roots in the vanity press, partisan newspapers of the nineteenth century and earlier, and twentieth-century gossip columns in newspapers and on radio.[20] A number of newspapers have published blogs by reporters on their Web site, a practice that has set off a debate about whether such material should be reviewed by editors in the same way as traditional content, or if doing so constitutes censorship.[21]

In television news programs, the viewer has also become a more active participant through e-mails that are read on-air, call-in voice mail, and instant polling. With a new generation of interactive television systems, all of these feedback mechanisms can be handled within the two-way television stream. The cell phone has also emerged as a significant conveyor of text-based news and gossip among individuals. Cell phones have been used to instantly relay breaking stories and also to spread gossip and unverified news that can be embellished at each point in a chain of text messages.[22] Collectively, these trends appear to signal a much more active role for citizens in future news services. The precise shape, quality of information and dialogue, and social effects of this expanded role are unclear.

Policy and Regulation

It began simply: "Congress shall make no law . . . abridging the freedom of speech, or of the press." The nation has mostly kept faith with the First Amendment's spirit, protecting an unfettered flow of individual expression and information. The business of news, on the other hand, is continually subjected to federal laws and rules that determine much about what we read, see, or hear. Although the regulations are intended to control business operations, they can have a profound effect on journalism.

Journalists pride themselves on a few big press-freedom successes. These began most famously with challenges to the Alien and Sedition Acts of 1798, under which ten editors were convicted for coverage preceding the nation's war with France. Thomas Jefferson's election brought repeal of those laws. More recently but before the secrecy rules put in place since September 11, the most notable confrontation centered on the Nixon administration's attempts to prevent publication of the Vietnam-era Pentagon Papers in 1971. Nixon failed. Freedom reigned.

Far more important, and more insidious, are a host of laws and policies affecting the way media companies do business. More often than not, this federal engineering creates a marketplace of winners and losers. Broadcast and cable operators are regulated, though less so than they had been. A number of laws also affect newspapers, which are less regulated than their broadcast and cable competition, but which must adhere to general rules governing commerce.

In earlier times, newspapers gained mightily, with special postal rates allowing cheap distribution though the mail. As media markets matured, Congress passed the Newspaper Preservation Act, allowing two dailies to combine business operations, as long as their news functions were separate and competitive. Each year, more of these combinations dissolve as unworkable, reducing further the number of cities publishing more than one daily. Other policies have been less helpful. The estate-tax structure encouraged the sale of smaller family-owned media properties to conglomerates because tax rates were so high. Those laws have eased, but the drumbeat toward bigger has been cast; the battle engaged.

The government cites several reasons for its tinkering: to encourage a diversity of community voices; to curb monopoly power or market dominance; to husband a limited electromagnetic spectrum, and generally to support the "public interest." But the policies of Congress, the Federal Communications Commission, and the Justice Department often do not support the vaulted "public interest," despite their great power:

- Government policy makers deregulated cable TV earlier and more completely than broadcast television, which is still trying to catch up. The result has been a growth spurt in paid television viewing at the expense of free-spectrum broadcasts, including the audience for evening network news.
- They continue to apply traditional antitrust standards to newspapers seeking to consolidate fractured markets while developing more liberal rules for broadcasters. In some cases, television owners can have two stations in the same market and radio owners multiple properties.
- To encourage local telephone competition and broadband Internet build-out, they allow megamergers among telecommunications companies that critics claim limit competition.
- To encourage high-definition television (HDTV), regulators granted additional free-channel spectrum to broadcasters, allowing them to develop niche audiences that print media cannot match.

This environment has created a land rush for owners seeking larger share in a market in which legacy media audiences are in decline, although most of the traditional media conglomerates are healthy financially. With so many new information outlets and loosening rules, the FCC allowed television broadcasters to own a growing number of local stations. Networks joined the fray because local stations are more profitable than national networks, which had been constrained in owning stations and cable networks under the old rules. Radio companies can own multiple properties in the same market as well. Newspapers, however, have been barred from owning television stations in their markets since the mid-1970s, and they wanted back the opportunity to produce news across the multiple platforms, serving a fracturing news audience market. Franchises grandfathered under the old rules, such as the *Dallas Morning News* and the *Chicago Tribune,* have been able to put together a daily newspaper, television and radio stations, cable TV, a robust Web site, and sometimes free dailies or city magazines. Such cohesion challenges the traditional definition of diversity, although it allows more resources to be concentrated on news and often results in more textured, sophisticated coverage.

Into this intense consolidation caldron came a new presidential administration in 2000, bent on more deregulation, with Michael Powell at FCC's helm. With much pulling and tugging—and some litigation—the commission reached a policy compromise that collapsed at the end of 2003. Consumer advocates claimed victory. So did congressional opponents. In fact, a more correct reading of the battles would be that station owners beat the networks, fearing their growing power. The long-term outcome in this struggle is far from clear.

It is also unclear what all of this activity means for the public good, the public's right to know or its knowledge base. The answers may have nothing to do with the historical watchdog roles of either regulation or journalism. The rules, following market and technological trends, may set in motion an information "wild west," as it were, bringing much uncertainty to the future landscape of media ownership.

Implications for the Future of News and Journalism

The changing technology and business environments for news organizations and journalists raise a number of questions about the future role of the press in a democracy and the relationship between news providers and citizens.

Time Compression and Space Expansion

In the future news environment, there will be even less time between gathering, analyzing, and reporting information than in the current environment. Technology will make this possible and competitive pressures may require it. In addition, citizens will have virtually twenty-four-hour access to news from multiple locations. This will provide less time for reporters and editors to think about what they should report. Consumers of news may react more and assess less, as the constant stream of news leaves them little time to reflect on what they have just seen or heard. At the same time, the constant stream of news will provide more opportunity to update a story, correct errors, and provide follow-up commentary.

The space to report news will expand in media such as the Web and television. News organizations will be able to provide virtually an unlimited amount of information on the Web. As television moves to storage on digital servers with video-on-demand, there will be less need to provide news in blocks of thirty or sixty minutes, as is the practice today. It is unclear, however, whether economic forces will support such expansions of news content or whether citizens will want more news.

What Is Reality?

One of the core functions of the press is to present citizens with a picture of reality that is factual and fair. This has always been a goal that can never be fully realized, since news organizations must inevitably choose what to report from the information that is available to them. Further, the opportunity to distort real-ity—always present—is much greater with digital technology, which makes it much easier to change the appearance of photos or video and much tougher for a viewer to detect bogus information. While there may be occasions where a news organization uses digital technology to deliberately distort reality, the greater danger is that they will be given a digitally manipulated photo or video by another organization with a malicious intent and the fraud will go unde-tected. Within news organizations, the temptation to change reality through dig-ital technology is likely to come not so much from a desire to deceive but a desire to entertain and enliven coverage of an event. Most examples of digital deception that we know about have involved removing a person or object from a photo so that the main subject of the photo stood out better. However, news organizations place themselves on a slippery slope once they decide that they have the right to alter reality through digital editing of a photo or video.

Technology presents a related problem for citizens. With higher-resolution cameras, more mobile equipment, and even 3-D video, the visual images that are captured may be so compelling that viewers will feel as if they are at the scene experiencing the event firsthand and fully understand it. The more complete real-ity that comes from an understanding of the context of the event and an assess-ment of the raw images could be lost. It can be argued that this issue was a prob-lem with some of the embedded reporting during the initial stages of the Iraq War in 2003. As reporters rode on tanks during battles and sent live images back home, viewers often felt that they understood what was happening. But did they?

Sources of News

In the future news environment, the sources of news will be more complex and the chances of their being unreliable will be greater. First, traditional sources of news from professional journalists will appear side by side with an explosion of nontraditional sources. There have always been nontraditional sources of news but in relatively small numbers. Research indicates that quality and reliability of a news source continue to be important to the public.[23] However, many people use both traditional and nontraditional sources, expecting different types of information from each. It is unclear where journalism as we know it will fit in the new landscape.

Second, establishing the authorship of a news story will be more problem-atic. In a digital environment, it is much easier to plagiarize from other sources. Also, as corporations and public relations firms feed more stories to news organ-izations, the source of an article may not always be clear. Third, the difficulty in authenticating some news stories may create a general uncertainty. Was the videotape really of Osama bin Laden, was he even alive when it was taped, and was it created by his people or shot by a journalist? In addition, the gatekeeper role of news organizations, selecting what is presented to citizens from original sources, will likely be diminished as the original sources, from the White House to the New York Yankees, will have more direct access to citizens through their own Web sites and video servers at cable systems.

Customized News

In the brave new information world, there are numerous ways for the news to be customized for citizens. As mentioned above, at some news Web sites, a person can choose what types of stories will be presented on the home page. Many news organizations will send readers an e-mail with links to only the subjects that interest them. And video-on-demand cable systems let people choose news stories from a menu, so that they watch only what they want. These examples merely scratch the surface of how news can be customized. However, where is this leading? Some have argued that such practices lead to *The Daily Me* news mindset, newspapers, Web sites, or video news sources of the future that present only what a person wants to know about. In this ultimate example of audience fragmentation, no two people might get the same news. It is unlikely that the extreme scenario will play out. However, customization raises an important question about democratic discourse when people do not share a common perspective on events. In the 1960s, many academics were concerned about the opposite social effect—that everyone saw the world the way CBS's veteran anchor Walter Cronkite saw it and that few would have sufficient access to alternate points of view. Clearly, the goal should be a balance of some common perspectives on events from shared mass media and some alternative perspectives from local sources and more narrowly defined media.

Future Journalists

In a future news environment, journalists are likely to need some additional skills. These include a broader working knowledge of technologies that will deliver the news and an understanding of how people use new media to get the news. The way people read Web news sites is quite different from how they read a newspaper. In addition, the "multimedia" journalist may emerge in greater numbers. Currently, many journalists cover stories for print, television, and the Web. This practice is likely to increase significantly in the future.

The role of journalists may also evolve from reporters to reporter-guides. A core communication function that has emerged on the Web is to guide people through hyperlinks and search engines to multiple sources of information on a topic.

Traditionally, reporters have served the role of "information guide" in certain types of stories. An article about a health topic, for example, may inform readers how to get more information or where to go for a medical screening. On news sites in the future, all stories may have this component.

Privacy

In recent years, privacy issues have arisen in relation to the computer and the Internet. Web news organizations gather information about people when readers register to use a site or customize settings to indicate the types of news they want to receive. Special software called "cookies" can also send back information about what content a person has viewed. This information is valuable to advertisers. While the greatest privacy concerns about the Web relate to identity theft, many individuals are concerned that information about them will be sold to third-party marketing groups or used by Web sites to manipulate them.

Privacy is a pervasive and thorny issue for any group, such as Web news organizations that seek to build a relationship of trust with citizens whose everyday experiences and exposure to media stories about privacy have taught them to be wary.

Some steps that may help to maintain a relationship of trust include: developing a written privacy code that addresses concerns about privacy and sets out professional standards of conduct about how information may be used; placing stronger emphasis on the confidentiality of information; and emphasizing a news organization's accountability to major industry associations that would not allow information about the household to be misused. Many news organizations have taken these steps.

Predicting the Future

In one of the reports accompanying the famous Hutchins Commission on Freedom of the Press in 1947, there were two predictions. The authors said that news would be dramatically changed in the future by (1) television and (2) radio fax newspapers.[24] One prediction was a home run and one a strikeout. We have tried to avoid predictions in this chapter. Inevitably, some of the trends and likely impacts that we have outlined will miss the mark. Fears about the future have been common among news organizations. In the mid-1990s, the industry's fear was that Microsoft would take over news and classified advertising. Bill Gates was the man to beat. But the threat was vacant. Gates, too, discovered what all publishers know: news, information, and advertising are difficult and expensive to procure. His company bowed out.

Consolidation of media businesses will probably continue. The results may be messy in the short term, as they are as each new technology takes hold. News may become more homogenized than is safe for a vibrant democracy. The sacred wall between the newsroom and marketing departments may tatter. A bigger gulf may develop between the old and the young in their news habits, with older Americans continuing to read daily newspapers and watch network news, and younger consumers watching cable, surfing the Web, and reading specialty magazines.

The American public has had a way of finding the right answers, at the right time, for policies that matter most. If we are a somnolent society when it comes to policy, history shows that we sleep with one eye open and pay attention when we must.

The core role of journalists and news organization in providing citizens with an accurate and informed picture of people and events is not likely to change, although there may be some adjustments to be made as new technologies take hold. And, while technology and business forces may shape how news is delivered and consumed—not always to the benefit of society—it will still be left to professional and committed journalists to determine the quality of what is created and how it serves the needs of citizens in a democracy.

Notes

1. U.S. Census Bureau, *Statistical Abstract of the United States, 2002* (Washington, D.C.: U.S. Census Bureau), 49.
2. Ibid., 29.
3. Suzanne Vranica, "U.S. Ad Spending Rose 6.1% in 2003," *Wall Street Journal,* March 9, 2004, B6.
4. For a more in-depth portrait of Newhouse, see Richard Meeker, *Newspaperman: S.I. Newhouse and the Business of News* (New Haven, Conn: Ticknor and Fields, 1983).
5. Katie Hafner, "The Camera Never Lies, But Software Can," *New York Times,* March 11, 2004, G1.
6. Peter Johnson, "This Just In: The Future of News," *USA Today*, March 15, 2004, A1.
7. Bob Tedeschi, "If You Liked the Web Page, You'll Love the Ad," *New York Times,* online edition, www.nytimes.com/2003/08/04/technology.
8. Alexander Stille, "Cameras Shoot Where Uzis Can't," *New York Times,* October 20, 2003, B9.
9. Adam Clayton Powell, "Getting the Picture: Trends in Television News Reporting," in *Demystifying Media Technology,* edited by Pavlik and Dennis.
10. Katharine Seelve, "Making of the Digital Press Corps, 2004," *New York Times,* January 29, 2004, G1.
11. Pavlik, *Journalism and New Media,* 54–57.
12. Eliot Jaspin, "The New Investigative Journalism: Exploring Public Records by Computer," in *Demystifying Media Technology,* edited by Pavlik and Dennis, 142.
13. Ken Kerschbaumer, "Still Photographers Take on Digital Video," *Broadcasting and Cable,* December 15, 2003, 36.
14. Katie Hafner, "If the Kitchen's Warm, It May Be the PC," *New York Times,* December 11, 2003, G1.
15. Byron Reeves and Clifford Nass, *The Media Equation: How People Treat Computers, Television, and New Media Like Real People and Places* (Stanford, Calif.: CSLI; Cambridge, U.K.: Cambridge University Press, 1996), 4–5.
16. Jacques Steinberg, "To Get Young Readers, Newspapers Print Free, Jazzy Editions," *New York Times,* December 1, 2003, A3.

17. See Bogart, *Press and Public,* 86–106.
18. Daniela V. Dimitrova et al., "Hyperlinking As Gatekeeping: Online Newspaper Coverage of the Execution of an American Terrorist," *Journalism Studies* 4, no. 3 (2003): 401–14.
19. Radio and Television News Directors Association, *A Seat at the Table: The Role of Journalism in the Digital Era* (Washington, D.C.: Radio and Television News Directors Association, 1995), 11.20.
20. Anthony Smith, "The Long Road to Objectivity and Back Again: The Truth We Get in Journalism," in *Newspaper History from the Seventeenth Century to the Present Day,* edited by George Boyce, James Curran, and Pauline Wingate (Beverly Hills, Calif.: Sage, 1978).
21. Michael Falcone, "Does an Editor's Pencil Ruin a Web Log?" *New York Times,* October 29, 2003, C9.
22. Dennis Redmont, "Newspapers See Danger in Text Messaging," *E-Week.Com,* May 8, 2004, 1.
23. John Carey, "The Web Habit: An Ethnographic Study of Web Usage," Online Publishers Association white paper (New York: Online Publishers Association, 2004), 14.
24. Commission on Freedom of the Press, *A Free and Responsible Press, A General Report on Mass Communication: Newspapers, Radio, Motion Pictures, Magazines, and Books,* edited by Robert Leigh (Chicago: University of Chicago Press, 1947), 34–35.

Bibliography

Bogart, Leo. *Press and Public: Who Reads What, When, Where, and Why in American Newspapers.* Hillsdale, N.J.: Lawrence Erlbaum, 1981.

Fidler, Roger. *Mediamorphosis: Understanding New Media.* Thousand Oaks, Calif.: Pine Forge, 1997.

Leonard, Thomas C. *News For All: America's Coming-of-Age with the Press.* New York: Oxford University Press, 1995.

Lippman, Walter. "The World Outside and the Picture in Our Heads." In *The Process and Effects of Mass Communication,* edited by Wilbur Schramm and Donald F. Roberts. Rev ed. Urbana: University of Illinois Press, 1972.

Maynard, Nancy. *Mega Media: How Market Forces Are Transforming News.* New York: Maynard Partners, 2000.

Pavlik, John V. *Journalism and New Media.* New York: Columbia University Press, 2001.

Pavlik, John V., and Everette E. Dennis, eds. *Demystifying Media Technology: Readings from the Freedom Forum Center.* Mountainview, Calif.: Mayfield, 1993.

Ritchin, Fred. *In Our Own Image: The Coming Revolution in Photography.* 2nd ed. New York: Aperture, 1999.

Rogers, Everett M. *Communication Technology: The New Media in Society.* New York: Free Press, 1986.

Zollman, Peter. *Interactive News: State of the Art.* Washington, D.C.: Radio and Television News Directors Association, 1997.

AFTERWORD

Geneva Overholser and Kathleen Hall Jamieson

THIS BOOK HAS SOUGHT TO TACKLE A LARGE AND COM-
plex subject, one whose reach extends throughout American society. It is
a subject of considerable discussion and debate. In four broad sections,
the book focuses on the press as an institution of American democracy. The first
asks what we mean by "journalism" and by "the press" in the context both of
U.S. history and of other models of journalism in a democratic state. In the second, we turn to press functions and ask how well they are performed. In a section
ranging from an exploration of the ways in which government supports the press
to a discussion of the ways in which government regulation serves or fails to
serve the public interest, our third section concentrates on the press-government
relationship. In the final section, we take a look at the nature and structure of the
press by focusing on journalistic practice and performance. A final essay looks at
the future of news and the future of journalism.

None of the questions raised in and by these chapters has simple answers.
There is widespread disagreement even about what constitutes the press, not to
mention precisely how we got to where we are today, or what are the best models for a press in a democratic nation. The first section of this book cautions that
there are many types of journalism, with wide-ranging and dissimilar audiences,
purposes, and functions. The book offers a number of optics through which one
can make sense of phenomena typically reduced to the words *media* and *press*.
Robert Entman, for example, parses journalism into mainstream journalism,
advocacy journalism, tabloid journalism, and entertainment journalism. Barbie
Zelizer notes the confusion created when one type of journalism is assumed to
be legitimate and others suspect. Rather than focusing on a static conception of
journalism, she invites us to see it and our conceptions of it as evolving. Daniel
Hallin and Robert Giles set the U.S. model of a democratic media system in the
context of two other models, each with its own relationships among democratic
party systems, electoral systems, and political cultures. In an increasingly inter-
connected world, journalism is no longer bound by national borders or national

interests. After tracing the impact of globalization on journalism and journalism on globalization, John Keane offers a new model of global journalism with new obligations and a new ethic.

One of our tasks in this book has been to explore how the press as we know it today came to be. Michael Schudson and Susan Tifft chart the changes in U.S. journalism from colonial times, marking the swing from the apolitical model of early colonial America, to the partisan press of the nineteenth century, and finally to the twentieth-century, profit-driven professional press.

Understanding the role of the press in giving voice to the concerns of all Americans is another emphasis of the book. Pamela Newkirk reminds us of the important role that the African American, Latino, Asian American, and Native American press has played in the country's history.

At the center of this book is a question: What should a democracy expect of the press? James Curran focuses on the news *system,* and suggests that various news outlets perform different functions which, taken as a whole, facilitate: representation, deliberation, conflict resolution, accountability, and information dissemination.

Our authors then turn to an exploration of the traditional functions of the press, asking how well they are served by journalism today. These include the press as a marketplace of ideas, examined by Robert Schmuhl and Robert Picard; the press as agenda setter, probed by Maxwell McCombs; the press as watchdog, analyzed by W. Lance Bennett and William Serrin; the press as the source of public information, assessed by Thomas Patterson and Philip Seib; and finally, the press as mobilizer, examined by Esther Thorson.

In the United States, government is both protected and held accountable by a constitutionally protected press. In the third section, on the government-press relationship, edited by Martha Joynt Kumar, Kumar and Alex Jones show that despite the complaint of government and elected officials about press coverage of them and their activities, the relationship between government and the press is more often than not a cooperative one. Timothy Cook charts the historical and contemporary ways in which the three branches have supported the press. This includes postal subsidies, support for development of new technologies, regulatory protection of intellectual property rights and corporate ownership, and support for governmental staff charged with easing the work of journalists reporting on government. Jane Kirtley tracks the social and legal changes affecting the relationship between government and the press. In their essay, "The First Amendment Tradition and Its Critics," Bruce Sanford and Kirtley chronicle two centuries of history to argue that the First Amendment "remains the heart of American democracy." Robert Horwitz examines the ways in which government regulation has balanced corporate and public interests and the tensions that have resulted. Daniel Schorr notes the complexity of the press-government relationship, with leaders often secretive and hostile toward the press, the public distrustful, media serving substantial private interests, and a shifting legal environment. William Prochnau asks how well the press has performed in reporting on wars in which the United States was engaged, and how the government-press relationship in times of war has changed over time.

Expressed memorably in A. J. Liebling's observation that "freedom of the press is guaranteed only to those who own one,"[1] the concentration of ownership in the hands of a few, explored in section four, raises important questions about whose voices will be heard and what the public will be told, particularly when the parent company has a stake in the debate. This section ponders such questions as: How well can corporate journalism "afflict the comfortable and comfort the afflicted"? How has government regulation responded to these changes in control, and with what effect? What has the demise of the fairness doctrine meant for the public and those who lead? Has consolidation constricted the range of voices, or has the proliferation of media channels increased the range of public debate? This section of the book explores the journalistic enterprise, its practice and performance. These essays document the market-driven nature of American journalism that produces news as a commodity; the ideals of the newsroom and their relation to the press as a democratic institution; and, finally, the inadequate ways in which mainstream journalism addresses and reflects minority communities. Robert Picard and James Hamilton focus on newsroom economics and the potential and actual conflicts between the financial self-interest of owners and the public interest of citizens. Hamilton argues that news coverage today "has shifted to an increasing emphasis on what people want to know and away from information that they may need as voters." Picard asks: In a marketplace model, how can the public hold owners accountable for the quality of the news product that they produce? Carolyn Marvin and Philip Meyer raise concerns over what happens when the needs of advertisers, whose revenue stream underwrites the press, collide with the needs of citizens. Mitchell Stephens and David Mindich focus on the African American press to examine "the inherent blind spots and prejudices" of the traditional mainstream media. Theodore Glasser and Marc Gunther ponder occasions when journalistic "autonomy trumps accountability; when autonomy *in* the newsroom threatens autonomy *for* the newsroom; and when autonomy—under the guise of competition—undermines the independence of judgment that good journalism demands." A final essay, by John Carey and Nancy Hicks Maynard, looks toward the future, considering how the many fast-paced demographic, economic, and technological changes will alter journalism—and what about it will remain the same.

Where does all of this leave us? The nineteenth-century model of a partisan press appears to be reemerging to some degree. The places in which news appears, and the contours of what is considered news, are changing. Throughout this volume, our authors have grappled with the changing nature and definition of news. In the early years of the country the press was partisan. By the 1920s, the independent press was alive and well, and "objectivity" was enshrined as a norm. In 1996 the *New Yorker* editor David Remnick captured the traditional notion of the press as one of "informed aggressive skepticism."[2] Even as the term *objectivity* gave way to the realization that the perspective of the reporter determines in part what is worthy of reporting and the frame within which it will be cast, as the author E. J. Dionne notes, "reporters still believed they should not be partisan, should present 'both sides' of a controversy and thereby allow the readers or listeners to make up their own minds."[3] Increasingly that assumption is being called into question by stories—in some cases labeled "interpretation" or "analysis" and in other cases not—that make explicit the views of the reporter or anchor. The rise and success of FOX News Channel, which frames its stories from conservative assumptions, and the institutionalization of cable talk shows, in which journalists from conservative Robert Novak to liberal Al Hunt express their views, raises the prospect of a return to the partisan model of the press that characterized the nineteenth century. Increasingly, as polls by the Pew Center for the People and the Press show, the public is choosing its news medium based on ideological preference. Acting as a brake on the apparent return to explicit partisanship may be another Pew finding—that the public considers objectivity as desirable, even if not totally achievable.

Another shift in contemporary journalism is the fusion of entertainment—comedy, in particular—and news, producing an unexpected increase in news consumption by the young. In 2004 Comedy Central's *The Daily Show* with Jon Stewart attracted over a million viewers a night Monday through Thursday.[4] Although social satire, the show imparts a great deal of both political information and opinion. Elected officials and candidates alike take the show seriously. It was on *The Daily Show* in 2003 that the Democratic hopeful John Edwards announced he was running for president. Stewart quipped, "I have to warn you we are a fake show, so you might have to do this again somewhere."

We also live in a world filled with twenty-four-hours-a-day access to news on cable and the Internet. Cable news channels such as CNN, MSNBC, and FOX News have not increased the amount of "news" but instead increased the speed with which political information and changing events move into the nation's living rooms and onto computer screens. Wire services have provided an around-the-clock news stream for decades. But while it was primarily editors who had access to wires, instant news is now available to anyone with cable or satellite service, or a computer and an Internet connection.

In each section of the book, scholars explore the implications of the Internet for the press as an institution of democracy. The effect of this massive new source of information, opinion, and news is hard to overstate—and impossible to predict over the long run: As a 2003 report in *Editor & Publisher* notes, "Eight of the top 20 news Web sites or groups in the U.S. during March were affiliated with newspapers, according to audience statistics from Nielsen//NetRatings. . . . Three individual newspaper sites were in the top 20: NYTimes.com, USAToday.com and washingtonpost.com. Newspaper chains on the list were Gannett Co. Inc., Knight Ridder, Tribune Co., Hearst Corp., and Advance Publications Inc."[5]

Where the major networks and newspapers once determined what the public saw and heard about their external political world, the Internet now makes available images that mainstream media won't air or print, including those of hostages beheaded in Iraq by Muslim extremists.

The Internet has also added new players to the news process. Bloggers alerted traditional media that Republican Trent Lott's approving statement in 2002 about then-segregationist Strom Thurmond's 1948 presidential bid was political dynamite (and eventually precipitated a change in leadership of the Republicans in the Senate as Lott stepped aside). Bloggers successfully challenged the validity of documents in a 2004 Dan Rather *60 Minutes II* report on President George W. Bush's service in the National Guard, prompting mainstream press investigations and, in turn, a CBS internal investigation and apology. The Internet has democratized the process of generating and vetting information. As a much-transmitted faked photo of John Kerry and Jane Fonda revealed during the 2004 presidential campaign, the Web has the potential to circulate fabrications widely—and also to circulate the "corrections."

The rise of the Internet has also created a way for those with resources to produce their own "spin sites." Charged with securities fraud and obstructing a federal investigation, Martha Stewart launched www.marthatalks.com in June 2003. Her staff then took out an ad in *USA Today* to draw viewers to the site. On it, one could find favorable news reports and e-mails from those supporting her case. When he was charged with child molestation, the pop singer Michael Jackson set his own website with a disclaimer indicating that only information about Jackson found on the site was trustworthy. Thus freedom of the press today, as Liebling would probably agree, exists not only for those who own one. It exists for anyone with an Internet connection and a computer.

This volume chronicles the changes in how news is produced and probes the implications of the changes. Competitive pressure can lead to getting things wrong. Similarly, unedited information can shape attitudes that would better have been left untouched until the facts were in. Like the famous 1948 headline "Dewey Defeats Truman," the rough draft of history written on the night of November 7, 2000, was rougher than most. "Bush Wins" declared the *Boston Herald* and *New York Post.* "Bush" affirmed the *Austin American Statesman.* The printed *New York Times,* at least, offered a qualifier: "Bush Appears to Defeat Gore." But the real havoc of election night and the morning after was wreaked by broadcast and cable with its call first that Gore had won in Florida and later that Bush had cinched the election. Whether the first call—for Gore—depressed

Bush votes in the area of Florida in which the polls were still open is difficult to know. Nor can we be sure about the effects, if any, on the postelection contest over vote counts that resulted from the second blunder, the one saying that it was instead Bush who had won.

Once the rare exception, specialized news outlets are now thriving throughout the country. Media proliferate for every demographic sector, and many of these are finding strong commercial success. "By the end of 2003, the United States had 655 Spanish-language stations, or 6 percent of the nation's 10,870 commercial stations, according to M Street, a radio research company owned by Clear Channel Communications. The Spanish language format is now the fifth most popular."[6] One example of the burgeoning ethnic press is the tale of Bengali newspapers in New York: "In the last decade, one or two new Bengali-language newspapers have appeared every year in New York City. Out of tiny offices dotted throughout Queens, and often with minuscule staffs, almost a dozen newspapers now issue forth every week."[7]

Regardless of the form the news takes or the medium that carries it, the well-being of a democracy requires that a press perform the functions identified in the sections of this book. How well is the press serving democracy and what challenges does this institution of democracy face at the dawn of the twenty-first century?

Looking back over the history of journalism in the United States, there are moments that vindicate Thomas Jefferson's confidence that it is "to the press alone, chequered as it is with abuses, the world is indebted for all the triumphs which have been gained by reason and humanity over errors and oppression." Journalism helped end slavery and lynching, and propelled the civil rights movements of the 1950s and 1960s. Journalists fought these battles at high personal cost. Ida B. Wells, whose crusade against lynching is a testament to the power of a determined individual, was herself threatened with death by defenders of the practice. Elijah Lovejoy's printing press was destroyed by a mob that objected to his pleas for justice after the lynching of an African American man. His presses were destroyed two more times before he was killed in 1837 by a mob as he tried to defend a fourth newspaper operation.

Harry Ashmore, Ralph McGill, Gene Patterson, Hodding Carter, Hazel Brannon Smith, and a handful of other courageous southern editors and reporters who were crusading for civil rights in the 1950s and 1960s paid a price as well. Smith's "editorials led to an economic boycott that, combined with the founding of an opposition paper, broke [her paper] the *Advertiser.*"[8]

It was after all small, underfunded papers that faced off against more powerful mainstream outlets to produce social change. Lost in our collective recollection of such heroic moments is the role of the established press in instigating them. It was the *Missouri Republican,* a paper in an adjoining town, that had argued before Lovejoy's murder that action was needed to quell the mischief of this minister-turned-publisher. And the papers that propelled the civil rights movement in the South were distinctly in the minority. Other editorial voices adamantly defended the status quo. Indeed, across the country, a majority of papers opposed the Supreme Court ruling in *Brown v. Board of Education*.

In its watchdog role, too, journalism has had both proud and shameful moments. *St. Louis Post-Dispatch* editor Joseph Pulitzer was embellishing when in 1878 he proclaimed, "More crime, immorality and rascality is prevented by the fear of exposure in the newspapers than by all the laws, morals and statutes ever devised."[9] How much wrongdoing has been prevented, we can never know. But it was the press that exposed the presidential deceptions of Vietnam and Watergate and Iran-Contra, alerted the nation to the dangers of pesticides, and shone a light on the cruelty of child labor.

At other times, however, the press has been less watchful. In January 2001, a bipartisan U.S. National Commission on National Security chaired by former senators Gary Hart and Warren Rudman warned that "the combination of unconventional weapons proliferation with the persistence of international terrorism will end the relative invulnerability of the U.S. homeland to catastrophic attack. A direct attack against American citizens on American soil is likely over the next quarter century." The commission argued that the "security of the American homeland" from terrorism "should be the primary national security mission of the U.S. government."

Articles based on wire-service stories about the report appeared on the inside pages of a few newspapers, while the story was ignored by many of the country's largest papers, including the *New York Times*. Although Hart and Rudman made appearances on CNN and MSNBC, none of the three large broadcast network news organizations did a story about their conclusions. A week later, Central Intelligence Agency director George Tenet told the Senate Intelligence Committee that "Osama bin Laden and his global network of lieutenants and associates remain the most immediate and serious threat" to American national security. Tenet's warnings did not prompt journalists to explore Bin Laden's network. The day after the September 11 attacks, the *New York Times* recalled the report and said that "the alarms have generally gone unheeded," but mentioned only the government's failure to address the warnings, leaving out the press's failure to do so.[10]

Nor did the press do its job in the face of claims by the Bush administration in the runup to the Iraq War that its leader, Saddam Hussein, had weapons of mass destruction, and implications that the Iraqi regime was tied to the September 11 terrorist attacks on the United States. The *New York Times* admitted as much when it wrote:

Over the last year this newspaper has shone the bright light of hindsight on decisions that led the United States into Iraq. We have examined the failings of American and allied intelligence, especially on the issue of Iraq's weapons and possible Iraqi connections to international terrorists. We have studied the allegations of official gullibility and hype. It is past time we turned the same light on ourselves. . . .

We have found a number of instances of coverage that was not as rigorous as it should have been. In some cases, information that was controversial then, and seems questionable now, was insufficiently qualified or allowed to stand unchallenged. Looking back, we wish we had been more aggressive in re-examining the claims as new evidence emerged—or failed to emerge.[11]

This was not the first or the only journalistic lapse in recent memory. Editors resigned at both the *New York Times* and *USA Today* after a reporter at each paper was caught fabricating material that was then published as news.

Amid the many disagreements about the press, there is widespread concurrence on one thing: The media in America are in a moment of profound transition. It was in recognition of this unsettlement that the editors of this volume brought together this commission to examine the press and its role in democracy. The book's walk through the history of the press, and its examination of contemporary media challenges, was not undertaken to settle disputes, but to create understanding. Consequently, along the way, we have offered competing views on some of the most critical questions and conclusions. In addition, we asked the authors not just to give us their views on what is, but also to say how it got to be that way, what else it could have been, and what it should be.

We confront at this point in the nation's history a media landscape in which the principle of objectivity is questioned, commercial pressures grow ever more powerful, legal and regulatory challenges increase, and public doubts about the press build, along with journalists' concerns about their own work. We now see more clearly the size and the range of the challenges we are facing. We know too that these press challenges arise amid great change in the American democracy itself. And we recognize that globalization makes any effort at understanding the press as an institution of democracy all the more complex. This volume's subject, the press, cannot be understood as separate from that of the other institutions of democracy. Public education and the three branches of government—addressed in four separate volumes, also underwritten by the Annenberg Foundation Trust at Sunnylands—are evolving at the same time, each influencing, and influenced by, the evolution of the press. The democracy that the American press is supposed to be assisting is a set of norms and institutions that are themselves in flux. The democratic polity that journalism is supposed to be serving is a moving target. The tools journalism has to work with are shaped not only by factors inside the press but by factors outside it, as well. What does Congress have to say about media ownership rules, or about enforcement of the Freedom of Information

Act? How open are congressional hearings? How well is government enabling the press to do its job, through campaign finance disclosure laws, or sunshine laws? How good are non-profits and think tanks at providing the information that serves good journalism? How well does public education equip citizens with an understanding of the media?

For all of the challenges, the importance of the function of the press in the American democracy remains undeniably clear. Whether the models in place are still working, the protections are effective, the function of the press as it has developed currently serves the nation's needs: These are questions of critical importance to our society. The threats to the press's capacity to perform effectively are real. Michael Schudson is right to caution, at the beginning of this volume's journey, that it ill-serves us to presume that journalism is in an unprecedented crisis. The press, as we have seen, is always in a time of change. Nonetheless, if this time is not one of earth-shattering change, it is surely one of earth-reshaping change.

What can be done to answer some of the unsettling questions raised in this volume? During the commission's discussions, this question frequently arose. Some participants recommended audits of journalism. Others spoke of spotlighting successes, or of raising public awareness of the challenge, or finding a way to give journalists a more powerful voice. Greater professionalization of the craft of journalism, a larger role for public-service broadcasting, and subsidies for ethnic and other alternative publications were mentioned. The proliferation of media criticism was welcomed, as was the increase in transparency shown by many media.

While arriving at solutions is not the purpose of this volume, the editors are indeed concerned about what happens next. The book makes clear that a rethinking of the press as an institution of democracy in America is needed. Just as we have seen that history is full of examples of how individuals and institutions have shaped the press, thoughtful people today can inform the current period of change. We have seen the forces at work in the past. The scholars and practitioners who have examined the press as an institution of democracy in this book offer the ideas found here to inform discussion of the changes to come.

Notes

1. A. J. Liebling, "Do You Belong in Journalism?" *New Yorker,* May 14, 1960, 109.
2. David Remnick, "Scoop," *New Yorker,* January 29, 1996, 42.
3. E. J. Dionne, *They Only Look Dead: Why Progressives Will Dominate the Next Political Era* (New York: Simon and Schuster, 1996), 246.
4. Bill Carter, "Comedy Central Sews Up Star for Four Years," *New York Times,* March 19, 2004, E3.

5. Carl Sullivan, "Papers Lure Web-Heads," *Editor & Publisher,* July 28, 2003.

6. Tim Race, "Most Wanted: Drilling Down/Radio Programming; Radio en Español," *New York Times,* January 12, 2004, C6.

7. Tripti LaHiri, "Immigrants with Ink in Their Blood: City's Bangladeshis Love to Read, and Many Newspapers Woo Them," *New York Times,* October 2, 2004, B1.

8. Judith and William Serrin, comps., *Muckraking!: The Journalism That Changed America* (New York: New Press, 2002), 106.

9. Ibid., xx.

10. David E. Rosenbaum, "A Day of Terror; The Warnings: Years of Unheeded Alarms," *New York Times,* September 12, 2001, A25.

11. "From the Editors: The *Times* and Iraq," *New York Times,* May 26, 2004, A10.

INDEX

Index

Index

Index

Index

Index

Index

Index

Index